teach®
yourself

gaelic dictionary
boyd robertson
and
ian macdonald

For over 60 years, more than
40 million people have learnt over
750 subjects the **teach yourself**
way, with impressive results.

be where you want to be
with **teach yourself**

For UK order enquiries: please contact Bookpoint Ltd, 130 Milton Park, Abingdon, Oxon OX14 4SB. Telephone: +44 (0) 1235 827720. Fax: +44 (0) 1235 400454. Lines are open 09.00–18.00, Monday to Saturday, with a 24-hour message answering service. Details about our titles and how to order are available at www.teachyourself.co.uk

For USA order enquiries: please contact McGraw-Hill Customer Services, PO Box 545, Blacklick, OH 43004-0545, USA. Telephone: 1-800-722-4726. Fax: 1-614-755-5645.

For Canada order enquiries: please contact McGraw-Hill Ryerson Ltd, 300 Water St, Whitby, Ontario L1N 9B6, Canada. Telephone: 905 430 5000. Fax: 905 430 5020.

Long renowned as the authoritative source for self-guided learning – with more than 40 million copies sold worldwide – the **teach yourself** series includes over 300 titles in the fields of languages, crafts, hobbies, business, computing and education.

British Library Cataloguing in Publication Data: a catalogue record for this title is available from the British Library.

Library of Congress Catalog Card Number: on file.

First published in UK 2004 by Hodder Arnold, 338 Euston Road, London, NW1 3BH.

First published in US 2004 by Contemporary Books, a Division of the McGraw-Hill Companies, 1 Prudential Plaza, 130 East Randolph Street, Chicago, IL 60601 USA.

This edition published 2004.

The **teach yourself** name is a registered trade mark of Hodder Headline Ltd.

Typeset by Transet Limited, Coventry, England.
Printed in Great Britain for Hodder Arnold, a division of Hodder Headline, 338 Euston Road, London NW1 3BH, by Cox & Wyman Ltd, Reading, Berkshire.

Hodder Headline's policy is to use papers that are natural, renewable and recyclable products and made from wood grown in sustainable forests. The logging and manufacturing processes are expected to conform to the environmental regulations of the country of origin.

Impression number   10 9 8 7 6 5 4 3 2
Year   2010 2009 2008 2007 2006 2005 2004

iii

contents

introduction

This *faclair* or dictionary was compiled in response to an invitation from the publishers to produce a publication that would complement the course book *Gaelic* in the Teach Yourself series and be useful to learners and to Gaelic speakers generally. The publishers were aware that there was a need and demand for a compact two-way dictionary of this kind.

One of the problems with a concise dictionary is that difficult decisions have to be taken as to what should be included and what left out. On occasion, therefore, there will be a noun here, but not the related adjective – and so on. This can be frustrating for the user, but within the constraints of the prescribed format we have tried to make the selection the most practically useful we could.

Anyone compiling a dictionary, whatever its length, must have recourse to the work of others, and we were grateful to have ready access to several existing dictionaries. The older Gaelic–English works by MacBain and Dwelly were consulted extensively, as were Derick Thomson's more recent *The New English–Gaelic Dictionary*, the all-Gaelic *Brìgh nam Facal* by Richard Cox and Clò Ostaig's *An Stòr-Dàta Briathrachais Gàidhlig*. We also drew on *Faclair na Pàrlamaid: Dictionary of Terms,* produced by the European Language Initiative and published by the Scottish Parliament, the Secondary Review Group's word list for schools, *Faclan Ùra Gàidhlig,* and two Irish dictionaries, Tomás de Bhaldraithe's *English–Irish Dictionary* and Séamus Mac Mathúna and Ailbhe Ó Corráin's *Pocket Irish Dictionary.*

Ian Quick read the dictionary in draft and contributed many useful suggestions. We are much obliged to him for his painstaking and perceptive commentary. Any shortcomings that remain are our responsibility. Katie Kennedy had the major task of keying in the text and formatting it onto disk. She has played a vital role in the production process, and we greatly appreciate her input and sustained commitment. We would also wish to acknowledge the support and encouragement given to us by Sheila Robertson and other members of our families, by John De Cecco of the University of Strathclyde and by Sue Hart and Ginny Catmur of the publishers, Hodder and Stoughton.

Detailed guidance on how to use the book is given in **the layout of the dictionary**. We hope it will prove a user-friendly work.

Tha sinn an dòchas gum bi am faclair feumail do luchd-labhairt na Gàidhlig, co-dhiù a tha iad fileanta no aig toiseach tòiseachaidh.

Boyd Robertson and Ian MacDonald

Selection and format of entries

For reasons of space, it has been possible to include only a small number of the many variants (including plurals) to be found in the language. These are indicated in the form used in 'Also **gàireachdaich**' under the main entry, **gàireachdainn**. Elsewhere, we have used oblique strokes, as in **neach-iùil/treòrachaidh**. In the case of hyphenated words like these, the oblique stroke indicates that the first element and the hyphen should also be added to the second word – ie, that the alternatives are **neach-iùil** and **neach-treòrachaidh**. Similarly, the oblique stroke in **gun toinisg/chiall** shows that the alternatives are **gun toinisg** and **gun chiall**.

We have also, to save space, usually given only the forms that are appropriate for the third person singular, masculine and feminine, in many phrases – eg, the translation of **awake** is given as **na d(h)ùisg**, *etc*, where the full paradigm would be **nam dhùisg, nad dhùisg, na dhùisg, na dùisg, nar dùisg, nur dùisg, nan dùisg**. Users should change the third person to another as required.

The language has more than one form of the prepositional pronouns that express 'to the, for the' etc and 'of the'/'off the', **don, dhan** and **dan** all being used for the first meaning and **den, dhen** and **dhan** for the second, but we have confined ourselves here to using only **dhan** for the first of these meanings and only **dhen** for the second.

We have used contractions throughout, as given in the **Abbreviations** section, and contracted forms of the headword are often used in entries. But the full headword is given where its form has changed – for example, where a consonant has been lenited (followed by h), and also if the word has fewer than four letters or if there may be ambiguity.

We have occasionally provided grammatical information – for instance, where a word or phrase should be followed by the genitive case – and short sections after the two main sections of the dictionary provide tabular information on the definite article, verbs and prepositional pronouns. These are intended to enable the user to have convenient access to basic forms, but it is not possible in any dictionary to provide the detailed guidance to be found in a grammar book. Similarly, the lists of personal and place names at the end are intended to be handy and useful, but they are necessarily selective.

A grammar book is also the best place in which to learn in detail where Gaelic greatly differs from English in the way certain meanings are expressed – for example, the fact that 'never' is not rendered by a separate word but is expressed by a negative form of a verb with one of the words used to render 'ever'. In such situations we have tried to give guidance as clear as space permitted, but we could not go into detail.

Nouns are nearly always listed before a related adjective, and an adjective before a related verb, but in cases in which, for example, an adjective is commoner than the noun, the adjective has been given first.

Headwords are in bold, translations are in roman and explanatory notes such as '+ *gen*' are in italics.

Current orthographic conventions are adopted throughout but earlier forms of spelling which users will encounter are provided as appropriate, and introduced by the term *Formerly*.

English words with one spelling but different meanings are included within one entry, but Gaelic ones are listed separately.

Layout of Gaelic–English section

All Gaelic text is in bold type.

Where a number of alternative translations of a Gaelic word are given, the order in which they appear aims to reflect currency and frequency of use.

When a Gaelic word has entirely distinct meanings, these are separated by semi-colons.

Some translations are glossed in brackets to clarify the context.

Alternative spellings of words are given either within the entry or as a separate entry:

eg **naoi** *n, a* nine *Also* **naodh**
    maith *v* *See* **math**

Secondary forms of entries show the element to be added to the basic form:

eg **màileid** *n* **-e, -ean** *f* bag, suitcase

In many cases, the secondary form involves an internal adaptation of the primary form. The secondary form begins with the last unchanged letter of the original or, sometimes, the last unchanged letter before h:

eg **mòinteach** *n* **-tich, -tichean** *f* moor, moorland
    easbhaidheach *a* **-dhiche** deficient, defective

The full secondary form is given in words where the primary form changes radically:

eg **sgian** *n* **sgeine, sgeinean** *f* knife

Where a secondary form of the word appears in the example, it is given in full.

Nouns

The gender of nouns is given after the last secondary form, usually the nominative plural. Some nouns can be feminine (*f*) in certain areas and masculine (*m*) in others.

Nouns are normally entered in their nominative singular form. The genitive singular and nominative plural forms are also indicated:

eg **faoileag** *n* **-eig, -an** *f* seagull

Where the genitive singular has the same form as the nominative singular, only the nominative plural form appears:

eg **slabhraidh** *n* **-ean** *f* chain

Where there are alternative forms of the genitive singular or nominative plural, these are given with an oblique:

eg **rathad** *n* **-aid/rothaid, -aidean/ròidean** *m* road, route, way

When nouns are normally accompanied by the definite article (*the* in English), the entry gives the full form:

eg **griùthrach** *n* **-aich** *f* **a' ghriùthrach** measles

In compound nouns, only the element that shows change from the basic form is shown in the genitive singular and nominative plural:

eg **ball-coise** *n* **buill-, buill-** *m* football

Where a noun and adjective have the same form, they are listed together under the same headword:

eg **ceithir** *n, a* four

Diùrach *n* -aich, -aich *m* someone from Jura *a* from, or pertaining to, Jura

Adjectives

The comparative/superlative form of the adjective is indicated along with the primary form except where the two are identical or in cases where they have little practical application.

Verbs

Verbs are entered in their root form, the second singular imperative or command form. The verbal noun (equivalent to the *-ing* ending in verbs in English) is also given where it differs from the root, but not otherwise:

eg **coisich** *v* -**seachd** walk

Where a verb is normally followed by a preposition, that is indicated thus:

eg **èist** *v* -**eachd** (+ **ri**) listen (to)

Common forms of irregular verbs are entered separately and most forms are listed in the **Grammar**.

Prepositions

Prepositions are usually followed by the dative case form of the noun. When the preposition is followed by the genitive case of the noun, this is indicated thus: (+ *gen*).

Prepositional pronouns

Each form of prepositional pronoun is included as a separate entry.

Layout of English–Gaelic section

The English headwords are in bold type.

Where a number of Gaelic words are given for an English headword, the order in which they appear reflects currency and frequency of use.

When an English word has entirely distinct meanings, these are separated by semi-colons and their sphere of application is specified in brackets.

Where a verb is intransitive, this is indicated thus: (*intrans*).

abbreviations

a	adjective	*def art*	definite article
abb	abbreviation	*def v*	defective verb
acad	academic	*dem a*	demonstrative
ad	advertisement		adjective
adj phr	adjectival phrase	*dem pron*	demonstrative
adv	adverb		pronoun
adv phr	adverbial phrase	*descr*	description
adv pref	adverbial prefix	*dom*	domestic
abstr	abstract		
agric	agriculture	*eccl*	ecclesiastical
anat	anatomical	*educ*	education(al)
atmos	atmosphere	*emph (pron)*	emphatic
aug conj	augmented		(pronoun)
	conjunction	*exam*	examination
aug prep	augmented	*exclam*	exclamation
	preposition		
		f	feminine
Bibl	Biblical	*fig*	figurative
biol	biological	*fin*	financial
bot	botanical		
		gen	genitive case
caps	capital letters	*geneal*	genealogical
coll	collective	*gen pl*	genitive plural
colloq	colloquial	*geog*	geography,
comp	comparative		geographical
comp a	comparative	*geol*	geology,
	adjective		geological
con	concrete	*gram*	grammar
conj	conjunction		
corresp	correspondence	*impl*	implement
contr	contraction	*ind*	industry,
cult	cultural		industrial
		infin part	infinitive particle
dat	dative case	*instit*	institution

intens	intensive	*pers pron*	personal pronoun
interj	interjection	*phil*	philosophical
interr	interrogative	*phot*	photographic
int part	interrogative particle	*phr*	phrase
		phys	physical
int pron	interrogative pronoun	*pl*	plural
		pol	polite
intrans	intransitive	*polit*	politics, political
irreg v	irregular verb	*pop*	population
		poss pron	possessive pronoun
jud	judicial		
		pref	prefix
lang	language	*prep*	preposition
leg	legal, legislation	*prep phr*	prepositional phrase
len	lenition		
ling	linguistics, linguistically	*prep pron*	prepositional pronoun
lit	literal(ly)	*pron*	pronoun
liter	literature, literary	*punct*	punctuation
m	masculine	*rel*	relative
math	mathematics	*rel part*	relative particle
mech	mechanical	*rel pron*	relative pronoun
med	medical	*relig*	religion, religious
met	metaphorical		
metr	metrical	*sg*	singular
mil	military	*stat*	statistics
mus	music(al)	*suff*	suffix
		sup a	superlative adjective
n	noun		
naut	nautical	*temp*	temperature
neg	negative	*topog*	topographical
neg conj	negative conjunction	*trad*	traditional(ly)
		trans	transitive
neg part	negative particle	*typ*	typographical
neg pref	negative prefix		
nf	noun feminine	*v*	verb
nm	noun masculine	*veg*	vegetable
nom	nominative case	*voc*	vocative case
num a	numerical adjective	*voc part*	vocative particle
		vn	verbal noun
num part	numerical particle	*v part*	verbal particle
		vulg	vulgar
org	organization	+	followed by
past part	past participle		
pej	pejorative		

Gaelic–English dictionary

A

a *num part* used before the numbers 1–19 in counting or when they are not followed by a noun **a h-aon, a dhà, a trì, a h-ochd, a h-aon deug, a dhà dheug, trithead 's a naoi, seachdad 's a ceithir**

a *voc part* when addressing someone **A Mhairead!** Margaret! **A Dhonnchaidh!** Duncan! **A Charaid/Bhanacharaid** Dear Sir/Madam (*at start of letter*)

a *prep* (*contraction of* **do**) to (*+ len*) **a' dol a Pheairt** going to Perth

a *prep* (*contraction of* **de**) of (*+ len*) **uair a thìde** an hour (*of time*)

a *rel part* who, whom, which, that **an tè a thachair rium** the one whom I met **an t-aodach a cheannaich sinn** the clothes that we bought

a *infin part* (*contraction of* **do**) to (*+ len*) **a bheil sibh a' dol a thadhal?** are you going to call? (*becomes* **a dh'** *before vowels*) **a' dol a dh'èirigh** going to get up

a *poss pron* her (*without len*); his (*+ len*) **a màthair 's a h-athair** her mother and father **a phiuthar is a bhràthair** his sister and brother

a' *def art* the (*See Forms of the article in Grammar*)

a' *v part* (*used before verbal nouns not beginning in vowels*) **a' ceannach** buying **a' suidhe** sitting

à *prep* from, out of

aba *n* -chan *m* abbot

abachadh *n* -aidh *m* ripening **gealach an abachaidh** the harvest moon *f*

abaich *v* abachadh ripen, mature

abaich *a* -e ripe, mature

abaid *n* -e *f* abbey

abair *irr v* ràdh say (*See irr v* **abair** *in Grammar*); used to give emphasis **a. sealladh!** what a sight!/some sight! **a. e!** indeed!/you can say that again!

abairt *n* -e, -ean *f* saying, expression, phrase

àbhachd *n f* fun, joking, mirth

àbhachdach *a* -aiche funny, given to joking

àbhachdas *n* -ais *m* fun, joking, mirth

abhag *n* -aig, -an *f* small dog, tyke

abhainn *n* **aibhne/-e, aibhneachan/aibhnichean** *f* river

àbhaist *n f* norm, custom, habit **'s à. dhomh ...** I usually ... **mar as à.** as usual

àbhaisteach *a* -tiche usual, normal

a-bhàn *adv* down, downward(s)

a bharrachd *adv phr* in addition, extra; either **fhuair mi £5 a bh.** I got £5 extra **chan eil sin fìor a bh.** that isn't true either *prep phr* (*+ air*) in addition to

abharsair *n* -ean *m* adversary **an t-A.** the Devil

a bhith *v* to be (*See verb* **to be** *in Grammar*)

a' bhòn-dè *adv phr* the day before yesterday

a' bhòn-raoir *adv phr* the night before last

a' bhòn-uiridh *adv phr* the year before last *Also* **a' bhèan-uiridh**

a-bhos *adv* (being) over here/on this side

abhsadh *n* -aidh *m* slackening **gun a.** non-stop, without halting

ablach *n* -aich, -aich/-aichean *m* carcase; person affected by illness or something suffering from wear and tear **tha e na a.** he is in poor shape **seann a. de chàr** an old wreck of a car

abstol *n* -oil, -oil/-an *m* apostle

aca(san) *prep pron* their; they **bha aca ri falbh** they had to go

acadamh *n* -aimh, -an *f* academy

acaid *n* -e, -ean *f* stabbing pain, stitch

acair(e) *n* (-e), acraichean *f m* anchor

acair(e) *n* (-e), acraichean *f m* acre

acarsaid *n* -(e), -ean *f* anchorage, harbour

acfhainn *n* -(e), -ean *f* equipment, instruments, tools **a. eich** horse harness

acfhainneach *a* -niche equipped; expert

ach *conj* but; (*after neg*) only, except **cha robh ann ach fathann** it was only a rumour

ach am/an *conj See* **feuch**

achadh *n* -aidh/acha, -aidhean/ **achannan** *m* field

a-chaoidh *adv* forever, always; (*after neg v*) never **cha tig iad a-ch.** they'll never come

achd *n* -a, -an *f* Act (*of Parliament*)

achdarra *a* skilful, expert, methodical

a-cheana *adv* already, previously

a-chianaibh *adv* recently, a short time ago

a chionn ('s) *adv phr* because, since **a ch. gu bheil mi sgìth** because I'm tired

achlais *n* -(e), -ean *f* armpit, oxter

achmhasan *n* -ain, -ain *m* rebuke, reprimand, reproach *v* **thoir a. do** rebuke, reprimand

a chum *prep phr* (+ *gen*) to **a chum an taighe** to the house *Also* **chum**

a chum is gu *conj* in order that **a chum is gum faic thu iad** in order that/so that you will see them

acrach *a* -aiche hungry

acraich *v* -achadh anchor

acras *n* -ais *m* hunger **a bheil an t-a. ort?** are you hungry?

actair *n* -ean *m* actor

ad(a) *n* aide, -(a)n/-(a)ichean *f* hat

adag *n* -aig, -an *f* haddock; stook (*eg of corn*)

a dh'aindeoin *prep phr* (+ *gen*) despite *adv phr* despite, even although, nevertheless **thig e a dh'. sin** he'll come despite that **a dheòin no (a) dh'.** willy-nilly/ like it or not

adha *n* àinean *m* liver

adhairc *n See* **adharc**

adhaltranach *a* -aiche adulterous

adhaltranas *n* -ais *m* adultery

adhar *n* -air sky *m*

adharc *n* -airc(e), -an/-aircean *f* horn

adhartach *a* -aiche progressive

adhartas *n* -ais *m* progress

adhbhar *n* -air, -air/-an *m* cause, reason **air an a. sin** for that reason, that being so, hence

adhbh(a)raich *v* adhbh(a)rachadh cause

a dh'ionnsaigh *prep phr* (+ *gen*) to, towards

adhbrann *n* -ainn, -ainnean/-an *f m* ankle

a dhìth *adv phr* needed; lost (forever) **tha sin a dh. orm** I need that **chaidh an streapadair a dh.** the climber perished

adhlacadh *n* -aidh, -aidh/-aidhean *m* funeral, burial, interment

adhlaic *v* -acadh bury, inter

adhradh *n* -aidh, -aidhean *m* worship, act of worship **a. teaghlaich** family worship **dèan a.** *v* worship

Afraganach *n* -aich, -aich *m* African *a* African

ag *v part* (*used before verbal nouns beginning in vowels*) **ag ithe 's ag òl** eating and drinking

agad(sa) *prep pron* your (*sg*) **a bheil càr agad?** do you have a car?

agaibh(se) *prep pron* your (*pl & pol*) **cò agaibh a bh' ann?** which of you were there?

againn(e) *prep pron* our **tha iad a' fuireach againne** they're staying with us

agair *v* -t petition, demand **ag agairt a chòraichean** demanding his rights

agallaich *v* -adh/-achadh interview; give abuse, quarrel with

agallaiche *n* -an *m* interviewer

agallamh *n* -aimh, -an *m* interview **dèan a.** *v* interview

agam(sa) *prep pron* my **cò th' agam an seo?** who's this?

agh *n* aighe, aighean *f m* heifer; hind

àgh *n* **àigh** *m* joy, bliss; good fortune **An ainm an Àigh!** For goodness's sake! **Gun sealladh an t-Àgh orm!** Goodness gracious me!

aghaidh *n* (-e), -ean *f* face (*human or geog*), facade **a. ri a.** face to face **nach ann ort a tha 'n a.!** what a cheek you've got! **bhithinn an a. sin** I'd be against that **air a.** forward **thug e an a. orm** *v* he (*verbally*) attacked/rebuked me

aghaidh-choimheach *n* -coimhich, **aghaidhean-coimheach** *f* mask, false-face

àghmhor *a* -oire happy; fortunate

a-ghnàth *adv* always (*past, present, future*), ever

agus *conj* and (*also contracted to* **is, 's**)

a h-uile *a* (*precedes n*) every, each, all **a h-uile h-oidhche** every night

àibheis *n* (-e), -ean *f* abyss, the deep; (*colloq*) large structure; ruin

àibheiseach *a* -siche large, huge; remarkable

aibidil *n* -ean *f* alphabet **òrdugh na h-a.** *m* alphabetical order

aice(se) *prep pron* her **an tèid aice air tighinn?** can she come?

àicheadh *n* -eidh, -eidhean *m* denial **rach às à.** *v* deny

àicheidh *v* -eadh deny

àicheil *a* negative

aideachadh *n* -aidh, -aidhean *m* admission, confession

aidh *excl* aye, yes

àidhear *n* See **èadhar**

aidich *v* **aideachadh** admit, confess

aidmheil *n* (-e), -ean *f* creed, faith

aifreann *n* -rinn(e), -rinnean *f m* Mass (*relig*)

aig *prep* at; (*also used to denote possession*) **tha càr aig Sìm** Simon has a car

aige(san) *prep pron* his **bidh fios aigesan** he'll know

àigeach *n* -gich, -gich *m* stallion

aigeann *n* -ginn *m* sea-bed *Also*

aigeal

aigeannach *a* -aiche spirited, lively

aighear *n* -eir *m* joy, high spirits, merriment

aighearach *a* -aiche joyful, in high spirits, merry

aigne *n* *f* mind, consciousness, spirits

ailbhean *n* -ein, -an *m* elephant

àile *n* *m* air, atmosphere

àileadh *n* *m* See **fàileadh**

aileag *n* -eig *f* hiccups **bha an a. orm** I had the hiccups

àilgheas *n* -eis *f* will, inclination, desire

àilgheasach *a* -aiche choosy, fussy, fastidious, hard to please

ailisich *v* -seachadh criticize strongly

àill *n* *f* wish, desire **dè b' àill leibh?** what is your wish? **b' àill leibh?/bàillibh?** pardon?

àilleachd *n* *f* beauty, loveliness

àilleag *n* -eig, -an *f* jewel

àilleagan *n* -ain, -ain *m* little jewel, treasure

àillidh *a* -e beautiful, lovely

aillse *n* *f* cancer **tha a. air** he has cancer **a. sgamhain** lung cancer

ailm *n* -e, -ean *f* elm tree

ailtire *n* -an *m* architect

ailtireachd *n* *f* architecture

aimhleas *n* -eis *m* harm, hurt; misfortune

aimhleasach *a* -aiche harmful, hurtful; unfortunate

aimhreit *n* (-e), -ean *f* argument, dispute

aimhreiteach *a* -tiche argumentative, disputatious

aimlisg *n* -e, -ean *f* confusion, disorder; mischief **'s e a. a th' ann** he's a mischief

aimlisgeach *a* -giche mischievous

aimsir *n* (-e), -ean *f* time, era; weather **san t-seann a.** in days gone by

aimsireil *a* -e temporal, of this world; climatic

ain-deòin *n* *f* unwillingness, reluctance

ain-deònach *a* -aiche unwilling, reluctant

aineol *n* **-oil** *m* stranger, foreigner; lack of acquaintance **bha mi air m' a. sa bhaile** I was a stranger in the town

aineolach *a* **-aiche** ignorant, unaware, ill-informed

aineolas *n* **-ais** *m* ignorance

aingeal *n* **-gil, ainglean** *m* angel

aingidh *a* **-e** wicked, heinous

aingidheachd *n* *f* wickedness, iniquity

ainm *n* **(-e), -ean/-eannan** *m* name **a. sgrìobhte** signature **dè an t-a. a th' ort?** what's your name?

ainmeachadh *n* **-aidh** *m* nomination; mention

ainmear *n* **-eir, -an** *m* noun **a. gnìomhaireach** verbal noun

ainmeil *a* **-e** famous

ainmhidh *n* **-ean** *m* animal

ainmich *v* **ainmeachadh** name, mention; announce

ainmichte *a* designated, nominated

ainmig *adv* seldom, rarely

ainmneach *a* nominative **an tuiseal a.** the nominative case

ainneamh *a* **-eimhe** rare, infrequent **gu h-a.** rarely, infrequently

ainneart *n* **-eirt** *m* oppression, violence

ainneartach *a* **-aiche** oppressive, violent

ainnir *n* **(-e), -ean** *f* maiden

ainnis *n* **-e** *f* need, poverty

ainniseach *a* **-siche** needy, indigent

aintighearn(a) *n* **(-a), -an** *m* tyrant, oppressor, abuser of power

aintighearnas *n* **-ais** *m* tyranny, oppression, abuse of power

air *adv* on **tha an solas air** the light is on

air *prep* on; by; about; at; however, no matter; (*used to describe feelings and states*) **tha an t-acras/an t-eagal orm** I'm hungry/I'm afraid (*sometimes with len*) **air chuairt** on a trip **rug mi air chois air** I caught him by the foot **a' bruidhinn air na rudan sin** speaking about these

things **bha sinn a' bruidhinn ort** we were speaking about you **air banais** at a wedding **math air ...** good at ... **air cho anmoch 's gum bi sinn** however late we are/will be

air *adv* after (*used before vn*) **tha iad air tilleadh** they've returned (*lit* they're after returning) **tha iad air an doras fhosgladh** they've opened the door

air(san) *prep pron* on him/it

air adhart *adv phr* ahead, forward(s), onwards **dol-air-adhart** *f* carry-on, undesirable behaviour

air aghaidh *adv phr* ahead, forward(s), onwards

air ais *adv phr* back, backwards **air ais 's air adhart** backwards and forwards

air ball *adv phr* at once, immediately

air beulaibh *prep phr* (+ *gen*) in front of **a. b. an taighe** in front of the house **air mo bheulaibh** in front of me

air bhog *adv phr* afloat **cuir a. b.** *v* launch

air bhonn *adv phr* in operation, up and running **cuir a. b.** *v* establish, set up

airc *n* **-e** *f* distress, want

àirc(e) *n* **(-e), -ean** *f* ark **À. Nòah** Noah's Ark

air chall *adv phr* lost

air chois *adv phr* in operation **cuir a. ch.** *v* establish, set up, institute

air choreigin *adv phr* or other **fear/tè a. ch.** someone or other

air chùl *adv phr* behind, rejected, lost

air cùl *prep phr* (+ *gen*) behind

air cùlaibh *comp prep* (+ *gen*) behind, at the back of **tha e air do chùlaibh** he/it is behind you

àird(e) *n* **-e, -ean** *f* height, high place, point, headland **sia troighean a dh'àirde** six feet tall

àird *n* **-e, -ean** *f* point of the compass, airt **an àird an iar** the west

air dheireadh *adv phr* behind, last; late **bha am bàta a. dh.** the boat was late

aire *n* heed, attention *f* **thoir an a.** notice; watch! look out! **thoir an a. ort fhèin** take care (of yourself)

air eagal ('s) gu *conj* lest, in case **a. e. gun tuit thu** in case you fall

àireamh *n f* **-eimh, -an** number **à. fòn** phone number

àireamhair *n* **-ean** *m* calculator

air fad *adv* altogether, in total

air falbh *adv* away, in a different place

air feadh *prep phr* (+ *gen*) throughout, all around

airgead *n* **-gid** *m* money, currency; silver **a.-pòcaid** pocket money **a. ullamh** cash

airidh *a* **-e** worthy, deserving **a. air duais** deserving a prize **'s math an a.** it's richly deserved

airidheachd *n f* merit

àirigh *n* **-ean** *f* sheiling, hill pasture; bothy

àirleas *n* **-eis, -an** *m* token **a.-clàir** record token *Also* **eàrlas**

air leth *adv* separate; exceptional, outstanding **cùm an dà rud sin a. l. o chèile** keep these two things separate from each other **duine a. l.** an exceptional man **a. l. math** exceptionally good

air-loidhne *a* online

air muin *prep phr* (+ *gen*) on top of, astride **a. m. eich** on horseback

àirne *n* **-an** *f* kidney

àirneis *n f* furniture **ball a.** an item of furniture

air neo *conj* or, or else

air sàillibh *prep phr* (+ *gen*) because of *Also* **air tàillibh**

air sgàth *prep phr* for the sake of, in the interests of **air mo sgàth-sa** for my sake **a. s. na sìthe** in the interests of peace

airson *prep* (+ *gen*) for, for the sake of; (*before a vn*) desirous of, wanting to **tha iad a. falbh** they want to go

airson gu *conj* because, since

air thoiseach *adv* ahead, in front; (*of a clock*) fast

air thoiseach *prep phr* ahead of

air thuaiream *adv* at random

airtneal *n* **-eil** *m* weariness, sorrow, dejection *Also* **airsneal**

airtnealach *a* **-aiche** weary, sorrowful, dejected *Also* **airsnealach**

aiseag *n* **-eig/-sig, -an** *m* ferry

aiseal *n* **-eil, -an** *m* axle

aisean *n* **-ein, aisnean** *f* rib *Also* **asna** *f pl* **asnaichean**

aiseirigh *n f* resurrection, resurgence

Àisianach *n* **-aich, -aich** *m* Asian *a* Asian

aisig *v* **aiseag** ferry; restore

aisling *n* **-e, -ean** *f* dream

aiste *prep pron* from/out of her/it

ait *a* **-e** glad, joyful; funny

àite *n* **-an/-achan/-tichean** *m* place **à.-fuirich** dwelling-place, accommodation, habitation **à.-obrach** workplace **à.-suidhe** seat **à. bàn** vacancy **an à.** (+ *gen*) in place of, instead of

àiteigin *n m* somewhere

àiteach *n* **-tich** *m* cultivation, farming **talamh-àitich** *m* arable land

àiteachas *n* **-ais** *m* agriculture

aiteal *n* **-eil, -an** *m* glimpse, ray; breeze; small quantity **a. grèine** a glimpse of sunshine

aiteamh *n* **-eimh** *f m* thaw **tha beagan aiteimh ann** it's thawing a little *Also vn* **ag aiteamh**

aiteann *n* **-tinn** *m* juniper

aitheamh *n* **-eimh, -an** *m* fathom

aithghearr *a* **-a** fast, swift, sudden; short, brief *f* **a dh'a.** *adv phr* soon, shortly **fhuair i bàs a.** she died suddenly

aithghearrachd *n f* shortness, brevity; shortcut **ann an a.** soon, swiftly; in brief

aithisg *n* **(-e), -ean** *f* report **a. bhliadhnail** annual report

àithn *v* **-e** command, ordain

aithne *n* knowledge; acquaintance **an a. dhut e?** do you know him? **cuir a. air** *v* get

to know **cuir an a. (a chèile)** *v*
introduce (to each other)

àithne *n* **-ntean** *f* order,
commandment **na Deich
Àithntean** the Ten Command-
ments

àithneach *a* imperative (*gram*)

aithnich *v* **-neachadh** know,
recognize, acknowledge **a bheil
thu ga h-aithneachadh?** do you
recognize her?

aithreachas *n* **-ais** *m* regret,
repentance **ghabh iad (an t-)a.**
they regretted it

aithris *n* **-ean** *f* account, report

aithris *v* relate, report, recite

àitich *v* **àiteach/àiteachadh**
cultivate; inhabit

aitreabh *n* **-eibh, -an** *m* building,
dwelling

àl *n* **àil, àil** *m* brood, young, litter

àlainn *a* **-e/àille** lovely, beautiful,
fine

Albàinianach *n* **-aich, -aich** *m*
Albanian *a* Albanian

Albais *n* *f* the Scots language,
Scots

Albannach *n* **-aich, -aich** *m* Scot
a Scottish

alcol *n* **-oil** *m* alcohol

allaban *n* **-ain** *m* wandering **air an
a.** wandering; homeless

allail *a* **-e** noble, illustrious

allmharach *n* **-aich, -aich** *m*
foreigner, alien

allaidh *a* **-e** wild, fierce

allt *n* **uillt, uillt** *m* stream, burn

alltan *n* **-ain, -ain** *m* little stream,
brook

alt *n* **uilt, -an/uilt** *m* joint (*of the
body*); aptitude, knack; article
(*liter, gram*) **tha alt aice air ceòl**
she has an aptitude for music

altachadh *n* **-aidh, -aidhean** *m*
grace (*before meals*) **dèan/gabh
a.** *v* say grace

altaich *v* **altachadh** relax the
joints; salute, thank **tha mi
airson mo chasan altachadh**
I want to stretch my legs (*See*
altachadh)

altair *n* **altarach, -ean/altraichean**
f altar

altraim *v* **-am/-amas** nurse,
dandle, foster, nurture

altram *n* **-aim** *m* fosterage,
fostering, nursing

am *def art* the (*used before b, f,
m, p*) (*See Forms of the article
in Grammar*)

am *poss pron* their (*used before
b, f, m, p*)

am *int part* **am pòs thu mi?** will
you marry me?

am *prep* equivalent to **an** in (*used
before b, f, m, p*) **am Peairt** in
Perth

àm *n* **ama, amannan** *m* time,
period of time **àm nam
Fuadaichean** the time of the
Clearances **tha an t-àm agad
falbh** it's time you went **tha an
t-àm agad!** it's high time! (you
did) **anns an eadar-àm** in the
meantime, at present **san àm ri
teachd** in future

a-mach *adv* out, outwards
(*implying motion*)

amadan *n* **-ain, -ain** *f* fool

amaideach *a* **-diche** foolish, silly,
ridiculous

amaideas *n* **-eis** *m* foolishness,
folly, silliness

a-màireach *adv* tomorrow

amais *v* **amas (+ air)** aim at;
chance on, chance to be **ag
amas air an targaid** aiming at
the target **dh'amais dhomh a
bhith ann** I happened/chanced
to be there

amar *n* **-air, -an** *m* container for
liquid, trough, bath **a.-snà(i)mh**
swimming pool

amas *n* **-ais, -an** *m* aim,
objective; chance **cha robh ann
ach a. gun d' fhuair mi e** it was
only by chance that I found it

ambaileans *n* **-ean** *f* ambulance

am bàrr *prep phr* **(+ gen)**, *adv* on
top of, on the surface of **chì
sinn dè thig am b.** we'll see what
comes to the surface/to light

ambasaid *n* **-ean** *f* embassy

am-bliadhna *adv* this year

am broinn *prep phr* **(+ gen)**
inside, within

Ameireaganach *n* -aich, -aich *m*
American *a* American
amen *exclam* amen, so let it be
am feast *adv phr* forever; (*after neg*) never **cha ruig iad a. f.**
they'll never get there
amh *a* aimhe raw; (*of a person*)
uncouth
amhach *n* -aich, -aichean *f* neck
Also **amhaich**
a-mhàin *adv* only, alone
àmhainn *n* -ean *f* oven
amhairc *v* amharc (+ air) see, look at, view
amharas *n* -ais *m* suspicion **fo a.**
under suspicion, suspect **tha a. agam gu bheil** I suspect so
amharasach *a* -aiche suspicious, distrustful
amharc *n* -airc *m* seeing, looking, view **dè th' agad san a. a-nis?**
what have you in view/in mind now?
àmhghar *n* -air, -an *f m* affliction, adversity, anguish, severe trouble
àmhghair *n* See **àmhghar**
amhlaidh *adv* as, in the way that
amhran *n* -ain, -ain *m* song
am measg *prep phr* (+ *gen*) among
a-muigh *adv* out, outside (*not implying motion*)
an *def art* the (*See Forms of the article in Grammar*)
an *poss pron* their
an *int part* **an tàinig iad?** have they arrived?
an *prep* in **an Èirinn** in Ireland
an-abaich *a* -e unripe
anabarr *n* -a *m* excess, too much
anabarrach *a* -aiche greatly, extremely, remarkably, excessively **a. mòr** extraordinarily large
ana-cainnt *n* -e *f* abusive language, verbal abuse
ana-caith *v* -eamh waste, misuse
ana-caitheanaich *n f* waste, misuse **a. air biadh math** a waste of good food
ana-ceartas *n* -ais *m* injustice
anacladh *n* -aidh *m* handling; protecting

anacothrom *n* -uim *m* injustice, hardship, handicap
ana-creideas *n* -eis *m* disbelief, scepticism
an aghaidh *prep phr* (+ *gen*) against
anail *n* -e/analach, -ean *f* breath; rest **a. na beatha** the breath of life **a. a' Ghàidheil am mullach** the Gael's rest is (*when he/she reaches*) the summit **leig d' a.** get your breath back/have a rest
an-àird(e) *adv* up, upwards
analachadh *n* -aidh *m* aspiration (*gram*)
a-nall *adv* over (*from the other side*), to this side
anam *n* -a, anman/anmannan *m* soul
anann *n* -ainn *m* pineapple
anarag *n* -aig, -an *f* anorak
anart *n* anairt *m* linen **anartan** clothes on a line **a.-leapa** bed linen **a.-bùird** table linen
an asgaidh *adv* free (of charge), for nothing **saor is an a.** free, gratis
an ath- *pref* (*usually lenites*) next **an ath-d(h)oras** *adv* next door **an ath-bhliadhna** *adv* next year, the following year **an ath-oidhch'** *adv* tomorrow night **an ath sheachdain** *adv* next week, the following week
an ceann *prep phr* (+ *gen*) after, at the end of
an ceartuair *adv* at present, just now; shortly **thig iad an c.** they'll come shortly/presently
an cois *prep phr* (+ *gen*) beside; (*met*) in the course of, as part of
an comhair *prep phr* (+ *gen*) in the direction of **an c. a chùil** backwards **an c. a chinn** forwards, head first
an còmhnaidh *adv* always, constantly
an-dè *adv* yesterday
an deaghaidh *prep phr* See **an dèidh**
an dèidh *prep phr* (+ *gen*) after; despite **cairteal an d. uair** quarter past one **is toigh leam e**

an d. sin I like him nevertheless/despite that **an d. sin 's na dhèidh** for all that, after all **an d. làimhe** afterwards, subsequently

an-diugh *adv* today **feasgar a.** this afternoon **san latha a.** these days

an-dràsta *adv* just now, now, at present **a. 's a-rithist** now and again

an ear *adv* east, eastern, eastwards **an àird an ear** the east

an-earar *adv* the day after next/tomorrow

an ear-dheas *adv* south-east, south-eastwards **gaoth an e.** a south-east wind

an ear-thuath *adv* north-east, north-eastwards **a' dol dhan ear-thuath** going north-eastwards

anfhann *a* -ainne weak, feeble, infirm

an-fhoiseil *a* -e restless, uneasy, ill-at-ease, troubled

an iar *adv* west, western, westwards **na h-Eileanan an Iar** the Western Isles

an iar-dheas *adv* south-west, south-westwards **oiteag on i.** a breeze from the south-west

an iar-thuath *adv* north-west, north-westwards

an impis *adv* about to, on the point of

an-iochdmhor *a* -oire unmerciful, unpitying, unfeeling

an làthair *adv* present *prep phr* (+ *gen*) in the presence of

an lùib *prep phr* (+ *gen*) among, involved in, in the course of, attached to

a-nìos *adv* up (*from below*)

a-nis *adv* now *Also* **a-nise, a-nist**

anmoch *a* -oiche late

ann(san) *rel pron* in him/it; he, it **'s e oileanach a th' ann** he's a student

ann *adv* in existence, there; in it **'s e latha math a th' ann** it's a fine day

ann *prep* in a (*followed by* **an,** *by*

am *before b, f, m, p, by* **a** *before h*) **ann an taigh** in a house **ann am bùth** in a shop **ann a Hiort** in St Kilda

annad(sa) *prep pron* in you (*sg*); you

annaibh(se) *prep pron* in you (*pl & pol*); you

annainn(e) *prep pron* in us; we

annam(sa) *prep pron* in me; I

annas *n* -ais, -an *m* rarity, novelty; unusual object/event **thug iad an t-a. às** the novelty wore off for them

annasach *a* -aiche unusual, novel; strange, odd

annlan *n* -ain *m* condiment, accompaniment to main food being eaten

anns *prep* (+ *art*) in (the) *Also used before* **gach** **a. gach taigh** in every house

annsa *a* better/best liked, preferred **an tè a b' a. leam** the woman I liked best

annsachd *n f* love, affection or object of these **m' a.** my beloved

ann(san) *prep pron* in him/it; he/it

annta(san) *prep pron* in them; they

a-nochd *adv* tonight

ànradh *n* -aidh *m* misfortune, distress

an seo *adv* here

anshocair *n* -ean/-ocran *f* unease; discomfort; illness

anshocrach *a* -aiche uneasy; discomforted, distressed, distressing; suffering from illness *Also* **anshocair**

an sin *adv* there

an siud *adv* over there

antaidh *n* -ean *f* aunt(ie)

an toiseach *adv* first, to begin with

an uair a *conj* when (*equivalent to* **nuair**)

an uair sin *adv phr* then, after that

a-nuas *adv* down (*from above*) *See also* **a-nìos**

an-uiridh *adv* last year

a-null *adv* over (*to the other side*)
  a-null 's a-nall hither and thither
a-nunn *adv See* **a-null**
aobhar *n See* **adhbhar**
aobrann *n See* **adhbrann**
aocoltach *a* -aiche unlike,
  unalike, dissimilar **glè a. ri
  chèile** very unlike one another
aodach *n* -aich/-aichean *m*
  clothes, cloth, material *pl*
  cloths of different kinds, clothes
  on a line **a.-leapa** bedclothes
  a.-oidhche night-clothes
aodann *n* -ainn *m* face (*human or
  geog*)
aodannan *n* -ain, -ain *m* false-
  face, mask
aodomhainn *a* -e shallow
aog *n* aoig *m* **an t-aog** death
aogas *n* -ais *m* face, appearance,
  countenance
aoibhinn *a* -e joyful, glad;
  pleasant
aoibhneach *a* -niche joyful,
  happy, glad; pleasant
aoidion *n* -a, -an *m* leak
aoidionach *a* -aiche leaky, leaking
aoigh *n* -ean *m* guest
aoigheachd *n f* hospitality **bha
  iad air a. againn** we had them as
  guests/they were our guests
aoigheil *a* -e hospitable; genial
aoir *n* -e, -ean *f* satire
aois *n* -e, -ean *f* age **dè an a. a tha
  i?** how old is she? **A. an Iarainn**
  the Iron Age
aol *n* aoil *m* lime
aom *v* -adh incline, bend **sna
  lathaichean a dh'aom** in days
  gone by
aomadh *n* -aidh *m* act of inclining
  or bending; inclination,
  tendency
aon *n* aoin *m* one (*of anything*)
  normally written a h-aon; each
  not an t-aon £1 each
aon *num a* one; only; same **sin an
  (t-)aon dath** that's the same
  colour *Also* **aona**
aonach *n* -aich, -aich *m* high or
  steep place, ridge **A. Eagach** the
  Serrated Ridge (in Glencoe)
aonach *n* -aich *f m* panting, state

of being out of breath **bha a.
orm** I was out of breath
aonachd *n f* unity
aonad *n* -aid, -an *m* unit
aonadh *n* -aidh, -aidhean *m*
  union, unity, merger **a. ciùird**
  (trade) union **an t-A. Eòrpach**
  the European Union
aonaich *v* -achadh unite,
  integrate, combine
aonaichte *a* united, integrated
aonan *n* -ain *m* one (*of
  anything*)
aonar *n* -air *m* one person; state
  of being alone **bha i na h-a.** she
  was alone *Also* **ònar**
aonaran *n* -ain, -ain *m* hermit,
  loner, recluse *Also* **ònaran**
aonar(an)ach *a* -aiche lonely,
  solitary
aonaranachd *n f* isolation,
  loneliness, solitude *Also*
  aonranas, ònrachd
aon-deug *n, a* eleven **aon duine
  deug** eleven men/persons
aon-ghuthach *a* -aiche
  unanimous
aonta *n* -n *m* agreement, assent,
  consent **cuir a. ri** *v* agree to,
  approve
aontachadh *n* -aidh *m* agreement,
  act of agreeing
aontaich *v* -achadh agree,
  consent
aontaichte *a* agreed
aoradh *n See* **adhradh**
aosta *a* old, elderly, aged
  Formerly **aosda**
aotraman *n* -ain, -ain *m* bladder
aotrom *a* -ruime light;
  light-hearted
aotromaich *v* -achadh lighten;
  alleviate
apa *n* -ichean *m* ape
aparan *n* -ain, -ain *m* apron
ar *poss pron* our **Ar n-Athair a tha
  air Nèamh** Our Father which art
  in Heaven
ar *def v* seems *in phr* **ar leam** it
  seems to me, I think
àr *n* àir *m* battle, battlefield,
  slaughter
ar-a-mach *n* rebellion, rising

A. nan Seumasach the Jacobite Rebellion/Rising
àra *n* **àrann, àirnean** *f* kidney
Arabach *n* **-aich, -aich** *m* Arab *a* Arabian, Arabic
àrachas *n* **-ais** *m* insurance
àrach *n* **-aich** *m* raising, upbringing, rearing
àradh *n* **-aidh, -aidhean** *m* ladder
àraich *v* **àrach** raise, bring up, rear
àraid(h) *a* **-e** certain, particular; odd, peculiar
Arainneach *n* **-nich, -nich** *m* someone from Arran *a* from, or pertaining to, Arran
àrainneachd *n* *f* environment
aran *n* **arain** *m* bread **a.-coirce** oat bread, oatcake **a.-cridhe** gingerbread
a-raoir *adv* last night
araon *adv* together, both **a. mise is tusa** both you and I
arbhar *n* **-air** *m* corn
àrc *n* **-a/àirce, -an** *f* cork, cork cap (*in bottle*)
Arcach *n* **-aich, -aich** *m* Orcadian *a* Orcadian
arc-eòlaiche *n* **-an** *m* archaeologist
arc-eòlas *n* **-ais** *m* archaeology
àrd *a* **àirde** high, tall; loud (*of sound*) *pref* principal, high, chief
àrd *n* See **àird(e)**
àrdachadh *n* **-aidh** *m* raising, increasing, elevation; promotion **fhuair sinn à. pàighidh** we got a pay rise
àrdaich *v* **-achadh** raise, increase, elevate; promote
àrdaichear *n* **-eir, -an** *m* lift
àrdan *n* **-ain** *m* pride, arrogance, haughtiness
àrdanach *a* **-aiche** proud, arrogant, haughty
àrd-chùirt *n* **-e, -ean** *f* high court
àrd-doras *n* **-ais** *m* lintel
àrd-easbaig *n* **-e, -ean** *m* archbishop
àrd-ghuthach *a* **-aiche** loud-voiced
àrd-ìre *n* **-an** *f* higher, higher grade/level **deuchainnean na h-Àrd Ìre** Higher exams **foghlam a.** *m* higher education
àrd-oifigear *n* **-eir, -an** *m* chief executive, senior officer
àrd-ollamh *n* **-aimh, -an** *m* professor
àrd-sgoil *n* **-e, -tean** *f* secondary school, high school
àrd-sheanadh *n* **-aidh, -aidhean** *m* general assembly (*eg of a Church*)
àrd-urram *n* **-aim, -an** *m* high honour, distinction; renown
àrd-ùrlar *n* **-air, -air** *m* stage, platform
a rèir *prep phr* (+ *gen*) according to **a. r. c(h)oltais** apparently
a-rèist(e) *adv* then, therefore, in that case
argamaid *n* **-e, -ean** *f* argument, dispute
argamaidich *v* **argamaid** argue
(a-)riamh *adv* ever, always
a-rithist *adv* again **an-dràsta 's a.** now and again, occasionally *Also* **a-rìs**
arm *n* **airm, airm** *m* army *Also* **armailt**
armachd *n* *f* arms, armour, weaponry
armaich *v* **-achadh** arm, equip with weapons
armaichte *a* armed
àrmann *n* **-ainn, -ainn** *m* hero, warrior
armlann *n* **-ainn, -an** *f* armoury, arsenal
ars *def v* said (**arsa** *before consonants*)
àrsaidh *a* **-e** ancient, antiquated
àrsair *n* **-ean** *m* antiquarian
àrsaidheachd *n* *f* quality of being ancient; antiquarianism; archaeology
artaigil *n* **-ean** *m* article
as *v rel form* of **is** (who/that) is **am fear as motha** the one that is biggest, the biggest one
as *prep* in *contraction of* **anns** *used in phrases* **as t-earrach, as t-samhradh, as t-fhoghar** in spring, in summer, in autumn

às *adv* out **chaidh an teine às** the fire went out **leig às e** let it go **rinn e às** he made off/ran for it/escaped **thàrr e às** he escaped

às *prep* out of

às(-san) *prep pron* from/out of him/it

asad(sa) *prep pron* out of you (*sg*)

asaibh(se) *prep pron* out of you (*pl & pol*)

asainn(e) *prep pron* out of us

asal *n* -ail, -ail *f m* ass, donkey **a.-stiallach** zebra *Also* **aiseal**

asam(sa) *prep pron* out of me

às aonais *prep phr* (+ *gen*) without, in the absence of

asbhuain *n f* stubble (*in field*)

às dèidh *prep phr* (+ *gen*) after, following *Also* **às deaghaidh**

às eugmhais *prep phr* (+ *gen*) without, lacking

asgaidh *n* -ean *f* gift *normally only used in phr* **an a.** free (*of charge*), for nothing

asgair *n* -ean *m* apostrophe

aslaich *v* -achadh supplicate, beseech

às leth *prep phr* (+ *gen*) on behalf of **rinn e sin às mo leth-sa** he did that on my behalf

asta(san) *prep pron* from/out of them

a-staigh *adv* in, inside; at home

astar *n* -air, -air/-an *m* distance; speed; journey **a. dheich mìle** a distance of ten miles **aig a.** at speed

a-steach *adv* in, into (*implying motion*) **thig a.** come in **chaidh iad a. dhan bhaile** they went into (the) town **cha tàinig e riamh a. orm** it never crossed my mind

Astràilianach *n* -aich, -aich *m* Australian *a* Australian

at *n* -an *m* swelling

at *v* at/-adh swell, puff up

ath *a* (+ *len*) (*preceded by def art*) next **an ath uair** the next time **an ath mhìos** next month

àth *n* -an *m* ford

àth *n* -a, -an *f* kiln; old barn/outhouse

ath- *pref* (+ *len*) re- **ath-aithris** *v*

repeat, reiterate **ath-chruthaich** *v* recreate

athair *n* athar, athraichean *m* father **a.-cèile** father-in-law **athraichean** forefathers

athaiseach *a* -siche dilatory, tardy

a thaobh *prep phr* (+ *gen*) concerning, regarding, on that account **na biodh dragh ort a th. sin** don't worry on that account

atharrachadh *n* -aidh, -aidhean/atharraichean *m* change, alteration **a. nan gràs** religious conversion **thàinig a. air** he changed

atharraich *v* -achadh change, alter **tha an t-àite air atharrachadh** the place has changed

atharrais *n f* imitation, mimicry **dèan a. air** *v* imitate

atharrais (+ **air**) *v* mimic, imitate **bha e ag a. orm** he was mimicking me

ath-bheothachadh *n* -aidh *m* revival, rejuvenation **Linn an Ath-Bheothachaidh** the Renaissance Period

ath-bheothaich *v* -achadh revive, rejuvenate, revitalize

ath-chruthaich *v* -achadh re-create

athchuinge *n* -an *f* entreaty, petition

ath-dhìol *v* -adh repay

ath-leasachadh *n* -aidh *m* reform, redevelopment, amendment **an t-A.** the Reformation

ath-leasaich *v* -achadh reform, redevelop, amend

ath-nuadhachadh *n* -aidh *m* renewal, renovation

ath-nuadhaich *v* -achadh renew, renovate, reinvigorate

àth-sgrìobh *v* -adh rewrite; transcribe

ath-sgrùdadh *n* -aidh, -aidhean *m* revision, review

a thuilleadh *prep phr* (+ **air**) in addition to, as well as

atmhorachd *n f* inflation **ìre na h-a.** inflation rate

B

b' *v part* shortened version of **bu**,
was (*used before vowels*)
bà-bà *n* soothing sound made to
child indicating sleep
bac *n* **baic/baca, -an** *m*
impediment, hindrance,
obstruction, restraint; rowlock;
bank
bac *v* **-adh** impede, hinder,
obstruct, restrain, prevent
bacach *n* **-aich, -aich** *m* lame
person, cripple
bacach *a* **-aiche** lame, crippled
bacadh *n* **-aidh, -aidhean** *m*
impediment, hindrance,
obstruction, restraint, delay,
handicap **cuir b. air** *v* obstruct,
hinder
bacan *n* **-ain, -ain** *m* stake, tether-
stake; crook, crooked staff;
hindrance **b.-dorais** hinge of a
door
bachall *n* **-aill, -aill/-an** *m* staff,
crozier
bachlach *a* **-aiche** curly, curled
bachlag *n* **-aig, -an** *f* curl, ringlet;
shoot (*of plant*)
bachlagach *a* **-aiche** curly, curled
bad *n* **baid, -an** *m* spot, place,
part, area; tuft, bunch, cluster;
clump, thicket **anns a' bhad** at
once, immediately
badan *n* **-ain, -anan/-ain** *m* a
small cluster or tuft, thicket;
nappy
badeigin *adv* somewhere
badhbh *n* **baidhbh, -an** *f* witch,
old hag
Badhlach *n* **-aich, -aich** *m*
someone from Benbecula
a from, or pertaining to,
Benbecula
baga *n* **-ichean/-nnan** *m* bag, case
bagaid *n* **-e, -ean** *f* cluster, bunch
bagair *v* **-t/bagradh** threaten,
menace
bagairt *n* **-e, -ean** *f* threat,
threatening
bagarrach *a* **-aiche** threatening,
ominous, menacing
bàgh *n* **bàigh, bàigh/-(ann)an** *m*

bay
bagradh *n* **-aidh, -aidhean** *m*
threat, threatening, menacing
baibheil *a* **-e** marvellous,
tremendous, terrific
baic *n* **-ichean** *m* bike, motorbike
bàidh *n* **-e** *f* kindness, affection,
tenderness
bàidheil *a* **-e** kind, affectionate,
friendly **b. ri** affectionate to,
well-disposed to
baidhsagal *n* **-ail, -an** *m* bicycle
baile *n* **bailtean** *m* town, village,
township **b. beag** village **b. mòr**
city **aig b.** at home
bailiùn *n* **-aichean** *m* balloon
bàillidh *n* **-ean** *m* factor; baillie,
magistrate
bainne *n* *m* milk **b. goirt** sour milk
baintighearna *n* **-n** *f* lady
bàirligeadh *n* **-gidh, -gidhean** *m*
summons of removal, eviction
order
bàirlinn *f* See **bàirligeadh**
bàirneach *n* **-nich, -nich** *f*
barnacle, limpet
baist *v* **-eadh** baptize
Baisteach *n* **-tich, -tich** *m* Baptist
a Baptist **an Eaglais Bhaisteach**
the Baptist Church
baisteadh *n* **-tidh, -tidhean** *m*
baptism, christening
bàl *n* **bàil, bàil/bàiltean** *m* ball,
dance
balach *n* **-aich, -aich** *m* boy, lad
bu tu am b.! well done, lad!
balachan *n* **-ain, -ain** *m* young
boy, young lad
balaist(e) *n* *f m* ballast
balbh *a* **-a/bailbhe** dumb, mute,
silent, quiet (*of weather*)
balbhachd *n* *f* dumbness,
muteness
balbhan *n* **-ain, -ain** *m* dumb
person, mute
balg *n* **builg, builg** *m* blister;
abdomen; leather bag **b.-sèididh**
bellows **b.-shaighead** quiver
balgair *n* **-e, -ean** *m* rogue, rotter,
scoundrel
balgam *n* **-aim, -(ann)an** *m*
mouthful (*of drink*), sip **b. tì** a
drop of tea

balgan-buachair *n* **balgain-b.,**
balgain-b. *m* mushroom
ball *n* **buill, buill** *m* member, limb
Ball Pàrlamaid, Buill Phàrlamaid
m Member of Parliament **B. P.**
na h-Alba Member of the
Scottish Parliament
ball *n* **buill, buill** *m* ball *Also*
bàl(l)a
balla *n* **-chan/-ichean** *m* wall,
rampart
ballach *a* **-aiche** spotted, speckled
ball-basgaid *n* **buill-, buill-** *m*
basketball
ball-coise *n* **buill-, buill-** *m*
football
ball-dòbhrain *n* **buill-** *m* mole (*on*
skin)
ball-lìn *n* **buill-, buill-** *m* netball
ball-maise *n* **buill-, buill-** *m*
accessory, ornament
ballrachd *n* *f* membership
ball-seirce *n* **buill-, buill-** *m*
beauty spot
ball-stèidhe *n* **buill-, buill-** *m*
baseball
bàn *a* **bàine** fair, fair-haired;
white, pale; vacant, fallow,
blank **talamh bàn** *m* fallow
ground **duilleag bhàn** *f* blank
sheet **eaglais bhàn** *f* vacant
charge (*relig*)
bàn- *pref* light, pale **bàn-dhearg**
light red
ban(a) *pref* used to give female
version of one's identity or
occupation, female, woman
ban-Albannach *f* Scotswoman
bana-chlèireach *f* clerkess
bana-bhuidseach *n* **-sich,**
-sichean *f* witch
banacharaid *n* **-ean** *f* female
friend, girlfriend
banachdach *n* **-aich** *f*
a' bhanachdach vaccination
bana-chliamhainn *n* **-chleamhna,**
-chleamhnan *f* daughter-in-law
banachrach *n* **-aich** *f*
a' bhanachrach smallpox
bànag *n* **-aig, -an** *f* grilse, sea
trout
bana-ghaisgeach *n* **-gich, -gich** *f*
heroine, female warrior

bana-ghoistidh *n* **-ean** *f*
godmother
banail *a* **-e/-ala** feminine,
womanly, modest
banais *n* **bainnse, bainnsean** *f*
wedding **bean na bainnse** *f* the
bride **fear na bainnse** *m* the
bridegroom
banaltram *n* **-aim, -an** *f* nurse
bana-mhaigh(i)stir-sgoile *n*
-mhaigh(i)stirean- *f* headmistress
bana-mhaigh(i)stir *n* **-ean** *f*
mistress (*figure of authority*)
banana *n* **-than** *m* banana
bana-phrionnsa *n* **-n** *f* princess
banas-taighe *n* *f* housekeeping;
home economics
banca *n* **-ichean** *m* bank (*fin*) **B.**
na h-Alba Bank of Scotland **B.**
Rìoghail na h-Alba Royal Bank
of Scotland **B. Dhail Chluaidh**
Clydesdale Bank
bancair *n* **-ean** *m* banker
bancaireachd *n* *f* banking
ban-diùc *n* **-an** *f* duchess
bangaid *n* **-ean** *f* banquet, feast
ban-iarla *n* **-n** *f* countess
bann *n* **-a, -an/-tan** *m* band, belt,
bandage; tie, hinge
bannal *n* **-ail, -an** *m* band, troupe,
group, panel (*of people*)
ban(n)trach *n* **-aich, -aichean** *f m*
widow, widower
ban-ogha *n* **-oghaichean/**
-oghachan *f* grand-daughter
banrigh *n* **-rean** *f* queen *Also* **ban-**
rìghinn
baobh *n* *See* **badhbh**
baoghalta *a* foolish, silly, idiotic
baoit *n* *f* bait
baoth *a* **baoithe** foolish, simple
(*of mind*)
bàr *n* **bàir, -aichean** *m* bar (*pub*)
bara *n* **-chan/-ichean** *m* barrow,
wheelbarrow
barail *n* **-e, -ean** *f* opinion **dè do**
bharail? what do you think?
baraille *n* **-ean** *m* barrel
barantaich *v* **-achadh** accredit
barantas *n* **-ais, -ais/-an** *m*
guarantee, authority, surety,
commission
bàrd *n* **bàird, bàird** *m* poet, bard

bàrdachd *n f* poetry
bargan *n* -ain, -ain/-an *f m* bargain
barganaich *v* -achadh bargain, make a deal
bàrr *n* barra, barran *m* top, surface, crest; cream **a bhàrr air** besides **thig am b.** *v* surface
Barrach *n* -aich, -aich *m* someone from Barra *a* from, or pertaining to, Barra
barrachd *n f* more **b. air** more than
barraichte *a* super, supreme, superlative, excellent
barraid *n* -e, -ean *f* terrace
barrall *n* -aill, -aillean *m* shoelace
bas *n* boise, -an *f* palm (*of hand*)
bàs *n* bàis, bàis *m* death **a' dol bàs** dying out
bàsaich *v* -achadh die
basgaid *n* -e, -ean *f* basket **b.-sgudail** waste-basket
bàsmhor *a* -a mortal
bàsmhorachd *n f* mortality
bata *n* -ichean *m* stick, staff
bàta *n* -ichean *m* boat **bàt'-aiseig** ferry **b.-cargu** cargo boat **bàt'-iasgaich** fishing boat **b.-sàbhalaidh** lifeboat **b.-siùil** sailing boat **b.-smùid** steamer, steamboat **b.-teasairginn** lifeboat **b.-tumaidh** submarine
batail *n* -ean *m* battle
bataraidh *n* -ean *f m* battery
bàth *v* -adh drown, extinguish, muffle (*sound*)
bàthach *n* bàthcha/-aich, bàthchannan/-aichean *f* byre, cowshed *Also* **bàthaich**
bàthadh *n* -aidh, -aidhean *m* drowning
bathais *n* -ean *f* forehead, brow
bathar *n* -air *m* goods, wares, merchandise **b. bog** software
bàthte *a* drowned
beachd *n* -a, -an *m* opinion, view, viewpoint; idea **dè do bheachd?** what do you think? **bha i a' dol às a b.** she was going crazy **gabh b. air** *v* consider
beachdaich *v* -achadh consider, think about, speculate, reflect

on
beachdail *a* -e reflective, meditative, observant
beachd-smaoinich/smuainich *v* -neachadh meditate, contemplate
beachd-smaoin/smuain *n* -tean *f* idea, theory
beachlann *n* -ainn, -annan *f* beehive
beadaidh *a* -e disrespectful, impudent, forward
beadradh *n* -aidh *m* flirting, fondling, caressing
beag *a* bige/lugha small, little, wee **b. air bheag** little by little **is b. orm ...** I dislike ...
beagaich *v* -achadh diminish, lessen **b. air** cut down on, reduce
beagan *adv* a little, a trifle, somewhat **b. tràth** a little early
beagan *n* -ain *m* a little, a few
beag-chuid *n* -chodach, -chodaichean *f* minority
beairt *n* -e, -ean *f* machine, equipment, engine **b.-fhighe** loom **b.-iasgaich** fishing tackle *Also* **beart**
beairteach *a* -tiche rich, wealthy *Also* **beartach**
beairteas *n* -eis *m* riches, wealth *Also* **beartas**
bealach *n* -aich, -aichean *m* mountain pass, way, gap
bealaidh *n* -ean *m* broom (*plant*)
Bealltainn *n* -e *f* May Day, first day of May, Beltane
bean *n* mnà/mnatha, mnathan *f* wife, woman *dat* mnaoi *gen pl* bhan **a mhnathan- 's a dhaoin' -uaisle!** ladies and gentlemen!
bean *v* -tainn (+ ri/do) touch, handle, meddle with
bean-bainnse *n f* bride **bean na bainnse** the bride
bean-ghlùine *n* mnà-glùine, mnathan-glùine *f* midwife
beannachadh *n* -aidh, -aidhean *m* blessing, benediction
beannachd *n* -an *f* blessing **b. leat** goodbye **mo bheannachd ort!** well done!

beannag *n* -aige, -an *f* shawl
beannaich *v* -achadh bless
beannaichte *a* blessed, religious
bean-phòsta *n* mnà-pòsta,
mnathan-pòsta *f* wife a' Bhean-
Phòsta (A' Bh) NicLeòid Mrs
MacLeod *Formerly* bean-phòsda
bean-sìthe *n* mnà-, mnathan- *f*
fairy *Also* bean-shìth
bean-taighe *n* mnà-, mnathan- *f*
housewife b. an taighe the lady
of the house
bean-teagaisg *n* mnà-, mnathan-
f teacher
bean-uasal *n* mnà-, mnathan- *f*
lady
beàrn *n* beàirn, -an *f m* gap,
space, hiatus, breach, cleft
beàrnan-brìde *n* beàrnain-,
beàrnain- *m* dandelion
Beàrnarach *n* -aich *m* someone
from Bernera(y) *a* from, or
pertaining to, Bernera(y)
beàrr *v* bearradh cut (*hair*),
shave, clip, shear, prune
bearradair *n* -ean *m* barber,
cutter
bearradaireachd *n f* sharp wit
bearradh *n* -aidh, -aidhean *m*
precipice, steep rockface;
shearing
beatha *n* -nnan *f* life 's e do
bheatha you're welcome
beathach *n* -aich, -aichean *m*
beast, animal b.-mara sea
mammal
beathachadh *n* -aidh, -aidhean *m*
living, sustenance, nourishment
beathadach *n* -aich *m* beaver
beathaich *v* -achadh feed,
nourish, sustain
beath-eachdraiche *n* -an *m*
biographer
beath-eachdraidh *n* (-e), -ean *f*
biography
bèibidh *n* -ean *m* baby
beic *n* -ean/-eannan *f* curtsy dèan
b. *v* curtsey
bèicear *n* -eir, -an *m* baker
bèicearachd *n f* baking
Beilgeach *n* -gich, -gich *m*
Belgian *a* Belgian
being *n* -e, -ean *f* bench

beinn *n* -e, beanntan *f* mountain,
ben
beinn-theine *n* -teine, beanntan-
teine *f* volcano
beir *irr v* breith/beireachdainn
bear, take, hold (*See irr v* beir *in
Grammar*) b. air catch (up with)
b. leanabh give birth to a child
b. ugh lay an egg
beirm *n* -e, -ean *f* yeast
beirmear *n* -an *m* enzyme
beithe *n* -an *f* birch, birch wood
craobh b. *f* birch tree
beithir *n* beathrach,
beathraichean *f m* thunderbolt
beò *a* beotha alive cha robh duine
b. ann there wasn't a soul there
beò *n m* lifetime rim bheò during
my life
beò-ghainmheach *n* -ghainmhich
f quicksand
beò-ghlacadh *n* -aidhean *m*
obsession
beòshlaint *n* -ean *f* livelihood,
living
beothachadh *n* -aidh *m*
animation, enlivening, kindling
beothaich *v* -achadh enliven,
animate, quicken, kindle, stir
beothail *a* -e/-ala lively, vital,
vivacious, animated
beothalachd *n f* liveliness,
vitality, animation
beuc *n* -an *m* roar, bellow
beuc *v* -adh/-ail roar, bellow
beud *n* -an *m* pity, shame; harm,
loss, damage is mòr am b.! what
a pity!
beugaileid *n* -ean *f* bayonet *Also*
bèigneid
beul *n* beòil, beòil *m* mouth,
opening dùin do bheul! be quiet!
b. an latha daybreak, dawn
b. na h-oidhche twilight, dusk
droch bheul verbal abuse air a
b(h)eul fodha face down
beulach *a* -aiche talkative,
plausible
beulaibh *n m* front (part) air b.
(+ *gen*) in front of
beul-aithris *n* beòil-, -aithrisean *f*
oral tradition, folklore
beum *n* -a, -an/-annan *m* blow,

stroke; reproach

beurla *n f* speech, language **Beurla** English **B. Ghallda** Scots (*lang*) **B. Shasannach** English

beus *n* -a, -an *f* virtue, conduct

beus *n* -a, -an *f* bass, bass (*instrument*)

beus *a* -a/bèise bass (*mus*)

beusach *a* -aiche virtuous, moral

beusail *a* -e/-ala ethical

beusalachd *n f* moral behaviour, ethics

bha *irr v* was, were (*See verb* **to be** *in Grammar*)

bhan *n* -aichean *f* van

bhàn *adv See* **a-bhàn**

bhàrr *prep* (+ *gen*) from, from off, down from

bhàsa *n* -ichean *f* vase

bhathar/bhathas *irr v* was, were (*passive form*) (*See verb* **to be** *in Grammar*)

bheat *n* -a, -aichean *m* veterinary surgeon

bheil *irr v* am? is? are? (*See verb* **to be** *in Grammar*)

bheir *irr v* will give, will bring, will take (*See irr v* **thoir** *in Grammar*)

bhidio *n* -than *f* video

bhiodh *irr v* would be (*See verb* **to be** *in Grammar*)

bhith *irr v See* **a bhith**

bhitheadh *irr v* would be (*See verb* **to be** *in Grammar*)

bho *conj* since

bho *prep* from

bho chionn *prep phr* since, ago (*equivalent to* **o chionn**) **b. c. mìos** a month ago **b. c. ghoirid** recently, a short time ago

bhod *aug prep* from your (*sg*)

b(h)olcàno *n* -than *m* volcano

bhom *aug prep* from my; from their

bhon *aug prep* from the; from their

bhon (a) *conj* since

bhor *aug prep* from our, from your

bhos *adv See* **a-bhos**

bhòt *n* -a, -aichean *f* vote

bhòt *v* -adh vote

bhòtadh *n* -aidh *m* voting, poll

bhuaibh(se) *prep pron* from you (*pl & pol*)

bhuainn(e) *prep pron* from us

bhuaipe(se) *prep pron* from her; from it

bhuaithe(san) *prep pron*; from him; from it *adv* **chaidh e bhuaithe** he/it deteriorated

bhuam(sa) *prep pron* from me

bhuapa(san) *prep pron* from them

bhuat(sa) *prep pron* from you (*sg*)

bhur *poss pron* your (*pl & pol*)

bi *irr v* be (*See verb* **to be** *in Grammar*)

biadh *n* bìdh, -an *m* food, meal

biadhlann *n* -ainne, -an *f* canteen, refectory, dining-hall

bian *n* bèin, bèin *m* hide, skin (*of animals*), pelt; fur

biast *n* bèiste, -an *f* beast; wretch

biastag *n* -aig, -an *f* beastie; insect

biast-dhubh *n* bèiste-duibhe, biastan-dubha *f* otter *Also* **biast-dubh**

biath *v* -adh feed

biathadh *n* -aidh *m* feeding; bait

bìd *n* -e, -ean *m* bite; cheep

bìd *v* -eadh bite

bìdeadh *n* -didh *m* biting, bite

bìdeag *n* -eig, -an *f* a little bit, morsel

bidean *n* -ein, -an *m* pinnacle

bidh *irr v* will be (*See verb* **to be** *in Grammar*)

bidse *n* -achan *f* bitch (*person*)

bigein *n* -ean *m* rock-pipit, any little bird; (*colloq*) willie (*penis*)

bile *n* -an *f* lip, rim, blade (*of grass etc*)

bile *n* -an *m* bill (*parliamentary*)

bileag *n* -eig(e), -an *f* little blade (*of grass etc*); label; leaflet

bile-bhuidhe *n* -buidhe, bilean-buidhe *f* marigold

binid *n* -e *f* rennet

binn *n* -e *f* judgement, sentence (*of court*), verdict

binn *a* -e melodious, harmonious, musical, sweet

binndich *v* -deachadh curdle, coagulate

binnean *n* -ein, -an *m* pinnacle, highest point, apex, high conical hill

binneas *n* -eis *m* melody, sweetness

Bìoball *n* -aill, -aill *m* Bible *Also* **Bìobla**

bìodach *a* -aiche minute, tiny

biodag *n* -aig(e), -an *f* dagger, dirk

biodh *irr v* would be (*See verb* **to be** *in Grammar*)

bìog *n* -a, -an *f* chirp, squeak, cheep

bìog *v* -ail chirp, squeak

bìogail *n f* chirping, squeaking

biolair *n* -ean *f* cress, water-cress

biona *n* -ichean *f m* bin

biona-sgudail *n f m* rubbish bin

bior *n* -a, -an *m* prickle; knitting needle

biorach *n* -aich, -aichean *f* dogfish

biorach *a* -aiche sharp, prickly

bioraich *v* -achadh sharpen, make pointed

bioran *n* -ain, -ain/-an *m* stick, kindler

biorgadh *n* -aidh, -aidhean *m* twitch, tingle, sensation of pain

biotais *n m* beet, beetroot

birlinn *n* -e, -ean *f* galley (*ship*)

bith *n* -e, -ean *f* life, being, existence **nì air b.** anything **às b.** whoever, whatever, wherever **sam b.** any **a' dol à b.** going out of existence

bìth *n* -e *f* gum, resin; bitumen, pitch

bith-beò *n f m* livelihood

bith-bhuan *a* -bhuaine eternal, everlasting *Also* **biothbhuan**

bith-bhuantachd *n f* eternity *Also* **biothbhuantachd**

bith-cheimigeachd *n f* biochemistry

bith-cheimigear *n* -eir, -an *m* biochemist

bitheadh *irr v* would be (*See verb* **to be** *in Grammar*)

bitheag *n* -eige, -an *f* microbe, germ

bitheanta *a* often, common, frequent **gu b.** often, regularly

bitheantas *n* -ais *m* frequency, generality, normality **am b.** generally, normally

bithear *irr v* am, is, are, will be (*passive form*) (*See verb* **to be** *in Grammar*)

bith-eòlas *n* -ais *m* biology

bith-eòlasach *a* biological

bithibh *irr v* be (*pl & pol command*) **b. sàmhach!** be quiet! (*See verb* **to be** *in Grammar*)

biùg *n m* sound; faint light

biùgan *n* -ain, -ain/-anan *m* torch, faint light

biùro *n* -than *m* bureau

biurocrasaidh *n* -ean *m* bureaucracy

blaigeard *n* -eird, -an *m* brat, blackguard, scoundrel *Also* **bleigeard**

blais *v* **blasad(h)** taste

blàr *n* **blàir**, -an *m* battle; plain, sward **cuir b.** *v* fight a battle

blas *n* **blais** *m* taste, flavour; accent

blasad *n* -aid *m* taste, tasting, bite **b. bìdh** a taste/bite of food

blasaich *v* -achadh add flavour to

blasta *a* tasty, savoury, delicious *Formerly* **blasda**

blàth *a* **blàithe** warm

blàth *n* **blàith**, -an *m* blossom, bloom **fo bhlàth** in bloom

blàthach *n* -aich *f* buttermilk

blàthaich *v* -achadh warm

blàths *n* **blàiths** *m* warmth

bleideag *n* -eig(e), -an *f* flake **bleideagan sneachda** snowflakes **bleideagan coirce** cornflakes

bleith *v* grind

bleoghain(n) *v* -an(n) milk

bliadhna *n* -chan/-ichean *f* year **am-b.** this year **a' Bhliadhn' Ùr** New Year **B. Mhath Ùr!** Happy New Year!

bliadhnail *a* annual, yearly **coinneamh bhliadhnail** *f* annual meeting

blian *a* -a insipid

blian *v* **-adh** sunbathe, bask in sun

blobhsa *n* **-ichean** *f m* blouse

bloc *n* **-a, -aichean** *m* block

bloigh *n* **-e, -ean** *f* fragment, scrap (of); incomplete state **dh'fhàg sibh e na bhloigh** you left it half-finished **rinn mi b. èisteachd ris** I half-listened to it

bloinigean-gàrraidh *n* **bloinigein-** *m* spinach

blonag *n* **-aig, -an** *f* lard *Also* **blonaig**

bò *n* **bà, bà** *f* cow *dat* **boin** *gen pl* **bò b. bhainne** milking cow, milch-cow

boban *n* **-ain, -ain/-an** *m* bobbin

bobhla *n* **-ichean** *m* bowl

bobhstair *n* **-ean** *m* bolster, mattress *Also* **babhstair**

boc *n* **buic, buic** *m* buck **boc-earba** roebuck

boc *v* **-adh/-ail** leap, skip

bòc *v* **-adh** swell, bloat, inflate

bocadaich *n* **-e** *f* leaping, skipping

bòcadh *n* **-aidh, -aidhean** *m* swelling, eruption

bòcan *n* **-ain, -ain** *m* hobgoblin, spectre, apparition, ghost

bochd *n* **-a** *m* poor person **na bochda** the poor *a* **-a** poor, wretched, ill

bochdainn *n* **-e** *f* poverty; ill-health

bod *n* **boid/buid, boid/buid** *m* penis

bodach *n* **-aich, -aich** *m* old man **b.-feannaig** scarecrow **b.-ruadh** cod **b.-sneachda** snowman **B. na Nollaig** Santa Claus

bodha *n* **-chan/-ichean** *m* submerged rock, reef

bodhaig *n* **-e, -ean** *f* body

bodhair *v* **bòdhradh** deafen

bodhar *n* **-air, -air** *m* deaf person

bodhar *a* **buidhre** deaf

bòdhradh *n* **-aidh** *m* deafening; boring

bòdhran *n* **-ain, -ain/-an** *m* bodhran (*drum*)

bodraig *v* **-eadh** bother **na b.** don't bother

bog *v* **-adh** dip, immerse, soak, steep

bog *a* **buige** soft, boggy, moist, damp (*of weather*) **b. fliuch** sodden, soaking wet

bogadaich *n* bobbing

bogadh *n* **-aidh** *m* dipping, immersing, steeping; bobbing

bogaich *v* **-achadh** soften, moisten; mellow

bog-chridheach *a* soft-hearted

bogha *n* **-chan** *m* bow; bulge

bogha-frois *n* **-froise, boghachan-** *m* rainbow

bog(l)ach *n* **-aich, -aichean** *f* bog, swamp, quagmire, marsh

bogsa *n* **-ichean** *m* box; accordion **b.-ciùil** acordion **b.-fòn** phone box **b.-litrichean** letter-box **b.-mhaidseachan** matchbox *Also* **bocsa**

bogsadh *n* **-aidh** *m* boxing *Also* **bocsadh**

bogsaig *v* **-eadh** box (*fight*) *Also* **bocsaig**

bogsaigeadh *n* **-gidh** *m* boxing *Also* **bocsaigeadh**

bogsair *n* **-ean** *m* boxer *Also* **bocsair**

bòid *n* **-e, -ean** *f* vow, oath

Bòideach *n* **-dich, -dich** *m* someone from Bute *a* from, or pertaining to, Bute

bòidhchead *n* **-chid** *f* beauty, comeliness

bòidheach *a* **bòidhche** beautiful, pretty, bonny

bòidich *v* **-deachadh** vow, swear

boil(e) *n* **-e** *f* frenzy, rage, madness **air bhoil(e)** in a frenzy

bòilich *n* *f* bawling, idle talk

boillsg *n* **-e, -ean** *m* gleam, shine, flash

boillsg *v* **-eadh** gleam, shine, flash

boillsgeach *a* **-giche** gleaming, shining

boillsgeadh *n* **-gidh, -gidhean** *m* gleam, shine, flashing

boineid *n* *See* **bonaid**

boinne *n* **-an/-achan** *f* drop (*of liquid*)

boinneag *n* **-eige, -an** *f* little drop (*of liquid*)

boireann *a* female, feminine (*gram*)
boireannach *n* -aich, -aich *m*
  woman
boireannta *a* effeminate; feminine
  (*gram*)
bois *n* -e, -ean *f* palm (*of hand*)
boiseag *n* -eige, -an *f* palmful,
  handful; slap **cuir b. air
  d' aodann** *v* wash your face
  quickly
boiteag *n* -eig, -an *f* worm *Also*
  baoiteag
boladh *n* -aidh, -aidhean *m* scent,
  smell
bolt *n* -a, -aichean *m* bolt, roll of
  wallpaper
boltaig *v* -eadh wallpaper
boltaigeadh *n* -gidh *m*
  wallpapering
boltrach *n* -aich, -aich *m* scent,
  fragrance
boma *n* -ichean *m* bomb
bonaid *n* -e, -ean *f m* bonnet
bonn *n* buinn, buinn *m* base,
  bottom, foundation; sole (*of
  foot*); coin, medal **b. airgid**
  silver coin, silver medal
  b.-cuimhne medal, medallion
  b.-dubh heel **b. òir** gold medal
bonnach *n* -aich, -aich *m*
  bannock, small cake
borb *a* **buirbe** fierce, barbaric,
  savage
borbair *n* -ean *m* barber, gents'
  hairdresser
bòrd *n* **bùird, bùird** *m* table,
  board **air b.** aboard **b. bàta** boat
  deck **b.-dubh** blackboard
  b.-geal whiteboard **b.-iarnaigidh**
  ironing table **b. locha** bank of
  loch **b.-sgeadachaidh** dressing
  table **b.-sgrìobhaidh** writing
  table, bureau **b.-stiùiridh** board
  of directors
bòst *n* -a, -an *m* boast *Formerly*
  bòsd
bòst *v* -adh boast *Formerly* **bòsd**
bòstail *a* -e boastful *Formerly*
  bòsdail
bòstair *n* -ean *m* boaster
  Formerly **bòsdair**
botal *n* -ail, -ail *m* bottle **b.-teth**
  hot-water bottle

bòtann *n* -ainn, -an *f m* boots,
  wellington boots
bothag *n* -aig, -an *f* bothy, small
  hut; hovel
brà *n* -than *f* quern
bracaist *n* -e, -ean *f* breakfast
  leabaidh is b. bed and breakfast
brach *v* -adh ferment, malt
brachadh *n* -aidh *m* fermenting,
  malting
bradan *n* -ain, -ain *m* salmon
brag *n* **braig,** -an *m* crack
  (*sound*), bang; report (*of gun*)
bragadaich *n m* crackling
  (*sound*), banging; gunfire
bragail *n f* crackling (*sound*),
  banging
bragail *a* -e cocky, self-confident
braich *n* -e *f* malt, fermented grain
braidhm *n* **brama, bramannan** *m*
  fart **leig b.** *v* break wind
braidseal *n* -eil, -an *m* roaring
  fire
bràigh *n* -e/**bràghad,** -eachan *m*
  brae, upper part; chest (*person*)
bràigh *n* -e, -dean *f m* hostage,
  captive
braighdeanas *n* -ais *m* captivity,
  bondage, confinement
bràiste *n* -an *f* brooch
bràmair *n* -ar, -ean *m* lover,
  boyfriend, girlfriend
branndaidh *n f* brandy
braoisg *n* -e, -ean *f* grin
braoisgeil *n f* grinning; giggling
braon *n* **braoin, braoin** *m* drop (*of
  liquid*)
bras *a* **braise** rash, impetuous,
  hasty
bras-shruth *n* -an *m* torrent
brat *n* -a, -an *m* cover, sheet,
  mantle **b.-làir/b.-ùrlair** carpet,
  rug, mat
bratach *n* -aich, -aichean *f* flag,
  banner
bratag *n* -aig, -an *f* caterpillar
brath *n* -a, -an *m* information,
  notice, message **b. naidheachd**
  press statement/release **cò aige
  tha b.?** who knows?
brath *v* -adh betray, inform on
brathadair *n* -ean *m* betrayer,
  informer

brathadh *n* -aidh *m* betraying, betrayal, treason

bràthair *n* -ar, bràithrean *m* brother **b.**-athar uncle (*father's brother*) **b.**-cèile brother-in-law **b.**-màthar uncle (*mother's brother*)

breab *n* -a, -an *f m* kick

breab *v* -adh kick, stamp

breabadair *n* -ean *m* weaver; daddy-longlegs

breac *n* brice *f* a' bhreac pox, smallpox

breac *n* bric, bric *m* trout; salmon (*in some dialects*)

breac *a* brice speckled, spotted, brindled

breacadh-seunain *n* breacaidh- *m* freckles *Also* breac-sheunain *f*

breacag *n* -aig, -an *f* scone, bannock, pancake

breacan *n* -ain, -ain/an *m* plaid, tartan

breacan-beithe *n* breacain-, breacain- *m* linnet, chaffinch

breac an t-sìl *n* bric-, bric- *m* wagtail

breac-bhallach *a* -bhallaiche freckled

breac-òtraich *n* bric- *f* a' bhreac-òtraich chickenpox

brèagha *a* beautiful, fine, lovely

Breatannach *n* -aich, -aich *m* Briton *a* British

brèid *n* -e, -ean *m* patch, kerchief

brèig *n* -e, -ean *f* brake (*as in car*)

breige *n* -gichean/-geachan *f* brick

brèige *a* false, deceiving, artificial

breisleach *n* -lich *f m* confusion, delirium ann am breislich in a state, delirious

breisleachail *a* confused, delirious

breislich *v* -leachadh rave, confuse

breith *n* *f* birth co-là-b. birthday

breith *v* bear, catch (*See irr v* beir *in Grammar*) **b.** air catch hold of

breith *n* *f* judgement, sentence, verdict thoir b. *v* pass judgement, give a verdict

breitheamh *n* *See* britheamh

breitheanas *n* -ais, -an *m* judgement thig b. ort *v* you'll suffer for it

breithneachadh *n* -aidh *m* judging, consideration

breithnich *v* -neachadh judge, consider

breòite *a* infirm, frail, sickly

breòiteachd *n* *f* infirmity, frailty

breoth *v* -adh rot, putrefy

breug *n* brèige, -an *f* lie, untruth

breug *v* -adh entice, coax, cajole

breugach *a* -aiche lying, dishonest, deceitful, false

breugaire *n* -an *m* liar

breugnaich *v* -achadh falsify; refute, rebut

breun *a* brèine putrid, stinking, nasty

briathar *n* -air, -thran *m* word, saying, term

briathrach *a* -aiche wordy, talkative, loquacious, verbose

briathrachas *n* -ais *m* terminology

brìb *n* -e, -ean/-eachan *f* bribe

brìb *v* -eadh bribe

brìbearachd *n* *f* bribery

brìgh *n* -ean *f* meaning; substance, essence; pith, juice do bhrìgh *conj* because (of)

briod *n* -a, -an/-aichean *m* breed, type

briod *v* -achadh/-adh breed

brìodal *n* -ail *m* expressions of endearment; flattery, lover's talk

briogais *n* -ean *f* trousers, breeches **b.**-snàimh swimsuit

brìoghmhor *a* -a meaningful; energetic, substantial, substantive; sappy, pithy

briosgaid *n* -e, -ean *f* biscuit

bris(t) *v* -(t)eadh break, smash

bris(t)eadh *n* -(t)idh *m* breaking, smashing, break, breach **b.** an latha daybreak **b.**-cridhe heartbreak **b.**-dùil disappointment

brisg *a* -e brittle, crisp

brisgean *n* -ein, -an *m* crisp; silverweed; gristle **brisgein** crisps

briste *past part* broken
britheamh *n* -eimh, -an *m* judge, adjudicator, umpire
broc *n* **bruic, bruic** *m* badger
brochan *n* -ain *m* gruel, porridge; hotch-potch **dèan b. de** *v* make a mess of
brod *n* **bruid, -an** *m* goad, prickle; the best of anything **brod na sìde** excellent weather
brod *v* -adh goad, poke; stimulate, spur
brodaich *v* -achadh stimulate, kindle
bròg *n* **bròige, -an** *f* shoe, boot **brògan-cleasachd** sports shoes, trainers **b. na cuthaig** pansy **brògan-spèilidh** skates
broidse *n* -sichean *m* brooch
broilleach *n* -lich, -lichean *m* breast, bosom, chest
bròinean *n* -ein *m* poor soul (*male*)
broinn *n* -e *f* belly **am b.** inside, within
bròn *n* **bròin** *m* sorrow, grief, sadness **fo bhròn** sad, sorrowful
brònach *a* -aiche sad, sorrowful, mournful
bhrònag *n* -aig *f* poor soul (*female*)
brosgal *n* -ail *m* flattery
brosnachadh *n* -aidh *m* encouragement, inspiration
brosnachail *a* -e encouraging, inspiring
brosnaich *v* -achadh encourage, inspire, spur, provoke
brot *n* -a, -an *m* broth, soup
broth *n* -a, -an *m* rash
brù *n* **broinne/bronn, brùthan** (*dat* **broinn**) *f* belly, womb
bruach *n* -aich(e), -aichean/-an *f* bank (*of river*), edge
bruadair *v* -ar dream
bruadar *n* -air, -an *m* dream
bruaillean *n* -ein *m* trouble, confusion
brùchd *v* -adh belch **b. a-mach** break out
brùchd *n* -a, -an *m* belch
brù-dhearg *n* **brùthan-dearga** *m* robin (redbreast)

bruich *v* boil, cook
bruich *a* -e boiled, cooked
bruid *n* -e, -ean *f* captivity
brùid *n* -e, -ean *f m* brute, beast
brùidealachd *n* *f* brutality
brùideil *a* -e brutal
bruidhinn *n* **bruidhne** *f* talk, conversation
bruidhinn *v* talk, speak, say **b. ri** talk/speak to
bruis *n* -e, -ean/-eachan *f* brush **b.-chinn/fuilt** hairbrush **b.-fhiaclan** toothbrush **b.-pheant** paintbrush
bruis(ig) *v* -eadh brush, sweep
brùite *a* bruised, oppressed
brùth *v* -adh bruise; press, push
bruthach *n* -aich, -aichean *f m* hillside, slope, brae **le b.** downhill **ri b.** uphill
bruthainn *n* -e *f* sultriness, sultry heat
bruthainneach *a* sultry
bu *v* was, were (*See verb* **to be** *in Grammar*)
buabhall *n* -aill *m* buffalo, unicorn
buachaille *n* -an *m* herdsman, cowherd, shepherd
buachailleachd *n* *f* herding
buachaillich *v* -leachd herd, tend cattle
buachar *n* -air *m* dung
buadh *n* **buaidh, -an/annan** *f* quality, property, attribute, virtue, talent
buadhach *a* -aiche victorious; talented; influential
buadhaich *v* -achadh win, triumph
buadhair *n* -ean *m* adjective
buadhmhor *a* -oire victorious; talented; influential
buaic *n* -e, -ean *f* wick
buaidh *n* -e, -ean *f* success, victory, sway, influence, effect, impact **fo bhuaidh** under the influence of **thoir b. air** *v* affect
buail *v* **bualadh** hit, strike, beat, thresh, crash into
buaile *n* -ltean *f* fold (*for animals*); circle, ring
buailteach *a* -tiche liable (to), apt

(to), inclined (to), susceptible (to)

buain *n* **buana** *f* harvest, reaping, cutting **b. mhòna** peat cutting

buain *v* reap, cut (*eg hay*), harvest

buair *v* **-eadh** tempt, lure, worry, trouble

buaireadh *n* **-ridh, -ridhean** *m* temptation, trouble

buaireas *n* **-eis, -an** *m* turbulence, trouble

buaireasach *a* **-aiche** turbulent, stormy, troublesome

bualadh *n* **-aidh** *m* hitting, striking, beating, threshing **b. bhasan** clapping, applause

buamastair *n* **-ean** *m* boor, blockhead, oaf

buan *a* **buaine** lasting, enduring

buannachd *n* **-an** *f* profit, gain, advantage

buannachdail *a* **-e** profitable, advantageous

buannaich *v* **-achadh** win, gain

buar *n* **-buair** *m* herd of cattle

buarach *n* **-aich, -aichean** *f* cow-fetter

bucaid *n* **-e, -ean** *f* bucket

bucall *n* **-aill** *m* buckle

bucas *n* **-ais, -ais** *m* box

bugair *n* **-ean** *m* bugger

buideal *n* **-eil** *m* bottle, flask, cask

buidhe *a* yellow **nach b. dhut!** aren't you lucky!

buidhe *pref* yellow-tinted **b.-ruadh** auburn

buidheach *a* **-iche** satisfied, grateful, thankful

buidheach *n* **-dhich** *f* **a' bhuidheach** jaundice

buidheachas *n* **-ais** *m* gratitude, thanks, thanksgiving

buidheag *n* **-eig, -an** *f* goldfinch

buidheagan *n* **-ain, -ain** *m* egg-yolk

buidheann *n* **buidhne/-dhinn, buidhnean** *f m* group, band, organization, agency **b.-ciùil** band **b.-obrach** working party

buidhinn *v* win, gain

buidhre *n* *f* deafness

buidseach *n* **-sich, -sichean/** **-seachan** *f m* wizard

bana-bhuidseach *f* witch

buidseachd *n* *f* witchcraft

bùidsear *n* **-eir, -an** *m* butcher

buidseat *n* **-eit, -an** *m* budget

buidsidh *n* **-ean** *m* budgie

buil *n* **-e, -ean** *f* effect, consequence, outcome, impact **thoir gu b.** *v* bring into effect, carry out, complete **bidh a' bhuil ann!** you'll see what will happen!

buileach *a* complete, absolutely, fully **nas miosa b.** worse still **gu b.** completely, entirely **chan eil e b. deiseil** it is not quite ready

buileann *n* **-linn, -an** *f* loaf

builgean *n* **-ein, -an** *m* bubble, blister

builgeanach *a* bubbly, blistered

builich *v* **-leachadh** bestow, grant

buille *n* **-an** *f* blow, hit, strike; emphasis, stress; beat (*mus*) **b.-cinn** header (*in football*)

buin *v* **buntainn/buntail** belong to **b. do** belong to; concern **b. ri** apply (to)

buinneach *n* **-eich** *f* **a' bhuinneach** diarrhoea

buinneag Bhruisealach *n* **buinneig Bruisealaich, buinneagan Bruisealach** *f* Brussels sprout

buinnig *v* **-eadh** win

buinteanas *n* **-ais** *m* relationship, connection

bùirean *n* **-ein, -ein/-an** *m* roar, bellow

bùirich *n* **-e, -ean** *f* roaring, bellowing *Also* **bùireanaich**

Bulgàirianach *n* **-aich** *m* Bulgarian *a* Bulgarian

bumailear *n* **-eir, -an** *m* boor, oaf, bungler

bumpair *n* **-ean** *m* bumper

bun *n* **-a/buin, -an/buin** *m* base, bottom, stump; root; mouth (*of river*) **b.-craoibhe** stump of tree

bunait *n* **-e, -ean** *f m* foundation, base, basis

bunaiteach *a* **-tiche** fundamental, basic

bunasach *a* **-aiche** original, fundamental

bun-bheachd *n* -a, -an *m*
concept, notion
bun-os-cionn *adv* upside-down,
topsy-turvy **cuir b.** *v* turn upside
down
bun-reachd *n* -a, -an *m*
constitution (*of org*)
bun-sgoil *n* -e, -tean *f* primary
school
bun-stèidh *n* buin-, buin- *m* basis,
constitution (*of org*)
buntainneach *a* -niche relevant
buntanas *n See* **buinteanas**
buntàta *n m* potato, potatoes
(*sg & pl*)
bùrach *n* -aich *m* mess, guddle,
shambles **abair b.!** what a
shambles!
bùrn *n* bùirn *m* water
burraidh *n* -ean *m* boor, oaf;
bully
burraidheachd *n f* bullying
burras *n* -ais, -ais *m* caterpillar
bùrt *v* mock, scoff, ridicule **bha e
gam bhùrt às** he was ridiculing
me
bus *n* -aichean *m* bus
bus *n* buis, -an/buis *m* mouth,
lip, snout, cheek **bha b. air** he
was sullen
busach *a* -aiche sullen, glum
butarrais *n f* hotch-potch **dèan b.
de** *v* make a mess of
bùth *n* -a, -an/bùith(t)ean *f* shop,
booth **b.-èisg** fish shop
b.-leabhraichean bookshop
buthaid *n* -e, -ean *f* puffin

C

cab *n* caib, -an *m* mouth (*colloq*)
dùin do chab! shut your trap!
cabach *a* -aiche talkative (*often
of a small child*), garrulous;
gap-toothed
cabadaich *n f* blethering,
chattering
càball *n* -aill, -aill *m* cable
cabar *n* -air, -air/-an *m* rafter; any
large piece of wood, eg caber
(*for tossing*); deer's antler **fo mo
chabair-sa** under my roof
cabhag *n* -aig *f* hurry, haste **a**

bheil c. ort? are you in a hurry?
dèan c.! *v* hurry! *Also* **cabhaig**
cabhagach *a* -aiche hurried,
hasty; impatient
cabhlach *n* -aich, -aich/-aichean
m fleet **an C. Rìoghail** the Royal
Navy
cabhsair *n* -ean *m* pavement,
sidewalk; causeway
cac *n* cac(a) *m* excrement, (*vulg*)
crap, shit
cac *v* cac/-adh excrete, defecate
caca *a* rotten, nasty
càch *pron* chàich (*of people*) the
rest, the others
cachaileith *n* -ean *f* gate, entrance
cadal *n* -ail, -ail/-an *m* sleep **tha an
c. orm** I'm sleepy **a bheil iad nan
c.?** are they asleep?
c.-deilgneach pins and needles
cadalach *a* -aiche sleepy
cafaidh *n* -ean *f m* cafe
cagailt(e) *n* (-e), -(e)an *f* hearth
cagainn *v* cagnadh chew, gnaw
cagair *v* -arsaich whisper
cagar *n* -air, -airean *m* whisper;
secret **a chagair** my darling **cuir
c. na chluais** whisper in his ear
caibeal *n* -eil, -eil/-an *m* chapel;
family burial area
caibideil *n* -ean *f m* chapter
caidil *v* cadal sleep
caidreachas *n* -ais, -an *m*
alliance, federation;
companionship
càil *n* -e, -ean *f* appetite,
disposition, desire; appearance;
anything **chan eil e a' tighinn
rim chàil** it doesn't appeal to me
c. an latha the first appearance
of day **chan eil c. ann** there's
nothing there **bheil c. às ùr?** is
there anything new/any news?
cailc *n* -e , -ean *f* chalk, piece of
chalk
caileag *n* -eig, -an *f* girl, lass,
young woman
càilear *a* -eire attractive, pleasing
cailin *n* -ean *f* maiden, young
woman
caill *v* call lose
cailleach *n* -lich(e), -an *f* old
woman **c.-dhubh** nun

c.-oidhche owl

càin *n* -e, -tean *f* fine **chaidh c. air** he was fined

càin *v* -eadh scold, criticize, denounce

cainb *n* -e *f* hemp, cannabis (*plant*)

càineadh *n* -nidh *m* criticism

caineal *n* -eil *m* cinnamon

cainnt *n* -e, -ean *f* speech, conversation, language **droch c(h)ainnt** bad language, swearing

caiptean *n* -ein, -an *m* captain, skipper, ship's master

cairbh *n* -e, -ean *f* carcase, corpse

càirdeach *a* -diche related (to) **tha i c. dhomh** she is related to me

càirdeas *n* -eis *m* kinship, relationship; friendship **tha c. fad' às eadarainn** we are distantly related **cha do mhair an c.** the friendship did not last

càirdeil *a* -e friendly

càirean *n* -ein, -an *m* palate

càirich *v* càradh repair, mend, arrange; place, lay **a' càradh na leapa** making the bed **c. an sin e** put it down there

cairt *n* -e, -ean *f* card; chart **c.-creideis** credit card **c.-iùil** chart **c. Nollaig** Christmas card **c.-p(h)uist** postcard

cairt *n* -e/cartach, -ean *f* cart

cairteal *n* -eil, -an/-eil *m* quarter **c. na h-uarach** quarter of an hour

caisbheart *n* -eirt *f* footwear

càis(e) *n* -an *f m* cheese

Càisg *n* -e *f* **a' Chàisg** Easter

caisg *v* casg/casgadh check, stop, proscribe

caismeachd *n* -an *f* march (*mus*), martial song; alarm

caisteal *n* -eil, -an/-eil *m* castle

càit(e) *int pron, adv* where **c. a bheil thu?** where are you? **chan eil fhios aca c. a bheil i** they don't know where she is

caith *v* -eamh/caith spend, use up; wear; throw

caitheamh *n* -eimh *f m* spending,

using up **a' chaitheamh** consumption, tuberculosis **c.-beatha** way of life, behaviour

caithris *v* watch at night, keep a vigil

caithriseach *a* watchful, vigilant; sleepless

Caitligeach *n* -gich, -gich *m* Catholic, Roman Catholic *a* Roman Catholic

càl *n* càil *m* cabbage, kail

caladh *n* -aidh, -aidhean *m* harbour, port; (*met*) place of rest *Also* **cala**

càl-colaig *n* càil-colaig *m* cauliflower

calg-dhìreach *adv* direct, directly **c. an aghaidh** completely against, diametrically opposed to

call *n* call(a) *m* loss; defeat **air chall** lost **'s e c. a bh' ann** it was a pity

callaid *n* -e, -ean *f* fence, hedge, partition

Callainn *n* -e *f* **a' Challainn** New Year's Day **Oidhche Challainn** Hogmanay

calltainn *n* -ean *m* hazel

calma *a* brave, strong, hardy

calman *n* -ain, -ain *m* dove, pigeon

calpa *n* -nnan *m* calf of leg; (*fin*) capital

calpachas *n* -ais *m* capitalism

cam *a* caime crooked, bent; one-eyed **cama-chasach** bow-legged

camag *n* -aig(e), -an *f* curl, ringlet of hair; (*in writing*) bracket

caman *n* -ain, -ain *m* stick for shinty, hockey etc.

camanachd *nf* shinty *Also vn* **a' c.** playing shinty

camara *n* -than *m* camera

camas *n* -ais, -ais/-an *m* wide bay

càmhal *n* -ail, -ail *m* camel

camhana(i)ch *n* -aich, -aich *f* dawn

campa *n* -ichean *m* camp

campaich *v* -achadh camp, encamp

can *v* -tainn/-tail/-ail say

cana *n* -ichean *m* can, tin

canabhas *n* -ais *m* canvas
canach *n* -aich *m* bog-cotton, cotton-grass
cànain *n See* **cànan**
canàl *n* -àil, -aichean *m* canal
cànan *n* -ain, -an *f m* language, tongue, speech **mion-chànan** minority language
canastair *n* -ean *m* canister, can, tin
Canèidianach *n* -aich, -aich *m* Canadian *a* Canadian
cangarù *n* -than *m* kangaroo
cànran *n* -ain *m* whingeing, grumbling, girning
cànranach *a* -aiche whingeing, grumbling, girning; fretful (*of small child*)
caoch *See* **cuthach**
caochail *v* **caochladh** change, alter; die, pass away
caochladh *n* -aidh *m* change, variation, different state; death **tha fhios agamsa air a chaochladh** I know different(ly)
caochlaideach *a* -diche changeable, variable, fickle
caog *v* -adh wink, close one eye (so as) to take aim
caogad *n* -aid, -an *m* fifty
caoidh *v* mourn, grieve, lament
caoin *a* -e kind, gentle, mild
caoin *v* -eadh weep, weep for, cry
caol *n* caoil, caoil/caoiltean *m* channel, narrows, kyle; narrow part of anything **Caol Loch Aillse** Kyle of Lochalsh **c.-shràid** lane, alley **c. an dùirn** the wrist
caol *a* caoile slender, thin, narrow
caolan *n* -ain, -ain/-an *m* gut, intestine
caolas *n* -ais, -ais *m* channel, narrows, kyle
caomh *a* caoimhe tender, kind, gentle; beloved, dear **is c. leam** I like
caomhain *v* **caomhnadh** save, economize on **ma bhios sinn air ar caomhnadh** if we are spared
caomhnadh *n* -aidh *m* saving, economizing
caora *n* -ch, -ich *f* sheep

caoran *n* -ain, -ain *m* small lump of peat; deeper part of a peat-bank
caorann *n* -ainn, -ainn/-ainnean *m* rowan, mountain ash
capall *n* -aill, -aill *m* mare; (*less commonly*) horse **c.-coille** capercaillie
car *n* **cuir**, -an *m* turn, twist, bend **cuir car dheth** capsize it/overturn it **a' cur charan** rolling/going round **car a' mhuiltein** somersault **thug e mo char asam** he got round me/tricked me **a' chiad char sa mhadainn** first thing in the morning
car *prep* during, for **car ùine** for some time *adv* about, somewhat **car daor** somewhat dear
càr *n* càr/càir, -aichean *m* car
carabhaidh *n* -ean *f* boyfriend
carabhan *n* -aichean *f m* caravan
carach *a* -aiche cunning, wily, sly, crafty, underhand
carachd *n f* wrestling
caractar *n* -air, -an *m* character
càradh *n* -aidh *m* mending, act of mending, repairing; condition, state
caraich *v* -achadh move, stir **cha do charaich e** he didn't budge
càraich *v See* **càirich**
caraid *n* (-e), -(e)an/càirdean *m* friend; relative (*especially in plural* **càirdean**) (*in corresp*) **A charaid/bhanacharaid** Dear ...
càraid *n* -e, -ean *f* couple, pair, married couple
caran *adv* somewhat, a little **c. anmoch** a bit late
carbad *n* -aid, -an *m* vehicle, car, conveyance, chariot, coach **c.-eiridinn** ambulance
Carghas *n* -ais *m* **an Carghas** Lent, any period of suffering
càrn *n* càirn/cùirn, càirn/cùirn *m* cairn, heap of stones (*often found in hill/mountain names*)
càrn *v* -adh heap, pile up; (*met*) accumulate **a' càrnadh airgid** accumulating/piling up money

càrnabhail *n* -ean *m* carnival

càrnan *n* -ain, -ain *m* small cairn; hill (*often found in place-names*)

carragh *n* -aigh, -aighean *m* pillar, erect stone **c.-cuimhne** memorial, monument

carraig *n* (-e), -ean *f* rock, pinnacle **C. nan Àl** the Rock of Ages

carraigean *n* -ein *m* carrageen (*seaweed used to make milk pudding*)

carson *int pron, adv* why

cartadh *n* -aidh *m* mucking out, clearing; clearance; tanning

carthannas *n* -ais *m* charity, compassion, tenderness **buidheann carthannais** *f m* a charity

cartùn *n* -ùin, -aichean *m* cartoon

cas *n* coise, casan *f* foot, leg; handle, shaft (*broom, spade, hammer etc*) **a bheil i air a cois?** is she up and about? **chaidh mi ann dhe mo chois** I went there on foot/I walked there **an cois** (+ *gen*) beside, as a result of, with **an cois na mara** close by the sea **an cois na litreach** enclosed with the letter **cuir air chois** *v* set up **thoir do chasan leat!** be off!/get off!

cas *a* **caise** steep, sudden, headlong; quick-tempered

càs *n* càis, -an *m* difficulty, emergency, predicament

casad *n* -aid, -an *m* cough **dèan c.** *v* cough

casadaich *n* *f* coughing *Also vn* **a' c.**

casa-gòbhlach, casa-gòbhlagain *adv* astride

casaid *n* -e, -ean *f* complaint, accusation, charge; prosecution **bha droch chasaid na aghaidh** he faced a serious accusation

cas-cheum *n* -chèim/-a, -an *m* path, footpath, track

cas-chrom *n* **coise-cruime, casan-croma** *f* foot-plough

casg/casgadh *n* **casg/casgaidh** *m* checking, stopping, preventing **casg/casgadh-gineamhainn** contraception **casg/casgadh-breith** abortion **cuir c. air** *v* stop, restrain, check

casruisgte *a* barefoot

cat *n* cait, cait *m* cat

catalog *n* -oig, -an *f m* catalogue

cath *n* (-a), -an/-annan *m* battle

cathadh *n* -aidh, -aidhean *m* snowstorm, snowdrift **c.-mara** sea-spray, spindrift *Also* **cabhadh**

cathag *n* -aig, -an *f* jackdaw

cathair *n* cathrach, cathraichean *f* chair; city **c.-bhaile** city **c.-chuibhle** wheelchair **c.-eaglais** cathedral

catharra *a* civil, civic

cathraiche *n* -an *m* chair (*person*)

ceacharra *a* awkward, perverse, cussed

cead *n* -a, -an *m* permission, permit **c.-siubhail** travel permit, passport **tha a chead aige** it serves him right, he well deserves it (*whether good or bad*) **c.-dealbha(cha)idh** planning permission

ceadaich *v* -achadh permit, allow

ceadaichte *a* permitted, allowed, permissible **chan eil e c. smocadh** smoking is not permitted

ceàird *n* -e, -ean *f* craft, trade, profession **fear-ceàirde** tradesman, craftsman

ceala-deug *n* *f* fortnight

cealg *n* ceilge *f* deceit, wiles, treachery

cealgach *a* -aiche deceitful, wily, treacherous, underhand

cealgair(e) *n* -e, -ean *m* deceiver, cheat

cealla *n* cille, -n/cilltean *f* cell (*biol*); cell, church, churchyard **Calum Cille** Columba

ceanalta *a* gentle, mild; comely, handsome

ceangail *v* -al tie, bind, connect, unite

ceangailte *a* tied up, connected, united

ceangal *n* -ail, -glaichean *m* tie, bond, connection, link

ceann *n* **cinn, cinn** *m* head; end; top **tha mo cheann goirt** I have a headache **cuir an c. dhan bhotal** put the top back on the bottle **c. an rathaid** the end of the road **o cheann gu c.** from end to end **air a' cheann thall** eventually **an c. mìos** in/after a month **ag obair air a c(h)eann fhèin** self-employed

ceannach *n* **-aich** *m* buy, purchase, buying, purchasing

ceannaich *v* **-ach** buy, purchase

ceannaiche *n* **-an** *m* merchant, dealer, buyer

ceannairceach *n* **-cich** *m* terrorist, rebel

ceannard *n* **-aird, -an** *m* head, chief, leader, commander

ceann-bhaile *n* **cinn-bhaile, -bhailtean** *m* capital city

ceann-bliadhna *n* **cinn-, cinn-** *m* birthday, anniversary

ceann-cinnidh *n* **cinn-, cinn-chinnidh** *m* clan chief

ceann-feadhna *n* **cinn-, cinn-** *m* clan chief

ceann-latha *n* **cinn-, cinn-** *m* deadline, day something is due, date

ceann-pholan *n* **cinn-pholain, -pholain** *m* tadpole

ceannruisgte *a* bare-headed

ceannsaich *v* **-achadh** subdue, conquer, master, control

ceann-suidhe *n* **cinn-, cinn-** *m* president **C. nan Stàitean Aonaichte** the President of the United States

ceann-uidhe *n* **cinn-, cinn-** *m* destination

ceap *n* **cip, -an/cip** *m* sod, piece of turf; block **c.-bròige** shoemaker's last

ceap *n* **-(a), -an** *m* cap

ceapaire *n* **-an** *m* sandwich

cearbach *a* **-aiche** awkward, inept, unfortunate, misguided

cearban *n* **-ain, -ain** *m* shark

cearc *n* **circe, -an** *f* hen **c.-fhraoich** grouse

cearcall *n* **-aill, -aill** *m* circle, hoop, ring **c. mun ghealaich** a ring round the moon

ceàrd *n* **ceàird, -an/-annan** *m* tinker

ceàrdach *n* **-aich, -aichean** *f* smithy, forge

ceàrn *n* **-a, -an/-aidhean** *f* quarter, particular area, zone, district

ceàrnach *a* square

ceàrnag *n* **-aig, -an** square *f* **C. Sheòrais** George Square

ceàrr *a* **-a** wrong, incorrect; left **an làmh cheàrr** the left hand

ceart *a* **-a** right, correct, just; (*before noun + len*) same **an uair cheart** the correct time **an làmh cheart** the right hand **cuir c.** *v* correct **an c. dhuine** the very same man **aig a' cheart àm** at the same time **a cheart cho ... ri ...** just as ... as ...

ceartachadh *n* **-aidh, -aidhean** *m* correction, marking, the act of correction

ceartaich *v* **-achadh** correct, put right, rectify

ceartas *n* **-ais** *m* justice **le c. ...** strictly speaking ...

ceart-cheàrnach *a* right-angled

ceartuair *adv* preceded by **an** at present, these days; shortly

ceas *n* **-a, -aichean** *m* suitcase

ceasnachadh *n* **-aidh, -aidhean** *m* questioning, interrogation; examination (*educ*)

ceasnaich *v* **-achadh** question, interrogate

ceatharnach *n* **-aich, -aich** *m* strongly built man, warrior

ceathrad *n* **-aid, -an** *m* forty

ceathramh *n* **-aimh, -an** *m* quarter; quatrain

ceathramh *a* fourth **an c. fear** the fourth one

ceathramh deug *a* fourteenth (*preceded by art* **an**) **an c. fear deug** the fourteenth one

ceathrar *n m* four (people)

cèic *n* **-e, -ichean** *f m* cake

cèidse *n* **-achan/-sichean** *f* cage

ceil *v* **ceil/-tinn/cleith** conceal, hold back information

cèile *n f m* spouse; fellow, match,

another **athair-c.** father-in-law
màthair-chèile mother-in-law
bu toigh leotha a chèile they
liked one another/each other
thuit e às a chèile it fell apart
ceileir *v* **-earadh** chirp, warble
(*usually of birds*)
cèilidh *n* **-idhean** *f m* ceilidh,
concert; visit **chaidh mi air
chèilidh orra** I paid them a visit
ceilp *n* **-e** *f* kelp
Ceilteach *n* **-tich, -tich** *m* Celt
a **-tiche** Celtic
ceimig *n* **-ean** *f* (a) chemical
ceimigeach *a* **-giche** chemical
ceimigeachd *n f* chemistry
ceimigear *n* **-eir, -an** *m* chemist
cèin *a* **-e** distant, foreign
cèir *n* **-e** *f* wax
ceirsle *n* **-an** *f* clew, ball (*of wool*)
Also **ceirtle**
cèis *n* **-e, -ean** *f* receptacle, case
c.-litreach envelope
cèiseag *n* **-eig, -an** *f* cassette
ceist *n* **-e, -ean** *f* question, query;
issue, problem; sum in
arithmetic **cuir c.** *v* ask a
question
ceisteachan *n* **-ain, -ain** *m*
questionnaire
ceistear *n* **-eir, -an** *m* questioner,
quizmaster; catechist
Cèitean *n* **-ein** *m* **an C.** the month
of May
ceithir *n, a* four **c.-chasach** four-
legged
ceithir-deug *n, a* fourteen **ceithir
taighean deug** fourteen houses
ceò *n* **ceò/ceotha, -than/
ceothannan** *f m* mist, fog;
smoke **Eilean a' Cheò** the Misty
Isle (the Isle of Skye)
ceòl *n* **ciùil** *m* music **c.-mòr**
pibroch **c.-beag** light music for
the pipes **c.-gàire** mirth **luchd-
ciùil** musicians
ceòlmhor *a* **-oire** musical, tuneful,
melodious
ceòthach *a* **-aiche** misty, foggy
ceud *n* **-an** *m* a hundred *a* a
hundred **bha c. cabhag orra**
they were in a great hurry **... sa
cheud ...** per cent **c. taing**

thanks a lot
ceudameatair *n* **-ean** *m*
centimetre
ceudamh *a* (*preceded by art* **an**)
hundredth
ceud-chasach *n* **-chasaich,
-chasaich** *m* centipede
ceudna *a* (*preceded by art* **an**)
same **air an dòigh cheudna** in
the same way **mar an c.** also,
likewise
ceum *n* **cèim/-a, -an/-annan** *m*
step; footpath; (*university*)
degree **c. air cheum** step by step
ceumnaich *v* **-achadh** graduate;
take a step
ceus *v* **-adh** crucify **chaidh Crìosd
a cheusadh** Christ was crucified
cha *neg part* not (*often lenites*)
cha bheag sin that is not small,
that's quite a lot
chaidh *irr v* went (*See irr v* **rach**
in Grammar)
chan *neg part* (*used before
vowels and fh*) **chan aithne
dhomh i** I don't know her **chan
fhuirich mi** I won't stay
chaoidh *See* **a-chaoidh**
cheana *See* **a-cheana**
chì *irr v* will see, can see (*See irr
v* **faic** *in Grammar*)
cho *adv* as, so, **cho dearg ris an
fhuil** as red as blood
chon *prep See* **chun**
chuala *irr v* heard (*See irr v*
cluinn *in Grammar*)
chum *See* **a chum**
chun *prep* (+ *gen*) to, towards, as
far as
chunnaic *irr v* saw (*See irr v* **faic**
in Grammar)
cia *int pron* who, which, what;
how *See* **cò**
ciad *a* first **an c. latha** the first
day (*often takes feminine form*)
a' chiad latha
ciad-fhuasgladh *n* **-fhuasglaidh** *m*
first aid
ciall *n* **cèille** *f* sense, reason,
understanding **dìth na cèille** lack
of sense **a' dol às a chiall** going
mad, losing his reason **a chiall!**
goodness!

ciallach *a* -aiche sensible, reasonable

ciallaich *v* -achadh mean, intend

ciamar *int pron, adv* how **c. a tha thu?** how are you?

cia mheud *int pron, adv* how many **cia mh. iasg a fhuair thu?** how many fish did you get? **cia mh. aca a bh' ann?** how many of them were there? Also **cò mheud**

cian *a* **cèine** distant, remote

cianail *a* -e mournful, melancholy; terrible **c. fuar** terribly cold

cianalas *n* -ais *m* nostalgia, homesickness, melancholy **bha an c. orm** I felt homesick/ nostalgic

ciar *v* -adh darken, grow dark

ciar *a* -a/**cèire** dusky, darkening; swarthy

ciatach *a* -aiche *m* pleasant, elegant, graceful, becoming, agreeable **bidh sin c.** that will be fine

cidhe *n* -achan *m* quay, pier

cidsin *n* -ean *m* kitchen

cileagram *n* -aim, -an *m* kilogram

cilemeatair *n* -ean *m* kilometre

cill *n* -e, -tean *f* church, churchyard (*common in place names*) **Cill Rìmhinn** St Andrews

cinn *v* -tinn grow, increase

cinneach *n* -nich *m* nation; gentile; a character **'s e c. a th' ann!** he's a hard case!

cinneadh *n* -nidh, -nidhean *m* clan, tribe, race; surname

cinnt *n* -e *f* sureness, certainty **le c.** definitely, certainly

cinnteach *a* -tiche sure, certain, reliable

cìobair *n* -ean *m* shepherd

cìoch *n* **cìche**, -an *f* female breast

cion *n* *m* lack, want, shortage **c. cosnaidh** unemployment

cionnas *adv* how **c. a fhuair e sin?** how did he get that?

ciont(a) *n* -(a), -(an) *m* guilt

ciontach *a* -aiche guilty

ciopair *n* -ean *m* kipper

ciorram *n* -aim *m* disability

ciorramach *n* -aich, -aich *m* disabled person

ciorramach *a* -aiche disabled, handicapped

ciotach *a* -aiche left-handed

cìr *n* -e, -ean *f* comb; cud **cìrmheala** honeycomb

cìr *v* -eadh comb

cìrean *n* -ein *m* comb or crest of a bird

cìs *n* -e, -ean *f* tax **Cìs Comhairle** Council Tax **cìs cosnaidh** income tax

ciste *n* -achan *f* chest **c.-dhràthraichean** chest of drawers **c.-laighe** coffin

ciùb *n* -an *m* cube

ciudha *n* -ichean *f m* queue

ciùin *a* -e calm, mild, meek **duine c.** an even-tempered man

ciùinich *v* -neachadh calm, pacify, appease

ciùrr *v* -adh hurt very painfully

ciutha *n* -chan *m* cue (*hair*)

ciùthran *n* -ain, -ain *m* drizzle

clach *n* **cloiche**, -an *f* stone **c.-ghràin** granite **c.-iùil** magnet **c.-mhuilinn** millstone **c.-sùla** eyeball

clach *v* -adh stone

clachair *n* -ean *m* stonemason

clachan *n* -ain, -ain *m* village, hamlet; stepping-stones

clach-mheallain *n* **cloichemeallain, clachan-meallain** *f* hailstone

cladach *n* -aich, -aichean *m* shore, coast

cladh *n* -a/**claidh**, -an/-annan *m* cemetery

cladhaich *v* -ach dig

cladhan *n* -ain, -ain *m* channel

clag *n* **cluig, cluig/-an** *m* bell

claidheamh *n* -eimh, -an/ **claidhmhnean** *m* sword **c.-mòr** claymore

claigeann *n* -ginn, -ginn *m* skull **ag èigheach àird a claiginn** shouting at the top of her voice

clais *n* -e, -ean *f* furrow, ditch, trench

claisneachd *n* *f* hearing **cùm cluas ri c.** keep an ear to the ground

clamhan *n* -ain, -ain *m* buzzard; kite

clann *n* **cloinne** *f* (*sg n*) children (*often lenited in gen*) **triùir chloinne** three children *Used in clan names, eg* **Clann Dòmhnaill** Clan Donald

clann-nighean *n* -nighinn *f* (*sg n*) girls, young women

claoidh *v* -eadh weary, oppress, vex, harass

claoidhte *a* exhausted, worn out

claon *a* -oine slanting, inclining, squint; (*met*) partial **c.-bharail** prejudice **c.-bhreith** prejudice, unjust verdict

claon *v* -adh slope, veer; (*met*) incline

clàr *n* -àir, -àir *m* board, table, level surface; table (*of figures*), programme (*of events*), form (*for filling*); record **c.-ama** timetable **c.-amais** index **c.-aodainn** brow, forehead **c.-bìdh** menu **c.-dùthcha** map **c.-gnothaich** agenda **c.-iarrtais** application form **c.-innse** contents list **c.-oideachais** curriculum

clàrachadh *n* -aidh *m* recording, registration

clàraich *v* -achadh record, register, tabulate, arrange into tables

clàrsach *n* -aich, -aichean *f* harp

clàrsair *n* -ean *m* harper, harpist

clas *n* -aichean *m* class (*in schools etc*)

clasaigeach *a* -giche classical

cleachd *v* -adh use, employ, deploy, practise, be accustomed (to), be used (to) **chleachd mi a bhith a' snàmh** I used to swim

cleachdadh *n* -aidh, -aidhean *m* use; custom, habit, practice, convention

cleachdte (ri) *past part* accustomed to, used to

cleamhnas *n* -ais *m* relationship by marriage

cleas *n* -an *m* play, trick, clever feat; way **rinn esan c. chàich** he

did what the others did

cleasachd *n* *f* play, playing

cleasaich *v* -achd play, perform feats

cleasaiche *n* -an *m* actor, performer, conjurer

clèir *n* -e, -ean *f* **a' chlèir** the clergy; presbytery

clèireach *n* -rich, -rich *m* cleric; clerk *a* presbyterian

cleith *See* **ceil**

cleòc(a) *n* -a, -aichean *m* cloak

clì *n* -the *f* strength, vigour

clì *a* left; wrong **an làmh chlì** the left hand

cliabh *n* clèibh, clèibh *m* creel, basket, hamper; person's chest

cliamhainn *n* cleamhna, cleamhnan *m* son-in-law **bana-chliamhainn** *f* daughter-in-law

cliath *n* clèithe, -an *f* grid; harrow **c.-chruidh** cattle grid

cliath *v* -adh harrow

cliatha(i)ch *n* -aich, -ean *f* side (*of person or thing*)

cliobach *a* -aiche clumsy, awkward

clis *a* -e quick, nimble, agile

clisg *v* -eadh move suddenly, start (*through fear or alarm*); **bi air do chlisgeadh** be very afraid of something **bha mi air mo chlisgeadh roimhe** I was terrified of it

clisgear *n* -eir , -an *m* exclamation (*gram*)

clisg-phuing *n* -phuing(e), -phuingean *f* exclamation mark

cliù *n* *m* fame, reputation; praise **c.-mhilleadh** *m* libel, slander

cliùiteach *a* -tiche famous, celebrated

clò *n* clò-/tha, clòith(n)tean *m* cloth (*especially tweed woven on looms*), a piece of tweed **an Clò Mòr/Hearach** Harris Tweed

clò *n* *m* print; press **cuir an c.** *v* print

clobha *n* -chan *m* pair of tongs

clòbhar *n* -air *m* clover

clobhd(a) *n* -(a), -an *m* cloth (*for wiping*), clout **c.-sgùraidh** scouring cloth

clobhsa *n* -n/-ichean close *m* (*in tenement*)

clò-bhuail *v* -bhualadh print (*a book*) -bhuailte (*past part*) printed

clò-bhualadair *n* -ean *m* printer, printing firm; publisher

clò-bhualadh *n* -aidh *m* printing, the work of printing

cloc *n* -aichean *m* clock

clogad *n* -aid, -an *m* helmet, headpiece *Also* **clogaid**

clòimh *n* -e, -ean *f* wool

closach *n* -aich, -aichean *f* carcase

clòsaid *n* (-e), -ean *f* closet, small back room

clostar *n* -air, -air *m* loud thump or noise of falling (*person or thing*); large specimen of something

cluain *n* -e, -tean *f* green plain, meadow, pasture

cluaineas *n* -eis *m* retirement **chaidh e air chluaineas** he retired (*from work*)

cluaran *n* -ain, -ain *m* thistle

clua(i)s *n* -e, -asan *f* ear

cluasag *n* -aig, -an *f* pillow

club *n* -aichean *m* club (*organization*) **c. òigridh** youth club

cluich *n* -e, -ean *m* play, game **c.-bùird** board game

cluich *v* cluich/-e/-eadh play (*sport or musical instrument*)

cluicheadair *n* -ean *m* player, actor **c.-chlàr** record-player

cluinn *irr v* hear, listen (*See irr v* **cluinn** *in Grammar*)

cnag *n* cnaig(e), -an *f* pin, peg, knob, piece of wood **c.-aodaich** clothes peg **c.-dealain** electric plug **sin c. na cùise** that's the nub of the matter

cnàimh *n* -e/cnàmha, -ean/cnàmhan *m* bone **c. an droma** the backbone

cnàimhneach *n* -nich, -nichean *m* skeleton

cnàimhseag *n* -eig, -an *f* pimple on face, acne

cnàmh *v* chew, digest; wear away,

decay **tha a' bhò a' c. a cìre(adh)** the cow is chewing the cud

cnap *n* cnaip, -an *m* knob; lump, small hill

cnapach *n* -aich, -aich *m* young boy (*not a small child*)

cnapach *a* -aiche lumpy

cnap-starra *n* cnaip-, cnapan- *m* obstacle, obstruction (*Also* met)

cnatan *n* -ain, -ain *m* common cold **bha an c. orm** I had the cold

cnead *n* -a, -an *m* groan **cha robh c. air** there was nothing wrong with him

cneasta *a* humane, moderate, decent, modest *Formerly* **cneasda**

cnò *n* cnò/cnotha, cnothan/cnòithtean *f* nut **c.-challtainn** hazelnut **c.-còco** coconut **gall-chnò** walnut

cnoc *n* cnuic, cnuic/-an *m* hill

cnocach *a* -aiche hilly

cnocan *n* -ain, -ain *m* hillock, small hill

cnot *n* -an *m* knot that is tied; door-bar

cnòthach *a* -aiche nutty

cnuasaich *v* -achadh reflect, ponder, ruminate; collect, accumulate

cnuimh *n* -e, -ean *f* worm, maggot **c.-thalmhainn** earthworm *Also* **cruimh**

cò *int pron, adv* who? which? **cò sibh?** who are you? **cò agaibh a dhèanadh sin?** which of you would do that? **tha fhios aicese cò iad** she knows who they are **cò às a tha thu?** where are you from?

co-aimsireil *a* -e contemporary

co-aois *n* See **comhaois**

cobhair *n* còbhrach *f* help, aid, succour, relief **rinn iad c. oirnn** they came to our rescue

co-bhann *n* -bhuinn, -an *f* bond, league, confederacy **an co-bhoinn/co-bhuinn ri** in co-operation/league with

co-bhanntachd *n* -an *f* coalition

cobhar *n* -air *m* foam, froth

còc *n* -an *m* coke (*drink & fuel*)
còcaire *n* -an *m* cook, chef
còcaireachd *n f* cooking, cookery
cochall *n* -aill, -aill *m* husk, shell;
hood **theab i a dhol à c.** a cridhe
she nearly died of fright
co-cheangail *v* -al connect, bind
together, involve with each
other
co-cheangal *n* -ail, -ail/-glan *m*
connection **an c. ri** in
connection with
co-cheangailte *a* (+ **ri**) connected
(to), in connection with, related
(to)
co-chomann *n* -ainn, -ainn *m*
society, association,
co-operative **C. Nis** Ness
Community Co-operative
co-chomhairle *n* -an *f*
consultation
co-chòrdadh *n* -aidh, -aidhean *m*
agreement, accord, alliance
co-chruinneachadh *n* -aidh,
-aidhean *m* assembly, gathering,
convention; compilation,
collection
còco *n m* cocoa
còd *n* -aichean *m* code **còd puist**
postcode
co-dheth *adv* See **co-dhiù**
co-dhiù *adv* anyway, whatever
happens **c. no co-dheth** anyway
co-dhùin *v* -dhùnadh conclude,
decide
co-dhùnadh *n* -aidh, -aidhean *m*
conclusion, decision
co-èignich *v* -èigneachadh urge,
persuade strongly, force, compel
cofaidh *n f m* coffee
co-fhaireachdainn *n f* sympathy
co-fharpais *n* (-e), -ean *f*
competition, contest
co-fhlaitheas *n* -eis *m*
confederation **An C.** The
Commonwealth
co-fhreagair *v* -t match,
correspond
cofhurtachd *n f* comfort
cofhurtaich *v* -achadh comfort,
console
cofhurtail *a* -e comfortable
cogadh *n* -aidh, -aidhean *m* war

an Dàrna C. the Second World
War
cogais *n* (-e), -ean *f* conscience
cogaiseach *a* -siche
conscientious, honest
co-ghin *v* -eadh/-tinn have sexual
intercourse, copulate
co-ghnìomhair *n* -ean *m* adverb
coibhneas *n* -eis, -an *m* kindness,
generosity
coibhneil *a* -e kind, kindly,
generous
coidse *n* -achan *f* coach
còig *n, a* five
còig-cheàrnach *n* -aich, -aichean
m pentagon
còig-deug *n, a* fifteen **còig
mìosan deug** fifteen months
còigeamh *n* -eimh *m* a fifth
a fifth **an c. fear** the fifth one
còignear *n m* five (people)
coigreach *n* -rich, -rich *m*
stranger, foreigner
coileach *n* -lich, -lich *m* cockerel
c.-gaoithe weathercock
coilean *v* -adh fulfil, accomplish,
complete *Formerly* **coimhlion**
coileanta *a* perfect, accomplished,
complete **an tràth c.** the perfect
tense
coilear *n* -eir, -an *m* collar
coilion *v* See **coilean**
coille *n* -ltean *f* wood, forest
coilleag *n* -eig, -an *f* cockle;
sand-dune
coimeas *n* -eis *f* comparison,
likeness **an c. ri** compared to, in
comparison to **chan eil a c. ann**
there's no-one like her **dèan c.
eatarra** *v* compare them
coimeas *v* compare
coimeasgaich *v* -achadh mix
together, mingle
coimheach *a* -mhiche foreign,
alien; shy, 'strange' (*of a small
child*), unfriendly
coimhead *v* look, look at; keep
watch over
coimhearsnach *n* -aich, -aich *m*
neighbour
coimhearsnachd *n f*
neighbourhood, vicinity,
community

coimisean *n* **-ein, -an** *m* commission **an C. Eòrpach** the European Commission

coimiseanair *n* **-ean** *m* commissioner

coimpiutair *n* **-ean** *m* computer

coimpiutaireachd *n f* computing

coineanach *n* **-aich, -aich** *m* rabbit

còinneach *n* **-nich** *f* moss

coinneachadh *n* **-aidh** *m* meeting, the act of meeting

coinneal *n* **coinnle, coinnlean** *f* candle

coinneamh *n* **-eimh, -an** *f* meeting, appointment; religious service **c. naidheachd** press conference

coinnich *v* **-neachadh** meet **c. ri** meet with

coinnlear *n* **-eir/-an** *m* candlestick *Also* **coinnleir**

co-ionann *a* equal, equivalent to

co-ionannachd *n f* state of being equal, equality **c. chothroman** equal opportunities (*policy*)

còir *n* **-e/còrach, -ean/còraichean** *f* what is right; obligation; right, privilege, claim **tha c. agad sin a dhèanamh** you ought to do that **bu chòir dhut fheuchainn** you should try it **ag agairt do chòraichean** claiming your rights

còir *a* **-e** worthy, decent; just, honest; kind, generous; gentle, docile **cho c. ris an fhaoileig** as kind as kind can be **cù c.** *m* a well-behaved dog

coirbte *a* corrupt

coirce *n m* oats **aran-c.** *m* oatmeal bread

coire *n* **-achan** *m* kettle, cauldron; corrie **C. a' Cheathaich** the Misty Corrie

coire *n* **-achan** *f* fault, wrongdoing; blame **na bi a' cur na c. ormsa** don't lay the blame on me

coireach *a* **-riche** at fault, blameworthy **'s tu fhèin as c.** you're the one who's to blame

coirich *v* **-reachadh** blame

coiridh *n* **-ean** *m* curry (*the food*)

coiseachd *n f* walking

coisich *v* **-seachd** walk

coisiche *n* **-an** *m* walker, pedestrian

coisinn *v* **cosnadh** earn, win, gain; deserve

còisir *n* **-e/còisre, -ean** *f* choir *Also* **c.-chiùil**

coisrig *v* **-eadh** consecrate, dedicate; sanctify

coisrigte *a* consecrated, sanctified **uisge c.** *m* holy water

coitcheann *a* **-chinne** common, public, general, standard

coitcheannas *n* **-ais** *m* generality

coitheanal *n* **-ail, -an** *m* congregation

coitich *v* **-teachadh** press, persuade; campaign, lobby

co-labhairt *n* **-ean** *f* conference, seminar

co-là-breith *n* **-làithean-/ -lathaichean-** *m* birthday

cola-deug *n f* fortnight

colag *n* **-aig, -an** *f* cauliflower

colaiste *n* **-an** *f m* college

colann *n* **-ainn, -an/-ainnean** *f* body

colbh *n* **cuilbh, cuilbh/-an** *m* pillar, column; column (*in newspaper*)

Colach *n* **-aich, -aich** *m* someone from Coll *a* from, or pertaining to, Coll

coltach *a* **-aiche** like, apparent, likely; healthy/robust-looking (*pronounced in some areas with the t silent*) **tha i c. riut** she's like you **tha e c. gu bheil i tinn** it seems she's ill **chan eil sin glè choltach** that's not very likely **duine mòr c.** a big robust-looking man

coltaich *v* **-achadh** (+ **ri**) liken (to)

coltas *n* **-ais** *m* appearance, likeness; expression (*on face*) **a rèir c(h)oltais** apparently, seemingly, by the looks of it **bha c. an acrais orra** they looked hungry

com *n* **cuim** *m* chest, upper part

of the body, trunk

coma *a* indifferent, unconcerned, uncaring **tha mi c. cò a thig** I don't care who comes **c. leat** never mind **tha mi c. dheth** I don't like it **c. co-dhiù/co-aca** couldn't care less, past caring, totally indifferent

comaig *n* -ean *f m* comic (*children's paper*)

comaig *a* -e comical, funny

comain *n* -ean *f* obligation for something done for one **tha mi fada nad chomain** I'm much obliged to you

comain *n* -ean *m* communion **a ciad chomain** her first communion

comanachadh *n* -aidh *m* communion; season of communion services

comanaich *v* -achadh take communion, be a communicant in church

comann *n* -ainn, -ainn *m* society, association; company, fellowship

comas *n* -ais, -an *m* ability **tha e gun chomas labhairt** he is without the power of speech

comasach *a* -aiche able, capable, talented **dèan c.** *v* enable, facilitate

comataidh *n* -ean *f* committee

combaist *n* -e, -ean *f* compass (*for direction*)

comhair *n* *f* direction **thuit mi an c. mo chùil** I fell backwards **an c. gach ama** now and then, from time to time **bha e fa chomhair na cùirt** he was before/in front of the court

comhairle *n* -an *f* advice, counsel; council **thug i deagh chomhairle orm** she gave me good advice **C. na Gàidhealtachd** the Highland Council

comhairleach *n* -lich, -lich *m* adviser, counsellor

comhairlich *v* -leachadh advise, guide

comhairliche *n* -an *m* councillor, adviser

comhaois(e) *n* (-e), (e)an *m* person the same age, peer, contemporary **tha iad nan comhaoisean** they are the same age

comharra(dh) *n* comharra/-aidh, comharran/-aidhean *m* mark, sign **c.-ceiste** question mark **c.-stiùiridh** landmark

comharrachadh *n* -aidh *m* marking

comharraich *v* -achadh mark, indicate, earmark, identify

comharraichte *a* noteworthy, special, exceptional

comhart *n* -airt, -an *m* dog's bark

comhartaich *n* *f* (*continuous*) barking

còmhdach *n* -aich *m* covering, cover

còmhdaich *v* -achadh cover, clothe

còmhdaichte *a* covered, clothed

còmhdhail *n* -dhala(ch), -ean *f* congress, convention; meeting, tryst; transport

cò mheud *See* **cia mheud**

còmhla *n* -chan/-idhean *f* door, door-leaf, door of cupboard

còmhla *adv* together **ràinig iad c.** they arrived together **c. ri** *prep phr* along/together with

còmhlan *n* -ain, -ain *m* group, band (*usually small*) **c.-ciùil** music group, band

còmhnaidh *n* -ean *f* residence, dwelling, house

còmhnaich *v* -aidh reside, live, stay; continue

còmhnard *a* -airde level, flat, even, smooth

còmhradh *n* -aidh, -aidhean *m* conversation, dialogue **dèan c.** *v* converse, chat

còmhrag *n* -aig, -an *f* fight, struggle, conflict, combat **c.-dhithis** duel

còmhraideach *a* -diche talkative, chatty, fond of conversation

còmhstri *n* -thean *f* strife, struggle, conflict; rivalry, disagreement

compàirt *n* (-e) *f* partnership, share, participation

compàirtich *v* **-teachadh** share, divide, take part, participate; communicate

companach *n* **-aich, -aich** *m* companion, partner; spouse

companaidh *n* **-ean** *f m* company (*org*), firm

companas *n* **-ais** *m* company (*personal*), companionship

comraich *n* **-ean** *f* sanctuary, protection **Comraich Ma-Ruibhe/a' Chomraich** Applecross **c. phoilitigeach** political asylum

còn *n* **-aichean** *m* cone

conair(e) *n* **(-e)** , **-(e)an** *f* rosary; path, way

conaltradh *n* **-aidh** *m* conversation, communication; company (*social*)

conas *n* **-ais** *m* contention, quarrel; teasing **chuir e c. orm** it annoyed me *Also vn* **a' c. bha iad a' c. rithe** they were teasing her

conasg *n* **-aisg** *m* whins, gorse

connadh *n* **-aidh, -aidhean** *m* fuel **c. làmhaich** ammunition, munitions

connlach *n* **-aich** *f* straw

connrag *n* **-aig, -an** *f* consonant

connsachadh *n* **-aidh** *m* quarrel, argument, dispute, feud

connsaich *v* **-achadh** quarrel, argue, dispute, feud, wrangle

connspaid *n* **(e)**, **-ean** *f* quarrel, dispute, strife, contention

connspaideach *a* **-diche** disputatious, quarrelsome, contentious, confrontational

conntraigh *n* **-ean** *f* neap tide

consal *n* **-ail, -an** *m* consul

co-obraich *v* **-obrachadh** work with, co-operate with, collaborate

co-obrachadh *n* **-aidh** *m* co-operation, collaboration

co-ogha *n* **-ichean** *m* cousin

co-òrdanaich *v* **-achadh** co-ordinate

co-òrdanaiche *n* **-an** *m* co-ordinator

cop *n* **coip** *m* foam, froth

còp *v* **-adh** tip up (*a load*);

capsize

copag *n* **-aig, -an** *f* dock, docken

copan *n* See **cupan**

copar *n* **-air** *m* copper (*metal*)

cor *n* **coir/cuir** *m* state, condition **cor an t-saoghail** the state the world is in **dè do chor?** how are you?/how are you doing? **air chor sam bith** under any circumstances

còrd *v* **-adh** agree, come to an agreement; (+ **ri**) give enjoyment/pleasure to **chòrd e rium** I enjoyed it

còrdadh *n* **-aidh, -aidhean** *m* agreement, pact

còrn *n* **cùirn, cùirn** *m* horn (*mus*), drinking horn; corn (*on foot*)

Còrnach *n* **-aich, -aich** *m* someone from Cornwall *a* Cornish

còrnair *n* **-ean** *m* corner

corp *n* **cuirp, cuirp** *m* body; corpse **c.-eòlas** anatomy

corporra *a* corporal, bodily; corporate

còrr *n* *f m* an excess; remainder, (*fin*) balance; more **na ith an c./a' chòrr** don't eat any more **còrr is mìle duine** over a thousand men

corra *a* odd, occasional, irregular **bidh c. dhuine a' dol ann** the odd person goes there **c. uair** occasionally, now and then

corra-biod(a) *n m* state of alertness/readiness; (*preceded by* **air**) on tiptoe **bha e air a chorra-biod(a)** he was on tiptoe

corrach *a* **-aiche** steep; rough; unsteady, unstable (*eg boat*)

corrag *n* **-aig, -an** *f* finger

corra-ghritheach *n* **-g(h)rithich, corrachan-gritheach** *f* heron

corran *n* **-ain, -ain** *m* sickle; point of land running into the sea; crescent

còrr-mhial *n* **-a, -an** *f* gnat, hornet

còs *n* **còis, -an** *m* cave, hollow, recess; any sheltered place

còsach *a* **-aiche** cavernous; porous, hollow; sheltered, snug, cosy

cosamhlachd *n* -an *f* parable
cosg *v* **cosg(adh)** cost; spend; run
out, be used up **dè a chosg sin?**
how much did that cost? **dè a
chosg thu air?** what did you
spend on it? **tha an t-airgead air
c.** the money has run out
cosgail *a* -e costly, expensive
cosgais *n* -e, -ean *f* cost,
expense
co-sheirm *n* -e, -ean *f* harmony
(*mus*)
co-shìnte *a* parallel
cosmhail *a* -e like, resembling
cosnadh *n* -aidh, -aidhean *m*
earnings, way of earning, work,
employment **gun chosnadh**
unemployed **ionad cosnaidh** *m*
job centre
cost(a) *n* -taichean *m* coast, shore
còta *n* -ichean *m* coat **c.-bàn**
petticoat
cotan *n* -ain *m* cotton, cotton-
wool
cothaich *v* -achadh contend with
cothlamadh *n* -aidh *m* mixture,
merger, merging
cothrom *a* -ruime even
cothrom *n* **cothruim,** -an *m*
chance, opportunity;
equilibrium, balance; fair play
C. na Fèinne fair play, a fair
opportunity, a sporting chance
chan eil c. air it can't be helped
a bheil thu air chothrom? are
you fit/able?
cothromach *a* -aiche just,
equitable, reasonable, fair,
balanced
cothromaich *v* -achadh weigh;
make equal, balance; consider
co-thuiteamas *n* -ais, -an *m*
coincidence
cràbhach *a* -aiche devout,
religious, pious
cràbhadh *n* -aidh *m* piety,
devoutness
crac *n* **craic** *f* chat, crack
cràdh *n* **cràidh** *m* pain, suffering
bha c. air he was in pain
craiceann *n* -cinn, -an *m* skin
cràidh *v* **cràdh(adh)** pain, torment
cràiteach *a* -tiche painful

crann *n* **cruinn/croinn,
cruinn/croinn/crainn** *m* mast or
other long rod; plough (*also*
crann-treabhaidh); bolt, bar,
beam; lot; cran (*measure for
herring*); tree **a' cur chrann**
casting lots **an C.-ceusaidh** the
Cross (*of Christ*) **c.-fiona** vine
c.-ola oilrig **c.-sneachd(a)**
snowplough
crannchur *n* -uir, -an *m* casting of
lots, lottery **an C. Nàiseanta** the
National Lottery **c.-gill** raffle
craobh *n* -oibhe, -an *f* tree **c.-
challtainn** hazel tree **c.-dharaich**
oak tree **c.-ghiuthais** pine tree
craobhag *n* -aig, -an *f* plant;
bush; small tree
craobh-sgaoil *v* -eadh broadcast,
transmit; promulgate,
propagate
craol *v* -adh broadcast, transmit;
promulgate, propagate
craoladair *n* -ean *m* broadcaster
craoladh *n* -aidh *m* broadcasting,
broadcast, transmission
craos *n* -ois, -an *m* large mouth,
maw; gluttony
craosach *a* -aiche wide-/large-
mouthed; gluttonous
crath *v* -adh shake, wave;
sprinkle
crathadh-làimhe *n* **crathaidhean-**
m handshake
creach *n* **creiche,** -an *f* plunder,
booty; ruin, destruction **Mo
chreach!** Alas! **Mo chreach-sa
thàinig!** Goodness gracious me!
creach *v* -adh plunder, rob, ruin
creachan(n) *n* -ain(n), -ain(n) *m*
scallop
crèadh *n* **crèadha/creadha** *f* clay
crèadhadair *n* -ean *m* potter
crèadhadaireachd *n* *f* pottery
creag *n* **creige,** -an *f* rock; crag,
cliff, precipice
creagach *a* -aiche rocky
creamh *n* -a *m* garlic **c.-gàrraidh**
leek, leeks
crèapailt(e) *n* -(e)an *m* garter *Also*
crèibilt(e)
creathail *n* (-e), -ean *f* cradle *Also*
creathall

creid *v* **-sinn** believe **chan eil mi ga chreidsinn** I don't believe it **cha chreid mi nach coisich mi** I think I shall walk

creideamh *n* **-eimh, -an** *m* faith; religion, religious belief

creideas *n* **-eis** *m* credit (*moral, fin*), credibility; faith, trust **chan eil cus creideis agam ann** I don't have much faith in him

creidhean *n* **-ein, -an** *m* crayon

creim *See* **criom**

creithleag *n* **-eig, -an** *f* cleg

creuchd *n* **-a, -an** *f* wound

creud *n* **(-a), -an** *f* creed; belief

creutair *n* **-ean** *m* creature, animal; (*Lewis*) female **an c.!** the poor thing!

criathar *n* **-air, -an** *m* sieve, riddle

criathraich *v* **-rachadh/-radh** sieve; (*met*) weigh up, assess

cridhe *n* **-achan** *m* heart **na biodh a chridh' agad ...!** don't dare ...!

cridhealas *n* **-ais** *m* heartiness, merriment, conviviality

cridheil *a* **-e** hearty, cheerful

crìoch *n* **crìche, -an** *f* end, conclusion; limit, boundary, border **na Crìochan** the Borders **cuir c. air** *v* finish it **thoir gu crìch** *v* bring to a close/an end **c.-ghrèine** tropic

crìochnaich *v* **-achadh** finish, complete, bring to an end

crìochnaichte *a* finished, completed, concluded

criogaid *n* *f* cricket (*sport*)

criom *v* **-adh** gnaw, nibble, chew; erode

criomag *n* **-aig, -an** *f* small bit, fragment, morsel

crìon *a* **crìne, -a** small, mean, trifling; withered, shrunken, dried up

crìon *v* **-adh** wither, fade, decay

crìonadh *n* **-aidh** *m* withering, decay, decline

crioplach *n* **-aich, -aich** *m* cripple

crios *n* **(-a), -an/-achan** *m* belt, strap **c.-sàbhalaidh** lifebelt

Crìosdachd *n* *f* **a' Chrìosdachd** Christianity; Christendom

Crìosdaidh *n* **-ean** *m* Christian *a* **-e** Christian

Crìosdail *a* **-e** Christian **an creideamh C.** the Christian religion

Crìosdalachd *n* *f* Christianity; Christian disposition

criostal *n* **-ail, -an** *m* crystal *a* crystal

cripleach *See* **crioplach**

crith *n* **(-e), -ean** *f* trembling, shaking, shivering **air chrith leis an eagal** trembling with fear

critheanach *a* **-aiche** shaky, unsteady; causing shaking

critheann *n* **-thinn, -an** *m* aspen tree

crith-thalmhainn *n* **crithe-talmhainn/-thalmhainn, crithean-talmhainn** *f* earthquake

crò *n* **-tha, -than** *m* pen for animals, fold; eye of a needle

croch *v* **-adh** hang (*person or thing*) **chaidh a chrochadh** he was hanged

crochadair *n* **-ean** *m* hangman; hanger

crochadh *n* **-aidh** *m* hanging (*of things or people*) **an c. air** dependent (on) **an c. air an t-sìde** depending on the weather

crochte *a* hung, hanging

crodh *n* **cruidh** *m* (*sg n*) cattle, kine **c.-bainne** dairy cows

crò-dhearg *a* crimson

cròg *n* **cròige, -an** *f* large hand; palm of the hand **làn cròige** a handful, fistful

crogall *n* **-aill, -aill** *m* crocodile

crogan *n* **-ain, -an** *m* jar, pitcher, tin **c.-silidh** jam-jar

cròic *n* **-e, -ean** *f* antlers; foam on liquids or on the sea

croich *n* **-e, -ean** *f* gallows

cròileagan *n* **-ain, -ain** *m* playgroup

crois *n* **-e, -ean** *f* cross; difficulty, mishap **c.-rathaid** crossroads **bha e ann an c.** he was in a fix **bha e ri c.** he was up to no good

croiseil *a* **-e** awkward, problematic

croit *n* **-e, -ean** *f* croft *Also* **crait,**

cruit
croit *n* -e *f* hump, hunch
croitear *n* -eir, -an *m* crofter
croitse *n* -achan *f* crutch
crom *a* **cruime** bent, crooked, curved **ceann c.** *m* a bowed head
crom *v* -adh bend, stoop; descend
cromag *n* -aig, -an *f* hook; shepherd's crook; apostrophe
cron *n* **croin**, -an *m* harm, damage, fault, crime **cha dèan e c. ort** it'll not harm you
cronaich *v* -achadh rebuke, reprimand, censure
cronail *a* -e harmful, damaging, pernicious
crònan *n* -ain, -ain *m* croon, low singing, humming, purring, any low murmuring sound **c. nan allt** the murmuring of the streams
crosgag *n* -aig, -an *f* starfish
crosta *a* cross, angry, irascible, irritable *Formerly* **crosda**
crotach *a* -aiche stooped, humpbacked
crotair(e) *n* -an *m* hunchback
crotal *n* -ail *m* lichen
cruach *n* **cruaiche**, -an *f* pile, heap, stack **c.-arbhair/fheòir/ mhòna(ch)** corn-/hay-/peat-stack *Also found in hill/mountain names*
cruach *v* -adh pile or heap up; make into a stack
cruachann *n* -ainn, -ainn/ **cruaichnean/-an** *f* hip, haunch *Also* **cruachan**
cruadal *n* -ail, -an *m* hardship, adversity, difficulty
cruadhaich *v* -achadh harden, solidify
cruaidh *n* -dhach, -ean *f* steel; stone (*used as anchor*)
cruaidh *a* -e hard; difficult; mean; hardy **c.-chàs** *m* danger, extremity, adversity
  c.-cheasnaich cross-examine
  c.-chridheach hard-hearted
cruas *n* -ais *m* hardness, hardihood; meanness
crùb *v* -adh crouch, squat

crùbach *a* -aiche lame or otherwise crippled
crùbag *n* -aig, -an *f* crab
crùbain *n* -ain *m* crouch, squat **dèan c.** *v* crouch, squat **na c(h)rùban** crouching, squatting
crudha *n* **cruidhe, cruidhean** *m* horseshoe
cruinn *a* -e round, circular; gathered together; compact, neat **c.-leum** *m* standing jump
cruinne *n m* the world (*f in gen na cruinne*); roundness
cruinneachadh *n* -aidh, -aidhean *m* gathering; function; collection
cruinne-cè *n m* **an C.** the world, the universe
cruinn-eòlas *n* **c.-eòlais** *m* geography (*subject*)
cruinnich *v* -neachadh collect, assemble, gather together; come together
crùisgean *n* -ein, -an *m* cruisie, oil-lamp
Cruithneach *n* -nich, -nich *m* Pict *a* Pictish
cruithneachd *n f m* wheat
crùn *n* **crùin, crùintean** *m* crown
crùn *v* -adh crown
crùnadh *n* -aidh *m* crowning, coronation
cruth *n* (-a), -an *m* form, shape, appearance **c.-atharrachadh** *m* transformation
cruthachail *a* -e creative
cruthaich *v* -achadh create, make
cruthaigheachd *n f* **a' Chruthaigheachd** Creation, the world **A Chruthaigheachd!** My goodness!
cruthaighear *n* -eir *m* **an C.** God, the Creator *Also* **cruthadair, cruithear**
cù *n* **coin, coin** *m* dog **cù- chaorach** sheepdog
cuach *n* **cuaiche, -an** *f* drinking cup, quaich; fold, curl of hair
cuagach *a* -aiche lame, limping
cuaille *n* -an *m* cudgel, club
cuairt *n* -e, -ean *f* circuit, round trip, trip (*generally*), excursion; round (*sport*); individual planks

in a clinker-built boat **chaidh sinn c. dhan Fhraing** we took a trip to France **c. dheireannach** final round **c.-ghaoth** eddying wind, whirlwind **c.-litir** circular, newsletter

cuairtich *v* **-teachadh** circulate

cuan *n* **cuain, cuain/-tan** *m* ocean, sea **an C. Siar** the Atlantic Ocean **an C. Sèimh** the Pacific Ocean

cuaraidh *n* **-ean** *f m* quarry

cuaran *n* **-ain, -an** *m* light shoe, sandal

cuartaich *v* **-achadh** surround, enclose; perform, conduct **a' cuartachadh an adhraidh** conducting worship

cùbaid *n* (**-e**), **-ean** *f* pulpit *Also* **cùbainn**

cubhaidh *a* **-e** fit, becoming, seemly, appropriate, fitting

cùbhraidh *a* **-e** fragrant

cucair *n* **-ean** *m* cooker

cudromach *a* **-aiche** important, weighty; heavy

cudthrom *See* **cuideam**

cudthromach *See* **cudromach**

cugallach *a* **-aiche** unstable (*also met*), wobbly, shoogly, unsteady; precarious

cuibheall *n* **cuibhle, cuibhleachan, cuibhlichean** *f* wheel **c.-stiùiridh** steering-wheel **c.-shnìomh** spinning-wheel

cuibheasach *a* **-aiche** sufficient; tolerable, middling

cuibhil *v* **cuibhleadh** wheel, roll along

cuibhle *n* **-an/-lichean** *f* wheel *See* **cuibheall**

cuibhlich *v* **-leachadh** *See* **cuibhil**

cuibhreann *n* **-rinn, -an** *f m* portion, part, instalment, allowance; (*met*) portion in life, fate

cuibhrig(e) *n* **-e, -ean/-an** *f m* cover, coverlet, bed-cover

cuid *n* **cuid/codach, -ean/ codaichean** *f* share, part; belongings, property, resources; *often used to indicate possession*; some (people) **c. na**

h-oidhche board and lodgings, bed and breakfast **mo chuid fhìn** my own/my own property/ resources **mo chuid airgid/aodaich/chloinne** my money/clothes/children **canaidh c. nach eil sin ceart** some people say that's not right **chan eil e an dara c. fuar no teth** it is neither hot nor cold **a' mhòr-chuid** the majority

cuideachadh *n* **-aidh** *m* help, assistance, aid

cuideachail *a* **-e** helpful

cuideachd *n* *f* company, group of people **bha e math a bhith nur c.** it was good to be in your company

cuideachd *adv* also, as well; together

cuideachdail *a* **-e** sociable, companionable

cuideam *n* **-eim, -an** *m* weight

cuideigin *pron* someone, somebody

cuide ri *prep* with, along with, in the company of

cuidhteag *n* **-eig, -an** *f* whiting

cuidhteas *n* receipt; riddance **fhuair mi c. an cnatan mu dheireadh thall** I finally got rid of the cold

cuidich *v* **-deachadh** help, assist, aid

cùil *n* (**-e**), **-tean** *f* corner, nook, recess, any secluded or private place **c.-chumhang** a tight spot, a fix

cuilbheart *n* **-eirt, -an** *f* wile, stratagem

cuilc *n* **-e, -ean** *f* reed

cuileag *n* **-eig, -an** *f* fly **a bheil a' chuileag ann?** are the midges out?

cuilean *n* **-ein, -an** *m* puppy

cuileann *n* **-linn, -an** *m* holly

cuimhne *n* *f* memory, remembrance **tha c. mhath aige** he has a good memory **an robh cuimhn' aice ort?** did she remember you? **mas math mo chuimhne** if my memory serves me right **chaidh e glan às mo chuimhne** I completely forgot (about it) **cuir nan c.** *v* remind them

cuimhneachan *n* -ain, -ain *m* memorial, remembrance, commemoration, keepsake **mar chuimhneachan ormsa** in remembrance of me

cuimhnich *v* -neachadh remember, recall, bear in mind, commemorate

cuimir *a* -e brief, concise; (*of person*) shapely, well-proportioned, handsome

Cuimreach *n* -rich, -rich *m* someone from Wales *a* Welsh

cuimse *n* -an *f* aim, mark; moderation

cuimseach *a* -siche moderate, reasonable; (*of person*) sure of aim **c. math** reasonably good

cuimsich *v* -seachadh aim; hit a mark or target, target

cuin(e) *int pron, adv* when **c. a thig iad?** when will they come? **chan eil fhios agamsa c. a thig iad** I don't know when they will come

cuing *n* -e, -ean *f* yoke, bond, restraint **c./a' chuing** (*pronounced* **a' chaoidh** *but nasally*) asthma

cuingealaich *v* -achadh restrict, limit

cuinneag *n* -eig, -an *f* pail, bucket

cuinnean *n* -ein, -an *m* nostril

cuip *n* -e, -ean/-eachan *f* whip

cuip *v* -eadh whip

cuir *v* cur put, place, lay; send; set; sow, plant; cast **c. buntàta** plant potatoes **c. clèibh/lìn** set creels/nets **c. fios/litir** send word/a letter **c. fios air ...** send for ... **c. gaoisid** shed coat **c. sneachda** snow *Also featured in many idioms eg* **c. air bhonn** set up **c. air chois** set up, establish **c. a-mach** issue; vomit, be sick **c. an aghaidh** oppose **c. an cèill** express, declare **c. an ìre** pretend **c. às do** abolish **c. às leth** accuse **c. dheth** postpone **c. fàilte air** welcome **c. geall** bet, lay wager **c. ìmpidh air** urge **c. ri**

add to **c. romhad** decide (to) **dè tha cur riut?** what's troubling you? **c. troimh-a-chèile** upset, confuse

cuireadh *n* -ridh, -idhean *m* invitation

cuirm *n* -e, -ean *f* feast, banquet **c.-chiùil** concert **c.-chnuic** picnic

cùirt *n* -e/cùrtach, -ean *f* court **c.-lagha** court of law

cùirtean *n* -ein, -an *m* curtain *Also* **cùirtear**

cùis *n* -e, -ean *f* matter, affair; cause; object, butt **sin mar a tha a' chùis** that's how things are/stand **c.-bhùirt/bhùrta** a laughing-stock **c.-eagail** something to be feared **c.-lagha** a court case **c.-mhaslaidh** a disgrace **an dèan thu a' chùis air?** will you manage it? **rinn iad a' chùis oirnn** they defeated us **nì sin a' chùis** that'll do/that'll suffice

cuisean *n* -ein, -an *f m* cushion

cuisle *n* -an *f* vein, blood-vessel, artery **c.-chiùil** pipe (*mus*)

cuislean *n* -ein, -an *m* flute

cuithe *n* -achan *f* pit, trench; fold for animals **c. sneachda** snowdrift

cùl *n* cùil, cùil/cùiltean *m* back; (*in poetry*) hair **c. an taighe** the back of the house **cuir c. ris** *v* abandon it/leave it/stop it **c.-chàin** *v* backbite, slander **c.-chàineadh** *n m* backbiting, slander **c.-taic** *n f* support **'s e Gàidheal gu chùl a th' ann** he's a Gael through and through

cùlaibh *n m* back, back part of anything **air do chùlaibh** behind you

culaidh *n* -e, -ean *f* garment, apparel; object, butt **c.-choimheach** fancy dress **c.-mhagaidh** object of scorn/mockery

cùlaist *n* -e, -ean *f* utility room, scullery

cularan *n* -ain, -ain *m* cucumber

cullach *n* -aich, -aich *m* male cat, tomcat; boar

cùl-mhùtaireachd *n* **cùil-** *f* smuggling; mutinying, plotting

cultar *n* **-air, -an** *m* culture

cultarach *a* **-aiche** cultural

cum *v* **-adh** shape, form, compose, fashion

cùm *v* **cumail** keep, retain; support; hold **a bheil thu a' cumail gu math?** are you keeping well? **dè na chumas e?** how much will it hold? **c. sin dhomh** hold that for me **c. a-mach** claim, make out **c. coinneamh** hold a meeting **c. grèim air** keep hold of **c. ort** keep going, carry on, keep at it **c. suas** keep up, maintain

cumadh *n* **-aidh, -aidhean** *m* shape, form; the act of shaping or forming

cumanta *a* common, ordinary

cumha *n* **-chan** *m* mourning, lamentation; elegy; condition, stipulation

cumhach *a* conditional (*gram*) **an tràth c.** the conditional tense

cumhachd *n* **-an** *f m* power, strength; authority

cumhachdach *a* **-aiche** powerful, mighty

cumhain *v See* **caomhain**

cumhang *a* **-ainge/cuinge** narrow, tight; narrow-minded

cùmhnant *n* **-aint, -an** *m* contract, agreement, covenant; condition **c.-obrach** contract of employment

cunbhalach *a* **-aiche** regular, constant, steady, consistent

cungaidh *n* **-ean** *f* ingredients; implement **c.-leighis** medicine, cure

cunnart *n* **-airt, -an** *m* danger, risk

cunnartach *a* **-aiche** dangerous, risky

cunnradh *n* **-aidh, -ean** *m* bargain, contract, deal, treaty

cunnt *v* **-adh/-as/-ais** count

cunntas *n* **-ais, -an** *f m* (*fin, general*) account; arithmetic **c.-beatha** CV **c.-bheachd** opinion poll **c.-sluaigh** census

cunntasachd *n* *f* accountancy, accounting

cunntasair *n* **-ean** *m* accountant

cuntair *n* **-ean** *m* counter (*in shop etc*) *Also* **cunntair**

cupa *n* **-nnan** *m* cup *Also* **cupan**

curaidh *n* **-ean** *m* hero, champion, warrior

cùram *n* **-aim, -an** *m* care, responsibility, charge, trust; anxiety, worry; religious conversion **ghabh mi c. a' ghille** I took care of/took responsibility for the boy **fo chùram** anxious/concerned **na biodh c. ort** don't be anxious/concerned **tha an c. oirre** she's been converted (*relig*)

cùramach *a* **-aiche** careful, responsible; anxious

cur na mara *n m* seasickness

currac *n* **-aic, -aicean** *m* cap, bonnet

curracag *n* **-aig, -an** *f* peewit, lapwing; haycock

curran *n* **-ain, -ain** *m* carrot

cùrsa *n* **-ichean** *f m* course

cur-seachad *n* **-an** *m* pastime, hobby

cus *n m* excess, too much, too many; (*less usual*) many **tha cus airgid aige** he has too much money **tha iad a' cur cus bheannachdan thugad** they send you lots of good wishes

cusbann *n f* customs, excise

cuspair *n* **-ean** *m* subject, topic

cut *v* **-adh** gut (*fish*)

cuthach *n* **-aich** *m* rage, fury; madness **duine-cuthaich** madman, wild man **bha an c. dearg oirre** she was mad with rage

cuthag *n* **-aig, -an** *f* cuckoo

D

dà *a* two (+ *dat sg & len*) **dà chaileig** two girls

da *aug prep* to his, for his

dachaigh *n* **(-e), -ean** *f* home **gun d.** homeless

dà-chànanach *a* bilingual

dà-chànanas *n* **-ais** *m*

bilingualism

dà-chasach *a* -aiche two-footed

dad *n f* anything **dad ort!** hang on! wait a minute!

dadaidh *n* -ean *m* dad, daddy

dadam *n* -aim, -an *m* atom

dadamach *a* atomic

dà-dheug *n, a* twelve (*nouns in their singular form are inserted between* **dà** *and* **dheug** *and are lenited*) **dà dhuine dheug** twelve men/persons

dà-dhualach *a* two-ply

dà fhichead *n, a* forty (*lit two score*)

dà-fhillte *a* two-fold, double, compound

daga *n* -ichean *m* pistol

dàibhear *n* -eir, -an *m* diver

dàibhig *v* -eadh dive

dail *n* dalach, -ean *f* dale, meadow

dàil *n* dàlach, dàlaichean *f* delay, procrastination; credit **cuir d. ann** *v* delay **air dhàil** on credit

dàimh *n* -e *f m* friendship, affinity, relationship

dàimheach *a* -mhiche related; relative (*gram*)

dàimhealachd *n f* friendliness

dàimheil *a* -e friendly

daingeann *a* daingne firm, steadfast, determined, committed

daingneach *n* -nich, -nichean *f* stronghold, fortification, fort

daingnich *v* -neachadh confirm, ratify; strengthen, consolidate

dàir *n* dàra/dàrach *f* breeding, heat, breeding together (*of cattle*) **tha an d. air a' bhoin** the cow is in heat/season

dall *n* doill, doill *m* blind person

dall *a* doille blind

dall *v* -adh blind

dallag an fheòir *n* dallaige an fh., dallagan an fh. *f* dormouse

dallag an fhraoich *n* dallaige an fh., dallagan an fh. *f* shrew

dalma *a* presumptuous; blatant

dalta *n* -n *m* foster-child

daltachd *n f* fosterage

daltag *n* -aig, -an *f* bat

dam *n* -a, -aichean *m* dam

dàmais *n f* draughts

damaiste *n f* damage; difficulty

damh *n* daimh, daimh *m* bullock, ox; stag

Dàmhair *n f* an D. October

damhan-allaidh *n* damhain-, damhain- *m* spider

dàn *n* dàin *m* fate, destiny **bha sin an dàn dhi** that was her destiny

dàn *n* dàin, dàin *m* poem

dàna *a* bold, intrepid, daring, presumptuous

dànachd *n f* boldness, daring

dànadas *n* -ais *m* boldness, daring

Danmhairgeach *n* -gich, -gich *m* Dane *a* Danish

danns *v* -a(dh) dance

dannsa *n* -ichean *m* dance

dannsa(dh) *n* (-aidh) *m* dancing

dannsair *n* -ean *m* dancer

daoimean *n* -ein, -an *m* diamond

daoine *n m See* **duine**

daolag *n* -aig(e), -an *f* beetle **d.-bhreac-dhearg** ladybird

daonna *a* human *Also* **daonda**

daonnachd *n f* humanity *Also* **daondachd**

daonnan *adv* always

daor *a* daoire dear, expensive, costly

daorach *n f* -aich intoxication, drunkenness **bha an d. air** he was drunk **air an daoraich** on a binge

daorsa *n f* bondage, captivity

dar *aug prep* to our, for our *conj* when

darach *n* -aich *m* oak (*tree*)

da-rìribh *adv* indeed, very, in earnest

dàrna *a* second *Also* **dara**

dà-sheaghach *a* -aiche ambiguous

dath *n* -a, -an *m* colour

dath *v* -adh colour; dye

dathadh *n* -aidh *m* colouring

dathte *a* coloured

dè *int pron* what? **dè an uair a tha e?** what's the time? **dè an t-ainm a th' ort?** what's your name? **dè cho fad' 's a tha e?** how far is it?

de *prep* of (+ *dat & len*)

deachd *v* **-adh** dictate

deachdadh *n* **-aidh, -aidhean** *m* dictation **inneal-deachdaidh** *m* dictaphone

deadhan *n* **-ain, -ain** *m* dean

deagh *a* (*precedes & lenites n*) good, fine, excellent **d. bhanais** a good wedding

deagh-bheus *n* **-a, -an** *f* virtue

deagh-ghean *n* **-a** *m* goodwill, benevolence

dealachadh *n* **-aidh** *m* parting, separation

dealaich *v* **-achadh** part, separate, differentiate **tha iad air dealachadh** they've separated (*a couple*)

dealaichte *a* separate, separated

dealain *a* electric **teine d.** *m* electric fire **post-d.** *m* e-mail

dealan *n* **-ain** *m* electricity

dealanach *n* **-aich, -aich** *m* lightning

dealanaich *v* **-achadh** electrify

dealanair *n* **-ean** *m* electrician

dealan-dè *n* **dealain-, dealain-** *m* butterfly

dealas *n* **-ais** *m* zeal, eagerness, commitment

dealasach *a* **-aiche** zealous, eager, committed

dealbh *n* **-a/deilbhe, -an/deilbh** *f* *m* picture, illustration, photograph, form, figure, outline **tog d.** *v* take a picture **d.-chluich(e)** play (*acted*) **d.-èibhinn** cartoon

dealbh *v* **-adh** design, plan

dealbhadair *n* **-ean** *m* photographer, designer

dealbhaiche *n* **-an** *m* draughtsman

dealg *n* **deilg, -an** *f* pin, prickle, skewer

dealgan *n* **-ain, -an** *m* spindle

deàlrach *a* **-aiche** shiny, shining

deàlradh *n* **-aidh, -aidhean** *m* shining, flashing

deàlraich *v* **-adh** shine, flash

dealt *n* **-a** *f m* dew

deamhais *n* **-ean** *f m* shears

deamhan *n* **-ain, -ain** *m* demon, devil **'s e d. a th' annad!** you're a devil!

deamhnaidh *a* **-e** devilish **tha fhios agad d. math** you know damned well

deamocrasaidh *n* **-ean** *m* democracy

deamocratach *n* **-aich, -aich** *m* democrat

deamocratach *a* **-aiche** democratic

dèan *irr v* **-amh** do, make **d. cabhag!** hurry! **d. gàire** laugh **d. air do shocair!** slow down! **d. an gnothach/a' chùis** suffice, manage (+ **air**) beat, overcome

dèanadach *a* **-aiche** industrious, hardworking

deann *n* **-a, -an** *f* force, haste

deannan *n* **-ain, -an** *m* a number, a good few **d. bhliadhnaichean** a good few years

deann-ruith *n* **-e** *f* movement at speed, travel at pace, headlong rush

deanntag *n* **-aige, -an** *f* nettle

dèanta *a* done, complete; stocky (*in build*)

dearbh *v* **-adh** prove, affirm

dearbh *a* (*precedes & lenites n*) certain, sure, identical **gu d. fhèin** indeed **an d. fhear/thè** the very one

dearbhadh *n* **-aidh** *m* proof, identification, trial

dearbhta *a* certain, sure, proven *Also* **dearbhte**

dearc *n* **-an** *f* berry

dearcag *n* **-aig, -an** *f* little berry, currant

dearg *a* **deirge** red, crimson (*also used as an intensive*) **d. amadan/òinseach** an utter fool **d. chuthach** mad rage **d. mhèirleach** a downright thief **d. rùisgte** stark naked

dearg- *pref* reddish **d.-dhonn** reddish brown

deargann *n* **-ainn, -an** *f* flea

dearmad *n* **-aid, -an** *m* omission, oversight (*error*), neglect **dèan d. air** *v* neglect, omit, overlook

dearmadach *a* **-aiche** negligent,

forgetful

dearmaid *v* -ad neglect

deàrrs *v* -adh shine

deàrrsach *a* -aiche shining, gleaming, glistening **d. uisge** *f* downpour

deàrrsadh *n* -aidh, -aidhean *m* shining

deas *n, a* deise *f* south; right; ready (to) **Uibhist a D.** South Uist **an taobh a d.** the south side **an làmh dheas** the right hand **air an làimh dheis** on the right

deasachadh *n* -aidh *m* preparation, editing **neach-deasachaidh** *m* editor

deasaich *v* -achadh prepare, edit

deasaichte *a* prepared, edited

deasbad *n* -aid, -an *f m* debate **dèan d.** *v* debate

deas-bhriathrach *a* -aiche eloquent

deas-chainnt *n* -e *f* eloquence

deasg *n* -a, -an *m* desk

deas-ghnàth *n* -ghnàith, -ghnàthan *m* ceremony, ceremonial

deatach *n* -aiche, -aichean *f* smoke, fumes, vapour

deatamach *a* -aiche necessary, crucial, essential

ded *aug prep* of your

deic *n* -e, -ichean *f m* deck (*of boat*)

deich *n, a* ten

deichead *n* -eid, -an *m* decade

deicheamh *n* -eimh *m* decimal *num a* tenth

deichnear *n m* ten (people) **d. fhear** ten men

dèideadh *n* -didh *m* toothache **a bheil an d. ort?** do you have toothache?

dèideag *n* -eig, -an *f* toy; pebble

dèidh *n* -e, -ean *f* desire; fondness; aspiration

dèidheil *a* -e fond **d. air …** fond of …

deifir *n See* diofar

deifrichte *See* diofraichte

deigh *n* -e *f* ice

dèile *n* -an/-achan *f* wooden board, plank **d.-bhogadain** see-

saw

dèilig *v* -eadh (*followed by* ri) deal (with), treat

deimhinn(t)e *a* certain, categorical, conclusive

dèine *n f* keenness, commitment; impetus

dèirc *n* -e, -ean *f* alms, charity

dèirceach *n* -cich, -cich *m* beggar

deireadh *n* -ridh, -ridhean *m* end, rear, stern; (*abstr*) finish, conclusion **air d(h).** late … **mu dheireadh** last **mu dheireadh thall** at (long) last, eventually

deireannach *a* -aiche last, latter, final, ultimate; backward

deis *a* deise ready, eager, willing

deisciobal *n* -ail, -ail *m* disciple

deise *n* -achan *f* suit, uniform **d. an Airm** Army uniform **d.-sgoile** school uniform **d.-snàimh** swimsuit

deiseil *a* -e/eala ready; finished (with); handy; clockwise

deit *n* -e, -ichean *f* date (*fruit*)

dem *aug prep* of my

den *aug prep* of the; of their

deò *n f* breath **thug e suas an d.** he breathed his last **d. gaoithe** a breath of wind

deoc *v* -adh suck

deoch *n* dighe/dibhe, -an/-annan *f* drink **d. an dorais** stirrup cup **d.-làidir** alcohol **d.-slàinte** toast (*with drink*)

deòin *n* -e *f* will, purpose

deònach *a* -aiche willing

deònaich *v* -achadh grant, vouchsafe, be willing to do

deothail *v* -al suck *Formerly* **deoghail**

der *aug prep* of/off our/your

deuchainn *n* -e, -ean *f* examination, test, trial; agony

deuchainneach *a* -niche trying, agonizing

deucon *n* -oin, -oin/-an *m* deacon

deud *n* -an *m* denture, tooth

deudach *a* -aiche toothy, dental

deug *suff* teen (*in numbers*) **sia-deug** sixteen

deugachadh *n m* a span of 13 to 19 years **d. bhliadhnaichean** a period of between 13 and 19 years

deugaich *v* -achadh enter teenage years

deugaire *n* -an *m* teenager

deur *n* deòir, deòir *m* tear (*drop*)

dha *prep See* **do**

dha *aug prep* to/for his

dha/dhàsan *prep pron* to/for him

dhà *n* two **a dhà** two **na dhà** the two

dhachaigh *adv* home (*ie homewards*)

dhad *aug prep* to/for your

dhà-dheug *n* twelve **a d.** twelve

dhaibh(san) *prep pron* to/for them

dham *aug prep* to/for my; to/for their

dhan *aug prep* to/for the/their

dha-rìribh *adv* indeed, very, in earnest **math d.** excellent, very good

dhe *aug prep* of/off him

dhed *aug prep* of/off your (*sg*)

dhem *aug prep* of/off my

dhen *aug prep* of/off the/their

dher *aug prep* of/off our/your

dheth *adv* off

dheth(san) *prep pron* of/off him

dhi/dhì(se) *prep pron* to/for her

dhibh(se) *prep pron* of/off you

dhinn(e) *prep pron* of/off us

dhìom(sa) *prep pron* of/off me

dhìot(sa) *prep pron* of/off you (*sg*)

dhith(se) *prep pron* of/off her

dhiubh(san) *prep pron* of/off them

dhòmh(sa) *prep pron* to/for me

dhuibh(se) *prep pron* to/for you

dhuinn(e) *prep pron* to/for us

dhuit *See* **dhut**

dhur *aug prep* to/for your

dhut(sa) *prep pron* to/for you (*sg*)

di/dì(se) *prep pron* to/for her

dia *n* dè, -than *m* god **Dia** God

diabhal *n* -ail, -ail/-bhlan *m* devil **an D.** the Devil

diabhlaidh *a* devilish, diabolical

diadhachd *n f* divinity, godhead; theology, study of divinity; godliness

diadhaidh *a* -e godly, devout; divine

diadhaire *n* -an *m* theologian, divine

diallaid *n See* **dìollaid**

dian *a* dèine keen, vehement, impetuous; intensive, intense

Diardaoin *n m* Thursday

dias *n* dèise, -an *f* ear of corn

diathad *n* -aid, -an *f* dinner, lunch

dibhearsain *n m* fun, entertainment, diversion

dìblidh *a* -e abject, wretched; in difficulty

dìcheall *n* dìchill *m* diligence, utmost **rinn iad an d.** they did their best/utmost

dìcheallach *a* -aiche diligent, conscientious

dì-chuimhnich *v See* **dìochuimhnich**

Diciadain *n m* Wednesday

Didòmhnaich *n m* Sunday

dìg *n* -e, -ean *f* ditch

digear *n* -eir, -an *m* digger

Dihaoine *n m* Friday

dìle *n* -ann, -an *f* deluge, flood **d. bhàthte** torrential rain

dìleab *n* -eib(e), -an *f* legacy, bequest

dìleas *a* dìlse faithful, loyal

dilleachdan *n* -ain, -an *m* orphan

dìlseachd *n f* faithfulness, loyalty

Diluain *n m* Monday

Dimàirt *n m* Tuesday

dìmeas *n* -a *m* disregard, disrespect **dèan d. air** *v* disregard, look down on

dìneasair *n* -ean *m* dinosaur

dinn *v* -eadh stuff, cram, squeeze in

dìnnear *n* -eir/-ach, -an *f* dinner

dinnsear *n* -eir *m* ginger

dìobair *v* -bradh desert, abandon; fail, come to nothing

dìobhair *v* (-t) vomit

dìochuimhne *n f* forgetfulness

dìochuimhneach *a* -niche forgetful

dìochuimhnich *v* -neachadh forget

diofar *n* **-air** *m* difference; variety **chan eil e gu d.** it doesn't matter

diofraichte *a* different

diog *n* **-an** *m* second (*unit of time*)

diogail *v* **-gladh** tickle

diogalach *a* **-aiche** tickly, ticklish

dìoghail *v* **-ghladh** avenge; pay back, compensate *Also* **dìol**

dìoghaltas *n* **-ais** *m* revenge, vengeance

dìoghras *n* **-ais** *m* enthusiasm

diogladh *n* **-aidh** *m* tickling

dìol *n m* abuse **dèan droch dhìol air** *v* badly abuse

dìolain *a* illegitimate (*as of child*)

dìol-dèirce *n* **diolacha/-an** *m* beggar, wretch, poor soul

dìollaid *n* **-e, -ean** *f* saddle

diomb *n m* displeasure, indignation, resentment

diombach *a* **-aiche** displeased, indignant, resentful

diombuan *a* **-uaine** transient, fleeting

dìomhain *a* **-e** vain; idle

dìomhair *a* **-e** mysterious; secret, confidential

dìomhaireachd *n f* mystery; secrecy, confidentiality

dìomhanas *n* **-ais** vanity; idleness

dìon *n* **-a** *m* protection, defence, security

dìon *v* protect, defend, guard

dìonach *a* **-aiche** watertight

dìosgan *n* **-ain, -ain** *m* creak

dìosganaich *n* **-e** *f* creaking

dìreach *a* **dìriche** straight, direct; upright

dìreach *adv* just **tha e d. air falbh** he has just gone **seadh d.** just so

dìreadh *n* **-ridh, -ridhean** *m* climb, ascent

dìrich *v* **dìreadh/dìreachadh** climb, ascend; straighten, make straight

Disathairne *n m* Saturday

dìsinn/dìsne *n* **dìsne, dìsnean** *m* dice, die

dìt *v* **-eadh** condemn, sentence

dìth *n* **-e** *f m* want, lack, deficiency **dè tha dhìth ort?** what do you want? **bha feadhainn a dhìth** there were some missing **a' dol a dhìth** perishing, dying

dìthean *n* **-ein, -ein/-an** *m* flower

dithis *n f* two (people); both; pair, couple **an d. aca** the two of them

diù *n m* worth, heed, attention **cha do chuir e d. ann** he paid no attention to it

diùc *n* **-an** *m* duke **ban-d.** *f* duchess

diùid *a* **-e** shy, bashful, reticent

diùlt *v* **-adh** refuse, reject

diùltadh *n* **-aidh, -aidhean** *m* refusal, rejection

Diùrach *n* **-aich, -aich** *m* someone from Jura *a* from, or pertaining to, Jura

dleastanas *n* **-ais, -an** *m* duty, obligation **mar dhleastanas** obligatory

dligheach *a* **-ghiche** due, legitimate

dlùth *n* **-a, dlùithe** *m* warp (*weaving*)

dlùth *a* **dlùithe** close (to), near

dlùthaich *v* **-achadh** approach, near; warp (*weaving*)

do *poss pron* your **d'** *before vowels* **d' athair** your father

do *prep* to, for (+ *dat*)

do *v part* (*indicates past tense*) **an do dh'èirich iad?** did they get up?

do *neg pref* in-, im-, un-

do-àireamh *a* innumerable, countless

dòbhran *n* **-ain, -ain** *m* otter

doca *n* **-n/-ichean** *m* dock; hollow, hole

docair *n* **-ean** *m* docker

dòcha *a* likely, probable **'s e sin as d.** that's most likely **'s d.** perhaps, maybe **is d. gun tig iad** perhaps they will come

dochainn *v* beat up, hurt, injure

dochann *n* **-ainn** *m* hurt, injury

dòchas *n* **-ais, -an** *m* hope **tha mi an d. gum faic mi iad** I hope I'll see them

dòchasach *a* **-aiche** hopeful

dod *aug prep* to your

do-dhèanta *a* impossible, impractical, impracticable

do-fhaicsinneach *a* **-niche** invisible

dòigh *n* **-e, -ean** *f* way, method, manner **d.-beatha** way of life, lifestyle **cuir air d.** *v* repair; arrange, organize **tha i air a d.** she is happy

dòigheil *a* **-e** well-arranged, contented, sensible, reasonable **tha e gu d.** he is well

doile *n* **-lichean** *f* doll

doileag *n* **-eig, -an** *f* (small) doll

doilgheas *n* **-eis** *m* affliction, vexation, sorrow

doille *n f* blindness

doilleir *a* **-e** dark, gloomy

doimhne *n f* depth **an d.** the sea

doimhneachd *n f* depth

doineann *n* **-ninn, -an** *f* tempest

doirbh *a* **-e/dorra** difficult

doire *n* **-an/-achan** *f m* grove, thicket

dòirt *v* **dòrtadh** pour; spill

dol *n m* going (*See irr v* **rach** *in Grammar*)

dol-a-mach *n m* exit; behaviour **anns a' chiad d.** initially **dè an d. a th' ort?** what are you up to?

dol-a-steach *n m* entrance

dolaidh *n f* harm, detriment **chaidh e a dholaidh** it perished/rotted

dolair *n* **-ean** *m* dollar

dol air adhart *n m* carry-on

dol-às *n m* escape **cha robh d. againn** we had no way out, we found it unavoidable

dom *aug prep* to/for my/their

domhainn *a* **doimhne/-e** deep; profound

domhan *n* **-ain** *m* universe

don *prep pron* to/for the/their

dona *a* **miosa** bad

donas *n* **-ais** *m* devil **an D.** the Devil **an D. ort!** Drat you!

donn *a* **duinne** brown, brown-haired

donnalaich *n f* howling

dor *aug prep* to/for you (*pl & pol*)

dòrainn *n* **-e, -ean** *f* anguish, agony

dòrainneach *a* **-niche** anguished, excruciating

doras *n* **-ais, dorsan** *m* door **d.-aghaidh** front door **d.-cùil** back door **d.-èiginn** emergency exit

dorch(a) *a* **duirch(e)** dark, dark-haired, dusky

dorchadas *n* **-ais** *m* darkness

dòrlach *n* **-aich, -aich** *m* handful

dòrn *n* **dùirn, dùirn** *m* fist

dorsair *n* **-ean** *m* doorman, janitor

dòrtadh *n* **-aidh, -aidhean** *m* pouring **bha d. uisge ann** it was pouring (with) rain

dos *n* **dois/duis, duis, -an** *m* bush, tuft; drone (*of bagpipe*)

dòs *v* **-adh** dose

do-sheachanta *a* unavoidable, inevitable

dotair *n* **-ean** *m* doctor

dòtaman *n* **-ain, -an** *m* spinning top

drabasta *a* lewd, obscene

dragh *n* **-a, -annan** *m* bother, trouble; worry **bha d. oirre** she was worried **na gabh d.** *v* don't worry/go to any trouble

dragh *v* **-adh** tug

draghadh *n* **-aidh, -aidhean** *m* a tug **thug i d. air** *v* she gave it a tug

draghail *a* **-e/-ala** worried, worrying, troublesome

dràibh *v* **-eadh** drive

dràibhear *n* **-eir, -an** *m* driver

dràibh(ig) *v* **-eadh** drive

drama *n* **-ichean** *m* dram (*of whisky*)

dràma *n f* drama

dranndan *n* **-ain** *m* murmur, drone; snarl

draoidh *n* **-ean** *m* wizard, sorcerer, druid

draoidheachd *n f* wizardry, sorcery; magic; druidism

drathair *n* **dràthraichean** *m* drawer (*in furniture*)

drathais *n* **-e, -ean** *f* drawers, pants, knickers *Also* **drathars**

dreach *n* **-a, -an** *m* appearance

dreachd *n* **-an** *f* draft

dreag *n* **dreige, -an** *f* meteor

dreagaire *n* **-an** *m* satellite

dreallag *n* -aige, -an *f* swing (*for play*)

dream *n* -a, -annan *m* people, tribe

drèana *n* -ichean *f* drain, ditch

dreas(a) *n* -(a)ichean *f m* dress

dreasair *n* -ean *m* dresser (*furniture*)

dreathan-donn *n* dreathain-duinn, **dreathain-donna** *m* wren

drèin *n* -e, -ean *f* scowl **chuir i d. oirre** *v* she pulled a face

dreuchd *n* -an *f* profession, occupation, office (*position*) **leig i dhith a d.** *v* she retired

driamlach *n* -aich, -aich/-aichean *f m* fishing line

drile *n* -lichean *f* drill (*mech*)

drilig *v* -eadh drill (*mech*)

drioftair *n* -ean *m* drifter (*fishing boat*)

drip *n* -e *f* bustle

dripeil *a* -e very busy, bustling

dris *n* -e, -ean *f* bramble

drithlinn *n m* malfunction **chaidh e d.** it malfunctioned

driùchd *n* -an *m* dew

dròbh *n* dròibh, -an *f m* drove

dròbhair *n* -ean *m* drover

droch *a* bad (*precedes & lenites n*) **d. shìde** bad weather **d. c(h)ainnt** bad language

drochaid *n* -e, -ean *f* bridge

droch-bheus *n* -a, -an *f* bad behaviour, immorality

droch-nàdarrach *a* -aiche bad-natured, ill-tempered

droga *n* -ichean *f* drug

droigheann *n* -ghinn *f* thorn

droman *n* -ain *m* elder tree

drudhag *n* -aig, -an *f* drop (*of liquid*); sip *Also* **drùdhag**

druid *n* -e, -ean *f* starling

druid *v* -eadh shut

drùidh *v* drùdhadh soak, penetrate; impress, influence **dhrùidh e orm** it impressed me

drùidhteach *a* -tiche penetrating; impressive

druim *n* droma, dromannan *m* back; ridge (*topog*)

druma *n* -chan/-ichean *f m* drum

duais *n* -e, -ean *f* prize, reward; wages

dual *n* duail, -an *m* lock (*of hair*), plait; strand

dual *n* duail *m* hereditary right, inherited character or quality **mar bu d. dha** as was his custom

dualach *a* -aiche curled, plaited

dualag *n* -aig, -an *f* curl (*of hair*), ringlet

dualchainnt *n* -e, -ean *f* speech of a particular area, dialect

dualchas *n* -ais *m* heritage, tradition

dualchasach *a* -aiche traditional

dual(t)ach *a* -aiche liable (to), inclined (to)

duan *n* duain, duain *m* poem

duanag *n* -aig, -an *f* ditty

duanaire *n* -an *m* anthology

dùbailte *a* double

dubh *n* duibh *m* black (*colour*); ink; pupil (*of eye*)

dubh *a* duibhe black **d. dorcha** pitch-dark/-black

dubh *v* -adh blacken **d. às** erase, excise

dubh- *pref* dark **d.-ghorm** dark blue

dubhach *a* -aiche sad, melancholy

dubhadh *n* -aidh *m* blackening, darkening, eclipse **d. na grèine/gealaich** eclipse of the sun/moon

dubhag *n* -aig, -an *f* kidney

dubhan *n* -ain, -ain *m* hook

dubhar *n* -air *m* shade

dubh-cheist *n* -cheistean *f* puzzle

dubh-fhacal *n* -ail, -ail/-fhaclan *m* riddle, enigma

Dùbhlachd *n f* **an D.** December

dùbhlan *n* -ain, -ain *m* challenge, defiance **thug i d. dha** she defied/challenged him

dùblaich *v* -achadh double, duplicate

dùdach *n* -aiche, -aichean *f m* horn (*in car*), hooter

dùil *n* -e, -ean *f* expectation **tha d. aice ri leanabh** she's expecting (a baby) **ma-tha, tha mi 'n d.** I should think so (too)

dùil *n* -e, -ean *f* element
duileasg *n* -lisg *m* dulse
duilgheadas *n* -ais, -an *m* difficulty, problem
duilich *a* duilghe sad, regrettable; difficult **tha mi d.** I'm sorry
duilleach *n* -lich, *m* foliage
duilleachan *n* -ain, -ain *m* leaflet
duilleag *n* -eige, -an *f* leaf; sheet (*of paper*); page **taobh-duilleig(e)** 6 page 6
duilleagach *a* -aiche leafy
dùin *v* dùnadh close, shut
duine *n* daoine *m* man, person, anyone; husband **a bheil d. a-staigh?** is there anyone in? **a h-uile d.** everyone, everybody **d.-uasal** gentleman, nobleman **d. sam bith** anyone
duinealas *n* -ais *m* manliness
duineil *a* -e manly
dùinte *a* closed, shut; reserved, withdrawn
duiseal *n* -eil, -an *f* flute
dùisg *v* dùsgadh wake, awaken, rouse
Dùitseach *n* -ich *m* Dutch person *a* Dutch
dùmhail *a* -e dense; crowded, congested
dùn *n* dùin, dùin *m* fort; heap
dùnadh *n* -aidh, -aidhean *m* closure, closing, ending
dùnan *n* -ain, -ain *m* small fort; small heap; dunghill
dùr *a* dùire dour; stubborn
dur *aug prep* to your (*pl & pol*)
dùrachd *n* -an *f* sincerity, earnestness, wish **le deagh dhùrachd** with best wishes/yours sincerely
dùrachdach *a* -aiche sincere, fervent, impassioned
dùraig *v* -eadh dare, venture; desire **dhùraiginn falbh** I'd like to go
durcan *n* -ain, -ain *m* cone (*on tree*)
dùrdail *n* -e *f* crooning, cooing
dusan *n* -ain *m* dozen (+ *sg*) **d. ugh** a dozen eggs **leth-d.** half a dozen
dùsgadh *n* -aidh, -aidhean *m* waking, awakening, rousing **d. spioradail** religious revival
duslach *n* -aich *m* dust; mortal remains
dust *n m* dust
dust/dustaig *v* -adh/-eadh dust
dustair *n* -ean *m* duster
dùthaich *n* dùthcha, dùthchannan *f* country **air an d.** in the countryside
dùthchail *a* -e rural
dùthchas *n* -ais *m* place of origin, homeland; heredity, heritage
dùthchasach *a* -aiche native, indigenous, hereditary

E

e *pron* he, him, it
eabar *n* -air *m* mud, mire
Eabhra *n f* Hebrew (*language*)
Eabhra(idhea)ch *n* -aich, -aich *m* Hebrew *a* Hebrew
eacarsaich *n* -e, -ean *f* exercise; capering about
each *n* eich, eich *m* horse **e.-aibhne** hippopotamus **e.-uisge** water-horse, kelpie
eachdraiche *n* -an *m* historian
eachdraidh *n* -e, -ean *f* history, chronicle
eachdraidheil *a* -e historic, historical
eaconamach *a* economic, economical
eaconamachd *n f* economics
eaconamaidh *n* -ean *m* economy
eaconamair *n* -ean *m* economist
eaconamas *n* -ais *m* economics **e. dachaigh** home economics
Eadailteach *n* -tich, -tich *m* Italian *a* Italian
Eadailtis *n f* Italian (*language*)
eadar *prep* (+ *len*) between **e. ... agus ...** both ... and ... **e. bheag is mhòr** both large and small **e. dhà bharail** in two minds *Does not always lenite*
eadaraibh(se) *prep pron* between you (*pl & pol*)
eadarainn(e) *prep pron* between us

eadar-àm *n* **-ama** *m* **-amannan** *m*
interim period, interval **anns an
e.** in the interim, meantime
eadar-bhreith *n* **-e, -ean** *f*
arbitration
eadar-bhreithnich *v* **-neachadh**
arbitrate
eadar-dhà-lionn *adv* floundering;
hesitating, undecided
eadar-dhà-shian *n f* a break in a
spell of adverse weather
eadar-dhealachadh *n* **-aidh,
-aidhean** *m* difference,
distinction, differentiation
eadar-dhealaich *v* **-achadh**
distinguish, differentiate,
discriminate
eadar-dhealaichte *a* different,
distinctive **e. bho** distinct from
eadar-ghuidhe *n* **-achan** *m*
intercession, mediation
eadar-lìon *n* **-lìn** *m* **an t-Eadar-lìon**
the Internet
eadar-mheadhanach *a*
intermediate
eadar-mheadhanair *n* **-ean** *m*
intermediary; Redeemer (*relig*)
eadar-nàiseanta *a* international
eadar-roinneil *a* inter-
departmental, inter-regional
eadar-sholas *n* **-ais** *m* twilight
eadar-theangachadh *n* **-aidh,
-aidhean** *m* translation (*of
languages*) **e. mar-aon**
simultaneous translation
eadar-theangaich *v* **-achadh**
translate
eadar-theangaiche *n* **-an** *m*
translator
eadar-ùine *n f* interval,
intermission
eadhon *adv* even
eadradh *n* **-aidh, -aidhean** *m*
milking time
eadraiginn *n* **-e, -ean** *f*
intervention, mediation **rach
san e.** *v* intervene, mediate
eag *n* **eige, -an** *f* nick, notch, jag
eagach *a* **-aiche** jagged, serrated,
notched
eagal *n* **-ail** *m* fear, fright **an robh
an t-eagal ort?** were you afraid?
bha e. mo bheatha orm I was

scared stiff **air e. 's gum faic iad
sinn** in case/lest they see us
eagalach *a* **-aiche** fearful, afraid;
frightful, dreadful **e. fuar**
fearfully cold
eag-eòlas *n* **-ais** *m* ecology
eaglais *n* **-e, -ean** *f* church **E. na
h-Alba** the Church of Scotland
an E. Bhaisteach the Baptist
Church **an E. Chaitligeach** the
Catholic Church **an E.
Easbaigeach** the Episcopal
Church **an E. Shaor** the Free
Church **an E. Shaor Chlèireach**
the Free Presbyterian Church **an
E. Stèidhichte** the Established
Church
eagnaidh *a* **-e** exact, precise
eagranaich *v* **-achadh** arrange,
organize, place in order
eala *n* **-chan** *f* swan
èalaidh *v* **-adh** creep, move
stealthily, steal away
ealain *n* **-e, -ean** *f* art **Comhairle
nan E.** the Arts Council
ealamh *a* **-aimhe** quick, swift,
ready
ealanta *a* skilful, skilled,
ingenious, expert, artistic
ealantas *n* **-ais** *m* skill, ingenuity
ealla *n f* watching **gabh e. ris** take
stock of it, watch him
eallach *n* **-aich, -aich** *m* burden,
load
ealt *n* **-a, -an** *f* flock of birds;
bird life
ealtainn *n* **-e, -ean** *f* razor
eanchainn *n* **-e, -ean** *f* brain **tha
deagh e. aice** she has a good
brain
eangarra *a* irritable, cross
eanraich *n* **-e** *f* soup
ear *n f* east **an ear** the east **Cille
Bhrìghde an Ear** East Kilbride
chaidh iad an ear 's an iar they
scattered **an ear-dheas** the
south-east **an ear-thuath** the
north-east **an Ear Mheadhanach**
the Middle East
earail *n* **-alach -alaichean** *f*
exhortation; warning
earalaich *v* **-achadh** exhort,
caution; warn

earalas *n* -ais *m* foresight,
precaution

earb *n* -a, -aichean *f* roe-deer

earb *v* **earbsa** trust, rely, confide

earball *n* -aill, -aill *m* tail

earbsa *n f* reliance, confidence,
trust **cha chuirinn e. ann**
I wouldn't trust him/it

earbsach *a* -aiche reliable,
trustworthy

eàrlas *n* -ais, -ais *m* pledge,
token **e. clàir** record token

eàrr *n* -a, -an *m* tail, end,
conclusion **e.-ràdh** *m* tailpiece

earrach *n* -aich, -aich *m* spring
as t-e. in spring

earrann *n* -ainn, -an *f* section,
portion, sector; (*fin*) share;
(*liter*) passage, verse *Also*
earrainn

earranta *a* limited (*as of
company*)

eas *n* -a, -an *m* waterfall,
cascade, cataract

easag *n* -aig, -an *f* pheasant

eas-aonta *n* -n *f* disagreement,
dissent, discord, disunity

eas-aontach *a* -aiche dissenting,
dissident, discordant

eas-aontachd *n* -an *f*
disagreement, dissent, discord,
disunity

eas-aontaich *v* -achadh disagree,
dissent

easaontas *n* -ais *m* disobedience,
transgression

easbaig *n* -e, -ean *m* bishop **àrd-
e.** archbishop

Easbaigeach *n* -gich, -gich *m*
Episcopalian *a* Episcopalian,
episcopal

easbhaidh *n* -e, -ean *f* want, lack,
defect **chan eil càil a dh'e. oirnn**
we lack for nothing

easbhaidheach *a* -dhiche
deficient, defective

eascaraid *n* -cairdean *m* enemy,
foe

èasgaidh *a* -e willing, ready (to),
keen, obliging; active

easgann *n* -ainn, -an *f* eel

eas-onair *n* -e *f* dishonour

eas-onarach *a* -aiche dishonest,
dishonourable

eas-umhail *a* -e disobedient,
insubordinate

eas-ùmhlachd *n f* disobedience,
insubordination

eas-urram *n* -aim *m* dishonour,
disrespect

eas-urramach *a* -aiche
dishonourable, disrespectful

eathar *n* -air, **eathraichean** *f m*
boat

eatarra(san) *prep pron* between
them

èibh *n* -e, -ean *f* shout, call, cry

èibh *v* -each shout, call, cry

èibhinn *a* -e funny, amusing,
humorous

èibhleag *n* -eige, -an *f* live coal,
cinder

èideadh *n* -didh, -didhean *m*
dress, clothing, garb, uniform

eidheann *n* **eidhne** *f* ivy

èifeachd *n f* effectiveness, efficacy

èifeachdach *a* -aiche effective,
effectual, efficient

èifeachdail *a* -e effectual,
effective

Eigeach *n* **Eigich, Eigich** *m*
someone from Eigg *a* from, or
pertaining to, Eigg

eigh *n* -e *f* ice

èigh *n* -e, -ean *f* shout, call, cry

èigh *v* -each shout, call, cry

eighe *n* -achan *f* file (*impl*)

èigheach *n* -ghich *f* shouting,
calling, proclamation *Also*
èigheachd

eighre *n f* ice

-eigin *suff* some **cuideigin**
someone **rudeigin** something

èiginn *n f* necessity, emergency,
straits **air è.** only just, with
difficulty **ann an è.** as a last
resort

èiginneach *a* -niche desperate,
essential *Also* **èigeannach**

èignich *v* **èigneachadh** compel,
force; rape

eil *irr v* was, were (*never used on
its own*) (*See verb* **to be** *in
Grammar*)

Eilbheiseach *n* -sich, -sich *m*
someone from Switzerland *a*

Swiss

èildear *n* **-eir, -an** *m* (church)
elder

eile *a* other, another, else **fear e.**
another one (*m*) **tè e.** another
one (*f*) **cò e.?** who else?

èileadh *n See* **fèileadh**

eileamaid *n* **-e, -ean** *f* element

eilean *n* **-ein, -an** *m* island, isle

eileanach *n* **-aich, -aich** *m*
islander

eileatrom *n* **-oim, -an** *m* hearse,
bier

eilid *n* **èilde, èildean** *f* hind

eilthireach *n* **-rich, -rich** *m* exile,
alien

eilthireachd *n f* exile

einnsean *n* **-ein, -an** *m* engine
e.-smàlaidh fire engine

einnseanair *n* **-ean** *m* engineer

Èipheiteach *n* **-tich, -tich** *m*
Egyptian *a* Egyptian

eireachdail *a* **-e** handsome,
comely

eireag *n* **-eige, -an** *f* pullet, young
hen

Èireannach *n* **-aich, -aich** *m* Irish
person *a* Irish

èirich *v* **èirigh** rise, arise, get up;
happen to, befall **dè dh'èirich
dhaibh?** what happened to
them? **chan eil càil ag èirigh
dhaibh** they are all right, they
are coming to no harm

èirig *n* **-e, -ean** *f* ransom, forfeit,
reparation

èirigh *n f* rising, arising, getting
up, uprising

Èirisgeach *n* **-gich, -gich** *m*
someone from Eriskay *a* from,
or pertaining to, Eriskay

eirmseach *a* **-siche** witty, sharp-
witted

èis *n* **-e, -ean** *f* need, want; delay,
impediment **Clann ann an Èis**
Children in Need

èiseil *a* **-e** needy, urgently
required

eisimeil *n* **-e** *f* dependence **an e.
air** dependent on **an e.
Dhòmhnaill** dependent on
Donald

eisimeileach *a* **-liche** dependent

eisimpleir *n* **-ean** *f m* example
mar e. for example

eisir *n* **-ean** *m* oyster

eisirean *n* **-ein, -an** *m* scallop,
clam

èislean *n* **-ein** *m* grief, sorrow **fo
è.** sorrowing, dejected

èist *v* **-eachd** (**+ ri**) listen (to)
Formerly **èisd**

èisteachd *n f* listening, audition;
confession (*relig*) **luchd-e.** *m*
audience *Formerly* **èisdeachd**

eòlach *a* **-aiche** knowledgeable,
acquainted (with) **a bheil thu e.
air?** do you know him/it?

eòlaiche *n* **-an** *m* expert **e.-inntinn**
psychologist

eòlas *n* **-ais, -an** *m* knowledge,
acquaintance **e.-bodhaig**
anatomy **e.-inntinn** psychology
cuir e. air *v* get to know

eòrna *n m* barley **Tìr an E.** *lit* the
Land of the Barley (*a poetic
name for the island of Tiree*)

Eòrpach *n* **-aich, -aich** *m*
European *a* **-aiche** European

esan *emph pron* he, him, it

eu- *neg pref* dis-, in-, mis-, un- *etc*

euchd *n* **-an** *m* feat, exploit,
achievement

eucoir *n* **eucorach, -ean** *f* crime,
misdemeanour, misdeed

eu-còir *a* **-e** unkind, stingy

eu-coltach *a* **-aiche** unlike,
dissimilar, unlikely

eu-coltas *n* **-ais** *m* unlikelihood,
dissimilarity

eu-comas *n* **-ais, -an** *m* inability

eu-comasach *a* **-aiche** (**+ do**)
unable (to)

eucorach *n* **-aich, -aich** *m*
criminal, miscreant, rascal **'s e
e. a th' ann** he's a rascal

eud *n m* zeal, jealousy

eudach *n* **-aich** *m* jealousy **bha e
ag e. rithe** he was jealous of her
a **-aiche** jealous

eudail *n* **-ean** *f* dear, darling,
treasure **m' eudail** my dear

eudar *n See* **feudar**

eudmhor *a* **-oire** zealous; jealous

eu-dòchas *n* **-ais** *m* hopelessness,
despair

eu-dòchasach *a* -aiche hopeless, despairing
eu-domhainn *a* -e shallow
eug *n* èig *m* death
eug *def v* die, decease **dh'eug e** he died
eugsamhail *a* -e/-mhla various, manifold, miscellaneous, incomparable
eun *n* eòin, eòin *m* bird, fowl **e. dubh an sgadain** guillemot **e.-eòlas** *m* ornithology **e.-Frangach** turkey **e.-fraoich** grouse, moorhen **e.-mara** seabird **e.-tràghad** wader **e.-tumaidh** diver **eunlann** *f m* cage, aviary
eunach *n* -aich *m* fowling
eunadair *n* -ean *m* fowler
eunlaith *n* -e *f* birds, fowls, bird life
euslaint *n* -e, -ean *f* ill-health, sickness
euslainteach *n* -tich, -tich *m* invalid, patient
euslainteach *a* -tiche ill, sickly, unhealthy

F

fàbhar *n* -air, -an *m* favour
fàbharach *a* -aiche favourable; providential
fabhra *n* -n *m* eyelid
facal *n* -ail, -ail/faclan *m* word **f. air an fhacal** word for word
fa chomhair *prep phr* (+ *gen*) opposite
faclair *n* -ean *m* dictionary
facs *n* -aichean *m* fax
factaraidh *n* -ean *f m* factory
fad *n* faid *m* length, distance **air f.** all, altogether **air fhad** lengthways **f. an latha** all day **f. an t-siubhail** all the time **fhad 's** while
fàd *n* fàid/fòid, -an *m* a peat
fada *a* faide long **dè cho f.?** how long? **fad' às** distant, remote **f. nas fheàrr** much better **gun èirigh** late getting up **fad-ùine** long term **'s fhada bhon uair sin** long time no see

fadachd *n* *f* longing, yearning **bha f. oirnn ...** we were longing for ... **a' gabhail f.** longing, wearying
fadalach *a* -aiche late, slow
fadhail *n* -ail/fadhlach, fadhlaichean *f* ford
fad-fhulangach *a* -fhulangaiche long-suffering
fa-dheòidh *adv* at last
fàg *v* -ail leave; depart, go **f. air** accuse, allege
fagas *a* faisge near **am f.** near
faghaid *n* -e, -ean *f* hunt
faic *v* -inn see (*See irr v* **faic** *in Grammar*)
faiceall *n* -cill *f* care, caution *Also* **faicill**
faiceallach *a* -aiche careful, cautious, wary **bi f.!** be careful! *Also* **faicilleach**
faiche *n* -an *f* lawn, plain, meadow
faicsinneach *a* -niche visible, conspicuous
fàidh *n* -e, -ean *m* prophet
faidhbhile *n* -an *f m* beech
fàidheadaireachd *n* -an *f* prophecy
faidhle *n* -achan *m* file
faigh *v* -inn get, obtain, acquire, receive **f. a-mach** find out, ascertain
faighean *n* -ein, -an *m* vagina
faighnich *v* -neachd question, ask, enquire **f. dhith** ask her
failbheachan *n* -ain *m* earring
failc *n* -e, -ean *f* guillemot
fàileadh *n* -(e)idh, -(e)idhean *m* smell
faileas *n* -eis, -an *m* shadow
faileasach *a* -aiche shadowy
fàil(l)idh *a* -e stealthy **gu f.** quietly
faillich *v* -leachadh (+ *air*) defeat **dh'fhaillich e orm** I failed to do it/I couldn't manage it/he got the better of me *Also* **fairtlich**
fàillig *v* -eadh fail
fàilligeadh *n* -gidh, -gidhean *m* failure; flaw, defect
failmean *n* -ein, -an *m* kneecap
fail-mhuc *n* failean- *f* pigsty
fàilneachadh *n* -aidh, -aidhean *m*

failing
fàilt(e) *n* -(e)an *f* welcome **cuir f.
air ...** *v* welcome **... ceud mìle f.**
a hundred thousand welcomes,
the warmest of welcomes
fàilteachadh *n* -aidh *m*
welcoming, reception
fàiltich *v* -teachadh welcome,
greet
fàiltiche *n* -an *m* receptionist
faing *n* -e, -ean *f* fank, sheep-pen
fàinne *n* -achan *f m* ring **f.-
cluaise** earring **f.-gealladh-
pòsaidh** engagement ring **f.-
pòsaidh** wedding ring
faire *n* -an *f* watch, watching,
guard **neach-f.** guard
fàire *n* -an *f* horizon **air f.** on the
horizon
faireachadh *n* -aidh *m* feeling,
sensation, sense
faireachdainn *n* -ean *f* feeling,
sensation, sense
fàireag *n* -eig, -an *f* gland
fairge *n* -achan/-annan *f* sea,
ocean
fairich *v* -reachdainn/-reachadh
feel, sense
fairtleachadh *n* -aidh *m* failing
faisg *a* -e near **nas fhaisge** nearer
f. air near/close (to)
fàisg *v* fàsgadh squeeze, press
fàisneachd *n* -an *f* prophecy
fàisnich *v* -neachadh prophesy
fàitheam *n* -eim, -an *m* hem
fàl *n* fàil, fàil *m* hedge, dyke **fàl an
rathaid** (*of road*) verge
falach *n* -aich *m* hiding-place,
concealment **cuir am f. e** *v* hide
it **chaidh iad am f.** they hid
f.-fead hide and seek
falaich *v* -ach, hide, conceal
falaichte *a* hidden, concealed,
secret
falamh *a* -aimhe empty, void
falamhachd *n f* emptiness,
vacuum
falbh *v* go **air f.** gone away
falbhanach *a* -aiche wandering,
unsettled
fallain *a* -e healthy, wholesome,
sound **slàn f.** safe and sound
fallaineachd *n f* health

fallas *n* -ais *m* sweat,
perspiration **bha (am) f. orm**
I was sweating
fallasach *a* -aiche sweaty
falmadair *n* -ean *m* helm
falmhaich *v* -achadh empty
falt *n* fuilt, fuilt *m* hair
famh *n* faimh, faimh/-an *f m* mole
(*animal*)
famhair *n* -ean *m* giant
fan *v* -tainn wait, stay, remain
fanaid *n* -e *f* mockery, mocking,
derision **a' dèanamh f. air** *v*
mocking him, deriding it
fànas *n* -ais *m* outer space **f.-long**
f spaceship
fa-near *adv* under consideration
thoir f. notice, observe, be
aware of
fang *n* faing, faing/-an *m* fank,
sheep-pen
fann *a* -a/fainne faint, feeble,
weak
fannaich *v* -achadh grow faint,
faint, weaken
fanntaig *v* -eadh faint
faobhar *n* -air, -an *m* edge (*as of
knife*) **cuir f. air** *v* sharpen it
faobharaich *v* -achadh sharpen
faochag *n* -aig, -an *f* whelk,
winkle
faod *def v* may, can **am f. mi
smocadh?** may I smoke?
faodaidh tu fuireach you
may/can wait/stay
faoileag *n* -eig, -an *f* seagull
faoilidh *a* -e generous, liberal,
hospitable
Faoilleach/Faoilteach *n* -lich/-tich
m am F. January
faoin *a* -e vain, silly, pointless,
futile
faoineas *n* -eis *m* vanity, futility
's e f. a th' ann it's pointless
faoinsgeul *n* -eil/-a, -an *m* idle
talk, fiction, myth
faoisid *n* -e, -ean *f* confession
(*relig*)
faoisidich *v* -deachadh confess
(*relig*)
fao(tha)chadh *n* -aidh *m* relief,
respite
far *prep See* **bhàrr**

far *conj* where **sin far a bheil iad** that's where they are

faradh *n* -aidh, -aidhean *m* fare (*price*)

fàradh *n* -aidh, -aidhean *m* ladder

far-ainm *n* -e, -ean *m* nickname

faram *n* -aim *m* loud noise; percussion

faramach *a* -aiche noisy, resounding

farasta *See* **furasta**

farchluais *n* -e *f* eavesdropping *Also vn* **a' f.**

fàrdach *n* -aich, -aichean *f* house, dwelling, lodging

farmad *n* -aid *m* envy

farmadach *a* -aiche envious

farpais *n* -e, -ean *f* competition

farpaiseach *n* -sich, -sich *m* competitor

farsaing *a* -e wide, wide-ranging, extensive **fad' is f.** far and wide

farsaingeachd *n* *f* width, extent, area **san fharsaingeachd** in general, on the whole

farsainn *a* -e *See* **farsaing**

farspag *n* -aig, -an *f* great black-backed gull

fàs *n* fàis *m* growth

fàs *a* -a empty, waste, desolate, fallow

fàs *v* grow, become **a' fàs sean** getting/growing old

fàsach *n* -aich, -an *f m* wilderness, desert

fàsachadh *n* -aidh, -aidhean *m* depopulation

fàsaich *v* -achadh depopulate, clear (*of people*), lay waste

fàsail *a* -e/-ala desolate (*of places*)

fasan *n* -ain, -ain/-an *m* fashion

fasanta *a* fashionable

fasgach *a* -aiche sheltered

fasgadh *n* -aidh, -aidhean *m* shelter

fa sgaoil *adv* loose

fasgnadh *n* -aidh *m* winnowing

fastadh *n* -aidh, -aidhean *m* hiring, employing, employment *Formerly* **fasdadh**

fastaidh *v* -adh hire, employ *Formerly* **fasdaidh**

fastaidhear *n* -an *m* employer *Formerly* **fasdaidhear**

fàth *n* *m* reason, cause, opportunity

fathann *n* -ainn, -an *m* rumour, hearsay

feabhas *n* -ais *m* improvement **a' dol am f.** getting better, improving, healing

feachd *n* -an *f* army, host **F. an Adhair** the (Royal) Air Force

fead *n* -an *f* whistle (*by person*) **dèan/geàrr f.** *v* whistle

fead *v* -ail/-alaich/-arsaich/ -aireachd whistle

feadag *n* -aige, -an *f* whistle, flute; plover

feadaireachd *n* *f* whistling

feadan *n* -ain, -ain *m* chanter (*of bagpipes*); water pipe, water duct

feadh *n* *m* length **air f.** throughout, during (+ *gen*) **am f.** while, whilst

feadhainn *n* feadhna/feadhnach *f* people, some **f. aca** some of them **an fheadhainn sin** those **an fheadhainn dhearg** the red ones

feagal *n* *See* **eagal**

feàirrde *a* better **'s fheàirrd' thu sin** you are the better of that **b' fheàirrde mi norrag** I'd be the better of a nap

fealla-dhà *n* *f* fun, jest **ri f.** in fun/jest

feall-fhalach *n* -aich, -aichean *m* ambush

feallsanach *n* -aich, -aich *m* philosopher

feallsanachd *n* -an *f* philosophy

feamainn *n* -ann/-mnach/ feamad *f* seaweed

feann *v* -adh skin, flay

feannag *n* -aige, -an *f* crow; lazybed (*for planting*), rig

feanntag *n* -aige, -an *f m* nettle

feansa *n* -ichean *f m* fence

fear *n* fir, fir *m* man, male, one (*referring to masculine subject*) **am f. sin** that one **f. sam bith** anyone **f. an taighe** chairman (*of concert*)

fearail *a* -e/-ala manly, manful, brave

fearalachd *n f* manliness, manfulness

fearann *n* -ainn *m* land, ground **am mòr-fhearann** the common grazing

fearas-chuideachd *n* fearais- *f* diversion, pastime

fearas-feise *n* fearais- *f* homosexuality

fear-bainnse *n* fir-, fir- *m* bridegroom *Also* **fear na bainnse**

fear-brèige *n* fir-bhrèige, fir- *m* puppet **na Fir Bhrèige** the Callanish Stones

fear-bùtha *n* fir-, fir- *m* shopkeeper *Also* **fear na bùtha**

fear-cathrach *n* fir-, fir- *m* chairman *Also* **fear na cathrach**

fear-ceàird *n* fir-, fir- *m* tradesman

fear-ciùil *n* fir-, fir- *m* musician

fear-deasachaidh *n* fir-, fir- *m* editor

fear-ealain *n* fir-, fir- *m* artist

feareigin *pron* someone (*male*)

fearg *n* feirge *f* anger, ire, wrath **cuir f. air** *v* anger, annoy **bha an fhearg air** he was angry/ annoyed

feargach *a* -aiche angry

fear-gnothaich *n* fir-, fir- *m* businessman

fear-labhairt *n* fir-, fir- *m* spokesman

fear-lagha *n* fir-, fir- *m* lawyer (*male*)

feàrna *n f* alder

fear-pòsta *n* fir-phòsta, fir-phòsta *m* married man

feàrr *a* better **nas fheàrr** better **is fheàrr leis ...** he prefers ... **is fheàrr dhi ...** she had better ...

fearsaid *n* -e, -ean *f* spindle

fear-smàlaidh *n* fir-, fir- *m* fireman

fear-stiùiridh *n* fir-, fir- *m* director (*male*)

feart *n* feirt, -an *f* notice, attention **na toir f. air** pay no heed to him/it

feart *n* -a, -an *m* quality, virtue, characteristic

fear-teagaisg *n* fir-, fir- *m* teacher (*male*)

fear-togail *n* fir-, fir- *m* builder

feasgar *n* -air, -air/-an *m* afternoon, evening *adv* in the afternoon/evening **F. math** Good afternoon/evening **f. Diluain** Monday afternoon/evening

fèath *n* -a, -an *f m* calm (*weather*) **bha f. ann** it was calm

fèathach *a* calm (*weather*)

fèileadh *n* -lidh, -lidhean *m* kilt

fèill *n* -e, -(t)ean *f* festival; fair, market, sale **bha f. mhòr air** it/he was in great demand

fèin *pron* self, selves

fèin-àicheadh *n* -eidh *m* self-denial

fèin-dhìon *n* -a *m* self-defence

fèin-eachdraidh *n* -e, -ean *f* autobiography

fèineil *a* -e, -eala selfish

fèin-ìobairt *n* -e, -ean *f* self-sacrifice

fèin-mheas *n m* self-respect

fèin-mhurt *n* -mhuirt *m* suicide

fèin-riaghladh *n* -aidh *m* self-government

fèin-spèis *n* -e *f* self-regard, conceit, egotism

fèis *n* -e, -ean *f* festival **f. ciùil** music festival **Fèisean nan Gàidheal** the Festivals of the Gaels

feis(e) *n* -e *f* sexual intercourse, copulation

fèist *n* -e, -ean *f* feast, banquet *Formerly* **fèisd**

fèith *n* -e, -ean *f* vein, sinew, muscle

fèith *n* -e, -ichean *f* bog, marsh; channel

feith *v* -eamh await, wait (for)

fèitheach *a* -thiche sinewy, muscular

feòil *n* feòla *f* meat **f.-caorach** *n* mutton **f.-muice** pork **f.-uan** lamb **mairt-fheòil** beef

feòirling *n* -ean *f* farthing

feòladair *n* -ean *m* butcher

feòlmhor *a* -a/-oire carnal, sensual

feòrag *n* -aig, -an *f* squirrel

feòraich *v* -ach/-achadh ask, inquire

feuch *v* **-ainn** try, test; see **f. ri ...** try to ... **f. gun tadhail thu** see and call/be sure to call **f. nach tuit thu** watch/see that you don't fall

feudar *def v* must **'s fheudar gu bheil ...** it would seem that ... **b' fheudar dhaibh** they had to

feum *n* **-a, -annan** *f m* use, need **a bheil f. agad air?** do you need it/him?

feum *def v* have to, need to, must **feumaidh mi falbh** I'll have to go **am f. thu sin a dhèanamh?** must you do that?

feumach *a* **-aiche** needy **bha sinn f. air** we needed it

feumail *a* **-e/-ala** useful

feumalachd *n f* use, utility, expediency

feur *n* **feòir** *m* grass, hay

feurach *n* **-aich** *m* pasture, grazing

feurach *a* **-aiche** grassy

feuraich *v* **-achadh** graze

feusag *n* **-aig, -an** *f* beard

feusagach *a* **-aiche** bearded

feusgan *n* **-ain, -ain** *m* mussel

fhad is a *conj* while, whilst

fhathast *adv* yet, still

fhèin *pron* self, selves (*often used with* **tha** *when returning question*) **leatha f.** by herself, alone

fhìn *pron Variation on* **fhèin** (*in first person only*)

fhuair *irr v* got (*See irr v* **faigh** *in Grammar*)

fiabhras *n* **-ais, -an** *m* fever

fiabhrasach *a* **-aiche** feverish

fiacail *n* **fiacla, fiaclan** *f* tooth **fiaclan fuadain** false teeth

fiach *n* **feich, -an** *m* worth, value; debt **fo fhiachaibh** indebted to, owing to **cuir mar fhiachaibh air** *v* oblige, compel **mar fhiachaibh oirnn(e)** incumbent upon us

fiach *a* **-a** worthwhile, worth **cha d' fhiach e** it's useless **is fhiach dhut seo fhaicinn** you should see this **'s fhiach e an t-saothair** it's worth the effort

fiach *v See* **feuch**

fiaclair *n* **-ean** *m* dentist

fiadh *n* **fèidh, fèidh** *m* deer

fiadhaich *a* **-aiche** wild, fierce; angry, furious

fialaidh *a* **-e** generous, liberal

fialaidheachd *n f* generosity, liberality

fiamh *n* **-a** tinge, hue; fear; expression **f. a' ghàire** a hint of a smile

fianais *n* **-ean** *f* witness, evidence, testimony **tog f.** *v* give evidence; profess faith publicly **thoir f.** *v* witness, testify **am f.** in sight/view

fiar *a* **-a** crooked, bent, squint, slanted **f.-shùileach** squint-eyed

fiaradh *n* **-aidh** *m* bend, squint, slant **air f.** slanting, askew

fiathachadh *n* **-aidh, -aidhean** *m* invitation

fiathaich *v* **-achadh** invite

fichead *n* **fichid, -an** *m* twenty (+ *sg*) **trì f.** sixty

ficheadamh *a* twentieth

fideag *n* **-eig, -an** *f* whistle

fidheall *n* **fìdhle, fìdhlean** *f* fiddle, violin

fìdhlear *n* **-eir, -an** *m* fiddler, violinist

fìdhlearachd *n f* fiddling

fìge *n* **-an** *f* fig

figear *n* **-eir, -an** *m* figure (*arithmetic*)

figh *v* **-e** knit, weave

fighe *n f* knitting, weaving

figheadair *n* **-ean** *m* knitter, weaver

fighte *a* knitted, woven

fileanta *a* fluent

fileantach *n* **-aich, -aich** *m* fluent speaker

fileantachd *n f* fluency

filidh *n* **-ean** *m* poet

fill *v* **-eadh** fold; wrap

filleadh *n* **-lidh, -lidhean** *m* fold, plait

fillte *a* folded, plaited, compound

fine *n* **-achan** *f* clan, tribe, kindred

fìnealta *a* fine, elegant

finn-fuainneach *a* all, entire **fad f. an latha** the livelong day, all day long

fiodh *n* **-a** *m* wood, timber

fìogais *n* -ean *f* fig
fiolan *n* -ain, -an *m* beetle, earwig
  f.-gòbhlach earwig
fìon *n* -a *m* wine **f. dearg** red
  wine **f. geal** white wine
  f.-dhearc *f* grape **f.-geur** vinegar
  f.-lios *m* vineyard
fìonan *n* -ain, -ain/-an *m* vine
fionn *a* -a white, fair
fionnach *a* -aiche hairy
fionnadh *n* -aidh *m* hair (*of
  animals*)
fionnairidh *n* -ean *f* evening **air an
  fhionnairidh** in the evening
fionnan-feòir *n* **fionnain-,
  fionnain-** *m* grasshopper
fionnar *a* -aire/-a cool (*temp*)
fionnarachadh *n* -aidh *m*
  refrigeration
fionnarachd *n* *f* coolness (*temp*)
fionnaradair *n* -ean *m* refrigerator
fionnaraich *v* -achadh cool,
  refrigerate
fionnsgeul *n* -eil/-eòil, -an *m* legend
fìor *a* -a/fìre (*precedes & lenites
  n*) true, real, genuine, actual;
  very/really **f. mhath** very good
  f. amadan a real fool
fios *n* -a *m* knowledge,
  information **tha f. aice** she
  knows **cò aige tha f.?** who
  knows? **fhuair sinn f.** we got
  word **gun fhios nach ...** in case,
  lest ... **cuir f. thuca** *v* send them
  word **tha f. gun tadhail iad**
  surely they'll call
fiosaiche *n* -an *m* fortune-teller,
  seer
fios-naidheachd *n* **fiosan-** *m* press
  release
fiosrach *a* -aiche knowledgeable,
  well-informed
fiosrachadh *n* -aidh, -aidhean *m*
  information; experience
fiosraich *v* -achadh experience
fiosraichte *a* knowledgeable,
  informed
fir chlis *n* *m* *pl* **na F.** the Aurora
  Borealis, Northern Lights
fìreanachadh *n* -aidh *m*
  justification
fìreanaich *v* -achadh justify
fireann *a* male, masculine

fireannach *n* -aich, -aich *m* man,
  male
fìreantachd *n* *f* righteousness
fìr-eun *n* -eòin, -eòin *m* eagle
fìrinn *n* -e, -ean *f* truth, fact **an
  fhìrinn a th' agam** I'm telling the
  truth, it's true **a dh'innse na f.** to
  tell the truth **an Fhìrinn** the
  Bible
fìrinneach *a* -niche truthful,
  factual
fitheach *n* **fithich, fithich** *m* raven
fiù *n* *m* worth, value **gun fhiù**
  worthless, useless
fiù *a* worth **fiù is/'s** even **cha robh
  fiù 's sèithear ann** there wasn't
  even a chair there
fiùdalach *a* -aiche feudal
fiùdalachd *n* *f* feudalism
flaitheanas *n* -ais *m* heaven,
  paradise
flaitheas *n* -eis *m* heaven, paradise
flat *n* -aichean *f* *m* flat; saucer
  (*Lewis*)
flath *n* **flaith, -an/flaithean** *m*
  prince, chief
flathail *a* -e princely, noble
fleadh *n* -a, -an *m* feast, banquet
fleasgach *n* -aich, -aich *m*
  bachelor, youth; best man (*at
  wedding*)
fleòdradh *n* -aidh *m* floating,
  buoyancy **air f.** afloat
fleòdraich *v* -radh float
flin(ne) *n* -(e) *m* sleet
fliuch *a* **fliche/fliuiche** wet
fliuch *v* -adh wet, moisten
flod *n* -a *m* floating, flotation **air
  f.** floating, afloat
flodach *a* -aiche lukewarm
  (*liquid*)
flùr *n* **flùir, -aichean** *m* flower
flùr *n* **flùir** *m* flour
flùranach *a* -aiche flowery
fo *prep* (+ *dat*) under, below,
  beneath; under the influence of
  fon bhòrd under the table **fo
  mhulad** sad
fo-aodach *n* -aich *m*
  underclothes, underwear
fochann *n* -ainn *m* corn in blade
fo-cheumnaiche *n* -an *m*
  undergraduate

fo-chomataidh *n* **-ean** *f* sub-committee
fod *aug prep* under your (*sg*)
fòd/fòid *n* **fòide, -ean** *f* turf, peat, clod **fon fhòid** underground, buried
fodar *n* **-air** *m* fodder, straw
fodha *adv* underneath, sunken **chaidh am bàta f.** the boat went down/sank
fodha(san) *prep pron* under him/it; below him/it
fodhad(sa) *prep pron* under/below you (*sg*)
fodhaibh(se) *prep pron* under/below you (*pl & pol*)
fodhainn(e) *prep pron* under/below us
fodham(sa) *prep pron* under/below me
fodhpa(san) *prep pron* under/below them
fògair *v* **fògradh/-t** expel, banish
fògairt *n* *f* expelling, expulsion, banishing, banishment
fògarrach *n* **-aich** *m* exile, refugee
foghain *v* **fòghnadh** suffice **fòghnaidh sin** that will suffice **fòghnaidh na dh'fhòghnas!** enough is enough!
foghar *n* **-air** *m* autumn, harvest **am f.** autumn **as t-fhoghar** in autumn
foghlaim *v* **-am** educate, learn
foghlaim(ich)te *a* educated, learned
foghlam *n* **-aim** *m* education **f. tron Ghàidhlig** Gaelic-medium education
fòghnan *n* **-ain** *m* thistle **F. na h-Alba** the Thistle of Scotland
fògradh *n* **-aidh** *m* expelling, expulsion, banishing, banishment
foidhpe(se) *prep pron* under/below her
foighidinn *n* **-e** *f* patience
foighidneach *a* **-niche** patient
foileag *n* **-eig, -an** *f* pancake
foill *n* **-e** *f* deceit, fraud, treachery
foillseachadh *n* **-aidh, -aidhean** *m* publishing, publication; revealing
foillsich *v* **-seachadh** publish; reveal
foillsichear *n* **-eir, -an** *m* publisher
foinne *n* **-an** *f m* wart
foirfe *a* perfect **dèan f.** *v* perfect
foirfeach *n* **-fich, -fich** *m* church elder
foirfeachd *n* *f* perfection
foirm *n* **-ean** *m* form (*document*)
foirmeil *a* **-e/-eala** formal
fòirneart *n* **-eirt** *m* violence, oppression
fois *n* **-e** *f* rest, leisure
follais *n* *f* openness, display, view, publicity **am f.** visible, displayed **thàinig e am f.** it became evident/public, it came to light
follaiseach *a* **-siche** obvious, evident, public
fom *aug prep* under my/their, below my/their
fòn *n* **-aichean** *f m* telephone
fòn/fònaig *v* **-adh/-eadh** telephone
fon *aug prep* under their, under the, below their, below the
fonn *n* **fuinn, fuinn** *m* tune, air; mood **dè 'm fonn a bh' air?** what form was he in?
fonnmhor *a* **-oire** *a* tuneful, melodious
for *aug prep* under our, below our; under your, below your
for *n* **foir** *m* awareness, alertness, attention **cha robh for aca gu ...** they had no idea that ...
forail *a* **-e** aware, alert
fo-rathad *n* **-aid/-rothaid, -an/-ròidean** *m* subway, underground route
forc(a) *n* **-a, -an/-aichean** *f* fork
fòr-chàin *n* **-e, -ean** *f* surtax
fòr-chìs *n* **-e, -ean** *f* surcharge
fòrladh *n* **-aidh** *m* leave, furlough
fo-roinn *n* **-e, -ean** *f* sub-division
forsair *n* **-ean** *m* forester
forsaireachd *n* *f* forestry
fortan *n* **-ain** *m* fortune, luck
fortanach *a* **-aiche** fortunate, lucky
fosgail *v* **-gladh** open
fosgailte *a* open, frank
fosgailteachd *n* *f* openness, frankness

fosgarra *a* open, frank, forthcoming, candid

fosgarrachd *n f* candour, openness

fo-sgiorta *n* **-ichean** *f* underskirt

fosgladh *n* **-aidh, -aidhean** *m* opening, aperture; opportunity

fosglair *n* **-ean** *m* opener (*implement*)

fo-thaghadh *n* **-aidh, -aidhean** *m* by-election

fo-thiotal *n* **-ail, -alan** *m* subtitle

fo-thìreach *a* subterranean

fradharc *n* **-airc** *m* eyesight, vision

Fraingis *n f* French (*language*)

Frangach *n* **-aich, -aich** *m* French person *a* French

fraoch *n* **-oich** *m* heather

fras *n* **froise, -an** *f* shower (*of rain*)

fras *v* **-adh** shower

frasach *a* **-aiche** showery

frasair *n* **-ean** *m* shower (*in bathroom*)

freagair *v* **-t/-gradh** answer, reply, respond; suit

freagairt *n* **-ean** *f* answer, reply, response

freagarrach *a* **-aiche** suitable, appropriate

frèam *n* **-a, -aichean** *m* frame, framework **f. streap** climbing frame

freastal *n* **-ail** *m* providence; service *Formerly* **freasdal**

freiceadan *n* **-ain, -ain/-an** *m* guard, watch

freumh *n* **-a, -an/-aichean** *m* root, source

freumhaich *v* **-achadh** root

frìde *n* **-an** *f* insect

frids *n* **-ichean** *m* fridge, refrigerator

frioghan *n* **-ain, -ain** *m* bristle, barb

frionas *n* **-ais** *m* fretfulness, vexation, over-sensitivity

frionasach *a* **-aiche** fretful, vexed, over-sensitive

frìth *n* **-e, -ean** *f* deer forest

frith-ainm *n* **-e, -ean** *m* nickname

frith-bhaile *n* **-ltean** *m* suburb

frithealadh *n* **-aidh** *m* service, attendance

fritheil *v* **-ealadh** attend, serve, wait on, minister (to)

frith-rathad *n* **-aid, -ròidean/-an** *m* lane, path

fròg *n* **fròige, -an** *f* hole, chink, niche, nook, den

froga *n* **-ichean** *m* frock

frogail *a* **-e** lively, cheerful

frois *v* **-eadh** scatter seed, thresh

fuachd *n* **-an** *m* cold (*atmos, med*) **bha am f. orm** I had the cold

fuadach *n* **-aich, -aichean** *m* banishment, expulsion **na Fuadaichean** the (Highland) Clearances

fuadaich *v* **-ach(adh)** expel, banish, chase away

fuadain *a* **-e** false, artificial

fuaigheal *n* **-eil** *m* seam, sewing

fuaigheil *v* **-eal** sew, stitch

fuaim *n* **-e, -ean** *f m* sound, noise

fuaimneach *a* **-niche** noisy

fuaimneachadh *n* **-aidh, -aidhean** *m* pronunciation

fuaimreag *n* **-eig, -an** *f* vowel

fuamhaire *n* **-an** *m* giant

fuar *a* **fuaire** cold

fuarachd *n f* dampness, mouldiness

fuaradair *n* **-ean** *m* refrigerator, fridge

fuaraich *v* **-achadh** cool, chill

fuaraidh *a* **-e** damp, chilly, mouldy

fuaralachd *n f* frigidity

fuaran *n* **-ain, -ain/-an** *m* spring (*water*), fountain

fuasgail *v* **-gladh** loosen, untie, release; solve, resolve

fuasgladh *n* **-aidh, -aidhean** *m* solution; release

fuath *n* **-a, -an** *m* hate, hatred, antipathy

fuathaich *v* **-achadh** hate, loathe, detest

fùc *v* **-adh** full (cloth), press, squeeze

fùdar *n* **-air, -an** *m* powder

fùdaraich *v* **-achadh** powder

fuidheall *n* **-dhill** *m* remainder, financial balance

fuigheall *n See* **fuidheall**
fuil *n* **fala** *f* blood, gore
  f.-mìos period (*menstrual*)
fuilear *n* necessity **chan fhuilear
  dhuinn** we need to **cha
  b' fhuilear dhaibh uile e** they
  would need it all
fuiling *v* **fulang** suffer, bear,
  endure
fuilteach *a* **-tiche** bloody
fuiltean *n* **-ein, -an** *m* single hair
fuin *v* **-e(adh)** bake
fuineadair *n* **-ean** *m* baker
fuireach *n* **-rich** *m* waiting,
  staying, dwelling
fuirich *v* **-reach** wait; stay, live
  f. rium wait for me **tha iad a' f.
  ann an Dùn Èideann** they live in
  Edinburgh
fùirneis *n* **-ean** *f* furnace
fulang *n* **-aing** *m* endurance,
  suffering
fulangach *a* **-aiche** suffering,
  patient; passive (*gram*) **fad-
  fhulangach** long-suffering
fulangas *n* **-ais** *m* suffering,
  passion (*of Christ*)
fulmair *n* **-e, -ean** *m* fulmar
furachail *a* **-e** watchful, vigilant,
  alert, attentive
furan *n* **-ain** *m* welcome,
  hospitality **fàilte is f.** a warm
  welcome
furasta *a* **fasa** easy **nas fhasa**
  easier *Formerly* **furasda**
furm *n* **fuirm, fuirm/furman** *m*
  form, bench; stool
furtachd *n* *f* relief, help,
  deliverance, solace
furtaich *v* **-achadh** relieve, aid,
  console

G

ga *aug prep* at his/its (+ *len*), at
  her/its **a bheil thu ga fhaicinn?**
  do you see him/it? **chan eil mi
  ga tuigsinn** I don't understand
  her
gabh *v* **-ail** take, hold; be possible
  an do ghabh sibh biadh? have
  you eaten? **g. brath air** take
  advantage of, exploit **g. os
  làimh** undertake **g. mo leisgeul**
  excuse me **g. ri** accept, adopt,
  approve **g. a-steach** include,
  encompass **g. òran** sing a song
  cha ghabh e (a) chreidsinn it's
  incredible **cho luath 's a
  ghabhas** as soon as possible
  gabhaidh e ceud it will hold a
  hundred
gàbhadh *n* **-aidh, -aidhean** *m*
  peril, danger
gàbhaidh *a* **-e** perilous,
  dangerous
gabhail *n* **-alach, -alaichean** *m*
  lease, tenure
gabhaltach *a* **-aiche** infectious,
  contagious
gabhaltas *n* **-ais** *m* tenancy,
  tenure
gach *a* each, every
gad *n* **goid, goid/-an** *m* withe;
  goad **gad èisg** a number of fish
  carried by a withe, wire or
  string
gad *aug prep* at your **chan eil mi
  gad chreidsinn** I don't believe
  you
gadaiche *n* **-an** *m* thief
gadhar *n* **-air, -air** *m* hound
gàg *n* **gàige, -an** *f* chink, fissure,
  chap in skin
gagach *a* **-aiche** stuttering,
  stammering
gàgail *n* **-e** *f* cackling
Gàidheal *n* **-eil, -eil** *m* Gael,
  Highlander
Gàidhealach *a* **-aiche** Highland
  crodh G. *m* Highland cattle
Gàidhealtachd *n* *f* **a'
  Ghàidhealtachd** the Highlands
Gàidhlig *n* **-e** *f* Gaelic **a bheil G.
  agad?** do you speak Gaelic?
  a Gaelic
gailbheach *a* **-bhiche** stormy
gailearaidh *n* **-ean** *m* gallery
gaileis *n* *f* braces *pl* **-ean** *Also*
  galais
gailleann *n* **-linn, -an** *f* storm,
  tempest
gainmheach *n* **-mhich/
  gainmhche(adh)** *f* sand
gainne *n* *f* scarcity, shortage,
  want

gainnead *n* **-nid** *m* scarcity, shortage, want

gain(n)eamh *n* **-eimh** *f* sand

gàir *n* **-e, -ean** *m* shout, roar

gàir *v* **-eachdainn/-eachdaich** laugh

gairbhe *n* *f* thickness; roughness

gàirdeachas *n* **-ais** *m* rejoicing, joy **dèan g.** *v* rejoice

gàirdean *n* **-ein, -an** *m* arm

gàire *n* *f* *m* laugh **dèan g.** *v* laugh

gàireachdainn *n* *f* laughter, laughing *Also* **gàireachdaich**

gairm *n* **-e, -ean/-eannan** *f* call, cry, proclamation **g. coilich** cockcrow

gairm *v* call (out), cry (out), crow (*as cockerel*); summon **g. coinneamh** convene meeting

gairmeach *a* vocative **an tuiseal g.** the vocative case

gàirnealair *n* **-ean** *m* gardener

gàirnealaireachd *n* *f* gardening

gaiseadh *n* **-sidh, -sidhean** *m* defect in crops, blight **g. a' bhuntàta** potato blight

gaisgeach *n* **-gich, -gich** *m* hero, warrior, champion

gaisge(achd) *n* *f* heroism, bravery, valour

gaisgeil *a* **-e** heroic, brave, valorous

galan *n* **-ain, -an** *m* gallon

galar *n* **-air, -an** *m* disease **an g. roilleach/ronnach** foot and mouth disease *Also* **galair**

Gall *n* **Goill, Goill** *m* Lowlander, stranger **Innse G.** the Hebrides

galla *n* **-chan** *f* bitch

gallan *n* **-ain, -ain/-an** *m* stalk; (*met*) lad, hero

gallda *a* foreign, strange **G. Lowland a' Mhachair Ghallda** the Lowlands *f*

Galldachd *n* *f* **a' Ghalldachd** the Lowlands

gam *aug prep* at my **a bheil thu gam chluinntinn?** do you hear me?

gamhainn *n* **gamhna/gaimhne, gamhna/gaimhne/gamhnaichean** *m* stirk, year-old calf

gamhlas *n* **-ais** *m* malice, hatred, revenge

gamhlasach *a* **-aiche** malicious, malevolent, vindictive

gan *aug prep* at their **cuin a tha thu gan coinneachadh?** when are you meeting them?

gann *a* **gainne** scarce, limited

gànraich *v* **-achadh** dirty, soil, besmirch

gaoid *n* **-e, -ean** *f* blemish, defect, flaw

gaoir *n* **-e, -ean** *f* noise, cry (*of pain*); thrill **chuir e g. nam fheòil** it made my flesh creep

gaoisid *n* **-e, -ean** *f* a hair

gaoisnean *n* **-ein, -einean** *m* a hair *Also* **gaoistean**

gaol *n* **gaoil** *m* love **tha g. agam ort** I love you **A ghaoil!** Love!

gaolach *a* **-aiche** loving, dear

gaoth *n* **gaoithe, -an** *f* wind **g. an iar** a westerly wind

gaothach *a* **-aiche** windy

gar *v* **-adh** warm, heat (*especially self*)

gar *aug prep* at our **chan eil e gar faicinn** he's not seeing us

gàradh *See* **gàrradh**

garaids *n* **-ean** *f* garage

garbh *a* **gairbhe** rough, rugged, coarse; thick; wild (*of weather*) *adv* extremely **g. trang** very busy

garbhlach *n* **-aich, -aichean** *m* rugged terrain

garg *a* **gairge** fierce, ferocious

ga-rìribh *adv See* **dha-rìribh**

gàrlach *n* **-aich** *m* nyaff, impudent fellow

gàrradair *n* **-ean** *m* gardener

gàrradaireachd *n* *f* horticulture

gàrradh *n* **-aidh, -aidhean** *m* garden, wall, dyke **g. margaidh** market garden

gartan *n* **-ain, -ain/-an** *m* tick (*insect*); garter

gas *n* **-an** *m* gas

gas *n* **gaise, -an/gaisean** *f* stalk, stem

gasta *a* fine, splendid *Formerly* **gasda**

gath *n* **-a, -an/annan** *m* sting, dart; ray, beam (*of light*) **g. grèine** sunbeam

ge *conj* although **ge b' e** whoever, whatever

gèadh *n* **geòidh, geòidh** *f m* goose

geal *a* **gile** white

gealach *n* **-aich, -aichean** *f* moon **g. ùr** new moon

gealag *n* **-aig, -an** *f* sea trout

gealagan *n* **-ain, -ain** *m* white of egg

gealbhonn *n* **-bhuinn, -an** *m* sparrow

geall *n* **gill, gill** *m* promise, pledge, bet, wager **cuir g.** *v* bet, wager

geall *v* **-tainn** promise, pledge; wager

gealladh *n* **-aidh, -aidhean** *m* promise, pledge **g.-pòsaidh** engagement (*to marry*), betrothal

gealltanach *a* **-aiche** promising, hopeful

gealltanas *n* **-ais, -ais** *m* promise, pledge

gealtach *a* **-aiche** cowardly, timorous, timid

gealtaire *n* **-an** *m* coward

gèam *n* **geama, geamannan/ geamachan/geamaichean** *m* game, match

geamair *n* **-ean** *m* gamekeeper

geamhrachail *a* **-e** wintry

geamhradh *n* **-aidh, -aidhean** *m* winter

geamhraich *v* **-achadh** winter, feed during winter

gean *n* **-a** *m* mood, humour **g. math/deagh ghean** goodwill

geanail *a* **-e** cheerful, pleasant

geanm-chnò *n* **-chnòtha, -chnòthan** *f* chestnut

geansaidh *n* **-ean** *m* jersey, sweater, jumper

gearain *v* **-an** complain, grumble, moan

gearan *n* **-ain, -an** *m* complaint, moan, objection **dèan g.** *v* complain *Also* **gearain**

gearanach *a* **-aiche** complaining, grumbling, moaning *Also* **gearaineach**

gearastan *n* **-ain, -ain** *m* garrison

Formerly **gearasdan**

geàrd *n* **geàird, -an** *m* guard

Gearmailteach *n* **-tich, -tich** *m* German *a* German

Gearmailtis *n* *f* German (*lang*)

geàrr *n* **-a, -an** *f* hare

geàrr *a* **giorra** short

geàrr *v* **gearradh** cut

gearradh *n* **-aidh** *m* cut, cutting **g. cainnte** sharp wit

geàrraidh *n* **-ean** *m* common grazing, pasture land

Gearran *n* **-ain** *m* **an G.** February

geàrr-chunntas *n* **-ais, -an** *m* minute (*of meeting*), summary

geas *n* **-a/geis, -an** *f* charm, spell **fo gheasaibh** under a spell, spellbound

geasachd *n* **-an** *f* enchantment, charm

geata *n* **-ichean/-chan** *m* gate

ged *conj* though, although

ged-thà *adv* though

gèile *n* **-achan/-an** *m* gale

gèill *v* **-eadh** submit, yield, give in/way

geilt *n* **-e** *f* terror, fear

geimheal *n* **-eil, -mhlean** *m* fetter

geimhleag *n* **-eig, -an** *f* crowbar, lever

geir *n* **-e** *f* tallow, suet; fat

gèire *n* *f* sharpness, acuteness; bitterness

geòcach *a* **-aiche** gluttonous, voracious

geòcaire *n* **-an** *m* glutton

geòcaireachd *n* *f* gluttony

geodal *n* **-ail** *m* flattery

geodha *n* **-chan/-ichean** *f m* creek, cove *Also* **geò**

geòla *n* **(-dh), -chan** *f* yawl, small boat

ge-tà *adv* though

geug *n* **gèige, -an** *f* branch (*of tree*)

geum *n* **-a/gèime, -an** *m* low, lowing, bellow

geum *v* **-naich** low, bellow

geur *a* **gèire** sharp. sharp-witted, discerning; bitter

geuradair *n* **-ean** *m* sharpener

geuraich *v* **-achadh** sharpen

geur-amhairc *v* **-amharc**

scrutinize, study closely
geurchuiseach *a* **-siche**
  perceptive, discerning, shrewd
geur-leanmhainn *n* **-ean** *m*
  persecution **dèan g.** *v* persecute
gheat *n* **-aichean** *f* yacht *Also*
  geat
gheibh *irr v* will get (*See irr v*
  faigh *in Grammar*)
ghia *exclam* Yuch!
giall *n* **-a/gèille, -an** *f* jaw, jowl
gibht *n* **-ean** *f* gift
Giblean *n* **-ein** *m* an **G.** April
gidheadh *adv* nevertheless, yet
gilb *n* **-e, -ean** *f* chisel *Also* **geilb**
gilead *n* **gilid** *m* whiteness
gille *n* **-an** lad, boy; servant
  g.-cruidh cowboy
  g.-frithealaidh waiter, servant
  g.-Caluim sword dance
gille-brìghde *n* **-bhrìghde, gillean-**
  m oystercatcher
gille-mirein *n* **gillean-** *m* whirlygig
gin *v* **-eadh/-eamhainn** beget,
  generate, reproduce
gin *pron* any, anyone, anything **a**
  bheil g. agad? do you have any?
gine *n* **-achan** *f* gene
gineachas *n* **-ais** *m* genesis,
  beginning
gineadh *n* **ginidh** *m* conception
ginealach *n* **-aich, -aich** *m*
  generation
gineamhainn *n m* conception,
  begetting
ginideach *a* genitive **an tuiseal g.**
  the genitive case
ginidh *n* **-ean** *m* guinea
gintinn *n m* reproduction
gintinneachd *n f* genetics
giobach *a* **-aiche** hairy, shaggy
gìodhar *n* **-air, -dhraichean** *m*
  gear (*in engine*)
gìogan *n* **-ain, -ain/-an** *m* thistle
giomach *n* **-aich, -aich** *m* lobster
gionach *a* **-aiche** greedy
giorna-giùirne *n* **-giùrnean** *f*
  helter-skelter (*slide*)
giorra *a See* **goirid, geàrr**
giorrachadh *n* **-aidh** *m*
  shortening, abbreviation;
  synopsis
giorrad *n* **-aid** *m* shortness,

brevity
giorraich *v* **-achadh** shorten,
  abbreviate
gìosg *n* **-an** *m* creaking, gnashing
gìosg *v* **-ail** creak, gnash
giotàr *n* **-àir, -an** *m* guitar
giùlain *v* **-an** carry, bear;
  comport, conduct (*oneself*)
giùlan *n* **-ain, -an** *m* carrying,
  carriage; conduct, behaviour;
  bier
giullachd *n f* handling, treatment
  droch ghiullachd maltreatment,
  being treated badly
giuthas *n* **-ais** *m* fir, pine
glac *n* **glaice, -an** *f* hollow (*in land*
  or hand); narrow valley, defile
glac *v* **-adh** catch, seize, grasp
glag *n* **glaig** *m* thud, noise of
  something falling
glag *n See* **clag**
glagadaich *n* **-e** *f* rattling;
  prattling, loud talk
glaine *n f* cleanliness, purity
glainne *n* **-achan/-nichean** *f* glass
  g.-sìde barometer
glainnichean *n f pl* spectacles,
  glasses *Also* **glainneachan**
glaisean *n* **-ein, -an** *m* sparrow
glaiste *a* locked
glamh *v* **-adh** gobble, devour
glan *a* **glaine** clean, pure;
  splendid, fine
glan *adv* completely, totally **g. às**
  a chiall absolutely crazy
glan *v* **-adh** clean, wash
glaodh *n* **-oidh, -an** *m* cry, call,
  shout
glaodh *v* **-ach/-aich** call, shout
glaodh *n* **-oidh** *m* glue
glaodh *v* **-adh** glue
glaodhaich *n m* shouting, calling,
  bawling
glaodhan *n* **-ain** *m* pith, pulp
glaoic *n See* **gloidhc**
glas *n* **glaise, -an** *f* lock **g.-làmh**
  handcuff
glas *a* **glaise** grey; (*of land*) green
glas *v* **-adh** lock
glas- *pref* grey-coloured
glasach *n* **-aich, -aichean** *m* green
  field
glasraich *n f* greens, vegetables

glè *adv* very, fairly (+ *len*) **g.**
  mhath very good/well, fairly
  good/well
gleac *v* **-adh** struggle, wrestle
gleadhraich *n f* din, excessive
  noise
gleann *n* **glinne, glinn/-tan** *m* glen
gleans *n* **-a, -an** *m* shine **bha g.**
  às it shone
glèidh *v* **gleidheadh** keep, retain,
  preserve, observe
glèidhte *a* preserved, reserved,
  kept
glèidhteachas *n* **-ais** *m*
  conservation, preservation
  neach-glèidhteachais *m*
  conservationist
gleoc *n* **-a, -aichean** *m* clock
gleus *n* **-a, -an** *f m* order, trim;
  tune, key **air ghleus** in tune
gleus *v* **-adh** prepare; adjust; tune
gleusta *a* prepared; tuned;
  skilled; shrewd *Formerly*
  gleusda
glic *a* **-e** wise, prudent, sensible
gliocas *n* **-ais** *m* wisdom,
  prudence
gliog *n* **-a, -an** *m* click, tick,
  tinkle
gliong *n* **-a, -an** *m* clink, clang,
  jingle
gliongarsaich *n f* clinking,
  clanging
gloc *v* **-ail** cluck (*as of hen*),
  cackle
gloidhc *n* **-e, -ean** *f* fool, idiot
  chan eil ann ach g. he's just a
  fool
gloine *n See* **glainne**
glòir *n* **-e/glòrach** *f* glory; speech
  droch ghlòir bad language
glòir-mhiann *n* **-a** *f m* ambition
glòir-mhiannach *a* **-aiche**
  ambitious
glòraich *v* **-achadh** glorify
glòrmhor *a* **-oire** glorious
gluais *v* **gluasad** move
gluasad *n* **-aid, -an** *m* movement,
  motion; gait, carriage
gluasadach *a* **-aiche** moving,
  mobile
glug *n* **gluig, -an** *m* glug, gurgle;
  gulp

glugan *n* **-ain** *m* bubbling,
  gurgling
glumag *n* **-aig, -an** *f* small pool,
  puddle; mouthful of bile
glùn *n* **glùine, glùinean/glùintean** *f*
  knee **bean-ghlùine** *f* midwife
  Also **glùin**
glutach *a* **-aiche** gluttonous
glutaire *n* **-an** *m* glutton
gnàth *n* **-a, -an/-annan** *m* habit,
  custom, practice **a-ghnàth** always
gnàth *a* usual, habitual, common
gnàthach *a* **-aiche** customary,
  habitual, usual
gnàthasach *a* **-aiche** idiomatic
gnàthas-cainnt *n* **-e, gnàthasan-**
  m idiom
gnàth-fhacal *n* **-ail, -clan** *m*
  proverb
gnàths *n m* usage
gnè *n f* kind, type, nature; sex,
  gender
gnìomh *n* **-an/-aran** *m* action, act,
  deed **cuir an g.** *v* put into
  practice, carry out
gnìomhach *a* **-aiche** active,
  industrious; executive
gnìomhachas *n* **-ais** *m* industry
gnìomhair *n* **-ean** *m* verb
gnoban *n* **-ein, -an** *m* little hill or
  knoll
gnog *n* **gnoig, -an** *m* knock
gnog *v* **-adh** knock
gnogadh *n* **-aidh, -aidhean** *m*
  knock, knocking
gnòsadaich *n f* grunting *Also vn*
gnothach *n* **-aich, -aichean** *m*
  business, matter **a dh'aon**
  ghnothach on purpose,
  deliberately **an dèan siud an g.?**
  v will that do? **na gabh g. ris** *v*
  don't have anything to do with
  it **rinn iad an g.** *v* they managed;
  they won *Also* **gnothaich**
gnù *a* surly, sullen
gnùis *n* **-e, -ean** *f* countenance,
  face
gò *n m* blemish, defect, fault **gun**
  ghò faultless, without guile
gob *n* **guib, guib/-an** *m* beak, bill
  (*of bird*); sharp point (*of*
  object); (*colloq*) gob, mouth
gobach *a* **-aiche** nebby, brash;

beaked

gobag *n* -aig, -an *f* nebby/brash female

gobha *n* -nn/-inn, goibhnean *m* smith, blacksmith

gobhal *n* -ail/goibhle, goibhlean *m* fork; crotch

gobhar *n* -air/goibhre, -air/goibhrean *f m* goat

gòbhlach *a* forked; astride

gòbhlag *n* -aig, -an *f* fork; earwig

gòbhlan-gainmhich *n* gòbhlain-, gòbhlanan/gòbhlain- *m* sand martin

gòbhlan-gaoithe *n* gòbhlain-, gòbhlanan-/gòbhlain- *m* swallow

goc *n* -a, -an/-aichean *m* tap, faucet, stopcock

gocan *n* -ain, -an *m* acolyte, pert little person; whinchat
g. cuthaige cuckoo's follower, titlark

gog *n m* cluck, cackle

gogaid *n* -e, -ean *f* coquette, flirt

gogail *n f* clucking, cackling

goid *n* -e *f* theft, stealing

goid *v* steal

goil *v* boil **air ghoil** boiling

goile *n* -an/-achan *f* stomach; appetite

goileach *a* -liche boiling **uisge g.** *m* boiling water

goir *v* -sinn call

goireas *n* -eis, -an *m* facility, amenity, resource, convenience

goireasach *a* -aiche convenient

goirid *a* giorra short, brief *adv* shortly **o chionn ghoirid** recently *prep* near **g. dhan bhaile** near the town

goirt *a* -e sore, painful; sour

goirtean *n* -ein, -an *m* small field, enclosure

goirtich *v* -teachadh hurt *Also* **gortaich**

goistidh *n* -ean *m* sponsor, godfather; gossip (*person*)

gonadh *n* -aidh *m* wounding, stinging **g. ort!** blast you!

gòrach *a* -aiche foolish, silly, daft, stupid

gòraiche *n f* folly, silliness, stupidity

gorm *a* guirme blue; green (*of grass*); (*met*) green, naive

gort *n* -a *f* famine, starvation

gràbhail *v* -al/-aladh engrave

gràbhalaiche *n* -an *m* engraver

grad *a* graide sudden, quick, swift, immediate **gu g.** suddenly, quickly

gràdh *n* gràidh *m* love **thugainn, a ghràidh** come on, love/dear

gràdhach *a* -aiche loving, dear, beloved

gràdhaich *v* -achadh love

gràdhag *n* -aig *f* love (*term of endearment applied to a woman*)

gràdhmhor *a* -oire loving

graf *n* -a, -aichean *m* graph

gràin *n* -e *f* loathing, abhorrence **bha g. aice air** she hated him/it

gràin-cinnidh *n* gràine-cinnidh *f* racism

gràineag *n* -eig, -an *f* hedgehog

gràineil *a* -e loathsome, abhorrent, disgusting, heinous

gràinich *v* -neachadh scunner, put one off, cause to hate/loathe

gràinne *n* -an *f* grain

gràinnean *n* -ein, -an *m* granule

gràisg *n* -e, -ean *f* rabble, mob

gram *n* -a, -an/-aichean *m* gram

gràmar *n* -air *m* grammar

gràn *n* gràin, gràin *m* grain, cereal

grànda *a* gràinde ugly

grannda *a See* **grànda**

gràpa *n* -n *m* graip, fork (*agric*)

gràs *n* gràis, -an *m* grace

gràsmhor *a* -oire gracious

greabhal *n* -ail *m* gravel

greadhnach *a* -aiche joyful, convivial; majestic

greadhnachas *n* -ais *m* joy, conviviality; pomp, majesty

greallach *n* -aiche *f* entrails, intestines

greann *n* greinn *m* scowl, irritation **bha g. air** he was scowling

greannach *a* -aiche wild, rough (*weather*); surly, crabbit, ill-tempered

greannmhor *a* **-oire** amusing, agreeable; comely

greas *v* **-ad** hasten, hurry **g. ort!** hurry up!

grèata *n* **-ichean** *m* grate

greideal *n* **-eil/-ach, -an** *f* griddle, girdle (*baking*)

grèidh *v* **-eadh** grill; groom (*eg horses*) **droch ghrèidheadh** bad treatment

greigh *n* **-e, -ean** *f* herd, stud

grèim *n* **-e, -ean/ -eannan** *m* hold, grip, grasp; custody; morsel; stitch (*of clothing*) **g. làimhe** handshake **g. bidh** bite of food **an g. aig a' phoileas** in police custody

greimeil *a* **-e** resolute, firm, persistent

greimich *v* **-meachadh** grip, grapple, grasp

greis *n* **-e, -ean** *f* a while, spell (*of time*)

grèis *n* **-e** *f* embroidery **obair-ghrèis** *f* embroidery

greiseag *n* **-eig** *f* a short while

Greugach *n* **-aich, -aich** *m* Greek *a* Greek, Grecian

Greugais *n* *f* Greek (*lang*)

greusaiche *n* **-an** *m* shoemaker, cobbler

grian *n* **grèine** *f* sun **èirigh na grèine** sunrise *f* **dol fodha na grèine** *m* sunset

grianach *a* **-aiche** sunny

grinn *a* **-e** fine, elegant; neat; pretty

grinneal *n* **-eil** *m* gravel

grinneas *n* **-eis** *m* elegance

grìob *n* **-a, -an** *m* coastal precipice

grìogag *n* **-aig, -an** *f* bead

Grioglachan *n* **-ain** *m* **an G.** Pleiades, constellation

Griomasach *n* **-aich, -aich** *m* someone from Grimsay *a* from, or pertaining to, Grimsay

grìos *n* **-a, -achan** *m* grill

grìos *v* **-ad/-adh** blaspheme, swear

grìosad *n* **-aid** *m* blasphemy, swearing

grìosaich *v* **-achadh** grill

griùthrach *n* **-aich** *f* **a' ghriùthrach** measles *Also* **griùthlach**

grod *a* **-a/groide** rotten, putrid

grod *v* **-adh** rot, putrefy

gròiseid *n* **-e, -ean** *f* gooseberry

gruag *n* **gruaig, -an** *f* hair; wig

gruagach *n* **-aiche, -aichean** *f* young woman, maiden

gruagaire *n* **-an** *m* hairdresser

gruaidh *n* **-e, -ean** *f* cheek (*of face*)

gruaim *n* **-e** *f* gloom, sullenness

gruamach *a* **-aiche** gloomy, sullen, stern

grùdadh *n* **-aidh** *m* brewing; distilling **taigh-grùdaidh** *m* brewery; distillery

grùdaire *n* **-an** *m* brewer; distiller

grùdaireachd *n* **-an** *f* brewing; distilling

grùid *n* **-e** *f* dregs

grunn *n* **gruinn** *m* several, a good number

grunnaich *v* **-achadh** wade, paddle (*in water*)

grunnan *n* **-ain, -annan** *m* a few, small group

grunnd *n* **gruinnd/-a, -an** *m* ground; bottom (*of sea*)

gruth *n* **-a** *m* crowdie, curds

grùthan *n* **-ain, -an** *m* liver

gu *adv pref* (*equivalent to -(i)ly in English adverbs*) *eg* **gu snog** nicely

gu *conj* that (*used to introduce positive subordinate clauses*) **chì mi gu bheil thu trang** I see that you're busy

gu *conj* so that; until **fuirich gu sia uairean** wait till six o'clock

gu *prep* to, towards

gual *n* **guail** *m* coal

gualaisg *n* **-e, -ean** *m* carbohydrate

gualan *n* **-ain, -an** *m* carbon

gualann *n* **-ainn/guailne, guailnean/guaillean** *f* shoulder *Also* **guala, gualainn**

guàna *n* *m* fertilizer

guanach *a* **-aiche** light, giddy

gu bràth *adv* forever

gucag *n* **-aig, -an** *f* bud, bubble

gucag-uighe *n* **gucaig-, gucagan-** *f* egg-cup

gud *aug prep* to your
gu dè? *interr pron* what?
gu dearbh *adv* indeed
gu deimhinn(e) *adv* certainly
guga *n* -ichean *m* young solan goose or gannet
guidh *v* -e wish; entreat, pray, implore
guidhe *n* -achan *f m* wish; entreaty; swear-word
guil *v* gul cry, weep *Also* a' gal
guilbneach *n* -nich, -nich *f m* curlew
guin *n* -ean *m* sting, pang, dart
guin *v* -eadh sting, wound
guineach *a* -niche stinging, venomous, wounding
guir *v* gur hatch, breed
guirean *n* -ein, -an *m* pimple, pustule
guirmean *n* -ein *m* indigo g. an fhraoich bluebell
guiseid *n* -e, -ean *f* gusset
gul *n* guil *m* crying, weeping
gu lèir *adv* altogether, completely, entirely
gu leòr *adv* enough, plenty, galore
gu leth *adj phr* and a half uair gu l. an hour and a half
gum *conj* that (*used to introduce positive subordinate clauses where verb begins in b, f, m, p*)
gum *aug prep* to my, to their
gùn *n* gùin, gùintean *m* gown gùn-oidhche nightgown, nightie
gun *conj* that (*used to introduce positive subordinate clauses*)
gun *prep* (+ *len*) without
gun *aug prep* to the; to their
gun fhios nach *conj* in case, lest
gun fhiosta *adv* unawares, inadvertently
gunna *n* -ichean/-chan *m* gun
gur *n* guir *m* brood, hatch
gur *aug conj* that (*used to introduce positive subordinate clauses before nouns and adjectives*)
gur *aug prep* to you (*pl & pol*)
gur *aug prep* at your (*pl & pol*)
gur *aug prep* to our, to your (*pl & pol*)

gurraban *n* -ain *m* crouching, hunkering bha e na ghurraban he was crouching
gu ruig(e) *prep* up to, as far as, until
gus *prep* so that, in order to
gus *prep* to, until
gus *conj* so that, until
guth *n* -a, -an *m* voice; word, mention cha chuala mi g. I didn't hear anything gun ghuth air ... not to mention ..., to say nothing of ...
gu tur *adv* entirely, completely, totally, altogether

H

h- *part* (*used before words beginning in a vowel when preceded by* a)
hàidridean *n, a* -ein *m* hydrogen
hallò *exclam* hello
ham(a) *n m* bacon
hamstair *n* -ean *m* hamster
hangair *n* -ean *m* hangar; hanger
heactair *n* -ean *m* hectare
Hearach *n* -aich, -aich *m* someone from Harris *a* from, or pertaining to, Harris *Also* Tearach
heileacoptair *n* -ean *m* helicopter
Hiortach *n* -aich, -aich *m* someone from St Kilda *a* from, or pertaining to, St Kilda *Also* Tiortach, Hirteach, Tirteach
hocaidh *n m* hockey
hòro-gheallaidh *n f m* celebration, fling, rave
hù-bhitheil *n f m* stramash

I

i *pron* she, her, it
iad *pron* they, them iad seo these iad sin those
iadh-shlat *n* -shlait *f* honeysuckle
iadsan *emph pron* they, them
iall *n* èill, -an *f* thong, leash, strap; shoelace
ialtag *n* -aig, -an *f* bat (*mammal*)
Iapanach *n, a* -aich, -aich *m* Japanese

iar *n f* west **an taobh an i.** the west side **i.-dheas** south-west **i.-thuath** north-west

iar- *pref* deputy, vice-, assistant **i.-cheann-suidhe** *m* vice-president

iarainn *a* iron

iarann *n* **-ainn, -an** *m* iron (*metal, impl*) **a bheil an t-i. air?** is the iron on?

iar-cheumnach *a* postgraduate

iar-cheumnaiche *n* **-an** *m* postgraduate

iargain *n f* sorrow, grief, pain

iargalt(a) *a* **-ailte/-alta** surly, forbidding

iarla *n* **-n/-chan** *m* earl

iarlachd *n f* earldom

iar-leasachan *n* **-ain** *m* suffix

iarmad *n* **-aid, -an** *m* remnant; offspring, race

iarmailt *n* **-e, -ean** *f* sky, firmament

iarnaig *v* **-eadh** iron

iar-ogha *n* **-chan/-ichean** *m* great-grandchild **tha iad anns na h-iar-oghachan** they are second cousins

iarr *v* **-aidh** ask (for), request, seek, want **i. orra tadhal** ask them to call (in)

iarrtach *a* demanding

iarrtas *n* **-ais, -an** *m* request, demand, application

iasad *n* **-aid, -an** *m* loan **air i.** on loan **am faigh mi i. dhen pheann agad?** may I borrow your pen?

iasg *n* **èisg, èisg** *m* fish **i. locha** freshwater fish **i. mara** seafish **i. òir** goldfish

iasgach *n* **-aich** *m* fishing, angling **bha e ris an i. fad a bheatha** he was a fisherman all his life

iasgaich *v* **-ach** fish, angle

iasgair *n* **-ean** *m* fisherman, angler

iath *v* **-adh** surround, envelop, encircle

iathaire *n* **-an** *m* aerial

'ic *contr* short for **mhic** of the son **mac Iain 'ic Sheumais** the son of John son of James

idir *adv* at all

ifrinn *n* **-e, -ean** *f* hell

Ìleach *n* **Ìlich, Ìlich** *m* someone from Islay *a* from, or pertaining to, Islay

ìm *n* **ime** *m* butter **ì. ùr** fresh butter **ì. saillte** salted butter

imcheist *n* **-ean** *f* anxiety, perplexity, doubt **fo i.** anxious **bha i. oirre mu dheidhinn** she was worried about it

imich *v* **imeachd** go, depart, leave

imleag *n* **-eige, -an** *f* navel

imlich *v* lick

impidh *n* **-e, -ean** *f* entreaty, petition, persuasion **chuir e i. oirnn fuireach** he implored us to stay/wait

impire *n* **-ean** *m* emperor *Also* **ìompaire**

impireachd *n* **-an** *f* empire *Also* **ìompaireachd**

impis *n f* imminence **an i.** on the point of, about to

imprig *n* **-ean** *f* removal (*house*), flitting **rinn iad i.** they flitted

imrich *n* **-e, -ean** *f* removal (*house*), flitting

inbhe *n* **-an** *f* rank, status, prestige

inbheach *n* **-bhich, -bhich** *m* adult

inbheach *a* **-bhiche** adult, mature

inbhir *n* **-e, -ean** *m* confluence, inver

inc *n f m* ink

ìne *n* **-an** *f* nail (*on finger*); claw, talon

in-imrich *n* **-e** *f* immigration

in-imriche *n* **-ean** *m* immigrant

inneal *n* **-eil, -an** *m* machine, instrument, engine **i.-ciùil** musical instrument **i.-fighe** knitting machine **i.-measgachaidh** mixer **i.-nigheadaireachd** washing machine

innean *n* **-ein, -an** *m* anvil

innear *n* **-arach** *f* dung, manure *Also* **inneir**

innidh *n f* bowel

innis *n* **innse, innsean** *f* island; meadow, pasture

innis *v* See **inns**

Innis-Tìleach *n* **-Tìlich, -Tìlich** *m*

Icelander *a* Icelandic

innleachd *n* **-an** *f* invention, device, mechanism, scheme; ingenuity; wile, tactic

innleachdach *a* **-aiche** ingenious, inventive; cunning, tactical

innleadair *n* **-ean** *m* engineer, inventor **i. dealain** electrical engineer

innleadaireachd *n f* engineering

innlich *v* **-leachadh** invent, devise, engineer

inns *v* **-e(adh)** (+ **do**) tell, relate **i. dhi** tell her

Innseanach *n* **-aich, -aich** *m* Indian *a* Indian

innte(se) *prep pron* in her(self), in it(self) **'s e cleasaiche a th' i.** she's an actress

inntinn *n* **-e, -ean** *f* mind, intellect

inntinneach *a* **-niche** interesting; encouraging, positive-minded

inntleachd *n* **(-a)** *f* intelligence, intellect

inntleachdail *a* **-e** intellectual

inntrig *v* **-eadh** enter

ìobair *v* **ìobradh/-t** sacrifice

ìobairt *n* **-e, -ean** *f* sacrifice, offering

ìoc *v* **-adh** pay, render

ìochd *n f* mercy, clemency, compassion

ìochdar *n* **-air, -an** *m* bottom, lower part

ìochdaran *n* **-ain, -an** *m* subject, inferior, subordinate

ìochdmhor *a* **-oire** merciful, clement, compassionate

ìocshlaint *n* **-e, -ean** *f* medicine, balm

iodhal *n* **-ail, -an** *m* idol **i.-adhradh** idolatry

iodhlann *n* **-ainn, -an** *f* stackyard, cornyard

iogart *n* **-airt, -an** *f m* yoghurt

ioghnadh *n See* **iongnadh**

iolach *n* **-aich, -aich** *m* shout, roar (*of triumph*)

iolair(e) *n* **-(e)an** *f* eagle **i.-uisge** osprey, sea eagle

iolra *n* **-n** *m* plural *a* plural

iomadach *a* (*precedes n*) many, many a, numerous

iomadh *a* (*precedes n*) many, many a, numerous

ioma-dhathach *a* **-aiche** multi-coloured

iomadh-fhillte *a* complex, compound, manifold

iomagain *n* **(-e), -ean** *f* worry, concern, anxiety **fo i.** worried, concerned

iomagaineach *a* **-niche** worried, concerned, anxious

ioma-ghaoth *n* **-ghaoith, -an** *f* whirlwind

iomain *n* **-e** *f* shinty; driving (*as of cattle*)

iomain *v* play shinty; drive (*as of cattle*)

iomair *n* **-e, -ean** *m* ridge (*ploughed*), piece of land

iomair *v* **iomradh** row (*boat*)

iomairt *n* **-e, -ean** *f* enterprise, initiative; campaign, venture **dèan i.** *v* campaign

iomall *n* **-aill, -aill** *m* border, limit, edge, margin, periphery **i. a' bhaile** the suburbs

iomallach *a* **-aiche** remote, isolated, peripheral

iomarra *a* plural

ioma-shruth *n* **-a, -an** *m* cross-current, eddying stream or tide

iomchaidh *a* **-e** suitable, appropriate, proper, fitting

iomchair *v* **-ar** carry, bear

ìomhaigh *n* **-ean** *f* image, statue; countenance

iomlaid *n* **-e, -ean** *f* change, exchange

iomlan *a* **-aine** complete, whole, total **gu h-i.** altogether, entirely

iomnaidh *n f* concern, anxiety **chuir e i. oirnn** it worried us

iompachadh *n* **-aidh, -aidhean** *m* religious conversion

iompachan *n* **-ain, -an** *m* convert (*relig*)

iompaich *v* **-achadh** convert (*relig*) **chaidh a h-iompachadh** she was converted

iomradh *n* **-aidh, -aidhean** *m* mention, report, reference; rowing (*boat*) **dèan i. air** *v* mention

iomraiteach *a* -tiche famous, renowned, celebrated

iomrall *n* -aill, -an *m* wandering, straying; error **chaidh sinn (air) i.** *v* we got lost

iomrallach *v* wandered, confused, mistaken

ionad *n* -aid, -an *m* place **i. fàilte** reception (*area*) **i. fiosrachaidh turasachd** tourist information centre **i. slàinte** health centre

ionadail *a* -e local **riaghaltas i.** *m* local government

ionaghailt *n* -e, -ean *f* pasture, grazing

ionaltair *v* -tradh pasture, graze

ionaltradh *n* -aidh, -aidhean *m* pasture, grazing

ionann *a* same, equal, alike, identical **chan i. iad idir** they are not at all alike

iongantach *a* -aiche surprising; wonderful

iongantas *n* -ais, -an *m* surprise; wonder

iongnadh *n* -aidh, -aidhean *m* surprise, wonder **chuir e i. orm** it surprised me **is beag an t-i.** little wonder

ionmhainn *a* -e/annsa beloved, dear

ionmhas *n* -ais, -an *m* finance, riches, treasure **Roinn an Ionmhais** the Finance Dept

ionmhasail *a* -e financial

ionmhasair *n* -ean *m* treasurer

ion-mhiannaichte *a* highly desirable

ionmholta *a* praiseworthy, laudable, commendable

ionnan *See* **ionann**

ionndrainn *n f m* missing, longing (for)

ionndrainn *v* miss, long (for)

ionnlaid *v* -ad wash, bathe **seòmar/rùm i.** *m* bathroom

ionnsachadh *n* -aidh *m* learning; instruction

ionnsaich *v* -achadh learn; (+ **do**) teach

ionnsaichte *a* learned, educated

ionnsaigh *n* -ean *f m* attack, assault, onslaught, invasion

thug iad i. oirnn *v* they attacked us **a dh'i.** (+ *gen*) to, towards

ionnsramaid *n* -e, -ean *f* instrument

ionracas *a* -ais *m* righteousness, integrity, probity

ionraic *a* -e righteous, honest, just

iorghail *n* -ean *f* tumult, uproar

iorram *n* -aim, -aim *m* rowing song; repetitive song or remarks

ìosal *a* ìsle low, lowly **gu h-ì.** down below

ìre *n* -an *f* level, stage, grade, rate; maturity **an ì. Choitcheann** Standard Grade (*exam*) **an Ard Ì.** Higher Grade (*exam*) **an ì. mhath** quite; almost **gu ì. mhòir** to a large extent **air tighinn gu ì.** having reached maturity

iriosal *a* -aile humble, lowly

irioslachd *n f* humility, lowliness

irioslaich *v* -achadh humble, humiliate

iris *n* -e, -ean *f* magazine, periodical

is *irr v* (*copula of verb* **to be**) am, is, are (*often abbreviated* to **'s**) **'s e oileanach a th' ann** he's a student

is *conj* and (*contr of* **agus**)

isbean *n* -ein, -an *m* sausage

ise *emph pron* she, her, it

ìseal *a* See **ìosal**

isean *n* isein, -an *m* chick, chicken; bird; young **droch i.** a bad egg (*colloq*), brat **i. deireadh linn** a tail-end baby

ìslich *v* ìsleachadh lower; humble

is mathaid *adv* perhaps, maybe

Israelach *n* -lich, -lich *m* Israeli *a* Israeli *Also* **Iosaraileach**

ist *interj* wheest, hist!, hush!, quiet!

ite *n* -an *f* feather; fin

iteach *n* itich *m* plumage

iteach *a* itiche feathered, feathery

iteachan *n* -ain, -ain/-an *m* weaver's bobbin

iteag *n* -eig, -an *f* small feather; flight **air (an) iteig** flying

iteagach *a* -aiche feathered, feathery

itealaich *v* **-achadh** fly
itealan *n* **-ain, -ain** *m* aeroplane
iteileag *n* **-eig, -an** *f* kite (*sport*)
ith *v* **-e** eat
iubailidh *n* **-ean** *f* jubilee
iubhar *n* **-air, -an** *m* yew
iuchair *n* **iuchrach, iuchraichean** *f*
  key; roe of fish
Iuchar *n* **-air** *m* **an t-I.** July
Iùdhach *n* **-aich, -aich** *m* Jew
  a Jewish
iùil-tharraing *n* **-e, -ean** *f*
  magnetism
iùil-tharraingeach *a* **-giche**
  magnetic
iùl *n* **iùil, iùilean** *m* guidance,
  direction **neach-iùil** *m* guide
Iupatar *n* **-air** *m* Jupiter
iutharn(a) *n* *f* hell

L

là *n* **làithean/lathaichean** *m* day
làbha *n* *f* lava
labhair *v* **-t** speak, talk
labhairt *n* *f* speaking, talking
  neach-l. *m* spokesperson
lach *n* **-a, -an/-ain** *f* wild duck
lachan *n* **-ain, -ain** *m* guffaw
  l.-gàire hearty laugh
lachanaich *n* *f* laughing heartily
lachdann *a* **-ainne** dun, tawny,
  swarthy
ladar *n* **-air, -an** *m* ladle
ladarna *a* bold, shameless,
  blatant, presumptuous
ladarnas *n* **-ais** *m* boldness,
  shamelessness,
  presumptuousness
ladhar *n* **-air/-dhra, -dhran** *m*
  hoof
lag *n* **laig/luig, -an** *f m* hollow
lag *a* **laige** weak, feeble, faint
lagaich *v* **-achadh** weaken,
  undermine *Also intrans*
lagais *n* **-ean** *f* slag heap, rubbish
  dump
lagan *n* **-ain, -an** *m* small hollow
lagchuiseach *a* **-siche** faint-
  hearted, unenterprising, weak-
  willed
lagh *n* **-a, -annan** *m* law **dèan l.** *v*
  legislate **l. baile** bye-law

laghach *a* **-aiche** nice, pleasant,
  fine
laghail *a* **-e** lawful, legal
laghairt *n* **-ean** *f m* lizard
Laideann *n* **-dinn(e)** *f* Latin
làidir *a* **-e** strong, robust
laige *n* *f* weakness, faintness
laigh *v* **-e** lie (down) **a' dol a
  laighe** going to bed
laigse *n* **-an/-achan** *f* weakness,
  defect **chaidh e ann an l.** he
  fainted
làimh ri *adv* near, close to
làimhsich *v* **-seachadh** handle,
  treat
laimrig *n* **-e, -ean** *f* landing-place,
  small harbour *Also* **laimhrig**
lainnir *n* **-e** *f* radiance, glitter
lainnireach *a* **-riche** radiant,
  glittering, gleaming
làir *n* **-e/làrach, -ean/-idhean/
  -ichean** *f* mare **l.-bhreabaidh**
  rocking-horse **l.-mhaide** see-saw
la(i)ste *a* lit
làitheil *a* daily
làmh *n* **làimhe, -an** *f* hand **l. ri
  làimh** hand in hand **an l.
  dheas/cheart** the right hand **an
  l. chlì/ cheàrr** the left hand **l.-an-
  uachdair** the upper hand **gabh
  os làimh** *v* undertake **ri làimh** at
  hand **obair-làimhe** *f* manual
  work **rug e air làimh oirre** he
  shook hands with her
làmhachas-làidir *n* **làmhachais-** *m*
  force
làmhagh *n* **-aigh, -aighean** *f*
  hand-axe *Also* **làmhag**
làmhchair *a* **-e** handy, dexterous
làmh-sgrìobhadh *n* **-aidh** *m*
  handwriting
làmh-sgrìobhainn *n* **-e, -ean** *f*
  manuscript
lampa *n* **-ichean** *f m* lamp
làn *a* **làine** full, complete **tha mi
  l.-chinnteach** I'm quite
  sure/certain **tha l.-earbs' agam
  ann** I have complete confidence
  in him **tha a l.-thìd' agad ...** it is
  high time you ... **làn-ùine** full-
  time
làn *n* **làin, làin** *m* tide **l. àrd** a high
  tide **l.-mara** (high) tide

langa *n* -an/-annan *f* ling (*fish*)
langan *n* -ain, -an *m* bellowing (*of deer*), bellow
langanaich *n* -e *f* lowing, bellowing (*of deer*)
langasaid *n* -e, -ean *f* sofa, couch, settee
lann *n* lainn, -an *f* enclosure, repository
lann *n* -a/lainne, -an *f* blade, sword; scale (*on fish*)
lannsa *a* -ichean *f* lance, lancet
lannsair *n* -ean *m* surgeon
lanntair *n* -ean *m* lantern *Also* **lainntear** *f*
laoch *n* laoich, laoich *m* hero, warrior, champion
laochan *n* -ain, -ain *m* little hero (*term of endearment*) **sin thu fhèin, a laochain** well done, my lad/little pal
laogh *n* laoigh, laoigh *m* calf
laoidh *n* -e, -ean *f m* hymn, anthem, lay
laoidheadair *n* -ean *m* hymnbook
lapach *a* -aiche weak, feeble, frail
làr *n* làir, làir/-an *m* floor, ground
làrach *n* -aich, -aichean *f m* site; ruin **l.-lìn** website **an l. nam bonn** on the spot, immediately
làraidh *n* -ean *f* lorry **l. an sgudail** the bin/refuse lorry
làrna-mhàireach *adv* the next day
las *v* -adh light
lasachadh *n* -aidh, -aidhean *m* slackening; discount, rebate
lasadair *n* -ean *m* match (*to light*)
lasadh *n* -aidh, -aidhean *m* lighting; flash
lasaich *v* -achadh slacken, ease off
lasair *n* lasrach, lasraichean *f* flame
lasgan *n* -ain, -ain *m* outburst **l. gàire** hearty laugh, peal of laughter
lasganaich *n* -e *f* hearty laughter
lasrach *a* -aiche flaming
lastaig *n, a* (-e) *f* elastic
lath *v* -adh numb **theabadh mo lathadh** I was nearly frozen
latha *n* làithean/-ichean *m* day

Latha na Sàbaid the Sabbath, Sunday **l.-breith** birthday
latheigin *adv* some day **l.-fèille** public holiday, fair day **L. Luain** Doomsday **làithean-saora/ saor-làithean** holidays **l. brèagha air choreigin** some fine day **nach ann oirnn a thàinig an dà l.!** how our circumstances have changed!
làthach *n* -aich/làthcha *f* mire, clay
làthair *n* -e *f* presence **an l.** present
le *prep* (+ *dat*) with, by **'s ann le Iain a tha e** it belongs to John **le chèile** both, together
lèabag *n* -aig, -an *f* flounder
leabaidh *n* leapa, leapannan *f* bed *Also* **leaba**
leabhar *n* -air, leabhraichean *m* book **L. Aithghearr nan Ceist** the Shorter Catechism **l.-iùil** guidebook **l.-latha** diary **l.-seòlaidh** address book **l.-sgrìobhaidh** notebook
leabharlann *n* -ainn, -an *f m* library
leabharlannaiche *n* -an *m* librarian
leabhrachan *n* -ain, -ain *m* pamphlet, brochure
leabhran *n* -ain, -ain/-an *m* booklet
leac *n* lic/lice, -an *f* flagstone, slab, flat stone; tombstone
leag *v* -ail knock down, fell, demolish **l. boma** drop a bomb
leagh *v* -adh melt, dissolve, smelt; liquidate
leaghadair *n* -ean *m* smelter
leam(sa) *prep pron* with me; by me **leam fhìn** alone **'s ann leamsa a tha e** it's mine **leam-leat** fickle, non-committal
leamh *a* -a vexing, sarcastic; importunate
leamhaich *v* -achadh vex, irk, irritate; importune
leamhan *n* -ain *m* elm
leamhnagan *n* -ain, -an *m* stye (*in eye*)
lean v -tainn/-tail follow,

continue, pursue **l. ort!** continue!, keep going! **ri**

leantainn to follow/be continued

leanabachd *n f* childhood, infancy, childishness

leanabail *a* **-e** childish, juvenile

leanaban *n* **-ain, -an** *m* infant, small child

leanabh *n* **-aibh, -an/leanaban** *m* child, infant

lèanag *n* **-aig, -an** *f* little meadow, lawn

leanailteach *a* **-tiche** continuous, lingering

leann *n* **-a, -tan** *m* beer, ale; (*any*) liquid

leannan *n* **-ain, -an** *m* lover, sweetheart

leannanachd *n f* courtship

leann-dubh *n* **-duibh** *m* melancholy

leantail/leantainn *n m* following, continuing

leantainneach *a* **-niche** continuous, lingering; sticky

leantainneachd *n f* continuity *Also* **leantalachd**

learag *n* **-aige, -an** *f* larch

learg *n* **-a** *f* black-throated diver

leas *n m* benefit, advantage **cha leig/ruig thu l.** *v* you needn't (bother)

leas- *pref* depute, deputy **l.-stiùiriche** *m* deputy director

leasachadh *n* **-aidh, -aidhean** *m* development, improvement, reformation, supplement **an t-Ath-L.** the Reformation **l.-fala** blood transfusion

leasaich *v* **-achadh** develop, improve, rectify; fertilize

leasaichte *a* developed, improved, rectified; fertilized

leasan *n* **-ain, -ain/-an** *m* lesson

leat(sa) *prep pron* with you; by you

leatas *n* **-ais, -an** *m* lettuce

leatha(se) *prep pron* with her, by her

leathad *n* **-aid/leothaid, -an/leòidean** *m* slope, brae

leathan(n) *a* **leatha/leithne** broad, wide *Also* **leathainn**

leathar *n* **-air** *m* leather

led *aug prep* with your, by your

leibh(se) *prep pron* with you; by you (*pl & pol*)

leibideach *a* **-diche** inept, defective; accidental, unfortunate

leig *v* **-eil** let, allow, permit **l. anail** draw breath, take a breather **l. leatha** leave her alone **na l. dad ort** don't let on **l. ort nach eil fhios agad** pretend you don't know **l. mu sgaoil** release **l. ris** reveal, show

leigeadh *n* **-gidh** *m* letting, allowing; discharge (*from boil etc*)

leigeil *n* **-ealach** *m* letting, allowing **l. fala** blood-letting

lèigh *n* **-e, -ean** *m* surgeon, physician **l.-lann** *f m* surgery

leigheas *n* **-eis, -an** *m* cure, remedy, healing **l.-inntinn** psychiatry

lèigh-eòlas *n* **-ais** *m* medicine (*science*)

leighis *v* **-gheas** cure, heal

lèine *n* **lèintean** *f* shirt **l.-mharbh** shroud

leinn(e) *prep pron* with us; by us

lèir *a* visible, clear

lèir *a* altogether **gu l.** altogether, in total

lèir *v* **-eadh** torment, pain

lèirmheas *n* **-eis, -an** *m* review (*liter*), overview

lèirsgrios *n* **-an** *m* total destruction, utter ruin

lèirsinn *n* **-e** *f* vision, sight; insight, perception

lèirsinneach *a* **-niche** discerning, perceptive, enlightened, visionary; visible

leis *prep* with, by (+ *def art*); his; downwards **l. an droch shìde** because of the bad weather **l. a' bhrutha(i)ch** down the brae/hill

leis(-san) *prep pron* with him; by him; his **an ann leis-san a tha e?** is it his?

leisg *a* **-e** lazy, slothful; reluctant

leisg(e) *n f* laziness, sloth, reluctance **bha l. air faighneachd** he was reluctant to ask

leisgeadair *n* -ean *m* lazy person, lazybones

leisgeul *n* -eil, -an *m* excuse, apology (*for absence*) **gabh mo l.!** excuse me!, pardon me!

leiteachas *n* -ais *m* partiality, bias

leithid *n* -e, -ean *f* such, the like **chan fhaca duine riamh a l.** no one has ever seen the like

leitir *n* -e/leitreach, -ean/ leitrichean *f* hillside, slope

lem *aug prep* with my, by my

len *aug prep* with their, by their

leòbag *n f See* **lèabag**

Leòdhasach *n* -aich, -aich *m* someone from Lewis *a* from, or pertaining to, Lewis

leòinteach *n* -tich, -tich *m* wounded person, casualty

leòm *n* **leòim(e)** *f* pride, conceit

leòmach *a* -aiche well-dressed, smart (*dress*); conceited

leòman *n* -ain, -ain *m* moth

leòmhann *n* -ainn, -ainn *m* lion **l.-mara** sea lion

leòn *n* **leòin**, -tan *m* wound

leòn *v* leòn/-adh wound

leònte *a* wounded, afflicted

leòr *n f* enough, sufficiency **an d' fhuair thu do l.?** did you get enough/your fill? **gu l.** plenty, enough **ceart gu l.** OK

l(e)òsan *n* -ain, -ain *m* window pane

leotha(san) *prep pron* with them; by them

ler *aug prep* with our, by our; with your, by your

leth *n m* half *a* separate **air l.** exceptional **às l.** on behalf of **fa l.** each one, individually **gu l.** and a half **l. mar l.** half and half, share and share alike

leth- *pref* half-, semi-

leth-aon *n* -aoin, -an *m* twin

lethbhreac *n* -ric, -ric *m* copy, photocopy, duplicate **dèan l.** *v* duplicate

leth-bhreith *n* -e *f* partiality, discrimination **dèan l.** *v* discriminate

leth-bhruich *v* (-eadh) parboil, half-boil

lethchar *adv* somewhat

leth-chas *n* -choise, -an *f* (only) one foot **air leth-chois** on one foot

lethcheann *n* -chinn, -chinn *n* temple, side of head, cheek (*phys*)

leth-chearcall *n* -aill, -aill/-an *m* semi-circle

leth-cheud *n* -an *m* fifty (+ *sg*) **l. bliadhna** fifty years

lethchiallach *n* -aich, -aich *m* half-witted person

leth-chruinne *n* -an *m* hemisphere

leth-chrùn *n* -chrùin, -chrùin/ -chrùintean *m* half-crown

leth-chuairt *n* -e, -ean *f* semi-circle

letheach *a* half **l. slighe** half-way

leth-fhacal *n* -ail, -ail/-fhaclan *m* byword

leth-làmh *n* -làimhe, -an *f* (only) one hand

leth-mhìle *n* -mhìltean *m* half-mile; five hundred

lethoireach *a* isolated, remote

leth-phinnt *n* -ean *m* half pint

leth-phunnd *n* -phuinnd, -phuinnd *m* half pound

leth-shùil *n* -shùla, -ean *f* (only) one eye

leth-uair *n* -uarach, -ean *f* half-hour **l. an dèidh uair** half past one

leud *n* **leòid**, -an *m* breadth, width

leudaich *v* -achadh broaden, widen, expand, enlarge

leug *n* **lèig**, -an *f* jewel, precious stone

leugh *v* -adh read

leughadair *n* -ean *m* reader

leughadh *n* -aidh *m* reading

leum *n* **lèim**/-a, -annan *f m* leap, jump, spring **l. àrd** high jump **l. droma** lumbago **l. fhada** long jump

leum *v* leum/-adaich leap, jump, spring **l. a sròn** she had a nosebleed

leumadair *n* -ean *m* jumper (*sport*); dolphin

leus *n* **leòis, leòis** *m* ray, light;
   blister
liac *v* **-radh** smear, spread
liagh *n* **lèigh, -an** *f* ladle; blade of
   oar
liath *a* **lèithe** grey, blue-grey, blue;
   grey-haired
liath *v* **-adh** make grey, become
   grey **tha fhalt air liathadh** his
   hair has gone grey
liath- *pref* grey-tinted
liath-reothadh *n* **-reothaidh** *m*
   hoar-frost
lìbhrig *v* **-eadh** deliver
lìbhrigeadh *n* **-gidh, -gidhean** *m*
   delivery (*not phys*)
lideadh *n* **lididh, lididhean** *m*
   syllable *Also* **lide**
lighiche *n* **-an** *m* doctor,
   physician **l.-inntinn** psychiatrist
lilidh *n* **-ean** *f* lily
lìnig *v* **-eadh** line (*clothes etc*)
lìnigeadh *n* **-gidh, -gidhean** *m*
   lining (*in clothes*) *Also* **lìnig**
linn *n* **-e, -tean** *f m* century, age,
   generation, era **ri l.** because of
   (+ *gen*)
linne *n* **-achan/linntean** *f* pool,
   pond
liodraig *v* **-eadh** beat up, leather
liogach *a* **-giche** sly, cunning
liomaid *n* **-e, -ean** *f* lemon *Also*
   liomain
lìomh *n* **-a** *f* polish, gloss
lìomh *v* **-adh** polish
lìomharra *a* polished, glossy
lìon *n* **lìn, lìn, -tan** *m* net, web **l.
   iasgaich** fishing net **lìn-mhòra**
   long-lines
lìon *n* **lìn** *m* flax, lint
lìon *v* **-adh** fill, replenish
lìonadh *n* **-aidh** *m* filling,
   replenishing; incoming tide
lìonmhor *a* **-a** numerous, plentiful
lionn *n* **-a, -tan** *m* (*any*) liquid
lios *n* **-a/lise, -an** *f m* garden
Liosach *n* **-aich, -aich** *m* someone
   from Lismore *a* from, or
   pertaining to, Lismore
liosta *n* **-ichean** *f* list (*written*)
liotach *a* **-aiche** lisping, slurring
liotair *n* **-ean** *m* litre
lip *n* **-e, -ean** *f* lip

lite *n* *f* porridge
litir *n* **litreach, litrichean** *f* letter
litreachadh *n* **-aidh** *m* spelling,
   orthography
litreachas *n* **-ais** *m* literature
litrich *v* **-reachadh** spell
liubhair *v* **-t** (*not phys*) deliver
liùdhag *n* **-aig, -an** *f* doll
liùg *v* **-adh** creep, steal, sneak a
   look at
liùgach *a* **-aiche** creeping, sneaking
liùgh *n* **-a, -achan** *f* lythe *Also*
   liugha
liut *n* **liuit** *f* knack, aptitude **l. air
   ...** aptitude for ...
liuthad *a* so many (*precedes n*)
lobh *v* **-adh** rot, putrefy
lobhadh *n* **-aidh** *m* rot
lobhar *n* **-air, -air** *m* leper
lobhta *n* **-ichean** *m* loft *Also*
   lobht
lobhte *a* rotten, putrid *Also*
   loibh(t)
locair *n* **-ean/locraichean** *f*
   carpenter's plane
locair *v* **locradh** plane
loch *n* **-a, -an** *f m* loch, lake
   l. mara sea loch
lochan *n* **-ain, -ain** *m* small loch
lochd *n* **-a, -an** *m* fault, defect,
   malice
lochdach *a* **-aiche** faulty, harmful,
   malicious
Lochlannach *n* **-aich, -aich** *m*
   Scandinavian, Viking
   a Scandinavian, Viking
lòchran *n* **-ain, -ain** *m* lantern,
   lamp
lod *n* **-a, -an** *m* load
lof *n* **-a, -aichean** *f m* loaf
logaidh *n* **-ean** *m* forelock, fringe
   (*of hair*), mane
loidhne *n* **-nichean** *f* line **l.-taice**
   helpline
loidseadh *n* **-sidh, -sidhean** *m*
   lodging
loidsear *n* **-eir, -an** *m* lodger
lòineag *n* **-eige, -an** *f* flake,
   snowflake; small tuft of wool
loingeas *n* **-eis** *m* ship; fleet, navy
   l.-cogaidh warship *Also*
   luingeas
loinid *n* **-e, -ean** *f* churn, whisk

lòinidh *n f m* **an I.** rheumatism, sciatica

loinn *n* **-e** *f* elegance, comeliness, fine finish **tha I. air** it is elegant

loinneil *a* **-e** elegant, comely

loireach *a* **-riche** soiled, bedraggled, messy

loireag *n* **-eig, -an** *f* untidy or messy female

loisg *v* **losgadh** burn, inflame, fire

loisgte *a* burnt

lom *a* **luime** bare, naked; thin, threadbare

lom *v* **-adh** make bare, shear, shave

lomadair *n* **-ean** *m* shears; shearer, shaver, mower

lomadh *n* **-aidh** *m* making bare, shearing, fleecing, shaving, mowing

lomair *v* **lomradh** mow, shear, fleece

lomaire *n* **-an** *m* mower, shearer

loma-làn *a* brimful, completely full

lomnochd *a* naked, bare, undressed *n f* nakedness, nudity

lon *n* **loin, loin** *m* elk

lòn *n* **lòin, lòintean** *m* pool; meadow

lòn *n* **lòin** *m* food, provisions, lunch; livelihood

lon-dubh *n* **loin-duibh, loin-dubha** *m* blackbird

long *n* **luinge, -an** *f* ship **l.-bhriseadh** *m* shipwreck **l.-chogaidh** warship **l.-fànais** spaceship **l.-fo-mhuir** submarine

lorg *n* **luirge, -an** *f* track, trace; staff, stick **a bheil I. agad air?** do you know where it/he is?

lorg *v* find, discover, trace, search for

los *conj* so that, because **air I.** for, on account of

losgadh *n* **-aidh, -aidhean** *m* burn, burning, combustion, firing **l.-bràghad** heartburn

losgann *n* **-ainn, -an** *m* toad; frog

lot *n* **-a, -aichean** *f* allotment, croft

lot *n* **-a, -an** *m* wound

lot *v* **-adh** wound

loth *n* **-a, -an** *f m* filly, colt

luach *n m* value, worth

luachair *n* **luachrach** *f* rushes

luachmhor *a* **-oire** valuable, precious

luadh *n* **luaidh, luaidh(ean)** *m* waulking (*of tweed*), fulling (*cloth*) **òran luaidh** waulking song *Also* **luadhadh**

luaidh *v* **luadh** waulk, full (*tweed*)

luaidh *n m* mention, praise; beloved person **dèan I. air** *v* make mention of **mo I.** my dear

luaidh *v* mention, praise

luaidh(e) *n* **-e** *f m* lead

luaineach *a* **-niche** restless, fickle

luaireag *n* **-eig, -an** *f* storm petrel

luaisg *v* **luasgadh** shake, toss, rock, wave, swing

luaisgeanach *a* **-aiche** shaking, tossing, swaying, unsettled

luamhan *n* **-ain, -an** *m* lever

luasgan *n* **-ain, -an** *m* shaking, tossing, swaying

luath *n* **luaith/-a** *f* ash, ashes *Also* **luaithre**

luath *a* **luaithe** fast, swift, speedy

luaths *n* **luaiths** *m* speed, swiftness, velocity

lùb *n* **lùib, -an** *f* bend, curve

lùb *v* **-adh** bend

lùbach *a* **-aiche** bending, winding; pliant

lùbte *a* bent

luch *n* **-a/-ainn, -an** *f* mouse **l.-fheòir** fieldmouse

luchag *n* **-aig, -an** *f* little mouse

lùchairt *n* **-e, -ean** *f* palace

lucharan *n* **-ain, -ain** *f* dwarf

luchd *n m* people *used to form collective nouns for groups of people eg* **neach-cunntais** accountant **l.-cunntais** accountants

luchd *n* **-a, -an** *m* load, cargo

luchdaich *v* **-achadh** load

luchd-aideachaidh *n m* professing Christians

luchd-amhairc *n m* spectators

luchd-casaid *n m* accusers, prosecution **l.-c. a' Chrùin** the

Crown prosecutors
luchd-ceanna(i)ch *n m* buyers
luchd-ciùil *n m* musicians
luchd-coimhid *n m* spectators,
observers
luchd-dàimh *n m* kindred
luchd-ealain *n m* artist(e)s
luchd-èisteachd *n m* audience,
listeners
luchd-eòlais *n m* acquaintances
luchd-foillseachaidh *n m*
publishers
luchd-fòirneirt *n m* terrorists,
oppressors
luchd-frithealaidh *n m* attendants;
waiters, waitresses
luchd-leughaidh *n m* readers,
readership
luchd-naidheachd *n m*
journalists, reporters
luchd-obrach *n m* workers, staff
luchd-riaghlaidh *n m* rulers
luchd-sàbhalaidh *n m* rescuers
luchd-seinn *n m* singers
luchd-sgrùdaidh *n m* inspectors
l.-s. nan sgoiltean school
inspectors
luchd-siubhail *n m* travellers
luchd-smàlaidh *n m* firefighters
luchd-stiùiridh *n m* directors
luchd-tagraidh *n m* pleaders,
advocates
luchd-trusaidh *n m* collectors
l.-t. nam fiach debt collectors
luchd-turais *n m* tourists
lùdag *n* **-aig, -an** *f* (the) little
finger, pinkie; hinge
luga *n* **-n/-ichean** *f* lugworm,
sandworm
lugha *a* less, least **is l. orm e**
I hate it/him
lùghdachadh *n* **-aidh** *m* decrease,
reduction, lessening,
diminution, downturn
lùghdaich *v* **-achadh** decrease,
reduce, lessen, diminish
luibh *n* **-e, -ean** *f m* plant, herb;
weed **l.-eòlaiche** *m* botanist
l.-eòlas *m* botany
Lugsamburgach *n* **-aich, -aich** *m*
someone from Luxemburg
a from, or pertaining to,
Luxemburg

luibhre *n f* an l. leprosy
luideach *a* **-diche** silly, daft;
shabby, untidy
luideag *n* **-eig, -an** *f* rag
luidhear *n* **-eir, -eirean** *f* vent,
chimney; ship's funnel
Luinneach *n* **-nich, -nich** *m*
someone from Luing *a* from,
or pertaining to, Luing
luinneag *n* **-eig, -an** *f* ditty, song
Lùnastal *n* **-ail** *m* an L. August
Formerly an Lùnasdal
lurach *a* **-aiche** lovely, beautiful,
pretty, attractive
lurgann *n* **-ainn, -an** *f* shin
lurmachd *a See* **lomnochd**
lus *n* **-a/luis, -an** *m* plant, herb
l. a' chrom-chinn daffodil **l. nam
ban-sìth** foxglove **l. nan cluas**
saxifrage
luthaig *v* **-eadh** wish, desire *Also*
lùig
lùth-chleas *n* **-a, -an** *m* athletics,
sport
lùth-chleasachd *n f* athletics,
sport
lùth-chleasaiche *n* **-an** *m* athlete,
sportsman, sportswoman
lùthmhor *a* **-oire** strong,
powerful, athletic, vigorous
lùth(s) *n* **lùith(s)** *m* strength,
power, vigour, energy **cion
lùith(s)** lack of power/energy
gun l. unable to move

M

m' *poss pron* my (*used before
words beginning in vowels or* **fh**)
ma *conj* if
ma *aug prep* about his/her/its
màb *v* **-adh** abuse, vilify
mabach *a* **-aiche** stammering,
stuttering, lisping
mac *n* **mic, mic** *m* son **m.
bràthar/peathar** nephew
mac-an-aba *n m* ring finger
macanta *a* meek, gentle, mild
macantas *n* **-ais** *m* meekness,
mildness
mach *adv* out (*used of motion*)
m. à seo! let's be off!; out you
go! **m. air a chèile** at odds

machair *n* e-/**machrach**,
machraichean *f m* machair,
sandy arable land near coast

machlag *n* -**aig**, -**an** *f* uterus,
womb, matrix

mac-meanmna *n* **mic-** *m*
imagination *Also* **mac-meanmainn**

mac-samhail *n* **mic-** *m* replica,
facsimile, duplicate; likeness

mac-talla *n* **mic-** *m* echo

madadh *n* -**aidh**, -**aidhean** *m*
hound, dog **m.-allaidh** wolf
m.-ruadh fox

madainn *n* **maidne**, **maidnean** *f*
morning **M. mhath!** Good
morning!

mag *v* -**adh** mock, scoff, laugh at,
jeer

magadh *n* -**aidh** *m* mocking,
scoffing, jeer **cùis-mhagaidh** *f*
object of ridicule

magail *a* -**e** scoffing, mocking;
apt to mock

magairle *n* -**an** *f m* testicle

màgaran *n* -**ain** *m* crawling on all
fours **air mhàgaran** on all fours

maghar *n* -**air**, -**airean** *m* bait
(*fishing*), artificial fly
vn **a' m.** fishing while moving

maide *n* -**an** *m* stick, wood
m.-tarsainn beam, cross-beam

maids *v* -**eadh**/-**igeadh** match

maids(e) *n* -**sichean** *m* match
(*light*); match (*game*)

màidsear *n* -**eir**, -**an** *m* major
M. na Pìoba Pipe Major

Màigh *n* -**e** *f* **a' Mhàigh** May

maighdeann *n* -**dinn**, -**an**/-**dinnean**
f maiden **m.-phòsaidh**
bridesmaid **m.-mhara** mermaid

maigheach *n* -**ghiche**, -**ghichean** *f*
hare

maigh(i)stir *n* -**ean** *m* master **Mgr**
MacÌomhair Mr MacIver **m.-sgoile** schoolmaster, headmaster

màileid *n* -**e**, -**ean** *f* bag, suitcase

maill(e) *n* *f* slowness, tardiness,
delay **chuireadh maill oirnn** we
were delayed

maille ri *prep* (along) with

mair *v* -**sinn**/-**eachdainn** last,
endure

maireann *a* living, extant ... **nach**
m. the late ... **ri do mhaireann**
during your lifetime, as long as
you live

maireannach *a* -**aiche** lasting,
enduring, everlasting,
permanent

mairg *a* woeful, pitiable

màirnealach *a* -**aiche** dilatory,
slow

màirnealachd *n* *f* slowness, delay

mairsinneach *a* -**niche** lasting,
long-lasting

mairtfheòil *n* -**òla** *f* beef

maise *n* *f* beauty, loveliness,
comeliness **ball-m.** beauty spot
(*on face*); ornament

maiseach *a* -**siche** beautiful,
lovely, comely

maistreadh *n* -**ridh** *m* churning
(*making butter*)

maith *v* *See* **math**

màl *n* **màil**, **màil** *m* rent **air mhàl**
rented

mala *n* -**idhean**/-**ichean**/**mailghean**
f eyebrow; brow

malairt *n* -**ean** *f* trade, exchange,
commerce, business

màlda *a* modest, coy; gentle, mild

mall *a* **maille** slow, tardy

mallachd *n* -**an** *f* curse

mallaich *v* -**achadh** curse

mallaichte *a* cursed, accursed

màm *n* **màim**, -**an** *m* large round
hill

mamaidh *n* -**ean** *f* mammy,
mummy

màm-slèibhe *n* **màim-**, **màman-** *m*
avalanche

manach *n* -**aich**, -**aich** *m* monk

manachainn *n* -**e**, -**ean** *f*
monastery

manadh *n* -**aidh**, -**aidhean** *m*
omen, warning (*supernatural*),
apparition; prophecy **cuir air**
mhanadh *v* prophesy

manaidsear *n* -**eir**, -**an** *m*
manager

Manainneach *n* -**nich**, -**nich** *m*
Manx person *a* Manx

mang *n* **mainge**, -**an** *f* fawn

mànran *n* -**ain**, -**an** *m* tuneful
sound, melody, crooning

mànranach *a* **-aiche** tuneful, melodious, crooning

maodal *n* **-ail, -an** *f* stomach, paunch

maoidh *v* **-eadh** threaten, reproach

maoidheadh *n* **-dhidh, -dhidhean** *m* threat, threatening

maoil *n* **-ean** *f* forehead, brow

maoin *n* **-e, -ean** *f* wealth, riches, fund

maoineachas *n* **-ais** *m* finance

maoinich *v* **-neachadh** finance, fund

maoiseach *n* **-sich, -sichean** *f* doe

maol *n* **maoil, maoil** *f m* rounded headland, mull; promontory **M. Chinn Tìre** Mull of Kintyre

maol *a* **maoile** blunt; bald; hornless; stupid

maor *n* **maoir, maoir** *m* bailiff, steward, constable **m.-cladaich** coastguard

maorach *n* **-aich** *m* shellfish

maoth *a* **maoithe** soft, tender

maothaich *v* **-achadh** soften; mitigate

mapa *n* **-ichean** *m* map

mar *a, adv, prep* (+ *len*), *conj* as, like **mar seo** *adv* like this, thus **mar sin** *adv* like that, therefore **mar sin leat/leibh** *adv* goodbye **mar a** *conj* as

mar *aug prep* about our

marag *n* **-aig, -an** *f* blood-pudding **m. dhubh** black pudding **m. gheal** white pudding

maraiche *n* **-an** *m* seaman, mariner

mar an ceudna *adv* also, likewise, too

mar-aon *adv* together, as one, in concert

marbh *n* **mairbh, mairbh** *m* dead person **na mairbh** the dead **m. na h-oidhche** the dead of night

marbh *a* **mairbhe** dead

marbh *v* **-adh** kill

mar-bhith *n* *f* fault **gun m.** without fault

marbhrann *n* **-ainn, -an** *m* elegy

marbhtach *a* **-aiche** deadly; mortal

marcachd *n* *f* riding, horsemanship

marcaich *v* **-achd** ride

marcaiche *n* **-an** *m* rider, horseman

marc-shluagh *n* **-aigh** *m* cavalry, horsemen

mar eisimpleir *adv* for example

margadh *n* **-aidh, -aidhean** *f* market **m. nan earrannan** stock exchange

margaid *n* **-e, -ean** *f* market

màrmor *n* **-oir** *m* marble

màrsail *n* **-e** *f* marching, march

marsanta *n* **-n** *m* merchant

mart *n* **mairt, mairt** *m* cow, steer

Màrt *n* **Màirt** *m* **am M.** March

mar-thà *adv* already

màs *n* **màis, -an** *m* buttock, bottom, posterior

mas *conj* *See* **mus**

maslach *a* **-aiche** disgraceful, shameful

masladh *n* **-aidh, -aidhean** *m* disgrace, reproach

maslaich *v* **-achadh** disgrace, put to shame

ma-tà *adv* then, in that case

matamataig *n* *m* mathematics

math *n* **maith** *m* good, benefit **m. a' phobaill** the public interest/good **dè (am) m. a bhith a' bruidhinn?** what's the use of talking?

math *a* **feàrr** good **gu m.** well **m. air ...** good at ... **gu m. fuar** quite cold **chan eil m. dhut ...** you must not ... **mas m. mo chuimhne** if I remember correctly **'s m. sin** that's good **m. dha-rìribh** very good indeed, excellent

math *adv* well

math *v* **-adh** forgive, pardon **m. dhuinn ar peacaidhean** forgive us our sins

ma-thà *adv* then, in that case

mathachadh *n* **-aidh** *m* manure, manuring

mathaich *v* **-achadh** manure

màthair *n* **-ar, màthraichean** *f* mother **m.-chèile** mother-in-law

mathan *n* -ain, -an *m* bear **m.-bàn** polar bear

mathanas *n* -ais *m* forgiveness, pardon *Also* **maitheanas**

mathas *n* -ais *m* goodness, virtue *Also* **maitheas**

math dh'fhaodte *conj* perhaps, maybe

meaban *n* -ain, -ain *m* upstart; something damaged

meacan-ruadh *n* **meacain-ruaidh, meacanan-ruadha** *m* radish

meadhan *n* -ain, -an *m* middle, centre; medium, means **na meadhanan** the media **teis-m.** the very centre **m.-aois** middle age **na M.-Aoisean** the Middle Ages **m.-chearcall** equator

meadhanach *a* -aiche middling, so-so, mediocre; intermediate, central

meadhan-là/latha *n* **meadhain-** *m* midday

meadhan-oidhche *n* **meadhain-** *m* midnight

meadh-bhlàth *a* lukewarm

meadhrach *a* -aiche glad, joyous, merry

meal *v* -tainn/-adh enjoy, relish **M. do naidheachd!** Congratulations! **m. is caith e** enjoy it and make good use of it

meal-bhuc *n* -bhuic, -an *f* melon

meall *n* **mill, mill** *m* lump; round hill; large number; shower (*of rain*) **m.-sgòrnain** Adam's apple

meall *v* -adh deceive ... **mura h-eil mi air mo mhealladh** ... if I'm not mistaken

mealladh *n* -aidh *m* deception, deceiving

meallta *a* deceptive, deceitful, misleading

meamhran *n* -ain *m* membrane

mean *a* little **m. air mhean** little by little, gradually

mèanan, mèananaich *n See* **mèaran, mèaranaich**

meanbh *a* -a minute, diminutive

meanbhchuileag *n* -eig, -an *f* midge

meang *n* -a/ming, -an *f* blemish,

flaw, abnormality **gun mheang** faultless

meang(l)an *n* -ain, -an *m* branch (*of tree*), bough

meanmnach *a* -aiche spirited, lively

meann *n* **minn, minn** *m* kid (*animal*)

meannt *n* -a *m* mint

meantraig *v* -eadh venture, dare

mear *a* -a merry, playful

mearachd *n* -an *f* mistake, error

mearachdach *a* -aiche mistaken, erroneous, inaccurate

mèaran *n* -ain, -an *m* yawn

mèaranaich *n* -e *f* yawning *Also* *vn* **a' m.**

mèarrs *v* -adh/-ail march

mèarrsadh *n* -aidh *m* march, marching

meas *n m* esteem, respect; evaluation, assessment **le m.** yours sincerely (*in letter*)

meas *n* -a, -an *m* fruit

meas *v* meas/-adh consider, esteem; reckon, estimate, value

measadh *n* -aidh, -aidhean *m* assessment, evaluation, appraisal, reckoning

measail *a* -e fond; respected, esteemed **m. air ...** fond of ...

measarra *a* temperate, moderate, sober

measarrachd *n f* temperance, restraint

measg *n* **am m.** (+ *gen*) among, amongst

measgachadh *n* -aidh, -aidhean *m* mixture, combination

measgaich *v* -achadh mix, mingle

meata *a* timid, faint-hearted, feeble

meatailt *n, a* -e, -ean *f* metal

meatair *n* -ean *m* metre (*length*)

meidh *n* -e, -ean *f* balance, scales **air mheidh** in the balance

meigeadaich *n f* bleating (*of goat or kid*)

meil *v* -ich/-eadh grind

mèil *v* -ich bleat

meileabhaid *n f* velvet

mèilich *n f* bleating

meilich *v* -leachadh chill, benumb

mèinn *n* -e, -ean *f* mine (*mil, ind*)

mèinn *n* -e *f* disposition,
temperament

mèinneadair *n* -ean *m* miner

mèinnear *n* -eir, -an *m* mineral;
miner

mèinnearachd *n* *f* mining,
mineralogy

mèinnearach *a* -aiche mineral,
mineralogical

mèinneil *a* -e placid, gentle,
refined

meirg *n* -e *f* rust

meirg *v* -eadh rust, corrode

meirgeach *a* -giche rusty

mèirle *n* *f* theft, thieving **ri m.**
thieving **dèan m.** *v* thieve, steal

mèirleach *n* -lich, -lich *m* thief

meòrachadh *n* -aidh, -aidhean *m*
meditation, deliberation

meòraich *v* -achadh meditate,
deliberate, reflect *Also*
meòmhraich

meòrachan *n* -ain, -ain *m*
memorandum

meud *n* -an *m* size, extent,
amount

meudachd *n* *f* size, bulk

meudaich *v* -achadh increase,
enlarge

meug *n* meòig *m* whey

meur *n* meòir, meòir/-an *f* finger,
digit; branch (*org*); knot (*in
wood*) **m.-lorg** fingerprint
m.-chlàr keyboard

meuran *n* -ain, -ain/-an *m*
thimble; knot (*in wood*)

mì- *neg pref* not, dis-, ill-, in-,
mis-, -less

mi(se) *pron* I, me

miadhail *a* -e respected, esteemed;
fond **m. air ...** fond of ...

miag *v* -ail mew

mial *n* -a, -an *f* louse; tick

mial-chù *n* -choin, -choin *m*
greyhound

mia(tha)laich *n* *f* mewing *Also vn*
a' m.

miann *n* -an *f m* desire, wish **bu
mhiann leam** I would like

miannaich *v* -achadh desire

mias *n* mias/mèise, -an *f* basin

miast(r)adh *n* -aidh *m* havoc,
vandalism

mì-bheusachd *n* *f* indecency,
impropriety

mì-chàilear *a* unpleasant,
disagreeable, distasteful

mì-chiatach *a* -aiche unseemly,
improper; outrageous

mì-chinnt *n* *f* uncertainty

mì-chinnteach *a* -tiche uncertain

mì-chliù *n* disrepute, dishonour

mì-chofhurtail *a* -e uncomfortable

mì-chùramach *a* -aiche careless

mì-dhòigh *n* *f* lack of method,
lack of care; deprivation

mì-dhòigheil *a* -e unmethodical,
disorganized

mì-fhaiceallach *a* -aiche careless

mì-fhallain *a* -e unhealthy,
unwholesome

mì-fhoighidneach *a* -niche
impatient

mì-fhortanach *a* -aiche
unfortunate, unlucky

mì-fhreagarrach *a* -aiche
unsuitable

mì-ghean *n* -a *m* discontent,
melancholy

mì-ghnàthaich *v* -achadh abuse

mì-ghoireasach *a* -aiche
inconvenient

mì-iomchaidh *a* -e improper

mì-laghail *a* -e unlawful, illegal

mil *n* meala/mealach, mealan *f*
honey

mìle *n* mìltean *f m* thousand; mile

milis *a* mìlse sweet; harmonious
(*mus*)

mill *v* -eadh spoil, mar, ruin

milleadh *n* -lidh *m* spoiling,
marring, ruining

millean *n* -ein/-an *m* million

millteach *a* -tiche destructive,
ruinous, prodigal,
detrimental

mìlseachd *n* *f* sweetness

mìlsean *n* -ein, -ein/-an *m* sweet,
dessert

mì-mhisneachadh *n* -aidh *m*
discouragement

mì-mhisneachail *a* -e
discouraging, disheartening

mì-mhisnich *v* -neachadh
discourage, dishearten

mì-mhodh *n* **-mhoidh, -a** *m*
impoliteness, misbehaviour,
impertinence **na bi ri m.!** don't
misbehave
mì-mhodhail *a* **-e** impolite,
misbehaved, rude, discourteous
min *n* **-e** meal *f* **m.-choirce**
oatmeal **m.-fhlùir** white flour
m.-sàibh sawdust
mìn *a* **-e** smooth, soft, delicate
mì-nàdarrach *a* **-aiche** unnatural
mìneachadh *n* **-aidh, -aidhean** *m*
interpretation, explanation
mìnich *v* **mìneachadh** interpret,
explain
minig *a* often, frequent
minig *v* **-eadh** mean
ministear *n* **-eir, -an** *m* minister
M. na Còmhdhail the Transport
Minister
ministrealachd *n f* ministry (*relig,
polit*) **M. an Dìon** the Ministry
of Defence
miogadaich *n See* **meigeadaich**
mion *a* **-a** minute, small, on a
small scale **m.-chunntas** *f m*
detailed account **m.-eòlach**
(**+ air**) fully conversant with,
expert in **m.-sgrùd** *v* scrutinize,
analyze
mionach *n* **-aich, -aichean** *m*
stomach, intestines, entrails
mionaid *n* **-e, -ean** *f* minute
fuirich m. bheag wait a second
mionaideach *a* **-diche** precise,
detailed, exact **gu m.** minutely,
in detail
mì-onarach *a* **-aiche** dishonest,
dishonourable
mion-chànan *n* **-ain, -an** *f m*
minority language
mionnachadh *n* **-aidh** *m* swearing
mionnaich *v* **-achadh** swear; curse
mionnaichte *a* convinced, certain
mionnan *n* **-ain, -ain/-an** *m* oath
mo mhionnan! I swear!
mions *n* **-a** *m* mince
mìorbhail *n* **-e, -ean** *f* marvel,
miracle
mìorbhaileach *a* **-liche**
marvellous, miraculous
mìos *n* **-a, -an** *f m* month
m. nam pòg honeymoon

miosa *a See* **dona**
mìosachan *n* **-ain, -ain** *m*
calendar
mìosail *a* monthly
miotag *n* **-aig, -an** *f* glove, mitten
mìr *n* **-e, -ean** *m* bit, piece,
fragment
mire *n f* merriment, mirth, frolic
mìrean *n* **-ein, -ein/-an** *m* particle,
small piece
mì-reusanta *a* unreasonable
mì-riaghailt *n* **-e, -ean** *f* disorder,
irregularity
mì-riaghailteach *a* **-tiche**
disorderly, unruly, irregular
mì-rian *n f* disorder,
disorganization
mì-rianail *a* **-e** disordered,
disorderly
mì-riaraichte *a* dissatisfied
mì-rùn *n* **-rùin** *m* malice, ill will
miseanaraidh *n* **-ean** *m*
missionary
misg *n* **-e** *f* drunkenness,
intoxication **air mhisg** drunk
misgear *n* **-eir, -an** *m* drunkard,
boozer
mì-sgiobalta *a* untidy
mì-shealbh *n* **-sheilbh** *m*
misfortune, ill-luck **gheibh thu
do mhì-shealbh** you'll catch it
(*met*)
mì-shealbhach *a* **-aiche**
unfortunate, unlucky
mì-shona *a* unhappy, discontent
misneachail *a* **-e** courageous,
encouraging; confident
misneachd *n f* courage,
encouragement, boldness;
confidence *Also* **misneach**
misnich *v* **-neachadh** encourage,
embolden
miste *a* worse **cha bu mhiste tu
sin** you would be none the
worse of that
mì-thaingealachd *n f* ingratitude
mì-thaingeil *a* **-e** ungrateful
mì-thaitneach *a* **-niche**
unpleasant, disagreeable
mì-thlachdmhor *a* **-oire**
unpleasant, disagreeable
mì-thoileachas *a* **-ais** *m*
displeasure, unhappiness,

discontent
mì-thoilichte *a* unhappy, displeased, discontent
mì-thuarail *a* **-e** ill-looking, looking off-colour
mo *poss pron* my, mine (+ *len*) **mo chreach!** Alas! **mo thogair!** who cares? (**m'** *before vowels or* **fh**)
moch *a* **moich(e)** early **o mhoch gu dubh** from dawn till dusk
mocheirigh *n f* rising early
mòd *n* **mòid, -an** *m* mod, assembly, court **am Mòd Nàiseanta** the National Mod
modail *n* **-e, -ean** *f* model
modal *n* **-ail, -an** *m* module
modh *n* **-a, -an/-annan** *f m* manner, mode, behaviour; procedure, process; mood (*gram*)
modhail *a* **-e** polite, mannerly, courteous
mogal *n* **-ail, -ail** *m* mesh (*of net*)
mogan *n* **-ain, -an** *m* stash (*of money*); slipper
mòine *n* **mòine/mòna(dh)/mònach** *f* peat, moss **buain na mòna** cutting peat
mòinteach *n* **-tich, -tichean** *f* moor, moorland
moit *n* **-e** *f* pride
moiteil *a* **-e** proud
mol *n* **moil/-a, -an** *m* shingle, shingle beach
mol *v* **-adh** praise; recommend, propose
molach *a* **-aiche** hairy, shaggy, rough
moladh *n* **-aidh** *m* praise; recommendation
molag *n* **-aig, -an** *f* pebble
moll *n* **muill** *m* chaff
molldair *n* **-ean** *m* mould
molt *n* **muilt, muilt** *m* wedder (*sheep*)
moltach *a* **-aiche (+ air)** praising, laudatory
mòmaid *n* **-e, -ean** *f* moment
monadail *a* **-e** hilly, mountainous
monadh *n* **-aidh, -aidhean** *m* moor, hill, mountain **am M. Ruadh** the Cairngorms

monaiseach *n* **-siche** slow, dull; self-effacing
monmhar *n* **-air, -an** *m* murmur
mòr *a* **motha/mò** big, great, large **tha iad mòr aig a chèile** they are great friends **cha mhòr gum faca sinn iad** we hardly saw them **cha mhòr nach do thuit mi** I almost fell **bha e mòr leam faighneachd** I was reluctant to ask **mòr às fhèin** haughty
mòrachd *n f* greatness, majesty
morair *n* **-ean** *m* lord, peer **Taigh nam Morairean** the House of Lords
moralta *a* moral
moraltachd *n f* morality
mòran *n* **-ain** *m* many, much, a lot *adv* much
mòr-bhùth *n* **-a, -an/-bhùithtean** *f* supermarket
mòr-chuid *n f* majority
mòrchuis *n* **-e** *f* pride, haughtiness, conceit
mòrchuiseach *a* **-siche** haughty, conceited, pompous
mòr-chuisle *n* **-an** *f* artery
mòr-dhail *n* **-ean** *m* convention, assembly, congress
morgaidse *n* **-an** *m* mortgage
morghan *n* **-ain** *m* gravel, shingle
mòr-ghath *n* **-a, -an** *m* harpoon, trident
mòr-roinn *n* **-e, -ean** *f* continent
mòr-shluagh *n* **-aigh, -an** *m* populace, host, multitude
mòr-thìr *n* **-e, -ean** *m* mainland, continent
mosach *a* **-aiche** miserable, nasty, inclement (*weather*); mean (*person*)
mosgaideach *a* **-diche** dilatory, slow, unreliable
mosgail *v* **-gladh** arouse, waken
motair *n* **-ean** *m* motor **m.-baic** motorbike **m.-baidhsagal** motorbicycle
motha *a See* **mòr**
mothachadh *n* **-aidh, -aidhean** *m* consciousness, awareness; sensation **gun mhothachadh** unconscious

mothachail *a* -e conscious, aware
mothaich *v* -achadh notice, perceive
mothar *n* -air, -air *m* loud shout Also **mòthar**
mu *prep* about, around
muc *n* muice, -an *f* pig, sow
mùch *v* -adh stifle, suppress, smother, extinguish
mu choinneamh *prep phr* (+ *gen*) opposite **mu ch. na bùtha** opposite the shop
mu chuairt *adv, prep phr* (+ *gen*) around **mu ch. an t-saoghail** around the world
muc-mhara *n* muic-mhara/muice-mara, mucan-mara *f* whale
mud *aug prep* about your (*sg*)
mu dheidhinn *prep phr* (+ *gen*) about, concerning **mu dh. na coinneimh** about the meeting
mu dheireadh *adv* eventually, finally, at last **mu dh. thall** at long last
muga *n* -nnan *f m* mug
mùgach *a* -aiche sullen, surly; gloomy
muicfheòil *n* -òla *f* pork
muigh *adv* a-muigh out, outside
Muileach *n* -lich, -lich *m* someone from Mull *a* from, or pertaining to, Mull
muileann *n* -linn/muilne, -an/muilnean *f m* mill **m.-gaoithe** windmill
muile-mhàg *n* muileacha-màg *f* toad
muilicheann *n* -chinn, -chinnean *m* sleeve (*clothing*) Also **muinichill**
muillear *n* -eir, -an *m* miller
muiltfheòil *n* -òla *f* mutton
muime *n* -achan *f* step-mother, foster mother
muin *n* *f* back **air m.** (+ *gen*) on top of **dèan m.** *v* have sexual intercourse
mùin *v* mùn urinate
muineal *n* -eil, -an *m* neck
muing *n* -e, -ean *f* mane
muinighin *n* -e *f* trust, confidence
muinntir *n* -e *f* people, folk
muinntireas *n* -eis *m* domestic service **air mhuinntireas** in service
muir *n* mara, marannan *f m* sea, ocean **m.-làn** high tide **m.-tràigh** low water
mùirn *n* -e *f* cheerfulness, joy; affection
mùirneach *a* -niche cheerful, joyful; beloved, precious
muirsgian *n* -sgein, -an *f m* razorfish
mulad *n* -aid *m* sadness, sorrow **fo mhulad** sad, sorrowful
muladach *a* -aiche sad, sorrowful; pitiful
mullach *n* -aich, -aich/-aichean *m* top, summit
mum *aug prep* about my; about their
mùn *n* mùin *m* urine
mun *aug prep* about the; about their
muncaidh *n* -ean *m* monkey
mun cuairt *adv* around
mur(a) *conj* unless, if not
mur *aug prep* about our; about your (*pl & pol*)
muran *n* -ain *m* marram grass, sea-bent, bent-grass
murt *n* muirt, muirt *m* murder
murt *v* murt/-adh murder
murtaidh *a* -e sultry
murtair *n* -ean *m* murderer
mus *conj* before
mu seach *adv* alternately; aside **tè mu s.** one after the other
mu sgaoil *adv* loose, at large **leig mu s.** *v* set free, release
mùth *v* -adh change, alter, mutate
mu thimcheall *prep phr* (+ *gen*) about, around, concerning
mu thràth *adv* already, before

N

na *def art* the (*used before pl forms not in gen case*), of the (*used before sg forms of feminine nouns in gen case*) **na h-ùbhlan** the apples **na h-uinneige** of the window
na *neg part* do not (*used in negative commands*) **na bi (cho)**

gòrach! don't be (so) silly! **na can an còrr!** don't say any more, say no more!

na *conj* than (*used in comparison of two items*) **tha an tè seo nas motha na an tè sin** this one is bigger than that one

na *rel pron* what, that (which), as much **sin na ghabhas e** that is as much as/all (that) it will take

na *aug prep* in her, in his (+ *len*), in it **na baga** in her bag **na bhaga** in his bag **tha i na dotair** she's a doctor **tha e na shaor** he's a joiner **bha i na cadal** she was asleep **bha e na chadal** he was asleep

na *contr of* **an do seo far na thachair e** this is where it happened

nàbachd *n f* neighbourhood

nàbaidh *n* -ean *m* neighbour; (*colloq*) mate

nach *neg conj* whom, that/those … not **an fheadhainn n. robh an làthair** those who were not present

nad *aug prep* in your (+ *len*) **nad phòcaid** in your pocket **a bheil thu nad dhùisg?** are you awake?

nàdar *n* -air *m* nature; type **bha n. de dh'eagal orm …** I was somewhat afraid to …

nàdarrach *a* -aiche natural

naidheachd *n* -an *f* news; story, anecdote **Dè do n.?** What's your news?

naidhlean *n* -ein *m* nylon

nàimhdeas *n* -eis *m* enmity, hostility

nàimhdeil *a* -e hostile

nàire *n f* shame, embarrassment **an robh nàir' ort idir?** were you not ashamed? **duine gun n.** a brazen man **mo nàir' ort!** shame on you!

nàisean *n* -ein, -an *m* nation

nàiseanta *a* national **Partaidh N. na h-Alba** the Scottish National Party **Dualchas N. na h-Alba** Scottish National Heritage

nàiseantach *n* -aich, -aich *m* nationalist

nàiseantachd *n f* nationalism, nationality

naisgear *n* -eir, -an *m* conjunction (*gram*)

nall *adv See* **a-nall**

nam *def art* of the (*used before words beginning in b, f, m, p in gen pl*)

nam *conj* if (*followed by the conditional form of verbs beginning in b, f, m, p*) **nam bruthadh tu am putan** if you pressed the button

nam *aug prep* in my (+ *len*) **nam thaigh fhèin** in my own house **bha mi nam chadal** I was asleep

nàmhaid *n* -ad, -ean *m* enemy, foe

nan *def art* of the (*used before words other than those beginning in b, f, m, p in gen pl*)

nan *conj* if (*followed by the conditional form of the verb*) **nan innseadh tu dhomh dè tha dhìth ort** if you'd tell me what you want

nan *aug prep* in their **nan obraichean** in their jobs **bha iad nan seasamh** they were standing

naochad *n* -aid, -an *m* ninety

naoi *n, a* nine *Also* **naodh**

naoi-deug *n, a* nineteen **naoi nota deug** nineteen pounds *Also* **naodh-deug**

naoidheamh *a* ninth *Also* **naodhamh**

naoidheamh-deug *a* nineteenth **an naoidheamh latha deug** the nineteenth day *Also* **naodhamh-d.**

naoidhean *n* -ein, -an *m* infant, baby

naoinear *n f m* nine (people) *Also* **naodhnar**

naomh *a* naoimhe holy, sacred, saintly

naomh *n* naoimh, naoimh *m* saint

naomhachadh *n* -aidh *m* sanctification

naomhachd *n f* holiness, saintliness, sanctity

naomhaich *v* **-achadh** sanctify

naosg *n* **naoisg, naoisg** *m* snipe

nar *aug prep* in our **nar cùram** in our care **bha sinn nar sìneadh** we were having a lie-down

nàr *a* **nàire** shameful, disgraceful

nàrach *a* **-aiche** ashamed, shamefaced; bashful

nàraich *v* **-achadh** shame, embarrass, disgrace **bha sinn air ar nàrachadh** we were ashamed

nas *aug pron* (*used with comparative forms of adjectives*) **nas motha na** bigger than

nathair *n* **nathrach, nathraichean** *f* snake, serpent

neach *n m* person, individual (**luchd** *is used as the pl of* **neach**) **n. sam bith** anyone

neach-casaid *n m* procurator **N.-c. a' Chrùin** Procurator Fiscal *pl* **Luchd-casaid**

neach-cathrach *n m* chairperson, chair

neach-ceàirde *n m* tradesperson

neach-ceasnachaidh *n m* questioner, interviewer, quizmaster, inquisitor

neach-ciùil *n m* musician

neach-comhairleachaidh *n m* adviser

neach-cuideachaidh *n m* helper, assistant, aide

neach-deasachaidh *n m* editor

neach-deilbh *n m* designer

neach-ealain *n m* artist(e)

neach-frithealaidh *n m* waiter, attendant

neach-gairm *n m* convener

neach-gnothaich *n m* business person

neach-ionaid *n m* proxy, agent, substitute

neach-iùil *n m* guide

neach-labhairt *n m* spokesperson, speaker

neach-lagha *n* **-a** *m* lawyer, solicitor

neach-obrach *n m* worker, employee

neach-riaghlaidh *n m* ruler, governor

neach-sàbhalaidh *n m* rescuer

neach-sgrùdaidh *n m* examiner, inspector

neach-stiùiridh *n m* director

neach-teagaisg *n m* teacher

neach-togail *n m* builder

neach-treòrachaidh *n m* guide

nead *n* **nid, nid/-an** *f m* nest

neadaich *v* **-achadh** nest, nestle

nèamh *n* **nèimh, -an** *m* heaven

nèamhaidh *a* heavenly

neamhnaid *n* **-e, -ean** *f* pearl, jewel

nèapaigin *n* **(-e), -ean** *f* napkin; handkerchief

nèapraigear *n* **-eir, -an** *m* handkerchief *Also* **nèapraige**

nearbha(sa)ch *a* **-a(sa)iche** nervous

neart *n* **neirt, -an** *m* strength, might, force

neartaich *v* **-achadh** strengthen

neartmhor *a* **-oire** strong, powerful

neas *n* **-a, -an** *m* weasel, stoat

neasgaid *n* **-e, -ean** *f* boil, ulcer

nèibhidh *n* **-ean** *m* navy

neo *conj* or

neo- *neg pref* in-, un-, -less

neo-abaich *a* **-e** unripe

neo-àbhaisteach *a* **-tiche** unusual, exceptional

neo-airidh *a* **-e** unworthy, undeserving

neo-ar-thaing *a* independent **air do n.** whether you like it or not **n. bruidhinn, ach cha dèan e dad** plenty talk but no action

neo-ar-thaingeil *a* independent-minded; ungrateful

neo-bhàsmhor *a* immortal

neo-chaochlaideach *a* unchangeable

neochoireach *a* **-riche** innocent, blameless

neo-chumanta *a* uncommon, unusual

neo-chùramach *a* **-aiche** negligent, careless, inattentive

neo-dhiadhachd *n f* atheism

neo-dhiadhaire *n* **-an** *m* atheist

neo-dhìlseachd *n f* infidelity, disloyalty

neo-eisimeileach *a* **-liche**

independent
neo-eisimeileachd *n f*
independence
neo-fhoirmeil *a* -e informal
neo-fhoirmeileachd *n f*
informality
neòghlan *a* -aine unclean
neoghlaine *n f* uncleanness,
uncleanliness
neo(i)chiontach *a* -aiche innocent
neo(i)chiontachd *n f* innocence
neòinean *n* -ein, -ein/-an *m* daisy
n.-grèine sunflower
neo-làthaireachd *n f m* absence
neo-mhearachdach *a* -aiche
unerring, infallible, correct
neònach *a* -aiche strange,
unusual, curious
neoni *n m* nothing, zero
neo-oifigeil *a* -e unofficial
neo-riaghailteach *a* -tiche
irregular
neo-thruacanta *a* pitiless,
unmerciful, implacable
neul *n* neòil, neòil *m* cloud; hue;
faint **chaidh e ann an n.** he
fainted
neulach *a* -aiche cloudy
nì *n* nithean *m* thing **nì sam bith**
anything **air sgàth Nì Math!** for
goodness's sake!
nì *irr v* will do, will make (*See irr
v* **dèan** *in Grammar*)
nic *n* daughter (of) (*used only in
surnames of women*) **Sìne
NicDhùghaill** Jean MacDougall
nigh *v* -e wash, clean
nigheadair *n* -ean *m* washing
machine
nigheadaireachd *n f* washing **an
do rinn thu an n.?** have you
done the washing?
nigheadair-shoithichean *n*
nigheadairean- *m* dishwasher
nighean *n* nighinne/ighne,
-an/ighnean *f* girl, daughter
n. bràthar/n. peathar niece
nìghneag *n* -eig, -an *f* young girl,
little girl *Also* **nìonag**
nimh *n* -e *m* poison, venom
nimheil *a* -e poisonous,
venomous, virulent
Nirribheach *n* -bhich, -bhich *m*

Norwegian *a* Norwegian
nis *adv* now *See* **a-nis**
nithear *irr v* will be done, will be
made (*See irr v* **dèan** *in
Grammar*)
nitheigin *pron* something
niùclas *n* -ais, -an *m* nucleus
niùclasach *a* nuclear
no *conj* or
nobhail *n* -e, -ean *f* novel
nochd *v* -adh appear; reveal,
show
nodha *a* new **ùr n.** brand new
nòisean *n* -ein, -ein *m* notion;
attraction **bha n. mòr aige dhi**
he was greatly attracted to her
Nollaig *n* -e, -ean *f* an N.
Christmas **N. Chridheil!** Merry
Christmas!
norra(dh) *n m* wink of sleep, nap
cha d' fhuair sinn n. cadail we
didn't get a wink of sleep
norradaich *n* -e *f* nodding off,
dozing *Also vn* **a' n.**
norrag *n* -aig, -an *f* nap, snooze,
forty winks
nòs *n* nòis, -an *m* habit, custom;
style **seinn san t-seann n.**
traditional style singing *f*
nota *n* -ichean *f* note; pound
sterling
nuadh *a* nuaidhe new **nuadh-
bhàrdachd** modern poetry **an
Tiomnadh N.** the New
Testament
nuair a *conj* when
nuairsin *adv See* **an uair sin**
nuallanaich *n* lowing, bellowing
(*of animals*)
nuas *adv* up, upwards *See* **a-nuas**
null *adv* over (*to the other side*)
See **a-null**
nur *aug prep* in your (*pl & pol*) **a
bheil sibh nur dùisg?** Are you
awake?
nurs *n* -aichean *f* nurse

O

ò *exclam* O! Oh!
o *prep* from **o cheann gu ceann**
from end to end *Also* **bho**

o (a) *conj* since **tha greis o thachair e** there's a while since it happened *Also* **bho**

òb *n* -a/òib, -an *m* bay, creek

obair *n* obrach/oibre, obraichean/oibrichean *f* work, job, employment, labour **o.-làimhe** handiwork **o.-taighe** housework **a dh'aon o./mar aon o.** intentionally, deliberately **gun o.** unemployed

òban *n* -ain, -ain *m* small bay, little creek

obann *a* obainne sudden **gu h-o.** suddenly

obh *exclam* **obh, obh!** Oh dear!

obraich *v* -achadh/obair work

obraiche *n* -an *m* worker *Also* **oibriche**

och *exclam* Alas! Ah!

ochanaich *n* (-e) *f* sighing

ochd *a* eight *n* **a h-ochd**

ochdad *n* -aid, -an *m* eighty

ochdamh *a* eighth

ochd-cheàrnach *n* -aich *m* octagon

ochd-deug *n*, *a* eighteen **ochd troighean deug** eighteen feet

ochdnar *n f m* eight (people)

o chionn *prep* since, ago **o ch. f(h)ada** a long time ago

od *aug prep* from your (*sg*)

odhar *a* -air/uidhre dun-coloured

ofrail *n* -e, -ean *f* offering, sacrifice

òg *a* òige young, youthful

ògail *a* -e youthful, young

òganach *n* -aich, -aich *m* youth, youngster

ogha *n* -ichean/-chan *m* grandchild **tha iad anns na h-oghaichean** they are cousins

Ògmhios *n* -ios(a) *m* **an t-Ò.** June

ogsaidean *n* -ein *m* oxygen

oide *n* -an *m* step-father; tutor

oideachas *n* -ais *m* education, tuition

oidhche *n* -annan *f* night **O. mhath** Good night **o. h-Aoine** Friday night **O. Challainn** Hogmanay **O. Shamhna** Halloween **air an o.** at night

oidhirp *n* -e, -ean *f* attempt, effort **dèan o.** *v* try

oifig *n* See **oifis**

oifigeach *n* -gich, -gich *m* official, officer

oifigear *n* -eir, -an *m* officer, official **àrd-o.** chief executive

oifigeil *a* -e official

oifis *n* -e, -ean *f* office **o. a' phuist** post office

òigear *n* -eir, -an *m* youth, youngster

òigh *n* -e, -ean *f* virgin, maiden

oighre *n* -achan *m* heir

oighreachd *n* -an *f* estate, inheritance

òigridh *n f* (*coll*) youth, youngsters

oilbheum *n* -eim, -an *m* offence

oilbheumach *a* -aiche offensive

oileanach *n* -aich, -aich *m* student

oilisgin *n* -ean *f m* oilskin

oillt *n* -e, -ean *f* horror, dread, terror

oillteil *a* -e horrific, horrid, dreadful, terrifying

oilltich *v* -teachadh horrify, terrify

oilthigh *n* -ean *m* university

òinseach *n* -siche, -sichean *f* fool (*female*), foolish woman

oir *n* -e, -ean *f m* edge, border, margin, fringe **air an o.** at the edge

oir *conj* for, because

oirbh(se) *prep pron* on you (*pl & pol*)

òirdheirc *a* -e glorious; illustrious

òirleach *n* -lich, -lich *f* inch

oirnn(e) *prep pron* on us

oirre(se) *prep pron* on her

oirthir *n* -e, -ean *f* coast, seaboard

oisean *n* -ein, -an *m* corner *Also* **oisinn**

oiteag *n* -eig, -an *f* breeze, gust of wind

oitir *n* -e/oitreach, -ean *f* bank in sea **o. gainmhich** sandbank

òl *v* drink

ola *n* -ichean *f* oil **clàr o.** oil production platform

olc *n* uilc *m* evil, wickedness

olc *a* evil, wicked, bad
ollamh *n* -aimh, -an *m* doctor (*acad*), professor **An t-Oll. MacLeòid** Dr MacLeod **àrd-o.** professor
om *aug prep* from my; from their
òmar *n* **òmair** *m* amber
on *aug prep* from their; from the
on a *conj* since
onair *n* -e, -ean *f* honour **air m' onair!** honestly!
onarach *a* -aiche honest, honourable
onfhadh *n* -aidh, -aidhean *m* blast, storm, raging sea
onghail *n* -e *f* uproar, tumult
ònrachd *n* *f* solitude **bha i na h-ò.** she was alone
òr *n* **òir** *m* gold
or *aug prep* from our, from your
òrach *a* -aiche golden
òraid *n* -e, -ean *f* speech, lecture, oration, talk **thoir seachad ò./dèan ò.** *v* give a talk/lecture
òraidiche *n* -an *m* speaker, lecturer
orainds *a* *See* **orains**
oraindsear *n* *See* **orainsear**
orains *a* -e orange
orainsear *n* -eir, -an *m* orange
òran *n* **òrain, òrain** *m* song **gabh ò.** *v* sing a song **ò. càraid** duet **ò. luaidh** waulking song *Also* **amhran**
òr-bhuidhe *a* golden yellow, auburn
òr-cheàrd *n* -chèird, -an *m* goldsmith, jeweller
òrd *n* **ùird, ùird/-an** *m* hammer
òrdag *n* -aig, -an *f* thumb, toe **an ò. mhòr** the big toe
òrdaich *v* -achadh order, ordain, decree
òrdail *a* -e orderly, methodical; ordinal
òrdan *n* -ain, -ain *m* order
òrdugh *n* -uigh, -uighean *m* order, command, decree; order (*arrangement*) **o. cùirte** court order, injunction **cuir an ò.** arrange *v* **na h-òrduighean** the communion services
òr-iasg *n* -èisg, -èisg *m* goldfish

orm(sa) *prep pron* on me
orra(san) *prep pron* on them
ort(sa) *prep pron* on you (*sg*)
osag *n* osaig, -an *f* breeze, gust
osan *n* osain/-an *m* hose, stocking
os cionn *prep phr* (+ *gen*) above, over **os ar cionn** above us
osgarra *a* audible
os ìosal *adv* secretly, covertly, quietly
os-nàdarra(ch) *a* supernatural
osna(dh) *n* osna(idh), -aidhean *f* *m* sigh **dèan/leig o.** *v* sigh
osnaich *n* -e, -ean *f* sighing *Also vn* **ag o.**
ospadal *n* -ail, -an *m* hospital
ostail *n* -ean *f* hostel **o.-òigridh** youth hostel
òstair *n* -ean *m* hotelier, innkeeper
Ostaireach *n* -rich, -rich *m* Austrian *a* Austrian
othail *n* -e, -ean *f* hubbub, tumult, uproar; rejoicing
othaisg *n* -e, -ean/ òisgean *f* year-old ewe, hog
òtrach *n* -aich, -aichean *m* dunghill, rubbish dump, midden *Also* **òcrach**

P

paca *n* -nnan *m* pack *Also* **pac**
pacaid *n* -e, -ean *f* packet
pacaig *v* -eadh pack
pacaigeadh *n* -gidh *m* packing *Also* **pacadh**
pàganach *n* -aich, -aich *m* pagan, heathen *a* pagan
pàganachd *n* *f* paganism, heathenism
paidh *n* -ean/-ichean *m* pie **p. ubhail** apple pie
paidhir *n* **pàidhrichean** *f m* pair **p. bhrògan** pair of shoes
paidirean *n* -rin, -rinean *m* rosary; string of beads
paidse *n* -sichean *f* patch
pàigh *v* -eadh pay
pàigheadh *n* -ghidh *m* pay, payment, wages
pàillean *n* -ein, -an *m* pavilion, marquee, tent

pailm *n* -e *f* palm (*tree*)
pailt *a* -e plentiful, abundant
pailteas *n* -eis *m* plenty, abundance **tha (am) p. againn** we have plenty
pàipear *n* -eir, -an *m* paper; newspaper **p.-balla** wallpaper **p.-gainmhich** sandpaper **p.-naidheachd** newspaper **am P. Beag** the West Highland Free Press
pàipearaich *v* -achadh paper, wallpaper
pàipeir *a* paper
pàirc(e) *n* -(e), -(e)an *f* park **p. chàraichean** car park
paireafain *n m* paraffin *Also* **parafan**
pairilis *n f m* paralysis, palsy
pàirt *n* -ean *m* part, portion **gabh p. an** *v* take part in, participate
paisean *n* -ein, -an *m* faint **chaidh e ann am p.** *v* he fainted *Also* **paiseanadh**
paisg *v* **pasgadh** fold, wrap
paisgte *a* folded, wrapped
pàiste *n* -an *m* infant, child *Formerly* **pàisde**
pait *n* -e, -ean *f* lump, swelling (*on body*)
pàiteach *a* -tiche thirsty, parched
pana *n* -ichean *m* pan
pannal *n* -ail, -an *m* panel **P. na Cloinne** the Children's Panel
Pàp(a) *n* -(a)n/-(a)chan *m* Pope **am Pàp(a)** the Pope
Pàpanach *n* -aich, -aich *m* Roman Catholic *a* Roman Catholic
paraist(e) *n* -an *m* parish *Formerly* **paraisd(e)**
pàrant *n* -an *m* parent
pàrlamaid *n* -e, -ean *f* parliament **P. na h-Alba** the Scottish Parliament **P. na h-Eòrpa** the European Parliament
Pàrras *n* -ais *m* Paradise
parsail *n* -ean *m* parcel
partaidh *n* -ean *f m* party **p. poilitigeach** political party
partan *n* -ain, -an *m* small crab
pasgan *n* -ain, -ain/-an *m* package, bundle

pathadh *n* -aidh *m* thirst **a bheil am p. ort?** are you thirsty?
pàtran *n* -ain, -an *m* pattern
peacach *n* -aich, -aich *m* sinner
peacach *a* -aiche sinful
peacadh *n* -aidh, -aidhean *m* sin
peacaich *v* -achadh sin
peall *n* **pill, pillean** *m* pelt, hide
peallach *a* -aiche hairy, shaggy
peanas *n* -ais, -an *m* punishment, penalty
peanasaich *v* -achadh punish, penalize
peann *n* **pinn, pinn/-tan** *m* pen
peansail *n* -ean *m* pencil
peant *n* -aichean/-an *m* paint
peant *v* -adh paint
peantair *n* -ean *m* painter, decorator
pearsa *n* -chan *m* person
pearsanta *a* personal, subjective
pearsantachd *n* -an *f* personality
pears-eaglais *n* **pearsan-/pearsachan-** *m* cleric, clergyman
peasair *n* -srach, -sraichean *f* pea, peas
peasan *n* -ain, -an *m* brat, imp
peata *n* -n/-aichean/-chan *m* pet **p.-ruadh** puffin
peatrail *n m* petrol *Also* **peatroil**
peighinn *n* -e, -ean *f* old penny; pennyland (*topog*)
peile *n* -lichean *m* pail *Also* **peidhil**
pèileag *n* -eig, -an *f* porpoise
peilear *n* -eir, -an *m* bullet **dh'fhalbh iad aig p. am beatha** they went off at high speed
pèin *See* **fhèin**
peinnsean *n* -ein *m* pension **p. na Stàite** the State pension
peirceall *n* -cill/-cle, -an/-clean *m* jaw, jawbone
peitean *n* -ein, -an *m* waistcoat, sweater
peitseag *n* -eig, -an *f* peach
peucag *n* -aig, -an *f* peacock
peur *n* -a, -an *f* pear
Pharasach *n* -aich, -aich *m* Pharisee
pian *n* **pèin, -tan** *f* pain, torment
pian *v* -adh pain, torment, annoy

piàna *n* -than *m* piano

piantach *a* -aiche painful *Also* **piantail**

pic *n* -e, -ean *m* pickaxe, pick

picil *n* -e *f* pickle

pige *n* -achan *m* pitcher, earthen jar *Also* **pigidh**

pile *n* **pilichean/-achan** *f m* pill

pillean *n* -ein, -an *m* pillion, cushion, saddle

pinc *a* -e pink

pinnt *n* -ean *m* pint **p. leann(a)** a pint of beer **leth-phinnt** half a pint

pìob *n* -a, -an *f* pipe; bagpipe **p.-analach** windpipe **p.-chiùil** bagpipe **p.-mhòr** Highland bagpipe **p.-uisge** water pipe

pìobair(e) *n* -(e)an *m* piper

pìobaireachd *n* *f* piping; pibroch

pìoban *n* -ain, -ain/, -an *m* tube, small pipe

piobar *n* -air *m* pepper

piobraich *v* -achadh incite, pep up, urge; pepper

pioc *v* -adh pick at, nibble

Piocach *n* -aich, -aich *m* Pict

piocach *n* -aich *m* saithe, coalfish

piorbhaig *n* -e, -ean *f* wig

piorna *n* -chan *f* pirn, bobbin, reel

pìos *n* -an *m* piece, section; sandwich; (*colloq*) talent **'s e pìos a th' innte** she's a bit of all right, she's a smasher

piseach *n* **pisich** *f* improvement, prosperity **thàinig p. mhòr air** he/it has improved greatly

piseag *n* -eig, -an *f* kitten

pit *n* -e, -ean *f* female genitalia, vulva

pitheid *n* -e, -ean *f* parrot; magpie *Also* **pioghaid**

piullach *a* -aiche untidy, unkempt, shabby; wan *Also* **piollach**

piuthar *n* **peathar, peathraichean** *f* sister **p.-athar** aunt (*on father's side*) **p.-chèile** sister-in-law **p.-màthar** aunt (*on mother's side*)

plaide *n* -an/-achan *f* blanket

plàigh *n* -e, -ean *f* plague **'s e p. a**

th' ann he's/it's a pest

plana *n* -ichean *m* plan

planaid *n* -e, -ean *f* planet

planaig *v* -eadh plan

plangaid *n* -e, -ean *f* blanket

plannt *n* -a, -aichean *m* plant

plaosg *n* -oisg, -an *m* husk, peel, shell, pod

plàst *n* -a, -an/-aidhean *m* plaster

plastaig *n* -e, -ean *f m* plastic *a* plastic

pleadhag *n* -aig, -an *f* paddle; dibble *Also* **pleadhan** *m*

pleadhagaich *v* paddle

plèan(a) *n* -(a)ichean *f m* aeroplane

plèastar *n* -an *m* plaster (*eg wall*)

plèastraig *v* -eadh plaster

pleata *n* -ichean *m* plait

ploc *n* **pluic**, -an *m* clod; block

plocan *n* -ain, -an *m* small clod; small block

plosg *v* -artaich/-adh palpitate, throb, gasp, pant

plub *n* -a, -an *m* plop (*sound*), splash

plubadaich *n* -e *f* plopping, splashing

plubarsaich *n* -e *f* plopping, splashing

plubraich *v* plop, splash, slosh, gurgle

plucan *n* -ain, -an *m* stopper (*as in bottle*), bung; pimple

pluga *n* -ichean *m* plug

pluic *n* -e, -ean *f* cheek

pluiceach *a* -ciche chubby-cheeked, having large cheeks

plumadaich *n* -e *f* plunging, plummeting

plumair *n* -ean *m* plumber

plumais *n* -e, -ean *f* plum

poball *n* -aill *m* people, public

poblach *a* -aiche public **gu p.** in public

poblachail *a* republican

poblachd *n* *f* republic **P. na h-Èireann** the Irish Republic

poca *n* -nnan *m* bag, sack **p.-cadail** sleeping bag **p.-droma** haversack

pòcaid *n* -e, -ean *f* pocket *Also* **pòca**

pòcair *n* -ean *m* poker

pòg *n* **pòige, -an** *f* kiss
pòg *v* **-adh** kiss
poidhleat *n* **-eit, -an** *m* pilot *Also* **pìleat**
poidsear *n* **-eir, -an** *m* poacher
poileas *n* **-lis, -lis** *m* police officer, police **ban-phoileas** *f* policewoman
poileasaidh *n* **-ean** *m* policy **p. àrachais** insurance policy
poileasman *n* **-ain, -ain** *m* policeman
poilitigs *n* *f* politics *Also* **poileataigs**
poilitigeach *a* **-giche** political
poirdse *n* **-an/-achan** *f m* porch
poit *n* **-e, -ean** *f* pot **p. tì/teatha** teapot **p.-dhubh** small whisky still
pòitear *n* **-eir, -an** *m* tippler, drinker, boozer
pòla *n* **-ichean** *m* pole; Pole **am P. a Deas** the South Pole **am P. a Tuath** the North Pole **p. aodaich** clothes-pole *Also* **pòile**
Pòlainneach *n* **-nich, -nich** *m* Pole *a* Polish
poll *n* **puill, puill** *m* mud, mire, bog; pool
pollag *n* **-aig, -an** *f* small peatbank; small pool; pollock, lythe
poll-mònach *n* **puill-mhònach, puill-mhònach** *m* peatbank *Also* **poll-mòna(dh)**
pònaidh *n* **-ean** *m* pony
pònair *n* **-arach** *f* bean, beans
pong *n* **puing, -an** *m* music note
pongail *a* **-e** methodical, punctilious; punctual; sensible
pòr *n* **pòir, -an** *m* seed; progeny; spore; pore (*in skin*)
pòrach *a* **-aiche** porous
port *n* **puirt, puirt** *m* port, harbour **p.-adhair** airport **p.-iasgaich** fishing port
port *n* **puirt, puirt** *m* tune **port-à-beul** mouth music
Portagaileach *n* **-lich, -lich** *m* Portuguese *a* Portuguese
portair *n* **-ean** *m* porter, janitor; porter (*drink*)
pòs *v* **-adh** marry
pòsadh *n* **-aidh, -aidhean** *m* marriage

post(a) *n* **(-a), puist** *m* postman, postwoman
post *n* **puist, puist** *m* post, stake, stob; post, mail **p.-adhair** airmail **p.-dealain** e-mail
pòsta *a* married **p. aig Eilidh** married to Helen **càraid phòsta** married couple *Formerly* **pòsda**
postachd *n* *f* postage; postal work
post-oifis *n* **puist-, puist-** *m* post office
prab *n* **praib, -an** *m* rheum (*in eye*)
praban *n* **-ain, -an** *m* shebeen
prab-shùileach *a* **-liche** bleary-eyed
prais *n* **-e, -ean** *f* pot, pan
pràis *n* **-e** *f* brass
pràiseach *a* brass
pram *n* **-a, -aichean** *m* pram
pràmh *n* **pràimh** *m* sorrow, sadness, dejection; slumber **fo phràmh** dejected, sorrowing
prann *See* **pronn**
preantas *n* **-ais, -an** *m* apprentice
preas *n* **pris, pris/-an** *m* bush, shrub
preas *n* **-a, -an** *m* wrinkle, crease, fold
preas *v* **-adh** fold, crease; furrow, wrinkle (*of humans*)
preas(a) *n* **-(a)ichean** *m* press, cupboard **p.-aodaich** wardrobe, clothes cupboard **p.-leabhraichean** bookcase
preasach *a* **-aiche** wrinkled, furrowed
preusant *n* **-an** *m* present, gift
prìne *n* **-nichean/-achan** *m* pin
priob *v* **-adh** wink, blink, twinkle
priobadh *n* **-aidh, -aidhean** *m* wink, winking, blinking **ann am p. na sùla** in the twinkling of an eye
prìobhaideach *a* **-diche** private **an roinn phrìobhaideach** *f* the private sector
prìomh *a* prime, primary, first, chief, principal **p. bhaile** capital city **am P. Mhinistear** the First Minister **p. oifis** head office, headquarters
prìomhaire *n* **-an** *m* prime minister, premier

prionnsa *n* -n/-ichean *m* prince
Am. P. Teàrlach Prince Charles
prionnsapal *n* -ail, -ail/-an *m*
principle **ann am p.** in principle
Also **prionnsabal**
prìosan *n* -ain, -ain/-an *m* prison
prìosanach *n* -aich, -aich *m*
prisoner, captive **p. cogaidh**
prisoner of war
prìs *n* -e, -ean *f* price **dè (a') phrìs
a tha e?** how much does it cost?
prìseil *a* -e precious, valuable,
priceless
pròbhaist *n* -e, -ean *m* provost
prògram *n* -aim, -an *m*
programme
proifeasair *n* -ean *m* professor
proifeiseanta *a* professional
pròis *n* -e *f* pride, haughtiness
pròiseact *n* -eict, -an *f m* project
Also **pròiseict**
pròiseil *a* -e proud, haughty
pronn *a* **pruinne** pounded,
mashed, ground, pulverized
buntàta p. *m* mashed potatoes
airgead p. *m* loose change
pronn *v* -adh pound, mash, grind,
pulverize **chaidh a phronnadh** he
was beaten up
pronnasg *n* -aisg *m* sulphur,
brimstone
pronnfheòil *n* -òla *f* mince
prosbaig *n* -ean *f* binoculars,
telescope
Pròstanach *n* -aich, -aich *m*
Protestant *a* Protestant
Formerly **Pròsdanach**
prothaid *n* -e, -ean *f* profit
puball *n* -aill, -an *m* marquee,
pavilion
pucaid *n* -e, -ean *f* bucket
pùdar *n* -air, -an *m* powder
pùdaraich *v* -achadh powder
pudhar *n m* harm, injury **cha do
chuir e p. orm** it didn't put me
up or down
puicean *n* -ein, -an *m* poke, small
bag; (*met*) small man
puing *n* -e, -ean *f* point; degree
(*of temperature*)
puinnsean *n* -ein, -an *m* poison,
venom
puinnseanaich *v* -achadh poison

puinnseanta *a* poisonous,
venomous **p. fuar** bitterly cold
pump(a) *n* -(a)ichean *m* pump
punnd *n* **puinnd, puinnd** *m* pound
(*weight*); pound (*money*)
p. Sasannach pound sterling
pupaid *n* -ean *m* puppet
purgadair *n* -e *m* purgatory;
purifier
purgaid *n* -e, -ean *f* purge,
purgative
purgaideach *a* -diche purgative
purpaidh *a* -e purple
put(a) *n* -a/-(a)ichean *m* buoy
put *v* -adh push, shove, jostle
putan *n* -ain, -an *m* button

R

rabaid *n* -e, -ean *f* rabbit
rabhadh *n* -aidh, -aidhean *m*
warning, alarm
rabhd *n* -a, -an *m* idle or far-
fetched talk, spiel
ràc *n* **ràic, -an** *m* rake (garden);
drake
ràc *v* -adh rake
racaid *n* -e, -ean *f* racket, noise;
racquet; skelp
ràcan *n* -ain, -ain/-an *m* rake
(*garden*); drake
ràc an t-sìl *n* **ràic-, ràcain-** *m*
corncrake
rach *irr v* **dol** go (*See irr v* **rach** *in
Grammar*) **r. an sàs an** tackle,
get involved in **r. an urras do**
assure **r. às àicheadh** deny **an
rachadh agad air?** could/
would you be able to do it?
radan *n* -ain, -ain *m* rat
ràdh *n* -an *m* saying, adage
rag *a* **raige** stiff, rigid; stubborn,
obstinate, inflexible **r.-mharbh**
stone dead
rag *v* -adh stiffen, benumb **bha
sinn air ar ragadh leis an
fhuachd** we were numb with
the cold
rag-mhuinealach *a* -aiche
obstinate, stubborn
raidhfil *n* -ean *f m* rifle
raige *n f* stiffness, rigidity;
obstinacy, stubbornness

raighd *v* -**eadh** ride
raighdeadh *n* -**didh** *m* riding **sgoil raighdidh** *f* riding school
raineach *n* -**nich** *f* fern, bracken *Also* **fraineach**
ràinig *irr v* came, reached, arrived (*See irr v* **ruig** *in Grammar*)
raip *n* -**e** *f* dribble, traces of food round mouth; refuse
ràith(e) *n* -**(e)an/-(e)achan** *f* quarter (*of year*), season
ràitheachan *n* -**ain**, -**ain** *m* quarterly (*magazine*)
ràmh *n* **ràimh**, **ràimh** *m* oar
ràn *n* **ràin**, **ràin** *m* cry; roar, yell
ràn *v* -**aich/-ail** cry; roar, yell
rann *n* **rainn**, -**an/rainn** *f* verse, stanza
rannsachadh *n* -**aidh**, -**aidhean** *m* research, investigation, survey
rannsaich *v* -**achadh** research, search, scrutinize, investigate, explore
raon *n* **raoin**, -**tan/raointean** *m* plain, field; area **r.-cluiche** playing field **r.-laighe** runway **r. ola** oilfield
rapach *a* -**aiche** slovenly, scruffy; inclement, dirty (*weather*)
ràsair *n* -**ean** *m* razor
ràsanach *a* -**aiche** tedious
ràth *n* -**a**, -**an** *m* raft
rath *n* -**a** *m* prosperity, fortune, luck
rathad *n* -**aid/rothaid**, -**aidean/ròidean** *m* road, route, way **r.-mòr** main road, trunk road, highway **r.-iarainn** railway, railroad **an r. sin** that way **tog às mo r.!** get out of my way! **chan eil e às an r.** it's not too bad **chaidh e às an r.** he perished
Ratharsach *n* -**aich**, -**aich** *m* someone from Raasay *a* from, or pertaining to, Raasay
rè *prep* (+ *gen*) during, throughout **rè na h-oidhche** during the night
rèaban *n* -**ain**, -**an** *m* beard, whiskers
reachd *n* -**an** *m* statute, law, ordinance
reamhar *a* **reamhra/reaimhre** fat,

plump
reamhraich *v* -**achadh** fatten
reic *n m* sale **fèill-reic** *f* sale of work
reic *v* sell
reiceadair *n* -**ean** *m* seller, salesman, vendor, auctioneer
rèidh *a* -**e** level, even, smooth; ready
rèidhleach *n* -**lich** *m* space, expanse
rèidhlean *n* -**ein**, -**an** *m* lawn, sward, green
rèidio *n* -**than** *m* radio
rèile *n* -**lichean** *f m* rail
rèilig *n* -**e**, -**ean** *f* grave, lair, graveyard, crypt *Also* **roilig**
reimhid *adv See* **roimhe**
rèis *n* -**e**, -**ean** *f* race (*sport*); span, lifetime
rèis *v* -**eadh** race
rèisimeid *n* -**e**, -**ean** *f* regiment
rèite *n* -**an** *f* accord, agreement, reconciliation
rèiteach *n* -**tich**, -**tichean** *m* betrothal; agreement, settlement
reithe *n* -**achan** *m* ram (*male sheep*)
rèitich *v* -**teachadh** reconcile, conciliate, arbitrate; settle, sort out
rèitire *n* -**an** *m* referee
reodh *v See* **reoth**
reòiteag *n* -**eig**, -**an** *f* ice cream
reoth *v* -**adh** freeze, become frozen
reothadair *n* -**ean** *m* freezer
reothadh *n* -**aidh** *m* frost, freezing
reothart *n* -**airt**, -**an** *f m* spring tide
reòthte *a* frozen *Also* **reòthta**
reub *v* -**adh** tear, rend, rip
reubal(t)ach *n* -**aich**, -**aich** *m* rebel
reubaire *n* -**an** *m* pirate, plunderer *Also* **reubadair**
reubte *a* riven, rent
reudan *n* -**ain**, -**an** *m* timber moth, woodlouse; dry rot
reul *n* **rèil**, -**tan** *f* star **r.-bhad** *m* constellation **r.-chearbach** *f* comet **r.-eòlas** *m* astronomy **r.-iùil** guiding star, Pole Star
reuladair *n* -**ean** *m* astronomer
reultag *n* -**aig**, -**an** *f* asterisk
reusan *n* -**ain** *m* reason, cause;

sanity

reusanaich *v* -achadh reason

reusanta *a* reasonable, rational
r. math reasonably good

ri *prep* to; engaged in **tha i ri bàrdachd** she composes poetry **bheil cus agad ri dhèanamh?** do you have a lot to do?

riabhach *a* -aiche brindled

riadh *n* **rèidh** *m* interest (*fin*) **chuir e r. mòr dheth** it returned high interest

riaghail *v* -ghladh rule, govern, regulate

riaghailt *n* -e, -ean *f* rule, regulation

riaghailteach *a* regular, orderly **r. bitheanta** fairly common

riaghaltas *n* -ais, -an *m* government **r. ionadail** local government **R. na h-Alba** Scottish Executive

riaghladair *n* -ean *m* ruler, governor, regulator

riaghladh *n* -aidh *m* ruling, governing

riamh *adv* ever, before *Also* **a-riamh**

rian *n* -an *m* order, method, organization; arrangement (*mus*) **tha e às a r.** he is mad, crazy **cuir r. air** *v* organize

rianachd *n* *f* administration

rianail *a* -e methodical, orderly; reasonable

riaraich *v* -achadh satisfy, please; share (out), distribute, allocate **doirbh a riarachadh** hard to please

riaraichte *a* satisfied

riasg *n* **rèisg** *m* sedge, dirk-grass, coarse grass, peat moss

riaslach *a* -aiche hectic, extremely busy

riasladh *n* -aidh *m* struggle, busy toing and froing **bha r. air a' bhoin** the cow was in heat

riatanach *a* -aiche necessary, essential; appropriate

ribe *n* -achan *f m* snare, trap

ribh(se) *prep pron* to you (*pl & pol*)

ribheid *n* -e, -ean *f* reed (*mus*)

rìbhinn *n* -e, -ean *f* maiden

rid *aug prep* to your (*sg*)

ridire *n* -an *m* knight, sir **An R.** Sir

rìgh *n* -rean *m* king **r.-chathair** *f* throne

righinn *a* **rìghne** tough, tenacious, durable

rim *aug prep* to my

rin *aug prep* to their

rinn *irr v* did, made (*See irr v* **dèan** *in Grammar*)

rinn(e) *prep pron* to us

rioban *n* -ain, -an *m* ribbon **r.-tomhais** measuring tape *Also* **ribinn** *f*

riochd *n* -a, -an *m* appearance, form

riochdaich *v* -achadh represent; produce (*eg programme*)

riochdail *a* -e beautiful, handsome

riochdair *n* -ean *m* pronoun

riochdaire *n* -an *m* representative, delegate; producer (*artistic*)

rìoghachd *n* -an *f* kingdom, country **an R. Aonaichte** the United Kingdom

rìoghaich *v* -achadh reign

rìoghail *a* -e royal, regal

rìomhach *a* -aiche beautiful, lovely, fine

rìomhachas *n* -ais *m* finery, beauty

rionnach *n* -aich, -aich *m* mackerel

rionnag *n* -aige, -an *f* star **r. (an) earbaill** shooting star

rionnagach *a* -aiche starry

rir *aug prep* to our; to your

ris *prep* to **dè tha thu ris?** what are you doing/up to?

ris *adv* exposed (*to view*) **bha a còta-bàn ris** her slip was showing

ris(-san) *prep pron* to him/it

ri taobh *prep phr* (+ *gen*) beside

rithe(se) *prep pron* to her/it

rium(sa) *prep pron* to me

riut(sa) *prep pron* to you

riutha(san) *prep pron* to them

ro *adv* too; very (+ *len*) **ro bheag** too small

ro *prep, adv* before **ro-làimh**

beforehand **ro-ainmichte** *a* aforementioned, aforesaid *Formerly* **roimh**

ro-aithris *a* **-ean** *f* forecast (*weather*); prediction

robach *a* **-aiche** slovenly, untidy, unkempt, squalid

robair(e) *n* **-(e)an** *m* robber

robh *irr v* was, were (*never used on its own*) (*See verb* **to be** *in Grammar*)

roc *n* **ruic/-a, -an** *f* wrinkle, crease; entanglement

roc *v* **-adh** wrinkle, crease

rocach *a* **-aiche** wrinkled, creased

rocaid *n* **-e, -ean** *f* rocket

ròcail *n* **-e** *f* croaking, croak

rocail *v* **rocladh** tangle, entangle

ròcais *n* **-ean** *f* rook **bodach-r.** scarecrow

rod *aug prep* before your (*sg*)

roghainn *n* **-ean** *f m* choice, selection, option **chan eil r. eile ann** there is no alternative **gheibh thu do r.** you can have your pick

roghnaich *v* **-achadh** choose, select

roid *n* **-e, -ean** *f* run before a leap **dh'fhalbh e aig r.** he went off at speed **thug iad r. a-steach dhan bhaile** they nipped into town

roile *n* **-lichean** *f* roll (*bread*)

roilear *n* **-eir, -an** *m* roller **roilearan-spèilidh** roller blades

roilig *v* **-eadh** roll

roimh *prep See* **ro**

roimhe *adv* before, formerly

roimhe(san) *prep pron* before him/it

roimhear *n* **-eir, -an** *m* preposition

roimhpe(se) *prep pron* before her/it

roimh-ràdh *n See* **ro-ràdh**

ròineag *n* **-eig, -an** *f* a single hair

roinn *n* **-e, -ean** *f* share, portion, division, department; region **an R. Eòrpa** Europe

roinn *v* divide, share (out)

roinneil *a* departmental, regional

ro-innleachd *n* **-an** *f* strategy

ròiseid *n* **-e, -ean** *f* resin

ròist *v* **ròstadh** roast

ro-leasachan *n* **-ain, -ain** *m* prefix

rola *n See* **roile**

ròlaist *n* **-e, -ean** *m* exaggeration, fanciful tale

ròlaisteach *a* **-tiche** prone to exaggeration or invention

rom *aug prep* before my

ròmach *a* **-aiche** hairy, shaggy, rough

Ròmàinianach *n* **-aich, -aich** *m* Romanian *a* Romanian

romhad(sa) *prep pron* before you

romhaibh(se) *prep pron* before you (*pl & pol*)

romhainn(e) *prep pron* before us

romham(sa) *prep pron* before me

romhpa(san) *prep pron* before them

ròn *n* **ròin, ròin** *m* seal

ron *aug prep* before the, before their

rong *n* **-a/roinge, -an** *f* rung, spar; boat-rib

rongach *a* **-aiche** dilatory

ronn *n* **roinn** *m* mucus, slaver, spittle

ròp(a) *n* **-(a), -(a)n/-(a)ichean** *m* rope **r.-anairt/-aodaich** clothes-line

ror *aug prep* before our, before your

ro-ràdh *n* **-ràidh, -an** *m* preface, preamble, prologue, introduction

ros *n* **rois, -an** *m* headland, promontory, peninsula

ròs *n* **ròis, -an** *m* rose

ròs *n* **ròis** knowledge **cha d'fhuair mi ròs air riamh** I never found any trace of him/it

ro-shealladh *n* **-aidh, -aidhean** *m* preview

rosg *n* **ruisg, -an** *m* prose

rosg *n* **ruisg, -an** *m* eyelash, eyelid

rosgrann *n* **-ainn, -an** *m* sentence

ròsta *n* **-ichean** *f m* roast, roast meat

ròsta *a* roasted, roast

roth *n* **-a, -an** *f m* wheel **r. mun ghealaich** a halo round the moon

rothaig *v* **-eadh** wind (*as clock*)

rothar *n* **-air, -an** *m* bicycle, cycle

ruadh *a* **ruaidhe** reddish-brown, ruddy, ginger **falt r.** red hair

ruaig *n* **-e, -ean** *f* chase, pursuit, flight, rout **chuireadh r. orra** *v* they were routed/put to flight

rua(i)g *v* **ruagadh/ruagail** chase, pursue, rout

ruamhair *v* **-ar** dig, delve; rummage

rubair *n* **-ean** *m* rubber

rùbarab *n* **-aib** *m* rhubarb

rubha *n* **-ichean** *m* point (*of land*), promontory, headland

rùchd *n* **-a, -an** *m* stomach rumble, belch **dèan r.** *v* belch *Also* **rùchdail**

rùchd *v* **-ail** rumble (*in stomach*)

rud *n* **-an** *m* thing **rud sam bith** anything

rùda *n* **-aichean/-n** *m* ram

rùdan *n* **-ain, -an** *m* knuckle

rudeigin *pron, adv* something, somewhat **tha i r. fuar** it's somewhat cold

rudhadh *n* **-aidh** *m* blush, blushing, flush **bha r. na gruaidh** she was flushed, she was blushing

rùdhan *n* **-ain, -ain** *m* small stack of peat, hay or corn

rug *irr v* caught, seized (*See irr v* **beir** *in Grammar*)

ruga *n* **-ichean** *m* rug

rugadh *irr v* was born (*See irr v* **beir** *in Grammar*) **r. is thogadh i ann am Barraigh** she was born and brought up in Barra

ruibh *prep pron See* **ribh**

r(u)idhil *v* **r(u)idhleadh** reel (*dance*)

r(u)idhle *n* **-an/-achan** *m* reel

ruig *irr v* **-hinn/-sinn/-heachd** reach, arrive at (*See irr v* **ruig** *in Grammar*)

ruighe *n* **-an** *f m* forearm; slope (*of hill*), plain

rùilear *n* **-eir, -an** *m* ruler (*measuring*)

ruinn *prep pron See* **rinn**

ruis *n* **-e** *f* elder (*tree*)

Ruiseanach *n* **-aich, -aich** *m*

Russian *a* Russian

rùisg *v* **rùsgadh** strip, peel; shear, fleece

rùisgte *a* naked, bare; shorn

ruiteach *a* **-tiche** ruddy

ruith *n* **-e, -ean** *f* running; run; rhythm

ruith *v* run, flow **tha 'n ùine air r. oirnn** we've run out of time

rùm *n* **rùim, rumannan** *m* room; space **rùm-cadail** bedroom **rùm-ionnlaid** bathroom **rùm-suidhe** sitting room **rùm-teagaisg** classroom

Rumach *n* **-aich, -aich** *m* someone from Rum *a* from, or pertaining to, Rum

rùmail *a* **-e** roomy, spacious

rùn *n* **rùin, rùintean** *m* desire, wish, intention, resolution; secret, love

rùnaich *v* **-achadh** desire, wish, intend, resolve

rùnaire *n* **-an** *m* secretary **R. na Stàite** the Secretary of State

rù-rà *a* untidy, topsy-turvy

rùraich *v* **-achadh** search (for); grope

rus *n* **ruis** *m* rice

rùsg *n* **rùisg, -an** peel, rind; bark; fleece

rùsgadh *n* **-aidh** *m* peeling; shearing

S

's *irr v* is (*See verb* **to be** *in Grammar*)

's *conj* and (*contraction of* **agus/is**)

sa *aug prep* in the

-sa *suff* (*used with* **mo, do** my, your *to give emphasis*)

sa *suff* this (*equivalent to* **seo**)

Sàbaid *n* **-ean** *f* Sabbath **Latha/Là na S.** Sunday *Also* **Sàboinn(t)**

sabaid *n* **(-e), -ean** *f* fight, fighting

sabaidich *v* **sabaid** fight

sàbh *n* **sàibh, sàibh/-an** *m* saw

sàbh *v* **-adh** saw

sàbhail *v* **-aladh** save, rescue

sàbhailte *a* safe

sàbhailteachd *n* *f* safety

sabhal *n* -ail, -an/**saibhlean** *m* barn

sàbhaladh *n* -aidh *m* saving, rescuing

sabhs *n* -a, -an *m* sauce

sac *n* **saic, saic/-an** *m* burden, load **an sac** asthma

sàcramaid *n* -e, -ean *f* sacrament

sad *v* -ail/-adh throw

sagart *n* -airt, -an *m* priest

sàibhear *n* -eir, -an *m* culvert

saideal *n* -eil, -an *m* satellite

saidhbhir *a* -e rich, wealthy

saidhbhreas *n* -eis *m* riches, wealth

saidheans *n* -an *m* science

saidhleafòn *n* -òin, -an *m* xylophone

saighdear *n* -eir, -an *m* soldier

saighead *n* **saighde/saighid, saighdean** *f* arrow

sail *n* -e, -thean *f* beam (*as in roof*), joist, large sawn piece of wood

sàil *n* **sàlach/sàla, -ean** *f* heel

sailead *n* -eid, -an *m* salad

saill *n f* -e fat; pickle, brine

saill *v* -eadh salt

saillear *n* -eir, -an *f* salt cellar

saillte *a* salty, salted

saimeant *n m* cement

sàirdseant *n* -an *m* sergeant

sàl *n* **sàil(e)** *m* salt water **an sàl** the sea

salach *a* -aiche/**sailche** dirty, filthy, foul

salaich *v* -ach/-achadh dirty, soil

salann *n* -ainn *m* salt

salchar *n* -air *m* dirt, filth

salm *n* **sailm, sailm** *f m* psalm **Leabhar nan S.** the Book of Psalms

salmadair *n* -ean *m* psalter; psalmist

salmaidh *n* -ean *m* psalmist

saltair *v* -t trample, tread

sam bith *adv phr* any **duine s. b.** anyone **rud s. b.** anything

samh *n* **saimh, -an** *m* odour, smell

sàmhach *a* -aiche silent, quiet **bi s.!** be quiet! **fan s.!** be quiet!, never! (*in surprise*)

samhail *n* **samhla, -ean** *m* likeness, like, equivalent **chan fhaca mi a shamhail** I've not seen his like

Samhain *n* **Samhna** *f* **an t-Samhain** November **Oidhche Shamhna** *f* Halloween

sàmhchair *n* -e *f* silence, quietness, quiet

samhla(dh) *n* -aidh, -aidhean *m* resemblance, likeness, allegory, figure; apparition

samhlachail *a* figurative; symbolic

samhlaich *v* -achadh liken, compare

samhradh *n* -aidh, -aidhean *m* summer **as t-s.** in summer

san *aug prep* in their

-san *suff used with* **a** his and **an** their *to give emphasis* **an coire-san** their fault

sanas *n* -ais, -an *m* notice, advertisement; whisper **s.-reic** advertisement

sannt *n* -a *m* greed, avarice, covetousness

sanntach *a* -aiche greedy, avaricious, covetous

sanntaich *v* -tachadh covet

saobh *a* -a/**saoibhe** erroneous, false, misguided

saobhaidh *n* -ean *m* den, fox's den, lair

saobh-chràbhadh *n* -aidh, -aidhean *m* superstition

saobh-chreideamh *n* -eimh, -an *m* heresy

saoghal *n* -ail, -ail/-an *m* world; lifetime **càit air an t-s. an robh sibh?** where on earth were you?

saoghalta *a* worldly, materialistic

saoibhir *a See* **saidhbhir**

saoil *v* -sinn/-tinn think, suppose **s. an tig iad** I wonder if they'll come **saoilibh?** do you think?

saoithean *n* -ein, -an/-ein *m* saithe

saor *n* **saoir, saoir** *m* joiner, carpenter

saor *a* **saoire** free; cheap **s. 's an asgaidh** free gratis, free of charge

saor *v* **-adh** free, liberate, exempt
saoradh *n* **-aidh** *m* liberation
saor-chlachair *n* **-ean** *m*
freemason
saor-latha *n* **-làithean/**
-lathaichean *m* holiday
saorsa *n f* freedom, liberty
s. chatharra civil liberty
saorsainn *n* **-e** *f* freedom, liberty
saorsainneachd *n f* joinery,
carpentry
saorsainneil *a* **-e** relaxed, at ease
saor-thoil *n* **-e** *f* free-will
saor-thoileach *a* voluntary
saothair *n* **saothrach** *f* labour, toil
saothraich *v* **-achadh** labour, toil
sàr *n* **sàir, sàir** *m* hero, excellent
person
sàr *a* (*precedes & lenites n*) very,
extremely, true **sàr sheinneadair**
a truly great singer
sàrachadh *n* **-aidh** *m* exhaustion,
annoyance, bother, harassment
sàraich *v* **-achadh** exhaust,
annoy, bother, harass
sàraichte *a* exhausted, exhausting
sàs *n* **sàis** *m* straits, restraint,
hold, grasp **an sàs an** involved
in, engaged in **chaidh an cur an**
sàs they were arrested
sàsachadh *n* **-aidh** *m* satisfaction
sàsaich *v* **-achadh** satisfy
sàsaichte *a* satisfied
Sasannach *n* **-aich, -aich** *m*
English person *a* English
sàsar *n* **-air, -an** *m* saucer
sàth *v* **-adh** thrust
sàth *n* **sàith** *m* plenty, surfeit,
satiety, abundance
's e *v* it is, he is (*See verb* **bi** *in*
Grammar)
seabhag *n* **-aig, -an** *f m* hawk
seac *v* **-adh** wither
seacaid *n* **(-e), -ean** *f* jacket
seach *conj* since, because **s. gu**
(+ *v*) since, because
seach *prep* instead of, rather
than; compared to
seachad *adv* past **san dol s.** in
passing **thoir s.** *v* give (away)
seachad air *prep phr* past, by
seachain *v* **seachnadh** avoid,
shun, abstain from

seachd *n, a* seven; (*also used as*
intensive) **tha mi s. sgìth dheth**
I'm absolutely fed up of it/him
seachdad *n* **-aid, -an** *m* seventy
seachdain *n* **-e/-donach, -ean** *f*
week
seachdamh *a* seventh
seachd-deug *n, a* seventeen
seachd latha deug seventeen
days
seachdnar *n f m* seven (people)
seachnadh *n* **-aidh** *m* avoiding,
avoidance, shunning
seachran *n* **-ain** *m* wandering
a' dol air s. wandering, going
astray
seach-rathad *n* **-aid, -aidean** *m*
bypass
seada *n* **-n/-ichean** *f m* shed
seadag *n* **-aig, -an** *f* grapefruit
seadh *adv* yes, indeed (*used to*
confirm or lend emphasis) **s.**
dìreach just so
seagal *n* **-ail** *m* rye
seagh *n* **-a, -an** *m* sense,
meaning
seàla *n* **-ichean** *f* shawl
sealastair *n* **-ean** *f m* iris (*plant*)
Also **seileastair**
sealbh *n* **seilbh, -an** *m* fortune;
possession, ownership **Aig an**
t-S. tha brath Goodness knows
Gu sealladh S. orm For
goodness's sake
sealbhach *a* **-aiche** fortunate,
lucky
sealbhadair *n* **-ean** *m* possessor,
owner
sealbhaich *v* **-achadh** possess,
own
sealg *n* **seilge, -an** *f* hunt
sealg *v* hunt
sealgair *n* **-ean** *m* hunter
sealgaireachd *n f* hunting
seall *v* **-tainn** look, see; show **s.**
seo! look at this! **s. dhomh sin**
show me that
sealladh *n* **-aidh, -aidhean** *m*
view, sight, vision, show,
spectacle **às an t-s.** out of sight
an dà shealladh second sight
Sealtainneach *n* **-nich, -nich** *m*
Shetlander *a* Shetland

seamrag *n* -aig, -an *f* shamrock
sean *a* sine old
seanadair *n* -ean *m* senator
seanadh *n* -aidh, -aidhean *m* senate, synod, assembly
seanailear *n* -eir, -an *m* general
seanair *n* -ar, -ean *m* grandfather; ancestor
seanchaidh *n* -ean *m* storyteller *Also* **seanachaidh**
seancharra *a* old-looking, old-fashioned *Also* **seangarra**
seanchas *n* -ais, -an *m* conversation, chat; lore *Also* **seanachas**
seanfhacal *n* -ail, -ail/-aclan *m* proverb
seang *a* -a slim, slender
seangan *n* -ain, -ain/-an *m* ant
seanmhair *n* -ar, -ean *f* grandmother
seann *a* old (*precedes & lenites n*) **s. chàr** an old car **s. fhear** an old one **s. nòs** traditional style **s. taigh** an old house **seann-fhasanta** old-fashioned
seantans *n* -an *m* sentence (*gram*)
sear *adv* east, eastern
searbh *a* -a/seirbhe bitter, sour, tart
searbhachd *n* *f* bitterness
searbhadair *n* -ean *m* towel
searbhag *n* -aig, -an *f* acid
searbhant(a) *n* -(a)n *f* servant
searg *v* wither, shrivel, decay
seargach *a* withered, shrivelled, deciduous
seargadh *n* -aidh *m* decay
searmon *n* -oin, -an *m* sermon
searmonaich *v* -achadh preach
searmonaiche *n* -an *m* preacher
searrach *n* -aich, -aich *m* foal, colt
searrag *n* -aig, -an *f* bottle, flask
seas *v* -amh stand
seasamh *n* -aimh, -an *m* standing, stand, stance
seasg *a* -a/seisge barren, sterile
seasgachd *n* *f* sterility
seasgad *n* -aid, -an *m* sixty
seasgaich *v* -achadh sterilize
seasgair *a* -e snug, comfortable, sheltered, protected

seasmhach *a* -aiche steadfast, firm, stable; durable
seat *v* -adh set (*except of sun*)
seic *n* -ean *f* cheque **leabhar-sheicichean** *m* chequebook
Seiceach *n* -cich, -cich *m* Czech *a* Czech
seiche *n* *f* hide, skin, pelt
sèid *v* -eadh blow
seilbh *n* -e, -ean *f* possession **gabh s. air** *v* take possession of
seilbheach *a* -bhiche possessive; genitive (*gram*)
seilbhich *v* -bheachadh possess, own
seilcheag *n* -eig, -an *f* snail, slug
seile *n* -an *m* spittle, saliva
seileach *n* -lich, -lich *m* willow
seillean *n* -ein, -an *m* bee
sèimh *a* -e gentle, mild, calm **an Cuan S.** the Pacific Ocean
sèimheachadh *n* -aidh *m* lenition, aspiration (*gram*)
sèine *n* -nichean *f* chain
seinn *n* *f* singing **s.-phàirteach** harmony
seinn *v* sing
seinneadair *n* -ean *m* singer
seirbheis *n* -ean *f* service **an t-S. Chatharra** the Civil Service
seirbheiseach *n* -sich, -sich *m* servant
seirc *n* -e *f* love, charity
seirm *n* -e *f* ring, chime, musical sound
seirm *v* ring, chime
seise *n* -an *m* one's match, one's equal **thachair a sheise ris** he met his match
seisean *n* -ein *m* session
sèist *n* -e, -ean *f m* chorus, refrain
sèist *n* -e, -ean *f m* siege
sèithear *n* -thir, sèithrichean *m* chair **s.-cuibhle** wheelchair **s.-putaidh** pushchair
seo *a* this
seo *pron* this (is); these (are)
seoclaid *n* -ean *f* chocolate
seòl *n* siùil, siùil *m* sail
seòl *n* siùil, siùil *m* method, way **s.-beatha** way of life, lifestyle
seòl *v* -adh sail, navigate; direct,

guide
seòladair *n* **-ean** *m* sailor
seòladh *n* **-aidh, -aidhean** *m*
sailing; address, direction
seòl-mara *n* **siùil-mara, siùil-mhara** *m* tide
seòlta *a* cunning, crafty
seòltachd *n* *f* cunning, craftiness, guile
seòmar *n* **-air, seòmraichean** *m*
room, chamber **s.-bìdh** dining-room **s.-cadail** bedroom
s.-còmhnaidh living-room
s.-fuirich waiting-room
s.-ionnlaid bathroom
s.-leughaidh reading-room, study **s.-sgeadachaidh** dressing-room **s.-suidhe** sitting-room
s.-teagaisg classroom, lecture room
seòrsa *n* **-chan/-ichean** *m* sort, kind, type, species, brand
seòrsaich *v* **-achadh** sort, classify
seotaire *n* **-an** *m* idler, lazybones
seud *n* **seòid, seòid/-an** jewel, gem; (*met*) hero
seudar *n* **-air** *m* cedar
seula *n* **-chan** *m* seal
seulaich *v* **-achadh** seal
seumarlan *n* **-ain, -ain** *m*
chamberlain, factor
seun *n* **-a, -an/-tan** *m* charm (*magical*)
seunta *a* charmed, enchanted
sgadan *n* **-ain, -ain** *m* herring
sgàil *n* **-e, -ean** *f* shade, shadow, veil, cover **s.-sùla** eyelid
sgàil *v* **-eadh** shade, screen, mask
sgailc *n* **-e, -ean** *f* slap, sharp blow, skelp, smack **s.-creige** echo
sgailc *v* slap, smack, skelp
sgàilean *n* **-ein, -an** *m* umbrella, screen **s.-grèine** parasol
sgàin *v* **-eadh** split, burst **tha mi gu s.** I've eaten too much/I'm over-full (*lit* I'm about to burst)
sgàineadh *n* **-nidh** *m* split, crack, bursting
sgainneal *n* **-eil, -an** *m* scandal
sgainnealaich *v* **-achadh**
scandalize

sgàird *n* **-e** *f* **an s.** diarrhoea
sgairt *n* **-e, -ean** *f* yell, loud cry
sgairt *n* **-e, -ean** *f* **an s.**
diaphragm, midriff **bhris(t) e a s.** he ruptured himself
sgairteil *a* **-e** vigorous, brisk, energetic
sgait *n* **-e, -ean** *f* skate (*fish*)
sgaiteach *a* **-tiche** sharp, cutting (*as in remark*); well-expressed, able
sgal *n* **-a, -an** *m* yell; blow
sgàl *n* **sgàil, sgàil** *m* tray
sgal *v* **-thart(aich)** howl, yell
sgalag *n* **-aig, -an** *f* servant, skivvy
sgall *n* **sgaill** *m* bald patch, baldness
sgallach *a* **-aiche** bald
Sgalpach *n* **-aich, -aich** *m*
someone from Scalpay *a* from, or pertaining to, Scalpay
sgamhan *n* **-ain, -an** *m* lung
sgannan *n* **-ain, -an** *m* film, membrane
sgaoil *v* **-eadh** spread, scatter, disperse, disseminate; become undone **leig mu s.** *v* free, liberate, loosen
sgaoth *n* **-oith/-otha, -an** *m*
swarm; multitude
sgap *v* **-adh** scatter
sgar *v* **-adh/-achdainn** separate, sever
sgaradh *n* **-aidh, -aidhean** *m*
separation **s.-pòsaidh** divorce
sgarbh *n* **sgairbh, sgairbh** *m*
cormorant
sgarfa *n* **-ichean** *f m* scarf
sgàrlaid *a* **-e** scarlet
Sgarpach *n* **-aich, -aich** *m*
someone from Scarp *a* from, or pertaining to, Scarp
sgath *n* *m* anything; part **cha robh s. airgid aice** she hadn't any money **a h-uile s. dheth** every bit of it
sgàth *n* **-a, -an** *m* sake; shade, protection **air s.** on account of, because of (+ *gen*)
sgath *v* **-adh** lop, cut, prune, slash
sgàthan *n* **-ain, -an** *m* mirror

sgeadaich *v* -achadh decorate, adorn, embellish; dress

sgeadaichte *a* decorated; dressed

sgealb *n* sgeilb, -an *f* splinter

sgealbag *n* -aig, -an *f* forefinger, index finger

sgeama *n* -ichean *f m* scheme

sgeap *n* sgeip, -an/-aichean *f* beehive

sgeig *n* -e *f* derision, ridicule

sgeigeil *a* -e derisive

sgeilb *n* -e, -ean *f* wood chisel

sgeileid *n* -e, -ean *f* saucepan, skillet

sgeilp *n* -ichean *f* shelf

sgèimhich *v* -mheachadh beautify, adorn

sgeir *n* -e, -ean *f* skerry, reef

sgeith *n* -e *m* vomit, vomiting

sgeith *v* sgeith/-eadh vomit, spew

sgèith *n* flying **air s.** flying

sgèith *v* fly

sgeith-rionnaig *n m* meteor

sgeul *n* sgeòil, sgeòil *m* story, tale; trace **a bheil s. orra?** is there any sign of them? *Also* **sgeula** *f*

sgeulachd *n* -an *f* story, tale

sgeulaiche *n* -an *m* storyteller

sgeunach *a* -aiche shy, timid, easily frightened

sgì *n* sgithe, sgithean *f* ski

sgì *v* -theadh ski

sgialachd *n See* **sgeulachd**

sgiamh *n* -a, -an *m* scream, squeal, shriek **dèan s.** *v* scream

sgiamh *v* -ail scream, squeal

sgiamhach *a* -aiche beautiful

sgiamhaich *v* -achadh beautify

sgiamhail *n f* screaming

sgian *n* sgeine, sgeinean *f* knife

sgiath *n* sgèithe, -an *f* wing; shield

sgiathach *a* winged

sgiathaich *v* -thadh fly

sgiathalaich *n f* flying about, fluttering *Also* **sgiathadaich**

Sgiathanach *n, a See* **Sgitheanach**

sgil *n* -ean *f m* skill

sgileil *a* -e skilful

sgillinn *n* -e, -ean *f* penny **deich sg.** 10 pence **chan eil s. ruadh agam** I don't have a single penny

sgioba *n* -n/-idhean *f m* crew, team

sgiobachd *n f* personnel, manpower

sgiobair *n* -ean *m* skipper, captain

sgiobalta *a* tidy, neat; quick

sgioblachadh *n* -aidh *m* tidying, tidying-up

sgioblaich *v* -achadh tidy, streamline

sgiorradh *n* -aidh, -aidhean *m* accident

sgiorrghail *n f* screaming, shrill crying

sgiort(a) *n* (-a), -(a)n/-(a)ichean *f* skirt

sgìos *n See* **sgìths**

sgìre *n* -an *f* district, parish **sgìr-easbaig** diocese

sgìreachd *n* -an *f* district, parish

sgìreil *a* -e district, parochial

sgìth *a* -e tired

sgitheach *n* -thich *m* hawthorn

sgitheadair *n* -ean *m* skier

sgitheadh *n* -thidh *m* skiing

Sgitheanach *n* -aich, -aich *m* someone from Skye *a* from, or pertaining to, Skye

sgìtheil *a* -e tiring, wearisome

sgìthich *v* -theachadh tire, make or become weary

sgìths *n f* tiredness, weariness, fatigue

sgiùrs *v* -adh scourge, lash

sgiùrsair *n* -ean *m* scourge

sglàib *n f* plaster

sglàibeadair *n* -ean *m* plasterer

sglàibrich *v* plaster

sglèat *n* -a, -an/-aichean *f m* slate

sglèat *v* -adh slate

sglèatair *n* -ean *m* slater

sgleog *n* -oig, -an *f* blow, slap

sgoch *v* -adh sprain, strain

sgòd *n* sgòid, -an *m* (*of sail*) sheet; piece of cloth or garment **cha robh s. aodaich orra** they were completely naked

sgoil *n* -e, -tean/-ean *f* school **àrd-s.** high school **bun-s.** primary school **s.-àraich** nursery school **s.-fhonn**

psalmody class

sgoilear *n* **-eir, -an** *m* pupil, scholar

sgoilearach *a* scholastic

sgoilearachd *n* *f* scholarship

sgoilt *v* **sgoltadh** split, cleave, slit

sgoinneil *a* **-e** terrific, super, superb, smashing, great; strapping (*of person*)

sgol *v* **-adh** rinse

sgoladh *n* **-aidh, -aidhean** *m* rinse, rinsing; (*met*) telling-off

sgolt *v* **-adh** split, cleave, slit

sgoltadh *n* **-aidh** *m* cleft, slit, split

sgona *n* **-ichean** *f m* scone

sgonn *n* **sgoinn/sguinn, -an** *m* block, lump **s. mòr de ghille** a big strapping lad

sgor *n* **sgoir, -an** *m* notch, cut, mark

sgòr *n* **sgòir, -an/-aichean** *m* score (*sport*)

sgorach *a* **-aiche** notched

sgòrnan *n* **-ain, -an** *m* gullet, throat

sgòrnanach *a* **-aiche** bronchial

sgot *n* **sgoit** *m* spot, plot of ground; fragment **cha robh s. aca** they hadn't a clue

sgoth *n* **-a, -an** *f* skiff, small boat

sgòth *n* **-a, -an** *f* cloud

sgòthach *a* **-aiche** cloudy

sgraing *n* **-e, -ean** *f* frown **chuir e s. air** *v* he frowned

sgreab *n* **-a, -an** *f* scab

sgread *n* **-a, -an** *m* shriek, screech

sgread *v* **-ail** shriek, screech **rinn i s.** *v* she shrieked

sgreadhail *n* **-e, -ean** *f* trowel

sgreamh *n* **-a/-eimhe** *m* disgust, loathing

sgreamhaich *v* **-achadh** disgust, nauseate

sgreamhail *a* **-e** disgusting, nauseating, horrible, loathsome

sgreataidh *a* **-e** ugly, horrible

sgreuch *n* **-a, -an** *m* scream, screech **dèan s.** *v* scream, screech

sgreuch *v* **-ail/-adh** scream, screech

sgriach *v* *See* **sgreuch**

sgrìob *n* **-a, -an** *n f* scrape, scratch; stripe; trip **chaidh sinn**

s. dhan bhaile we went on a trip to town

sgrìob *v* **-adh** scrape, scratch

sgrìobach *a* **-aiche** striped

sgrìobag *n* **-aig, -an** *f* note (*written*)

sgrìoban *n* **-ain, -an** *m* hoe, rake

sgrìob-cheangail *n* **sgrìoban- ceangail** *f* hyphen

sgrìobh *v* **-adh** write

sgrìobhadair *n* **-ean** *m* writer *Also* **sgrìobhaiche**

sgrìobhadh *n* **-aidh, -aidhean** *m* writing, inscription

sgrìobhte *a* written

sgriobtar *n* **-air, -an** *m* scripture

sgriobtarail *a* **-e** scriptural

sgrios *n* **-a, -an** *m* destruction, ruin

sgrios *v* **sgrios/-adh** destroy, ruin

sgriosail *a* **-e** destructive, ruinous; terrible, awful, dreadful **s. daor** terribly expensive

sgriubha *n* **-ichean** *f m* screw

sgriubhaire *n* **-an** *m* screwdriver

sgròb *v* **-adh** scratch

sgròbadh *n* **-aidh, -aidhean** *m* scratch, scratching

sgrùd *v* **-adh** scrutinize, examine, inspect, audit

sgrùdadh *n* **-aidh, -aidhean** *m* examination, scrutiny, inspection, audit **dèan s. air** *v* scrutinize, examine **neach- sgrùdaidh** *m* examiner, inspector

sguab *n* **-aibe, -an** *f* broom, brush, sweep; sheaf **s. arbhair** a sheaf of corn **s.-fhliuch** mop

sguab *v* **-adh** sweep, brush

sguabadair *n* **-ean** *m* sweeper

sgud *v* **-adh** lop, chop, cut; (+ **leis** *etc*) snatch

sgudal *n* **-ail** *m* rubbish, trash, garbage **làraidh an sgudail** *f* the refuse lorry

sguir *v* **sgur** cease, stop **s. dheth** stop it **s. i a smocadh** she stopped smoking

sgùirt *n* **-e, -ean** *f* lap

sgur *n* **sguir** *m* ceasing, stopping **gun s.** endlessly, constantly, non-stop

sgùr *v* -adh scour, cleanse

sgùrr *n* sgurra, sgurran *m* steep hill, peak, pinnacle

shìos *adv* down (*stationary*)

shuas *adv* up (*stationary*)

sia *n, a* six

siab *v* -adh blow (away), drift

siaban *n* -ain *m* sand-drift, sea-spray

siabann *n* -ainn, -ainn *m* soap

sia-cheàrnach *n* -aich, -an *m* hexagon *a* hexagonal

sia-deug *n, a* sixteen **sia bliadhna deug** sixteen years

sian *n* sìne, -tan *f* weather, storm **na siantan** the elements

sian *n* See **sìon**

sianar *n f m* six (people)

siar *a* west, western **an Cuan S.** the Atlantic Ocean

siathamh *a* sixth

sibh(se) *pron* you (*pl & pol*)

sìde *n f* weather **deagh shìde** good weather **droch shìde** bad weather

sil *v* -eadh drip, drop, rain **a bheil i a' sileadh?** is it raining?

sileadh *n* -lidh, -lidhean *m* dripping; rainfall, precipitation

sileagan *n* -ain, -an *m* jar

silidh *n m* jam **crogan s.** jam-jar

similear *n* -eir, -an *m* chimney

sìmplich *v* -leachadh simplify

sìmplidh *a* -e simple, easy

sin *a* that, those

sin *pron* that **an sin** there; then

sìn *v* -eadh stretch; pass **sìn a-mach** extend, prolong **sìn dhomh an salann** pass me the salt

sinc *n m* zinc

sinc(e) *n* -(e)achan/-(e)an *f m* sink

sine *n* -an *f* teat, nipple

sineach *n* sinich, sinich *m* mammal

sìneadh *n* sìnidh *m* stretch, stretching

singilte *a* single, singular

sinn(e) *pron* we, us

sinn-seanair *n* -ar, -ean *m* great-grandfather

sinn-seanmhair *n* -ar, -ean *f* great-grandmother

sinnsear *n* -sir, -sirean *m* ancestor, forefather

sinnsearachd *n f* ancestry

sìnteag *n* -eig, -an *f* hop, bound, stride; stepping-stone

siobhag *n* -aig, -an *f* wick

sìobhalta *a* civil, courteous, polite

sìobhaltachd *n f* civility; civilization

sìobra *n* -than *m* zebra

sìochail *a* -e peaceful, peaceable

sìoda *n* -chan *m* silk

siogàr *n* -air, -an *m* cigar

sìol *n* sìl *m* seed; sperm; progeny

sìolag *n* -aig, -an *f* sand-eel

sìolaich *v* -achadh seed; beget, propagate; (*intrans*) multiply

sìolaidh *v* subside, settle; filter, strain **s. às** peter out

siolandair *n* -ean *m* cylinder

sìol-chuir *v* -chur sow

siolp *v* -adh slip away, slink off, skulk

sìol(t)achan *n* -ain, -ain *m* filter, strainer

sìoman *n* -ain, -an *m* rope of straw or hay; line for clothes

sìon *n* anything, something **a h-uile s.** everything

Sìonach *n* -aich, -aich *m* Chinese *a* Chinese

sionnach *n* -aich, -aich *m* fox

sionnsar *n* -air, -an *m* bagpipe chanter

sìor *a* ever, always, continual **s.-mhaireannach** perpetual, everlasting **s.-uaine** evergreen

sioraf *n* -aif, -an *m* giraffe

siorc *n* -a, -an *m* shark

siorrachd *n* -an *f* shire, county *Also* **siorramachd**

sìorraidh *a* ever **gu s.** forever

sìorraidheachd *n f* eternity *Also* **sìorrachd**

siorram *n* -aim, -an *m* sheriff *Also* **siorraidh**

sìos *adv* down, downwards

siosar *n* -air, -an *f m* scissors

siosarnaich *n f* hissing, hiss

siostam *n* -aim, -an *m* system

siota *n* -ichean *f* sheet

sir *v* -eadh seek, search for

siris(t) *n* -ean *f* cherry

sìth *n* -e *f* peace, reconciliation
sitheadh *n* -thidh, -thidhean *m*
speed, onrush, impetuosity
sithean *n* -ein, -ein/-an *m* hillock,
knoll, fairy knoll; flower
sitheann *n* sithinn/sìthne *f*
venison, game; flesh of fowls
sìtheil *a* -e peaceful, tranquil,
peaceable
sìthich *v* sìtheachadh pacify
sìthiche *n* -an *m* fairy
sitig *n* -e, -ean *f* dunghill,
midden; outdoors
sitir *n* -e *f* neighing, braying
sitrich *n* -e *f* neighing, braying
Also vn **a' s.**
siubhail *v* -al travel, journey; die,
pass away
siubhal *n* -ail, siùbhlaichean *m*
travel **cosgaisean siubhail** *f pl*
travel expenses **fad an**
t-siubhail all the time
siùbhlach *n* -aiche, -aichean *m*
traveller; nomad
siùbhlach *a* -aiche swift, speedy;
wandering; fluent (*speech*)
siùcar *n* -air, -an *m* sugar; sweet
siud *pron* that **an siud** there, over
there
siùdan *n* -ain, -an *m* swing
siuga *n* -nnan *f m* jug
siùrsach *n* -aich, -an *f* prostitute
siuthad *def v* go on! *pl*
siuthadaibh/siùdaibh
slabhraidh *n* -ean *f* chain
slaic *n* -ean *f* blow **thug iad s. air**
an Riaghaltas they hit out at the
Government
slaic *v* -eadh thrash, beat, strike
slaighd *v* -eadh slide
slaightear *m* -eir, -an *m* rogue
Also **slaoightear, slaightire**
slàinte *n f* health **bòrd s.** *m* health
board **Seirbheis na S.** the
Health Service **Slàinte!** Cheers!
S. Mhath! Good Health! Cheers!
slàinteachail *a* -e hygienic
slàinteachas *n* -ais *m* hygiene
slàintealachd *n f* sanitation
slaman *n* -ain *m* curds, curdled
milk **s.-milis** jelly
slàn *a* slàine whole, complete,
wholesome **s. leat** goodbye,

farewell
slànaich *v* -achadh heal, cure
slànaighear *n* -air *m* saviour **an S.**
the Saviour
slaod *n* slaoid, -an *m* sledge, raft
slaod *v* -adh pull, drag, haul
slaodach *a* -aiche slow, tardy,
sluggish
slaodair *n* -ean *m* sluggard
slapag *n* -aig, -an *f* slipper
slat *n* slait, -an *f* rod; yard (length)
s.-iasgaich fishing rod
s.-t(h)omhais measuring rod;
criterion, yardstick
sleagh *n* -a, -an *f* spear, javelin
sleamhainn *a* -e/-mhna slippery
sleamhnag *n* -aig, -an *f* slide
sleamhnaich *v* -achadh slip, slide
sleids *n* -ichean *m* sledge
sleuchd *v* -adh kneel, prostrate
self; submit
sliabh *n* slèibh(e), slèibhtean *m*
mountain, hillside, moor
sliasaid *n* -e, -ean *f* thigh
slige *n* -an/-achan *f* shell
sligeach *a* -giche shelled, having
a shell, shelly
sligeanach *n* -aich *m* tortoise
slighe *n* -an *f* way, path,
direction, track, route
slinnean *n* -ein, -an *m* shoulder,
shoulder-blade
slìob *v* -adh stroke; (*met*) flatter
sliochd *n* -a, -an *m* offspring,
progeny, descendants
slìogach *a* -aiche sly, sleekit
slios *n* -a, -an *m* side, slope, flank
slis *n* -e, -ean *f* slice, rasher
sliseag *n* -eig, -an *f* slice, small
slice
slisnich *v* -neadh slice
sloc *n* sluic, sluic/-an *m* pit,
cavity, hollow
sloinn *v* -eadh give/trace
genealogy/family tree
sloinneadh *n* -nidh, -nidhean *m*
surname; genealogy
sloinntearachd *n f* (*act of giving*
a) genealogy
sluagh *n* sluaigh, slòigh *m*
people, host, crowd
sluagh-ghairm *n* -e, -ean *f* war-
cry, slogan

sluasaid *n* -e, -ean *f* shovel
slugadh *n* -aidh *m* swallowing, gulping, devouring; capacity **tha s. mòr aig an talla** the hall has a large capacity
slugan *n* -ain, -an *m* gullet
sluig *v* -eadh/slugadh swallow
slupraich *n* -e *f* slurping; splashing through water
smachd *n f* discipline, authority, control **fo s.** under control **cùm s. air** *v* keep control of
smachdaich *v* -achadh discipline
smachdail *a* -e authoritative, commanding, disciplinary
smal *n* smail *m* spot, stain **gun s.** without blemish **màireach gun s. dhut** have a good day tomorrow
smàl *v* -adh extinguish, quench
smàladair *n* -ean *m* firefighter
smalan *n* -ain *m* grief, sorrow, melancholy
smaoin *n* -e, -tean *f* thought, idea
smaoineachadh *n* -aidh *m* thinking
smaoin(t)ich *v* smaoin(t)eachadh/smaointinn think
smàrag *n* -aig, -an *f* emerald
smèid *v* -eadh wave, beckon
smeòrach *n* -aich, -aichean *f* thrush
smeur *n* -a, -an *f* bramble
smeur *v* -adh smear, daub
smid *n* -e, -ean *f* syllable, word **cha tuirt e s.** he didn't utter a word
smig *n* -ean *f m* chin
smiogaid *n* -ean *f m* chin
smior *n* smir/-a *m* marrow, pith; strength, pluck, vigour; best part **'s e s. an duin'-uasail a th' ann** he's a real/true gentleman **s.-caillich** spinal marrow
smiorail *a* -e/-ala strong, vigorous, doughty, plucky *Also* **smearail**
smiùr *v* -adh *See* **smeur**
smoc *v* -adh smoke *Also* **smocaig**
smocadh *n* -aidh *m* smoking
smodal *n* -ail *m* fragments, crumbs; smattering **s. airgid** loose change
smuain *n* -e, -tean *f* thought, idea
smuainich *v* -neachadh think
smug *n* smuig, -an *m* phlegm
smugadaich *n f* spitting
smugaid *n* -e, -ean *f* spit, spittle **tilg s.** *v* spit
smùid *n* -e, -ean *f* smoke, vapour; intoxication **ghabh e droch s.** *v* he got very drunk
smùirnean *n* -ein, -ein *m* mote, atom
smùirneanach *a* atomic
smùr *n* smùir *m* dross, dust
sna *aug prep* in the (*before pl nouns*)
snag *n* snaig, -an *m* knock, crack
snagadaich *n* -e *f* gnashing, grating, chattering (*of teeth*)
snàgail *n* -e *f* crawl, crawling
snàgair *n* -ean *m* crawler; reptile
snagan-daraich *n* snagain-, snagain-/snaganan- *m* woodpecker
snaidhm *n* -ean, -eannan *m* knot **cuir s. air** *v* tie a knot in it *Also* **snaoim**
snàig *v* snàgadh/snàgail creep, crawl
snàigeach *a* -giche creeping, crawling
snàigeadh *n* -gidh *m* creeping, crawling
snaigh *v* -eadh sculpt, carve, hew
snaigheadair *n* -ean *m* sculptor
snaigheadh *n* -ghidh, -ghidhean *m* sculpture, carving **bha iad a' s. ris an uair** they were cutting it fine
snàithlean *n* -ein, -an *m* thread
snàmh *v* swim
snaoisean *n* -ein *m* snuff
snas *n* snais *m* accomplishment, elegance, finesse
snasail *a* -e accomplished, elegant, well-finished
snasmhor *a* -oire accomplished, elegant, well-finished
snàth *n* -a/snàith, snàithean *m* thread
snàthad *n* -aid, -an *f* needle
snàthainn *n* -e/snàithe, -ean/snàithean *m* thread, single

thread
snàthlainn *n See* **snàithlean**
sneachd(a) *n m* snow **a' cur an t-s.** *v* snowing **bodach-s.** snowman
snèap *n* **snèip, -an** *f* turnip, neep *Also* **snèip**
snigh *v* **-e** leak, drip, seep
snighe *n m* rain penetration from roof, seeping, seepage, drip
snìomh *n* **-a, -an** *m* spinning, twist
snìomh *v* **snìomh/-adh** spin, twist **shnìomh i a h-adhbrann** she twisted/sprained her ankle
snìomhaire *n* **-an** *m* wimble, drill
snìomhan *n* **-ain, -an** *m* spiral
snodhach *n* **-aich** *m* sap
snodha-gàire *n* **snodhan-** *m* smile, quick smile
snog *a* **snoige** nice, lovely, attractive; likeable
snot *v* **-adh** smell, sniff
snuadh *n* **-aidh** hue, complexion, appearance, aspect
so *a See* **seo**
sòbarra *a* sober
sòbhrach *n* **-aich, -aichean** *f* primrose *Also* **seòbhrach**
socair *n* **-e/socrach** *f* ease, rest **gabh air do shocair** take it easy
socair *a* **socraiche, -e** at ease, quiet, tranquil, mild; comfortable
sochair *n* **-(e), -ean** *f* benefit, privilege **s. chloinne** child benefit **s. cion-cosnaidh** unemployment benefit
socharach *a* **-aiche** laid back, easy-going, bashful
socrach *a* **-aiche** at ease, comfortable, sedate
socraich *v* **-achadh** settle; determine, fix
sodal *n* **-ail** *f m* flattery, fawning
sòfa *n* **-than** *f* sofa
soidhne *n* **-achan** *m* sign *Also* **soighne**
soilire *n m* celery
soilleir *a* **-e** clear, bright
soilleireachd *n f* clearness, clarity, clarification, brightness
soilleirich *v* **-reachadh** clear,

clarify, illuminate, brighten
soillse *n* **-an** *m* light
soillseach *a* **-siche** bright, clear, shining
soillsich *v* **-seachadh** light, enlighten
soirbh *a* **-e** easy
soirbheachadh *n* **-aidh, -aidhean** *m* success, prosperity
soirbheachail *a* **-e** successful, prosperous
soirbheas *n* **-eis, -eis** *m* success, prosperity; favourable breeze
soirbhich *v* **-bheachadh** succeed, prosper
soircas *n* **-ais, -an** *m* circus
sòisealach *n* **-aich, -aich** *m* socialist
sòisealach *a* **-aiche** socialist
sòisealachd *n f* socialism, social work
sòisealta *a* social **na seirbheisean s.** the social services
sòisealtas *n* **-ais** *m* society
soisgeul *n* **-eil, -an** *m* gospel
soisgeulach *a* **-aiche** evangelical
soisgeulaiche *n* **-an** *m* evangelist
soitheach *n* **-thich, -thichean** *f m* dish; vessel, ship **nigh na soithichean** wash the dishes **s.-sgudail** rubbish bin
soitheamh *a* **-eimhe** tame, docile, tractable, gentle
sòlaimte *a* solemn, dignified
solair *v* **-ar/-aradh** provide, supply, cater for, procure
solarachadh *n* **-aidh** *m* provision, supply, catering, procurement
solaraich *v* **-achadh** provide, supply, cater for, procure
solas *n* **-ais, -ais** *m* light; traffic lights
sòlas *n* **-ais** *m* happiness, joy, solace
sòlasach *a* **-aiche** happy, joyful
so-leaghadh *a* dissoluble
so-leughadh *a* legible
so-loisgeach *a* combustible
solt(a) *a* mild, gentle, placid
so-lùbadh *a* flexible
somalta *a* placid, docile; inactive
son *n m* cause, account **air mo shon-sa** on my behalf

son *prep See* **airson**
sona *a* happy, content
sonas *n* **-ais** *m* happiness, contentment
sònraich *v* **-achadh** specify, stipulate
sònraichte *a* special, particular, specific; remarkable **gu s.** particularly, especially
sop *n* **suip, suip/-an** *m* wisp
soraidh *n* *f* farewell **s. leibh** farewell (*to you*) (*pl & pol*)
sòrn *n* **sùirn** *m* flue, vent
so-ruighinn *a* accessible *Also* **so-ruigsinn**
so-thuigsinn *a* intelligible, clear
spàgach *a* **-aiche** splay-footed
spàgail *n* *f* walking awkwardly
spaid *n* **-e, -ean** *f* spade
spaideil *a* **-e** well-dressed, smart
spaidsirich *v* **-searachd** parade, saunter
spàin *n* **-e, -ean/-tean/-eachan** *f* spoon **s.-tì/teatha** teaspoon
Spàinn(t)each *n* Spaniard *a* Spanish
Spàinn(t)is *n* *f* Spanish (*lang*)
spàirn *n* **-e** *f* effort, exertion, struggle, stress **rinn e s. mhòr** he made a great effort
spàl *n* **spàil, -an** *m* shuttle **s.-fànais** space shuttle **s.-ite** shuttlecock
spanair *n* **-ean** *m* spanner
spàrdan *n* **-ain, -ain/-an** *m* roost
spàrr *n* **sparra, sparran** *m* joist, beam; roost
spàrr *v* **sparradh** thrust, force
spastach *n* **-aich, -aich** *m* spastic
spastach *a* **-aiche** spastic
speach *n* **-a, -an** *f* wasp
speal *n* **-a, -an** *f* scythe
spealg *n* **speilg, -an** *f* splinter, fragment
spealg *v* **-adh** splinter, smash
spèil *n* **-e, -ean** *f* skate
spèil *v* **-eadh** skate
spèileabord *n* **-buird, -buird** *m* skateboard, skateboarding
spèile-deighe *n* *f* ice skating
spèiliche *n* **-an** *m* skater
speireag *n* **-eig, -an** *f* sparrow-hawk; spitfire, nippy sweetie

spèis *n* **-e** *f* esteem, affection, regard, fondness, attachment **bha s. mhòr aige dhi** he held her in great esteem, he was very fond of her
spèisealta *a* specialist
speuclairean *n* *m* *pl* spectacles, glasses **s.-grèine** sunglasses *Also* **speuclair** (*sg*)
speur *n* **-a, -an** *m* sky **na speuran** the heavens, the firmament **s.-sheòladair** spaceman, astronaut **s.-shiubhal** *m* space travel
speur(ad)air *n* **-ean** *m* astronaut, spaceman
speuradaireachd *n* *f* space exploration
spìc *n* **-e, -ean** *f* spike
spideag *n* **-eig, -an** *f* nightingale; nippy female
spìocach *a* **-aiche** mean, miserly, stingy
spìocaire *n* **-an** *m* miser
spìocaireachd *n* *f* meanness, miserliness
spìon *v* **-adh** pluck, tug, snatch, wrench
spionnadh *n* **-aidh** *m* strength, vigour
spiorad *n* **-aid, -an** *m* spirit **an S. Naomh** the Holy Spirit
spioradail *a* **-e** spiritual
spioradalachd *n* *f* spirituality
spìosrach *a* **-aiche** spicy
spìosradh *n* **-aidh, -aidhean** *m* spice
spìosraich *v* **-achadh** spice; embalm
spìosraidh *n* *f* spices
spiris *n* **-e, -ean** *f* roost, perch
spitheag *n* **-eig, -an** *f* chuckie (*small flat pebble*), skimmer
splais *n* **-ean** *f* splash
splais *v* **-eadh** splash
spleadhach *a* **-aiche** splay-footed *Also* **spliathach**
spleuchd *n* **-a, -an** *m* smarm; stare, gaze
spleuchd *v* spread out, plaster all over; stare, gaze
spliùchan *n* **-ain, -an** *m* tobacco pouch *Also* **spliuchan**
spòg *n* **spòig, -an** *f* paw; claw,

spoke; hand (*of watch/clock*)
spong *n* **spuing, -an** *m* sponge
spor *n* **spuir, -an** *m* spur; claw,
talon; flint
sporan *n* **-ain, -ain** *m* purse
sporghail *n* *f* noisy scramble/
scrabble, rustling
spòrs *n* **-a** *f* sport, fun
spòrsail *a* **-e** sporting, sporty;
funny, in fun
spot *n* **-an** *f m* spot
spoth *v* **spoth, -adh** castrate, geld
spreadh *v* **-adh** explode, burst
spreadhadh *n* **-aidh, -aidhean** *m*
explosion, burst
sprèidh *n* **-e** *f* cattle, livestock
spreig *v* **-eadh** incite
sprochd *n* *f* dejection, sadness **fo
s.** dejected
sprùilleach *n* **-lich** *m* crumbs,
fragments, debris
spùill *v* **-eadh** plunder
spùinn *v* **-eadh** plunder
spùinneadair *n* **-ean** *m* plunderer
s.-mara pirate
spuir *n* **-ean** *m* claw, talon
spùt *n* **-a, -an** *m* spout; very
small particle **chan eil s. aige** he
has no idea
spùt *v* **-adh** spout, squirt
sràbh *n* **sràibh, -an** *m* straw
srac *v* **-adh** tear, rend
sracadh *n* **-aidh, -aidhean** *m* tear,
tearing
sradag *n* **-aig, -an** *f* spark **tha s.
innte** she has a quick temper
sràid *n* **-e, -ean** *f* street
srainnsear *n* **-eir, -an** *m* stranger
srann *n* **srainn, -an** *f* snore, hum
dèan s. *v* snore
srath *n* **-a, -an** *m* wide valley
(*usually with river*)
sreang *n* **-a/sreinge, -an** *f* string
sreap *v* *See* **streap**
sreath *n* **-a, -an** *f m* row, series **an
s. a chèile** in a row, in
succession
sreothart *n* **-airt, -an** *m* sneeze
dèan s. *v* sneeze *Also* **sreathart**
sreothartaich *n* *f* sneezing *Also*
sreathartaich
srian *n* **srèine, -tan/srèinean** *f*
stripe; bridle **cùm s. air do
theanga** *v* watch what you say
srianach *a* **-aiche** striped
sròl *n* **sròil, -an** *m* satin
sròn *n* **sròine, -an/sròinean** *f*
nose; promontory **ghabh iad san
t-sròin e** they took offence at it
sròin-adharcach *n* **-aich** *m*
rhinoceros
srùb *n* **srùib, -an** *m* spout
srùbag *n* **-aig, -an** *f* a small
drink, a cuppa
srùban *n* **-ain, -ain** *m* cockle
sruth *n* **-a/sruithe, -an** *m* stream,
burn; current **leis an t-s.** with
the current; (*met*) downhill
sruth *v* **-adh** stream, flow
sruthail *v* **-thladh/srùthladh** wash,
rinse
sruthan *n* **-ain, -ain** *m* streamlet,
small stream
stàball *n* **-aill, -aill/-an** *m* stable
staca *n* **-nnan** *m* stack
stad *n* *m* stop, halt, pause **na s.**
stationary **chuireadh s. oirnn** *v*
we were stopped
stad *v* stop, halt, pause
stad-phuing *n* **-e, -ean** *f* full stop
staid *n* **(-e), -ean** *f* state,
condition
staidhre *n* **-richean** *f* stair **shuas
an s.** upstairs **shìos an s.**
downstairs *Also* **staidhir**
staigh *adv See* **a-staigh**
stail *n* **-e, -ean** *f* still (*for
whisky*)
stailc *n* **-ean** *f* strike (*labour*)
stàile *n* **-lichean** *f* stall
stàilinn *n* **-e** *f* steel
staing *n* **-e, -ean** *f* difficulty,
predicament **ann an s.** in a
quandary/fix
stàirn *n* **-e** *f* loud noise, clamour
stairs(n)each *n* **-s(n)ich, -s(n)ichean**
f threshold; stone steps/stone path
stais *n* **-e, -ean** *f* moustache
stàit *n* **-e, -ean** *f* state **na Stàitean
Aonaichte** the United States
stàiteil *a* **-e/-eala** stately
stàitire *n* **-an** *m* statesman
stàitireachd *n* *f* statesmanship
stalc *n* **stailc** *m* starch
stalla *n* **-chan** *m* overhanging
rock, precipice

stamag *n* -aig, -an *f* stomach
stamh *n* **staimh** *m* tangle (*on shore*)
stamp *v* -adh stamp, trample
stamp(a) *n* -(a)ichean *f* (*postage*) stamp
staoig *n* -ean *f* steak
staoin *n* -e *f* tin, pewter
stapag *n* -aig, -an *f* mixture of meal and cold water
staran *n* -ain, -an *m* path (*to house*)
starrag *n* -aig, -an *f* hoodie crow
steach *adv* See **a-steach**
steall *n* still, -an *f* spout, squirt
steall *v* -adh spout, squirt
steallair *n* -e, -ean *m* syringe
steapa *n* -ichean *f m* step
steatasgop *n* -oip, -an *f m* stethoscope
stèidh *n* -e, -ean *f* foundation, base, basis
stèidheachadh *n* -aidh, -aidhean *m* foundation, establishment
stèidheachd *n* *f* foundation, institute
stèidhich *v* -dheachadh found, establish, set up
steigeach *a* -giche sticky
stèisean *n* -ein, -an *m* station **s. peatrail** petrol station **s. rèidio** radio station **s. thrèanaichean** train station
stiall *n* **stèill**, -an *f* strip, stripe, streak **cha robh s. orra** they hadn't a stitch on
stiall *v* -adh thrash, lash; tear into strips; stripe
stiallach *a* -aiche streaky
stìopall *n* -aill, -aill *m* steeple
stiorap *n* -aip, -an *m* stirrup
stiùbhard *n* -aird, -an *m* steward
stiùir *n* -e/stiùrach, -ean/-ichean *f* rudder, helm
stiùir *v* -eadh steer, direct, guide
stiùireadair *n* -ean *m* steersman, helmsman
stiùireadh *n* -ridh, -ridhean *m* steering; direction, guidance, management, supervision
stiùiriche *n* -an *m* director **S. an Fhoghlaim** the Director of Education
stob *n* **stuib**, -an *m* stump;

protrusion **bha mi nam s.**
a' feitheamh riutha I was left standing around waiting for them
stob *v* -adh stab, thrust
stobach *a* -aiche prickly, barbed
stòbha *n* -ichean *f m* stove
stoc *n* **stuic, stuic** *m* trunk, stump (*of tree*); stock, livestock
stoc *n* **stuic, stuic** *m* scarf
stoc *v* -adh stock
stocainn *n* (-e), -ean *f* stocking
stoc-mhargaid *n* -ean *f* stock-exchange
stoidhle *n* -lichean *f* style
stoighle *n* See **stoidhle**
stò(i)r *v* **stòradh** store
stòiridh *n* -ean *f m* story *Also* **stòraidh**
stoirm *n* -e, -ean *f m* storm
stoirmeil *a* -e stormy
stòl *a* -a/stòil, -an *m* stool
stòlda *a* steady, sedate, settled, staid
stòr *n* **stòir**, -an/-aichean *m* store **s.-dàta** database
stòradh *n* -aidh *m* storage, storing
stòras *n* -ais, -ais *m* riches, wealth, resources
stràc *n* -àic, -an *f m* stroke; accent (*in writing*)
strèan *n* -èin *m* strain, stress
streap *v* **streap/-adh** climb
streapadair *n* -ean *m* climber
strì *n* *f* strife, struggle, conflict, contention **dèan s.** *v* strive
strì *v* strive, struggle, compete, contest
strìoch *n* -a, -an *f* streak; line; hyphen
strìochd *v* -adh submit, yield, give in, surrender
strìopach *n* -aich(e), -aichean *f* prostitute, whore
strìopachas *n* -ais *m* prostitution
stròdhail *a* -e prodigal, extravagant, lavish *Also* **strùidheil**
stròdhalachd *n* *f* prodigality *Also* **strùidhealachd**
structair *n* -ean *m* structure
structarail *a* -e structural

strùidhear *n* -eir, -an *m*
spendthrift
strùpag *n* See **srùbag**
struth *n* -a, -an *f m* ostrich
stuadh *n* See **stuagh**
stuagh *n* stuaigh, -an/-annan *f*
wave; gable
stuaim *n* -e *f* moderation,
temperance, abstemiousness
stuama *a* stuaime moderate,
temperate, sober, abstemious
stuamachd *n f* temperance,
abstemiousness
stùirceach *n* -ciche surly, scowling
stuig *v* -eadh incite, prompt
stùr *n* stùir *m* stour, dust
stuth *n* -a, -an *m* stuff, matter;
material **s.-fhiaclan** toothpaste
stuthaigeadh *n* -gidh *m* starch
sù *n* -than *m* zoo Also **sutha**
suaicheanta *a* remarkable,
notable, prominent
suaicheantas *n* -ais, -ais *m*
badge, emblem
suaimhneach *a* -niche tranquil,
quiet
suaimhneas *n* -eis *m* rest,
tranquillity, quiet
suain *n* -e *f* deep sleep, slumber
suain *v* -eadh wrap
suainealachadh *n* -aidh *m*
hypnotism
suainealaiche *n* -an *m* hypnotist
suainealas *n* -ais *m* hypnosis
Suaineach *n* -nich, -nich *m* Swede
a Swedish
suaip *n* -e, -ean *f* slight
resemblance
suairce *a* affable; gentle,
courteous
suairceas *n* -eis *m* affability;
gentility, courteousness
suarach *a* -aiche insignificant,
trifling; mean, contemptible,
despicable
suarachas *n* -ais *m*
insignificance; meanness,
contemptibility
suas *adv* up, upwards
suath *v* -adh rub, wipe; massage
suathadh *n* -aidh, -aidhean *m*
rub, rubbing, massage, friction
sùbailte *a* supple, flexible, elastic

Also **subailte**
sùbailteachd *n f* suppleness,
flexibility Also **subailteachd**
sùbh *n* sùibh, -an *m* berry
s.-craoibh raspberry **s.-làir**
strawberry Also **subh**
subhach *a* -aiche merry
subhailc *n* -e, -ean *f* virtue
subhailceach *a* -ciche virtuous
subsadaidh *n* -ean *m* subsidy
sùgach *a* -aiche joyous
sùgh *n* -a/sùigh, -an *m* juice, sap
sùgh *v* -adh suck, absorb, soak
up Also **sùigh**
sùghach *a* -aiche absorbent
sùghadh *n* -aidh *m* absorption,
suction
sùghmhor *a* -oire juicy
sùgradh *n* -aidh *m* mirth **dèan s.**
v make merry
suidh *v* -e sit **dèan suidhe** *v* take
a seat
suidhe *n* -an/-achan *m* sitting
àite-s. *nm* seat
suidheachadh *n* -aidh, -aidhean
m situation, site; state,
condition, circumstances
suidheachan *n* -ain, -ain *m* seat
suidhich *v* -dheachadh settle,
place, situate, set, appoint
suidhichte *a* situated, settled, set
suidse *n* -sichean *f* switch **cuir s.**
ri *v* set on fire
suids-chlàr *n* -chlàir *m*
switchboard
suigeart *n* -eirt *m* jollity,
cheerfulness, chirpiness
suigeartach *a* -aiche jolly,
cheerful, chirpy
sùil *n* sùla, -ean *f* eye **s.-bheag**
wink **s.-dhubh** black eye **thug e**
s. air he had a look at it
s.-chritheach quagmire
suilbhir *a* -e cheerful
sùilich *v* -leachadh expect,
anticipate
sùim *n* -e, -eannan *f* sum,
amount; regard, esteem, interest
cha do ghabh e mòran s. dheth
he didn't pay much regard to it
suipear *n* -eir/-ach, -an *f* supper
suirghe *n f* courtship, wooing,
love-making

suirghiche *n* -an *m* wooer, lover
sùist *n* -e, -ean *f* flail
sùist *v* -eadh flail
suiteas *n* -eis, -eis *m* sweet *Also* **suitidh**
sùith *n* -e *f m* soot
sùlaire *n* -an *m* gannet
sult *n* suilt *m* fat; joy
Sultain *n* -e *f* an t-S. September
sultmhor *a* -oire fat, plump; joyful, jolly
sumainn *n* -e, -ean *f* surge (*of sea*), billow
sumanadh *n* -aidh *m* summons
sunnd *n m* mood, humour **bha iad ann an deagh shunnd** they were in good spirits
sunndach *a* -aiche lively, contented, hearty, in good spirits
sùrd *n* sùird *m* cheerfulness; eagerness
sùrdag *n* -aig, -an *f* leap, bound, skip
sùrdail *a* -e energetic
susbaint *n* -e *f* substance, content
susbainteach *a* -tiche substantial
suth *n* -a, -an *m* embryo
suthainn *a* eternal **gu s. sìor** forever and ever, eternally

T

tà *conj* though, although
tàbh *n* tàibh, -an *m* spoon net, fishing net
tàbhachd *n f* efficacy, effectiveness; substance; benefit
tàbhachdach *a* -aiche effectual, effective; substantial; beneficial
tabhainn *v* -ann offer, tender *Also* **tathainn**
tabhair *irr v* give, bestow (*See irr v* tabhair *in Grammar*)
tabhairtiche *n* -an *m* donor, giver
tabhann *n* -ainn *m* offer, offering *Also* **tathann**
tabhannaich *v* bark, yelp
tabhartach *a* liberal; dative **an tuiseal t.** the dative case
tabhartas *n* -ais *m* donation, grant, offering, presentation
tac *n* -a/taic, -annan/-aichean *f* tack (*of land*)
tac(a) *n f* time, season **mun t. seo an-uiridh** about this time last year **an t. ri** in comparison with
tacaid *n* -e, -ean *f* tack
tacan *n* -ain, -an *m* a while, a short time
tachair *v* -t happen; meet **t. do** happen to (*someone*) **t. ri** meet (with)
tachas *n* -ais *m* itch, itchiness *Also* **tachais**
tachais *v* -as/-ais scratch
tàcharan *n* -ain, -an *m* sprite, ghost; changeling
tachartas *n* -ais, -an *m* event, incident, occurrence
tachasach *a* -aiche itchy
tachd *v* -adh choke, smother, strangle
tacsa *n m* support **an t. ri balla** leaning against a wall
tadhail *v* -al call (on), visit
tadhal *n* -ail, -aichean *m* visit, call; goal, hail (*in sport*)
tagach *a* -aiche stocky
tagair *v* -t/tagradh plead, claim, advocate
tagairt *n* -e *f* claim
tagh *v* -adh choose, select, elect
taghadh *n* -aidh, -aidhean *m* choice, selection, election **T. Pàrlamaid** General Election
taghta *a* splendid, fine, chosen, choice
tagradh *n* -aidh, -aidhean *m* plea, pleading, claim, submission
tagraiche *n* -an *m* advocate, applicant, candidate (*polit*)
tagsaidh *n* -ean *f m* taxi
taibhs(e) *n* -(e)an *f m* ghost, apparition
taic *n* -e *f* support; proximity **t. airgid** financial support **cuir t. ri/thoir t. do** *v* support
taiceil *a* -e supportive
taidh *n* -ean *f* tie (*necktie*)
taidhr *n* -ichean *f* tyre *Also* **taidhear**
taigeis *n* -e, -ean *f* haggis
taigh *n* -e, -ean *m* house **aig an t.** at home **T. nan Cumantan** the House of Commons **T. nam**

Morairean the House of Lords
t.-beag toilet **t.-bìdh** restaurant
t.-ceàirde factory **t.-chearc**
henhouse **t.-chon** kennel
t.-cluiche theatre **t.-cuibhle**
wheelhouse **t.-cùirte** courthouse
t.-dhealbh cinema **t.-dubh** black
house, thatched cottage
t.-eiridinn hospital, infirmary
t.-faire watch-house, vigil;
mortuary **t.-fuine** bakery
t.-glainne glasshouse
t.-grùide brewery **t.-òsta** hotel
t.-seinnse bar, inn, hotel
t.-solais lighthouse **t.-spadaidh**
slaughterhouse **t.-staile** distillery
t.-tasgaidh museum **t.-tughaidh**
thatched cottage
taigheadas *n* -ais *m* housing
tàileasg *n* -eisg *m* chess;
backgammon
tàillear *n* -eir, -an *m* tailor
taing *n* -e *f* thanks, gratitude
mòran t. many thanks, thanks
very much
taingealachd *n f* gratitude,
thankfulness
taingeil *a* -e thankful, grateful
tàinig *irr v* came (*See irr v* **thig** *in*
Grammar)
tàir *n* -e, -ean *f* contempt;
difficulty **dèan t. air** *v* deride,
scoff at, disparage
tairbeart *n* -eirt, -an *f* isthmus
tairbhe *n f* profit, advantage,
benefit
tàireil *a* -e insulting, disparaging;
contemptible, mean
tairg *v* -sinn/-se(adh) offer, tender
tairgse *n* -an *f* offer, tender
tàirneanach *n* -aich, -aich *m*
thunder
tàirnge *n See* **tarrang**
tais *a* -e moist, damp
taisbean *v* -adh reveal, show,
exhibit, demonstrate, manifest
taisbeanadh *n* -aidh, -aidhean *m*
exhibition, display, show
taisbein *v See* **taisbean**
taiseachd *n f* moisture,
dampness, humidity
taisg *v* **tasgadh** deposit, store,
hoard

taisich *v* -seachadh moisten,
dampen
taitinn *v* **taitneadh** please, delight
(+ **ri**)
taitneach *a* -niche pleasant,
pleasing, agreeable
taitneas *n* -eis, -an *m* pleasure
tàl *n* **tàil**, -an *m* adze
tàladh *n* -aidh, -aidhean *m*
lullaby; enticing, attracting;
soothing
tàlaidh *v* -adh entice, attract;
soothe; lull
talamh *n* -aimh/talmhainn, -an *m*
(*the gen sg* **talmhainn** *f is more*
common) earth, land, soil **t.**
àitich arable land **t. bàn** fallow
ground
tàlant *n* -tan *m* talent *Also* **tàlann**
tàlantach *a* -aiche talented
talla *n* -chan/-ichean *f m* hall
t. a' bhaile the town/village hall
t. ciùil music hall
tallan *n* -ain, -an *m* partition
(*phys*)
talmhaidh *a* -e earthly, terrestrial;
worldly (*of person*)
tàmailt *n* -e, -ean *f* chagrin,
humiliation, shame,
embarrassment; offence, insult
tàmailteach *a* -tiche humiliating,
embarrassing; humiliated,
embarrassed; indignant,
insulted
tamall *n* -aill, -aill *m* a while,
length of time
tàmh *n* **tàimh** *m* rest, repose **a**
bheil i na t. an-dràsta? is she
idle/out of work at present?
tàmh *v* rest; stay, dwell
tamhasg *n* -aisg, -an *m*
blockhead, fool; ghost
tana *a* **taine** thin, slender, slim;
shallow
tanaich *v* -achadh thin
tànaiste *n* -an *m* regent
tanalach *n* -aich *m* shallow water
tanca *n* -ichean *f m* tank
tancair *n* -ean *m* tanker
tannasg *n* -aisg, -aisg *m*
apparition, ghost, spectre
taobh *n* **taoibh**, -an *m* side; way **ri**
t. (+ *gen*) beside **t. an fhasgaidh**

taobh

the lee side **t. an fhuaraidh** the windward side **t.-duilleig(e)** page (*in book*) **a thaobh** (+ *gen*) concerning, regarding **tha t. aice ri Ìle** she is fond of Islay

taobh *v* **-adh** (+ **ri**) side with, favour

taod *n* **taoid, taoid** *m* halter

taois *n* **-e, -ean** *f* dough

taoisnich *v* **-neachadh** knead

taom *v* **-adh** pour out; bale

tap *n* **-a, -aichean** *f m* tap

tapachd *n f* boldness, sturdiness

tapadh *n* **-aidh** *m* courage **tapadh leat/leibh** thank you

tapaidh *a* **-e** bold, active; well-built

tapais *n* **-ean** *f* carpet

Tarasach *n* **-aich, -aich** *m* native of Taransay *a* from, or pertaining to, Taransay

tarbh *n* **tairbh, tairbh** *m* bull

tarbhach *a* **-aiche** beneficial, advantageous

tarbh-nathrach *n* **tairbh-, tairbh-** *m* dragonfly

tarcais *n* **-e, -ean** *f* contempt, scorn **dèan t. air** *v* scorn, despise *Also* **tarchais**

tarchaiseach *a* **-siche** contemptuous, scornful

targaid *n* **-e, -ean** *f* target

tàrmachan *n* **-ain, -ain** *m* ptarmigan

tàrmaich *v* originate, derive; breed, propagate

tàrmasach *a* **-aiche** fussy, hard to please

tàrr *v* **-sainn/-adh** flee, take off; be in time for **tàrr às** flee, escape **cha do thàrr sinn an t-aiseag** we didn't make the ferry

tarrag *n* **-aig, -an** *f* nail *Also* **tar(r)aig**

tarraing *v* draw, pull, attract **t. anail** draw breath, breathe **t. dealbh** draw a picture **t. à/às** tease **t. air ais** withdraw **a bheil an tì air t.?** has the tea infused?

tarraing *n* **-ean** *f m* attraction; drawing, drag; mention **thoir t. air** mention, refer to

tarraingeach *a* **-giche** attractive

tarrainn *v See* **tarraing**

tarrang *n* **tàirn(g)e, tàirn(g)ean** *f* nail

tarsaing *adv See* **tarsainn**

tarsainn *adv* across, transversely **t. air** *prep* across, over

tarsannan *n* **-ain, -an** *m* cross-beam, transom

tart *n* **tairt** *m* extreme thirst, parchedness; drought

tartmhor *a* **-oire** *m* thirsty, parched

tasgadh *n* **-aidh** *m* deposit, reserve, hoard

tastan *n* **-ain, -an** *m* shilling *Formerly* **tasdan**

tataidh *v* **-adh** attract

tàth *v* **-adh** join together, cement, weld

tàthag *n* **-aig, -an** *f* pointed remark, dig

tathaich *v* frequent, visit

tàthan *n* **-ain, -an** *m* hyphen

tè *n f* one (*f/female*), woman **tè bheag** a whisky ('*a small one*')

teachd *n m* coming, arrival **t.-a-steach** income, revenue **t.-an-tìr** livelihood, subsistence

teachdaire *n* **-an** *m* messenger, courier

teachdaireachd *n f* message, tidings

teacsa *n* **-ichean** *f m* text

teadaidh *n* **-ean** *m* teddy

teadhair *n* **-dhrach, -dhraichean** *f* tether

teagaisg *v* **-asg** teach, instruct; preach

teagamh *n* **-aimh, -an** *m* doubt **gun t.** without a doubt, undoubtedly, indeed

teagasg *n* **-aisg** *m* teaching, instruction, pedagogy; preaching

teaghlach *n* **-aich, -aichean** *m* family

teagmhach *a* **-aiche** doubtful, dubious

teallach *n* **-aich, -aichean** *m* hearth, fireplace, forge

teampall *n* **-aill, -aill** *m* temple

teanas *n* **-ais** *m* tennis

teanchair *n* -ean *m* pincers, tongs; vice

teanga *n* teanga/-dh, -n/-nnan *f* tongue

teann *a* **teinne** tight, tense **t. air** near to

teann *v* -adh move; commence, begin **t. às an rathad** get out of the way **theann iad ri seinn** they began to sing **t. a-nall** come over here

teannaich *v* -achadh tighten

teanntachd *n* -an *f* strait, difficulty, austerity

teanta *n* -ichean *f m* tent

tèarainte *a* safe, secure

tèarainteachd *n f* safety, security

tearb *v* -adh separate (*eg sheep*), part

tearc *a* **teirce** rare, scarce, few

tèarmann *n* -ainn, -ainn *m* protection, refuge, sanctuary **t. nàdair** nature reserve

teàrn *v* -adh deliver (from), save, rescue *Also* **tèarainn**

teàrr *n* **tearra(dh)** *f* tar

teàrr *v* **tearradh** tar

teas *n m* heat **t.-mheidh** *f* thermometer

teasach *n* -aich, -aichean *f* fever

teasadair *n* -air, -ean *m* heater

teasaich *v* -achadh heat

teasairg *v* -inn save, rescue, deliver (from) *Also* **teasraig**

teatha *n f* tea **copan t.** *m* cup of tea

teich *v* -eadh flee, escape, retreat

teicneòlach *a* -aiche technological

teicneòlas *n* -ais *m* technology **t. fiosrachaidh agus conaltraidh** information and communication technology

teicnigeach *a* -igiche technical

tèid *irr v* go (*See irr v* **rach** *in Grammar*)

tèile *pron* another one (*f/female*)

teileagram *n* -aim, -an *m* telegram

teileasgop *n* -oip, -an *f m* telescope

teine *n* **teintean** *m* fire **na theine** on fire **cuir t. ri** *v* set fire to **t.-aighir/t.-èibhinn** bonfire

teinn *n* -e *f* strait, predicament

teinntean *n* -ein, -ein *m* hearth, fireplace

teip *n* -ichean *f* tape, cassette **t.-chlàradair** *m* tape recorder

teirig *v* -eachdainn/teireachdainn expire, run out

teirinn *v* **teàrnadh** descend

teirm *n* -ichean *f* term *Also* **tearm**

teis-meadhan *n* -ain *m* very centre, epicentre

teist *n* -e, -ean *f* testimony

teisteanas *n* -ais, -an *m* testimony, testimonial, certificate

telebhisean *n* -ein, -an *m* television

teò-chridheach *a* -dhiche affectionate, warm-hearted

teòclaid *n* -ean *f* chocolate

teòma *a* skilful, expert

teòmachd *n f* skill, expertise

teòth *v* -adh warm, heat *Also* **teò**

teòthachd *n f* temperature

teothaich *v* -achadh warm, heat

teth *a* **teotha** hot

teud *n* -a/tèid, -an *m* string (*mus*), chord

tha *irr v* am, is, are; yes (*See verb* **to be** *in Grammar*)

thàinig *irr v* came (*See irr v* **thig** *in Grammar*)

thairis *adv* across, over **a' cur t.** overflowing **a' toirt t.** becoming exhausted

thairis (air) *prep pron* over him

thairis air *prep phr* across, over

thairte *prep pron* over her

thall *adv* over, yonder, on the other side **air a' cheann t.** in the end, ultimately **t. 's a-bhos** here and there **t. thairis** abroad

thalla *v* go!, away!, be off! **t. seo** come here (*Islay*)

thar *prep* (+ *gen*) across, over

tharad(sa) *prep pron* over you (*sg*)

tharaibh(se) *prep pron* over you (*pl & pol*)

tharainn(e) *prep pron* over us

tharam(sa) *prep pron* over me

tharta(san) *prep pron* over them
theab *def v* nearly (did) **t. mi
tuiteam** I almost fell **theabadh a
bhàthadh** he was almost
drowned
theagamh *adv* perhaps
thèid *irr v* (will) go (*See irr v* **rach**
in Grammar)
their *irr v* (will) say (*See irr v*
abair *in Grammar*)
theirig *irr v* go! (*See irr v* **rach** *in
Grammar*)
thig *irr v* (will) come **t. a-steach**
come in **t. orra falbh** they will
have to go
thoir *irr v* give, bestow, take **t.
leat** take away (with you) **t. air**
force, compel **t. an aire** take
care **t. gu buil** effect, implement
t. seachad duais present a prize
t. do chasan leat! clear off! **t. a
thaobh** persuade, beguile **t. am
follais** reveal, make public **t.
breith** judge **t. sùil (air)** look (at)
thu(sa) *pron* you (*sg*)
thubhairt *irr v* said (*See irr v* **abair**
in Grammar)
thuca(san) *prep pron* to them
thug *irr v* gave; brought (*See irr v*
beir *in Grammar*)
thugad(sa) *prep pron* to you (*sg*)
thugaibh(se) *prep pron* to you (*pl
& pol*)
thugainn *def v* come on! let's go!
pl **thugnaibh, thugainnibh**
thugainn(e) *prep pron* to us
thugam(sa) *prep pron* to me
thuice(se) *prep pron* to her
thuige(san) *prep pron* to him
thuige seo to date, until now
thuirt *irr v* said (*See irr v* **abair** *in
Grammar*)
tì *n f* tea **cupa tì** a cup of tea
tiamhaidh *a* -e plaintive,
poignant, melancholy
ticead *n See* **tiogaid**
tìde *n* -ean *f* time **fad na t.** all the
time **ri t./tro thìde** through time,
eventually **uair a thìde** an hour
tha a thìd' agad sgur it's time
you stopped
tìde-mhara *n* -mara, **tìdean-mara**
f tide

tidsear *n* -eir, -an *m* teacher
tig *irr v* come (*See irr v* **thig** *in
Grammar*)
tigear *n* -eir, -an *m* tiger
tigh *n See* **taigh**
tighead *n* -eid *m* thickness
tighearna *n* -n *m* lord **an T.** the
Lord (*God*)
tighearnas *n* -ais *m* lordship
T. nan Eilean the Lordship of
the Isles
tighinn *irr v* coming (*See irr v* **thig**
in Grammar) **Dihaoine seo t.**
this coming Friday
tilg *v* -eil/-eadh throw, cast **thilg
iad air ...** they accused him ...
till *v* -eadh return
tìm *n* -e, **-ean** *f* time
timcheall *adv* around
timcheall *prep* (+ *gen*) round,
around, about **t. an taighe**
around the house **t. air** around,
about
timcheallan *n* -ain, -ain *m*
roundabout
timcheall-ghearradh *n* -aidh *m*
circumcision
tinn *a* -e sick, ill
tinneas *n* -eis, -an *m* illness,
sickness, disease **an t.-busach**
mumps **an t.-mara** seasickness
an t. tuiteamach epilepsy,
dropsy **t. inntinn** mental illness
t. an t-siùcair diabetes
tiodhlac *n* -aic, -an *m* gift,
present, donation **t. Nollaig**
Christmas present
tiodhlacadh *n* -aidh, -aidhean *m*
burial, funeral
tiodhlaic *v* -acadh inter, bury
tiogaid *n* -e, -ean *f* ticket *Also*
tigead, tigeard
tiomnadh *n* -aidh *m* will, bequest,
testament **an Seann T.** the Old
Testament **an T. Nuadh** the New
Testament
tiompan *n* -ain, -ain/-an *m*
cymbal
tiona *n* -ichean *m* tin, can
tionail *v* -al gather, collect,
assemble
tional *n* -ail, -an *m* collection,
assembly

tionndaidh *v* -adh turn

tionnsgal *n* -ail/-an *m* industry; ingenuity, invention

tionnsgalach *a* -aiche industrial; inventive

tìoraidh *exclam* cheerio!

tìorail *a* -e cosy, sheltered, comfortable

tioram *a* -a/tiorma dry

tiormachadh *n* -aidh *m* drying **tha t. math ann** there are good drying conditions

tiormachd *n f* dryness, drought

tiormadair *n* -ean *m* dryer

tiormaich *v* -achadh dry

tiota *n* -n/-idhean *m* a moment, a short while

tiotal *n* -ail, -an *m* title

tiotan *n* -ain, -ain *m* a moment, a short while

tìr *n* -e, -ean *f* land **Tìr nan Òg** the Land of (Eternal) Youth

Tiristeach *n* -tich, -tich *m* someone from Tiree *a* from, or pertaining to, Tiree *Formerly* **Tirisdeach** *Also* **Tiridheach**

tìr-mòr *n m* mainland **air t.** on the mainland

titheach *a* tithiche fond (of) **t. air** keen (on)

tiugainn *def v* come on!, let's go! *pl* **tiugnaibh, tiugainnibh**

tiugh *a* tighe thick, fat, dense

tiùrr(a) *n m* seaware left by tide, mark of sea on shore; confused heap **bha t. phàipearan air a' bhòrd** there was a heap of papers on the table

tlachd *n f* pleasure

tlachdmhor *a* -oire pleasant, pleasing

tlàth *a* tlàithe mild, mellow, soft

toban *n* -ain, -an *m* tuft (*of hair, wool etc*)

tobar *n* -air/tobrach, tobraichean *f m* well, source (*gen sg* **tobrach** *is f*)

tobhaig *v* -eadh tow *Also* **tobh**

tobhta *n* -ichean *f* roofless walls, ruin; thwart (*in boat*)

todha *n* -ichean *m* hoe *Also* **tobha**

todhaig *v* -eadh hoe

todhar *n* -air *m* fertilizer, manure, dung **cuir t. air** *v* fertilize, manure

tofaidh *n* -ean *m* toffee

tog *v* -ail lift, raise, build, construct **thog iad taigh ùr** they built a new house **thogadh i ann an Lios Mòr** she was brought up in Lismore **thog iad orra** they set off **tog às an rathad!** get out of the way! **thog e a' Ghàidhlig ann am Barraigh** he acquired Gaelic in Barra **thog mi ceàrr e** I misunderstood him/it

togair *v* togradh/-t wish, desire **a' dèanamh mar a thogras e** doing as he pleases

togalach *n* -aich, -aichean *m* building

togarrach *a* -aiche keen, willing, enthusiastic

togsaid *n* -ean *f* cask, drum *Also* **tocasaid**

toibheum *n* -eim, -an *m* blasphemy

toidh *n* -ean *m* toy

toigh *a* agreeable, pleasing **is t. leam ...** I like ...

toil *n* -e, -ean *f* will, wish **mas e do thoil e** please, if it is your will

toileach *a* -liche willing, voluntary

toileachadh *n* -aidh *m* pleasure, satisfaction

toileachas *n* -ais *m* pleasure, contentment **t.-inntinn** pleasure, contentment

toilich *v* -leachadh please

toilichte *a* pleased, happy, glad

toil-inntinn *n* -(e), -ean *f* pleasure, contentment, satisfaction

toill *v* -sinn/-tinn deserve, merit; be contained in **cha toill e sa bhaga** it's too big for the bag

toillteanas *n* -ais, -an *m* deserts, merit

tòimhseachan *n* -ain, -ain *m* riddle, puzzle **t.-tarsainn** crossword puzzle

toimhsean *n pl* scales, balances, measures

toinisg *n* -e *f* sense, common sense, wit

toinisgeil *a* -e sensible

toinn *v* -eadh/-eamh twist, twine

toinneamh *n* -eimh *m* twist, twisting

toinnte *a* twisted, complex

tòir *n* -e/tòrach, -ean/-ichean *f* pursuit **an t. air** (+ *gen*) in pursuit of

toir *irr v* give (*See irr v* **thoir** *in Grammar*)

toirm *n* -e, -ean *f* loud murmuring sound, hubbub; hum

toirmeasg *n* -misg *m* prohibition, ban; harum-scarum **'s e t. cianail a th' ann** he's a terrible harum-scarum

toirmisg *v* -measg forbid, prohibit, ban, proscribe

toirmisgte *a* forbidden, prohibited, banned, proscribed

toirsgeir *n* -ean *f* peat iron, peatcutter *Also* **troidhsgeir**

toirt *irr v* giving, bestowing, taking (*See irr v* **thoir** *in Grammar*)

toiseach *n* -sich, -sichean *m* beginning, start, front **an t.** at first **air thoiseach** in front **t. tòiseachaidh** at the very beginning

tòiseachadh *n* -aidh *m* beginning, starting, start

tòisich *v* -seachadh begin, start, commence, initiate **t. air** begin to

toit *n* -e, -ean *f* smoke, vapour

toitean *n* -ein, -ein/-an *m* cigarette

toll *n* tuill, tuill *m* hole, perforation, cavity

toll *v* -adh hole, bore, pierce, perforate

tom *n* tuim, -annan *m* round hillock/knoll

tomadach *a* -aiche bulky, large

tomàto *n* -than *m* tomato

tombaca *n m* tobacco

tomhais *v* -as/-ais measure; guess

tomhas *n* -ais, -an/toimhsean *m* measure, measurement, gauge **t.-teas** thermometer

tòn *n* tòine, -an/tòinean *f* buttocks, bottom

tonn *n* tuinn/tuinne, tuinn/-an *f m* wave (*in sea*)

topag *n* -aig, -an *f* skylark

toradh *n* -aidh, -aidhean *m* produce, fruit(s); result, outcome, consequence **a thoradh sin** because of that

torc *n* tuirce, tuirc *m* boar

torman *n* -ain, -an *m* murmur, hum, rumbling

tòrr *n* torra, torran *m* mound, heap, conical hill; large quantity or number

torrach *a* -aiche fertile, fruitful; pregnant

tòrradh *n* -aidh, -aidhean *m* burial, funeral

tosgaire *n* -an *m* ambassador, envoy

tosgaireachd *n f* embassy

tost *n* -a *m* toast (*bread*)

tost *n m* silence **bha i na t.** she was silent *Formerly* **tosd**

tostair *n* -ean *m* toaster

tràchdas *n* -ais, -ais *m* thesis, treatise

tractar *n* -air, -an *m* tractor

trafaig *n* -e *f* traffic

traidhsagal *n* -ail, -an *m* tricycle

traidiseanta *a* traditional

tràigh *n* -e/tràghad, -ean/tràghannan *f* beach, strand **bha t. mhòr ann an-dè** there was a very low tide yesterday

tràigh *v* tràghadh ebb

tràill *n* -ean *f m* slave; addict; scoundrel **'s e t. a th' ann** he's a rotter/nasty piece of work

tràillealachd *n f* slavery, servitude, servility

tràilleil *a* slavish, servile

traisg *v* trasgadh fast

tràlair *n* -ean *m* trawler

tramasgal *n* -ail *m* trash; (*met*) confused mess

trang *a* trainge busy

trannsa *n* -ichean *f* corridor, passage, lobby, aisle

traogh *v* -adh subside, abate; drain

traon *n* traoin, traoin *m* corncrake

trasg *n* traisg, -an *f* fast **latha traisg** *m* fast day

trasgadh *n* **-aidh** *m* fasting
trasta *a* diagonal
trastan *n* **-ain, -ain** *m* cross-beam, diagonal
tràth *a, adv* **tràithe** early
tràth *n* **-a/tràith, -an** *m* time, season; tense **mu thràth** already **an t. caithte** the past tense **an t. làthaireach** the present tense **an t. teachdail** the future tense
tre *prep* through
treabh *v* **-adh** plough
treabhaiche *n* **-an** *m* ploughman
treal(l)aich *n* **-ean** *f* trash; lumber, bits and pieces **bha t. aig a' choinneimh** there were quite a few at the meeting
trèan(a) *n* **-(a)ichean** *f* train
trèanadh *n* **-aidh** *m* training
trèanaig *v* **-eadh** train
treas *a* third
treibhdhireach *a* **-riche** sincere, upright, honest
treibhdhireas *n* **-eis** *m* sincerity, uprightness, honesty
trèiceil *n m* treacle
treidhe *n* **-achan** *f* tray
trèig *v* **-sinn** forsake, quit, desert
trèilear *n* **-eir, -an** *m* trailer
treis *n* **-ean** *f* a while
treiseag *n* **-an** *f* a short while
treòrachadh *n* **-aidh** *m* guidance, direction, leading
treòraich *v* **-achadh** guide, direct, lead
treubh *n* **-a/trèibh, -an** *f* tribe
treud *n* **-a/trèid, -an** *m* flock, herd
treun *a* **treasa/treise** strong, brave, valiant
trì *n, a* three
triall *v* go, journey, depart
trian *n m* third (*part*)
Trianaid *n f* Trinity
triantan *n* **-ain, -ain/-an** *m* triangle
triath *n* **-a, -an** *m* lord, chief
trì-bhileach *n* **-lich** *m* trefoil
tric *a, adv* **-e** often, frequent
trì-cheàrnach *a* triangular
trì-cheàrnag *n* **-aig, -an** *f* triangle
trìd *prep* (+ *gen*) through, by
trì-deug *n, a* thirteen **trì coin dheug** thirteen dogs

trì-dhualach *a* three-ply
trìd-shoilleir *a* **-e** transparent
trì fichead *n, a* sixty
trì-fillte *a* threefold, triple, treble
trìlleachan *n* **-ain, -ain** *m* oyster-catcher
trioblaid *n* **-e, -ean** *f* trouble, tribulation
trì-rothach *a* three-wheeled
trithead *n* **-eid, -an** *m* thirty
trìtheamh *a* third
triubhas *n* **-ais, -an** *m* trews, trousers
triùir *n f m* three (people) **t. ghillean** three boys
triuthach *n* **-aich** *f* **an t.** whooping cough
tro *prep* through
trobhad *def v* come, come on, come here
tròcair *n* **-e, -ean** *f* mercy
tròcaireach *a* **-riche** merciful
trod *n* **troid, troid/-an** *f m* quarrel; reproof
trod *aug prep* through your (*sg*)
troich *n* **-e, -ean** *f m* dwarf
troid *v* **trod** quarrel; scold
troigh *n* **-e, -ean** *f* foot (*on body & in length*)
troimh *prep* See **tro**
troimh-a-chèile *adv* mixed-up, confused
troimhe(san) *prep pron* through him/it
troimhpe(se) *prep pron* through her/it
trom *a* **truime** heavy, onerous; pregnant
trom *aug prep* through my; through their
tromalach *n* **-aich** *f* preponderance, majority
tromb *n* **-a, -an** *f* jew's harp
trombaid *n* **-e, -ean** *f* trumpet
tromhad(sa) *prep pron* through you (*sg*)
tromhaibh(se) *prep pron* through you (*pl & pol*)
tromhainn(e) *prep pron* through us
tromham(sa) *prep pron* through me
tromhpa(san) *prep pron* through them

trom-inntinneach *a* **-niche** depressed, melancholy

trom-laighe *n* **-an** *f m* nightmare

trom-neul *n* **-neoil, -neoil/-an** *m* coma

tron *aug prep* through the; through their

tror *aug prep* through our; through your

trosg *n* **truisg, truisg** *m* large cod

trotan *n* **-ain** *m* trot, trotting **dèan t.** *v* trot

truacanta *a* compassionate, merciful, pitying

truacantas *n* **-ais** *m* pity, compassion

truagh *a* **-aighe** miserable, wretched, pitiful, poor (*unfortunate*)

truaghag *n* **-aig, -an** *f* wretch (*female*), poor soul **A thruaghag bhochd!** You poor soul!

truaghan *n* **-ain, -ain/-an** *m* wretch (*male*), poor soul

truaighe *n* **-an** *f* misery, woe **mo thruaighe!** Oh dear!, Alas!

truaill *n* **-e, -ean** *f* scabbard

truaill *v* **-eadh** pollute, contaminate, defile; corrupt

truailleadh *n* **-lidh** *m* pollution, contamination; corruption

truaillte *a* polluted, contaminated, defiled; corrupt

truas *n* **truais** *m* pity, compassion, sympathy **gabh t. ri** *v* pity **tha t. agam rithe** I am sorry for her

truasail *a* **-e** compassionate, sympathetic

truileis *n* *f* trash, junk

truinnsear *n* **-eir, -an** *m* plate

trus *v* **-adh** gather, collect

trusgan *n* **-ain, -an** *m* garb, clothes, clothing, apparel, garment

trustar *n* **-air, -airean** *m* rotter, scoundrel

tu(sa) *pron* you

tuagh *n* **tuaigh(e), -an** *f* axe

tuaileas *n* **-eis, -an** *m* scandal, slander

tuaileasach *a* **-aiche** defamatory, slanderous, scurrilous

tuaineal *n* **-eil** *m* dizziness, giddiness

tuainealach *a* **-aiche** dizzy, giddy

tuainealaich *n* **-e** *f* dizziness, giddiness

tuaiream *n* **-eim, -an** *f* guess, conjecture **air thuaiream** at random **mu thuaiream** about

tuairisgeul *n* **-eil, -an** *m* description, report

tuairisgeulach *a* **-aiche** descriptive

tuairmeas *n* **-eis, -an** *m* guess, conjecture

tuairmse *n* **-an** *f* guess, estimate, conjecture **dèan t.** *v* guess

tuam *n* **tuaim, -an** *m* tomb

tuar *n* **tuair, -an** *m* hue, complexion

tuarastal *n* **-ail, -ail/-an** *f* wages, salary, earnings *Formerly* **tuarasdal**

tuasaid *n* **-e, -ean** *f* quarrel, squabble, fight

tuath *n* **-a** *f* tenantry, country people **air an t.** in the countryside

tuath *n, a* north, northern **t. air ...** north of ... **mu thuath** in the north, northwards **an ceann a tuath** the north end

tuathal *a* **-aile** anti-clockwise; confused

tuathanach *n* **-aich, -aich** *m* farmer

tuathanachas *n* **-ais** *m* agriculture, farming

tuathanas *n* **-ais, -an** *m* farm

tuba *n* **-nnan** *f m* tub

tubaist *n* **-e, -ean** *f* accident, mishap

tubhailte *n* **-an** *f* towel; tablecloth **t.-shoithichean** dish towel **t.-bùird** tablecloth

tùchadh *n* **-aidh** *m* hoarseness **tha an t. air** he is hoarse

tùchan *n* **-ain** *m* hoarseness; cooing

tùchanach *a* **-aiche** hoarse

tud *interj* tut!

tug *irr v* gave, brought (*See irr v* **thoir** *in Grammar*)

tugainn *def v* come, come on *pl* **tiugainnibh**

tugh *v* **-adh** thatch

tughadair *n* -ean *m* thatcher
tughadh *n* -aidh *m* thatch, thatching
tuig *v* -sinn understand,
   comprehend
tuigse *n* *f* understanding, insight
tuigseach *a* -siche understanding,
   perceptive
tuil *n* -e, -ean/-tean *f* flood,
   deluge, downpour
tuilleadh *adv* more, any more;
   again **a thuilleadh air** in addition
   to, as well as
tuilleadh *n* *m* more, additional
   quantity/number **t. 's a' chòir**
   too much
tuireadh *n* -ridh, -ridhean *m*
   lament, mourning
tui(r)neap *n* -an *m* turnip
tuirt *irr v* said (*See irr v* **abair** *in
   Grammar*)
tùis *n* -e, -ean *f* incense
tuiseal *n* -eil, -an *m* case (*gram*)
   an t. ainmneach the nominative
   case **an t. ginideach** the genitive
   case **an t. tabhartach** the dative
   case
tuisleadh *n* -lidh, -lidhean *m*
   stumbling, stumble, fall; (*met*)
   mistake, lapse
tuislich *v* -leachadh stumble, fall;
   (*met*) make a mistake, lapse
tuit *v* -eam fall
tuiteamach *a* -aiche fortuitous,
   contingent; epileptic
tuiteamas *n* -ais, -an *m* chance
tulach *n* -aich, -aichean *m*
   hillock, knoll
tulg *v* -adh rock (to and fro)
tulgach *a* -aiche rocking
tum *v* -adh dip, immerse, plunge
tunail *n* -ean *f m* tunnel
tunna *n* -chan *m* ton
tunnag *n* -aig, -an *f* duck
tùr *n* tùir, tùir *m* sense **duine gun
   t.** *a* reckless man
tùr *n* tùir, tùir *m* tower
tur *a* complete, whole, absolute
   gu t. entirely, completely,
   absolutely
turadh *n* -aidh *m* dry weather, dry
   spell **tha t. ann** it's dry **tha i air t.
   a dhèanamh** the rain has
   stopped

turaid *n* -e, -ean *f* turret
tùrail *a* -e sensible
turas *n* -ais, **tursan/-an** *m*
   journey, trip; time, occasion **t.
   malairt** trade mission **aon t.**
   once **t. eile** another time
turasachd *n* *f* tourism
Turcach *n* -aich, -aich *m* Turk
   a Turkish
tursa *n* -chan *m* standing stone
   Tursachan Chalanais the
   Callanish Stones
tùrsach *a* -aiche sad, sorrowful
tùs *n* tùis *m* start, beginning,
   origin **(bh)o thùs** from the
   beginning, originally
tùsaire *n* -an *m* pioneer,
   innovator
tùsanach *n* -aich *m* aborigine
tuthag *n* -aig, -an *f* patch

U

uabhar *n* -air *m* pride,
   haughtiness
uabhas *n* -ais *m* a lot; terror,
   dread, horror **bha an t-uabhas
   dhaoine ann** there were an
   awful lot of people there
uabhasach *a* -aiche terrible,
   dreadful *adv* very, terribly
   u. math very/terribly good
uachdaran *n* -ain, -ain *m*
   landlord, laird; governor,
   superior
uachdranachd *n* *f* landlordism;
   sovereignty, superiority,
   presidency
uachdranas *n* -ais *m* sovereignty,
   jurisdiction
uaibh(se) *prep pron* from you (*pl
   & pol*)
uaibhreach *a* -riche proud,
   haughty
uaibhreas *n* -eis *m* pride,
   haughtiness
uaigh *n* -e/uaghach, -ean *f* grave,
   tomb
uaigneach *a* -niche lonely,
   solitary, remote, secret
uaigneas *n* -eis *m* loneliness,
   solitude, secrecy, privacy
uaill *n* -e *f* pride, vanity; dignity

uaim *n* **-e** *f* alliteration
uaimh *n* **-e/uamha, -ean/uamhan** *f*
cave
uaine *a* green
uainn(e) *prep pron* from us
uaipe(se) *prep pron* from her
uair *n* **uarach, -ean** *f* hour, time
u. an uaireadair an hour **tha e u.**
it is one o'clock **u. is u.** time
and time again, repeatedly
u. dhan robh saoghal once upon
a time
uaireadair *n* **-ean** *m* watch
u.-grèine sundial
uaireannan *adv* sometimes, at
times
uaireigin *adv* sometime
uaisle *n f* nobility (*of nature*)
uaithe(san) *prep pron* from him
uallach *n* **-aich, -aichean** *m*
concern, worry, burden;
responsibility (*duty*) **na gabh u.**
don't be concerned
uàlras *n* **-ais, -asan** *m* walrus
uam(sa) *prep pron* from me
uamh *n* *See* **uaimh**
uamhann *n* **-ainn** *m* dread, terror,
horror
uamhas *n* *See* **uabhas**
uamhasach *a* *See* **uabhasach**
uan *n* **uain, uain** *m* lamb
uanfheòil *n* **-òla** *f* lamb (*meat*)
uapa(san) *prep pron* from them
uasal *a* **uaisle** noble
uasal *n* **-ail, uaislean** *m*
nobleman, gentleman **na**
h-uaislean the nobility,
aristocracy
uat(sa) *prep pron* from you (*sg*)
ubhal *n* **-ail, ùbhlan** *f m* apple
ubhalghort *n* **-oirt, -an** *m* orchard
ucas *n* **ucais, ucais** *m* coalfish
uchd *n* **-a, -an** *m* chest, breast,
bosom; brow of ... **ri u. bàis** at
the point of death **u.-leanabh** *m*
adopted child
uchd-mhacachd *n f* adoption
uchd-mhacaich *v* **-achadh** adopt
ud *dem a* that, yon, yonder
ud *exclam* away!, get away!
(*dismissive*)
udalan *n* **-ain** *m* swivel **air u.**
moving to and fro

ùdlaidh *a* **-e** gloomy
uèir *n* **-ichean** *f* wire **u.-bhiorach**
barbed wire
ugan *n* **-ain, -nan** *m* upper breast
ugh *m* **uighe, uighean** *m* egg
ughach *m* **-aiche** oval
ughagan *n* **-ain** *m* custard
ùghdar *n* **-air, -an** *m* author
ùghdarras *n* **-ais, -an/-ais** *m*
authority, mandate **u. ionadail**
local authority
ùghdarrasail *a* **-e** authoritative
Uibhisteach *n* **-tich, -tich** *m*
someone from Uist *a* from, or
pertaining to, Uist
ùidh *n* **-e, -ean** *f* interest, desire
uidh *n* **-e** *f* degree, gradation **u.**
air n-u. bit by bit, gradually
uidheam *n* **-eim, -an** *f* machine,
utensil; gear, apparatus,
equipment
uidheamachd *n* **-an** *f* equipment,
apparatus
uidheamaich *v* **-achadh** equip; get
ready
uidheamaichte *a* equipped,
geared up
ùidheil *a* **-e** interesting, interested
uile *a* every, each, all **u.-gu-lèir**
adv all, altogether, completely **a**
h-uile duine everyone **na h-eòin**
uile all the birds
uilebheist *n* **-ean** *f m* monster
uile-chumhachdach *a* **-aiche** all-
powerful, almighty, omnipotent
uilinn *n* **uilinn/uilne, uilnean** *f*
elbow *Also* **uileann**
uill *interj* well, indeed
uime(san) *prep pron* about him
uime sin *adv* therefore, thereupon
uimhir *n f* number, quantity;
certain amount, measure
uimpe(se) *prep pron* about her
ùine *n* **ùinichean/-achan** *f* time
(*span of*), period **anns an u.**
fhada in the long term
uinneag *n* **-eige, -an** *f* window
uinnean *n* **-ein, -an** *m* onion
uinnseann *n* **-sinn, -an** *m* ash tree
ùir *n* **-e/ùrach** *f* soil, earth
uircean *n* **-ein, -an** *m* piglet
uiread *n f* a certain amount,
measure, so much, as much

uireasbhach *a* **-aiche** suffering discomfort, sore; defective, inadequate

uireasbhaidh *n* **-ean** *f* deficiency, want, need, lack, inadequacy

uirsgeul *n* **-eil, -an** *f m* fable, legend; novel

uirsgeulach *a* **-aiche** fabulous, legendary

uiseag *n* **-eig, -an** *f* lark, skylark

uisge *n* **-achan/-gichean** *m* water; rain **a bheil an t-u. ann?** is it raining?

uisge-beatha *n m* whisky

uisgich *v* **-geachadh** water, irrigate

ulaidh *n* **-e, -ean** *f* treasure **m' u.** my dear, my precious one

ulbhag *n* **-aig, -an** *f* boulder

ulfhart *n* **-airt** *m* howl (*as dog*)

ullachadh *n* **-aidh** *m* preparation

ullaich *v* **-achadh** prepare

ullamh *a* ready, prepared; finished

ultach *n* **-aich, -aichean** *m* armful, lapful, load

umad(sa) *prep pron* about you (*sg*)

umaibh(se) *prep pron* about you (*pl & pol*)

ùmaidh *n* **-e, -ean** *f* blockhead, dolt, boor

umainn(e) *prep pron* about us

umam(sa) *prep pron* about me

umha *n m* brass; bronze **Linn an U.** the Bronze Age

umhail *a* **-e** obedient; humble

ùmhlachd *n f* obedience; humility; obeisance, homage **dèan u.** *v* pay homage

ùmhlaich *v* **-achadh** (*intrans*) obey, submit; (*trans*) humble, subdue

umpa(san) *prep pron* about them

uncail *n* **-ean** *m* uncle

ung *v* **-achadh/-adh** anoint

ungadh *n* **-aidh** *f* anointing, unction, ointment

Ungaireach *n* **-rich** *m* Hungarian *a* Hungarian

unnsa *n* **-chan/-idhean** *m* ounce

ùpag *n* **-aig, -an** *f* push, elbowing

ùpraid *n* **-e, -ean** *f* uproar, confusion, bustle

ùr *a* **ùire** new, fresh **a bheil càil às ùr?** anything fresh? **tòisich às ùr** *v* start again **talc-ùr** brand new

ur *poss pron* your (*pl & pol*)

ùrachadh *n* **-aidh** *m* renewal, refreshment; modernization

ùraich *v* **ùrachadh** renew, refresh; modernize

urchair *n* **-e/urchrach, -ean** *f* bullet, shot, report of gun

urchasg *n* **-aisg, -an** *m* antibiotic, antidote

ùr-fhàs *n* **-ais** *m* bloom, fresh growth

ùr-fhàs *v* **ùr-fhàs** grow afresh

ùr-ghnàthach *a* **-aiche** innovative

ùr-ghnàthaich *v* **-achadh** innovate

ùrlar *n* **-air, -an** *m* floor

ùrnaigh *n* **-ean** *m* prayer **Ù. an Tighearna** the Lord's Prayer **dèan ù.** *v* pray *Also vn* **ag ù.**

urra *n* **-cha(n)** *f* person **not an u.** a pound each **tha sin an u. riut fhèin** that is up to you **na h-urracha mòra** those and such as those, the high heid yins **gun u.** anonymous

urrainn *n* ability **is u. dhomh** I can

urram *n* **-aim** *m* honour, respect, reverence **cuir u. air** *v* honour

urramach *a* **-aiche** honourable, revered, venerable **an t-Urr** the Rev

urras *n* **-ais, -an** *m* surety, security, bond; trust **cha rachainn an u.** *v* I wouldn't bet against it, I bet

urrasair *n* **-ean** *m* trustee; sponsor

ursainn *n* **-ean** *f* doorpost, jamb

ùruisg *n* **-e, -ean** *m* water spirit; diviner

usgar *n* **-air/-grach, -an/ usgraichean** *m* bracelet, necklace, ornament, jewel

uspag *n* **-aig, -an** *f* light gust

ùth *n* **-a, -an/-annan** *m* udder

ùtraid *n* **-e, -ean** *f* access road, track

English–Gaelic dictionary

A

abandon *v* trèig, fàg

abate *v* lùghdaich, sìolaidh, lasaich

abbey *n* abaid *f*

abbot *n* aba *m*

abbreviation *n* giorrachadh *m*

abdicate *v* leig dheth/dhith *etc*, dìobair

abdomen *n* brù *f*, balg *m*

abduct *v* goid air falbh

abhor *v* she abhors it is lugha oirre e/tha dubh-ghràin aice air

abhorrent *a* gràineil, sgreamhail

abide *v* fuirich; (*tolerate*) fuiling

ability *n* comas *m*

abject *a* truagh, dìblidh

able *a* comasach **are you a. to ...?** an urrainn dhut ...? an tèid agad air ...?

abnormal *a* mì-nàdarra, neo-àbhaisteach, às a' chumantas, annasach

abnormality *n* mì-ghnàthas *m*, meang *f*

aboard *adv* air bòrd

abolish *v* cuir às (do)

abolition *n* cur às (do) *m*

aborigine *n* tùsanach *m*

abortion *n* casg-breith *m*

about *prep* mu, mu dheidhinn (+ *gen*), mu thimcheall (+ *gen*) mun cuairt air, timcheall air *adv* timcheall, mun cuairt **a. to** gus

above *prep* os cionn (+ *gen*) **a. all** gu seachd àraidh *adv* shuas, gu h-àrd

abrasive *a* sgrìobach; (*nature*) ceacharra, amh

abreast *adv* gualainn ri gualainn

abroad *adv* thall thairis **going a.** a' dol a-null thairis

abrupt *a* cas, aithghearr

abscess *n* neasgaid *f*

absence *n* neo-làthaireachd *f* **in the a. of** às aonais (+ *gen*)

absent *a* neo-làthaireach, nach eil an làthair

absolute *a* làn- (*precedes & len n*), iomlan

absolutely *adv* gu tur, gu h-iomlan

absolve *v* math, saor (o)

absorb *v* sù(i)gh, deothail, gabh a-steach

abstain (from) *v* seachain; (*eg drink*) na gabh

abstemious *a* stuama

abstinence *n* stuamachd *f*, seachnadh *m*

abstract *a* eas-chruthach

absurd *a* gun toinisg/chiall

abundance *n* pailteas *m*, (*in numbers*) lìonmhorachd *f*

abundant *a* pailt, lìonmhor

abuse *n* mì-bhuileachadh *m*, ana-caitheamh *f m*; (*phys*) droch dhìol *f*, (*verbal*) càineadh *m*, droch bheul *m* *v* mì-bhuilich; (*phys*) dèan droch dhìol air; (*verbally*) càin, thoir droch bheul do

abysmal *a* sgriosail, muladach

academic *a* sgoilearach

academy *n* acadamaidh *f*, àrd-sgoil *f*

accelerate *v* luathaich, greas

accent *n* (*voice*) blas *m*; (*stress*) buille *f*; (*speech mark*) stràc *f m*

accept *v* gabh ri

acceptable *a* iomchaidh, furasta gabhail ris

access *n* (*phys*) rathad *m*, slighe *f*; (*opportunity*) cothrom (air) *m* *v* ruig air

accessible *a* ruigsinneach, so-ruigsinn, fosgailte

accident *n* tubaist *f*, sgiorradh *m*; (*chance*) tuiteamas *m*

accidental *a* tuiteamach

accidentally *adv* gun fhiosta

accommodate *v* thoir àite-fuirich do; (*hold*) gabh

accommodation *n* àite-fuirich *m*, rùm *m*; (*abstr*) còrdadh *m*

accompany *v* rach còmhla ri, còmhdhalaich; (*mus*) thoir taic do

accompanying *a* an cois (+ *gen*) **a. the letter** an cois na litreach

accomplish *v* coilean, thoir gu buil

accomplished *a* coileanta, deas

accord *n* aonta *m*, co-chòrdadh *m* **in a. with** a rèir (+ *gen*)

accordingly *adv* mar sin, uime sin

according to *prep phr* a rèir (+ *gen*)

accordion *n* bogsa(-ciùil) *m*

account *n* iomradh *m*; (*fin*) cunntas *f m*

accountable *a* cunntachail

accountant *n* cunntasair *m*, neach-cunntais *f m*

accumulate *v* cruinnich

accurate *a* neo-mhearachdach, ceart

accusation *n* casaid *f*

accuse *v* tog casaid an aghaidh, cuir às leth, fàg air

accused *a* fo chasaid

accustomed *a* gnàthach, àbhaisteach **a. to** cleachdte ri

ace *n* an t-aon *m* *a* (*colloq*) sgoinneil

ache *n* cràdh *m*, goirteas *m*, pian *f v* **it aches** tha cràdh ann **my back aches** tha cràdh nam dhruim

achieve *v* coilean, thoir gu buil

achievement *n* euchd *m*

acid *n* searbhag *f* **a. rain** uisge-searbhaig *m*, uisge searbhagach *m* *a* searbh, geur

acknowledge *v* aithnich; (*admit*) aidich, gabh ri

acknowledgement *n* aithneachadh *m*; (*admission*) aideachadh *m*; (*reply*) freagairt *f*, fios-freagairt *m*

acquaint *v* cuir eòlas air, thoir eòlas do

acquainted *a* eòlach **a. with** eòlach air

acquire *v* faigh, coisinn

acre *n* acair(e) *f m*

across *adv* tarsainn, thairis, a-null *prep* tarsainn air, thairis air, thar (+ *gen*)

act *n* gnìomh *m*; (*legal*) achd *f*; (*in play*) earrann *f v* obraich, dèan gnìomh; (*conduct oneself*) giùlain thu fhèin *etc*; (*in a play*) cluich

action *n* gnìomh *m*; (*legal*) cùis-lagha *f* **a. plan** plana-gnìomha *m*

active *a* gnìomhach, dèanadach; (*gram*) spreigeach

activity *n* gnìomhachd *f*, obair *f*; (*pastime*) cur-seachad *m*

actor *n* cleasaiche *m*, actair *m*

actress *n* bana-chleasaiche *f*, ban-actair *f*

actual *a* dearbh, fìor (*both precede & lenite n*)

acute *a* geur; (*intense*) dian **a. accent** stràc gheur *f*

adapt *v* atharraich, ceartaich, dèan freagarrach **a. to** fàs suas ri

add *v* cuir ri, meudaich

adder *n* nathair(-nimhe) *f*

addict *n* tràill *f*

addicted *a* (**to**) fo smachd, na t(h)ràill do *etc*

addiction *n* tràilleachd *f*

addition *n* meudachadh *m*; (*sum*) cur-ris *m* **in a. to** a bharrachd/thuilleadh air

additional *a* a bharrachd, a thuilleadh

address *n* seòladh *m*; (*talk*) òraid *f v* cuir seòladh air; (*talk*) dèan òraid, labhair ri; (*tackle*) cuir aghaidh air

adept *a* sgileil, ealanta, teòma

adequate *a* gu leòr, iomchaidh

adhesive *n* tàthair *m* *a* leanailteach **a. tape** teip-tàthaidh *f*

adjacent (**to**) *a* faisg (air), dlùth (do/ri), ri taobh (+ *gen*)

adjective *n* buadhair *m*

adjourn *v* cuir dàil an, sgaoil, sguir de

adjust *v* ceartaich, rèitich, atharraich

administration *n* rianachd *f* **this A.** an Riaghaltas seo

administrator *n* rianadair *m*, rianaire *m*, neach-riaghlaidh *m*

admirable *a* ionmholta

admiration *n* meas *m*, sùim *f*

admire *v* saoil mòran de **I a. her** tha mi saoilsinn mòran dhith **I a. them** tha meas agam orra

admission *n* leigeil a-steach *m*; (*confession*) aideachadh *m*

admit *v* leig a-steach; (*confess*) aidich

adolescent *n* òigear *m*

adopt *v* uchd-mhacaich; (*policy*) gabh ri

adoption *n* uchd-mhacachd *f*; (*policy*) gabhail ri *m*

adore *v* bi fo throm-ghaol; (*relig*) dèan adhradh do **she adored him** bha gaol a cridhe aice air

adult *n*, *a* inbheach *m*

adultery *n* adhaltranas *m* **commit a.** dèan adhaltranas

advance *n* dol air adhart *m*, ceum air thoiseach *m*; (*of money*) eàrlas *m* *v* rach air adhart; (*rank*) àrdaich; (*money*) thoir eàrlas

advanced *a* adhartach

advantage *n* buannachd *f* **she took a. of me** ghabh i brath orm

advantageous *a* buannachdail

adventure *n* dàn'-thuras *m*

adventurous *a* dàna

adverb *n* co-ghnìomhair *m*

adverse *a* mì-fhàbharach, calltach

adversity *n* cruaidh-chàs *m*, teinn *f*

advertise *v* cuir sanas, sanasaich

advertisement *n* sanas *m*, sanas-reic *m*

advice *n* comhairle *f*

advise *v* comhairlich, earalaich **be advised** gabh comhairle

adviser *n* comhairleach *m*, neach-comhairleachaidh *m*

advocate *n* neach-tagraidh *m* *v* mol

aesthetic *a* tarraingeach, maiseach

affable *a* aoigheil, ceanalta

affair *n* gnothach *m*, cùis *f* **he had an a.** bha e a' falbh le tèile

affect *v* thoir buaidh air, drùidh air; (*pretend*) leig air/oirre *etc*

affection *n* gaol *m*, spèis *f*

affectionate *a* gaolach, teò-chridheach

affirm *v* dearbh, daingnich

affliction *n* doilgheas *m*, àmhghar *f m*

affluent *a* beairteach, saidhbhir

afford *v* ruig air; (*provide*) builich **I can't a. the time** chan urrainn dhomh ùine a chosg air

afloat *adv* air bhog, air flod

afraid *a* fo eagal, eagalach

African *n*, *a* Afraganach *m*, (*female*) ban-Afraganach *f*

after *prep* (+ *gen*) an dèidh, às dèidh *adv* an dèidh làimhe **a. all** an dèidh a h-uile rud/càil

afternoon *n* feasgar *m* **in the a.** feasgar

afterwards *adv* an dèidh sin

again *adv* a-rithist

against *prep* an aghaidh (+ *gen*)

age *n* aois *f*; (*period*) linn *f m* **it took ages** thug e ùine chianail *v* fàs sean/aosta

aged *a* sean, aosta

agency *n* (*body*) buidheann *f m*

agenda *n* clàr-gnothaich *m*

agent *n* àidseant *m*, neach-ionaid *m*; (*means*) dòigh *f*

aggravate *v* dèan nas miosa

aggregate *n* iomlan *m* *v* cuir còmhla

aggression *n* ionnsaigh *f m*

aggressive *a* ionnsaigheach

agile *a* sùbailte, subailte

agitate *v* cuir troimh-a-chèile, luasganaich; (*polit*) piobraich

ago *adv* o chionn; ... air ais **five years ago** o chionn c(h)òig bliadhna **long ago** o chionn f(h)ada **a short time ago** o chionn ghoirid

agony *n* dòrainn *f*

agree *v* aontaich, còrd, rach le

agreeable *a* taitneach, ciatach

agreement *n* aonta *m*, còrdadh *m*, cùmhnant *m*

agriculture *n* àiteachas *m*

aground *adv* air tìr

ahead *adv* air adhart **a. of** *prep phr* air thoiseach air

aid *n* cobhair *f*, cuideachadh *m*, còmhnadh *m* *v* cuidich, dèan cobhair air **First Aid** Ciad Fhuasgladh *m*

aim *n* cuimse *f*; (*intention*) amas *m*, rùn *m* *v* cuimsich (+ air); (*intend*) amais

air *n* àile *m*, èadhar *f*; (*breath of*) deò *f*; (*mus*) fonn *m* *v* leig an t-àile gu; (*opinion*) cuir an cèill

airline *n* companaidh phlèanaichean *f m*

airmail *n* post-adhair *m*
airport *n* port-adhair *m*
aisle *n* trannsa *f*
ajar *adv* leth-fhosgailte
alarm *n* rabhadh *m* **a. clock** cloc-
   rabhaidh *m*
alarming *a* eagalach, draghail
alas *exclam* Och!, Mo chreach!,
   Mo thruaighe!
alcohol *n* alcol *m*, deoch-làidir *f*
alcoholic *n* alcolach *m* *a*
   alcolach
ale *n* leann *m*
alert *a* furachail, forail, deas *v*
   (to) cuir na f(h)aireachadh (mu)
alien *n* coigreach *m*, neach-
   fuadain *m* *a* coimheach
alienate *v* gràinnich
alight *a* na t(h)eine
alike *adv* co-ionann, coltach ri
   chèile
alive *a* beò
all *a* uile, iomlan, gu h-iomlan,
   gu lèir
allegation *n* cur às leth *m* *a*
   serious a. casaid chudromach *f*
allege *v* cuir às leth, fàg air
alleviate *v* aotromaich, lùghdaich
alliance *n* caidreachas *m*, co-
   chòrdadh *m*
allocate *v* suidhich, sònraich;
   (*distribute*) riaraich
allow *v* leig le, ceadaich
allowance *n* cuibhreann *f m*
allude (to) *v* thoir tarraing/
   iomradh (air)
ally *n* caraid *m*, caidreabhach *m*;
   (*mil*) co-chòmhragaiche *m*
almost *adv* gu bhith, an ìre
   mhath, gu ìre bhig, cha mhòr
   nach, theab **it is a. finished** tha e
   gu bhith ullamh, tha e an ìre
   mhath ullamh, cha mhòr nach
   eil e ullamh **I a. fell** cha mhòr
   nach do thuit mi, theab mi
   tuiteam
alone *a* na (h-)aonar, leis/leatha
   fhèin *etc*
along (*with*) *adv* còmhla ri, cuide
   ri, maille ri, le, an cois (+ *gen*)
aloud *adv* gu h-àrd-ghuthach
   read a. leugh a-mach
alphabet *n* aibidil *f*

alphabetical *a* a rèir na h-aibideil
   in a. order an òrdugh na
   h-aibideil
already *adv* mar thà, mu thràth,
   cheana
also *adv* cuideachd, mar an ceudna
alter *v* atharraich; (*intrans*)
   caochail
alteration *n* atharrachadh *m*
alternate *a* mu seach
alternative *n* roghainn eile *f*
   a eile, eadar-roghnach
alternatively *adv* air an làimh eile
although *conj* ged; (*before a*) ge
altitude *n* àirde *f*
altogether *adv* gu lèir, uile-gu-lèir,
   gu h-iomlan, gu tur
always *adv* an còmhnaidh,
   daonnan
am *v* tha **am not** chan eil (*See
   verb* **to be** *in Grammar*)
amalgamate *v* cuir ri chèile,
   amalaich, measgaich; (*intrans*)
   rach còmhla
amateur *n* neo-dhreuchdair *m*
   a neo-dhreuchdail
amaze *v* cuir iongnadh air
amazement *n* iongantas *m*,
   iongnadh *m*
amazing *a* iongantach **amazingly
   good** iongantach fhèin math
ambassador *n* tosgaire *m*
ambiguous *a* dà-sheaghach
ambition *n* glòir-mhiann *f m*,
   miann-adhartais *f m* **I have an
   a. to ...** tha miann agam ...
ambitious *a* glòir-mhiannach,
   miannach air adhartas
ambulance *n* carbad-eiridinn *m*,
   ambaileans *f*
ambush *n* feall-fhalach *m*
   v dèan feall-fhalach
amenable *a* fosgailte (ri, do)
amend *v* atharraich, leasaich
amendment *n* atharrachadh *m*,
   leasachadh *m*
amenity *n* goireas *m*
American *n, a* Ameireaganach *m*,
   (*female*) ban-Ameireaganach *f*
amiable *a* càirdeil, bàidheil,
   ceanalta
amicable *a* càirdeil, suairce,
   geanail

amid(st) *prep* am measg, am meadhan (*both* + *gen*)
amiss *adv* gu h-olc, ceàrr
ammunition *n* connadh làmhaich *m*; (*met*) cothrom-losgaidh *m*
among(st) *prep* am measg, air feadh (*both* + *gen*)
amount *n* meud *m*, uimhir *f*; (*money*) sùim *f*
ample *a* pailt; (*in size etc*) mòr, tomadach
amplify *v* meudaich, leudaich air
amputate *v* geàrr dheth *etc*, sgath
amuse *v* toilich, thoir gàire air
amusing *a* èibhinn, ait
anaesthetic *n* an-fhaireachair *m*
analyze *v* mion-sgrùd, sgrùd
analysis *n* mion-sgrùdadh *m*, sgrùdadh *m*, anailis *f*
anarchy *n* ain-riaghailt *f*, ceannairc *f*
anatomy *n* (*body*) bodhaig *f*; (*science*) eòlas bodhaig *m*, corp-eòlas *m*
ancestor *n* sinnsear *m*
anchor *n* acair(e) *f m* **at a.** air (an) acair(e) *v* acraich
anchorage *n* acarsaid *f*
ancient *a* àrsaidh
and *conj* agus, is, 's
anecdote *n* naidheachd *f*, sgeula *f*
angel *n* aingeal *m*
anger *n* fearg *f*, corraich *f* *v* cuir fearg air
angle *n* uilinn *f*, ceàrn *f m*
angry *a* feargach **he was a.** bha an fhearg air
anguish *n* àmhghar *f m*, dòrainn *f*
animal *n* ainmhidh *m*, beathach *m*
animated *a* beothail, meanmnach
animosity *n* gamhlas *m*, mì-rùn *m*
ankle *n* adhbrann *f m*
annihilate *v* sgrios, cuir às do
anniversary *n* ceann-bliadhna *m*, cuimhneachan bliadhnail *m*
announce *v* ainmich, cuir an cèill, leig fhaicinn
announcement *n* teachdaireachd *f*, fios *m*
annoy *v* cuir dragh air, leamhaich
annoyance *n* dragh *m*, buaireas *m*

annoyed *a* diombach, mì-thoilichte
annoying *a* leamh, buaireanta
annual *a* bliadhnail **a. report** aithisg bhliadhnail *f* **A. General Meeting** Coinneamh Bhliadhnail *f*
annually *adv* gach bliadhna
anonymous *a* gun ainm, gun urra(inn)
another *pron* neach/tè eile *a* eile **one a.** a chèile
answer *n* freagairt *f* *v* freagair, thoir freagairt (do)
ant *n* seangan *m*
antagonize *v* dèan nàmhaid de
anthem *n* laoidh *f m* **national a.** laoidh nàiseanta/na rìoghachd
antibiotic *n* antibiotaig *f*
anticipate *v* sùilich; (*prepare for*) deasaich airson
anti-clockwise *a* tuathal
antidote *n* urchasg *m*
antipathy *n* fuath *m*
antique *n* seann rud *m* *a* àrsaidh
antler *n* cabar (fèidh) *m*
anxiety *n* dragh *m*, iomagain *f*, imcheist *f*
anxious *a* draghail, iomagaineach, fo imcheist
any *a* sam bith, air bith; (*pron*) aon/fear/tè sam bith, aon, gin **any at all** gin idir **any other business** gnothach sam bith eile
anyone *n* neach/duine sam bith *m*
anything *n* dad/sìon/rud/nì (sam bith) *m*, càil (sam bith) *f*
anywhere *adv* àite sam bith
apart *adv* air leth; (*distance, motion*) (bh)o chèile
apartment *n* (*suite*) àros *m*; (*room*) seòmar *m*
apathy *n* cion ùidh *m*
ape *n* apa *f*
apologize *v* dèan leisgeul, iarr do/a *etc* leisgeul a ghabhail
apology *n* leisgeul *m*
apostrophe *n* asgair *m*
appal *v* cuir uabhas air
appalling *a* sgriosail, cianail, eagalach
apparent *a* soilleir, follaiseach, faicsinneach

appeal *n* tarraing *f*; (*leg*) ath-agairt *m*, ath-thagradh *m*
v tarraing; (*leg*) ath-agair **a. against** tagair an aghaidh
appear *v* nochd, thig am fianais/follais
appearance *n* (*phys*) coltas *m*, dreach *m*, aogas *m*
appendicitis *n* an grèim mionaich *m*
appetite *n* càil *f*, càil bìdh *f*; (*desire*) miann *f m*
applause *n* bualadh bhas *m*; (*met*) moladh *m*
apple *n* ubhal *f m* **a. of eye** dearc na sùla *m* **a.-tree** craobh-ubhail *f*
appliance *n* uidheam *f*, inneal *m*
applicant *n* tagraiche *m*
application *n* iarrtas *m*, tagradh *m*; (*use*) cur an sàs *m* **a. form** foirm/clàr-iarrtais *m*
apply (for) *v* cuir a-steach (airson); (*use*) cuir gu feum, cuir an gnìomh **a. to/with** (*phys*) cuir air
appoint *v* suidhich, cuir an dreuchd
appointment *n* coinneamh *f*, àm suidhichte *m*; (*to post*) cur an dreuchd *m*
apposite *a* freagarrach, iomchaidh
appraise *v* meas, dèan measadh air, thoir beachd air
appreciate *v* cuir luach air; (*understand*) tuig gu math; (*fin*) meudaich, rach suas an luach
apprehensive *a* gealtach, draghail
apprentice *n* preantas *m*, foghlamaiche-ciùird *m*
approach *n* dòigh *f*; (*entry*) slighe *f v* dlùthaich ri, teann ri
appropriate *a* freagarrach, iomchaidh, cubhaidh
approval *n* riarachadh *m*, toileachadh *m*; (*official*) aonta *m*, ceadachadh *m* **win a. of ...** riaraich
approve *v* gabh beachd math air; (*of plan etc*) aontaich ri, ceadaich
approximately *adv* timcheall air, mu thuairmeas, faisg air

April *n* an Giblean *m*
apron *n* aparan *m*
apt *a* deas **a. to** buailteach ri/do
aptitude *n* alt *m*, sgil *m* **an a. for ...** alt air ...
Arab *n* Arabach *m*, (*female*) ban-Arabach *f*
Arabic *a* Arabach **a. numerals** figearan Arabach *n m pl*; (*lang*) Arabais *f*
arable *a* àitich **a. land** talamh àitich *m*
arbitrary *a* neo-riaghailteach, neo-chunbhalach
arbitration *n* eadar-bhreith *f*, breith-rèite *f*
arch *n* stuagh *f*, bogha *m*
archaeologist *n* arc-eòlaiche *m*, àrsair *m*
archaeology *n* arc-eòlas *m*, àrsaidheachd *f*
architect *n* ailtire *m*
architecture *n* ailtireachd *f*
archive(s) *n* tasglann *f*
arduous *a* doirbh, cruaidh, spàirneil
are *v* tha **are not** chan eil (*See verb* **to be** *in Grammar*)
area *n* farsaingeachd *f*; (*topic*) raon *m*; (*geog*) ceàrnaidh *f*
argue *v* dèan argamaid, connsaich *Also vn* ag argamaid
argument *n* argamaid *f*, connsachadh *m*
argumentative *a* connspaideach, connsachail, aimhreiteach
arise *v* èirich
aristocracy *n* na h-uaislean *pl*
arithmetic *n* àireamhachd *f*, cunntas *m*
arm *n* gàirdean *m*
armed *a* fo armachd, armaichte
armful *n* achlasan *m*, ultach *m*
armour *n* armachd *f*
armpit *n* achlais *f*, lag na h-achlaise *f*
army *n* arm *m*, armailt *m*, feachd *f m*
aroma *n* boladh *m*
around *prep* timcheall, mu chuairt, mu thimcheall (*all + gen*) *adv* mun cuairt
arouse *v* dùisg

arrange *v* suidhich, cuir air
dòigh; *(put in order)* cuir rian
air
arrangement *n* òrdachadh *m*;
(met) aonta *m*; *(mus)* rian *m*
arrest *v* cuir an grèim, cuir an sàs
arrival *n* teachd *m*, tighinn *m*,
ruighinn *m* **on my a.** nuair a
ràinig mi
arrive *v* ruig, thig
arrogance *n* àrdan *m*, ladarnas *m*
arrogant *a* àrdanach, ladarna
arrow *n* saighead *f*
art *n* ealain *f*; *(pictorial)*
dealbhadaireachd *f* **the arts** na
h-ealain(ean)
artery *n* cuisle *f*
arthritis *n* tinneas nan alt *m*
article *n* *(lit, gram)* alt *m*, artaigil
m; *(of clothing)* ball aodaich *m*;
(leg) bonn *m*
articulate *a* pongail, deas-
bhriathrach, siùbhlach
artificial *a* brèige, fuadain
artist *n* dealbhadair *m*;
(performer) neach-ealain *m*
artistic *a* ealanta
as *adv* cho ... ri (+ *n*), cho ... (+
v) is **as white as snow** cho geal
ris an t-sneachda **as long as you
like** cho fad' 's a thogras tu *conj*
mar; *(time)* nuair
ascend *v* dìrich, streap, rach suas
ascent *n* dìreadh *m*
ascertain *v* faigh a-mach, fiosraich
ash(es) *n* luath *f*, luaithre *f*
ashamed *a* air mo/a *etc*
nàrachadh, nàraichte
ashore *adv* air tìr
ashtray *n* soitheach-luaithre *f m*
Asian *n, a* Àisianach *m*, *(female)*
ban-Àisianach *f*
aside *adv* gu aon taobh, an
dàrna taobh, air leth
ask *v* *(request)* iarr; *(enquire)*
faighnich, feòraich, farraid
asleep *adv* nam chadal, na
c(h)adal *etc*
aspect *n* snuadh *m*, aogas *m*; *(of
topic)* taobh *m*; *(view)* sealladh *m*
aspiration *n* miann *f m*, rùn *m*;
(ling) analachadh *m*
aspire *v* rùnaich, miannaich

ass *n* asal *f m*
assassinate *v* murt
assault *n* ionnsaigh *f m* *v* thoir
ionnsaigh air
assemble *v* cruinnich
assembly *n* co-chruinneachadh
m, tional *m*; *(eccl)* àrd-
sheanadh *m*; *(polit)* seanadh *m*
assent *n* aonta *m*, aontachadh *m*
assess *v* meas
assessment *n* meas *m*, measadh
m
asset *n* maoin *f*
assiduous *a* dìcheallach,
leanmhainneach
assign *v* cuir air leth, sònraich
assignment *n* obair shònraichte *f*,
dleastanas sònraichte *m*
assist *v* cuidich, dèan cobhair air
assistance *n* cuideachadh *m*,
cobhair *f*
assistant *n* neach-cuideachaidh *m*
association *n* comann *m*,
caidreabh *m*
assume *v* bi dhen bheachd; *(take
control)* gabh sealbh air
assurance *n* dearbhachd *f*, cinnt
f; *(insurance)* àrachas *m* **self-a.**
dànachd *f*
assure *v* dearbh, dèan cinnteach
do **I a. you he'll come** thèid mi
an urras dhut gun tig e
asthma *n* a' chuing *f*, an sac *m*
astonish *v* cuir iongnadh air
astonishment *n* mòr-iongnadh *m*,
mòr-iongantas *m*
astray *adv* air seachran, air
iomrall
astride *adv* casa-gòbhlach
astrology *n* reuladaireachd *f*
astronaut *n* speuradair *m*,
speurair *m*
astronomy *n* reul-eòlas *m*
asylum *n* comraich *f*, tèarmann
m; *(instit)* ospadal inntinn *m*
at *prep* aig **a. all** idir
atheism *n* neo-dhiadhachd *f*
atheist *n* neo-dhiadhaire *m*,
ana-creidmheach *m*
athlete *n* lùth-chleasaiche *m*
athletic *a* *(person)* lùthmhor;
(game, feat) lùth-chleasach
athletics *n* lùth-chleasachd *f*

atlas *n* atlas *m*
atmosphere *n* àile *m*; (*met*)
faireachdainn *f*
atom *n* dadam *m*, smùirnean *m*,
atam *m*
atomic *a* dadamach, smùirneach,
atamach
atrocious *a* uabhasach, eagalach,
cianail, sgriosail
atrocity *n* buirbe *f*
attach *v* ceangail, greimich air/ri
attached *a* ceangailte, an lùib
(+ *gen*), an cois (+ *gen*) **very a.**
to ... fìor mheasail air ...
attachment *n* dàimh *f m*, ceangal
m; (*document*) faidhle *m*
attack *n* ionnsaigh *f m* **she had**
an attack of ... bhuail ... i
v thoir ionnsaigh (air)
attain *v* ruig, coisinn, faigh
attainable *a* ruigsinneach, so-
ruighinn, a ghabhas f(h)aighinn
attempt *n* oidhirp *f v* dèan
oidhirp, feuch ri
attend *v* fritheil **a. to** dèan, gabh
os làimh
attendant *n* neach-frithealaidh *m*
attention *n* aire *f*, feairt *f* **pay a.**
to thoir an aire do
attentive *a* furachail, suimeil
attic *n* seòmar-mullaich *m*
attitude *n* seasamh *m*, beachd *m*
attract *v* tarraing, tàlaidh
attraction *n* tarraing *f*, tàladh *m*
attractive *a* tarraingeach,
tlachdmhor, bòidheach
auburn *a* buidhe-ruadh
auction *n* rup *f* **up for a.** ga reic
audible *a* osgarra, ri chluinntinn
audience *n* luchd-èisteachd *m*;
(*a hearing*) èisteachd *f*
audit *n* sgrùdadh *m v* sgrùd,
dèan sgrùdadh air
auditor *n* sgrùdaire *m*, neach-
sgrùdaidh *m*
August *n* an Lùnastal *m*
aunt *n* piuthar-athar/màthar *f*,
antaidh *f* **my a.** piuthar m'
athar/mo mhàthar, m' antaidh
auspicious *a* gealltanach,
fàbharach, rathail
austere *a* teann, cruaidh
Australian *n, a* Astràilianach *m*,

(*female*) ban-Astràilianach *f*
authentic *a* fìor (+ *len*),
cinnteach, dearbhte, dhà-rìribh
author *n* ùghdar *m*
authority *n* ùghdarras *m*, smachd
m; (*warrant*) barantas *m* **the**
Local A. an t-Ùghdarras
Ionadail
authorize *v* thoir ùghdarras,
ceadaich
autobiography *n* fèin-eachdraidh
f
automatic *a* fèin-ghluasadach
autonomous *a* neo-eisimeileach
autumn *n* am foghar *m*
auxiliary *n* neach-cuideachaidh *m*,
neach-taic(e) *m a* taiceil
available *a* ri fhaighinn/fhaotainn
avenge *v* dìol
average *n* cuibheas *m*, meadhan
m a cuibheasach, gnàthach
on a. anns a' chumantas
avoid *v* seachain
await *v* fuirich ri
awake *a* na d(h)ùisg *etc*
award *n* duais *f v* thoir duais
aware *a* mothachail, forail
awareness *n* mothachadh *m*
away *adv* air falbh
awful *a* eagalach, uabhasach,
sgràthail
awkward *a* leibideach, clobhdach
axe *n* tuagh *f*, làmhagh *f*, làmhag
f
axle *n* aiseal *f m*
aye *interj* seadh, aidh!

B

baby *n* leanabh *m*, bèibidh *m*
bachelor *n* baidsealair *m*,
fleasgach *m*, seana-ghille *m*
back *n* cùl *m*, cùlaibh *m v* rach
air ais; (*support*) seas, cuidich;
(*bet on*) cuir airgead air *adv* air
ais
background *n* cùl-raon *m*, bun-
fhiosrachadh *m*
backside *n* tòn *f*, màs *m Also*
tòin
backward(s) *adv* an comhair a
c(h)ùil *etc*
backward *a* fad' air ais

bacon *m* muicfheòil *f*
bad *a* dona, droch (*precedes &
len n*), olc **bad-tempered** *a*
greannach, eangarra
badge *n* suaicheantas *m*, baidse
m
badger *n* broc *m*
baffle *v* dubh-fhaillich air,
fairtlich air **b. someone** dèan
a' chùis air
bag *n* baga *m*, màileid *f*; (*sack*)
poca *m*
baggage *n* bagaichean *m pl*
bagpipe *n* pìob *f* **great Highland
b.** pìob-mhòr
bail *n* urras *m* **on b.** air urras
v fuasgail air urras, thoir urras
air
baillie *n* bàillidh *m*
bait *n* biathadh *m*, baoit *f*,
maghar *m* *v* biadh, cuir
biathadh/maghar air; (*taunt*)
leamhaich, mag air
bake *v* fuin; (*in oven*) bruich san
àmhainn
baker *n* bèicear *m*, fuineadair *m*
bakery *n* taigh-fuine *m*
baking *n* bèicearachd *f*, fuine *m*
b. powder pùdar/fùdar-fuine *m*
balance *n* meidh *f*; (*abstr*)
cothrom *m*, co-chothrom *m*;
(*fin*) còrr *m* **b. sheet** clàr
cothromachaidh *m* *v* cuir air
mheidh; (*abstr*) cothromaich
balanced *a* cothromach
balcony *n* for-uinneag *f*
bald *a* maol, le sgall
ball *n* ball *m*, bàl(l)a *m*; (*wool*)
ceirtle *f*; (*dance*) bàl *m*
ballast *n* balaist(e) *f m*
balloon *n* bailiùn *m*
ballot *n* baileat *m*, bhòtadh *m*
ban *n* toirmeasg *m*, casg *m*,
bacadh *m* *v* toirmisg, caisg, bac
band *n* bann *m*; (*of people*)
buidheann *f m*; (*mus*) còmhlan-
ciùil *m*
bandage *n* bann *m*
bang *n* brag *m* *v* thoir brag air,
buail
banish *v* fuadaich, fògair
bank *n* banca *m*; (*topog*) bruach
f m, bac *m*

bank *v* cuir dhan bhanca **b. on**
theirig an urras air
banker *n* bancair *m*
bankrupt *a* briste **the company
went b.** bhris(t) air
a' chompanaidh
banned *a* toirmisgte
banner *n* bratach *f*
banquet *n* fèist *f*, fleadh *m*,
bangaid *f*
banter *n* tarraing-às *f*
baptism *n* baisteadh *m*
Baptist *n*, *a* Baisteach *m*
baptize *v* baist
bar *n* crann-tarsainn *m*; (*pub*)
bàr *m*, taigh-seinnse *m*;
(*hindrance*) bacadh *m* **b. chart**
clàr-cholbh *m* **b. graph** graf-
bann *m*
barbaric *a* borb
barbed *a* gathach **b. wire** uèir
bhiorach/stobach *f*
barber *n* borbair *m*, bearradair *m*
bard *n* bàrd *m*, filidh *m*
bare *a* lom, rùisgte
bargain *n* bargan *f m*;
(*agreement*) cùmhnant *m*
barge *n* bàirdse *f*
bark *n* rùsg *m*; (*of dog*) comhart
m
barking *n* comhartaich *f* *Also vn*
a' comhartaich
barley *n* eòrna *m*
barn *n* sabhal *m*
barnacle *n* giùran *m*,
bàirneach *f*
barometer *n* glainne-sìde *f*
barrel *n* baraille *m* *Also* barailte
barren *a* neo-thorrach, seasg;
(*land*) fàs
barrier *n* bacadh *m*, cnap-starra
m
barrow *n* bara *m*
barter *n* malairt *f* *v* dèan
malairt/iomlaid, malairtich
base *n* stèidh *f*, bonn *m*, bun *m*,
bunait *f m*
bashful *a* nàrach, diùid
basic *a* bunaiteach, bunasach
basin *n* mias *f*
basis *n* bun *m*, bunait *f*, bun-
stèidh *f*
bask *v* blian

basket n basgaid f
bass a beus
bat n slacan m, bat m; (mammal) ialtag f
batch n baidse m, grunn m, dòrlach m
bath n amar m
batter v liodraig, pronn
battery n bataraidh f m
battle n cath m, blàr m, batail m
bay n bàgh m, camas m, òb m
be v bi (See verb **to be** in Grammar)
beach n tràigh f **shingle b.** mol m
bead n grìogag f **beads** (relig) paidirean m
beak n gob m
beam n (of wood) sail f; (of light) gath m, boillsgeadh m; (apparatus) crann m
bean n pònair f (normally used as coll) **beans** pònairean
bear n mathan m
bear v giùlain; (suffer) fuiling; (a child) beir
beard n feusag f
beast n beathach m, ainmhidh m; (pej) biast f
beat n buille f
beautiful a brèagha, bòidheach, maiseach, riochdail
beauty n bòidhchead f, maise f, sgèimh f, àilleachd f **b. spot** ball-seirce m
because conj airson, a chionn, seach, ri linn **b. of** air sàillibh (+ gen)
become v fàs, cinn **b. a ...** rach na ... etc
bed n leabaidh f **bed and breakfast** leabaidh is bracaist
bedroom rùm/seòmar-cadail m
bee n seillean m, beach m
beef n mairtfheòil f
beer n leann m
beetle n daolag f
beetroot n biotais m
before prep ro; (in front of) air beulaibh (+ gen) adv roimhe conj mus
beforehand adv ro-làimh
beg v guidh; (for money etc) iarr dèirc (air)

beggar n dèirceach m
begin v tòisich
beginner n neach-tòiseachaidh m
beginning n toiseach m, tòiseachadh m, tùs m **the very b.** toiseach tòiseachaidh
behalf n **on b. of** às leth (+ gen) **on my b.** às mo leth(-sa)
behave v bi modhail
behaviour n giùlan m
behind adv air d(h)eireadh prep air cùlaibh, air c(h)ùl (both + gen) **b. them** air an cùlaibh
belch v dèan brùchd
belief n (relig) creideamh m
believe v creid, thoir creideas do
bell n clag m
bellow v beuc, geum, dèan geum, bùir
belly n brù f, broinn f
belong v buin **b. to** buin do **that belongs to me** 's ann leamsa a tha sin
beloved a ionmhainn, gràdhach, gràdhaichte
below adv shìos; (down here) a-bhos; (downwards) sìos prep fo (+ len)
belt n crios m, bann m
bench n being(e) f
bend n lùb m, fiaradh m v lùb, aom, fiaraich; (stoop) crom
beneath prep fo (+ len)
beneficial a feumail, buannachdail
benefit n feum m, buannachd f, tairbhe f
benevolent a coibhneil, le deagh-ghean
benign a coibneil, fial; (med) neo-aillseach, neo-chronail
bent a lùbte, fiar, cam; (stooped) crom
bequest n dìleab f
berry n dearc f, dearcag f, sùbh m
beseech v guidh, dèan guidhe (ri)
beside prep phr ri taobh (+ gen), làimh ri
besides adv a bhàrr air, a bharrachd air, a thuilleadh air; (anyway) co-dhiù
best a, adv (as) fheàrr

bestow *v* builich
bet *n* geall *m* *v* cuir geall
betray *v* brath; (*feelings*) leig ris
better *a* nas fheàrr, (*past*) na b' fheàrr
between *prep* eadar *adv* eadar
beware *v* thoir an aire, bi air d' fhaiceall
beyond *prep* air taobh thall, thar (*both* + *gen*); (*time*) seachad air; (*exceeding*) os cionn (+ *gen*)
bias *n* leiteachas *m*; claon-bhàidh *f*; (*phys*) claonadh *m*
Bible *n* Bìoball *m*
bibliography *n* leabhar-chlàr *m*; (*activity*) leabhar-chlàradh *m*
bicycle *n* baidhsagal *m*, rothair *m*
bid *n* tairgse *f*, iarrtas *m* **bid for** dèan tairgse airson, cuir a-steach airson
big *a* mòr, tomadach
bigot *n* dalm-bheachdaiche *m*
bigotry *n* dalm-bheachd *m*
bile *n* domblas *m*
bilingual *a* dà-chànanach
bill *n* cunntas *f m*; (*of a bird*) gob *m*; (*leg*) bile *m*
billion *n* billean *m*
bin *n* biona *f m*
bind *v* ceangail, naisg; (*fetter*) cuibhrich
binoculars *n* prosbaig *f*, glainneachan *f pl*
biography *n* eachdraidh-beatha *f*
biology *n* bith-eòlas *m*
birch *n* beithe *f*
bird *n* eun *m*
birth *n* breith *f* **b. certificate** teisteanas-breith *m* **birthday** co-là-breith *m*, ceann-bliadhna *m*
biscuit *n* briosgaid *f*
bishop *n* easbaig *m*
bit *n* bìdeag *f*, mìr *m*, pìos *m*, criomag *f*; (*horse's*) cabstair *m*, mìreanach *m*
bitch *n* galla *f*, saigh *f*
bite *n* bìdeadh *m*, bìdeag *f*; (*of food*) grèim *m* *v* bìd, thoir grèim/bìdeag à
bitter *a* geur, searbh (*also met*)
black *a* dubh, dorch(a); (*mood*) gruamach **blackbird** lon-dubh *m* **blackboard** bòrd-dubh *m*

blacken *v* dubh, dèan dubh; (*reputation*) mill cliù
blacksmith *n* gobha *m*
bladder *n* aotroman *m*
blade *n* (*of knife*) lann *f*; (*on tool*) iarann *m*; (*of grass*) bileag *f*
blame *n* coire *f* *v* cuir coire air, coirich, faigh coire/cron do
blameless *a* neo-chiontach, gun choire
bland *a* mìn, tlàth, staoin
blank *a* bàn, falamh
blanket *n* plaide *f*, plangaid *f*
blatant *a* dalma, gun chleith
blaze *n* teine lasrach *m*, caoir *f*; (*domestic*) braidseal *m*
bleak *a* lom, aognaidh; (*met*) gun dòchas
bleat *v* dèan mèilich, dèan meigeadaich *Also vn* a' mèilich, a' meigeadaich
bleed *v* caill/sil fuil; (*drain*) leig
blemish *n* gaoid *f*, smal *m*
blend *n* coimeasgadh *m* *v* coimeasgaich
bless *v* beannaich
blessing *n* beannachd *f*, beannachadh *m*
blethering *n* bleadraich *f*, bleadaireachd *f*
blight *n* gaiseadh *m*
blind *n* sgàil(e) *f*
blind *a* dall **the b.** na doill *n m pl*
blindness *n* doille *f*
blink *v* caog, priob
bliss *n* sòlas *m*, sonas *m*, làn-aoibhneas *m*
blissful *a* sòlasach, sona, làn-aoibhneach
blister *n* builgean *m*, balg *m*, leus *m*
blizzard *n* cathadh-sneachda *m*
block *n* bloc *m*, sgonn *m*, ceap *m* *v* caisg, cuir bacadh air, dùin
blond(e) *a* bàn *n* tè bhàn *f*, fear bàn *m*
blood *n* fuil *f* **b. pressure** bruthadh-fala *m* **b. transfusion** leasachadh-fala *m* **bloodshed** dòrtadh-fala *m*
bloody *a* fuilteach **you b. idiot** amadain na mallachd/croiche *m*

bloom n blàth m, ùr-fhàs m
v thig fo bhlàth
blossom n blàth m
blouse n blobhs(a) f m
blow n buille f, bualadh m, beum
m; (weather) sèideadh m v sèid
blue a gorm **light blue** liath
bluff v meall, thoir an car à(s)
blunder n mearachd mhòr f
blunt a maol
blurred a doilleir, a-mach à fòcas
blush n rudhadh (gruaidhe) m
v fàs dearg **she blushed** thàinig
rudhadh na gruaidh
blushing a rudhach, ruiteach
boar n torc m
board n bòrd m, clàr m; (plank)
dèile f v rach air bòrd
boast n bòst m v dèan bòst,
bòstaich
boasting n bòstadh m
boat n bàta m; (open) eathar f m
fishing b. bàt'-iasgaich **sailing b.**
bàta-siùil
body n corp m, bodhaig f; (of
people) buidheann f m,
còmhlan m
bog n bog(l)ach f, fèithe f
boil n neasgaid f
boil v goil; (food) bruich **it's on
the b.** tha e a' goil
boiled a bruich
boisterous a gailbheach; (person)
iorghaileach
bold a dàna, tapaidh, dalma
b. type (liter) clò trom m
boldness n dànadas m, dànachd
f, tapachd f
bolster v cùm taic ri, misnich
bolt n bolt(a) m
bomb n bom(a) m v leag bom
air, bom(aig)
bond n ceangal m, bann m,
gealladh m
bone n cnàimh m
bonfire n tein-aighir m, tein-
èibhinn m
bonnet n bonaid f m
bonny a bòidheach, brèagha,
buaidheach
bonus n leasachadh (duaise) m
it was a real b. 's e fìor
bhuannachd a bh' ann

book n leabhar m **bookshop** bùth
leabhraichean f
booklet n leabhran m
boot n bròg f
booth n bùth f, bothan m
booze n deoch-làidir f v òl, gabh
steall
border n crìoch f; (edge) oir f,
iomall m
bore v cladhaich, dèan toll; (met)
bòraig, sàraich
boring a ràsanach, sàraichte
borrow v faigh (air) iasad
bosom n broilleach m
boss n ceannard m
botany n luibh-eòlas m
both a dà; (of people) dithis **with
b. hands** leis an dà làimh
b. sons an dithis mhac adv le
chèile **b. great and small** eadar
bheag is mhòr
bother n bodraigeadh m, dragh
m v bodraig, cuir dragh air
bottle n botal m
bottom n ìochdar m, bonn m;
(sea) aigeann m, grunnd m;
(of person) màs m, tòn f **b. up**
bhon bhonn suas
bounce v bunsaig, buns
bound n sìnteag f, cruinn-leum m
boundary n crìoch f
bow n bogha m; (ship) toiseach
m; (bending) cromadh-cinn m
v (bend) crom, lùb
bowel(s) n innidh f
bowl n bobhla m, cuach f
bowling n bòbhladh m **b. alley**
ionad bòbhlaidh m
box n bogsa m, bucas m; (blow)
buille f v cuir am bogsa; (fight)
bogs(aig)
boxer n bogsair m
boxing n bogsadh m
boy n balach m, gille m
boycott v seachain, na gabh
gnothach ri
boyfriend n carabhaidh f m,
bràmair m
brace n uidheam-teannachaidh
m; (pair) dithis m, càraid f,
caigeann f
bracelet n bann-làimhe m
braces n gaileis f

bracken *n* raineach *f*
bracket *n* bracaid *f*; (*in writing*) camag *f*
brae *n* bruthach *f*, leathad *m*
brag *v* bòst, dèan bòst
brain *n* eanchainn *f*
brake *n* brèig *f*, casgan *m*
bramble *n* (*berry*) smeur *f*; (*bush*) dris *f*
branch *n* geug *f*, meangan *m*; (*abstr*) meur *f*
brand *n* seòrsa *m*; (*of fire*) aithinne *m* **b. new** talc-ùr, ùr nodha
brandy *n* branndaidh *f*
brass *n* pràis *f*
brat *n* isean *m*, peasan *m*
brave *a* gaisgeil, calma
bravery *n* gaisge *f*, gaisgeachd *f*, misneachd *f*
brawl *n* tuasaid *f*, còmhrag *f*
brazen *a* ladarna, gun nàire; (*metal*) pràiseach
breach *n* bris(t)eadh *m*, bealach *m*, beàrn *f m*
breach *v* dèan bris(t)eadh/beàrn
bread *n* aran *m*
breadth *n* leud *m*, farsaingeachd *f*
break *n* bris(t)eadh *m*; (*abstr*) fois *f* *v* bris(t); (*of word, promise*) rach air ais air
breakfast *n* bracaist *f*
breast *n* broilleach *m*, uchd *m* **a b.** cìoch *f*
breath *n* anail *f*, deò *f*
breathe *v* tarraing anail
breathless *a* gun anail, goirid san anail
breed *n* seòrsa *m*, gnè *f*, sìol *m* *v* gin, tàrmaich, briod(aich)
breeding *n* briodachadh *m*; (*met*) togail *f*, modh *f*
breeze *n* oiteag *f*, osag *f*, soirbheas *m*
brew *v* dèan grùdaireachd; (*tea*) tarraing
brewery *n* taigh-grùide *m*
bribe *n* brìb *f* *v* brìb
brick *n* breige *f m*
bride *n* bean-bainnse *f* **the b.** bean na bainnse
bridegroom *n* fear-bainnse *m* **the b.** fear na bainnse

bridesmaid *n* maighdeann-phòsaidh *f*, bean-chomhailteachd *f*
bridge *n* drochaid *f*
bridle *n* srian *f*
brief *v* leig brath gu, thoir fiosrachadh do
brief *a* goirid, geàrr
bright *a* soilleir; (*clever*) comasach
brighten *v* soillsich, soilleirich
brilliant *a* boillsgeach, lainnireach; (*very clever*) air leth comasach
brim *n* oir *f m*, bile *f* **full to the b.** làn gu bheul
bring *v* thoir, bheir **b. up** (family) àraich, tog (teaghlach)
brink *n* oir *f m*, bruach *f m*
brisk *a* beothail, sunndach, clis
bristle *n* calg *m*, frioghan *m* *v* cuir calg air, tog frioghan air
British *a* Breatannach
Briton *n* Breatannach *m*, (*female*) ban-Bhreatannach *f*
brittle *a* pronn, brisg
broad *a* leathan(n), farsaing
broadcast *n* craoladh *m* *v* craobh-sgaoil, craol
broadcaster *n* craoladair *m*
broadcasting *n* craoladh *m*
brochure *n* leabhran(-shanas) *m*
broken *past part* briste
bronchitis *n* at-sgòrnain *m*
bronze *n* umha *m* **B. Age** Linn an Umha *f m*
brooch *n* bràiste *f*, broidse *m*
brood *n* àl *m*, sìol *m*
brook *n* sruthan *m*, alltan *m*
broom *n* sguab *f*; (*bot*) bealaidh *m*
broth *n* brot *m*, eanraich *f*
brothel *n* taigh-siùrsachd *m*
brother *n* bràthair *m* **b.-in-law** bràthair-cèile *m*
brow *n* mala *f*, bathais *f*, maoil *f*; (*topog*) bruach *f m*
brown *a* donn, ruadh
bruise *n* bruthadh *m*, pat *m* *v* brùth
brunette *a* donn *n* tè dhonn *f*
brush *n* sguab *f*, bruis *f* *v* sguab, bruis(ig)

brutal *a* brùideil, garg
brutality *n* brùidealachd *f*
brute *n* brùid *f m*, beathach *m*
bubble *n* builgean *m*, gucag *f*
bucket *n* bucaid *f*, cuinneag *f*
buckle *n* bucall *m*
bud *n* gucag *f*
budge *v* caraich, gluais
budget *n* buidseat *m* **the B.** am
  Buidseat **b. for** comharraich
  ionmhas (airson)
budgie *n* buidsidh *m*
bug *n* (*illness*) treamhlaidh *f*;
  (*computer*) biastag *f*
build *v* tog
builder *n* neach-togail *m*
building *n* togalach *m*, aitreabh *m*
  b. society comann thogalach *m*
bulb *n* bolgan *m*; (*bot*) meacan *m*
bulge *v* brùchd a-mach
bulky *a* mòr, tomadach
bull *n* tarbh *m*
bullet *n* peilear *m*
bullock *n* damh *m*
bully *n* burraidh *m*
bullying *n* burraidheachd *f*
bungalow *n* bungalo *m*
buoy *n* puta *m*
burden *n* eallach *m*
bureaucracy *n* biurocrasaidh *m*
bureaucratic *a* biurocratach
burgh *n* baile *m*, borgh *m*
burglar *n* gadaiche *m*
burial *n* adhlacadh *m*,
  tiodhlacadh *m*, tòrradh *m*
burly *a* tapaidh, dòmhail
burn *n* losgadh *m*; (*stream*)
  sruthan *m*, alltan *m* *v* loisg
  they suffered burns chaidh an
  losgadh
bursary *n* bursaraidh *m*
burst *v* spreadh, sgàin
bury *v* adhlaic, tiodhlaic
bus *n* bus *m* **b. stop** stad-bus *m*
  b. station stèisean bhusaichean
  m
bush *n* preas *m*, dos *m*
business *n* gnothach *m*,
  gnothachas *f*, malairt *f* **it's none
  of your b.** chan e do ghnothach-
  sa e
businessman *n* neach-gnothaich
  m

bustle *n* drip *f*, trainge *f*
busy *a* trang, dripeil
but *conj*, *prep* ach **b. for that**
  mura b' e sin
butcher *n* bùidsear *m*, feòladair
  m
butler *n* buidealair *m*
butter *n* ìm *m* *v* cuir ìm air
buttercup *n* buidheag an
  t-samhraidh *f*
butterfly *n* dealan-dè *m*
buttermilk *n* blàthach *f*
buttock *n* màs *m*
button *n* putan *m* *v* dùin na
  putanan, putanaich
buy *v* ceannaich
buyer *n* ceannaiche *m*, neach-
  ceanna(i)ch *m*
buzz *n* srann *f*, crònan *m* **it gave
  me a real b.** thug e fìor thogail
  dhomh
buzzard *n* clamhan *m*
by *prep* le; (*near*) faisg air, ri
  taobh (+ *gen*) **by herself** leatha
  fhèin **by degrees** mean air
  mhean **by night** tron oidhche **by
  now** thuige seo **a picture by
  Picasso** dealbh le Picasso
by *adv* an dara taobh, seachad
  **we'll need to put a little money
  by** feumaidh sinn beagan airgid
  a chur an dara taobh **she went
  by** chaidh i seachad **by and by**
  a dh'aithghearr, ri ùine
by-election *n* fo-thaghadh *m*
bypass *n* seach-rathad *m*
byproduct *n* far-stuth *m*
byre *n* bàthach *f*
byway *n* frith-rathad *m*

C

cab *n* caba *m*; (*taxi*) tagsaidh *f m*
cabbage *n* càl *m*
cabin *n* bothan *m*; (*on ship*)
  cèaban *m*
cabinet *n* caibineat *m*, preasa *m*
  the C. an Caibineat
cable *n* càball *m*
cackle *n* glocail *f*
café *n* cafaidh *f m*
cage *n* cèidse *f*, eunlann *f*
cairn *n* càrn *m*

cajole *v* coitich, breug
cake *n* cèic *f m*
calamity *n* dosgainn *f*, mòr-chall *m*, truaighe *f*
calculate *v* meas, tomhais, obraich a-mach
calculator *n* àireamhair *m*
calendar *n* mìosachan *m*
calf *n* laogh *m*; (*of leg*) calpa *m*
calibre *n* cailibhear *m*, meudachd baraille *f*; (*of person*) stuth *m*, feartan *f pl*
call *n* èigh *f*, gairm *f*, glaodh *m* *v* èigh, glaodh, gairm; (*visit*) tadhail air; (*send for*) cuir fios air **they called her Jean** thug iad Sìne (mar ainm) oirre
calling *n* èigheach *f*; (*vocation*) dreuchd *f*, gairm *f*
callous *a* cruaidh(-chridheach), an-iochdmhor
calm *a* ciùin, sèimh *n* ciùine *f*; (*weather*) fèath *f m*
calorie *n* calaraidh *m*
calve *v* beir laogh
camel *n* càmhal *m*
camera *n* camara *m*
camp *n* campa *m* **c. site** àite-campachaidh *m* *v* campaich
campaign *n* iomairt *f*; (*in war*) còmhrag *f* *v* dèan iomairt
can *n* cana *m*, crogan *m*
can *v* is urrainn do; (*may*) faod **can you do that?** an urrainn dhut sin a dhèanamh? **can she go?** am faod i a dhol ann?
Canadian *n*, *a* Canèidianach *m*, (*female*) ban-Chanèidianach *f*
canal *n* clais-uisge *f*, canàl *m*, faoighteach *m*
cancel *v* dubh a-mach/às; (*event*) cuir dheth
cancer *n* aillse *f* **breast c.** aillse broillich
candid *a* fosgarra
candidate *n* tagraiche *m*
candle *n* coinneal *f* **candlestick** coinnlear *m*
candy *n* candaidh *m*, suiteis *m pl*
cane *n* cuilc *f*; (*stick*) bata *m*
canister *n* canastair *m*
canker *n* cnuimh *f*, cnàmhainn *f*
cannabis *n* cainb *f*, cainb-lus *m*

cannon *n* gunna-mòr *m*, canan *m*
canny *a* cùramach, gleusta
canoe *n* curachan *m*, curach Innseanach *f*
canopy *n* sgàil-bhrat *m*
canteen *n* biadhlann *f*, ionad bìdh *m*
canter *n* trotan *m*
canvas *n* canabhas *m*
canvass *v* (*views*) sir beachdan; (*votes*) sir bhòtaichean; (*support*) sir taic
cap *n* currac *m*, ceap *m*, bonaid *f m*; (*limit*) cuibhreachadh *m*, cuingealachadh *m* *v* (*cover*) còmhdaich; (*limit*) cuibhrich, cuingealaich; (*surpass*) thoir bàrr air
capability *n* comas *m*
capable *a* comasach
capacity *n* na ghabhas rud/ionad; (*role*) dreuchd *f*; (*mental*) comas *m*
cape *n* rubha *m*, maol *m*; (*cloak*) cleòc(a) *m*, guailleachan *m*
capital *n* prìomh-bhaile *m*, ceanna-bhaile *m*; (*fin*) calpa *m*; (*profit*) buannachd *f* *a* (*fin*) calpa **c. expenditure** caiteachas calpa *m* **c. letter** litir mhòr *f*
capitalism *n* calpachas *m*
capitalist *n* calpaire *m*
capsize *v* còp, cuir thairis
captain *n* caiptean *m*, sgiobair *m*
caption *n* fo-thiotal *m*, tiotal *m*
captive *n* prìosanach *m*, ciomach *m*, bràigh *f m*
captivity *n* ciomachas *m*, braighdeanas *m*
capture *n* glacadh *m*
car *n* càr *m* **car ferry** aiseag chàraichean *f* **car park** pàirc(e)-chàraichean *f*
caramel *n* carra-mheille *f*, caramail *m*
caravan *n* carabhan *f m* **c. site** ionad charabhanaichean *m*
caraway *n* lus MhicCuimein *m*, carabhaidh *f m*
carbohydrate *n* gualaisg *m*
carbon *n* gualan *m* **c. dioxide** gualan dà-ogsaid *m*
carbuncle *n* guirean *m*
carcase *n* closach *f*, cairbh *f*

card *n* cairt *f* **cardboard** cairt-bhòrd *m*

cardiac *a* cridhe **c. arrest** stad cridhe *m*

cardigan *n* càrdagan *m*, peitean *m*

cardinal *n* càirdineal *m*

cardinal *a* prìomh; (*numbers*) àrdail

care *n* cùram *m*, aire *f*, faiceall *f* **in my c.** air mo chùram(-sa) **take c.** thoir an aire **c. for** *v* gabh cùram (+ *gen*), gabh sùim (do)

career *n* cùrsa-beatha *m*, dreuchd *f* **careers convention** fèill-dhreuchdan *f*

careful *a* cùramach, faiceallach, furachail

careless *a* mì-chùramach, mì-fhaiceallach; (*indifferent*) coma

carelessness *n* mì-chùram *m*, cion cùraim *m*, dìth cùraim *f m*

caress *v* cnèadaich, cionacraich

caretaker *n* neach-aire *m*

cargo *n* luchd *m*, cargu *m* **c. boat** bàta cargu/bathair *m*

carnage *n* àr *m*, casgradh *m*

carnal *a* feòlmhor, corporra

carnation *n* càrnaid *f*

carnival *n* càrnabhail *m*, àrd-fhèill *f*

carol *n* laoidh *f m*, coireal *m*

carpenter *n* saor *m*

carpentry *n* saorsainneachd *f*

carpet *n* brat-ùrlair *m*, tapais *f*

carriage *n* (*person*) giùlan *m*; (*vehicle*) carbad *m*

carrier *n* neach-giùlain *m*; (*company*) buidheann giùlain *f m*

carrot *n* curran *m*

carry *v* giùlain, iomchair **c. out** (*fulfil*) coilean **c. over** thoir air adhart

cart *n* cairt *f*

cartilage *n* maoth-chnàimh *m*

carton *n* cartan *m*

cartoon *n* cartùn *m*, dealbh-èibhinn *f m*

cartridge *n* catraids(e) *f*

carve *v* snaigh; (*meat*) geàrr

carving *n* gràbhaladh *m*, snaigheadh *m*; (*meat etc*) gearradh *m*

case *n* màileid *f*, ceas *m*; (*abstr*)

staid *f*, cor *m*; (*leg*) cùis(-lagha) *f*; (*gram*) tuiseal *m* **nominative c.** an tuiseal ainmneach **gen c.** an tuiseal ginideach **dat c.** an tuiseal tabhartach **if that is the c.** mas ann mar sin a tha **in any c.** co-dhiù

cash *n* airgead ullamh *m*, airgead làimhe *m*

cask *n* buideal *m*, baraille *m*

cassette *n* cèiseag *f* **c. recording** clàradh cèiseig *m*

cast *n* (*performers*) sgioba *f*; (*plaster*) còmhdach plàsta *v* caith/tilg (air falbh); (*moult*) cuir; (*mould*) molldaich **c. lots** tilg croinn

castigate *v* cronaich

castle *n* caisteal *m*

castrate *v* spoth

casual *a* tuiteamach; (*employment*) sealach

casualty *n* leòinteach *m*

cat *n* cat *m*

catalogue *n* catalog *f m*

catapult *n* tailm *f*, lungaid *f*

cataract *n* eas *m*; (*on eye*) meamran sùla *m*

catarrh *n* an galar smugaideach *m*

catastrophe *n* mòr-chreach *f*, lèirsgrios *m*

catch *n* glacadh *m*; (*latch*) claimhean *m* **a good c.** deagh mhurrag *f*, deagh iasgach *m* *v* glac, beir air, greimich air

catchy *a* tarraingeach, fonnmhor

categorical *a* deimhinnte, mionnaichte

category *n* gnè *f*, seòrsa *m*

cater *v* thoir biadh do, solair, ullaich

catering *n* solarachd *f*

caterpillar *n* burras *m*, bratag *f*

cathedral *n* cathair-eaglais *f*, àrd-eaglais *f*

Catholic *n*, *a* Caitligeach *m*, (*female*) ban-Chaitligeach *f*

catholic *a* coitcheann

cattle *n* crodh *m*, sprèidh *f* **c. grid** cliath chruidh *f* **c. show** fèill-chruidh *f*

cauliflower *n* colag *f*, càl-colaig *m*

cause *n* adhbhar *m*

v adhbhraich
causeway *n* cabhsair *m*
caustic *a* loisgeach; (*wit*) geur,
guineach
caution *n* faiceall *f*, cùram *m*;
(*warning*) rabhadh *m* *v* thoir
rabhadh, cuir air *etc* fhaicill,
earalaich
cautious *a* faiceallach, cùramach
cavalry *n* eachraidh *m*, marc-
shluagh *m*
cave *n* uaimh *f*
cavern *n* uaimh *f*, talamh-toll *m*
cavity *n* sloc *m*, toll *m*, lag *f m*
cease *v* sguir, stad
cease-fire *n* fois-losgaidh *m*
ceaseless *a* gun sgur/stad/
abhsadh
ceiling *n* mullach *m*, mullach
rùm/seòmair
celebrate *v* dèan subhachas;
(*mark*) comharraich, cùm;
(*laud*) cuir an cèill cliù;
(*sacrament*) cuartaich
celebrated *a* iomraiteach,
cliùiteach
celebration *n* subhachas *m*;
(*marking*) comharrachadh *m*
celebrity *n* neach iomraiteach *m*;
(*fame*) iomraiteachd *f*
celery *n* soilire *f*
celestial *a* nèamhaidh
cell *n* (*church*) cill *f*; (*biol*) cealla
f; (*prison*) cealla prìosain *f*
cellar *n* seilear *m*
cello *n* beus-fhidheall *f*
cellular *a* ceallach
Celt *n* Ceilteach *m*
Celtic *a* Ceilteach
cement *n* saimeant *m* *v* tàth,
cuir ri chèile; (*met*) neartaich
cemetery *n* cladh *m*
censor *v* caisg
censorious *a* achmhasanach,
coireachail, cronachail
censure *n* achmhasan *m*,
cronachadh *m* *v* cronaich,
coirich
census *n* cunntas *m*; (*pop*)
cunntas-sluaigh *m*
cent *n* seant *m* **it didn't cost me a
c.** cha do chosg e sgillinn
(ruadh) dhomh

centenary *n* ceud *m*, ceud bliadhna
f, cuimhneachan ceud *m*
centimetre *n* ceudameatair *m*
centipede *n* ceud-chasach *m*
central *a* meadhain, meadhanach,
anns a' mheadhan
centralize *v* cuir/thoir dhan
mheadhan
centre *n* meadhan *m*
century *n* linn *f m*, ceud *m*, ceud
bliadhna *f*
cereal *n* gràn *m*; (*food*) biadh
grànach *m*
cerebral *a* eanchainneach
ceremony *n* deas-ghnàth *m*;
(*event*) seirbheis *f*
certain *a* cinnteach, deimhinnte
absolutely c. mionnaichte
certainly *adv* gu cinnteach, gu
deimhinn, dha-rìribh
certainty *n* cinnt *f*, dearbhadh *m*
certificate *n* teisteanas *m*,
barantas *m*
certify *v* teistich, dearbh
chaff *n* moll *m*, càth *f*
chain *n* sèine *f*, slabhraidh *f*,
cuibhreach *m* *v* cuibhrich, cuir
slabhraidh air
chair *n* cathair *f*, sèithear *m*;
(*person*) cathraiche *m* **chairlift**
beairt-dhìridh *f* **chairman** fear-
cathrach *m*, fear na cathrach *m*
chairperson neach-cathrach *m*,
cathraiche *m* **chairwoman** bean-
chathrach *f*, bean na cathrach *f*
v gabh cathair
chalk *n* cailc *f*
challenge *n* dùbhlan *m* *v* thoir
dùbhlan do; (*oppose*) cuir an
aghaidh
chamber *n* seòmar *m*
champion *n* gaisgeach *m*, curaidh
m, laoch *m*; (*winner*)
buadhaiche *m*
chance *n* cothrom *m*,
seansa/teans *m* **c. event**
tuiteamas *m* **by c.** le turchairt/
tuiteamas
chancellor *n* seansalair *m*
change *n* atharrachadh *m*,
caochladh *m*; (*money*) iomlaid
f, airgead pronn *m*
v atharraich, caochail, mùth

changeable *a* caochlaideach
channel *n* cladhan *m*, clais *f*;
(*topog*) caolas *m*; (*means*)
modh *f m*
chant *v* seinn
chanter *n* (*of pipes*) feadan *m*,
sionnsar *m*
chaos *n* mì-riaghailt *f*
chapel *n* caibeal *m*
chaplain *n* seaplain *m*; (*mil*)
ministear-feachd *m*
chapter *n* caibideil *f m*
character *n* beus *f*, mèinn *f*,
nàdar *m*; (*liter*) caractar *m*,
pearsa *m*; (*typ*) litir *f* **he's a real
c.** 's e cinneach a th' ann
characteristic *n* feart *m*, dual-
nàdair *m a* coltach,
samhlachail
charge *n* (*cost*) prìs *f*, cosgais *f*;
(*attack*) ionnsaigh *f m*;
(*accusation*) casaid *f* **in c. of** air
ceann (+ *gen*) *v* (*attack*)
dèan/thoir ionnsaigh; (*accuse*)
cuir às leth, fàg air **how much
did they c. for it?** dè na chuir
iad ort e? **take c. of** gabh os
làimh
charisma *n* tarraing pearsa *f*
charitable *a* carthannach,
coibhneil
charity *n* carthannas *m*,
coibhneas *m*; (*alms*) dèirc *f*;
(*agency*) buidheann carthannais
f m
charm *v* cuir seun air, cuir fo
dhraoidheachd
charming *a* taitneach, meallach
chart *n* cairt-iùil *f*; (*mus*) clàr *m*
charter *n* cairt *f*, còir-sgrìobhte *f*;
(*hire*) fastadh *m v* fastaidh
chase *n* sealg *f*, tòir *f*, faghaid *f*
v ruith (às dèidh) **c. away** ruaig,
fuadaich
chasm *n* mòr-bheàrn *m*
chat *n* còmhradh *m*, crac *m v*
dèan còmhradh/crac/conaltradh
cheap *a* saor; (*remark*) suarach
cheat *n* mealltair *m v* meall,
thoir an car à, dèan foill air
check *v* dèan cinnteach, thoir
sùil air; (*stop*) caisg, bac;
(*reprove*) cronaich

checklist *n* liosta-sgrùdaidh *f*
cheek *n* gruaidh *f*, lethcheann *m*;
(*met*) mì-mhodh *m* **some cheek!**
abair aghaidh!
cheeky *a* aghach, mì-mhodhail
cheer *v* tog spiorad, dèan
sunndach **c. on** brosnaich,
misnich
cheerful *a* sunndach, aighearach,
ait
cheese *n* càise *f m*; (*one*)
mulchag *f* **cheesecake** càis-
chèic *f*
chef *n* còcaire *m*
chemical *n* ceimig *f a* ceimigeach
chemist *n* ceimigear *m*;
(*pharmacist*) cungaidhear *m* **c.'s
shop** bùth-cungaidheir *f*
chemistry *n* ceimigeachd *f*, ceimig
f
cheque *n* seic *f* **c.-book** leabhar-
sheicichean *m*
cherry *n* siris(t) *f*
chess *n* tàileasg *m*, fidhcheall *m*
chest *n* ciste *f*; (*human*) cliabh *m*,
broilleach *m* **c. of drawers** ciste-
dhràthraichean *f*
chestnut *n* geanm-chnò *f*
chew *v* cagainn, cnàmh
chick(en) *n* isean *m*; (*pullet*)
eireag *f*; (*food*) cearc *f*, sitheann
f m
chickenpox *n* a' bhreac-òtraich *f*
chief *n* ceannard *m*; (*clan*) ceann-
feadhna *m* **c. executive** àrd-
oifigear *m a* prìomh, àrd
(*precedes n*)
chieftain *n* ceann-feadhna/cinnidh
m
child *n* leanabh *m*, pàiste *m*
c. benefit sochair chloinne *f*
c. care cùram-chloinne *m*
childhood *n* leanabas *m*
childish *a* leanabail, leanabaidh
children *n* clann *f*
chill(y) *a* fuar, aognaidh
chimney *n* similear *m*, luidhear *m*
chin *n* smig *f m*, smiogaid *f m*
Chinese *n, a* Sìonach *m*, (*female*)
ban-S(h)ìonach *f*
chip *n* mìr *m*, sgealb *f*, sliseag *f*
chips sliseagan (buntàta) *f pl*
v sgealb, snaigh

chisel *n* (s)geilb *f*, sgathair(e) *m*
chlorine *n* clòrain *m*
chocolate *n* seoclaid *f*, teòclaid *f*
choice *n* roghainn *m*, taghadh *m*
choir *n* còisir(-chiùil) *f*
cholesterol *n* coileastarail *m*
choke *v* tachd, mùch
choose *v* tagh, roghnaich
chop *v* sgud
chord *n* còrd(a) *m*
chore *n* car-obrach *m*
chorus *n* sèist *f m*, co-sheirm *f*
Christ *n* Crìosd(a) *m*
christen *v* baist
christening *n* baisteadh *m*
Christian *n* Crìosdaidh *m a*
    Crìosdail **C. name** ainm baistidh
    m
Christianity *n* Crìosdaidheachd *f*,
    Crìosdalachd *f*, an creideamh
    Crìosdaidh/Crìosdail *m*
Christmas *n* Nollaig *f* **C. Day**
    Là/Latha na Nollaig(e) *m* **C.**
    Eve Oidhche Nollaig *f* **Merry C.!**
    Nollaig Chridheil!
chronic *a* fìor dhona, trom;
    (*med*) buan, leantalach; (*slang*)
    cianail
chum *n* companach *m*, caraid *m*
chunk *n* caob *m*, cnap *m*
church *n* eaglais *f* **C. of Scotland**
    Eaglais na h-Alba **Catholic C.**
    an Eaglais Chaitligeach
    Episcopal C. an Eaglais
    Easbaigeach **Baptist C.** an
    Eaglais Bhaisteach **Free C.** an
    Eaglais Shaor **Free Presbyterian**
    C. an Eaglais Shaor Chlèireach
churchyard cladh *m*, cill *f*
churlish *a* mosach, neo-fhialaidh
churn *n* crannachan *m*, muidhe
    m
cider *n* leann-ubhal *m*
cigar *n* siogàr *m*
cigarette *n* toitean *m*, siogarait *f*
cinder *n* èibhleag *f*
cinema *n* taigh-dhealbh *m*
cinnamon *n* caineal *m*
circle *n* cearcall *m*, cuairt *f*,
    buaile *f v* cuairtich, cuartaich,
    iadh
circuit *n* cuairt *f*
circular *n* cuairt-litir *f a* cruinn,

cearclach, cuairteagach
circulate *v* cuir mun cuairt, cuir
    timcheall, cuairtich
circumference *n* cearcall-thomhas
    m
circumspect *a* faiceallach, aireach
circumstance *n* cùis *f*, cor *m*,
    staid *f*, suidheachadh *m*
circus *n* soircas *m*
cistern *n* tanca *f m*
cite *v* ainmich, tog; (*leg*) thoir
    sumanadh do, gairm
citizen *n* saoranach *m*, neach-
    àiteachaidh *m*, neach-dùthcha
    m
city *n* cathair-bhaile *f*, cathair *f*,
    baile-mòr *m*
civic *a* cathaireach, catharra
civil *a* catharra; (*behaviour*)
    sìobhalta, modhail, rianail **the**
    Civil Service an t-Seirbheis
    Chatharra *f* **c. servant**
    seirbheiseach catharra *m*
    c. rights còraichean catharra *f*
    pl **c. war** cogadh catharra *m*
civilian *n* sìobhaltach *m*, neach
    nach eil san Arm *m*
    a sìobhaltach
civilization *n* sìobhaltachd *f*
civilize *v* sìobhailich, cuir fo rian
claim *n* tagradh *m*, còir *f* **c. form**
    foirm-tagraidh *m v* (t)agair
clam *n* creachan(n) *m*
clamour gleadhraich *f*, othail *f*
clan *n* fine *f*, cinneadh *m*
    clansman fear-cinnidh *m*
clap *n* bas-bhualadh *m*; (*of*
    thunder) brag *m v* buail
    boisean, bas-bhuail
clarify *v* soilleirich, dèan soilleir
clarinet *n* clàirneid *f*
clarity *n* soilleireachd *f*
clash *n* (*dispute*) connsachadh *m*;
    (*sound*) glagadaich *f*
clasp *n* cromag *f*, dealg *m*;
    (*embrace*) cnèadachadh *m*
class *n* (*educ*) clas *m*; (*type*)
    seòrsa *m* **social c.** eagar
    sòisealta *m* **classroom**
    rùm/seòmar-teagaisg *m*
classic(al) *a* clasaigeach
classified *a* (*information*)
    dìomhair, glaiste

classify v seòrsaich
clause n (gram) clàs m; (condition) cumha f m
claw n spuir m, ionga f
clay n crèadh f, crè f
clean a glan v glan
cleaner n glanadair m, neach-glanaidh m
cleanliness n glainead m
cleanse v glan, ionnlaid
clear v (clarify) soilleirich; (tidy) rèitich, sgioblaich; (free) saor a soilleir
clearance n fuadach m **the Highland Clearances** na Fuadaichean
cleg n creithleag f
clemency n tròcair f, iochd f
clench v teannaich, dùin
clergy n clèir f **clergyman** pears-eaglais m
clerk n clèireach m **township c.** clàrc a' bhaile m
clever a deas, clis
click v gliog; (met) thig air a chèile
client n neach-dèiligidh m
cliff n creag f, bearradh m
climate n gnàth-shìde f
climax n àirde f
climb v dìrich, streap
climber n streapadair m
climbing n dìreadh m, streap m
clinch v daingnich, teannaich, dùin
cling v claon (ri)
clinic n clionaig f
clink v dèan gliong
clip n cliop m v geàrr, bearr; (sheep) rùisg; (shorten) giorraich
cloak n cleòc(a) m, fallainn f
clock n cloc m
clockwise a deasail, deiseil
close n (closure) dùnadh m, crìoch f, ceann m; (in tenement) clobhsa m v dùin; (end) crìochnaich
close a faisg, teann, dlùth; (atmos) dùmhail, murtaidh
closed a dùinte
closing n dùnadh **c. date** ceann-latha m
cloth n aodach m **dish-c.**

searbhadair-shoithichean m, tubhailt(e)-shoithichean f m **table-c.** tubhailt(e)-bùird f m
clothe v còmhdaich, èid
clothes n aodach m **c.-peg** bioran-anairt m, cnag-aodaich f
clothing n aodach m, èideadh m, trusgan m
cloud n sgòth f, neul m
cloudy a sgòthach, neulach
clover n clòbhar m; (single plant) seamrag f
clown n tuaistear m; (met) amadan m
club n cuaille m; (in sport) caman m; (association) club m **clubhouse** taigh-club m
cluck v dèan gogail
clue n tuairmse f **he hasn't a c.** chan eil sgot/poidhs aige
clump n bad m
clumsy a cliobach, cearbach, liobasta
cluster n bagaid f, cluigean m
clutch v greimich (air), glac
clutter n frachd m
coach n coidse f, bus m; (instructor) oide m v oidich, teagaisg, ionnsaich
coal n gual m **c. mine** mèinn(e)-guail f, toll-guail m
coalition n co-bhanntachd f; aonachadh m, tàthadh m **c. government** riaghaltas co-bhanntachd m
coarse a (texture) garbh; (manners) curs, neo-fhìnealta, amh
coast n oirthir f, costa m **coastguard** maor-cladaich m
coat n còta m **c. of arms** gearradh arm m v còmhdaich, cuir còta air
coax v coitich, tàlaidh
cobweb n eige f, lìon damhain-allaidh m
cocaine n coicèan m
cock n (bird) coileach m **c.-crow** gairm coilich f **haycock** coc fheòir f
cockle n coilleag f, srùban m
cocktail n earball a' choilich m, geinealag f

cocky *a* bragail
cocoa *n* còco *m*
coconut *n* cnò-còco *f*
cod *n* bodach(-ruadh) *m*, (*large*)
   trosg *m*
code còd *m*, riaghailt *f*; (*rule*)
   c. of conduct riaghailt obrach *f*
coerce *v* èignich, ceannsaich
co-exist *v* bi beò le
coffee *n* cofaidh *f m*
coffin *n* ciste(-laighe) *f*
cog *n* fiacail *f*, roth *f m*
cogent *a* làidir, cumhachdach
coherent *a* pongail, rianail,
   ciallach
cohesion *n* co-cheangal *m*,
   leantalachd *f*, co-thàthadh *m*
cohesive *a* co-cheangailte,
   leantalach, co-thàthach
coil *n* cuibhle *f*, cuairteag *f*
coin *n* bonn (airgid) *m*
coincide *v* co-thuit; (*agree*)
   co-aontaich, thig ri chèile
coincidence *n* tuiteamas *m*,
   co-thuiteamas *m*; (*agreement*)
   co-aontachadh *m*
coke *n* còc *m*
cold *n* fuachd *m*; (*common*)
   cnatan *m* **she had the c.** bha an
   cnatan oirre *a* fuar
colic *n* grèim-mionaich *m*
collaborate *v* co-obraich
collaboration *n* co-obrachadh *m*
collapse *v* tuit (am broinn a
   chèile); (*of person*) rach ann an
   laig(s)e
collar *n* coilear *m*; (*on horse*)
   braighdean *m* **c.-bone** ugan *m*,
   cnàimh an uga *m*
collate *v* cuir ri chèile
colleague *n* co-obraiche *m*,
   companach *m*
collect *v* cruinnich, tionail, trus;
   (*money*) tog
collection *n* cruinneachadh *m*,
   tional *m*
collector *n* cruinniche *m*, neach-
   tionail *m*
college *n* colaiste *f m*
collision *n* bualadh *m*, sgleog *f*
colon *n* caolan mòr *m*; (*gram*)
   còilean *f*
colonel *n* còirneal *m*, còirnealair *m*

colonial *a* colòiniach
colony *n* coloinidh *m*, eilthir *f*
colossal *a* àibheiseach
colour *n* dath *m* **c.-blind** dath-
   dhall *v* dath, cuir dath air;
   (*blush*) rudhadh *m*
coloured *a* dathte
colourful *a* dathach
column *n* colbh *m*; (*rock
   formation*) stac *m*
coma *n* trom-neul *m*, còma *m*
comb *n* cìr *f*; (*coxcomb*) cìrean *m*
   honeycomb cìr-mheala *f v* cìr
combine *v* cuir/rach còmhla
come *v* thig, ruig **where do you c.
   from?** cò às a tha thu? **if it
   comes to the bit** ma thig e gu
   h-aon 's gu dhà **c. on!** trobhad!
   t(h)ugainn! **c. to pass** tachair
comedy *n* comadaidh *m*, mear-
   chluich *f*
comet *n* reul chearbach *f*,
   rionnag an earbaill *f*
comfort *n* cofhurtachd *f
   v* cofhurtaich
comfortable *a* cofhurtail, socair
comic *n* comaig *f m*
comic(al) *a* èibhinn, ait, comaig
comma *n* cromag *f* **inverted
   commas** cromagan turrach
command *n* òrdugh *m*;
   (*authority*) ùghdarras *m*,
   smachd *f v* thoir òrdugh
   (seachad), òrdaich, àithn, bi an
   ceann; (*eg respect*) dleas
commander *n* ceannard *m*
commandment *n* òrdugh *m*;
   (*Bibl*) àithne *f*
commemorate *v* cuimhnich,
   comharraich
commence *v* tòisich
commend *v* mol
commendable *a* ionmholta, ri
   mholadh, airidh air moladh
comment *n* iomradh *m*, facal *m*,
   luaidh *m*, aithris *f v* thoir
   tarraing (air), dèan
   luaidh/aithris (air)
commentary *n* cunntas *m*, aithris
   f
commentator *n* neach-aithris *m*
commerce *n* malairt *f*
commercial *a* malairteach

commiserate *v* nochd co-fhaireachdainn/truas ri
commission *n* coimisean *m*; (*warrant*) barantas *m* **the European C.** an Coimisean Eòrpach *m* *v* barantaich
commissioner *n* coimiseanair *m*
commit *v* cuir an gnìomh; (*undertake*) cuir roimhe/roimhpe *etc*; (*entrust*) earb (ri)
committed *a* dealasach, daingeann **c. to/for ...** (*fin*) air a ghealltainn airson ...
commitment *n* dealas *m*
committee *n* comataidh *f* **sub-c.** fo-chomataidh
common *a* cumanta, coitcheann
common sense *n* toinisg *f*
commonwealth *n* co-fhlaitheas *m*
commotion *n* ùpraid *f*
communal *n* coitcheann
communicant *n* comanaiche *m*, neach-comanachaidh *m*
communicate *v* compàirtich, aithris, cuir an cèill, dèan conaltradh
communication *n* compàirteachadh *m*, conaltradh *m*
communion *n* co-chomann *m*; (*relig*) comanachadh *m*, comain *m* **take c.** comanaich *v*
communism *n* comannachas *m*, co-mhaoineas *m*
communist *n* comannach *m*, co-mhaoineach *m* *a* comannach, co-mhaoineach
community *n* coimhearsnachd *f*, co-chuideachd *f* **c. centre** ionad coimhearsnachd *m* **c. council** comhairle coimhearsnachd *f* **c. service** seirbheis coimhearsnachd *f*
commute *v* (*travel*) siubhail
compact *a* teann, dùmhail, daingeann
compact disc *n* meanbh-chlàr *m*
companion *n* companach *m*
company *n* cuideachd *f*, comann *m*; (*firm*) companaidh *f* *m*
comparable *a* cosmhail, a ghabhas coimeas **they're not c.**

chan ionann iad
compare *v* coimeas, dèan coimeas (ri/eadar)
comparison *n* coimeas *m*
compartment *n* earrann *f*; (*room*) seòmar *m*
compass *n* combaist *f*, cairt-iùil *f*; (*ambit*) raon *m*
compassion *n* truas *m*, iochd *f*
compassionate *a* truasail, iochdmhor
compatible *a* co-chòrdail, co-fhreagarrach
compel *v* co-èignich, thoir air
compensate *v* dìol, ìoc, cuidhtich
compensation *n* dìoladh *m*, cuidhteachadh *m*
compete *v* strì, dèan farpais
competent *a* comasach
competition *n* co-fharpais *f*, farpais *f*
competitive *a* farpaiseach, strìtheil **c. tendering** tairgseachadh farpaiseach *m*
competitor *n* farpaiseach *m*
compile *v* cuir ri chèile, co-chruinnich
complacency *n* somaltachd *f*
complacent *a* somalta
complain *v* gearain, dèan gearan, dèan casaid
complaint *n* gearan *m*, casaid *f*; (*med*) treamhlaidh *f*
complement *n* làn *m* **a full c. of staff** làn-sgioba *f m*
complete *v* crìochnaich; (*form etc*) lìon *a* iomlan, coileanta
completely *adv* gu h-iomlan, gu tur, buileach
complex *a* iomadh-fhillte, casta
complexion *n* tuar *m*, dreach *m*
complicated *a* toinnte
compliment *n* moladh *m* **with compliments** le dùrachd *f* *v* mol, dèan moladh
comply *v* thig/dèan a rèir, cùm ri
component *n* pàirt *f m*, pìos *m*
compose *v* dèan, cuir ri chèile, sgrìobh; (*oneself*) socraich/ stòldaich (e/i *etc* fhèin)
composed *a* socraichte, ciùin, stòlda
composer *n* (*mus*) sgrìobhaiche

ciùil *m*; (*liter*) ùghdar *m*
composition *n* sgrìobhadh *m*;
(*essay*) aiste *f*
compost *n* todhar gàrraidh *m*
composure *n* suaimhneas *m*,
socrachd *f*
compound *n* coimeasgadh *m*,
co-thàthadh *m*
comprehend *v* tuig
comprehension *n* tuigse *f*
comprehensive *a* coitcheann,
farsaing, iomlan, ioma-
chuimseach **c. education**
foghlam coitcheann *m* **c. school**
sgoil choitcheann *f*
compromise *n* co-rèiteachadh *m*
compulsory *a* èigeantach,
èigneachail **c. purchase**
ceannach èigneachail *m*
compute *v* coimpiut, àireamhaich
computer *n* coimpiutair *m*
computing *n* coimpiutaireachd *f*
comrade *n* companach *m*
concave *a* fo-chearclach
conceal *v* ceil, cleith, falaich
concede *v* gèill, aidich, strìochd
conceit *n* fearas-mhòr(a) *f*,
mòrchuis *f*
conceited *a* baralach,
mòrchuiseach
conceive *v* fàs torrach/trom;
(*think*) gabh a-steach, tuig
concentrate *v* thoir dlùth-aire do
concentration *n* (*heed*) dlùth-aire
f; (*density*) dùmhlachd *f*
concentric *a* co-mheadhanach
concept *n* bun-bheachd *m*,
smaoineas *m*
conception *n* gineamhainn *m*;
(*thought*) beachd *m*
concern *n* cùram *m*, iomagain *f*;
(*business*) gnothach *m* *v* cuir
uallach/iomagain air; (*oneself
with*) gabh gnothach ri
concerning *prep* mu, mu
thimcheall (+ *gen*), mu
dheidhinn (+ *gen*)
concert *n* cuirm-chiùil *f*, consairt
f **c.-hall** talla-ciùil *m*
concession *n* strìochdadh *m*;
(*fin*) lasachadh *m*; (*licence etc*)
ceadachd *f*
conciliation *n* rèiteachadh *m*

concise *a* sgiobalta, goirid, geàrr
conclude *v* co-dhùin; (*finish*)
crìochnaich
conclusion *n* co-dhùnadh *m*;
(*finish*) crìoch *f*
concoct *v* dèan suas; (*mix*)
measgaich
concord *n* còrdadh *m*,
co-chòrdadh *m*
concrete *n* cruadhtan *m*, concrait
f m *a* rudail, nitheil; (*substance*)
concrait, de chruadhtan
concur *v* aontaich
concurrent *a* co-cheumnach,
co-ruitheach
concussion *n* criothnachadh-
eanchainn *m*
condemn *v* dìt
condensation *n* (*moisture*) taise *f*
condense *v* co-dhlùthaich,
sùmhlaich
condescend *v* deònaich,
irioslaich; (*be patronizing*) bi
mòrchuiseach
condescending *a* neo-uallach;
(*patronizing*) mòrchuiseach
condition *n* cùmhnant *m*, cumha
f; (*state*) cor *m*, staid *f* **on c.
that** air chùmhnant gu
conditional *a* air chùmhnant;
(*gram*) cumhach **c. tense** an
tràth cumhach *m*
condom *n* casgan-gin *m*
condone *v* leig seachad
conduct *n* giùlan *m*, dol-a-mach
m *v* stiùir, treòraich; (*oneself*)
giùlain
conductor *n* stiùiriche *m*; (*agent*)
stuth-giùlain *m*
conduit *n* cladhan-uisge *m*
cone *n* còn *m*; (*pine*) durcan *m*
confederation *n* co-chaidreachas *m*
confer *v* cuir comhairle ri; (*grant*)
builich
conference *n* co-labhairt *f*
confess *v* aidich; (*relig*)
faoisidich
confession *n* aideachadh *m*,
aidmheil *f*; (*relig*) èisteachd *f*,
faoisid *f*
confide *v* leig rùn ri
confidence *n* misneachd *f*,
dànadas *m*, earbsa *f*

confident *a* misneachail, dàna, bragail

confidential *a* dìomhair, fo rùn

confine *v* cùm a-staigh, cuir crìochan ro

confinement *n* cùbadh *m*, braighdeanas *m*; *(pregnancy)* ùine air leabaidh-shiùbhla *f*

confirm *v* daingnich, dearbh

confirmation *n* daingneachadh *m*; *(relig)* dol fo làimh easbaig *m*

conflict *n* strì *f*, còmhstri *f*, còmhrag *f*

conform *v* rach le, co-fhreagair, gèill, dèan/rach a rèir

confront *v* seas mu choinneimh, còmhlaich, cuir aghaidh air

confrontation *n* cur aghaidh air *m*

confuse *v* cuir troimh-a-chèile

confused *a* troimh-a-chèile

confusion *n* breisleach *m*, troimh-a-chèile *m*

congeal *v* reoth

congenial *a* taitneach, ri a c(h)àil *etc*

congestion *n* dùmhlachd *f*

congratulate *v* cuir meal-a-naidheachd air

congratulation(s) *n* co-ghàirdeachas *m* **c.!** meal do naidheachd!

congregate *v* cruinnich

congregation *n* coitheanal *m*, co-chruinneachadh *m*

congress *n* còmhdhail *f*

conifer *n* craobh-durcain *f*

conjecture *n* barail *f*, tuairmeas *m*

connect *v* ceangail

connected *a* ceangailte

connection *n* ceangal *m*, co-bhann *f* **in c. with** a thaobh (+ *gen*)

conquer *v* ceannsaich, cìosnaich

conquest *n* buaidh *f*, ceannsachadh *m*

conscience *n* cogais *f*, cuinnseas *f*

conscientious *a* cogaiseach

conscious *a* mothachail

consecrate *v* coisrig

consecration *n* coisrigeadh *m*

consecutive *a* co-leantaileach, às dèidh a chèile

consensus *n* co-aontachd *f*

consent *n* aonta *m*, cead *m* *v* aontaich

consequence *n* buil *f*, buaidh *f*, toradh *m*

consequently *adv* uime sin, ri linn sin

conservation *n* glèidhteachas *m*, gleidheadh *m*, dìon *m*

conservationist *n* neach-glèidhteachais *m*

Conservative *n* Tòraidh *m* **the C. Party** am Partaidh Tòraidheach *m*

conservative *a* caomhnach, glèidhteach, stuama

conserve *v* glèidh, taisg, dìon

consider *v* smaoinich, beachdaich, meòraich

considerable *a* cudromach, fiùghail

considerate *a* suimeil, mothachail, coibhneil

consideration *n* suimealachd *f*, coibhneas *m*; *(of matter)* beachdachadh *m*

consistency *n* cunbhalachd *f*

consistent *a* cunbhalach **c. with** co-chòrdail (ri)

consolation *n* furtachd *f*

consolidate *v* daingnich, neartaich

consonant *n* connrag *f*

consortium *n* co-bhanntachd *f*

conspicuous *a* follaiseach, nochdte

conspiracy *n* co-fheall *f*, gùim *m*

conspire *v* dèan co-fheall/gùim

constable *n* constabal *m*, maor-sìthe *m*

constant *a* seasmhach, daingeann, cunbhalach, dìleas

consternation *n* clisgeadh *m*, uabhas *m*

constituency *n* roinn-phàrlamaid *f*

constitution *n* *(phys)* aorabh *m*, dèanamh *m*; *(org)* bonn-stèidh *m*; *(polit)* bun-reachd *m*

constrain *v* co-èignich, thoir air

constrict *v* teannaich, tachd

construct *v* dèan, tog, cuir ri chèile

construction *n* cur ri chèile *m*;
(*building*) togail *f*, togalach *m*
under c. ga t(h)ogail, gan togail
constructive *a* cuideachail,
adhartach
consul *n* consal *m*
consult *v* cuir comhairle ri, gabh
comhairle
consultant *n* co-chomhairliche *m*
consultation *n* co-chomhairle *f*
c. paper pàipear co-
chomhairleachaidh *m*
consultative *a* co-
chomhairleachaidh
c. committee comataidh co-
chomhairleachaidh *f*
consume *v* (*use*) caith; (*food*) ith;
(*burn*) loisg
consumer *n* neach-cleachdaidh
m, caitheadair *m* *pl* luchd-
caitheimh/cleachdaidh
consummate *a* barraichte
consumption *n* caitheamh *f*;
(*med*) a' chaitheamh *f*
contact *n* (*abstr*) co-cheangal *m*;
(*phys*) suathadh *m*, beantainn
m *v* cuir fios gu, bi an tobha ri
contagious *a* gabhaltach
contain *v* cùm; (*keep in check*)
bac, caisg
container *n* soitheach *f m*; (*for
cargo*) bogsa-stòraidh *m*
contaminate *v* truaill, salaich,
gànraich
contemplate *v* beachd-smaoinich,
meòraich, gabh beachd air
contemporary *a* co-aimsireil; (*in
age*) co-aoiseach *n* comhaois *m*
contempt *n* tàir *f*, tarcais *f* **he
was held in c.** bha e air a chur
ann an suarachas
contemptible *a* suarach
contemptuous *a* tàireil,
tarcaiseach
contend *v* cathaich, dèan strì an
aghaidh (+ *gen*); (*maintain*) cùm
a-mach
content *n* susbaint *f*
content(ed) *a* riaraichte, toilichte
contention *n* còmhstri *f*,
connspaid *f*, aimhreit *f*,
argamaid *f*
contentious *a* connspaideach

contentment *n* toileachas
(-inntinn) *m*, riarachadh *m*
contents *n* na tha ann, na tha am
broinn ... **list of c.** clàr-innse *m*
contest *n* strì *f*, farpais *f* *v* dèan
strì; (*election*) seas
contestant *n* farpaiseach *m*
context *n* co-theacs(a) *m*
continent *n* mòr-thìr *f*
continually *adv* gun sgur,
a-ghnàth **c. asking** a' sìor
fhaighneachd
continue *v* lean (air)
continuing *a* leantainneach,
a' leantainn
continuity *n* leantalachd *f*
continuous *a* leantainneach
c. assessment measadh
leantainneach *m*
contraception *n* casg-
gin(eamhainn) *m*
contraceptive *a* casg-
gineamhainneach
contract *n* cùmhnant *m*,
cunnradh *m* **c. of employment**
cùmhnant-obrach *m* *v* (*lessen*)
lùghdaich; (*enter into*) dèan
cùmhnant; (*illness*) gabh
contraction *n* teannachadh *m*,
crìonadh *m*, giorrachadh *m*,
lùghdachadh *m*
contractor *n* cunnradair *m*
contradict *v* cuir an aghaidh
(+ *gen*)
contrary *a* an aghaidh (+ *gen*)
contrast *n* eadar-dhealachadh *m*,
ao-coltas *m* *v* cuir an aghaidh
a chèile, dèan iomsgaradh eadar
contravene *v* bris(t), rach an
aghaidh
contribute *v* cuir ri, cuidich le
c. to thoir ... do
contribution *n* tabhartas *m*,
cuideachadh *m*
contrite *a* fo aithreachas
control *n* (*abstr*) smachd *m*,
ùghdarras *m* **controls** uidheam-
stiùiridh *f* *v* ceannsaich **gain c.**
faigh smachd air
controller *n* neach-riaghlaidh *m*,
rianadair *m*
controversial *a* connspaideach,
connsachail

controversy *n* connspaid *f*, connsachadh *m*
conundrum *n* tòimhseachan (toinnte) *m*
convene *v* tionail, cruinnich, gairm
convener *n* neach-gairm *m*
convenience *n* goireas *m* **public c.** goireasan poblach
convenient *a* goireasach
convent *n* taigh-cràbhaidh *m*, clochar *m*
convention *n* (*norm*) cleachdadh *m*, gnàthas *m*; (*body*) co-chruinneachadh *m*; (*agreement*) cùmhnant *m*
conventional *a* gnàthach
conversant with *a* fiosrach (mu), eòlach (air)
conversation *n* còmhradh *m*
converse *v* dèan còmhradh
conversion *n* (*relig*) iompachadh *m*; (*building*) atharrachadh *m*
convert *n* iompachan *m*
convert *v* (*relig*) iompaich; atharraich
convex *a* os-chearclach
convey *v* giùlain, iomchair
convict *v* dìt
conviction *n* dìteadh *m*; (*feeling*) faireachdainn làidir *f*
convince *v* dearbh (do)
convivial *a* cuideachdail
convoy *n* comhailteachd *f*; (*naut*) luing-dhion *f pl*
coo *v* dèan dùrdail/tùchan
cook *n* còcaire *m* *v* còcairich, deasaich biadh, bruich
cooker *n* cucair *m*
cookery, cooking *n* còcaireachd *f*
cool *a* fionnar; (*colloq*) smodaig *v* fuaraich, fionnaraich
co-operate *v* co-obraich
co-operation *n* co-obrachadh *f*
co-operative *a* co-obrachail, cuideachail
co-opt *v* co-thagh
co-opted *a* co-thaghte
co-option *n* co-thaghadh *m*
co-ordinate *v* co-òrdanaich
co-ordinated *a* co-òrdanaichte
co-ordination *n* co-òrdanachadh *m*

co-ordinator *n* co-òrdanaiche *m*
cope *v* dèan an gnothach/a' chùis
copious *a* lìonmhor, pailt
copper *n* copar *m*
copse *n* badan *m*, frith-choille *f*
copulate *v* cuplaich
copy *n* lethbhreac *m*, copaidh *f* *m* *v* copaig, dèan lethbhreac, ath-sgrìobh
copyright *n* còraichean (foillseachaidh) *f pl*, dlighe-sgrìobhaidh *f*
coral *n* corail *m*
cord *n* còrd *m*, bann *m*
cordial *a* cridheil, càirdeil
core *n* cridhe *m*, eitean *m*
cork *n* àrc *f*, corcais *f*
corkscrew *n* sgriubha-àrc *m*
cormorant *n* sgarbh *m*
corn *n* arbhar *m*; (*on foot*) còrn *m* **c. on the cob** dias Innseanach *f*
corncrake *n* traon *m*, ràc an arbhair *m*
corner *n* oisean *m*, cùil *f*, còrnair *m* **c. kick** breab-oisein *f* **c. stone** clach-oisein/-oisne *f*
cornflakes *n* bleideagan coirce *f*
Cornish *a* Còrnach **C. person** *n* Còrnach *m*, (*female*) ban-Chòrnach *f*
coronation *n* crùnadh *m*
corporal *n* corpailear *m*
corporal *a* corporra, bodhaige
corporate *a* corporra
corporation *n* corporaid *f*, comhairle baile-mòr *f*
corpse *n* corp *m*, marbhan *m*
correct *v* ceartaich *a* ceart
correction *n* ceartachadh *m*
correlation *n* co-dhàimh *f*
correspond *v* co-fhreagair; (*write*) sgrìobh
correspondence *n* litrichean *f pl*, sgrìobhadh *m*; (*match*) co-fhreagradh *m*
corridor *n* trannsa *f*
corroborate *v* daingnich, co-dhearbh
corrode *v* meirg
corrosion *n* meirg *f*, meirgeadh *m*
corrugated *a* preasach **c. iron** iarann liorcach *m* **c. paper**

pàipear preasach *m*

corrupt *a* coirbte, breun, truaillte *v* coirb, truaill

corrupted *a* coirbte, truaillte

corruption *n* coirbeachd *f*, truaillidheachd *f*

cosmetic *n* cungaidh maise *f* **c. surgery** lannsaireachd cruth *f* *a* (*met*) air an uachdar

cosmonaut *n* speur(ad)air *m*

cosmopolitan *a* os-nàiseanta

cost *n* cosgais *f* **c. of living** cosgais bith-beò *f* *v* cosg

costly *a* cosgail, daor

costume *n* culaidh *f*

cosy *a* seasgair

cot *n* cot *m*

cottage *n* taigh-còmhnaidh beag *m*

cotton *n* cotan *m* **bog-c.** an canach *m* **c.-wool** snàth-cotain *m* *a* cotain

couch *n* sèidhs(e) *f*, langasaid *f*

cough *n* casad *m* *v* dèan casad

coughing *n* casadaich *f* *Also vn* a' casadaich

council *n* comhairle *f* **C. of Europe** Comhairle na h-Eòrpa *f* **C. Tax** Cìs Comhairle *f*

councillor *n* comhairliche *m*

counsel *v* comhairlich

counsellor *n* neach-comhairle *m*, comhairleach *m*

count *v* cunnt, cunntais, àireamh(aich)

countenance *n* gnùis *f*

counter *n* cuntair *m*

counter *v* rach an aghaidh (+ *gen*)

countess *n* ban-iarla *f*

counting *n* cunntadh *m*, cunntais *f m*

countless *a* gun àireamh, do-àireamh

country *n* dùthaich *f*, tìr *f*, rìoghachd *f*

countryside *n* dùthaich *f* **in the c.** air an dùthaich/tuath

county *n* siorrachd *f*, siorramachd *f*

couple *n* càraid *f*, dithis *f* **a c. of hours** dà uair

courage *n* misneach(d) *f*,

smior *m*

courageous *a* misneachail, smiorail, tapaidh

courier *n* teachdaire *m*

course *n* cùrsa *m*; (*route*) slighe *f*, cùrsa *m*

court *n* cùirt *f* **courthouse** taigh-cùirte/cùrtach *m*

court *v* dèan suirghe *vn* a' suirghe

courteous *a* cùirteil, modhail, suairce

courtesy *n* modh *f m*, modhalachd *f*

courtship *n* suirghe *f*, leannanachd *f*

cousin *n* co-ogha *m*

covenant *n* cùmhnant *m*

cover *n* còmhdach *m*, brat *m*; (*for bed*) cuibhrig(e) *f m* *v* còmhdaich; (*deal with*) dèilig ri

covering *n* còmhdach *m*, brat *m*

covert *a* dìomhair, falaichte, os ìosal

covet *v* sanntaich

cow *n* bò *f*, mart *m*

coward *n* gealtaire *m*, cladhaire *m*

cowardice *n* gealtachd *f*, cladhaireachd *f*

coy *a* nàrach, màlda

crab *n* crùbag *f*, partan *m*

crabbed/crabbit *a* greannach

crack *n* sgàineadh *m*, sgoltadh *m* *v* sgàin, sgoilt

cradle *n* creathail *f*

craft *n* ceàird *f*; (*cunning*) seòltachd *f*; (*boat*) bàta *m*

craftsman neach-ceàirde *m*

crafty *a* seòlta, carach

crag *n* creag *f*, stalla *f*, carraig *f*

cram *v* dinn

crammed *a* dinnte, dùmhail

cramp *n* an t-orc *m*, cramb *f*

crane *n* crann *m*; (*bird*) corra-mhonaidh *f*

cranny *n* cùil *f*, fròg *f*

crash *n* stàirn *f*, bualadh *m* *v* buail na chèile, craisig

crate *n* cliath-bhogsa *m*, creat *m*

craving *n* cìocras *m*, miann *f m*

crawl *v* snàig, crùb

crayon *n* creidhean *m*, cailc dhathte *f*

craze *n* fasan *m*, annas *m*
crazy *a* cracte, às a c(h)iall *etc*
creak *n* dìosgan *m* *v* dìosg, dèan
dìosgan *Also vn* a' dìòsganaich
cream *n* uachdar *m*, bàrr *m*;
(*cosmetic*) cè *m*
crease *n* filleadh *m*, preas *m*
v preas(aich)
create *v* cruthaich
creation *n* cruthachadh *m*
Creation an Cruthachadh *m*,
a' Chruthaigheachd *f*
creative *a* cruthachail
creator *n* neach-cruthachaidh *m*
the C. an Cruthaighear *m*
creature *n* creutair *m*
credibility *n* creideas *m*
credible *a* creideasach, a ghabhas
creidsinn
credit *n* creideas *m* **c. card** cairt-
creideis *f* **that's to his c.** tha e ri
mholadh airson sin *v* creid
creditable *a* teisteil, measail
creditor *n* neach-fiach *m*,
creideasaiche *m*
creed *n* creud *f*, creideamh *m*
creek *n* geodha *m*, òb *m*, òban *m*
creel *n* cliabh *m*
creep *v* snàig, èalaidh, liùg
cremate *v* luaithrich
crematorium *n* luaithreachan *m*
crescent *n* corran *m*; (*of moon*)
corran-gealaich *m*
cress *n* biolair *f*
crest *n* suaicheantas *m*; (*bird*)
cìrean *m*; (*topog*) mullach *m*,
bàrr *m*
crevice *n* sgoltadh *m*, sgàineadh
m
crew *n* sgioba *f m*, criutha *m*
cricket *n* (*game*) criogaid *m*
crime *n* eucoir *f*
criminal *n, a* eucorach *m*
crimson *n, a* crò-dhearg *m*
cringe *v* crùb, gìog
cripple *n* crioplach *m*, bacach *m*
crippled *a* bacach, na
c(h)rioplach *etc*
crisis *n* càs *m*, èiginn *f*, gàbhadh
m
crisp *n* brisgean *m pl* brisgeanan
a brisg
criterion *n* slat-t(h)omhais *f*

critic *n* sgrùdair *m*, breithniche *m*
critical *a* (*vital*) deatamach,
èiginneach; (*liter*) sgrùdail,
breitheach; (*adversely*) beumach
criticism *n* càineadh; (*liter*)
sgrùdadh *m*, breithneachadh *m*
criticize *v* càin
croak *v* dèan gràgail
crockery *n* soithichean *m pl*
crocodile *n* crogall *m*
croft *n* croit *f*, lot(a) *m*
crofter *n* croitear *m* **Crofters
Commission** Ùghdarras nan
Croitearan
crony *n* seann charaid *m*, dlùth-
chompanach *m*
crook *n* cromag *f*; (*person*)
rògaire *m*
crooked *a* cam, crom, fiar
crop *n* (*harvest*) bàrr *m*; (*of bird*)
sgròban *m*; (*haircut*) bearradh
m v geàrr, buain; (*hair etc*)
beàrr
cross *n* crois *f*; (*crucifixion*)
crann-ceusaidh *m* **the Red C.**
a' Chrois Dhearg *a* crosta
v rach tarsainn/thairis **c. oneself**
dèan comharra na croise **c. a
cheque** cros seic
cross-beam *n* spàrr *f*, trastan *m*
cross-examine *v* cruaidh-
cheasnaich
cross-eyed *a* cam, cam-shùileach,
fiar-shùileach
crossfire *n* eadar-theine *m*
cross-legged *a* casa-gòbhlach
crossroads *n* crois (an) rathaid *f*
crossword *n* tòimhseachan-
tarsainn *m*
crotch *n* gobhal *m*
crouch *v* crom, crùb
crow *n* feannag *f*, starrag *f*
crowbar *n* geimhleag *f*
crowd *n* sluagh *m*; (*pej*) gràisg *f*
crowded *a* dùmhail
crowdie *n* gruth *m*
crown *n* crùn *m*; (*of head*)
mullach a' chinn *m*, bàrr
a' chinn *m v* crùn
crucial *a* deatamach
crucifix *n* crois *f*
crucify *v* ceus
crude *a* amh; (*met*) drabasta,

curs(a)

cruel *a* an-iochdmhor, neo-thruacanta

cruelty *n* an-iochd *f*, neo-thruacantachd *f*

cruise *n* cuairt-mara *f*, turas-cuain *m*

crumb *n* criomag *f*, sprùilleag *f*, mìr *m* **crumbs** sprùilleach *m*

crumple *v* rocaich

crunch *n* **when it comes to the c.** nuair a thig e gu h-aon 's gu dhà

crusade *n* iomairt *f* **the Crusades** Cogaidhean na Croise *m pl*

crush *n* bruthadh *m* *v* pronn; (*met*) ceannsaich, mùch

crust *n* rùsg *m*, plaosg *m*

crutch *n* crasg *f*, croitse *f*

crux *n* cnag (na cùise) *f*

cry *n* èigh *f*, glaodh *f m*, gairm *f*; (*tears*)ràn *m* *v* èigh, glaodh, gairm; (*shed tears*) caoin, guil

crying *n* èigheach(d) *f*, glaodhaich *f*; (*tears*) caoineadh, gal/gul *m*, rànaich *f*

crystal *n* criostal *m* *a* criostail

cube *n* ciùb *m*

cubic *a* ciùbach

cuckoo *n* cuthag *f*

cucumber *n* cularan *m*

cuddle *v* dèan cionacraich air

cue *n* (*sport*) slat-chluiche *f*, ciù *m*; (*stage*) cagar *m*; (*hair*) ciutha *m*

cuisine *n* modh còcaireachd *m*

cull *v* tanaich

culpable *a* ciontach, coireach **c. homicide** marbhadh le coire *m*

culprit *n* ciontach *m*

cultivate *v* àitich

cultivation *n* àiteach *m*

cultural *a* cultarach

culture *n* cultar *m*

cumbersome *a* trom, liobasta

cunning *a* seòlta, carach

cup *n* cupa *m*, copan *m* **cup final** cuairt dheireannach a' chupa *f*

cupboard *n* preas(a) *m*

curb *v* ceannsaich, bac, cuir srian air

curdle *v* binndich

cure *n* leigheas *m*; (*specific*) cungaidh-leigheis *f* *v* leighis,

slànaich; (*fish*) saill, ciùraig

curious *a* ceasnachail, farraideach, feòrachail; (*odd*) annasach, neònach

curl *n* dual *m*, bachlag *f*, cam-lùb *f* *v* bachlaich, caisich

curlew *n* guilbneach *f m*

curling *n* (*sport*) curladh *m*

curly *a* dualach, bachlagach, camagach

currant *n* dearc(ag) thiormaichte *f*

currency *n* airgead *m*

current *n* sruth *m*, buinne *f* **electric c.** sruth-dealain *m*

current *a* gnàthaichte, làithreach **c. account** cunntas làitheil *m*, cunntas-ruith *m* **c. affairs** cùisean an latha *f pl*

currently *adv* an-dràsta, an ceartuair

curriculum *n* curraicealam *m*, clàr-oideachais *m* **c. vitae** cunntas-beatha *m*

curry *n* coiridh *m*

curse *n* mallachd *f* *v* mallaich; (*swear*) mionnaich, bi ri na mionnan/guidheachan

cursory *a* cabhagach, gun aire

curtail *v* giorraich

curtain *n* cùirtear *m*, cùirtean *m*

curve *n* lùb *f*, camadh *m*

curved *a* lùbte, le camadh

cushion *n* cuisean *f m*, pillean *m*

custard *n* ughagan *m*

custody *n* grèim *m*, cùram *m*

custom *n* cleachdadh *m*, àbhaist *f*, gnàths *m*, nòs *m*

customary *a* àbhaisteach, gnàthach

customer *n* neach-ceanna(i)ch *m*

Customs *n* seirbheis na Cusbainn *f* **C. duty** cìs Cusbainn *f*

cut *n* gearradh *m* *v* geàrr, giorraich **cut hair** beàrr **his work is cut out for him** tha a dhìol/leòr aige ri dhèanamh

cutlery *n* uidheam-ithe *f*

cycle *n* cuairt *f*, cùrsa *m*; (*bicycle*) baidhsagal *m*, rothair *m*

cyclist *n* baidhsaglair *m*, rothaiche *m*

cyclone *n* toirm-ghaoth *f*, cuairt-gaoithe *f*
cygnet *n* isean eala *m*
cylinder *n* siolandair *m*
cymbal *n* tiompan *m*, ciombal *m*
cynic *n* sgaitear *m*, searbh-neach *m*
cynical *a* sgaiteachail, searbhasach
cyst *n* ùthan *m*, balgan *m*
Czech *n, a* Seiceach *m*, (*female*) ban-S(h)eiceach *f*

D

dab *v* suath
dad *n* dadaidh *m*
daffodil *n* lus a' chrom-chinn *m*
daft *a* gòrach, baoghalta
dagger *n* biodag *f*
daily *a* làitheil *adv* gach latha, gu làitheil
dainty *n* grinn, mìn
dairy *n* taigh-bainne *m* **d.-farm** tuathanachas bainne *m*
daisy *n* neòinean *m*
dale *n* dail *f*, gleann *m*
dam *n* dam *m*
damage *n* dìol *m*, dochann *m*, milleadh *m* *v* dèan dìol air, dèan dochann air, mill
damn! *interj* daingit!, gonadh!
damnable *a* damainte, mallaichte
damnation *n* dìteadh (sìorraidh) *m*, sgrios *m* *interj* daingit!
damp *a* tais
dampness *n* fuarachd *f*; (*weather*) taiseachd *f*
dance *n* dannsa *m* *v* danns, dèan dannsa
dancer *n* dannsair *m*
dancing *n* dannsa(dh) *m*
dandelion *n* beàrnan-brìde *m*
dandruff *n* sgealpaich *f*, càrr *f*
dandy *n* spaidire *m*
danger *n* cunnart *m*, gàbhadh *m*
dangerous *a* cunnartach
dangle *v* bi air bhogadan/udalan
Dane *n* Danmhairgeach *m*, (*female*) ban-D(h)anmhairgeach *f*
Danish *a* Danmhairgeach
dank *a* tungaidh

dapper *a* speiseanta
dare *v* dùraig; (*challenge*) thoir dùbhlan do **don't you d.** na gabh ort
daring *a* dàna
dark *a* dorch(a), doilleir **d. blue** dubh-ghorm
darken *v* dorchnaich
darkness *n* dorchadas *m*
darling *n* gaol *m*, gràdh *m*, eudail *f*, luaidh *f m* **my d.** a ghaoil, m' eudail a gaolach, gràdhach
darn *v* càirich
dart *n* gath *m*; (*move*) siorradh *m*
dash *n* ruith *f*, leum *m*, ruith is leum; (*punct*) strìochag *f*, sgrìob *f* *v* ruith, leum; (*break*) spealg, buail air **d. to pieces** spealt
data *n* dàta *m*
date *n* latha *m*; (*deadline*) ceann-latha *m*; (*appointment*) deit *f*; (*fruit*) deit *f* **up-to-d.** ùr-nòsach **to d.** gu ruige seo **d. of birth** latha-breith **out-of-d.** seann-fhasanta **past sell-by d.** seach an ceann-latha **she had a d. with Allan** bha deit aice fhèin 's Ailean *v* cuir latha air, comharraich an latha; (*intrans*) fàs seann-fhasanta
dative *a* tabhartach **the d. case** an tuiseal tabhartach *m*
daub *v* smeur, buaic
daughter *n* nighean *f* **d.-in-law** ban(a)-chliamhain *f*
dawn *n* camhana(i)ch *f*, beul an latha *m*
day *n* latha *m*, là *m* **the day after tomorrow** an-earar **the day before yesterday** a' bhòn-dè **d. centre** ionad latha *m* **daybreak** bris(t)eadh an latha *m* **daylight** solas an latha *m*
daze *v* cuir bho mhothachadh
dazzle *v* deàrrs, boillsgich
deacon *n* deucon *m*
dead *a* marbh **d. centre** teis-meadhan *m*
deadly *a* marbhtach
deaf *a* bodhar **d.-mute** balbhan *m*
deafen *v* bodhair, dèan bodhar
deafness *n* buidhre *f*
deal *n* cùmhnant *m*, cunnradh *m*

a great d. (*much*) tòrr *m* **a good
d.** deagh bhargan *m* *v* dèilig
(ri); (*in business*) dèan gnothach
ri; (*cards*) roinn
dealer *n* neach-malairt *m*; (*of
cards*) neach-roinn *m*
dean *n* deadhan *m*
dear *a* ionmhainn, gràdhach,
gaolach; (*expensive*) daor *n*
luaidh *f m*, gràdh *m*, eudail *m*
dearth *n* gainne *f*, dìth *f m*
death *n* bàs *m*, caochladh *m*, eug
m, aog *m*
debate *n* deasbad *f*,
deasbaireachd *f* *v* bi
a' deasbad, deasbair
debauched *a* neo-mheasarra,
stròdhail
debauchery *n* neo-mheasarrachd
f, mì-gheanmnachd *f*,
geòcaireachd *f*
debility *n* laige *f*, anfhainneachd *f*
debit(s) *n* fiachan *f pl* *v* thoir à
(cunntas)
debris *n* sprùilleach *m*
debt *n* fiachan *m pl*; (*met*)
comain *f* **in d.** ann am fiachan
debtor *n* neach-fhiach *m*
debut *n* ciad nochdadh *m*
decade *n* deichead *m*
decadence *n* claonadh *m*,
coirbeachd *f*
decadent *a* coirbte
decant *v* taom; (*move*) gluais
decay *n* crìonadh *m*, seargadh *m*,
lobhadh *m* *v* crìon, searg, caith
decayed *a* seargte, crìon, lobhte
decease *n* caochladh *m*, bàs *m*
the deceased am fear/tè nach
maireann
deceit *n* cealgaireachd *f*, cealg *f*,
foill *f*
deceitful *a* cealgach, foilleil
deceive *v* meall, thoir an car à
December *n* an Dùbhlachd *f*
decency *n* beusachd *f*,
cubhaidheachd *f*
decent *a* beusach, cubhaidh
decentralize *v* sgaoil a-mach,
gluais (bh)on mheadhan
deception *n* mealladh *m*, foill *f*
deceptive *a* meallta
decide *v* socraich/suidhich (air),

co-dhùin, cuir romhad
deciduous *a* seargach
decimal *n*, *a* deicheamh *m*
decipher *v* mìnich, fuasgail
decision *n* breith *f*, co-dhùnadh
m
decisive *a* dearbhachail,
cinnteach
deck *n* deic *f*, clàr-uachdair *m*;
(*of cards*) paca *m*
declaration *n* cur an cèill *m*
declare *v* cuir an cèill, inn(i)s
declension *n* cromadh *m*,
teàrnadh *m*; (*gram*) tuisealadh
m
decline *n* cromadh *m*, crìonadh
m, dol air ais *m*, dol sìos *m*
v crom, crìon, rach air ais, rach
sìos; (*gram*) claoin
decompose *v* lobh
decorate *v* sgeadaich, maisich
decoration *n* sgeadachadh *m*,
maiseachadh *m*
decorator *n* sgeadaiche *m*
decorum *n* stuaim *f*, deagh-bheus
f
decrease *n* lùghdachadh *m*, dol
sìos *m* *v* lùghdaich, beagaich,
rach sìos
decree *n* òrdugh *m*, reachd *m*,
breith *f* *v* òrdaich, reachdaich,
thoir breith
decrepit *a* breòite, anfhann
decry *v* cuir sìos air, càin
dedicate *v* coisrig **d. to** ainmich
air
dedicated *a* coisrigte;
(*committed*) dìcheallach
dedication *n* coisrigeadh *m*;
(*commitment*) dìcheall *f m*
deduce *v* dèan a-mach, tuig
deduct *v* thoir air falbh (bh)o
deed *n* gnìomh *m*, euchd *m*; (*leg*)
sgrìobhainn lagha *f*
deem *v* meas
deep *a* domhainn *n* doimhne *f*
deep-freeze *n* cruaidh-reothadair
m
deer *n* fiadh *m* **d.-forest** frìth *f*
deface *v* mill
defamation *n* tuaileas *m*, mì-chliù
m
defamatory *a* tuaileasach

defeat *n* call *m* *v* gabh air, faigh buaidh (air)
defect *n* easbhaidh *f*, uireasbhaidh *f*
defective *a* easbhaidheach, uireasbhach
defence *n* dìon *m*, dìdean *f*; (*excuse*) leisgeul *m* **d. mechanism** dòigh dèiligidh (ri) *f*
defend *v* dìon
defender *n* neach-dìon(a) *m*, dìonadair *m*
defensive *a* dìonadach
defer *v* cuir air dàil, dàilich **d. to** thoir inbhe/urram do
deference *n* ùmhlachd *f*, urram *m*
defiance *n* dùbhlan *m*
defiant *a* dùbhlanach
deficiency *n* easbhaidh *f*, dìth *f m*
deficient *a* easbhaidheach
deficit *n* easbhaidh *f*, call *m*
defile *v* salaich, truaill, gànraich
define *v* seall brìgh, mìnich
definite *a* cinnteach, deimhinn(t)e
definition *n* mìneachadh *m*, comharrachadh *m*; (*audio-visual*) gèire *f*, soilleireachd *f*
deflate *v* traogh, leig gaoth às; (*met*) thoir a' ghaoth à siùil
deflect *v* cuir air falbh bho; (*intrans*) aom, claon
deformity *n* mì-chumadh *m*, mì-dhealbh *f m*
defraud *v* dean foill (air)
deft *a* ealamh, deas
defunct *a* à bith, (bh)o fheum
defy *v* thoir dùbhlan do, cuir gu dùbhlan
degenerate *v* rach bhuaithe, meath
degrade *v* ìslich, truaill
degrading *a* maslach, truaillidh
degree *n* inbhe *f*, ìre *f*; (*acad*) ceum *m*; (*temp*) puing *f* **to some d.** gu ìre **by degrees** beag air bheag, mean air mhean
dehydration *n* sgreubhadh *m*
deity *n* diadhachd *f*; (*a god*) dia *m*
dejected *a* fo bhròn/phràmh/sprochd
dejection *n* sprochd *m*, smuairean *m*
delay *n* dàil *f*, maill(e) *f* *v* cuir dàil/maill(e) an/air, cùm air ais
delayed *a* (*late*) fadalach, air dheireadh
delegate *n* neach-ionaid *m*, teachdaire *m*
delegate *v* thoir ùghdarras do
delegation *n* buidheann-riochdachaidh *m*, luchd-tagraidh *m*
delete *v* dubh às/a-mach
deliberate *v* beachdaich, meòraich
deliberate *a* a dh'aon ghnotha(i)ch; (*pace*) mall
delicacy *n* fìnealtas *m*, grinneas *m*
delicate *a* fìnealta, grinn; (*health*) meata, lag
delicious *a* fìor bhlasta
delight *n* aighear *m*, aoibhneas *m*, sòlas *m* *v* toilich, dèan aoibhneach **d. in** gabh tlachd an
delightful *a* aoibhneach, sòlasach, ciatach
delineate *v* dealbh, dealbhaich, tarrainn crìoch eadar
delinquent *n* eucorach *m*, ciontach *m* *a* ciontach, coireach
delirious *a* breisleachail, bruailleanach
delirium *n* breisleach *f*, bruaillean *m*
deliver *v* (*save*) saor, fuasgail, teàrn; (*an address, services*) lìbhrig, liubhair; (*child*) asaidich
deliverance *n* saoradh *f*, fuasgladh *m*, teàrnadh *m*
delivery *n* teàrnadh *m*; (*an address, services*) lìbhrigeadh *m*, liubhairt *m*; (*manner of speech*) cainnt *f*, dòigh-labhairt *f*; (*childbirth*) asaid *f*; (*mail*) post *m*
delude *v* meall, thoir an car à
deluge *n* tuil *f*, dìle *f* *v* cuir fodha
delusion *n* mealladh *m*, dalladh *m*
delve *v* cladhaich, ruamhair, àitich

demand *n* iarrtas *m*, tagradh *m*
v iarr, tagair

demanding *a* iarrtach

demean *v* ìslich, dìblich

demeanour *n* giùlan *m*, modh *f*
m, beus *f*

demented *a* air bhoil(e), às a rian

dementia *n* boile *f*; (*senility*)
seargadh-inntinn *m*

demise *n* deireadh *m*; (*gradual*)
crìonadh; (*death*) bàs *m*

demit *v* leig dheth/dhith *etc*

democracy *n* deamocrasaidh *m*

democrat *n* deamocratach *m*

democratic *a* deamocratach

demolish *v* leag

demolition *n* leagail (gu làr) *f*

demon *n* deamhan *m*

demonstrate *v* seall, soilleirich,
taisbean

demonstration *n* taisbeanadh *m*,
soilleireachadh *m*; (*protest*)
sluagh-fhianais *f*

demonstrative *a* comharraichte,
suaicheanta

demoralize *v* mì-mhisnich gu tur,
thoir an cridhe (bh)o

demur *v* cuir an aghaidh (+ *gen*),
cuir teagamh an

demure *a* stuama

den *n* saobhaidh *m*, garaidh *m*,
faiche *f*, còs *m*

denial *n* àicheadh *m*;
(*withholding*) diùltadh *m*

denigrate *v* dì-mol, cuir sìos air

denomination *n* ainm *m*,
ainmneachadh *m*; (*relig*) seòrsa
m, buidheann *f m*

denote *v* comharraich

denounce *v* càin; (*accuse*) tog
casaid an aghaidh (+ *gen*)

dense *a* dùmhail, tiugh; (*not
intelligent*) maol

density *n* dùmhlachd *f*, dlùths *m*

dent *n* lag *f m* *v* dèan lag an

dental *a* fiaclach, deudach

dentist *n* fiaclair *m*

dentistry *n* fiaclaireachd *f*

dentures *n* fiaclan fuadain *f pl*

denunciation *n* càineadh *m*;
(*accusation*) casaid *f*

deny *v* àich, rach às àicheadh;
(*withhold*) diùlt, cùm (bh)o

depart *v* falbh, triall, tog air *etc*

department *n* roinn *f*

departure *n* falbh *m*, fàgail *f*

depend *v* bi an eisimeil/am
freastal (+ *gen*) **d. on** (**someone**)
cuir earbsa an, earb à **it
depends on ...** tha e an
crochadh air ... **you can d. on it**
faodaidh tu bhith cinnteach às

dependent *a* eisimealach **d. on** an
eisimeil (+ *gen*), an eisimeil air,
an crochadh air, an urra ri

depict *v* dealbh, tarraing dealbh
de

depleted *a* falmhaichte, falamh

deplorable *a* sgriosail, muladach,
maslach

deplore *v* faic/meas maslach **we
d. what you've done** tha an rud
a rinn sibh a' cur uabhas oirnn

depopulation *n* fàsachadh *m*

deport *v* fuadaich, fògair, cuir às
an tìr

deportment *n* giùlan *m*, gluasad
m

depose *v* cuir à dreuchd

deposit *n* tasgadh *m* **d. account**
cunntas tasgaidh *m* *v* taisg

depot *n* ionad-stòraidh *m*

depraved *a* aingidh, coirbte

depravity *n* truaill(idh)eachd *f*,
aingidheachd *f*

depreciate *v* ìslich (ann an
luach), rach sìos

depreciation *n* ìsleachadh (luach)
m, tuiteam (ann an luach) *m*

depress *v* cuir trom-inntinn (air);
(*phys*) brùth sìos

depressed *a* airtnealach, fo
sprochd, dubhach, trom-
inntinneach

depression *n* airtneal *m*, sprochd
m, trom-inntinn *f*, smalan *m*

deprivation *n* easbhaidh *f*, toirt
air falbh *m*

deprive *v* thoir (air falbh) (bh)o,
cùm (bh)o

depth *n* doimhneachd *f*, doimhne
f

deputation *n* buidheann-tagraidh
f m

depute *a* iar- (+ *len*) **d. director**
iar-stiùiriche

deputy n neach-ionaid m a iar-
(+ len) **d. head** iar-cheannard m
derail v cuir bhàrr an rèile; (met)
cuir drithleann
deranged a às a c(h)iall etc,
air/fon chuthach
derelict a trèigte, fàs
deride v dèan fanaid air
derision n fanaid f, sgeig f
derivation n freumhachadh m,
bun m
derive v freumhaich, bunaich
derogatory a tarcaiseach, suarach
descend v teirinn, crom, thig
a-nuas
descendant n fear/tè de shliochd
f m **descendants** (coll) sliochd
m, sìol m
descent n teàrnadh m, cromadh
m
describe v thoir tuairisgeul air,
dèan dealbh (de)
description n tuairisgeul m
descriptive a tuairisgeulach
desecrate v mì-naomhaich,
truaill
desert n fàsach f m
desert v trèig, dìobair **d. from**
teich à, ruith à
deserter n neach-teichidh m,
neach-trèigsinn m
deserve v coisinn, toill, bi airidh
air
deserving a airidh, toillteanach
design n dealbh f, dealbhadh m;
(intent) rùn m **by d.** a dh'aon
ghnotha(i)ch
design v dealbhaich, deilbh;
(intend) rùnaich
designate v sònraich, ainmich
designer n dealbhaiche m, neach-
deilbh m
desirable a ion-mhiannaichte
desire n miann f m, dèidh f, toil
f, iarrtas m v miannaich
desirous a miannach, dèidheil
(air)
desk n deasg m
desolate a fàsail, aonranach
desolation n fàsalachd f,
aonranachd f
despair n eu-dòchas m
v leig/thoir thairis dòchas

despatch v cuir air falbh
desperate a èiginneach, nam/na
èiginn, na h-èiginn etc
desperation n èiginn f
despicable a suarach
despise v dèan tàir air
despite prep a dh'aindeoin
(+ gen)
despondency n eu-dòchas m,
dubhachas m
despondent a eu-dòchasach,
dubhach
despot n aintighearna m
despotism n aintighearnas m
dessert n mìlsean m
destination n ceann-uidhe m
destiny n dàn m **he was destined
to ...** bha e/sin an dàn dha
destitute a falamh, ainniseach
n dìol-dèirce m
destroy v mill, sgrios
destruction n milleadh m, sgrios
m, lèirsgrios m
destructive a sgriosail, millteach
detach v dealaich, cuir air leth
detached a dealaichte, air leth
detail n mion-phuing f v thoir
mion-chunntas air
detailed a mionaideach
detain v cùm air ais
detect v (notice) thoir an aire;
lorg; (discover) faigh a-mach
detective n lorg-phoileas m
detention n cumail air ais m;
(imprisonment) cumail an grèim
m
deter v cuir bacadh ro
detergent n stuth-glanaidh m
deteriorate v rach bhuaithe
deterioration n dol bhuaithe m,
dol am miosad m
determination n diongmhaltas m,
cruaidh-bharail f
determine v cuir ro, faigh
a-mach; (decide) cuir romhad
determined a diongmhalta,
daingeann
deterrent n casg m, bacadh m
detest v fuathaich, dubh-
ghràinich **I d. it** tha gràin (an)
uilc agam air
detonate v leig dheth, spreadh;
(intrans) spreadh

detour *n* cam-rathad *m*
detract *v* thoir air falbh (bh)o (luach)
detrimental *a* cronail, millteach
devaluation *n* lùghdachadh luach *m*, dì-luachadh *m*
devalue *v* lùghdaich luach, dì-luachaich
devastate *v* lèirsgrios, dèan lèirsgrios air
devastation *n* lèirsgrios *m*
develop *v* (*trans*) leasaich; (*intrans*) fàs
development *n* leasachadh *m*; (*growth*) fàs *m*
deviate *v* claon (bho)
device *n* innleachd *f*, cleas *m*
devil *n* diabhal *m*, deamhan *m*, donas *m*
devilish *a* diabhlaidh, deamhnaidh
devious *a* carach
devise *v* dealbh, innlich
devoid (of) *a* falamh (de), às eugmhais (+ *gen*)
devolution *n* sgaoileadh-cumhachd *m*
devolved *a* tiomnaichte
devote *v* cosg, thoir (ùine) do
devotion *n* dìlseachd *f*, ionmhainneachd *f*; (*relig*) cràbhadh *m*; (*devotions*) adhradh *m*
devour *v* sluig, glamh
devout *a* cràbhach
dew *n* dealt *f m*, dr(i)ùchd *m*
dewy *a* dealtach, dr(i)ùchdach
dexterity *n* deisealachd *f*, làmhchaireachd *f*
diabetes *n* tinneas an t-siùcair *m*
diabetic *n* diabaiteach *m*
diabolical *a* diabhlaidh, deamhnaidh
diagnose *v* lorg adhbhar
diagnosis *n* lorg-adhbhair *m*
diagonal *a* trasta(nach)
diagram *n* diagram *m*
dial *n* (*watch*) aodann (uaireadair) *m* **sun-d.** uaireadair-grèine *m*
dialect *n* dualchainnt *f*
dialogue *n* còmhradh *m*
diameter *n* trast-thomhas *m*

diamond *n* daoimean *m*
diaper *n* badan *m*
diaphragm *n* sgairt *f*
diarrhoea *n* an spùt *m*, a' bhuinneach *f*
diary *n* leabhar-latha *m*
dice *n* dìsinn *m pl* dìsnean
dictate *v* deachd, òrdaich
dictator *n* deachdaire *m*
dictatorial *a* ceannsalach, deachdaireach
dictatorship *n* deachdaireachd *f*
diction *n* modh-cainnt *f m*
dictionary *n* faclair *m*
die *v* caochail, bàsaich, eug, siubhail
diesel *n* dìosail *m*
diet *n* daithead *f* **regular d.** riaghailt bìdh *f*
differ *v* bi eadar-dhealaichte; (*disagree*) eas-aontaich
difference *n* eadar-dhealachadh *m*, diofar *m*, caochladh *m*
different *a* eadar-dhealaichte, diofraichte, air leth, air a' chaochladh
differentiate *v* diofaraich, eadar-sgar, dèan sgaradh eadar
differentiation *n* eadar-sgarachdainn *f*, eadar-dhealachadh *m*
differing *a* diofraichte
difficult *a* doirbh, duilich
difficulty *n* duilgheadas *m*, dorradas *m*
diffident *a* socharach, mì-mhisneachail, eu-dàna
diffuse(d) *a* sgaoilte *v* sgaoil
dig *v* cladhaich, ruamhair
digest *v* cnàmh, cnuasaich
digestion *n* (an) cnàmh *m*
digger *n* ruamhaire *m*, digear *m*
digit *n* meur *f m*; (*number*) figear *m*
digital *a* meurach; (*number*) figearail, didsiotach
dignified *a* le uaisleachd
dignify *v* urramaich, àrdaich
dignity *n* urram *m*, inbhe *f*
digress *v* rach a thaobh, rach thar sgeula
digression *n* fiaradh-sgeula *m*
digs *n* taigh/àite-loidsidh *m*

dilapidated *a* air a dhol bhuaithe
dilatory *a* màirnealach
dilemma *n* imcheist *f*, ceist *f*
diligence *n* dìcheall *f m*
diligent *a* dìcheallach, dèanadach
dilute *v* tanaich, lagaich
diluted *a* tanaichte, lagaichte
dim *v* doilleirich, duibhrich
dimension *n* tomhas *m*, meud *m*; (*aspect*) modh *f m*, taobh *m*
diminish *v* lùghdaich, beagaich (air); (*intrans*) lùghdaich
diminutive *a* meanbh, bìodach, beag bìodach
dimple *n* lagan-maise *m*
din *n* gleadhraich *f m*, toirm *f*, othail *f*
dine *v* gabh dìnnear/biadh
dinghy *n* geòla-bheag *f*
dingy *a* duainidh, gruamach
dining-room *n* seòmar-bìdh *m*
dinner *n* dìnnear *f*, diathad *f*
   d.-time àm dìnnearach *m*
dinosaur *n* dìneasair *m*
diocese *n* sgìr-easbaig *f*
dip *n* tumadh *m*, bogadh *m*; (*for sheep*) dup *m* *v* tùm, bog, dup
diploma *n* teisteanas *m*
diplomacy *n* gleustachd *f*; (*polit*) dioplòmasaidh *f m*
diplomat *n* gleustair *m*; (*polit*) riochdaire dioplòmasach *m*
diplomatic *a* gleusta, faiceallach; (*polit*) dioplòmasach
dire *a* eagalach, uabhasach, cianail **in d. straits** ann an cruaidh-chàs
direct *a* dìreach *v* stiùir, seòl
direction *n* stiùireadh *m*; (*point of compass*) àird *f*
directive *n* òrdugh *m*
directly *adv* air ball, dìreach
director *n* stiùiriche *m*, neach-stiùiridh *m*
dirt *n* salchar *m*
dirty *a* salach *v* salaich
disability *n* ciorram *m*
disabled person *n* ciorramach *m*
disadvantage *n* anacothrom, mì-leas *m*
disadvantaged *a* beag cothrom **the d.** na feumaich *m pl*
disaffected *a* diombach,

mì-riaraichte
disagree *v* rach an aghaidh, eas-aontaich
disagreeable *a* mì-thaitneach, mì-thlachdmhor
disagreement *n* eas-aonta *f*, mì-chòrdadh *m*
disallow *v* diùlt, na ceadaich
disappear *v* rach à sealladh
disappoint *v* bris(t) dùil, leig sìos
disappointment *n* bris(t)eadh-dùil *m*
disapprove *v* bi an aghaidh **her parents d. of him** chan eil a pàrantan air a shon
disarm *v* dì-armaich
disarmament *n* dì-armachadh *m*
disaster *n* mòr-thubaist *f*, calldachd *f*
disastrous *a* sgriosail
disband *v* (*intrans*) sgaoil; (*trans*) leig mu sgaoil
disbelief *n* eas-creideamh *m*
disburse *v* caith/cuir a-mach airgead
disc *n* clàr *m*
discard *v* cuir dheth, dhith *etc*/bhuaithe, bhuaipe *etc*
discerning *a* lèirsinneach, tuigseach, geurchuiseach
discernment *n* lèirsinn *f*, tuigse *f*
discharge *n* sileadh *m*; (*release*) leigeil mu sgaoil *m*, fuasgladh *m*; (*debt*) ìoc *m*, pàigheadh *m* *v* sil; (*release*) leig mu sgaoil, fuasgail; (*debts*) ìoc, pàigh; (*obligation*) coilean; (*cargo*) falmhaich, cuir air tìr
disciple *n* deisciobal *m*
discipline *n* smachd *m*; (*acad*) cuspair *m* *v* smachdaich
disclose *v* foillsich, leig ris
disco *n* diosgo *m*
discomfort *n* mì-chofhurtachd *f*, anshocair *f*
disconcerting *n* buaireasach
disconnect *v* fuasgail, dealaich (bh)o chèile
disconsolate *a* brònach, dubhach, tùrsach
discontent *n* mì-riarachadh *m*, mì-thoileachadh *m*
discontented *a* mì-riaraichte, mì-

thoilichte
discontinue *v* leig seachad, sguir de, cuir stad air
discord *n* mì-chòrdadh *m*, aimhreit *f*; (*mus*) dì-chòrdadh *m*, eas-aonta *m*
discount *n* lasachadh (prìse) *m*
discourage *v* mì-mhisnich
discouragement *n* mì-mhisneachadh *m*
discourteous *a* mì-spèiseil, eas-urramach, gun mhodh
discourtesy *n* cion modh(a) *m*, cion spèis *m*
discover *v* faigh a-mach, lorg
discovery *n* lorg *f*
discredit *v* mì-chliùthaich, thoir creideas (bh)o
discreet *a* faiceallach, cùramach
discrepancy *n* diofar *m*
discrete *a* air leth
discretion *n* faiceall *f*, cùram *m*; (*judgement*) toil *f*, toinisg *f* **at your d.** a rèir do thoil (fhèin)
discriminate *v* dèan dealachadh eadar **d. in favour of** dèan leth-bhreith air
discrimination *n* eadar-dhealachadh *m*, leth-bhreith *f*
discuss *v* deasbair, bi a' deasbad, beachdaich (air/mu)
discussion *n* deasbaireachd *f*, deasbad *m*, cnuasachadh *m*, beachdachadh *m*
disdain *n* tàir *f*, dìmeas *m*
disease *n* tinneas *m*, galar *m*
disembark *v* rach air tìr, thig bhàrr/far (+ *gen*)
disengage *v* dealaich ri, fuasgail
disentangle *v* fuasgail, rèitich
disfigure *v* mill (cruth), cuir à cruth
disgrace *n* masladh *m*, tàmailt *f*, cùis-mhaslaidh *f v* maslaich, nàraich
disgraceful *a* maslach, nàr
disgruntled *a* mì-riaraichte, diombach
disguise *n* breug-riochd *m* **in d.** ann an riochd ... *v* cuir breug-riochd air/oirre *etc*
disgust *n* sgreamh *m*, gràin *f v* sgreamhaich, gràinich

disgusting *a* sgreamhail, gràineil
dish *n* soitheach *f m* **washing the dishes** a' nighe nan soithichean
dishearten *v* mì-mhisnich
disheartening *a* mì-mhisneachail
dishevelled *a* mì-sgiobalta
dishonest *a* eas-onarach
dishonesty *n* eas-onair *f*
dishonour *n* eas-onair *f*, eas-urram *m*, mì-chliù *m*
dishwasher *n* nigheadair-shoithichean *m*
disillusion *n* bris(t)eadh-dùil *m*, fosgladh sùla *m*
disinclined *a* neo-thoileach, leisg (gu)
disinfectant *n* dì-ghalaran *m*
disingenuous *a* carach, neo-fhosgarra
disintegrate *v* rach às a chèile
disinterested *a* gun fhèin-chùis
disjointed *a* (*met*) neo-thàthach, briste
disk *n* clàr *m*
dislike *v* dislikes cha toigh/toil (le), cha chaomh (le), is beag air
dislocate *v* cuir à(s) àite, cuir às an alt
dislodge *v* cuir à(s) àite, fuasgail
disloyal *a* neo-dhìleas
dismal *a* dubhach, gruamach; (*poor*) truagh, leibideach
dismantle *v* thoir às a chèile
dismay *n* uabhas *m*
dismiss *v* cuir air falbh, cuir à dreuchd
dismissal *n* cur à dreuchd *m*
dismount *v* teirinn (bh)o, thig de
disobedience *n* eas-ùmhlachd *f*
disobedient *a* eas-umhail
disobey *v* bi eas-umhail do, rach an aghaidh
disorder *n* mì-rian *m*, buaireas *m*, troimh-a-chèile *f m*
disorderly *a* mì-rianail
disorganized *a* mì-dhòigheil, gun rian
disown *v* diùlt gabhail ri, cuir cùl ri
disparage *v* cuir sìos air, dì-mol
disparate *a* diofraichte, neo-ionann

disparity n diofar m,
neo-ionannachd f
dispassionate a ceart-
bhreitheach, neo-chlaon
dispatch v cuir air falbh
dispel v sgaoil, fògair
dispensary n ìoclann f
dispense v (*issue*) riaraich; (*drugs
etc*) dèan suas cungaidh **d. with**
faigh cuidhteas
dispersal n sgapadh m,
sgaoileadh m
disperse v sgap, sgaoil
dispersed a sgapte, sgaoilte
dispirited a neo-shunndach, gun
s(h)unnd
displace v cuir à àite, fògair
display n taisbeanadh m,
foillseachadh m v taisbean,
foillsich
displease v mì-thoilich
displeased a mì-thoilichte,
diombach
displeasure n mì-thoileachas m,
diomb f m
disposal n toirt seachad f,
riarachadh m **d. of** faighinn
cuidhteas f
dispose v thoir seachad, riaraich
d. of faigh cuidhteas
dispossess v cuir à seilbh
disproportionate a neo-
chuimseach, mì-chothromach
disprove v breugnaich
dispute n connspaid f, aimhreit f
v connsaich, tagair
disqualify v dì-cheadaich, cuir à
(farpais)
disquiet n iomagain f, iomnaidh f
disregard v cuir an neo-shùim,
dèan dìmeas air
disrepair n droch c(h)àradh m
in a state of d. feumach air
a c(h)àradh
disreputable a le droch ainm
disrepute n droch ainm m,
mì-chliù m
disrespect n dìmeas m,
eas-urram m
disrespectful a eas-urramach
disrupt v cuir troimh-a-chèile;
(*break up*) bris(t)
disruption n cur troimh-a-chèile

m; (*breaking up*) bris(t)eadh m
the Disruption Bris(t)eadh na
h-Eaglaise
dissatisfaction n mì-riarachadh m
dissatisfied a mì-riaraichte
dissect v sgrùd; (*phys*) geàrr às a
chèile
disseminate v sgaoil
dissent n eas-aonta m
dissertation n tràchdas m
disservice n cron m
dissident n eas-aontaiche m
dissimilar a eu-coltach (ri)
dissimilarity n eu-coltas m
dissociate v sgar, na gabh
gnotha(i)ch ri
dissolute a stròdhail
dissolution n leaghadh m,
eadar-sgaoileadh m; (*eg
Parliament*) sgaoileadh m
dissolve v leagh, eadar-sgaoil;
(*eg Parliament*) sgaoil
dissuade v thoir à beachd
distance n astar m, fad m
distant a fad' air falbh, cian;
(*manner*) fad' às; (*relationship*)
fada a-mach
distaste n mì-thlachd f
distasteful a mì-chàilear,
mì-thaitneach
distil v tarraing, dèan
grùdaireachd
distillery n taigh-staile m
distinct a eadar-dhealaichte;
(*clear*) soilleir
distinction n eadar-dhealachadh
m; (*quality*) cliù m
distinctive a sònraichte,
eadar-dhealaichte
distinguish v dèan dealachadh
eadar, aithnich (bh)o chèile
distinguished a òirdheirc,
cliùiteach
distort v fiaraich
distorted a fiar
distortion n fiaradh m
distract v tarraing aire (bh)o,
buair
distress n àmhghar f m, teinn f,
sàrachadh m
distressing a àmhgharach
distribute v sgaoil, roinn, riaraich
distribution n sgaoileadh m,

riarachadh *m*
district *n* ceàrn *m*, sgìre *f*
distrust *n* cion earbsa *m*,
　mì-earbsa *f*, amharas *m*
distrustful *a* mì-earbsach,
　amharasach
disturb *v* cuir dragh air, buair
disturbance *n* buaireadh *m*,
　aimhreit *f*
disturbing *a* draghail
disunity *n* eas-aonachd *f*
disuse *n* dìth cleachdaidh *f m* **it
　fell into d.** chaidh e à cleachdadh
ditch *n* clais *f*, dìg *f*
ditto *adv* mar an ceudna
dive *v* dàibhig, rach fon uisge
diver *n* dàibhear *m*; (*bird*) eun
　tumaidh *m*
diverge *v* gabh caochladh slighe
diverse *a* eugsamhail, eadar-
　mheasgte, de chaochladh
　sheòrsa
diversify *v* eugsamhlaich, sgaoil
diversion *n* claonadh *m*; (*detour*)
　cam(a)-rathad *m*; (*distraction*)
　tarraing aire *f*; (*pastime*) cur-
　seachad *m*
diversity *n* eugsamhlachd *f*,
　iomadachd *f*
divert *v* claon; (*detour*) gabh
　cam(a)-rathad
divide *v* roinn, pàirtich
divided *a* roinnte, air a/an roinn
　etc
dividend *n* earrann *f*, roinn *f*
divine *a* (*relig*) diadhaidh **the d.
　will** toil Dhè *f*
divinity *n* diadhachd *f*
division *n* roinn *f*, earrann *f*; (*act
　of*) pàirteachadh *m*
divorce *n* sgaradh-pòsaidh *m*
　v sgar o chèile
divot *n* ceap *m*, sgrath *f*
divulge *v* foillsich, leig ris,
　taisbean
dizziness *n* tuaineal *m*,
　tuainealaich *f*, luairean *m*
dizzy *a* ann an tuaineal/luairean
do *v* dèan **do away with** cuir às
　do **do your best** dèan do
　dhìcheall **do what you can** dèan
　na 's urrainn dhut
docile *a* soitheamh, solta

dock *n* doca *m*; (*plant*) copag *f*
docken *n* copag *f*, cuiseag ruadh
　f
docker *n* docair *m*
doctor *n* dotair *m*, lighiche *m*;
　(*acad*) ollamh *m*
doctrinaire *a* rag-bharaileach
doctrine *n* teagasg *m*
document *n* sgrìobhainn *f*
documentary *n* aithriseachd *f*
　a aithriseach
documentation *n* pàipearan *m pl*
dodge *n* cleas *m* *v* (*avoid*)
　seachain
doe *n* (*deer*) maoiseach *f*
dog *n* cù *m*, madadh *m* **dog-tired**
　cho sgìth ris a' chù **dogfish**
　biorach *f*
dogged *a* leanailteach, ruighinn
doggerel *n* rannghal *m*,
　rabhd(aireachd) *f*
dogma *n* gnàth-theagasg *m*
dogmatic *a* dìorrasach,
　baraileach
dole *n* dòil *m*
doll *n* liùdhag *f*, doile(ag) *f*
dollar *n* dolair *m*
dolphin *n* leumadair-mara *m*
dolt *n* burraidh *m*, ùmaidh *m*
domain *n* raon *m*
dome *n* cuach-mhullaich *f*
domestic *a* dachaigheil
domesticate *v* callaich
domesticated *a* callaichte
dominance *n* làmh-an-uachdair *f*
dominant *a* ceannasach,
　smachdail
dominate *v* ceannsaich,
　smachdaich, faigh làmh-an-
　uachdair air
domination *n* ceannsachadh *m*,
　smachdachadh *m*, làmh-an-
　uachdair *f*
domineering *a* maigh(i)stireil,
　ceannsalach
dominion *n* uachdranachd *f*
donate *v* thoir tabhartas/tiodhlac
donation *n* tabhartas *m*, tiodhlac
　m
donkey *n* asal *f m*
donor *n* tabhartaiche *m*
doom *n* bàs *m*, sgrios *m*;
　(*judgement*) binn *f*, dìteadh *m*

doomsday *n* Latha Luain *m*
door *n* doras *m* **front d.** doras-aghaidh **back d.** doras-cùil
d.-handle làmh dorais *f*
doorpost ursainn *f* **doorstep** maide-buinn *m*, leac an dorais *f*
dormant *n* na c(h)adal *etc*, na t(h)àmh *etc*, falaichte
dormitory *n* seòmar-cadail *m*
dormouse *n* dall-luch *f*
dose *n* dòs *m*; (*measure*) tomhas *m*
dot *n* dotag *f*; (*punct*) puing *f*
dote *v* gabh mòr-mhiadh air
dotted *a* dotagach
double *n* a dhà uimhir *f*, uimhir eile *f*; (*person*) mac-samhail *m*
d. chin sprogan *m*, sprogaill *f*
d.-decker bus bus dà-ùrlair *m*
d. glazing uinneag dhùbailte *f* *a* dùbailte, dà-fhillte *v* dùblaich
doubt *n* teagamh *m*, imcheist *f* *v* cuir an teagamh, cuir teagamh an
doubtful *a* teagmhach
doubtless *adv* gun teagamh, gu cinnteach
dough *n* taois *f*; (*slang*) airgead *m*
dour *a* dùr
douse *v* smàl
dove *n* calman *m*
dowdy *a* seann-fhasanta, sgleòideach, duainidh
down *n* clòimhteach *f*
down *prep* shìos; (*motion*) sìos, a-nuas **are they d. there?** a bheil iad shìos an sin? **come d. here** thig a-nuas an seo
downcast *a* smuaireanach, dubhach
downfall *n* tuiteam *m*, leagadh *m* **that was his d.** 's e sin a dh'fhoghain dha
downhill *adv* leis/sìos an leathad, leis a' bhrutha(i)ch
downpour *n* dìle (bhàthte) *f*, deàrrsach *f*
downright *adv* dìreach
downstairs *adv* shìos an staidhre; (*motion*) sìos an staidhre
downward(s) *adv* sìos, a-nuas **going d.** a' dol sìos **coming d.** a' tighinn a-nuas

dowry *n* tochradh *m*
doze *v* dèan norrag/snuachdan
dozen *n* dusan *m*
dozy *a* cadalach
drab *a* duainidh
draft *n* dreach *m*, (*mil*) foireann *m*
drag *v* slaod, dragh, tarraing
dragon *n* dràgon *m*
drain *n* drèana *f*, clais *f* *v* drèan, sìolaidh, traogh
drainage *n* drèanadh *m*
drake *n* (d)ràc *m*, ràcan *m*
dram *n* dram(a) *m*
drama *n* dràma *f m*
dramatic *a* dràmadach
drat (it)! *interj* gonadh air!
draught *n* gaoth *f*; (*of ship*) tarraing-uisge *f* **d.-beer** leann baraille *m*
draughts *n* dàmais *f*
draughtsman *n* neach-tarraing *m*
draw *v* (*pull*) tarraing, dragh, slaod; (*picture*) dèan dealbh **d. lots** cuir croinn
drawer *n* drathair *m*
drawing *n* dealbh *f m*
drawing-pin *n* tacaid *f*
drawl *v* bruidhinn gu slaodach/sgleogach
dread *n* oillt *f*, uamhann *m*, sgàth *m*
dreadful *a* eagalach, cianail
dream *n* aisling *f*, bruadar *m* *v* bruadair, faic aisling *Also vn* ag aisling
dreary *a* muladach, dorcha, gruamach
dredge *v* sgrìob/glan grunnd
dregs *n* druaip *f*, grùid *f*
drenched *a* bog fliuch
dress *n* dreasa *f m*; (*clothes*) aodach *m*
dress *v* cuir aodach air/oirre *etc*, cuir uime/uimpe *etc*
dresser *n* (*furniture*) dreasair *m*
dressing *n* (*med*) bann lota *m*; (*salad*) sùgh saileid *m*
dressing-table *n* bòrd-sgeadachaidh *m*
dribble *v* dèan ròill; (*in football*) drioblaig
drift *n* siabadh *m*; (*argument*)

brìgh *f* **sand-d.** siaban *m* **snow-
d.** cuithe sneachd(a) *f* *v* siab,
falbh le gaoith; (*of snow*) rach
na chuithe
drill *n* (*tool*) snìomhaire *m*; (*mil*)
drile *f*; (*veg*) sreath *m* *v* drilich,
drilig
drink *n* deoch *f* *v* òl, gabh deoch
drinker *n* neach-òil *m*, pòitear *m*
drip *n* boinne *m*, sileadh *m*,
snighe *m*
drive *v* dràibh; (*animals*) iomain
d. away ruaig
drivel *n* sgudal *m*
driver *n* dràibhear *m*; (*of
animals*) neach-iomain *m*
driving *n* dràibheadh *m*; (*of
animals*) iomain *f*
drizzle *n* ciùthran *m*,
ciùthranaich *f*, smugraich *f*
droll *a* neònach; (*amusing*) ait
droop *v* crom, aom
drop *n* boinne *f*, braon *m*,
drudhag *f*, deur *m*; (*fall*) tuiteam
m
drop *v* leig às; (*give up*) leig
seachad; (*fall*) tuit; (*liquid*) sil
d. me a line cuir sgrìobag
thugam **d. in any time** tadhail
uair sam bith
dross *n* (*coal*) smùr *m*; (*met*)
smodal *m*
drought *n* mòr-thiormachd *f*,
tartmhorachd *f*
drove *n* dròbh *m*, treud *m*
drover *n* dròbhair *m*
drown *v* bàth; (*intrans*) bi air a
b(h)àthadh *etc*
drowning *n* bàthadh *m*
drowsy *a* cadalach
drudgery *n* dubh-chosnadh *m*,
tràilleachd *f*
drug *n* droga *f*, cungaidh-leighis *f*
d. addict tràill-dhrogaichean *f*
druid *n* draoidh *m*
drum *n* druma *f* *m*
drummer *n* drumair *m*
drunk *a* air an daoraich, air
mhisg **he was d.** bha an
deoch/daorach air
drunkard *n* drungair *m*, misgear *m*
drunkenness *n* misg *f*, daorach *f*
dry *a* tioram; (*thirsty*) pàiteach

v tiormaich **dry-clean** tioram-
ghlan
dryer *n* tiormadair *m*
drying *n* tiormachadh *m* **good d.
weather** turadh math *m*
dry-rot *n* mosgan *m*
dual *a* dùbailte **d.-carriageway**
rathad dùbailte *m*
dubious *a* teagmhach
duchess *n* ban-diùc *f*
duck *n* tunnag *f*, (*wild*) lach *f*
duct *n* pìob-ghiùlain *f*
dud *n* rud gun fheum *m*
due *n* còir *f*, dlighe *f* *a*
(*deserved*) dligheach, cubhaidh;
(*of debt*) ri phàigheadh **when is
it d.?** cuin a tha dùil ris? **d. back**
ri th(i)lleadh *etc*
duel *n* còmhrag-dithis *f*
duet *n* òran-càraid/dithis *m*
duke *n* diùc *m*
dulcet *a* binn, fonnmhor
dull *a* dorch(a), gruamach,
doilleir; (*of hearing*) bodhar;
(*personality*) trom, somalta
dulse *n* duileasg *m*
duly *adv* gu riaghailteach
dumb *a* balbh **d. person** balbhan *m*
dumbness *n* balbhachd *f*;
(*silence*) tostachd *f*
dummy *n* neach-brèige *m*
dump *n* òtrach *m*, lagais *f*, sitig *f*
v caith air falbh, cuir bhuat
dumpling *n* turraisg *f*, duf *m*
dun *a* ciar, odhar, lachdann
dung *n* innear *f*, buachar *m*, todhar
m **dunghill** sitig *f*, dùnan *m*
dungeon *n* toll-dubh *m*, sloc *m*
duodenum *n* beul a' chaolain *m*
dupe *v* meall, thoir an car à
duplicate *n* lethbhreac *m*,
mac-samhail *m*
durable *a* maireannach, buan,
seasmhach
duration *n* ùine *f*, fad *m*
during *prep* rè (+ *gen*)
dusk *n* ciaradh (an fheasgair) *m*,
beul na h-oidhche *m*, eadar-
sholas *m*
dusky *a* ciar
dust *n* dust *m*, duslach *m*, stùr
m; (*human remains*) dust *m*
v dust(aig)

dustbin _n_ soitheach-sgudail _f m_
duster _n_ dustair _m_
dusting _n_ dustadh _m_
dusty _a_ dustach
Dutch _n_ (lang) Dùitsis _f_
_a_ Dùitseach
Dutchman _n_ Dùitseach _m_
Dutchwoman ban-D(h)ùitseach
_f_
duty _n_ dleastanas _m_; (_excise_) cìs _f_
d.-free saor o chìsean
dux _n_ ducs _m_
dwarf _n_ troich _f m_
dwelling _n_ àite/ionad-còmhnaidh
_m_, fàrdach _f_ **d. house**
taigh-còmhnaidh _m_
dye _n_ dath _m_ _v_ dath
dyke _n_ (_wall_) gàrradh _m_
dynamic _a_ fiùghantach
dynamics _n_ daineamaig _f_
dynamite _n_ daineamait _m_
dynamo _n_ daineamo _m_
dynasty _n_ sliochd rìoghail _m_
dysentery _n_ a' bhuinneach mhòr _f_

E

each _a_ gach _adv_ an urra, an
duine, an ceann **e. other** a chèile
each one is different tha gach
fear/tè eadar-dhealaichte **they
cost £20 each** tha iad a' cosg
£20 am fear/an tè
eager _a_ dealasach
eagerness _n_ dealas _m_
eagle _n_ iolair(e) _f_
ear _n_ cluas _f_; (_of corn_) dias _f_
earl _n_ iarla _m_
early _a_ tràth, moch
earmark _v_ (_met_) comharraich,
sònraich; (_phys_) cuir comharra
air
earphone _n_ cluasan _m_, fòn-
cluaise _m_
earn _v_ coisinn
earnest _a_ dùrachdach
earning(s) _n_ tuarastal _m_, cosnadh
_m_
earring _n_ fàinne-cluaise _f m_
earth _n_ talamh _f m_; (_soil_) ùir _f_
the E. an Talamh, an Cruinne-
cè _m_ **where on e. were you?** càit
air an t-saoghal an robh thu?

earthly _a_ talmhaidh
earthquake _n_ crith-thalmhainn _f_
earthworm _n_ boiteag _f_
earwig _n_ gòbhlag(-stobach) _f_,
fiolan-gòbhlach _m_
ease _n_ fois _f_, tàmh _m_
east _n_ ear _f_, an àird an ear _f_
Easter _n_ a' Chàisg _f_ **e. egg** ugh
Càisge _m_
easterly _a_ an ear, (bh)on ear
easy _a_ furasta, soirbh
eat _v_ ith
eavesdropping _n_ farchluais _f_
ebb _n_ tràghadh _m_ **ebb-tide** sruth-
tràghaidh _m_ _v_ tràigh, traogh
eccentric _a_ àraid, annasach,
neònach
ecclesiastic _a_ eaglaiseil
echo _n_ mac-talla _m_
eclectic _a_ roghainneach
eclipse _n_ dubhadh grèine/
gealaich _m_
ecology _n_ eag-eòlas _m_
economic _a_ eaconamach
economical _a_ cùramach,
caomhnach/cùmhnach
economics _n_ eaconamas _m_,
eaconamachd _f_
economist _n_ eaconamair _m_
economize _v_ caomhain/
cumhain
economy _n_ eaconamaidh _m_
ecstasy _n_ àrd-aoibhneas _m_, mire
_f_; (_drug_) eacstasaidh _m_
ecstatic _a_ àrd-aoibhneach, air
mhire
ecumenical _a_ uil-eaglaiseil,
aont'-eaglaiseil
edge _n_ oir _f m_, iomall _m_, bruach
_m_; (_blade_) faobhar _m_; (_verge_) fàl
_m_
edible _a_ so-ithe, a ghabhas ithe
edict _n_ reachd _m_
edit _v_ deasaich
edition _n_ deasachadh _m_, eagran _m_
editor _n_ neach-deasachaidh _m_,
deasaiche _m_
editorial _n_ colbh deasaiche _m_
educate _v_ foghlaim, teagaisg,
ionnsaich
educated _a_ foghlaim(ich)te **a
well-e. person** neach a fhuair
deagh fhoghlam

education *n* foghlam *m*,
oideachas *m* **e. authority**
ùghdarras foghlaim *m*
educational *a* oideachail,
foghlaim
eel *n* easgann *f*
eerie *a* iargalta, gaoireil
effect *n* buaidh *f*, buil *f*, toradh
m v thoir gu buil, coilean
effective *a* èifeachdach, buadhach
effectively *adv* gu h-èifeachdach,
le èifeachd
effeminate *a* boireannta
effervescent *a* beothail,
suigeartach, làn sunnd
efficacy *n* èifeachd *f*
efficiency *n* èifeachdas *f*
efficient *a* èifeachdach, (*person*)
gnothachail
effort *n* oidhirp *f*, dìcheall *f m*,
spàirn *f*
effrontery *n* bathais *f*, ladarnas *m*
egg *n* ugh *m* **boiled egg** ugh air a
bhruich **egg-cup** glainne/gucag-
uighe *f* **egg-white** gealagan *m*
egg-yolk buidheagan *m*
ego *n* fèin *f*, an fhèin *f*
egotism *n* fèin-spèis *f*
egotist *n* fèin-spèisiche *m*, fèinear
m
egotistical *a* fèin-spèiseach
Egyptian *n, a* Èipheiteach *m*,
(*female*) ban-Èipheiteach *f*
eider duck *n* lach mhòr *f*
eight *n* a h-ochd *a* ochd **e. people**
ochdnar *f m*
eighth *a* ochdamh
eighteen *n, a* ochd-deug **e. years**
ochd bliadhna deug
eighty *n* ceithir fichead *f m*,
ochdad *m*
either *a, pron, conj, adv* **on e.
side of it** air gach taobh
dheth/dhith **e. of them** an
dara/dàrna fear/tè dhiubh, fear
seach fear dhiubh, tè seach tè
dhiubh **e. go or stay** an dara
cuid falbh no fuirich **that's not
right e.** chan eil sin ceart a
bharrachd/nas mò
eject *v* cuir/tilg a-mach
elaborate *a* mionaideach, toinnte
v leudaich (air)

elapse *v* rach seachad
elastic *n, a* lastaig *f* (*supple*)
sùbailte, subailte
elation *n* mòr-aoibhneas *m*
elbow *n* uileann *f*, uilinn *f*
elder *n* (*eccl*) èildear *m*, foirfeach
m; (*tree*) droman *m a* nas/as
sine, na/a bu shine
elderly *a* sean, aosta
elect *v* tagh
elected *a* air a t(h)aghadh, taghte
election *n* taghadh *m* **e. day** latha
taghaidh *m*
elector *n* neach-taghaidh *m*,
neach-bhòtaidh *m*
electorate *n* luchd-taghaidh *m*
electric(al) *a* dealain
electrician *n* dealanair *m*
electricity *n* dealan *m*
electronic *a* dealanta(ch),
eileagtronaigeach
elegance *n* grinneas *m*,
eireachdas *m*, snas *m*, loinn *f*
elegant *a* grinn, eireachdail,
snasail, loinneil
elegy *n* marbhrann *m*, tuireadh
m, cumha *f m*
element *n* eileamaid *f*; (*in nature*)
dùil *f*
elementary *a* bunasach, sìmplidh
elephant *n* ailbhean *m*
elevate *v* àrdaich, tog suas
elevation *n* àrdachadh *m*; (*height*)
àirde *f*; (*plan*) dealbh *f m*
elevator *n* àrdaichear *m*
eleven *n, a* aon-deug **e. men** aon
duine deug
elf *n* màileachan *m*
elicit *v* faigh/lorg a-mach
eligible *a* airidh air roghainn,
iomchaidh, dligheach
eliminate *v* cuir às do, geàrr às
elk *n* lon *m*
elm *n* leamhan *m*
elocution *n* deas-chainnt *f*,
uirgheall *m*
elongate *v* fadaich, tarraing/sìn
a-mach
elope *v* teich, ruith air falbh
eloquence *n* deas-bhriathrachd *f*
eloquent *a* deas-bhriathrach
else *a, adv* eile **or e.** air neo
elucidate *v* soilleirich

elude *v* seachain, èalaidh às
elusive *a* èalaidheach
emaciated *a* reangach, seargte
e-mail *n* post-dealain *m*
emanate *v* sruth/thig (bh)o
embargo *n* bacadh *m*
embark *v* (*board*) rach air bòrd
   e. on tòisich air
embarrass *v* nàraich, tàmailtich
embarrassed *a* air mo/a *etc*
   nàrachadh
embarrassing *a* nàrach,
   tàmailteach
embarrassment *n* nàrachadh *m*,
   tàmailt *f*
embassy *n* ambasaid *f*
embellish *v* sgeadaich, sgèimhich
ember *n* èibhleag *f*
embezzle *v* dèan foill le airgead
embittered *a* searbh
emblem *n* suaicheantas *m*
embrace *v* glac nad ghàirdeanan;
   (*accept*) gabh ri
embroider *v* cuir obair-ghrèis air
embroidery *n* obair-ghrèis *f*
embryo *n* suth *m*, tùs-ghinean *m*
emerald *n* smàrag *f*
emerge *v* thig am bàrr/am follais
emergency *a* suidheachadh-
   èiginn *m*, èiginn *f* e. exit doras-
   èiginn *m*
emigrant *n* eilthireach *m*
emigrate *v* fàg an dùthaich, dèan
   eilthireachd
emigration *n* eilthireachd *f*,
   às-imrich *f*
eminent *a* àrd, inbheil,
   iomraiteach
emit *v* leig a-mach
emotion *n* faireachdainn làidir *f*
emotional *a* làn faireachdainn
empathy *n* co-fhaireachdainn *f*
emperor *n* ìmpire *m*
emphasis *n* cudrom *m*; (*in
   speech*) sìneadh *m*
emphasize *v* cuir cudrom air; (*in
   speech*) cuir sìneadh an
emphatic *a* neartmhor, làidir
empire *n* ìmpireachd *f*
employ *v* fastaidh, thoir obair do;
   (*use*) cleachd
employee *n* neach-obrach *m*,
   obraiche *m*, cosnaiche *m*

employer *n* fastaiche *m*
employment *n* obair *f*, cosnadh *m*
empower *v* thoir comas/
   ùghdarras do
emptiness *n* falamhachd *f*
empty *a* falamh *v* falmhaich
emulate *v* bi a' comharspaidh ri
enable *v* dèan comasach, thoir
   comas do
enact *v* cuir an gnìomh, coilean;
   (*leg*) dèan lagh de
enamel *n* cruan *m*
enchanted *a* fo gheasaibh, seunta
encircle *v* cuartaich
enclose *v* cuartaich, iath mun
   cuairt; (*in letter etc*) cuir an cois
enclosed *a* cuartaichte; (*of
   document etc*) an cois ...
enclosure *n* crò *m*, geàrraidh *m*;
   (*document etc*) na tha an cois
   ...
encompass *v* cuartaich, iath;
   (*include*) gabh a-steach
encounter *n* coinneachadh *m*,
   tachairt *f* *v* coinnich (ri),
   tachair (ri)
encourage *v* misnich, brosnaich
encouragement *n* misneachadh
   m, brosnachadh *m*
encouraging *a* brosnachail
encyclopedia *n* leabhar mòr-
   eòlais *m*
end *n* deireadh *m*, crìoch *f*, ceann
   m in the end aig a' cheann thall
   from end to end (bh)o cheann
   gu ceann we will never hear the
   end of it cha chluinn sinn a
   dheireadh (gu bràth/sìorraidh)
   come to an end thig gu
   ceann/crìch *v* crìochnaich, cuir
   crìoch air, thoir gu ceann
endanger *v* cuir an cunnart
endangered *a* an cunnart
endear *v* coisinn meas/spèis
endeavour *n* spàirn *f*, oidhirp *f*
   v oidhirpich
endless *a* gun cheann, gun
   chrìoch, sìorraidh, neo-
   chrìochnach
endorse *v* (*support*) cuir aonta ri,
   thoir taic do; (*sign*) cuir ainm ri
endow *v* builich, bàirig
endowment *n* buileachadh *m*,

bàirigeadh *m*
endurance *n* fulang(as) *m*
endure *v* fuiling; (*last*) seas, mair
enemy *n* nàmhaid *m*, eascaraid *m*
energetic *a* lùthmhor, sgairteil
energize *v* cuir brìgh/spionnadh
an
energy *n* lùth *m*, neart *m*,
spionnadh *m*, brìgh *f*
enforce *v* cuir an gnìomh;
(*compel*) spàrr (air)
enforcement *n* cur an gnìomh *m*,
sparradh *m*
engage *v* (*hire*) fastaidh **e. with**
rach an sàs an
engaged *a* (*to be married*) fo
ghealladh-pòsaidh; (*of phone*)
trang; (*of toilet*) ga
c(h)leachdadh **e. in** an sàs an
engagement *n* (*marriage*)
gealladh-pòsaidh *m*;
(*commitment*) dleastanas *m*
engaging *a* taitneach,
tarraingeach
engine *n* einnsean *m*, inneal *m*,
beairt *f*
engineer *n* einnseanair *m*,
innleadair *m* **chief e.** prìomh
innleadair **civil e.** innleadair-
togail
engineering *n* einnseanaireachd *f*,
innleadaireachd *f*
English *n* (*lang*) Beurla
(Shasannach) *f a* Sasannach
Englishman *n* Sasannach *m*
Englishwoman ban-
S(h)asannach *f*
engrave *v* gràbhail
engrossed *a* beò-ghlacte
enhance *v* leasaich, thoir feabhas
air; (*add to*) cuir ris
enjoy *v* còrd (ri), gabh tlachd an,
meal **they enjoyed the holidays**
chòrd na làithean-saora riutha
enjoyment *n* tlachd *f*, toileachas
m, toil-inntinn *f*
enlarge *v* leudaich, meudaich
enlargement *n* leudachadh *m*,
meudachadh *m*; (*phot*)
meudachadh *m*
enlighten *v* soilleirich (do), thoir
soilleireachadh (do)
enlist *v* (*mil*) liost(aig), gabh san

Arm; (*support*) sir
enliven *v* beothaich
enmity *n* nàimhdeas *m*
enormous *a* ana-mhòr,
àibheiseach
enough *n* leòr *f a, adv* gu leòr
did you get e.? an d' fhuair thu
do leòr/gu leòr? **e. is e.**
fòghnaidh na dh'fhòghnas **do
you have e. money?** a bheil
airgead gu leòr agaibh? **I wasn't
fast e.** cha robh mi luath gu
leòr
enquire *v* faighnich, feòraich
enquiry *n* ceist *f*
enrage *v* cuir caoch/fearg air
enrich *v* dèan beairteach; (*soil
etc*) neartaich
enrol *v* clàraich
en route *adv* air an t-slighe, air
an rathad
ensemble *n* (*mus*) co-cheòltairean
m pl; (*dress*) èideadh *m*
ensign *n* (*flag*) bratach *f*
ensue *v* lean, tachair (ri linn)
ensure *v* dèan cinnteach
entangle *v* rib, cuir an sàs, amail,
rocail
entangled *a* an grèim, air
amaladh, air rocladh
enter *v* rach/thig a-steach, inntrig
enterprise *n* iomairt *f*
enterprising *a* adhartach,
iomairteach
entertain *v* dèan cur-seachad do,
dèan dibhearsain; (*hospitality*)
thoir aoigheachd do
entertainer *n* fèistear *m*, aisteach
m
entertainment *n* fèisteas *m*, cur-
seachadachd *f*, dibhearsain *m*;
(*hospitality*) aoigheachd *f*
enthusiasm *n* dealas *m*, dìoghras
m
enthusiastic *a* dealasach,
dìoghrasach
entice *v* tàlaidh, meall, thoir a
thaobh, breug
enticing *a* tarraingeach,
tàlaidheach
entire *a* iomlan, slàn, uile
entirely *adv* gu lèir, gu tur
entitlement *n* còir *f*, làn-chòir *f*

entrails *n* mionach *m*, caolain *m pl*; (*animals*) greallach *f*
entrance *n* dol/tighinn a-steach *m*, inntrigeadh *m*; (*way in*) slighe a-steach *f* **main e.** doras-mòr *m*, prìomh dhoras *m*
entreat *v* guidh (air)
entreaty *n* guidhe *f m*, achanaich *f*
entrepreneur *n* neach-tionnsgain *m*
entrust *v* fàg an urra ri, cuir air cùram
entry *n* teachd a-steach *m*, inntrigeadh *m*
enumerate *v* àirmhich, cunnt
enunciate *v* cuir an cèill, aithris
envelop *v* còmhdaich, cuartaich
envelope *n* cèis-litreach *f*
envious *a* farmadach
environment *n* àrainneachd *f*
environmentalist *n* neach-àrainneachd *m*
envoy *n* tosgaire *m*
envy *n* farmad *m*, eud *m v* bi ri farmad **I envied her** bha farmad agam rithe
epic *n* euchd-dhàn *m*, mòr-dhuan *m*
epidemic *n* galar sgaoilte *m*, ruathar *m*
epilepsy *n* an tinneas tuiteamach *m*
episcopal *a* easbaigeach
Episcopalian *n, a* Easbaigeach *m*
episode *n* eadar-sgeul *m*, tachartas *m*
epitome *n* sàr eisimpleir *f m* **the e. of laziness** dealbh na leisge *f m*
equable *a* cothrom, rèidh, ciùin
equal *a* ionann, co-ionann **e. opportunities** co-ionannachd chothroman *f n* seise *m v* bi co-ionann
equality *n* co-ionannachd *f*, cothromachd *f*
equalize *v* dèan co-ionann
equation *n* co-ionannachadh *m*; (*maths*) co-aontar *m*
equator *n* meadhan-chearcall (na talmhainn) *m*, Crios-meadhain *m*

equestrian *n* marcaiche *m*
equilateral *a* co-shliosach **e. triangle** triantan ionann-thaobhach *m*
equinox *n* co-fhreagradh nan tràth *m*
equip *v* uidheamaich, beairtich
equipment *n* uidheam *f*, acfhainn *f*
equipped *a* uidheamaichte, acfhainneach
equivalent *a* co-ionann
era *n* linn *f*
eradicate *v* cuir às do, spìon à bun
erase *v* dubh às/a-mach
erect *v* tog, cuir suas *a* dìreach
erode *v* creim, bleith; (*intrans*) cnàmh, crìon
erosion *n* (*act*) creimeadh *m*, bleith *f*; (*state*) cnàmh *m*, crìonadh *m*
erotic *a* earotach
err *v* rach ceàrr, dèan mearachd, rach air seachran
errand *n* gnothach *m*, ceann-gnothaich *m*
erroneous *a* mearachdach, iomrallach
error *n* mearachd *f*, iomrall *m*
eruption *n* brùchdadh *m*; (*volcanic*) spreadhadh *m*
escalator *n* streapadan *m*
escape *n* teicheadh *m*, tàrrsainn às *m v* teich, tàrr às
escort *n* coimheadachd *f*, freiceadan *m v* coimheadaich, bi mar chompanach
Eskimo *n, a* Easgiomach *m*, (*female*) ban-Easgiomach *m*
especially *adv* gu h-àraidh, gu sònraichte
espionage *n* beachdaireachd *f*
esplanade *n* àilean *m*
espouse *v* nochd/thoir taic do, taobh ri
essay *n* aiste *f*
essence *n* brìgh *f*, sùgh *m*
essential *a* deatamach
establish *v* stèidhich, suidhich, cuir air bhonn
establishment *n* stèidheachadh *m*, cur air bhonn *m* **the E.** na

h-urracha mòra *m pl*
estate *n* oighreachd *f* **e. agent**
reiceadair thaighean *m*
esteem *n* meas *m*, spèis *f*
v meas, cuir luach air
estimate *n* tuairmse *f v* thoir
tuairmse air, meas luach
estuary *n* inbhir *m*
eternal *a* sìorraidh, maireannach,
bith-bhuan, suthainn
eternally *adv* gu sìorraidh, gu
bràth
eternity *n* sìorr(aidhe)achd *f*,
bith-bhuantachd *f*,
biothbhuantachd *f*
ether *n* adhar fìnealta *m*, èatar *m*
ethical *a* beusanta, modhannach;
(*of conduct*) beusach
ethics *n* beus-eòlas *m*; (*personal*)
beusan *m pl*
ethnic *a* cinneachail
ethos *n* nòs *m*, feallsanachd *f*
etiquette *n* modh *f m*, dòigh-
giùlain *f*
eulogy *n* moladh *m*, òraid-
mholaidh *f*; (*poem*) dàn
molaidh *m*
euphemism *m* caomh-ràdh *m*,
maoth-fhacal *m*
euro *n* euro *f m*, ìuro *f m*
European *n, a* Eòrpach *m* **E.**
Commission an Coimisean
Eòrpach *m* **E. Parliament**
Pàrlamaid na h-Eòrpa *f* **E.**
Union an t-Aonadh Eòrpach *m*
evacuate *v* falmhaich
evade *v* seachain, faigh às
evaluate *v* meas, tomhais
luach
evaluation *n* measadh *m*,
luachadh *m*, tomhas luach *m*
evangelical *a* soisgeulach
evaporate *v* deataich
evaporation *n* deatachadh *m*
evasion *n* seachnadh *m*
even *a* rèidh, còmhnard
e.-tempered ciùin **e. number**
àireamh chothrom *f*
even *adv* eadhon, fiù 's **he didn't
e. have a coat** cha robh fiù 's
còta aige **e. the old folk were
there** bha na seann daoine fhèin
ann

evening *n* feasgar *m* **early e.**
fionnairidh *f*
event *n* tachartas *m*
eventually *adv* mu dheireadh
thall
ever *adv* uair sam bith; (*past
only*) riamh; (*fut only*) gu
bràth, gu sìorraidh **he was as
stubborn as e.** bha e cho rag 's
a bha e riamh
everlasting *a* sìorraidh, bith-
bhuan **e. life** a' bheatha
mhaireannach *f*
every *a* a h-uile, gach
everyday *a* làitheil; (*routine*)
àbhaisteach
everyone *pron* a h-uile
duine/neach, gach duine/neach
everything *pron* a h-uile nì/rud,
gach nì/rud
everywhere *pron* (anns) a h-uile
(h-)àite, (anns) gach àite
evict *v* fuadaich, cuir à seilbh
eviction *n* fuadach *m*, cur à
seilbh *m*
evidence *n* fianais *f*,
teisteanas *m*
evident *a* soilleir, follaiseach
evil *n* olc *m*, aingidheachd *f*
a olc, aingidh
evoke *v* thoir gu cuimhne
evolve *v* thoir gu bith; (*intrans*)
thig gu bith
ewe *n* caora *f*
exacerbate *v* dèan nas miosa
exact *a* ceart, mionaideach,
pongail
exactly *adv* dìreach, gu
mionaideach
exaggerate *v* àibheisich, cuir ris
(an fhìrinn)
examination *n* deuchainn *f*,
ceasnachadh *m*; (*scrutiny*)
sgrùdadh *m*
examine *v* ceasnaich; (*scrutinize*)
sgrùd, dèan sgrùdadh air
examiner *n* neach-ceasnachaidh
m; (*scrutineer*) neach-sgrùdaidh
m, sgrùdaire *m*
example *n* eisimpleir *f m*, ball-
sampaill *m*
excavate *v* cladhaich, ruamhair
exceed *v* rach thairis air

exceedingly *adv* glè (+ *len*), anabarrach

excel *v* dèan math (an), bi sònraichte/barraichte air; (*surpass*) thoir bàrr (air) **she excelled at music** bha i sònraichte/barraichte air ceòl

excellence *n* feabhas *m*, sàr-mhathas *m*

excellent *a* sàr-mhath, barrail, sgoinneil

except *prep* ach, a-mach air **e. for one or two** a-mach air fear/tè no dhà

exception *n* mura-bhith *f*, fàgail a-mach *f*, nì eadar-dhealaichte *m* **with the e. of** ach a-mhàin **everyone without e.** a h-uile duine riamh **take e. to** nochd diomb (mu) *v*

exceptional *a* air leth, sònraichte

excess *n* (*surplus*) còrr *m*; (*too much*) anabarr *m*, cus *m*, tuilleadh 's a' chòir *m*

excessive *a* neo-chuimseach, mì-choltach

exchange *n* iomlaid *f*, malairt *f* **e. rate** co-luach an airgid *m*, luach-iomlaid *m* *v* dèan iomlaid, malairtich

exchequer *n* stàit-chiste *f* **the E.** Roinn an Ionmhais *f*

excise *v* geàrr às/de

excite *v* brosnaich, gluais

excited *a* air bhioran, air bhoil

excitement *n* brosnachadh *m*, spreagadh *m*, boil *f*

exclaim *v* glaodh

exclamation *n* glaodh *m*, clisgeadh *m* **e. mark** clisg-phuing *f*

exclude *v* cùm a-muigh, dùin a-mach, toirmisg

exclusion *n* cumail a-muigh *m*, dùnadh a-mach *m*, toirmeasg *m*

exclusive *a* toirmeasgach; (*expensive*) fìor chosgail

excruciating *a* creadhnachail, fìor chràiteach

excursion *n* cuairt *f*, sgrìob *f*

excuse *n* leisgeul *m* *v* gabh leisgeul (+ *gen*)

execute *v* cuir an gnìomh, thoir gu buil; (*person*) cuir gu bàs

execution *n* cur an gnìomh *m*; (*person*) cur gu bàs *m*

executive *n* (*person*) neach-gnìomh *m*, gnìomhaiche *m*; (*body*) roinn-ghnìomha *f* **the Scottish E.** Riaghaltas na h-Alba

exemplar *n* eisimpleir *f m*

exemplify *v* bi mar/nad eisimpleir de

exempt *a* saor (bh)o, neo-bhuailteach

exemption *n* saoradh (bh)o *m*

exercise *n* eacarsaich *f* **e. book** leabhar-obrach *m* *v* gnàthaich, cleachd; (*work out*) dèan eacarsaich

exertion *n* spàirn *f*, dìcheall *f m*

exhaust *v* traogh; (*tire out*) claoidh

exhausted *a* traoghte, air teirigsinn; (*of person*) claoidhte

exhaustion *n* traoghadh *m*; (*of person*) claoidheadh *m*

exhaustive *a* iomlan, mion

exhibit *v* taisbean

exhibition *n* taisbeanadh *m*

exhilarating *a* meanmnach, aighearach

exhort *v* earalaich, brosnaich

exile *n* fògarrach *m*, eilthireach *m v* fògair, fuadaich

exist *v* bi beò, bi ann **it doesn't e.** chan eil e ann/ann am bith

exit *n* dol a-mach *m*; (*way out*) slighe a-mach *f*

exorbitant *a* mì-choltach, ana-cuimseach

exotic *a* cian-annasach, cian-thìreach

expand *v* sgaoil, meudaich, leudaich

expansion *n* sgaoileadh *m*, meudachadh *m*, leudachadh *m*

expect *v* bi an dùil (gu), sùilich **expects** tha dùil aig …

expectant *a* dòchasach, fiughaireach

expectation *n* dùil *f*, dòchas *m*, fiughair *f*

expedient *a* deiseil do, freagarrach san àm

expedite *v* luathaich, cuir cabhag air

expedition *n* turas *m*; (*speed*) cabhag *f*, luaths *m*

expel *v* cuir às, fògair, fuadaich

expend *v* caith, cosg

expenditure *n* caiteachas *m*, cosgais *f*

expense *n* cosgais *f*

expensive *a* cosgail, cosgaiseach, daor

experience *n* eòlas *m*, fiosrachadh *m*, fèin-fhiosrachadh *m* *v* fiosraich, fairich

experienced *a* eòlach

experiment *n* deuchainn *f*, dearbhadh *m*

expert *n* eòlaiche *m* *a* fiosrach, eòlach, ealanta, teòma

expertise *n* ealantas *m*, teòmachd *f*

explain *v* mìnich

explanation *n* mìneachadh *m*

explicit *a* soilleir, follaiseach, gun chleith

explode *v* spreadh

exploit *n* euchd *m* *v* gabh an cothrom air, cleachd airson prothaid **e. unfairly** gabh brath air

exploitation *n* gabhail a' chothruim air *m*, cleachdadh airson prothaid *m*; (*unfair*) gabhail brath air *f*

explore *v* rannsaich, lorg a-mach

explosion *n* spreadhadh *m*

explosive *n* stuth spreadhaidh *m* **e. device** inneal/uidheam spreadhaidh *m*

export *n* às-mhalairt *f*, às-bhathar *m* **e. market** margadh às-mhalairt *m* *v* cuir a-null thairis, às-mhalairtich

expose *v* leig ris, nochd, thoir am follais

exposed *a* am follais; (*skin*) ris; (*site*) fosgailte

expound *v* mìnich, soilleirich

express *v* cuir an cèill; (*send quickly*) luathaich

express *a* luath **e. train** trèan-luath *f* **with the e. purpose** a

dh'aon ghnotha(i)ch

expression *n* dòigh/modh-labhairt *f*; (*phrase*) abairt *f*; (*facial*) coltas *m*, fiamh *m*

expulsion *n* fògradh *m*

exquisite *a* loinneil, fìor àlainn

extempore *a* an làrach nam bonn, gun ullachadh

extend *v* sìn, leudaich, cuir ri **e. to** ruig (air)

extension *n* sìneadh *m*, leudachadh *m* **e. work** obair-leudachaidh *f*

extensive *a* farsaing, leathan(n)

extent *n* farsaingeachd *f*, leud *m*, meud *m*

exterior *n* taobh a-muigh *m*

exterminate *v* cuir às do, sgrios

external *a* (bh)on/air an taobh a-muigh

extinct *a* à bith; (*volcano*) marbh

extinguish *v* cuir às, smàl, mùch

extol *v* àrd-mhol

extort *v* foireignich

extra *a* fìor (+ *len*), ro (+ *len*); (*additional*) a chòrr *adv* a bharrachd, a thuilleadh

extract *n* earrann *f*, cuibhreann *f* *m* *v* tarraing/thoir/tog à

extraordinary *a* anabarrach, iongantach (fhèin)

extravagance *n* ana-caitheamh *m*, stròdhalachd *f*

extravagant *a* ana-caitheach, stròdhail

extreme *a* fìor (+ *len*), ro (+ *len*), anabarrach *n* iomall *m*, ceann thall *m*

extremely *adv* dha-rìribh **e. good** math dha-rìribh

extricate *v* saor, fuasgail

extrovert *n* neach fosgarra *m*

eye *n* sùil *f*; (*of needle*) crò (snàthaid) *m* **eye-opener** fosgladh sùla *m*, sùileachan *m* **eyebrow** mala *f* **eyelash** fabhra *m*, rosg *m* **eyelid** sgàile sùla *f*, fabhra *m* **eyesight** fradharc *m*, lèirsinn *f* **eyesore** cùis sgreamh *f*

eyrie *n* nead iolaire *m*

F

fable n uirsgeul m, sgeulachd f
fabric n aodach m, eige f;
(structure) dèanamh m
fabulous a uirsgeulach;
(wonderful) iongantach,
mìorbhaileach
face n aodann m, aghaidh f;
(human only) gnùis f f.-cloth
clobhd aodainn m v cuir/toir
aghaidh air; (be opposite) bi mu
choinneamh
facet n taobh m
facetious a saobh-spòrsail,
magail
facile a furasta; (superficial)
staoin
facilitate v dèan nas fhasa do,
dèan comasach, cuidich
facility n goireas m f. in alt (air)
m
facing adv mu choinneamh
(+ gen)
fact n fìrinn f
faction n buidheann f m
factor n adhbhar m, eileamaid f;
(agent) bàillidh m, seumarlan
m; (math) factar m
factory n factaraidh f m, ionad
ceàirde m, ionad tionnsgain m
faculty n ciad-fàth f, comas m,
bua(i)dh f; (acad) dàmh she had
all her faculties bha a buadhan
uile aice
fade v searg, crìon, meath
fail v fàillig; (intrans) fàilnich,
dìobair
failing n fàilligeadh m, fàillinn f
failure n fàilligeadh m,
fàilneachadh m
faint n neul m, laigse f, luairean
m v fannaich, fanntaig, rach an
laigse
faint a fann, lag; (unclear)
neo-shoilleir f.-hearted lag-
chridheach, meata
fair n fèill f, faidhir f
fair a bàn, fionn; (beautiful)
maiseach; (just) ceart,
cothromach
fairly adv an ìre mhath, gu math
fairness n bàinead f; (beauty)

maisealachd f; (justness) ceartas
m, cothromachd f
fairy n sìthiche m; (female) bean-
shìth f
faith n creideamh m; (trust)
earbsa f, muinighin f, creideas
m
faithful a dìleas, treibhdhireach
faithfulness n dìlseachd f,
treibhdhireas m
falcon n seabhag f
fall n tuiteam m, leagail m f. out
dol a-mach air a chèile m
v tuit; (in level) sìolaidh
fallow a bàn
false a meallta, brèige; (wrong)
ceàrr f. teeth fiaclan fuadain f pl
falsehood n breug f
falter v lagaich, tuislich
fame n cliù m, ainm m
familiar a eòlach (air); (manner)
faisg
familiarize v cuir eòlas air, cuir
aithne air
family n teaghlach m f. tree
craobh-teaghlaich f
famine n gort(a) f
famous a ainmeil, iomraiteach
fan n gaotharan m
fanatic n eudmhoraiche m,
dìoghrasaiche m
fanatical a eudmhorach,
dìoghrasach
fanaticism n eudmhorachd f,
dìoghrasachd f
fancy a àraid, annasach
fancy v smaoinich, beachdaich;
(desire) miannaich
fancy dress n aodach-brèige m,
culaidh choimheach f
fank n (agric) faing f, fang m
fantastic a mìorbhaileach;
(incredible) do-chreidsinn
fantasy n sgeul mhìorbhail m;
(delusion) sgeul gun bhrìgh
far a, adv fada f. away fad' air
falbh f. more tòrr a bharrachd
f.-fetched ràbhartach f.-sighted
fad-fhradharcach
farce n baoth-chluich f,
sgeig-chluich f
fare n faradh m; (food) biadh m,
lòn m

farewell *n* soraidh *f*, slàn *m*, beannachd (le) *f*
farm *n* tuathanas *f*, baile-fearainn *m* **farmhouse** taigh-tuathanais *m*
farmer *n* tuathanach *m*
farming *n* tuathanachas *m*
fart *n* braidhm *m*; (*soundless*) tùt *m* *v* dèan braidhm/tùt
farther *adv* nas fhaide, na b' fhaide *a* as fhaide, a b' fhaide
fascinate *v* tàlaidh, tog aire/ùidh
fascinating *a* tarraingeach, ùidheil
fascism *n* faisisteachd *f*
fascist *n, a* faisisteach *m*
fashion *n* fasan *m*; (*habit*) cleachdadh *m*, gnàths *m*, dòigh *f* **in f.** san fhasan **out of f.** às an fhasan *v* cum, dealbh
fashionable *a* fasanta, nòsail
fast *n* trasg *f*, trasgadh *m* **f.-day** latha-traisg/trasgaidh *m* *v* traisg
fast *a* luath; (*firm*) daingeann, teann
fasten *v* ceangail, dùin **f. on to** gabh grèim air
fat *n* saill *f*, sult *m*, geir *f*, blona(i)g *f*; (*state*) reamhrachd *f* *a* reamhar, tiugh
fatal *a* marbhtach, bàsmhor
fate *n* dàn *m*
father *n* athair *m* **F.** (*relig*) an t-Athair **F. Christmas** Bodach na Nollaig *m* **f.-in-law** athair-cèile
fathom *n* aitheamh *m*
fathom *v* (*understand*) tuig, ruig air, dèan a-mach
fatigue *n* sgìths *m*
fatten *v* reamhraich
fault *n* coire *f*, cron *m*, lochd *m*; (*geog*) sgàineadh *m* *v* faigh coire do
faultless *a* neo-choireach, gun mheang
faulty *a* easbhaidheach
fauna *n* ainmhidhean *m pl*
favour *n* fàbhar *m*, bàidh *f*; (*decoration*) suaicheantas *m* *v* bi fàbharach do, nochd fàbhar do

favourable *a* fàbharach
favourite *n* annsachd *f*, neach as annsa/docha (le) *m* *a* ... as annsa/docha (le)
fawn *n* mang *f*
fax *n* facs *m* *v* cuir facs (gu)
fear *n* eagal *m*, fiamh *m*
fear *v* gabh eagal, bi fo eagal
fearful *a* eagalach
fearless *a* gun eagal, gun athadh
feasibility *n* comasachd *f* **f. study** sgrùdadh comasachd *m*
feasible *a* comasach, a ghabhas dèanamh
feast *n* fèist *f*, fleadh *m*, cuirm *f*
feat *n* euchd *m*
feather *n* ite *f*, iteag *f*
feature *n* (*aspect*) comharra *m*; (*facial features*) aogas *m*; (*landscape*) feart-tìre *m*; (*article*) alt sònraichte *m*
February *n* an Gearran *m*
federal *a* feadarail
federation *n* caidreachas *m*
fee *n* (*payment*) duais *f*; (*charge*) cìs *f*
feeble *a* fann, anfhann, breòite
feed *v* biadh, beathaich
feedback *n* fios air ais *m*
feeding *n* beathachadh *m*; (*for animals*) fodradh *m*
feel *v* fairich, mothaich; (*touch*) làimhsich, feuch
feeling *n* faireachdainn *f*, mothachadh *m*
feign *v* leig air/oirre *etc*
fell *v* leag, geàrr sìos
fellow *n* companach *m*, duine *m*
fellow *pref* co-
fellowship *n* comann *m*, companas *m*, caidreabh *m*
felony *n* eucoir *f*
felt *n* teàrr-anart *m*
female *n* bean *f*, boireannach *m* *a* boireann
feminine *a* banail, màlda; (*gram*) boireannta
feminist *n* boireannaiche *m*
fence *n* feansa *f m*, callaid *f* *v* feans(aig)
ferment *n* (*confusion*) troimh-a-chèile *f m* *v* (*alcohol*) brach
fern *n* raineach *f*

ferocious *a* garg
ferocity *n* gairge *f*
ferret *n* feòcallan *m*, neas *f*
ferry *n* aiseag *m*; (*boat*) bàt'-aiseig *m*
fertile *a* torrach
fertility *n* torrachas *m*
fertilizer *n* todhar *m*, mathachadh *m* **artificial f.** todhar Gallda
fervent *a* dùrachdach, dian, eudmhor
fervour *n* dèine *f*, dùrachd *f*, dìoghras *m*, eud *m*
fester *v* lionnraich, grod
festival *n* fèis *f*, fèill *f*
festive *a* fleadhach, cuirmeach, meadhrach **f. season** àm a' ghreadhnachais *m*
festivity *n* subhachas *m*, greadhnachas *m*
fetch *v* faigh, thoir gu
fetching *a* tarraingeach, taitneach
fetter *n* cuibhreach *m*, geimheal *m*
feu *n* gabhail *m*
feud *n* falachd *f*, strì *f*, connsachadh *m* *v* connsaich
feudal *a* fiùdalach
feudalism *n* fiùdalachd *f*
fever *n* fiabhras *m*, teasach *f*
few *n* beagan *m*, deannan *m* *a* ainneamh, gann, tearc
fiance(e) *n* leannan *m*
fibre *n* (*textile*) snàithleach *m*; (*in diet*) freumhag *f*
fickle *a* caochlaideach, gogaideach, leam-leat
fiction *n* uirsgeul *m*, ficsean *m*
fictional *a* uirsgeulach, ficseanail
fiddle *n* fidheall *f* *v* bi ri fìdhlearachd, cluich air an fhidhill; (*be dishonest*) bi ri foill **don't f. with it** na bi a' fideis ris
fiddler *n* fìdhlear *m*
fidelity *n* dìlseachd *f*
fidgety *a* idrisgeach, fideiseach, beag-fois
field *n* achadh *m*, raon *m* **f.-mouse** luch-fheòir *f*
fiend *n* deamhan *m*
fierce *a* fiadhaich, garg
fiery *a* teinnteach, loisgeach *f*; (*temper*) sradagach, aithghearr/cas (san nàdar)

f. cross crann-tàra *m*
fifteen *n* còig-deug **f. pence** còig sgillinn deug
fifth *a* còigeamh
fiftieth *a* leth-cheudamh
fifty *n* leth-cheud *m*, caogad *m* **f. pounds** leth-cheud/caogad not
fight(ing) *n* sabaid *f*, còmhrag *f* *v* sabaidich, dèan sabaid, còmhraig
figure *n* figear *m*; (*shape*) cumadh *m*, cruth *m*; (*of speech*) samhla *m*, ìomhaigh *f*
file *n* (*tool*) eighe *f*; (*office*) faidhle *m* *v* lìomh; (*papers*) faidhl(ig), cuir ann am faidhle
filing *n* faidhleadh *m* **f. cabinet** preasa faidhlidh *m*
fill *n* lìon *m*, sàth *m* *v* lìon; (*intrans*) lìon, fàs làn
filling *a* sàthach
filling-station *n* stèisean connaidh/peatrail *m*
filly *n* loth *f m*
film *n* film *m*; (*membrane*) sgannan *m* **f.-star** reul *m*, reultag film *f*
filter *n* sìoltachan *m*
filth *n* salchar *m*
filthy *a* salach
fin *n* ite *f*
final *a* deireannach *n*; (*sport*) cuairt dheireannach *f*
finalize *v* thoir gu crìch, crìochnaich
finally *adv* mu dheireadh thall
finance *n* ionmhas *m*, maoineachas *m*, airgead *m* **F. Department** Roinn an Ionmhais *f* *v* maoinich, pàigh, ionmhasaich
financial *a* ionmhasail, ionmhasach **f. year** bliadhna-ionmhais *f*
financier *n* maoiniche *m*
find *v* faigh, lorg
fine *n* càin *f* *v* cuir càin (air)
fine *a* (*quality*) grinn; (*smooth*) mìn; (*weather*) brèagha **that's f.** tha sin taghta/glan
finesse *n* snas *m*, fìnealtachd *f*
finger *n* meur *f*, corrag *f* **f.-nail** ìne *f* **f.-print** lorg-meòire *f*

v làimhsich, cuir meur air
finish *n* crìoch *f*, ceann *m*
  v crìochnaich, cuir crìoch air
finished *a* crìochnaichte, deiseil,
  ullamh
Finn *n* Fionnlannach *m*, (*female*)
  ban-Fhionnlannach *f*
Finnish *a* Fionnlannach
fir *n* giuthas *m*
fire *n* teine *m* **f. alarm** inneal-
  rabhaidh teine *m*, clag teine *m*
  f.-engine einnsean-smàlaidh *m*
  f.-escape slighe teichidh *f* **f.-**
  extinguisher inneal-smàlaidh *m*
  firefighter neach-smàlaidh *m*,
  smàladair *m* **firework** teine-
  ealain *m* **fireworks** teintean-
  ealain **firelighter** lasadair-teine
  m **fireside** teallach *m* **firewood**
  fiodh-connaidh *m* **by the f.** an
  tac an teine *v* (*weapons*) loisg
  set f. to cuir teine ri, cuir na
  t(h)eine *etc*
firm *n* companaidh *f m*
firm *a* daingeann, cruaidh;
  (*steadfast*) seasmhach,
  diongmhalta
firmness *n* daingneachd *f*, cruas
  m; (*steadfastness*) seasmhachd
  f, diongmhaltas *m*, cruas *m*
first *a* ciad, a' chiad, prìomh
  f. thing in the morning a' chiad
  char sa mhadainn **First Minister**
  Prìomh Mhinistear *m* *adv* an
  toiseach, anns a' chiad àite **from**
  f. to last bho thùs gu èis
first aid *n* ciad-fhuasgladh *m*
firth *n* linne *f*, caol *m*, caolas *m*
fiscal *n* fiosgail *m* *a* fiosgail; (*fin*)
  ionmhasail
fish *n* iasg *m* **f.-farm** tuathanas-
  èisg *m* **f.-market** margadh-èisg
  m **f.-shop** bùth-èisg *f*
  v iasgaich, bi ag iasgach
fisherman *n* iasgair *m*
fishing *n* iasgach *m* **f.-line**
  driamlach *f m* **f.-rod** slat-
  iasgaich *f*
fishmonger *n* reiceadair èisg *m*
fissure *n* sgoltadh *m*, sgàineadh *m*
fist *n* dòrn *m*
fit *n* cuairt *f*, taom *m* **he took a fit**
  thàinig cuairt air

fit *a* fallain; (*suitable*) iomchaidh,
  cubhaidh *v* dèan freagarrach,
  cuir an òrdugh; (*suit*) freagair
fitful *a* plathach
fitness *n* fallaineachd *f*;
  (*suitability*) freagarrachd *f*
fitting *a* iomchaidh, cubhaidh
five *n*, *a* còig *a* còig **f. people**
  còignear *f m*
fix *v* suidhich, socraich; (*mend*)
  càirich **that'll fix him** bheir siud
  air
fixture *n* rud suidhichte *m*;
  (*sport*) gèam *m*, maids *m* **f. list**
  clàr-gheamannan *m*
flabby *a* plamach, bog
flag *n* bratach *f* **flagpole** brat-
  chrann *m*
flagrant *a* dalma, ladarna
flagship *n* prìomh long *f*
  a suaicheanta
flail *n* sùist *f*
flair *n* liut *m*, alt *m*
flake *n* bleideag *f*
flame *n* lasair *f*
flammable *a* lasanta
flan *n* flana *m*
flank *n* slios *m*, taobh *m*
flap *n* flapa *m* **in a f.** na b(h)oil
  etc *v* crath
flare *n* lasair-bhoillsg *m*
flash *n* lasadh *m*, boillsgeadh *m*
  v deàlraich, boillsg, las
flashback *n* ais-shealladh *m*
flashing *a* boillsgeach
flask *n* flasg *m*, searrag *f*, buideal *m*
flat *n* còmhnard *m*; (*residence*)
  flat *f m* **f. calm** fèath nan eun *f*
  m *a* còmhnard, rèidh; (*met*)
  neo-bheothail; (*mus*) maol, flat
flatten *v* dèan rèidh; (*mus*)
  maolaich
flatter *v* dèan brosgal/miodal/
  sodal
flattering *a* brosgalach, sodalach
flattery *n* brosgal *m*, miodal *m*,
  sodal *m*
flatulence *n* gaothaireachd *f*
flavour *n* blas *m*
flaw *n* meang *f*, gaoid *f*
flax *n* lìon *m*
flea *n* deargann *f*, deargad *f*
flee *v* teich, tàrr às

fleece n rùsg m; (garment)
seacaid-bhlàth f
fleet n cabhlach m, loingeas m
flesh n feòil f
flex n fleisg f, càball m
flexibility n sùbailteachd f,
subailteachd f
flexible a sùbailte, subailte,
so-lùbach
flicker v priob
flight n (in air) iteag m, iteal(adh)
m; (on plane) turas-adhair m;
(escape) teicheadh m, ruaig f;
(of imagination) ruith-inntinn f
flimsy a tana, lag **f. excuse**
leisgeul bochd m
flinch v clisg
fling v tilg, caith
flint n ailbhinn f, spor m
flippant a beadaidh
flirt n beadrach f, gogaid f
v beadraich, dèan beadradh
flit v èalaidh; (move house) dèan
imrich
flitting n (moving house) imprig f,
imrich f
float n puta m, fleòdragan m
float v flod, bi a'/air fleòdradh, bi
air bhog
flock n treud m, (birds) ealt(a) f
flood n tuil f, dìle f **f.-gate** tuil-
dhoras m v còmhdaich le uisge
flooded a fo uisge, bàthte
flooding n tuileachadh m
floor n làr m, ùrlar m **f.-board**
clàr ùrlair m, bòrd an ùrlair m
floppy disc n clàr-bog m
floral a flùr(an)ach, dìtheanach
florid a ruiteach
florist n reiceadair-fhlùraichean m
flounder n lèabag f, leòbag f
flour n flùr m, min-fhlùir f
flourish v fàs, rach gu math le;
(brandish) steòrn le
flow n sruth m, sileadh m **f. chart**
sruth-chlàr m, clàr-ruith m
f.-tide sruth-lìonaidh v sruth,
ruith, sil
flower n flùr m, dìthean m, blàth
m
flowery a flùr(an)ach, dìtheanach
flu n an cnatan mòr m
fluctuate v luaisg, atharraich

(bho àm gu àm)
fluent a fileanta, siùbhlach
f. speaker fileantach m
fluid n lionn m
fluke n (chance) turchairt m,
tuiteamas m; (of anchor) fliùt
m, pliuthan m; (worm) cnuimh
f, cruimh f
fluoride n fluoraid m
flurry n othail f
flush n (facial) rudhadh m v fàs
dearg; (toilet) sruthlaich
fluster v cuir an cabhaig, cuir
troimh-a-chèile
flute n duiseal f, cuisle-chiùil f
flutter v (fly) dèan itealaich,
sgiathalaich
flux n sruthadh m, ruith f
fly n cuileag f; (fishing) maghar
m
fly a carach, seòlta
fly v rach/falbh air iteig, itealaich;
(escape) teich
flying n itealaich f, sgiathalaich f
foal n searrach m, loth f m
foam n cop m, cobhar m
focus n fòcas m v dèan fòcas air,
cuimsich air
fodder n fodar m
foe n nàmhaid m, eascaraid m
foetus n ginean m, toircheas m
fog n ceò f m
foggy a ceòthach
foible n laigse bheag f
foil v cuir casg air, bac
fold n filleadh m, preas m;
(animal) buaile f, crò m
v paisg, fill
folder n pasgan m
foliage n duilleach m
folk n muinntir f, sluagh m,
poball m, daoine m pl **f. music**
ceòl dùthchasach m **folksong**
mith-òran m **folktale** mith-sgeul
m, sgeulachd f **folklore** beul-
aithris f
follow v lean, thig an dèidh **as**
follows mar a leanas
following a **the f. ...** an/am/an t-/
a' ... a leanas **a f. wind** gaoth na
c(h)ùl etc
folly n gòraiche f, amaideas m
fond a (of) dèidheil/measail/

miadhail air **a f. mother** màthair chaomh *f*
fondle *v* cnèadaich, tataidh
font *n* amar(-baistidh) *m*; (*type*) clò *m*
food *n* biadh *m*, lòn *m*
fool *n* amadan *m*, gloidhc *f* **female f.** òinseach *f v* meall, thoir an car à
foolish *a* gòrach, amaideach
foot *n* cas *f*, troigh *f*; (*of hill*) bonn *m*, bun *m*; (*in length*) troigh *f* **f. and mouth disease** an galar roil(l)each/ronnach *m*
football ball-coise *m* **footpath** frith-rathad *m* **footprint** lorg-coise *f* **footstep** cas-cheum *m*
for *prep* do, ri, airson (+ *gen*), fad **he left this for you** dh'fhàg e seo dhut **wait for me** fuirich rium **they'll be here for a week** bidh iad an seo airson/fad seachdain **we paid £100 for it** phàigh/thug sinn ceud not air
forbearance *n* foighidinn *f*
forbid *v* toirmisg
forbidden *a* toirmisgte
force *n* neart *m*, cumhachd *f m* **the Armed Forces** Feachdan na Dùthcha *f pl* **undue f.** làmhachas-làidir *m v* co-èignich, thoir air, spàrr (air) **she forced her to do it** thug i oirre a dhèanamh
forceful *a* neartmhor
ford *n* àth *m*; (*between islands*) fadhail *f*
forecast *n* ro-aithris *f*, ro-amas *m* **weather f.** tuairmse sìde *f v* dèan ro-aithris, dèan ro-amas; (*weather*) dèan tuairmse air an t-sìde
forefather *n* sinnsear *m* **forefathers** na h-athraichean *m pl*
forefront *n* fìor thoiseach *m* **in the f. of the campaign** air ceann na h-iomairt
forego *v* leig seachad, dèan às aonais
forehead *n* bathais *f*, maoil *f*, mala *f*
foreign *a* coimheach, cian **F. Office** Oifis nan Dùthchannan

Cèin *f*
foreigner *n* coigreach *m*
forelock *n* dosan *m*, logan *m*
foreman *n* gafair *m*
foremost *a* prìomh *adv* air thoiseach
forenoon *n* ro mheadhan-latha *m*, ro-nòin *m*
forensic *a* foireansach
foresee *v* faic ro-làimh
foresight *n* ro-shealladh *m*; (*met*) lèirsinn *f*
forest *n* coille *f* **deer f.** frìth *f*
forester *n* forsair *m*, coilltear *m*
forestry *n* forsaireachd *f*, coilltearachd *f* **F. Commission** Coimisean na Coille *m*
foretaste *n* blasad ro-làimh *m*, ro-aithne *f*
foretell *v* fàisnich
forever *adv* gu bràth, gu sìorraidh, a-chaoidh **f. more** gu bràth tuilleadh
forewarn *v* cuir air earalas
foreword *n* ro-ràdh *m*
forfeit *v* caill (còir air)
forge *n* teallach *m*, ceàrdach *f v* dealbh à meatailt; (*document etc*) feall-dheilbh, sgrìobh gu fallsa; (*links etc*) stèidhich
forgery *n* fallsaidheachd *f*, meall-sgrìobhadh *m*
forget *v* dìochuimhnich
forgetful *a* dìochuimhneach
forgive *v* math, thoir mathanas
forgiveness *n* mathanas *m*
fork *n* forc(a) *f*, greimire *m*; (*in road*) gobhal *m*
form *n* cumadh *m*, cruth *m*, riochd *m*, dealbh *f m*; (*document*) foirm *m*; (*mood*) cor *m*, triom *f m*; (*seat*) furm *m* **in good f.** an deagh shunnd *v* dealbh, cum, cruthaich, cuir ri chèile
formal *a* foirmeil, riaghailteach
formality *n* foirmealachd *f*, deas-ghnàth *m* **a f.** gnàths *m*
format *n* cruth *m*
formation *n* cumadh *m*, eagar *m*
former *a* a chaidh seachad, a bha ann (roimhe)
formidable *a* foghainteach

formula *n* foirmle *f*
formulate *v* riaghailtich, cuir ri chèile
fornication *n* strìopachas *f*
forsake *v* trèig, dìobair, cuir cùl ri
fort *n* dùn *m*, daingneach *f*
forth *adv* a-mach, air adhart **from this time f.** o seo a-mach/suas
forthcoming *a* a' tighinn, ri teachd; (*open*) fosgarra
forthright *a* dìreach, fosgailte
forthwith *adv* gun dàil
fortieth *a* dà fhicheadamh
fortify *v* daingnich, neartaich
fortitude *n* tapachd *f*, fiùghantachd *f*
fortnight *n* cola-deug *f*, ceala-deug *f*
fortress *n* daingneach *f*
fortuitous *a* tuiteamach
fortunate *a* fortanach, sealbhach
fortune *n* fortan *m*, sealbh *m*, àgh *m*
forty *n, a* dà fhichead *m*, ceathrad *m* **f. winks** norrag *f*
forum *n* fòram *m*
forward *a* iarrtach, aghach
forward(s) *adv* air adhart *v* adhartaich, cuir air adhart
fossil *n* fosail *f* **f.-fuel** connadh-fosail *m*
foster *v* altraim, àraich
foster-father *n* oide *m*
fosterling *n* dalta *m*
foster-mother *n* muime *f*
foul *n* fealladh *m*
foul *a* salach, gràineil, breun *v* salaich, gànraich; (*sport*) dèan fealladh
found *v* stèidhich, suidhich, bunaitich
foundation *n* stèidh *f*, bunait *f m*; (*org*) stèidheachd *f*
founder *v* theirig fodha
foundry *n* leaghadair *m*, ionad leaghaidh *m*
fountain *n* fuaran *m*
four *n* a ceithir *a* ceithir **f. people** ceathrar *f m*
fourteen *n, a* ceithir-deug **f. fish** ceithir iasg deug
fourteenth *a* ceathramh deug
fourth *a* ceathramh
fowl *n* eun *m*

fox *n* sionnach *m*, madadh-ruadh *m*
foxglove *n* lus nam ban-sìth *m*
foyer *n* for-thalla *m*
fraction *n* mìr *m*, bloigh *f*
fracture *n* bris(t)eadh *m v* bris(t), bloighdich
fragile *a* brisg, lag
fragment *n* fuidheall *m*, bloigh *f*, criomag *f*, mìr *m*
fragmented *a* bìdeagach, às a chèile
fragrance *n* cùbhraidheachd *f*
fragrant *a* cùbhraidh
frail *a* lag, anfhann
frame *n* frèam *m*, cèis *f*; (*of mind*) staid-inntinn *f*
framework *n* frèam *m*
franchise *n* còir *f*, còrachd *f*, ceadachd *f*
frank *a* faoilidh, fosgailte
frantic *a* air bhoil(e), air chuthach
fraternal *a* bràithreil
fraud *n* foill *f*
fraudulent *a* foilleil, fealltach
fray *v* bleith, sgaoil
freak *n* cùis-iongnaidh *f* **a f. event** fìor thuiteamas *m*
freckled *a* breac-bhallach
freckles *n* breacadh-seunain *m*
free *a* saor; (*of charge*) an asgaidh *v* saor, leig fa sgaoil
freedom *n* saorsa *f*, saorsainn *f*, cead *m*
freelance *a* ag obair air a c(h)eann fhèin
freemason *n* saor-chlachair *m*
freeze *n* reothadh *m v* reoth; (*stop*) cuir casg air
freezer *n* reothadair *m*
freight *n* luchd *m*; (*charge*) faradh *m*
French *n* **the F.** na Frangaich *m pl a* Frangach; (*lang*) Fraingis *f*
Frenchman *n* Frangach *m*
Frenchwoman ban-Fhrangach *f*
frenetic *a* air bhoil(e)
frenzy *n* boil(e) *f*
frequent *a* tric, minig, bitheanta
frequent *v* tadhail, tathaich
frequently *adv* gu tric, gu minig
fresh *a* (*produce*) ùr; (*atmos*) fionnar

freshen *v* ùraich
freshness *n* ùrachd *f*, ùralachd *f*
fret *v* luaisg, bi frionasach
friction *n* suathadh (ri chèile) *m*,
  bleith *f*; (*discord*) eas-aonta *m*
Friday *n* Dihaoine *m*
fridge *n* fuaradair *m*, frids *m*
friend *n* caraid *m* **female f.**
  banacharaid *f*
friendly *a* càirdeil, dàimheil
friendship *n* càirdeas *m*, dàimh *f m*
fright *n* eagal *m*, clisgeadh *m*
frighten *v* cuir eagal air **were you**
  frightened? an robh an t-eagal
  ort?
frightening *a* eagalach
frightful *a* eagalach, oillteil
frigid *a* fuar
frill *n* fraoidhneas *m* **without any**
  frills gun spaidealachd sam bith
fringe *n* fraoidhneas *m*, oir *f m*,
  iomall *m*; (*hair*) logaidh *f* **the**
  Festival F. Iomall na Fèise
frisky *a* mear, mireagach
frivolous *a* faoin, luideach
frock *n* froga *m*
frog *n* losgann *m*
from *prep* (bh)o, à **f. time to time**
  (bh)o àm gu àm **f. dawn till dusk**
  o mhoch gu dubh, **a man from**
  Uist fear à Uibhist
front *n* aghaidh *f*, aodann *m*,
  toiseach *m*, beulaibh *m* **in f.** air
  thoiseach **in f. of** air beulaibh
  (+ *gen*)
frontier *n* crìoch *f*
frost *n* reothadh *m*
frosty *a* reòthte **a f. reception**
  fàilte glè fhuar
froth *n* cop *m*
frown *n* gruaim *f*, sgraing *f*,
  greann *f*
frozen *a* reòthte, reothta
frugal *a* glèidhteach, caomhntach
fruit *n* meas *m*; (*produce*) toradh
  m **f.-cake** cèic-mheasan *f m*
  f. juice sùgh mheasan *m*
fruitful *a* torrach; (*successful*)
  soirbheachail
fruition *n* buil *f* **come to f.** thig gu
  buil *v*
fruitless *a* neo-thorrach; (*met*)
  gun tairbhe **a f. expedition/**

exercise siubhal gun siùcar
frustrate *v* leamhaich; (*hinder*)
  cuir bacadh air
fry *v* ròst, fraighig, praighig
frying-pan *n* aghann *f*,
  praigheapan *m*
fuel *n* connadh *m*
fugitive *n* fògarrach *m*
fulfil *v* coilean
fulfilled *a* coileanta, sàsaichte
full *a* làn, iomlan **f. to the brim**
  loma-làn **f. moon** gealach
  (sh)làn *f* **f.-time** làn-thìde,
  làn-ùine
full stop *n* (*punct*) stad-phuing *f*
fulmar *m* fulmair *m*
fumble *v* làimhsich gu cearbach,
  bi cliobach
fumes *n* deatach *f*, smùid *f*
fun *n* fealla-dhà *f*, dibhearsain *m*,
  spòrs *f*
function *n* feum *m*; (*of person*)
  dreuchd *f*; (*event*)
  cruinneachadh *m* *v* obraich
fund *n* maoin *f*, stòr *m* **funds**
  ionmhas *m*, airgead *m*
  v maoinich
fundamental *a* bunaiteach
fundraising *n* togail-airgid *f*
funeral *n* tiodhlacadh *m*,
  adhlacadh *m*, tòrradh *m*
  f. procession giùlan *m*
funnel *n* pìob-tharraing *f*; (*on*
  ship) luidhear *m*
funny *a* èibhinn, ait
fur *n* bian *m*
furious *a* fiadhaich, air/fon
  chuthach
furnace *n* fùirneis *f*
furnish *v* cuir àirneis an;
  (*provide*) thoir do, uidheamaich
furniture *n* àirneis *f* **item of f.** ball
  àirneis *m*
furrow *n* clais *f*, sgrìob *f*;
  (*wrinkle*) roc *f*, preas *m*
furry *a* molach, ròmach
further *v* cuir air adhart,
  adhartaich *a*, *adv* a bharrachd
further education *n* foghlam
  adhartach *m*
furthermore *adv* rud eile, a
  thuilleadh air sin, cho math ri
  sin, a bhàrr/bharrachd air sin

furtive *a* fàil(l)idh
fury *n* cuthach *m*
fuse *n* fiùs(a) *m*
fusion *n* leaghadh *m*, aonadh *m*
fuss *n* othail *f*, ùpraid *f*
fussy *a* àilgheasach, tàrmasach
futile *a* dìomhain, faoin
future *n* àm ri teachd *m* *a* ri teachd, teachdail **f. tense** an tràth teachdail *m*

G

gadget *n* uidheam *f*, magaid *f*
Gael *n* Gàidheal *m*, (*female*) bana-Ghàidheal *f*
Gaelic *n, a* Gàidhlig *f* (*usually with def art*) a' Ghàidhlig
gag *v* cuir glas-ghuib air
gain *n* buannachd *f* *v* buannaich, coisinn; (*reach*) ruig
gait *n* dòigh-gluasaid *f*
galaxy *n* Slighe Chlann Uisnich *f*, reul-chrios *m*
gale *n* gèile *m*, gaoth mhòr *f*
gallant *a* (*chivalrous*) flathail; (*spirited*) meanmnach **a g. effort** oidhirp thapaidh
gallery *n* gailearaidh *f m*, lobhta *m*
galley *n* birlinn *f*; (*kitchen*) cidsin *m*
galling *a* leamh, doimheadach
gallon *n* galan *m*
gallop *v* falbh aig roid; (*on horseback*) luath-mharcaich
gallows *n* croich *f*
galore *adv* gu leòr
gamble *v* cuir airgead air gheall, dèan ceàrrachas
gambler *n* ceàrraiche *m*
gambling *n* ceàrrachas *m*
game *n* gèam *m*, cluiche *f*; (*food etc*) sitheann *f*
gamekeeper *n* geamair *m*
gander *n* gànradh *m*, gèadh fireann *m*
gang *n* buidheann *m*, foireann *m*
gannet *n* sùlaire *m* **g. chick** guga *m*
gap *n* beàrn *f m*; (*topog*) bealach *m*
garage *n* garaids *f* *v* cuir ann an garaids
garbage *n* sgudal *m*

garbled *a* troimh-a-chèile
garden *n* gàrradh *m*, lios *m*
gardener *n* gàirnealair *m*, gàrradair *m*
gardening *n* gàirnealaireachd *f*, gàrradaireachd *f*
gargle *v* sruthail
garlic *n* creamh *m*
garment *n* bad aodaich *m*
garrison *n* gearastan *m*
garrulous *a* cabach, goileamach
gas *n* gas *m* **gas cooker** cucair gas *m* **gas fire** teine gas *m* *v* mùch le gas, sgaoil gas
gash *n* gearradh *m*, lot domhainn *m*, beum *m* *v* geàrr, sgor
gasp *n* plosg *m*, ospag *f* *v* plosg
gastric *a* meirbheach
gastronomic *a* sòghail
gate *n* geata *m*, cachaileith *f*
gather *v* cruinnich, tionail, trus; (*money*) tog
gathering *n* cruinneachadh *m*, co-chruinneachadh *m*
gaudy *a* bastalach
gauge *n* tomhas *m* *v* tomhais, meas
gaunt *a* caol, seang, tana, lom
gay *a* sunndach, sùgach, aighearach; (*homosexual*) co-ghnèitheach, co-sheòrsach
gaze *v* dùr-amhairc
gear *n* uidheam *f*, àirneis *f*; (*clothes*) trusgan *m*; (*in engine*) giodhar *f*
gem *n* seud *m*, neamhnaid *f*, leug *f*
gender *n* (*gram*) gnè *f*; (*sex*) gin *f*
gene *n* gine *f*
genealogical *a* sloinnteachail
genealogist *n* sloinntear *m*
genealogy *n* sloinntearachd *f*
general *n* seanailear *m*
general *a* coitcheann, cumanta **in g. sa bhitheantas, sa chumantas G. Election** Taghadh Coitcheann *m*, Taghadh Pàrlamaid *m*
generalize *v* coitcheannaich
generally *adv* am bitheantas, sa bhitheantas
generate *v* gin, tàrmaich
generation *n* ginealach *m*, glùn *f*;

(*creation*) gineamhainn *m*
g. gap sgaradh nan ginealach *m*
generator *n* gineadair *m*
generic *a* gnèitheach, coitcheann
generosity *n* còiread *f*,
fialaidheachd *f*, fiùghantachd *f*
generous *a* còir, fialaidh, faoilidh
genesis *n* gineachas *m*, toiseach *m*
genetic *a* ginteil
genetics *n* ginntinneachd *f*
genial *a* dàimheil, cridheil,
aoigheil
genitals *n* buill-gineamhainn *m pl*
genitive *a* ginideach **the g. case**
an tuiseal ginideach/seilbheach *m*
genius *n* (*person*) sàr-ghin *m*;
(*quality*) sàr-ghineachas *m*,
sàr-chomas *m*
gentle *a* ciùin, socair, soitheamh
gentleman *n* duin(e)-uasal *m*
genuine *a* fìor, dha-rìribh
geography *n* cruinn-eòlas *m*
geologist *n* clach-eòlaiche *m*
geology *n* clach-eòlas *m*
geometry *n* geoimeatraidh *m*
germ *n* bitheag *f*
German *n, a* Gearmailteach *m*,
(*female*) ban-Ghearmailteach *f*;
(*lang*) Gearmailtis *f*
germinate *v* ginidich, thoir fàs;
(*intrans*) fàs
get *v* faigh; (*grow*) fàs **g. away!**
thalla! **get dressed** cuir aodach
ort **get rid of** faigh cuidhteas
getting on for ... a' streap ri ...
get the better of faigh làmh-an-
uachdair air **get used to** fàs
cleachdte ri
ghastly *a* oillteil, sgriosail
ghost *n* taibhs(e) *f m* tannasg *m*,
bòcan *m* **the Holy G.** an Spiorad
Naomh *m*
ghostly *a* taibhseil
giant *n* famhair *m*, fuamhaire *m*
giddy *a* tuainealach; (*met*)
guanach, faoin
gift *n* tiodhlac *m*, gibht *f*
gifted *a* comasach, tàlantach
gigantic *a* àibheiseach mòr
giggle *v* dèan braoisgeil *Also vn*
a' braoisgeil, a' cireaslaich
gimmick *n* innleachd *f*
gin *n* (*drink*) sine *f*, Sineubhar *f*;

(*trap*) ribe *m*
ginger *n* dinnsear *m*
gingerbread *n* aran-crì/cridhe *m*
giraffe *n* sioraf *m*
girl *n* caileag *f*, nighean *f*
girlfriend *n* leannan *f*, bràmair *m*
gist *n* brìgh *f*
give *v* thoir, tabhair **g. up** leig
seachad/thoir thairis
glacier *n* eigh-shruth *m*
glad *a* toilichte, aoibhinn
gladden *v* toilich, dèan
aoibhneach
gladness *n* toil-inntinn *f*,
aoibhneas *m*, toileachas *m*
glamour *n* riochdalachd *f*
glance *n* sùil aithghearr *f*
v grad-amhairc
gland *n* fàireag *f*
glare *n* deàrrsadh *m*, dalladh *m*;
(*look*) sùil fhiadhaich *f*; (*of
publicity*) làn-fhollais *f v* thoir
sùil fhiadhaich
glaring *a* (*obvious*) làn-
fhollaiseach
glass *n* glainne *f* **g.-house** taigh-
glainne *m*
glasses *n* glainneachan *f pl*,
speuclairean *m pl*, speuclair *m*
gleam *n* boillsgeadh *m v* boillsg,
soillsich, deàrrs
gleaming *a* boillsgeach, deàrrsach
glee *n* mire *f*, cridhealas *m*
glen *n* gleann *m*
glib *a* mìn-chainnteach, cabanta
glide *v* sigh, gluais gu ciùin
glider *n* glaidhdear *m*, plèan-
seòlaidh *m*
glimmer *n* fann-sholas *m*
glimpse *n* aiteal *m*, boillsgeadh
m, plathadh *m v* faigh sealladh
(aithghearr) de
glisten *v* deàlraich, boillsg
glitter *n* lainnir *f v* deàrrs, boillsg,
dèan lainnir/drithleann
glittering *a* boillsgeach,
lainnireach
global *a* domhanta, cruinne,
cruinneil **g. warming**
blàthachadh na cruinne *m*
globe *n* cruinne *m* (*f in gen*)
gloom *n* duibhre *f*; (*dejection*)
gruaim *f*, smalan *m*

gloomy *a* doilleir, gruamach; (*dejected*) fo ghruaim, smalanach
glorious *a* glòrmhor, òirdheirc
glory *n* glòir *f*
gloss *n* lìomh *f*; (*explanation*) mìneachadh *m* *v* lìomh; (*explain*) mìnich
glossy *a* gleansach, lìomharra
glove *n* miotag *f*
glow *n* lasadh *f*, blàthachadh *m* *v* deàrrs, las
glue *n* glaodh *m* *v* glaodh, tàth
glum *a* tùrsach, gruamach
glut *n* cus *m*, tuilleadh 's a' chòir *m*
glutton *n* glutaire *m*, geòcaire *m*, craosaire *m*
gnarled *a* meallach, plucach
gnash *v* gìosg
gnat *n* corr-mhial *f*
gnaw *v* creim, cagainn
go *v* falbh, imich, rach, theirig **go away!** thalla! **let him go** leig às e **go on/ahead** siuthad
goad *v* brod, greas; (*met*) stuig, cuir thuige
goal *n* ceann-uidhe *m*; (*in sport*) gòil *m*; (*score*) tadhal *m*, gòil *m* **goalkeeper** neach-gleidhidh *m*
goat *n* gobhar *f m*
God, god *n* Dia, dia *m*
goddess *n* ban-dia *f*
godly *a* diadhaidh
gold *n* òr *m*
gold(en) *a* òir, òrail, òrdha, òr-bhuidhe
golden eagle *n* fìr-eun *m*, iolaire-bhuidhe *f*
goldfish *n* iasg òir *m*, òr-iasg *m*
golf *n* goilf *m* **g.-club** caman goilf *m*; (*org*) comann goilf *m* **g.-course** raon goilf *m*
golfer *n* goilfear *m*
good *a* math, deagh (*precedes & len n*) **g.-natured** dòigheil, mèinneil **g.-looking** brèagha, eireachdail *n* math *m*
goodbye *n*, *interj* slàn le, beannachd le **g. (to you)** slàn leat, beannachd leat **she said g. to them** dh'fhàg i slàn aca
Good Friday *n* Dihaoine na

Ceusta/a' Cheusaidh/na Càisge *m*
goodness *n* mathas *m*, deagh-bheus *f* (**My**) **g.!** A chiall!
goods *n* bathar *m*, cuid *f*, maoin *f* **g. train** trèan bathair *m*
goodwill *n* deagh-ghean *m*, deagh mhèin *f*
goose *n* gèadh *m*
gorge *n* (*topog*) clais mhòr *f*, mòr-ghil *f*; (*gullet*) slugan *m* *v* lìon craos
gorgeous *a* eireachdail, greadhnach, rìomhach
gorse *n* conasg *m*
gospel *n* soisgeul *m*
gossip *n* geodal *m*, fothal *m*; (*person*) goistidh *m* *v* bi a' gobaireachd, bi a' fothal
gouge (out) *v* buin à, cladhaich à
govern *v* riaghail, seòl
government *n* riaghaltas *m*, riaghladh *m* **the G.** an Riaghaltas *m*
governor *n* riaghladair *m*
gown *n* gùn *m*
grab *v* faigh/gabh grèim air
grace *n* gràs *m*; (*prayer*) altachadh *m*; (*quality*) loinn *f*, eireachdas *m* *v* sgeadaich, maisich, cuir loinn air
graceful *a* grinn
grade *n* ìre *f* *v* cuir an òrdugh, rangaich
gradient *n* àrdachadh *m*, ìsleachadh *m*, caisead *m*
gradual *a* beag air bheag, ceum air cheum, mean air mhean
gradually *adv* beag air bheag, ceum air cheum, mean air mhean
graduate *v* ceumnaich
graft *n* nòdachadh *m*; (*fin*) slaightearachd *f* *v* nòdaich
grain *n* gràinne *f*, gràinnean *m*, sìlean *m*; (*coll*) gràn *m*, sìol *m*
gram *n* gram *m*
grammar *n* gràmar *m*
grammatical *a* gramataigeach, gràmarach
grand *a* mòr, prìomh (*precedes & len n*) **that's g.** tha sin gasta
grandchild *n* ogha *m*
grandfather *n* seanair *m*

grandmother *n* seanmhair *f*
granite *n* clach-ghràin *f*, eibhir *f*
grant *n* tabhartas *m* *v* (*allow*)
  ceadaich, deònaich; (*bestow*)
  builich **g. aid** thoir tabhartas-
  cuideachaidh
granule *n* gràinean *m*, gràineag *f*
grape *n* fìon-dhearc *f*
grapefruit *n* seadag *f*
graph *n* graf *m*
grasp *v* dèan grèim air, greimich,
  glac
grass *n* feur *m*
grasshopper *n* fionnan-feòir *m*
grassroots *n* ìre an t-sluaigh *f* **at
  the g.** aig ìre an t-sluaigh
grate *n* grèata *m* *v* sgrìob, thoir
  sgreuch air; (*met*) bi mì-
  thaitneach
grateful *a* taingeil
grater *n* sgrìoban *m*
gratify *v* toilich, sàsaich
gratifying *a* riarachail, sàsachail
grating *a* sgreuchach, sgreadach
gratitude *n* taingealachd *f*,
  buidheachas *m*
grave *n* uaigh *f* **graveyard** cladh *m*
grave *a* stòlda, suidhichte
grave accent *n* stràc fhada *m*
gravel *n* greabhal *m*, grinneal *m*,
  morghan *m*
gravity *n* (*force*) iom-tharraing *f*;
  (*mass*) dùmhlachd *f*;
  (*seriousness*) sòlaimteachd *f*
gravy *n* sùgh feòla *m*, grèibhidh *m*
graze *v* feuraich, ionaltraich, bi
  ag ionaltradh; (*touch*) suath
  (an)
grease *n* saill *f*, crèis *f*
greasy *a* crèiseach
great *a* mòr, àrd
great-grandchild *n* iar-ogha *m*
great-grandfather *n* sinn-seanair
  m
great-grandmother *n* sinn-
  seanmhair *f*
greatness *n* mòrachd *f*; (*size*)
  meudachd *f*
greed *n* sannt *m*, gionaiche *m*
greedy *a* sanntach, gionach
Greek *n*, *a* Greugach *m*, (*female*)
  ban-Ghreugach *f*; (*lang*)
  Greugais *f*

green *a* uaine; (*of grass*) gorm,
  glas; (*inexperienced*) gorm *n*
  (dath) uaine *m*; (*grass*)
  rèidhlean *m*, faiche *f* **G. Party**
  am Partaidh Uaine *m*
greenhouse *n* taigh-glainne *m*
greet *v* fàiltich, cuir fàilte air,
  beannaich do
greeting *n* fàilte *f*, beannachadh
  m
grey *a* glas, liath **g. area** cùis neo-
  chinnteach *f* **g.-haired** liath
grid *n* cliath *f*
grief *n* bròn *m*, mulad *m*
grievance *n* cùis-ghearain *f*
grieve *v* caoidh
grill *n* (*cooking*) grìosach *f*
  v grìosaich
grim *a* mùgach, gnù
grimace *n* drèin *f*, gruaim *f*, mùig
  m
grin *n* braoisg *f* *v* cuir braoisg
  air/oirre *etc*
grind *v* meil, bleith, pronn
grip *n* grèim *m*
grisly *a* oillteil, dèisinneach
grit *n* grinneal *m*, garbhan *m*; (*of
  character*) tapachd *f*
groan *n* cnead *m*, osann *m*, osna
  f *v* dèan cnead/osna
grocer *n* grosair *m*
groin *n* loch-bhlèin *f*
groom *n* gille-each *m*;
  (*bridegroom*) fear na bainnse *m*
groove *n* clais *f*, eag *f*
grope *v* fairich, rùraich
gross *a* garbh, dòmhail; (*whole*)
  iomlan; (*disgusting*) sgreamhail
grotesque *a* suaitheanta, mì-
  dhealbhach, mì-nàdarrach
ground *n* grunnd *m*, talamh *m*,
  fonn *m*; (*foundation*) (bonn-)
  stèidh *f*; (*in piping*) ùrlar *m*
  grounds adhbhar *m* **g. floor** làr
  ìosal *m* *a* pronn
groundwork *n* stèidh *f*,
  deasachadh *m*
group *n* buidheann *f m*, còmhlan
  m **g. work** obair-buidhne *f*
group *v* cuir am buidhnean
grouse *n* cearc-fhraoich *f*,
  coileach-fraoich *m*; (*complaint*)
  gearan *m*

grovel 188

grovel v snàig, liùg
grow v fàs, cinn, cinnich, meudaich; (*trans*) thoir fàs air
growl n dranndan m, grùnsgal m v dèan dranndan
growth n fàs m, cinneas m, toradh m
grudge n diomb f m, doicheall m v sòr, talaich
gruff a gnuadh, durg(h)a, neo-aoigheil; (*voice*) greannach
grumble v gearain, talaich, dèan cànran
grumbling n gearan m
grunt n gnòsail f, gnòsad f v dèan gnòsail/gnòsad
guarantee n urras m, barantas m v rach an urras, barantaich
guard n (*person*) geàrd m, freiceadan m; (*watch*) faire f, dìon m v geàrd, glèidh, dìon
guardian n neach-gleidhidh m, neach-cùraim m
guess n tomhas m, tuairmse f, tuaiream f v tomhais, thoir tuairmse/tuairmeas
guest n aoigh m **g.-house** taigh-aoigheachd m
guidance n stiùireadh m, iùl m, treòrachadh m, seòladh m **g. teacher** tidsear treòrachaidh m
guide n neach-iùil/treòrachaidh m **guide-book** leabhar-iùil m v seòl, stiùir, treòraich
guidelines n seòladh m, stiùireadh m
guile n foill f, cealg f
guilt n ciont(a) m
guilty a ciontach
guinea-pig n gearra-mhuc f; (*met*) ball-sampaill m
guise n riochd m
guitar n giotàr m
gulf n camas mòr m, bàgh mòr m; (*met*) astar mòr m
gull n faoileag f
gullet n goile f, sgòrnan m, slugan m
gullible a so-mheallta, furasta an car a thoirt às/aiste *etc*
gulp n slugadh m, glacadh m v sluig, glac, glut
gum n càirean m, bannas m; (*glue*) glaodh m, bìth f **chewing gum** guma cagnaidh m
gumption n ciall f, toinisg f
gun n gunna m
gunwale n beul(-mòr) m
gurgle n glugan m v dèan glugan/plubraich
gush n spùt, brùchd
gust n oiteag f, osag f, cuairt-ghaoth f
gusty a oiteagach, gaothar
gut n caolan m **you've got guts** tha misneach(d) agad v cut, thoir am mionach à
gutter n guitear m; (*of fish*) cutair m
guy n fear m **come on, guys** siuthadaibh, fhearaibh
gymnasium n lann lùth-chleas f, talla spòrs m
gymnast n lùth-chleasaiche m
gymnastics n lùth-chleasachd f
gynaecology n lèigh-eòlas bhan m
gypsy n siopsach m, giofag f, rasaiche m

H

habit n cleachdadh m, fasan m, àbhaist f, nòs m; (*clothing*) earradh m, èideadh m
habitable a freagarrach airson còmhnaidh
habitat n àrainn f
habitual a gnàthach *adv* daonnan, gu gnàthach
hack v geàrr, spòlt, sgolt, sgoch
haddock n adag f
haemorrhage n sileadh/dòrtadh-fala m
hag n badhbh f, sgroidhd f
haggis n taigeis f
haggle v barganaich, dèan còmhstri mu phrìs
hail n clach-mheallain f, (*hailstones*) clachan-meallain pl
hair n falt m, gruag f; (*one*) gaoisnean m, fuiltean m, ròineag f; (*of animals*) gaoisid f, fionnadh m **h.-brush** bruis-chinn/fhuilt f **h.-dryer** tiormadair gruaige m

haircut *n* cliop *m*, bearradh fuilt *m*

hairdresser *n* gruagaire *m*

hairy *a* gaoisideach, molach, ròmach, fionnach

hale *a* slàn, fallain **h. and hearty** slàn fallain

half *n* leth *m* **h. past one** leth-uair an dèidh uair **h. a pound** leth-phunnd **h. a dozen** leth-dusan **h.-bottle** leth-bhotal *m* **h.-hearted** meadh-bhlàth **h.-pint** leth-phinnt *m* **halfway** *a, adv* letheach-slighe **h.-wit** gloidhc *f*, lethchiallach *m* **six and a h.** sia gu leth

halibut *n* lèabag/leòbag leathan(n) *f*

hall *n* talla *f m*; (*hallway*) trannsa

hallmark *n* comharra *m*

hallow *v* coisrig, naomhaich

Halloween *n* Oidhche Shamhna *f*

hallucination *n* mearachadh *m*, breug-shealladh *m*

halo *n* fàinne solais *f*; (*eg round moon*) buaile *f*, roth *f*, riomball *m*

halt *n* stad *m* *v* stad

halter *n* aghastar *m*

halve *v* dèan dà leth air

ham *n* hama *f*

hamlet *n* clachan *m*

hammer *n* òrd *m* *v* buail le òrd

hamper *n* basgaid *f* **food h.** basgaid bìdh

hamper *v* bac, cuir bacadh air

hamster *n* hamstair *m*

hamstring *n* fèith na h-iosgaid *f*

hand *n* làmh; (*large*) cròg *f m* **handloom** beart-làimhe *f* **the upper h.** làmh-an-uachdair *f* *v* sìn (+ do)

handbag *n* baga-làimhe *m*

handcuff *n* glas-làmh *f* *v* cuir glas-làmh air

handful *n* làn dùirn *m*; (*number*) dòrlach *m*

handicap *n* bacadh *m*; (*phys*) ciorram *m*

handicapped *a* ciorramach, ana-cothromach

handicraft *n* ceàird *f*

handiwork *n* obair-làimhe *f*

handkerchief *n* nèapraige *f*, nèapraigear *f*

handle *n* (*of door etc*) làmh *f*; (*of impl*) cas *f*; (*of cup, dish*) cluas *f* *v* làimhsich

handless *a* (*met*) cliobach

handshake *n* crathadh-làimhe *m*

handsome *a* eireachdail, maiseach, riochdail

handwriting *n* làmh-sgrìobha(i)dh *m*

handy *a* deas, ullamh; (*good with hands*) làmhchair(each); (*nearby*) deiseil, goirid

hang *v* croch **h. on!** fuirich!, dèan air do shocair!

hanging *n* crochadh *m*

hangover *n* ceann-daoraich *m*, ceann goirt *m*

hanker *v* miannaich

haphazard *a* tuiteamach; (*untidy*) rù-rà

happen *v* tachair

happiness *n* sonas *m*, toileachas *m*, àgh *m*

happy *a* sona, toilichte, àghmhor

harangue *n* òraid-ghearain *f*

harass *v* sàraich, leamhaich

harassed *a* sàraichte

harassment *n* sàrachadh *m* **sexual h.** sàrachadh gnè *m*

harbour *n* caladh *m*, port *m* **h.-master** ceannard-calaidh/puirt *m* *v* thoir fasgadh do, ceil

hard *a* cruaidh; (*of understanding*) doirbh *adv* cruaidh, dian **h.-hearted** cruaidh-chridheach **h.-working** dìcheallach

harden *v* cruadhaich, fàs cruaidh

hardly *adv* (bi) gann; cha mhòr gu(n) **there was h. any food left** is gann gun robh biadh air fhàgail **she could h. reach it** cha mhòr gun ruigeadh i air

hardship *n* cruadal *m*, cruaidh-chàs *m*, teinn *f*

hardware *n* bathar cruaidh *m*

hardy *a* cruaidh, calma

hare *n* geàrr *f*, maigheach *f*

harm *n* cron *m*, milleadh *m*, beud *m* *v* mill, dèan cron/milleadh air

harmful *a* cronail, millteach
harmless *a* gun lochd, neo-lochdach, gun chron
harmonious *a* co-sheirmeach, co-chòrdach, leadarra
harmonize *v* cuir an co-chòrdachd, ceòl-rèim, dèan ceòl-rèimeadh
harmony *n* co-sheirm *f*, co-cheòl *m*, ceòl-rèimeadh *m*
harness *n* acfhainn *f*, uidheam *f* *v* beairtich; (*utilize*) dèan feum de
harp *n* clàrsach *f*
harper *n* clàrsair *m*
harpoon *n* mòr-ghath *m*
Harrisman *n* Hearach *m*
Harriswoman ban-Hearach *f*
Harris Tweed *n* an Clò Mòr/ Hearach *m*
harrow *n* cliath *f* *v* cliath
harrowing *a* gaoirsinneach
harsh *a* garg, borb; (*sound*) neo-bhinn
harvest *n* buain *f*, foghar *m*
h. moon gealach an abachaidh *f*
haste *n* cabhag *f*
hasten *v* greas, dèan cabhag; (*trans*) cuir cabhag air
hasty *a* cabhagach, bras, cas
hat *n* ad(a) *f*
hatch *n* gur *m*; (*on ship*) haidse *f* *v* guir; (*met*) tàrmaich
hatchet *n* làmhagh *f*, làmhag *f*, tuagh *f*
hate *n* fuath *m*, gràin *f* *v* fuathaich, gràinich she hated them bha gràin aice orra
hatred *n* fuath *m*, gràin *f*
haughtiness *n* àrdan *m*, uabhar *m*
haughty *a* àrdanach, uaibhreach
haul *n* tarraing *f* a big h. meall mòr *m* *v* tarraing, slaod
haulage *n* tarraing bathair *f*, gluasad bathair *m*
haunch *n* leis *f*, leth-deiridh *m*, ceathramh *m*
haunt *n* àite-tathaich *m* *v* tathaich, tadhal
have *v* bi aig, seilbhich; (*take*) gabh; (*must*) feumaidh do you h. money? a bheil airgead agad?

will you h. a drink? an gabh thu deoch? you'll h. to call feumaidh tu tadhal
haven *n* caladh *m*, acarsaid *f*
havoc *n* sgrios *m*, miast(r)adh *m*
hawk *n* seabhag *f m*
hawthorn *n* sgitheach *m*
hay *n* feur *m* haystack cruach-fheòir *f* haycock coc *f*
hazard *n* cunnart *m*, gàbhadh *m*
hazardous *a* cunnartach
haze *n* ceò *f m*, smùid *f*
hazel *n* calltainn *m* hazelnut cnò-challtainn *f* *a* (*colour*) buidhe-dhonn
hazy *a* ceòthach, sgleòthach, culmach
he *pron* e, (*emph*) esan
head *n* ceann *m*; (*person*) ceannard *m* *a* àrd-, prìomh
h. office prìomh oifis *f* *v* stiùir
h. for dèan air headfirst an comhair a c(h)inn *etc* headlong an comhair a c(h)inn *etc*; (*met*) (gu) bras headstrong fada na c(h)eann (fhèin) *etc*, ceann-làidir, ceannasach
headache *n* ceann goirt *m*
header *n* (*football*) buille-cinn *f*
heading *n* ceann *m*
headland *n* rubha *m*
headline *n* ceann-naidheachd *m*
headmaster *n* maigh(i)stir-sgoile *m*, ceannard-sgoile *m*
headmistress *n* bana-mhaigh(i)stir-sgoile *f*, ceannard-sgoile *m*
headphone *n* fòn-cluaise *m*
headquarters *n* prìomh-oifis *f*
headsquare *n* beannag *f*
headteacher *a* ceannard-sgoile *m*
headway *n* adhartas *m*
heal *v* leighis, slànaich Also intrans
health *n* slàinte *f* h. board bòrd slàinte *m* h. centre ionad slàinte *m*
healthy *a* fallain, slàn
heap *n* tòrr *m*, càrn *m*, dùn *m* *v* càrn, cruach
hear *v* cluinn, èist
hearing *n* (*faculty*) claisneachd *f*; (*listening*) èisteachd *f* h.-aid

inneal claisneachd *m*
hearsay *n* fathann *m*, iomradh *m*
hearse *n* carbad-tiodhlacaidh *m*
heart *n* cridhe *m*; (*centre*)
meadhan *m*; (*met*) spiorad *m*
h.-attack grèim-cridhe *m*
heartbreak bris(t)eadh-cridhe *m*
heartburn losgadh-bràghad *m*
heartfelt *a* dùrachdach, (bh)on
chridhe, dha-rìribh
hearten *v* misnich, cùm cridhe ri
hearth *n* cagailt *f*, teinntean *m*,
leac an teinntein *f*
hearty *a* cridheil, sunndach
heat *n* teas *m*   *v* teasaich
heated *a* teth, air a theasachadh
heater *n* teasadair *m*, uidheam
teasachaidh *f*
heath *n* (*topog*) blàr-fraoich *m*;
(*bot*) fraoch *m* **h. burning**
falaisg *f*
heathen *n* cinneach *m*, pàganach
m   *a* pàganta
heather *n* fraoch *m*
heating *n* teasachadh *m*
heaven *n* nèamh *m*, flaitheanas *m*
the heavens na speuran *m pl*
Good heavens! Gu sealladh
orm!
heavenly *a* nèamhaidh
heavy *a* trom; (*of spirit*)
airtnealach
Hebrew *n, a* Eabhra(idhea)ch *m*;
(*lang*) Eabhra *f*
Hebridean *n, a* Innse-Gallach *m*
heckle *v* buair, piobraich
heckler *n* buaireadair *m*
hectare *n* heactair *m*
hectic *a* riaslach
hedge *n* callaid *f*
hedgehog *n* gràineag *f*
heed *n* feart *f*, aire *f* **pay no h. to
him!** na toir feart air! *v* thoir
feart/aire
heel *n* sàil *f*, bonn(-dubh) *m*
v cuir sàil air **h. (over)** rach air
fiaradh
hefty *a* garbh, tapaidh
heifer *n* agh *f m*
height *n* àirde *f*; (*topog*) mullach
m, binnean *m*
heighten *v* àrdaich, tog suas
heinous *a* aingidh, gràineil

heir *n* oighre *m* **heiress** ban-
oighre *f*
heirloom *n* seud *m*, ball-
sinnsearachd *m*
helicopter *n* heileacoptair *m*
helium *n* hilium *m*
hell *n* ifrinn *f*, iutharna *f*
hellish *a* ifrinneach, iutharnail,
diabhlaidh
helm *n* falmadair *m*, stiùir *f*
helmsman stiùireadair *m*
helmet *n* clogad *f m*
help *n* cuideachadh *m*, cobhair *f*
helpline loidhne-taice *f*
v cuidich, thoir cobhair (do)
helper *n* neach-cuideachaidh *m*,
cuidiche *m*
helpful *a* cuideachail
helpless *a* gun chuideachadh,
gun naire
helter-skelter *n* giorna-gùirne *m*
go h. rach na ruith 's na leum
hem *n* fàitheam *m* *v* **hem in** crò,
druid
hemisphere *n* leth-chruinne *m*
(*f in gen sg*)
hemp *n* cainb *f*
hen *n* cearc *f* **hen-house** bothag-
chearc *f*
hence *adv* (*time*) à seo suas;
(*place*) às a seo; (*for that
reason*) air an adhbhar sin, mar
sin
henceforth *adv* o seo a-mach
henpecked *a* fon spòig
heptagon *n* seachd-shliosach *m*,
seachd-cheàrnach *m*
her *pron* i, (*emph*) ise *poss pron*
a, a h- (*before vowels*)
herald *n* teachdaire *m*, earraid *m*
heraldic *a* suaicheantach,
earraideach
heraldry *n* earraideas *m*
herb *n* lus *m*, luibh *f m*
herbal *a* lusragach
herd *n* treud *m*, greigh *f*, buar *m*;
(*person*) buachaille *m*
v buachaillich
herdsman *n* buachaille *m*
here *adv* an seo, seo
hereafter *adv* (bh)o seo a-mach,
san àm ri teachd
hereby *adv* le seo, leis a seo

hereditary *a* dùth, dùthchasach
h. right còir oighre *f*
herein *adv* an seo
heresy *n* saobh-chreideamh *m*,
eiriceachd *f*
heretic *n* saobh-chreidmheach *m*
heretical *a* saobh-chreidmheach
herewith *adv* seo, le seo, leis a
seo
heritable *n* oighreachail
heritage *n* dualchas *m*,
oighreachd *f*
hermit *n* aonaran *m*,
dìthreabhach *m*
hernia *n* màm-sic(e) *m*
hero *n* laoch *m*, gaisgeach *m*,
curaidh *m* **heroine** bana-
ghaisgeach *f*, ban-laoch *f*
heroic *a* gaisgeil
heroin *n* hearoin *m*
heroism *n* gaisgeachd *f*
heron *n* corra-ghritheach *f*
herring *n* sgadan *m*
herself *pron* ise, i fhèin
hesitate *v* stad; (*mental*) bi
teagmhach
hesitation *n* stad *f*; (*mental*)
teagamh *m*
heterogeneous *a* iol-ghnèitheach,
ioma-sheòrsach
hew *v* geàrr, snaigh
hexagon *n* sia-shliosach *m*,
sia-cheàrnach *m*
hexameter *n* sia-chasach *m*,
meadrachd shia-chasach *f*
hey! *interj* hoigh!
heyday *n* treise *f* **in his/her h.** an
trèine a neairt
hiatus *n* beàrn *f*, bris(t)eadh *m*
hibernation *n* cadal
a' gheamhraidh *m*
hiccup *n* (an) aileag *f*
hidden *a* falaichte, am falach
hide *n* seiche *f*, bian *m*; (*place*)
àite-falaich *m* *v* cuir am falach,
falaich, ceil, cleith; (*intrans*)
rach am falach
hide-and-seek *n* falach-fead *m*
hideous *a* oillteil, gràineil
hiding *n* falach *m*; (*beating*)
liodraigeadh *m*, loineadh *m*
in h. am falach **h.-place** àite-
falaich *m*

hierarchy *n* rangachd *f*, siostam
rangachaidh *m*; (*eccl*) riaghladh
eaglais *m* **the h.** na
h-urracha mòra *pl*
higgledy-piggledy *adv* dromach-
air-thearrach, triomach-air-
thearrach, rù-rà
high *a* àrd **h. and dry** tioram
tràighte **h. court** àrd-chùirt *f*
h. jump leum-àrd *f m* **h. tide**
làn-àrd/mòr *m* **at h. tide** aig
muir-làn **h.-powered** mòr-
chumhachdach **h. priest** àrd-
shagart *m* **h.-profile** follaiseach
h. school àrd-sgoil *f* **h.-spirited**
aigeannach, sùrdail **h. spirits**
àrd-aigne *f*, sùrd *m* **h. water**
muir-làn *f m*
Higher *n* (*exam*) Àrd Ìre *f*
Highland *a* Gàidhealach **the H.
Council** Comhairle na
Gàidhealtachd *f*
Highlander *n* Gàidheal *m*,
(*female*) ban-Ghàidheal *f*
Highlands, the *n*
a' Ghàidhealtachd *f* **H. and
Islands Enterprise** Iomairt na
Gàidhealtachd is nan Eilean *f*
highlight *v* cuir/leig cudrom air,
soillsich
highway *n* rathad-mòr *m*
hilarity *n* àbhachd *f*, àbhachdas *m*
hill *n* cnoc *m*
hillock *n* cnocan *m*, tulach *m*
hillside *n* taobh cnuic *m*, slios
beinne *m*, leitir *f*, leacann *f*
hilly *a* cnocach, monadail
him *pron* e, (*emph*) esan
himself *pron* e fhèin
hind *n* eilid *f*
hinder *v* cuir bacadh air, bac
Hindi *n* (*lang*) Hindidh *f*
hindrance *n* bacadh *m*
Hindu *n, a* Hindeach *m*, (*female*)
ban-Hindeach *f*
hinge *n* bann *m*, lùdag *f*
hint *n* sanas *m*, leth-fhacal *m*,
oidheam *m* *v* thoir sanas, thoir
tuairmeas
hip *n* cruachan(n) *f m*
hippopotamus *n* each-aibhne *m*
hippy *n* hipidh *m*
hire *n* fastadh *m* *v* fastaidh,

tuarastalaich **hire-purchase**
ceannach-iasaid *m*, ceannach
air dhàil *m*
hirsute *a* molach
his *poss pron* a (+ *len*)
Hispanic *a* Spàinn(t)each
hiss(ing) *n* siosarnaich *f*
historian *n* eachdraiche *m*, neach-
eachdraidh *m*
historical *a* eachdraidheil
history *n* eachdraidh *f*
hit *n* buille *f*; (*on target*) bualadh
m v buail
hitch *n* (*snag*) amaladh *m*,
tuisleadh *m v* ceangail **h.-hike**
sir lioft **h. up** slaod suas
hither *adv* an seo **h. and thither**
an siud 's an seo, a-null 's a-nall
hitherto *adv* gu ruige seo,
fhathast
hive *n* sgeap *f*, beachlann *f*
hoard *n* tasgaidh *f*; (*treasure*)
ulaidh *f v* taisg, glèidh
hoar-frost *n* liath-reothadh *m*
hoarse *a* tùchanach **he was h.**
bha an tùchadh air
hoarseness *n* tùchadh *m*
hoary *a* liath
hoax *n* cleas-meallaidh *m*
hobble *v* cuagail
hobby *n* cur-seachad *m*
hockey *n* hocaidh *m*
hoe *n* todha *m*, sgrìoban *m*
v todhaig
Hogmanay *n* a' Challainn *f*,
Oidhche Challainn *f*,
a' Chullaig *f*
hoist *v* tog suas
hold *n* grèim *m*; (*of ship*) toll *m*
v cùm, cùm grèim air **h. back**
cùm air ais **h. on** (*wait*) fuirich
tiotan
hole *n* toll *m v* toll, tollaich
holiday *n* latha-saor *m*, saor-latha
m, latha-fèille *m*
holiness *n* naomhachd *f*
hollow *n* lag *f m*, còs *m*
a falamh, fàs; (*met*) gun bhrìgh
holly *n* cuileann *m*
holy *a* naomh, coisrigte
homage *n* ùmhlachd *f*
home *n* dachaigh *f* **h.-help**
cuidiche-taighe *m adv*

dhachaigh
home economics *n* eaconamas
dachaigh *m*
homeless *a* gun dachaigh *n*
daoine gun dachaigh *m pl*
home rule *n* fèin-riaghladh *m*
homesick *a* leis a' chianalas **she
was h.** bha an cianalas oirre
homesickness *n* cianalas *m*
homespun *a* gun leòm
homicide *n* murt *m*
homogeneous *a* aon-ghnèitheach,
aon-sheòrsach
homosexual *n, a* co-ghnèitheach
m, co-sheòrsach *m*
homosexuality *n* fearas-feise *f*
hone *v* faobhraich
honest *a* onarach,
treibhdhireach, ionraic
honesty *n* onair *f*, treibhdhireas
m, ionracas *m*
honey *n* mil *f* **honeycomb** cìr-
mheala *f*
honeymoon *n* mìos nam pòg *f* **h.
period** àm nam pòg *m*
honeysuckle *n* iadh-shlat *f*
honorary *a* urramach
honour *n* onair *f*, urram *m*
v onaraich, cuir urram air;
(*fulfil*) coilean
honourable *a* onarach, urramach
hoodie-crow *n* feannag *f*
hoodwink *v* meall, thoir an car às
hoof *n* ladhar *m*, crubh *m*
hook *n* dubhan *m*, cromag *f*
v glac le/air dubhan
hooligan *n* miastair *m*, ùpraidiche
m
hooliganism *n* miast(r)adh *m*
hoop *n* cearcall *m*
hoot *v* goir, glaodh; (*vehicle*)
seinn dùdach
hoover *n* sguabadair *m*
hop *n* sìnteag *f v* geàrr sìnteag,
falbh air leth-chois
hop(s) *n* lus an leanna *m*
hope *n* dòchas *m v* bi an dòchas
I h. tha dòchas agam
hopeful *a* dòchasach
hopeless *a* eu-dòchasach, gun
dòchas
horde *n* dròbh *m*, greigh dhaoine
f

horizon *n* fàire *f*, am bun-sgòth *m*
on the h. air fàire
horizontal *a* còmhnard
hormone *n* hòrmon *m*, brodag *f*
horn *n* adharc *f*, cabar *m*;
(*drinking, mus*) còrn *m*; (*car*)
dùdach *m*
hornet *n* connspeach *f*
horoscope *n* reul-fhrith *f*
horrible *a* sgreamhail, oillteil
horrid *a* sgreataidh
horror *n* uamhann *m*, oillt *f*,
cùis-uabhais *f*
horse *n* each *m* **h. racing**
rèiseadh-each *m* **horseshoe**
crudha (eich) *m* **on horseback**
air muin eich
horse-fly *n* crcithleag *f*
horseman *n* marcaiche *m*
horsemanship *n* marcachd *f*
horse-radish *n* meacan ruadh *m*,
racadal *m*
horticulture *n* gàrradaireachd *f*,
tuathanas gàrraidh *m*
hose *n* (*stocking*) osan *m*,
stocainn *f*; (*for water*) pìob-
uisge *f*
hospitable *a* aoigheil, fialaidh
hospital *n* ospadal *m*, taigh-
eiridinn *m*
hospitality *n* aoigheachd *f*, fàilte
's furan
host *n* fear-an-taighe *m*, neach-
aoigheachd *m*; (*of people*)
sluagh *m*
hostage *n* bràigh *f m*, giall *m*,
neach am bruid *m*
hostel *n* ostail *f*
hostess *n* bean-an-taighe *f*
hostile *a* nàimhdeil
hostility *n* nàimhdeas *m*
hot *a* teth **hot-water bottle** *n*
botal-teth *m*
hotch-potch *n* brochan *m*,
butarrais *f*
hotel *n* taigh-òsta *m*
hotelier *n* òstair *m*
hound *n* gadhar *m*, cù-seilge *m*
hour *n* uair *f*
hourly *adv* gach uair, san uair
house *n* taigh *m* **H. of Commons**
Taigh nan Cumantan **H. of
Lords** Taigh nam Morairean

v thoir/faigh taigh do
housekeeping banas-taighe *f*
housewife bean-taighe *f*
housework obair-taighe *f*
household *n* teaghlach *m*
householder *n* ceann-taighe *m*
housing *n* taigheadas *m* **h.
scheme** sgeama-thaighean *f*
hovel *n* bruchlag *f*, bothan *m*
hovercraft *n* bàta-foluaimein *m*
how *adv, int part* ciamar, cionnas
(*before a or adv*) **how are you?**
ciamar a tha thu? dè (cho), cia
how old is she? dè an aois a tha
i? **how often?** dè cho tric? **how
many are there?** cia mheud a
th' ann?
however *adv* ge-ta, gidheadh;
co-dhiù
howl *n* donnal *m*, ulfhart *m*
v dèan donnalaich/ulfhart
hubbub *n* othail *f*, coileid *f*
huddle *v* crùb còmhla
hue *n* dath *m*, tuar *m*, snuadh *m*
hue and cry othail is èigheach
huff *n* stuirt *f* **in the h.** ann an stuirt
hug *v* glac teann thugad
huge *a* ana-mhòr
hulk *n* (*naut*) bodhaig luinge *f*;
(*person*) sgonn mòr (duine) *m*,
liodar *m*
hull *n* slige soithich *f*
hum *n* srann *f*, crònan *m* *v* dèan
torman/crònan
human *a* daonna **h. rights**
còraichean daonna *f pl*
humane *a* caomh, truacanta,
daonnadach
humanism *n* daonnachas *f*
humanist *n* daonnaire *m*
humanity *n* daonnachd *f*, nàdar
a' chinne-daonna *m*
humble *a* iriosal *v* (*oneself*)
irioslaich, ùmhlaich; (*subdue*)
thoir fo smachd
humbug *n* amaideas *m*; (*person*)
buamastair *m*
humid *a* bruthainneach, tais
humidity *n* bruthainneachd *f*,
taiseachd *f*
humiliate *v* tàmailtich, nàraich
humiliating *a* tàmailteach
humiliation *n* irioslachadh *m*,

ùmhlachadh *m*
humility *n* irioslachd *f*
humorous *a* ait, àbhachdach,
èibhinn
humour *n* àbhachdas *m*; (*mood*)
sunnd *m*, càil *f* **in good h.** an
deagh thriom/shunnd **to h.**
someone airson neach a
thoileachadh
hump *n* croit *f* **humpbacked** *a*
crotach
hunch *n* giùig *f*, meall *m*; (*idea*)
beachd *m*
hundred *n, a* ceud *m*
hundredth *a* ceudamh
Hungarian *n, a* Ungaireach *m*,
(*female*) ban-Ungaireach *f*
hunger *n* acras *m* **h.-strike** *n*
stailc acrais *f*, diùltadh-bìdh *m*
hungry *a* acrach
hunt *n* sealg *f v* sealg
hunter *n* sealgair *m*
hunting *n* sealg *f*, sealgaireachd *f*
hurdle *n* cliath *f*
hurl *v* tilg
hurley/hurling *n* iomain
Èireannach *f*
hurly-burly *n* uirle-thruis *f*
hurricane *n* doineann *f*
hurried *a* cabhagach
hurry *n* cabhag *f* **they were in a h.**
bha cabhag orra *v* cuir cabhag
air, luathaich; (*intrans*) dèan
cabhag, greas (ort/air/oirre *etc*)
hurt *n* goirteachadh *m*, leòn *m*
 v goirtich, leòn
hurtful *a* goirt, cronail
husband *n* fear-pòsta *m*, cèile *m*
husbandry *n* àiteachas *m*
hush *v* sàmhaich, tostaich *interj*
ist!
husk *n* cochall *m*, plaosg *m*
husky *a* plaosgach; (*voice*)
tùchanach
hustle *n* drip *f v* cuir cabhag air,
spursaig
hut *n* bothan *m*
hutch *n* bothag coineanaich *f*
hydrant *n* tobar-sràide *f m*
hydro-electric *a* dealan-uisgeach
hydro-electricity *n* dealan-uisge *m*
hydrogen *n* hàidridean *m*
hyena *n* hièna *m*

hygiene *n* slàinteachas *m*
hygienic *a* slàinteachail
hymn *n* laoidh *f m*, dàn
spioradail *m* **hymnbook**
laoidheadair *m*
hype *n* haidhp *f*
hyperbole *n* spleadhachas *m*,
àibheiseachadh *m*
hypercritical *a* trom-bhreitheach
hyphen *n* sgrìob-cheangail *f*,
tàthan *m*
hypnosis *n* suainealas *m*
hypnotic *a* suainealach
hypnotism *n* suainealachadh *m*
hypnotist *n* suainealaiche *m*
hypochondriac *a* leann-dubhach
hypocrisy *n* breug-chràbhadh *m*,
cealg *f*, gò *m*
hypocrite *n* breug-chràbhaiche *m*,
cealgair(e) *m*
hypocritical *a* breug-chràbhach,
dà-aodannach, cealgach
hypothesis *n* beachd-bharail *f*
hypothetical *a* baralach
hysterical *a* r(e)achdail
hysterics *n* r(e)achd *f*

I

I *pron* mi, (*emph*) mise
ice *n* deigh *f*, eigh *f*, eighre *f* **the
Ice Age** Linn na Deighe *f*
iceberg beinn-deighe *f*, cnoc-
eighre *m* **ice-cream** reòiteag *f*
ice-rink rinc-deighe *f* **ice-skating**
spèileadh-deighe *m*
Icelander *n* Innis-Tìleach *m*,
(*female*) ban Innis-Tìleach *f*
Icelandic *a* Innis-Tìleach
icicle *n* caisean-reòthta *m*, stob
reòthta *f*
icing *n* còmhdach-siùcair *m*
icon *n* ìomhaigh *f*
icy *a* reòthte, deighe
idea *n* smaoineas *m*, smaoin *f*,
smuain *f* **I've no i.!** chan eil
càil/sìon a dh'fhios agam!
ideal *a* taghta, sàr, barrail, sàr-
inbheach
identical *a* ionann, co-ionann,
ceudna
identification *n* aithneachadh *m*,
dearbhadh-ionannachd *m*

identify *v* comharraich, dearbh-aithnich

identity *n* dearbh-aithne *f*, ionannachd *f* **i. card** cairt-aithneachaidh *f*

ideology *n* smaoineasachd *f*, creud *f*

idiom *n* gnàthas-cainnt *m*

idiosyncracy *n* nòsarachd *f*

idiosyncratic *a* nòsarach

idiot *n* amadan *m*, gloidhc *f*

idiotic *a* amaideach

idle *a* dìomhain; (*lazy*) leisg; (*at rest*) na t(h)àmh *etc*; (*thought*) faoin

idol *n* iodhal *m*, ìomhaigh *f*

idolize *v* dèan iodhal de, bi ag adhradh do

idyllic *a* eireachdail

if *conj* ma, nan, nam; (*if not*) mur(a); (*whether*) a/an/am **if they come** ma thig iad **if she does not come** mur(a) tig i **if you had come earlier** nan robh sibh air tighinn na bu tràithe **ask him if he is playing** faighnich dha/dheth a bheil e a' cluich

igloo *n* taigh-sneachda *m*

ignite *v* cuir teine ri, las

ignition *n* lasadh *m*, losgadh *m*; (*car*) adhnadh *m*

ignoble *a* suarach, neo-uasal

ignorance *n* aineolas *m*

ignorant *a* aineolach

ignore *v* leig seachad

ill *a* tinn, bochd, meadhanach; (*bad*) olc, dona **ill-informed** aineolach, beag-fios **ill-natured** droch-nàdarrach **ill-health** euslaint *f* **ill-treatment** droch làimhseachadh *m*

illegal *a* mì-laghail

illegible *a* do-leughadh, nach gabh leughadh

illegitimate *a* neo-dhligheil; (*person*) dìolain

illiberal *a* (*mean*) neo-fhialaidh; (*met*) cumhang

illicit *a* neo-cheadaichte, mì-laghail

illiterate *a* neo-litearra

illness *n* tinneas *m*, euslaint *f*

illogical *a* mì-sheaghach

illuminate *v* soilleirich

illumine *v* soillsich, soilleirich

illusion *n* mealladh *m*, mearachadh *m*

illustrate *v* dealbhaich; (*show*) seall, nochd

illustrated *a* dealbhaichte

illustration *n* dealbh *f m*; (*example*) eisimpleir *f*

illustrator *n* dealbhadair *m*

illustrious *a* cliùiteach, òirdheirc

image *n* ìomhaigh *f*; (*liter only*) samhla *m*

imagery *n* ìomhaigheachd *f*

imaginary *a* mac-meanmnach, ìomhaigheach

imagination *n* mac-meanmna *m*, mac-meanmainn *m*

imaginative *a* mac-meanmnach

imagine *v* smaoinich, smuainich (air); (*wrongly*) gabh na c(h)eann *etc*

imbecile *n* lethchiallach *m*

imbibe *v* òl, deothail

imbue *v* lìon

imitate *v* (*mimic*) dèan atharrais air; (*follow*) lean (eisimpleir, dòigh *etc*)

imitation *n* atharrais *f*, breug-shamhail *m*; (*copying*) leantainn *f m*

immaculate *a* gun smal, fìorghlan

immaterial *a* coma **it is i.** chan eil e gu diofar; (*without matter*) neo-nitheach

immature *a* an-abaich; (*person*) leanabail

immaturity *n* an-abaichead *m*; (*person*) leanabalachd *f*

immediate *a* grad, ealamh

immediately *adv* gun dàil, anns a' bhad, air ball

immense *a* àibheiseach, ana-mhòr

immerse *v* cuir am bogadh, tùm, bog

immersion *n* tumadh *m*, bogadh *m*, cur am bogadh *m* **i. course** cùrsa bogaidh *m*

immigrant *n* in-imrich *m*

immigration *n* in-imriche *f*, imrich a-steach *f*

imminent *a* gus teachd, an impis
  (+ *vn*)
immobile *a* neo-ghluasadach
immodest *a* mì-nàrach,
  mì-bheusach
immoral *a* mì-mhoralta
immorality *n* mì-mhoraltachd *f*
immortal *a* neo-bhàsmhor
immovable *a* neo-ghluasadach,
  nach gabh gluasad
immune *a* saor (bh)o, air a
  d(h)ìon (bh)o
immunisation *n* banachdach *f*
immunity *n* (*med*) dìonachd *f*,
  dìon *m*; (*leg*) saorsa *f*
immunize *v* dìon (bh)o ghalar,
  cuir a' bhanachdach air
imp *n* peasan *m*, deamhain *m*,
  spealg (dhen donas) *f*
impact *n* buaidh *f* *v* **i. on** thoir
  buaidh air
impair *v* mill, lùghdaich
impart *v* compàirtich
impartial *a* ceart-bhreitheach,
  cothromach, gun leth-bhreith
impasse *n* staing *f*
impassioned *a* lasanta,
  dùrachdach
impassive *a* do-fhaireachadh,
  socair, a' cleith faireachdainn
impatience *n* mì-fhoighidinn *f*,
  cion na foighidinn *m*
impatient *a* mì-fhoighidneach
impeach *v* casaidich (às leth na
  Stàite)
impeccable *a* gun smal, gun
  mheang, foirfe
impede *v* bac, cuir maill air
impediment *n* bacadh *m*, cnap-
  starra *m*
impenetrable *a* do-inntrig; (*met*)
  do-thuigsinn
imperative *n* (*command*) cruaidh-
  òrdugh *m*; (*urgency*) deatamas
  m **the i. mood** am modh
  àithneach *f* *a* (*urgent*)
  deatamach; (*gram*) àithneach
imperfect *a* neo-choileanta,
  easbhaidheach
imperial *a* ìmpireil
impersonal *a* neo-phearsanta
impersonate *v* gabh riochd
  (cuideigin)

impertinent *a* mì-mhodhail,
  beadaidh, bleideil
imperturbable *a* ciùin, somalta,
  sona
impetuous *a* bras, cas
impetus *n* gluasad *m*, sitheadh *m*
impinge *v* buail (air), suath (ri)
implacable *a* do-rèiteachail,
  neo-thruacanta
implant *v* suidhich, cuir a-steach
implausible *a* mì-choltach
implement *n* inneal *m*, uidheam *f*
implement *v* thoir gu buil, cuir an
  sàs
implicate *v* cuir an lùib
implication *n* (*impact*) buaidh *f*
  m, buil *f*
implicit *a* fillte, a' gabhail
  a-steach
implied *a* fillte, air a ghabhail
  a-steach, ri thuigsinn
implore *v* guidh, aslaich
imply *v* ciallaich, gabh a-steach
impolite *a* mì-mhodhail
import *n* brìgh *f*, ciall *f*; (*imports*)
  bathar a-steach *m*, in-mhalairt *f*
  v thoir a-steach bathar
importance *n* cudrom/cuideam *m*
important *a* cudromach,
  brìoghmhor
impose *v* cuir air, leag air, spàrr air
imposition *n* leagail *f*, sparradh *m*
impossible *a* do-dhèanta,
  eu-comasach
impostor *n* mealltair *m*
impotence *n* eu-comas *m*
impotent *a* eu-comasach
impound *v* punnd
impoverish *v* dèan/fàg bochd
impractical *a* nach obraich;
  (*person*) mì-dhòigheil
impress *v* (*someone*) fàg làrach
  air, coisinn deagh bheachd,
  drùidh air
impression *n* (*view*) beachd *m*;
  (*mark*) làrach *f m*; (*book*)
  deargadh *m*
impressive *a* ri m(h)oladh *etc*,
  drùidhteach
imprison *v* cuir dhan phrìosan
improbable *a* mì-choltach
impromptu *a* gun ullachadh, an
  làrach nam bonn

improper *a* mì-iomchaidh
improve *v* leasaich, cuir am
feabhas; (*intrans*) tog air/oirre
etc, thig air adhart, rach am
feabhas
improvement *n* leasachadh *m*,
feabhas *m*, piseach *f*
improvise *v* dèan gun ullachadh
impudence *n* beadaidheachd *f*,
ladarnas *m*
impudent *a* beadaidh, ladarna
impulse *n* spreigeadh *m*, togradh *m*
impulsive *a* spreigearra, bras
impurity *n* neòghlaine *f*,
truailleadh *m*
impute *v* cuir às leth
in *prep* ann, an, am, ann an/am/a
in the anns an/a'/na, sa *adv*
(*inside*) a-staigh; (*at home*)
a-staigh, aig an taigh; (*motion*)
a-steach
inability *n* neo-chomas *m*, dìth
comais *f m*
inaccessible *a* do-ruigsinn,
do-ruighinn
inaccurate *a* mearachdach
inactive *a* neo-ghnìomhach, na
t(h)àmh *etc*
inadequate *a* easbhaidheach
inadvertently *adv* gun fhiosta
inane *a* faoin
inanimate *a* marbh, gun bheatha
inappropriate *a* mì-choltach, mì-
fhreagarrach, neo-iomchaidh
inarticulate *a* mabach, gagach
inattention *n* cion aire *m*,
neo-aire *f*
inattentive *a* neo-aireil, cion-
aireachail
inaudible *a* nach gabh cluinntinn
inaugurate *v* tòisich; (*with
ceremony*) coisrig
inauspicious *a* bagarrach
inbred *a* eadar-ghinte; (*ingrained*)
nàdarra, dualchasach
incalculable *a* do-àireamh, thar
tomhais
incapable *a* neo-chomasach
incapacity *n* neo-chomas *m*
incendiary *a* loisgeach
incense *n* tùis *f*
incense *v* cuir an cuthach/fhearg
air

incentive *n* brosnachadh *m*
inception *n* tùs *m*, toiseach *m*
incessant *a* sìor, daonnan, gun
sgur/stad
incessantly *adv* gun sgur/stad
incest *n* col *m*
inch *n* òirleach *f*; (*island*) innis *f*
incident *n* tachartas *m*
incinerate *v* dubh-loisg
incision *n* gearradh *m*
incisive *a* geur, geurchuiseach
incite *v* brosnaich, gluais, spreig
incitement *n* brosnachadh *m*,
piobrachadh *m*
incivility *n* mì-shìobhaltachd *f*,
mì-mhodhalachd *f*
inclement *a* an-iochdmhor;
(*weather*) mosach
inclination *n* (*tendency*) aomadh
m, claonadh *m*; (*desire*) iarraidh
m, togradh *m*, deòin *f*
incline *n* leathad *m v* aom,
claon; (*desire*) togair
inclined (to) *a* buailteach
include *v* gabh/thoir a-steach
inclusion *n* gabhail a-steach *m*,
in-ghabhail *m* **social i.**
in-ghabhail sòisealta
inclusive *a* a ghabhas a-steach,
in-ghabhalach
incoherent *a* neo-leanailteach,
sgaoilte, mabach
income *n* teachd-a-steach *m*
i. support taic teachd-a-steach *f*
i. tax cìs cosnaidh *f*
incomparable *a* gun choimeas
incompatible *a* nach freagair,
nach tig air a chèile
incompetence *n* neo-chomasachd
f
incompetent *a* neo-chomasach
incomplete *a* neo-choileanta,
neo-iomlan
incomprehensible *a* do-thuigsinn
inconceivable *a*
do-smaoineachaidh, thar tuigse
inconclusive *a* neo-chinnteach,
neo-dhearbhte
incongruous *a* mì-fhreagarrach,
mì-choltach
inconsiderate *a* beag-diù,
neo-shuimeil, neo-mhothachail
inconsistency *n* neo-

chunbhalachd *f*
inconsistent *a* neo-chunbhalach
inconsolable *a* nach gabh
cofhurtachadh
incontinent *a* (*phys*)
neo-dhìonach
inconvenience *n* neo-
ghoireasachd *f*
inconvenient *a* mì-ghoireasach
incorporate *v* co-cheangail, gabh
a-steach
incorporation *n* co-cheangal *m*,
gabhail a-steach *m*
incorrect *a* mearachdach, ceàrr
incorrigible *a* thar leasachaidh
incorruptible *a* neo-thruaillidh,
do-choirbte, nach gabh
coirbeadh/truailleadh
increase *n* meudachadh *m*,
cinntinn *m* *v* meudaich, cuir
am meud; (*intrans*) fàs
lìonmhor, rach am meud
incredible *a* do-chreidsinn(each)
incredulity *n* cion creidsinn *m*
increment *n* leasachadh *m*,
meudachadh *m*
incremental *a* beag air bheag,
mean air mhean
incriminate *v* cuir ciont(a) air
incubate *v* guir
incubation *n* gur *m*
incumbent (on) *a* mar fhiachaibh
(air)
incur *v* tarraing (air/oirre fhèin
etc), bi buailteach do
incurable *a* do-leigheas, thar
leigheas, nach gabh leigheas
indebted *a* an comain (+ *gen*), fo
fhiachan (do)
indecency *n* mì-chuibheasachd *f*,
mì-bheus *m*, drabastachd *f*
indecent *a* mì-chuibheasach, mì-
bheusach, drabasta
indecision *n*
neo-dheimhinnteachd *f*
indecisive *a* neo-dheimhinnte,
eadar dà bheachd
indeed *adv* gu dearbh(a), gu
deimhinne
indefensible *a* neo-leisgeulach,
nach gabh dìon
indefinite *a* neo-shònraichte, neo-
chinnteach

indelible *a* nach gabh
dubhadh/suathadh às
indelicate *a* neo-ghrinn,
neo-cheanalta
indented *a* eagach, gròbach
independence *n* neo-
eisimeileachd *f*; (*polit*) saorsa *f*
independent *n* neo-eisimeileach *m*
a neo-eisimeileach; (*polit*) saor
indescribable *a* do-aithris **it's i.**
cha ghabh eachdraidh/luaidh
dèanamh air
indestructible *a* nach gabh sgrios
indeterminate *a* neo-chinnteach,
gun sònrachadh
index *n* clàr-amais *m* **i. finger**
sgealbag/calgag *f* **i.-card** cairt-
comharrachaidh *f*
Indian *n*, *a* Innseanach *m*,
(*female*) ban-Innseanach *f*
indicate *v* comharraich, taisbean
indication *n* comharra *m* **there is
every i. that ...** tha a h-uile
coltas gu ...
indicator *n* taisbeanair *m*
indict *v* cuir às leth, tog casaid an
aghaidh (+ *gen*)
indifference *n* neo-shùim *f*, cion-
diù *m*
indifferent *a* coma, neo-shuimeil,
coingeis
indigenous *a* dùthchasach
indigent *a* ainniseach
indigestion *n* cion-cnàmh *m*,
dìth-cnàmhaidh *f*
indignant *a* diombach,
feargach
indignation *n* diomb *f m*, corraich
f
indignity *n* tàmailt *f*
indigo *n* guirmean *m*
indirect *a* neo-dhìreach, fiar
indiscipline *n* cion smachd *m*,
mì-rian *m*
indiscreet *a* neo-chrìonna,
mì-chùramach
indiscretion *n* neo-chrìonnachd *f*
indiscriminate *a* (*random*)
neo-chuimsichte; (*jumbled*) am
measg a chèile
indispensable *a* riatanach,
neo-sheachanta
indisposed *a* tinn, bochd

indistinct *a* neo-shoilleir
indistinguishable *a* nach gabh
aithneachadh/dealachadh (bh)o
chèile; (*vision*) doilleir
individual *n* urra *f*, neach (air
leth) *m*, pearsa *m* *a* fa leth, air
leth, pearsanta
individually *adv* air leth, fa leth
indolent *a* leisg, dìomhain
indomitable *a* do-chlaoidhte
indoor(s) *a, adv* a-staigh
induce *v* adhbhraich, thoir air;
(*birth*) thoir air adhart
inducement *n* brosnachadh *m*
induct *v* (*educ*) oidich; (*eccl*) pòs
(ri coitheanal)
induction *n* (*educ*) oideachadh *m*,
inntrigeadh *m*; (*eccl*) pòsadh *m*
indulge *v* leig le, toilich
indulgence *n* gèilleadh *m*,
toileachadh *m*; (*favour*) cead *m*
i. in tromachadh air
industrial *a* tionnsgalach,
gnìomhachasach **i. estate** raon
gnìomhachais *m*
industrialist *n* tionnsgalaiche *m*,
neach-gnìomhachais *m*
industrious *a* dèanadach,
gnìomhach
industry *n* gnìomhachas *m*,
tionnsgal *f*; (*effort*) saothair *f*
inebriated *a* air mhisg, fo/air
dhaorach
inedible *a* nach gabh ithe
ineffective *a* neo-èifeachdach,
neo-bhuadhach
ineffectual *a* neo-tharbhach
inefficiency *n* neo-èifeachdas *m*
inefficient *a* neo-
èifeachdach/tharbhach
inelegant *a* mì-loinneil
ineligible *a* neo-cheadaichte,
neo-iomchaidh
inept *a* leibideach
inequality *n* neo-ionannachd *f*
inequitable *a* mì-cheart,
mì-chothromach
inert *a* na t(h)àmh *etc*,
marbhanta
inertia *n* tàmhachd *f*; (*in person*)
leisg(e) *f*

inevitable *a* do-sheachanta
inexcusable *a* neo-leisgeulach
inexpensive *a* saor
inexperience *n* cion eòlais *m*
inexperienced *a* neo-eòlach, gun
eòlas, neo-chleachdte
inexplicable *a* do-thuigsinn, nach
gabh tuigsinn
infallible *a* neo-mhearachdach
infamous *a* maslach,
mì-chliùiteach
infamy *n* masladh *m*, mì-chliù *m*
infant *n* naoidhean *m*, pàiste beag
m, leanaban *m*
infantry *n* coisridh *f*, saighdearan-
coise *m pl*
infatuation *n* dalladh *m*, cur fo
gheasaibh *m* **he had an i. for her**
bha e air a dhalladh leatha
infect *v* cuir galar/tinneas air,
truaill
infection *n* galar-ghabhail *m*
infectious *a* gabhaltach **i. disease**
tinneas gabhaltach *m*
infer *v* co-dhùin
inference *n* co-dhùnadh *m*
inferior *a* nas miosa; (*in quality*)
bochd, truagh; (*in status*)
ìochdarach
infertile *a* neo-thorrach, aimrid
infidel *n* ana-creidmheach *m*
infidelity *n* neo-dhìlseachd *f*
infiltrate *v* eàlaidh (a-steach)
infinite *a* neo-chrìochnach,
suthainn
infinity *n* neo-chrìochnachd *f*
infinitive *n* neo-fhinideach *m* **the
i. mood** am modh neo-
fhinideach *f m*
infirm *a* anfhann
infirmary *n* taigh-eiridinn *m*
infirmity *n* laige *f*, anfhannachd *f*,
breòiteachd *f*
inflame *v* (*met*) fadaidh, cuir
suidse ri; (*lit*) cuir teine ri
inflammable *a* lasarra, lasanta
inflammation *n* (*med*) at *m*, teas-
at *m*, ainteas *m*; (*lit*) lasadh *m*
inflammatory *a* (*met*)
buaireasach; (*med*) le at; (*lit*)
loisgeach
inflate *v* sèid (suas), cuir gaoth
an; (*intrans*) at

inflated *a* air at
inflation *n* sèideadh *m*; *(fin)* atmhorachd *f*
inflexible *a* rag, neo-lùbach
inflict *v* leag … air
influence *n* buaidh *f* **under the i. of alcohol** fo bhuaidh na dibhe, fon mhisg *v* thoir buaidh air, buadhaich air
influential *a* buadhach, aig a bheil buaidh
influenza *n* an cnatan mòr *m*
influx *n* sruth (a-steach) *m*
inform *v* innis (do), thoir brath (do), cuir/leig/thoir fios (gu/do)
informal *a* neo-fhoirmeil
information *n* fiosrachadh *m*, brath *m* **i. centre** ionad fiosrachaidh *m* **i. and communications technology (ICT)** teicneòlas fiosrachaidh agus conaltraidh (TFC) *m*
informed *a* fiosrach, fiosraichte
informer *n* neach-brathaidh *m*, brathadair *m*
infrastructure *n* bun-structair/eagar *m*
infrequent *a* ainneamh
infringe *v* bris(t) a-steach air
infringement *n* bris(t)eadh a-steach *m*
infuriate *v* cuir air bhoil(e), cuir corraich/cuthach air
infuse *v* lion (le), cuir … air feadh
ingenious *a* innleachdach, teòma
ingenuity *n* innleachd *f*, teòmachd *f*
ingrained *a* fuaighte
ingratiate *v* lorg fàbhar
ingredient *n* tàthchuid *f*
inhabit *v* àitich, tuinich, tàmh (an)
inhabitant *n* neach-àiteachaidh *m pl* luchd-àiteachaidh, muinntir (an àite) *f*
inhale *v* tarraing anail, gabh a-steach leis an anail
inherent *a* dualach, in-ghnèitheach
inherit *v* sealbhaich/faigh mar oighreachd
inheritance *n* oighreachd *f*, sealbh

m; *(cult)* dualchas *m*
inhibit *v* caisg, cùm air ais, cuir stad air
inhibition *n* casg *m*, bacadh *m*, cuing (san nàdar) *f* **she had no inhibitions about singing on stage** cha robh leisge sam bith oirre seinn air àrd-ùrlar
inhospitable *a* mosach, neo-fhialaidh
inhuman *a* mì-dhaonna
inhumane *a* an-iochdmhor
inhumanity *n* an-iochdmhorachd *f*
inimitable *a* gun choimeas
iniquitous *a* aingidh
iniquity *n* aingidheachd *f*, olc *m*
initial *n* ciad litir *f* **my initials** ciad litrichean m' ainm *a* ciad, tùsail
initially *adv* sa chiad dol a-mach, aig toiseach gnothaich
initiate *v* tòisich, cuir air bhonn/chois; *(into an order)* gabh a-steach; *(into a skill)* teagaisg, oidich
initiative *n* iomairt *f*, tionnsgnadh *m*
inject *v* *(med)* sàth-steallaich; *(met)* cuir a-steach do, cuir ri
injection *n* sàth-stealladh *m* **i. of** cur a-steach *m*, cur ris *m*
injunction *n* àithne *f*, òrdugh *m*
injure *v* goirtich, ciùrr, dèan dochann air, leòn
injury *n* goirteachadh *m*, dochann *m*, leòn *m*
injustice *n* ana-ceartas *m*
ink *n* dubh *m*, inc *f m*
inland *a* a-staigh san tìr
inmate *n* neach fo chùram/ghlais *m*
inn *n* taigh-seinnse/òsta *m*
innate *a* dualach, nàdarra
inner *a* as fhaide/a b' fhaide a-staigh
innocence *n* neo(i)chiontachd *f*, ionracas *m*
innocent *a* neo(i)chiontach, ionraic
innocuous *a* neo-lochdach, neo-choireach
innovation *n* ùr-ghnàthachadh *m*, nuadhas *m*
innovative *a* ùr-ghnàthach

innovator n ùr-ghnàthadair m, nuadhasair m

innuendo n fiar-shanas m, leth-iomradh m

innumerable a gun àireamh, do-àireamh

inoculate v cuir a' bhreac air

inoculation n cur na brice m

inoffensive a neo-lochdach

inoperable a (med) do-leigheas, nach gabh leigheas

inopportune a mì-thràthail

inordinate a neo-chuimseach **an i. length of time** ùine gun chiall f

input n cur a-steach m v cuir a-steach

inquest n rannsachadh m, sgrùdadh m

inquire v feòraich, faighnich

inquiring a rannsachail

inquiry n rannsachadh m; (query) ceist f **public i.** rannsachadh poblach

inquisitive a ceasnachail, farraideach

insane a às a c(h)iall etc, às a rian etc

insanity n cuthach m, dìth-cèille f m; (slang) crac m

insatiable a nach gabh sàsachadh/riarachadh

inscribe v sgrìobh air

inscription n sgrìobhadh m; (statue etc) snaigheadh m

insect n biastag f, meanbh-fhrìde f

insecure a neo-thèarainte

insecurity n neo-thèarainteachd f

insemination n sìolachadh m

inseparable a do-sgaradh, nach gabh dealachadh

insert v cuir a-steach

inside n an taobh/leth a-staigh m **i.-out** caoin air ascaoin, an taobh a-staigh a-muigh prep am broinn (+ gen) adv a-staigh

insidious a lìogach, sniagach; (dangerous) cunnartach

insight n lèirsinn f

insignia n suaicheantas m

insignificant a suarach, beag-seagh

insincere a neo-threibhdhireach, neo-dhùrachdach

insincerity n neo-threibhdhireas m, neo-dhùrachd f

insinuate v leth-thuaileasaich

insipid a blian, gun bhlas

insist v cùm a-mach **i. on** sìor iarr **he insists on a dram every night** feumaidh e drama fhaighinn a h-uile h-oidhche

insolence n stràicealachd f

insolent a stràiceil

insoluble a do-sgaoilte; (problem) do-rèite, nach gabh rèiteach/ f(h)uasgladh

insolvent a briste, air bris(t)eadh air/oirre etc

insomnia n bacadh-cadail m

inspect v sgrùd

inspection n sgrùdadh m

inspector n neach-sgrùdaidh m, sgrùdaire m

inspiration n sàr-smaoin f; (source of) brosnachadh m

inspire v brosnaich, spreag

inspiring a brosnachail, spreagail

instability n cugallachd f, neo-sheasmhachd f

instal v (object) cuir a-steach; (person) cuir an dreuchd, suidhich

installation n (of object) cur a-steach m; (person) cur an dreuchd m, suidheachadh m

instalment n cuibhreann f m, earrann f

instance n eisimpleir f m **for i.** mar eisimpleir **in the first i.** anns a' chiad àite **in this i.** an turas seo

instant n tiota m a grad, an làrach nam bonn

instantly adv sa bhad, san spot

instead adv an àite, an àite sin

instigate v cuir air bhonn, tòisich; (incite) piobraich

instigation n cur air bhonn m, tòiseachadh m; (incitement) piobrachadh m

instil v teagaisg, cuir an inntinn

instinct n gnèithealachd f, nàdar m

instinctive a gnèitheach, nàdarrach, a rèir gnè

institute *n* stèidheachd *f* *v* cuir
air chois, stèidhich
institution *n* (*act of*) stèidheachadh
m; (*place*) ionad *m*, stèidheachd
f; (*practice*) riaghailt *f*
instruct *v* teagaisg, ionnsaich
instruction *n* teagasg *m*,
ionnsachadh *m*; (*order*) òrdugh
m, stiùireadh *m*
instructor *n* neach-teagaisg *m*
instrument *n* (*tool*) inneal *m*;
(*mus*) ionnsramaid *f*, inneal-
ciùil *m*; (*means*) meadhan *m*
instrumental *a* (*mus*)
ionnsramaideach **i. in** mar
mheadhan air
insubordinate *a* eas-umhail
insufferable *a* doirbh a ghiùlan,
doirbh cur suas leis; (*met*)
maslach
insufficient *a* goirid, geàrr, gann
insular *a* eileanach; (*met*)
cumhang
insulate *v* còmhdaich **i. from**
dealaich, cuir air leth
insulated *a* còmhdaichte **i. from**
dealaichte, air a chur air leth
insult *n* ailis *f*, beum *m* *v* ailisich,
thoir beum/droch bheul do
insulting *a* beum(n)ach, tàireil
insurance *n* àrachas *m* **i. claim**
tagradh àrachais *m* **i. company**
companaidh àrachais *f m* **i. policy**
poileasaidh àrachais *m*
insure *v* thoir àrachas air,
faigh/thoir urras air
insured *a* fo àrachas
insurrection *n* ar-a-mach *m*
intact *a* slàn, iomlan
intake *n* gabhail a-steach *f*
intangible *a* nach gabh
làimhseachadh/fhaicinn,
do-bheantainn
integral *a* slàn, coileanta,
riatanach
integrate *v* aonaich **i. with** fill
a-steach còmhla ri
integrated *a* aonaichte, fighte-
fuaighte
integrity *n* treibhdhireas *m*,
ionracas *m*; (*wholeness*)
iomlanachd *f*
intellect *n* inntinn *f*

intellectual *a* inntleachdail
n innleachdach *m*
intelligence *n* tuigse *f*; (*report*)
aithris *f*, fiosrachadh *m*;
(*covert*) fàisneis *f*
intelligent *a* inntleachdach, tùrail
intelligible *a* so-thuigsinn
intemperate *a* mì-stuama,
ana-measarra
intend *v* dùilich, cuir
roimhe/roimhpe *etc*, rùnaich
intended *a* san amharc
intense *a* dian, teann
intensify *v* teinnich, geuraich
intensity *n* dèine *f*, teinne *f*
intensive *a* dian **i. care** dlùth-
chùram *m*
intent *n* rùn *m*
intention *n* rùn *m*
intentional *a* a dh'aon
obair/ghnotha(i)ch
intentionally *adv* a dh'aon
ghnotha(i)ch
inter *v* adhlaic, tiodhlaic
inter- *pref* eadar
interaction *n* eadar-obrachadh *m*
intercede *v* dèan eadar-ghuidhe
intercept *v* ceap, stad san t-slighe
interchange *n* iomlaid *f*, malairt *f*
interchangeable *a* co-
iomlaideach, co-mhalairteach,
a ghabhas iomlaid/malairt
intercourse *n* (*social*) co-
chomann *m*, comhluadar *m*;
(*sexual*) feis(e) *f*
interdependent *a* eadar-
eisimeileach, an eisimeil a chèile
interdict *n* toirmeasg/bacadh
(lagha) *m*
interest *n* ùidh *f*; (*fin*) riadh *m*;
(*stake*) earrann *f*, pàirt *f m*
i. rate ìre an rèidh *f* *v* gabh/tog
ùidh
interesting *a* ùidheil, inntinneach
interface *n* eadar-aghaidh *f*
interfere *v* gabh gnotha(i)ch ri,
buin ri
interference *n* gabhail
gnotha(i)ch ri *m*, buntainn ri *m*;
(*atmos*) riasladh *m*
interim *n* eadar-àm *m* *a* eadar-
amail **in the i.** anns an eadar-àm
interior *n* an leth/taobh a-staigh *m*

interject v geàrr a-steach, caith
a-steach
interlacing a eadar-fhighte
interlink v naisg, ceangail ri chèile
interlocking a co-naisgte,
co-cheangailte
interlude n eadar-chluiche f
intermediate a eadar-
mheadhanach, meadhanach
interment n adhlacadh m,
tiodhlacadh m
interminable a neo-chrìochnach,
gun chrìoch
intermittent a (bh)o àm gu àm,
air is dheth
internal a a-staigh
international n eadar-nàiseanail m
a eadar-nàiseanta
internecine a co-sgriosail
internet n eadar-lìon m **the I.** an
t-Eadar-lìon
interpret v mìnich; (translate)
eadar-theangaich
interpretation n mìneachadh m;
(translation) eadar-
theangachadh m
interpreter n neach-mìneachaidh
m, mìniche m; (translator)
eadar-theangaiche m
interrogate v cruaidh-cheasnaich
interrogation n cruaidh-
cheasnachadh m
interrupt v bris(t) a-steach (air);
(halt) cuir casg/stad air
interruption n bris(t)eadh a-steach
m; (halting) casg m, stad m
intersect v geàrr tarsainn
(a chèile), trasnaich
intersperse v sgap am measg
intertwined a eadar-thoinnte
interval n eadar-ùine f, eadar-àm
m; (school) àm-cluiche m,
pleidhe m
intervene v rach san eadraiginn,
thig eadar
intervention n tighinn eadar m
interview n agallamh m v dèan
agallamh le
interviewer n agallaiche m,
ceasnaiche m, neach-
ceasnachaidh m
intestine(s) n caolan(an) m;
(animal only) greallach f

intimacy n dlùth-chaidreabh m
intimate a dlùth-chaidreach, fìor
eòlach
intimate v ainmich, inn(i)s
intimation n ainmeachadh m, fios
m
intimidate v cuir fo eagal
into adv do, a-steach do
intolerable a do-ghiùlan, nach
gabh fhulang **i. pain** cràdh
eagalach/thar tomhais m
intolerant a neo-fhulangach,
cumhang na s(h)ealladh etc
intonation n fonn cainnt m
intoxicated a air mhisg, air an
daoraich, fo bhuaidh na dibhe
intoxication n misg f, daorach f
intractable a nach gabh
f(h)uasgladh, neo-fhuasglach
intrepid a dàna, gaisgeil, tapaidh
intricate a toinnte, mion
intrigue n cluaineas m, cuilbheart
f
intrinsic a gnèitheach, ann fhèin
etc
introduce v cuir an aithne;
(subject) tog, thoir iomradh air
introduction n cur an aithne m;
(of subject) togail f; (in book)
ro-ràdh m
introvert a neo-fhosgarra, dùr
intrude v bris(t)/brùth a-steach
intuition n im-fhios m
inundate v cuir fo uisge **we were
inundated with requests** bha
sinn a' dol fodha le iarrtasan
invade v thoir ionnsaigh air,
bris(t) a-steach
invalid n euslainteach m
invalid a neo-bhrìgheil,
neo-dhligheach
invalidate v cuir an neo-bhrìgh
invaluable a thar luach, nach
gabh luach a chur air
invariably adv an còmhnaidh,
daonnan; (very frequently) mar
as trice
invasion n ionnsaigh f,
bris(t)eadh a-steach m
inveigle v meall, thoir a thaobh
invent v innlich, tionnsgail
invention n innleachd f, tionnsgal
m

inventive *a* innleachdach, tionnsgalach
inventor *n* innleadair *m*, tionnsgalair *m*
inventory *n* cunntas *f m*, clàr-seilbhe/stuthan *m*
invert *v* cuir bun-os-cionn, tionndaidh
invest *v* (*fin*) cuir an seilbh, cuir airgead an
investigate *v* rannsaich, sgrùd
investigation *n* rannsachadh *m*, sgrùdadh *m*
investment *n* (*fin*) cur an seilbh *m*, airgead-seilbhe/tasgaidh *m*
investor *n* neach-tasgaidh *m*
invidious *a* fuath-dhùsgach; (*unfair*) mì-cheart
invigilate *v* cùm sùil air, bi ri faire
invincible *a* do-cheannsachail, nach gabh ceannsachadh
invisible *a* neo-fhaicsinneach
invitation *n* cuireadh *m*, fiathachadh *m*
invite *v* iarr, thoir cuireadh (do), thoir fiathachadh (do)
inviting *a* tarraingeach
invoice *n* cunntas *f m*
involuntary *a* neo-shaor-thoileach, an aghaidh toil
involve *v* gabh a-steach **were you involved in it?** an robh thusa na lùib/an sàs ann?
irascible *a* crosta, feargach, greannach
irate *a* feargach, fiadhaich
ire *n* fearg *f*, corraich *f*
iris *n* (*of eye*) cearcall na sùla *m*; (*plant*) sealastair *f m*, seileastair *f m*
Irish *n* (*lang*) a' Ghaeilge *f*, Gàidhlig na h-Èireann *f* *a* Èireannach
Irishman *n* Èireannach *m*
Irishwoman ban-Eireannach *f*
irksome *a* leamh, sàraichte
iron *n* iarann *m* *a* iarainn **I. Age** Linn an Iarainn *f* **i. ore** clach-iarainn *f* *v* iarnaig
ironic(al) *a* ìoranta
irony *n* ìoranas *m*
irrational *a* neo-reusanta
irreconcilable *a* do-rèiteachail,

nach gabh toirt gu chèile
irregular *a* neo-chunbhalach, neo-riaghailteach **i. verb** gnìomhair neo-riaghailteach *m*
irregularity *n* neo-chunbhalachd *f*, neo-riaghailteachd *f*
irrelevant *a* nach buin dhan/ris a' ghnothach, neo-bhointealach, mì-fhreagarrach
irreparable *a* nach gabh càradh/leasachadh
irrepressible *a* nach gabh casg(adh)
irresistible *a* nach gabh diùltadh
irrespective *adv* a dh'aindeoin
irresponsible *a* neo-chùramach, gun chùram
irresponsibility *n* cion cùraim *m*, dìth cùraim *f*
irretrievable *a* nach gabh lorg/sàbhaladh
irreverence *n* eas-urram *m*
irreverent *a* eas-urramach
irreversible *a* nach gabh atharrachadh
irrevocable *a* nach gabh tilleadh/atharrachadh
irrigation *n* uisgeachadh *m*
irritable *a* crosta, frionasach, greannach
irritate *v* cuir caise/frionas air
irritation *n* crostachd *f*, frionas *m*
is *v* tha, is (*See verb* **to be** *in Grammar*)
Islam *n* an creideamh Ioslamach *m*; (*people*) a' mhuinntir Ioslamach *f*
Islamic *a* Ioslamach
island *n* eilean *m*, innis *f*
islander *n* eileanach *m*
Islay person *n* Ìleach *m*, (*female*) ban-Ìleach *f*
isolated *a* air leth, iomallach, lethoireach
isolation *n* aonarachd *f*, lethoireachd *f* **in i.** leis fhèin
Israeli *n*, *a* Israelach/Iosaraileach *m*
issue *n* ceist *f*, cùis *f*; (*offspring*) clann *f*, sliochd *m*; (*liter*) iris *f* *v* bris(t)/thig/cuir a-mach, lìbhrig
isthmus *n* tairbeart *f*, aoidh *f*

it *pron* e, i
Italian *n, a* Eadailteach *m*,
 (*female*) ban-Eadailteach *f*;
 (*lang*) Eadailtis *f*
italics *n* clò eadailteach *m*
itch *n* tachas *m*; (*desire*) miann *f*
 m
itchy *a* tachasach
item *n* nì *m*, rud *m*
itinerant *a* siùbhlach, siubhail
itinerary *n* clàr-siubhail *m*
its *poss pron* a
itself *pron* e/i fhèin
ivory *n* ìbhri *f*
ivy *n* eidheann *f*

J

jackdaw *n* cathag *f*
jacket *n* seacaid *f*
Jacobite *n* Seumasach *m*
 J. Rebellion/Rising Ar-a-mach
 nan Seumasach *m*
jade *n* sèad *f*
jaded *a* seachd sgìth
jag *n* briogadh *m*; (*notch*) eag *f*
jagged/jaggy *a* eagach
jail *n* prìosan *m*
jam *n* silidh *m*; (*congestion*)
 dùmhlachd *f* **in a jam** ann an
 staing **jam-jar** crogan-silidh *m*,
 sileagan *m v* brùth, dùmhlaich
 my fingers got jammed chaidh
 mo mheòirean a ghlacadh
jangle *v* dèan gleadhraich/
 gliongadaich
janitor *n* dorsair *m*, neach-cùraim
 sgoile *m*
January *n* am Faoilleach/
 Faoilteach *m*
Japanese *n, a* Iapanach, (*female*)
 ban-Iapanach *f*
jar *n* crogan *m*, sileagan *m*
jargon *n* ceàird-chainnt *f*
jaundice *n* a' bhuidheach *f*, an
 tinneas buidhe *m*
jaunt *n* sgrìob *f*, splaoid *f*
javelin *n* sleagh *f*
jaw *n* peirceall *m*, giall *f*
jealous *a* eudmhor **she was j. of
 her** bha i ag eudach rithe
jealousy *n* eud *m*, eudmhorachd *f*
jeans *n* dinichean *f pl*

jeer *v* mag (air), dèan magadh
 (air)
Jehovah *n* Iehòbhah *m*
jelly *n* slaman-milis *m*
jellyfish *n* muir-tiachd *f m*
jeopardy *n* cunnart *m*, gàbhadh
 m
jerk *n* tarraing obann *f*, tulgag *f*
 v tarraing gu h-obann
jersey *n* geansaidh *m*
jest *n* abhcaid *f*, fealla-dhà *f*
jet *n* steall *m*; (*plane*) seit
 (-phlèan) *m*
jettison *v* tilg a-mach, cuir bhuat
jetty *n* cidhe *m*, laimrig *f*
Jew *n* Iùdhach *m* **Jewess**
 ban-Iùdhach *f*
jewel *n* seud *m*, leug *f*, àilleag *m*
jeweller *n* seudair *m*
jewellery *n* seudraidh *f*
Jewish *a* Iùdhach
jig *n* (*tune*) port-cruinn *m*;
 (*dance*) sige *f*
jigsaw *n* mìrean-measgaichte *f pl*
jilt *v* trèig, faigh cuidhteas
 (leannan)
jingle *n* gliong *m*; (*ad*) rannag *f*
job *n* obair *f*, cosnadh *m* **job-
 centre** ionad obrach *m* **job
 description** dealbh-obrach *f m*
jockey *n* marcach *m*, marcaiche
 m
jocular *a* spòrsail, abhcaideach
jog *v* bi a' trotan, ruith; (*nudge*)
 put; (*memory*) brod cuimhne
join *v* ceangail, aonaich, cuir ri
 chèile, tàth; (*eg club*) gabh
 ballrachd an
joiner *n* saor *m*
joinery *n* saorsainneachd *f*
joint *n* alt *m*; (*of meat*) spòlt *m*
 a co-, coitcheann, co-phàirteach
jointly *adv* cuideachd, le chèile,
 an co-bho(i)nn
joist *n* sail *f*, spàrr *m*,
 cas-ceangail *f*
joke, joking *n* abhcaid *f*, fealla-
 dhà *f* **I was only joking** cha robh
 mi ach ri spòrs
jolly *a* cridheil, aighearach
jolt *n* crathadh *m*, tulgadh *m*
jostle *v* put, brùth (a-null 's
 a-nall)

jotter *n* diotar *m*, leabhran-sgrìobhaidh *m*

journal *n* (*diary*) leabhar-latha *m*; (*magazine*) iris *f*

journalism *n* naidheachdas *m*

journalist *n* neach-naidheachd *m*, naidheachdair *m*

journey *n* turas *m*, cuairt *f*

jovial *a* fonnmhor, suilbhir

jowl *n* giall *f*, bus *m*

joy *n* aoibhneas *m*, gàirdeachas *m*, sòlas *m*

joyful *a* aoibhneach, ait, sòlasach

jubilant *a* lùth-ghaireach

jubilee *n* iubailidh *f*

judge *n* britheamh *m* *v* thoir breith, breithnich, meas

judgement *n* breith *f*, breithneachadh *m*, binn *f* **J. Day** Latha a' Bhreitheanais *m*, Latha Luain *m*

judicial *a* laghail, a rèir an lagha, breitheach

judicious *a* tuigseach, geurchuiseach

jug *n* siuga *f m*

juggle *v* làmh-chleasaich

jugular *n* fèith sgòrnain *f*

juice *n* sùgh *m*; (*essence*) brìgh *f*

juicy *a* sùghmhor; (*pithy*) brìoghmhor

July *n* an t-Iuchar *m*

jumble *n* measgachadh *m*, brochan *m* **j. sale** reic treal(l)aich *m* *v* cuir troimh-a-chèile, measgaich

jump *n* leum *m*, sùrdag *f* **standing j.** cruinn-leum *m* *v* leum

jumper *n* (*sport*) leumadair *m*; (*garment*) geansaidh *m*

junction *n* snaidhm *m*, comar *m*, ceangal *m*

June *n* an t-Ògmhios *m*

jungle *n* dlùth-choille *f*

junior *a* as òige, a b' òige

juniper *n* aiteann *m*

junk *n* smodal *m*, truileis *f*; (*naut*) long Shìonach *f*

Jupiter *n* Iupatar *m*

jury *n* diùraidh *m*

just *a* cothromach, ceart, fìrinneach *adv* (*recently*) dìreach; (*with difficulty*) air

èiginn *j.* **now** an-dràsta, an ceartuair **it is j.** **amazing** tha e dìreach iongantach **the shop has j. closed** tha a' bhùth dìreach air dùnadh **they only j. escaped** 's ann air èiginn a thàrr iad às

justice *n* ceartas *m*

justifiable *a* reusanta, a ghabhas seasamh/dìon

justify *v* seas, dìon; (*relig*) fìreanaich

juvenile *n* òganach *m* *a* òigridh

K

kangaroo *n* cangarù *m*

keel *n* druim *m*

keen *a* dian, dealasach; (*sharp*) geur

keenness *n* dealas *m*, eudmhorachd *f*

keep *v* cùm, glèidh

keeper *n* neach-gleidhidh *m*

keepsake *n* cuimhneachan *m*

kelpie *n* each-uisge *m*, ùruisg *m*

kennel *n* taigh-chon *m*

kerb *n* oir a' chabhsair *f m*, cabhsair *m*

kernel *n* eitean *m*

kestrel *n* speireag ruadh *f*, clamhan ruadh *m*

kettle *n* coire *m*

key *n* iuchair *f*; (*mus*) gleus *f m*; (*on keyboard*) meur *f*; (*solution*) fuasgladh *m* *a* cudromach, prìomh (*precedes n*)

keyboard *n* meur-chlàr *m*

kick *n* breab *f m* *v* breab

kid *n* meann *m*; (*child*) pàiste *m*

kidnap *v* goid air falbh

kidney *n* dubhag *f*, àra *f*, àirne *f*

kill *v* marbh, cuir gu bàs

killer *n* murtair *m*

killing *n* marbhadh *m*, spadadh *m*

kilogram(me) *n* cileagram *m*

kilometre *n* cilemeatair *m*

kilowatt *n* cileabhat *m*

kilt *n* (f)èileadh *m*

kin(dred) *n* dàimhean *f m pl*, càirdean *m pl*

kind *n* gnè *f*, seòrsa *m*

kindle v las, fadaich; (met)
beothaich, brosnaich
kind(ly) a coibhneil, còir, bàidheil
kindness n coibhneas m,
caomhalachd f, bàidhealachd f
kindred a co-aigneach **they were
k. spirits** bha iad a dh'aon aigne
kinetic a gluaiseach
king n rìgh m
kingdom n rìoghachd f
kinsman n fear-dàimh m
kinswoman bean-dàimh f
kipper n ciopair m, sgadan
rèisgte m
kirk n eaglais f
kiss n pòg f v pòg, thoir pòg
kit n acfhainn f, uidheam f;
(clothes) èideadh m
kitchen n cidsin m
kite n iteileag f; (bird) clamhan m
kitten n piseag f
knack n alt m, liut f
knead v fuin, taoisnich
knee n glù(i)n f **k.-cap** failmean
(na glùine) m
kneel v lùb glù(i)n, sleuchd
knickers n drathais/drathars f
knife n sgian f
knight n ridire m
knit v figh **k. together** (after
injury) ceangail, slànaich
knitting-needle n bior-fighe m
knob n cnap m, cnag f
knock n buille f, sgailc f, sgleog f;
(at door) gnogadh m v (door)
gnog **k. down** leag
knocking n gnogadh m
knoll n tom m, tolman m, tulach
m **fairy k.** sìthean m
knot n snaidhm/snaoim m;
(nautical mile) mìle mara m; (in
wood) meuran m
v snaidhmich/snaoimich, cuir
snaidhm/snaoim air
know v **knows** tha fios aig;
(person) is aithne do;
(recognize) aithnich **k. well** bi
eòlach air
knowledge n eòlas m, aithne f
knowledgeable a fiosrach
knuckle n rùdan m
kyle n caol(as) m

L

label n bileag f v cuir bileag air
laboratory n obair-lann f,
deuchainn-lann f
laborious a saothrachail, deacair
labour n saothair f, obair f; (med)
saothair chloinne f **in l.** air
leabaidh-shiùbhla **the L. Party**
am Partaidh Làbarach m
v saothraich, obraich
labourer n obraiche m, dubh-
chosnaiche m
labyrinth n ioma-shlighe f
lace n sròl m; (shoe) barrall m
v ceangail
lack n easbhaidh f, dìth f m, cion
m v bi a dh'easbhaidh **he lacks
... tha ... a dhìth air**
lacklustre a marbhanta, gun
spionnadh
laconic a geàrr-bhriathrach
lad n gille m, balach m
ladder n (f)àradh m
ladle n ladar m, liagh f
lady n bean-uasal f,
baintighearna f, leadaidh f
ladybird n an daolag dhearg-
bhreac f
lager n làgar m
lair n saobhaidh f, garaidh m;
(grave) rèilig f
laird n uachdaran m
lake n loch m
lamb n uan m; (meat) uanfheòil f,
feòil uain f
lame a cuagach, bacach, crùbach
lament n cumha m, tuireadh m,
caoidh f v caoidh, dèan
tuireadh
lamentable a cianail, tùrsach,
muladach
laminated a lannaichte
lamp n lampa f m **l.-post** post-
lampa m **l.-shade** sgàil-lampa f
lampoon n aoir f v aoir
lance n sleagh f; (med) lannsa f
v leig fuil, geàrr le lannsa
land n fearann m, talamh m;
(country) tìr f, dùthaich f **the L.
Court** Cùirt an Fhearainn f
v (go ashore) rach air tìr; (of
plane) laigh; (goods) cuir air tìr

landlady *n* bean an taighe *f*
landlord *n* (*estate*) uachdaran *m*; (*property, pub etc*) fear an taighe *m*
landmark *n* comharra-stiùiridh *m*
landowner *n* uachdaran *m*
landscape *n* dealbh-tìre *f m*, cruth tìre *m*; (*picture*) sealladh tìre *m*
landslide *n* maoim-slèibhe *f*, maoim-talmhainn *f*
lane *n* frith-rathad *m*, caolshràid *f*; (*on motorway*) sreath *f m*
language *n* cànan *f m*; (*speech*) cainnt *f*
languid *a* anfhann, gun sunnd
languish *v* fannaich, crìon
lanky *a* fada caol
lantern *n* lanntair *f m*, lainntear *f m*, lòchran *m*
lap *n* uchd *m*, sgùird *f*; (*sport*) cuairt *f v* (*slurp*) slupairich, bileagaich; (*waves*) sruthail
lapel *n* liopaid *f*, fillteag *f*
lapse *n* sleamhnachadh *m*, mearachd *f v* sleamhnaich, tuislich, dèan mearachd; (*expire*) thig gu ceann **she lapsed into English** thionndaidh i gu Beurla
lapwing *n* curracag *f*
larceny *n* goid *f*, gadachd *f*
larch *n* learag *f*
lard *n* blona(i)g *f*
larder *n* preas/seòmar-bìdh *m*
large *a* mòr, tomadach
lark *n* uiseag *f*, topag *f*; (*play*) cleas *m*
larynx *n* bràigh an sgòrnain *m*
laser *n* leusair *m* **l. beam** gath leusair *m* **l. printer** clò-bhualadair leusair *m*
lash *v* sgiùrs, stiall
lass *n* nighean *f*, caileag *f*
last *a* deireannach, mu dheireadh **l. week** an t-seachdain seo chaidh **l. night** a-raoir **the night before l.** a' bhòn-raoir **l. year** an-uiridh **the l. person** an duine mu dheireadh *adv* air deireadh **at (long) l.** mu dheireadh (thall) *v* mair, seas
lasting *a* maireannach, buan

latch *n* clàimhean *m*, dealan-dorais *m*
late *a* anmoch, fadalach, air deireadh; (*evening, night*) anmoch; (*deceased*) nach maireann **they arrived l.** bha iad fada gun tighinn
lately *adv* o chionn ghoirid
latent *a* falaichte, neo-fhollaiseach
lateral *a* taobhach, leth-taobhach
lathe *n* beairt-thuairnearachd *f*
lather *n* cop *m*
Latin *n* Laideann *f*
latitude *n* domhan-leud *m*; (*scope*) saorsa *f*
latter *a* deireannach, mu dheireadh
laud *v* àrd-mhol
laudable *a* ionmholta, ri m(h)oladh *etc*
laugh *n* gàire *f m* **loud l.** lachan *m*, lasgan *m v* gàir, dèan gàire
laughing-stock *n* culaidh/cùis-mhagaidh *f*
laughter *n* gàireachdaich *f* **loud l.** lasganaich *f*
launch *n* cur air bhog *m*; (*product*) foillseachadh *m v* cuir air bhog; (*product*) foillsich; (*begin*) tòisich air
laundry *n* taigh-nighe *m*
lava *n* làbha *f*
lavish *a* fialaidh, strùidheil, cosgail
law *n* lagh *m* **lawsuit** cùis-lagha *f*
lawful *a* laghail
lawless *a* mì-riaghailteach, gun spèis do lagh
lawn *n* rèidhlean *m*, faiche *f* **l.-mower** lomaire-feòir *m*
lawyer *n* neach-lagha *m*
lax *a* slac, sgaoilte, gun chùram
laxative *n* purgaid *f*
lay *v* càirich, cuir **lay egg** breith ugh **lay foundation** leag stèidh **lay off** (*staff*) leig mu sgaoil **lay wager** cuir geall **lay waste** sgrios, cuir fàs
layer *n* filleadh *m*, sreath *f m*
layout *n* cruth *m*; (*of page*) coltas-duilleig *m*
laziness *n* leisg(e) *f*

lazy *a* leisg
lazybones *n* leisgeadair *m*
lead *n* (*metal*) luaidhe *f m*
lead *n* stiùir *f*; (*dog's*) taod *m*
v stiùir, treòraich
leader *n* ceannard *m*, ceannbhair *m*
leadership *n* ceannas *m*
leaf *n* duilleag *f*
leaflet *n* duilleachan *m*, bileag *f*
league *n* dionnasg *m*; (*sport*) lìog
f **the Premier L.** a' Phrìomh Lìog
leak *n* aoidion *m* *v* leig
a-steach/a-mach; (*intrans*) bi
aoidionach; (*reveal*) leig mu
sgaoil
leaking, leaky *a* aoidionach
lean *v* leig do thaic air, leig
cudrom air
lean *a* caol, tana
leap *n* leum *m* **standing l.** cruinn-
leum *m* **l. year** bliadhna-lèim *f*
v leum, thoir leum
learn *v* ionnsaich, foghlaim
learned *a* foghlaim(ich)te,
ionnsaichte
learner *n* neach-ionnsachaidh *m*
pl luchd-ionnsachaidh
lease *n* gabhail *m*, còir *f* *v* gabh
air mhàl
leash *n* iall *f*
least *sup* *a* as lugha **at l.** co-dhiù,
aig a' char as lugha
leather *n* leathar *m* *a* leathair
leave *n* (*permission*) cead *m*;
(*from duty*) fòrladh *m*
leave *v* fàg, trèig **l. alone** leig le
l. off sguir de
lecherous *a* drùiseil
lecture *n* òraid *f* *v* dèan òraid,
thoir (seachad) òraid; (*tell off*)
cronaich
lecturer *n* òraidiche *m*
ledge *n* leac *f*; (*topog*) palla *m*
ledger *n* leabhar-cunntais *m*
lee *n* taobh an fhasgaidh *m*
leek *n* creamh-gàrraidh *m*
leer *v* claon-amhairc
left *n* an taobh clì/ceàrr *m*, an
làmh chlì/cheàrr *f* **the l. hand** an
làmh chlì *f*, a' chearrag *f*
l.-handed ciotach, cearragach
a clì **l. over** air fhàgail **leftovers**
corran *m* *pl*

leg *n* cas *f*; (*of meat*) ceathramh
feòla *m*
legacy *n* dìleab *f*
legal *a* laghail, dligheach,
ceadaichte
legalize *v* dèan laghail
legend *n* uirsgeul *m*, fionnsgeul
m
legendary *a* uirsgeulach; (*famous*)
iomraiteach
legible *a* so-leughte, a ghabhas
leughadh
legislate *v* dèan lagh(an),
reachdaich
legislation *n* reachdas *m*
legitimate *a* dligheach
leisure *n* saor-ùine *f* **l. activity**
cur-seachad *m*
lemon *n* liomaid *f* **l. sole** lèabag
cheàrr *f*
lemonade *n* liomaineud *m*
lend *v* thoir iasad (de), thoir an
iasad
length *n* fad *m*, faid *f*
lengthen *v* cuir fad ri/às, dèan
nas fhaide, sìn; (*intrans*) fàs nas
fhaide, sìn
leniency *n* tròcair *f*, iochdalachd
f, iochd *f*
lenient *a* tròcaireach, iochdail
lenition *n* sèimheachadh *m*
lens *n* lionsa *f*
Lent *n* an Carghas *m*
lentil *n* leantail *m*, peasair nan
luch *f*
leopard *n* liopard *m*
leper *n* lobhar *m*
leprosy *n* luibhre *f*
lesbian *n*, *a* leasbach *f*
less *comp* *a* nas lugha, na bu
lugha
lessen *v* lùghdaich, beagaich
(air); (*intrans*) lùghdaich
lesson *n* leasan *m*
let *v* leig le, ceadaich; (*property*)
thoir air ghabhail **let go** leig às
let on leig ort/air/oirre *etc*
lethal *a* marbhtach, bàsmhor
lethargic *a* trom, slaodach
letter *n* litir *f* **capital l.** litir mhòr
l.-box bogsa-litrichean *m*
lettuce *n* leatas *f*
leukaemia *n* bànachadh-fala *m*

level *n* còmhnard *m*; (*grade*) inbhe *f*, ìre *f a* còmhnard, rèidh *v* dèan còmhnard/rèidh **l. an accusation at** cuir às leth (+ *gen*)

lever *n* geimhleag *f*, luamhan *m* **gear l.** stob nan giodhraichean *m*

levy *n* cìs *f v* (*tax etc*) leag

lewd *a* draosta

Lewis person *n* Leòdhasach *m*, (*female*) ban-Leòdhasach *f*

liability *n* (*fin*) fiach *m*; (*tendency*) buailteachd *f* **it was just a l.** cha robh ann ach call

liable *a* buailteach (do), dualtach

liaise *v* dèan ceangal (ri)

liaison *n* ceangal *m*, co-cheangal *m*

liar *n* breugaire *m*, breugadair *m*

libel *n* tuaileas *m*, cliù-mhilleadh *m v* cuir tuaileas air, mill cliù **he libelled me** chuir e na breugan orm

libellous *a* tuaileasach

liberal *a* fial, fialaidh; (*phil*) libearalach

Liberal *n*, *a* Libearalach *m* **L. Democratic Party** am Partaidh Libearalach Deamocratach *m*

liberate *v* saor, cuir mu sgaoil

liberation *n* saoradh *m*, leigeil/cur mu sgaoil *m*

liberty *n* saorsa *f*

libidinous *a* ana-miannach, drùiseil

librarian *n* leabharlannaiche *m*

library *n* leabharlann *f m*

licence *n* cead *m*

license *v* ceadaich, thoir cead do/seachad

licensed *a* fo cheadachd, le cead, ùghdarraichte

licentious *a* mì-bheusach

lick *v* imlich

lid *n* ceann *m*, mullach *m*

lie *n* breug *f* **I had a lie-down** chaidh mi nam shìneadh *v* (*tell untruth*) inn(i)s breug; (*phys*) laigh

lieutenant *n* leifteanant *m*; (*associate*) neach-ionaid *m*

life *n* beatha *f*; (*vitality*)

beothalachd *f* **l.-insurance** àrachas beatha *m* **l.-style** dòigh-beatha *f* **lifebelt** crios-teasairginn *m* **lifeboat** bàta-teasairginn *m* **lifeguard** neach-teasairginn *m* **l.-jacket** seacaid-teasairginn *f* **lifeline** loidhne-teasairginn *f*; (*met*) cothrom eile *m*

lifeless *a* marbh, gun deò; (*met*) trom

lifetime *n* rè *f*, beò *m*, saoghal *m*

lift *n* togail *f*; (*elevator*) àrdaichear *m v* tog

ligament *n* ball-nasg *m*, ceanglachan *m*

light *n* solas *m*; (*daylight*) soilleireachd *f* **l.-house** taigh-solais *m v* las **l. up** (+ *met*) soillsich

light *a* aotrom; (*of daylight*) soilleir **l.-headed** aotrom, mear **l.-hearted** sunndach, suigeartach, aighearach

lighten *v* deàlraich, soillsich; (*weight*) aotromaich

lighter *n* lasadair *m*

lightning *n* dealanach *m*

like *v* **likes** is toigh/toil (le), is caomh le **be l.** bi coltach ri

like *n* leithid *f*, samhail *f*, mac-samhail *m a* coltach (ri), mar (+ *len*) *adv* mar

likelihood *n* coltas *m*

likely *a* coltach, dòcha

liken *v* samhlaich, coimeas

likeness *n* (*similarity*) coltas *m*, ìomhaigh *f*; (*picture*) dealbh *f m*

likewise *adv* cuideachd, mar an ceudna

lilac *n* liath-chorcra *f a* bàn-phurpaidh

lily *n* lilidh *f*

limb *n* ball *m*

lime *n* aol *m*; (*fruit/tree*) teile *f*

limit *n* crìoch *f*, iomall *m v* cuingealaich, cuir crìoch ri

limited *a* cuingealaichte, cuibhrichte **l. company** companaidh earranta *f m*

limp *n* ceum *m* **he has a l.** tha ceum ann, tha e cuagach *a* bog *v* bi bacach/cuagach/crùbach

limpet n bàirneach f
line n loidhne f; (in writing)
sreath f m; (clothes) ròp anairt;
(fishing) driamlach f; (geneal)
sìol m, gineal f m **l.-fishing**
dorghach m **on-l.** air loidhne
v lìnig
linear a sreathach, loidhneach
linen n anart m, lìon-aodach m
ling n (fish) langa f
linger v dèan dàil, rongaich, gabh
ùine
lingerie n aodach-cneis m
linguistic a cànanach
lining n lìnig(eadh) m
link n ceangal m; (in chain) tinne
f, dul m **linkspan** alt-aiseig m
v dèan co-cheangal
lint n lìon m, caiteas m
lintel n àrd-doras m
lion n leòmhann m **the l.'s share**
an ceann reamhar m
lip n bile f, lip f; (geog) oir f m
lip-service beul bòidheach m
lipstick dath-lipean m, peant
bhilean m
liqueur n liciùr m
liquid n lionn m a lionnach,
sruthach
liquidate v (company) sgaoil;
(kill) cuir às do
liquidation n (of company)
sgaoileadh m
liquidize v lionnaich
liquor n deoch(-làidir) f
liquorice n carra-mheille m
lisp n liotaiche m, liotachas m
v bi liotach
lisping a liotach
list n liosta f; (to side) fiaradh m
v dèan liosta; (of ship) liost(aig)
listen v èist (ri)
listening n èisteachd f
listless a gun lùths/sunnd
literacy n litearrachd f, litearras m
literal a litireil
literary a litreachail
literate a litearra
literature n litreachas m **oral l.**
litreachas beòil
lithe a sùbailte, subailte
litigate v rach gu lagh, agair lagh
air

litigation n agartachd f, cùis-
lagha f
litre n liotair m
litter n sgudal m; (of animals)
cuain f, iseanan m pl v fàg na
bhùrach **discard l.** fàg sgudal
little n beagan m, rud beag m
a beag, meanbh
liturgy n ùrnaigh choitcheann f
live v bi beò
live a beò
livelihood n beòshlaint f, teachd-
an-tìr m, bith-beò m
lively a beothail, frogail,
sunndach
liver n adha m, grùthan m
livid a (met) **he was l.** bha an
cuthach dearg air
living n beòshlaint f, teachd-an-tìr
m, bith-beò m a beò
lizard n laghairt f m, dearc-
luachrach f
load n luchd m, eallach m; (on
mind) uallach m v luchdaich,
lìon; (gun) cuir urchair an
loaf n lof f m
loan n iasad m **loanword** facal-
iasaid m v thoir iasad do, thoir
... air iasad
loath a ain-deònach
loathe v fuathaich **I loathed it** bha
gràin (an) uilc agam air
loathing n gràin uilc f, sgreamh m
loathsome a gràineil, sgreamhail,
sgreataidh
lobby n lobaidh f, trannsa f;
(pressure group) luchd-
coiteachaidh m v coitich
lobster n giomach m **l.-pot**
cliabh-ghiomach f
local a ionadail **l. authority**
ùghdarras ionadail m
l. government riaghaltas
ionadail m
locality n àite m, coimhearsnachd
f, sgìre f
locate v suidhich, cuir na àite
location n suidheachadh m, àite
m
loch n loch m
lock n glas f; (of hair) dual m,
ciabh f, cuailean m v glas
locker n preasa glaiste m

locus *n* lòcas *m*, àite *m*
locust *n* lòcast *m*
lodge *n* loidse *f m*, taigh-geata *m*
lodge *v* (*submit*) cuir a-steach, càirich; (*stay*) gabh còmhnaidh
lodger *n* loidsear *m*
lodging *n* loidseadh *m* **l. house** taigh-loidsidh *m*
loft *n* lobhta *m*
log *n* sail *f*, loga *f m*; (*book*) leabhar-aithris *m*; (*math*) log *m*
logic *n* loidsig *f*
logical *a* loidsigeach
log off *v* thig dheth, tarraing às
log on *v* rach air, dèan ceangal
loin *n* blian *m* **the loins** an leasraidh *f*
loiter *v* dèan màirneal, rongaich
lollipop *n* loiliopop *f*
Londoner *n* Lunnainneach *m*, neach à Lunnainn *m*
lone *a* aonarach, na (h-)aonar *etc*, leis/leatha fhèin *etc*
loneliness *n* aonaranachd *f*
lonely *a* aonaranach
loner *n* aonaran *m*
long *a* fada **l. ago** o chionn f(h)ada **l.-lasting** buan, maireannach **l.-suffering** fad-fhulangach **l.-term** fad-ùine *v* **l. for** miannaich; (*weary for*) gabh fadachd ri
long division *n* roinn fhada *f*
longing *n* miann *f m*, togradh *m*, fadachd *f*
longitude *n* domhan-fhad *m*
long jump *n* leum-fada *m*, leum-fhada *f*
look *n* sùil *f*; (*appearance*) coltas *m*, fiamh *m* *v* seall, coimhead, amhairc **l. for** coimhead airson, lorg, sir
loom *n* beairt(-fhighe) *f*
loop *n* lùb *f*
loophole *n* beàrn *f*, dòigh às *f*
loose *a* fuasgailte, sgaoilte, gun cheangal **l. change** airgead pronn *m*
loose(n) *v* fuasgail, cuir/leig mu sgaoil
loot *n* creach *f* *v* creach
lop *v* sgud, sgath, geàrr
lopsided *a* leathoireach, gu aon taobh

loquacious *a* briathrach
lord *n* tighearna *m*, triath *m*, morair *m* **House of Lords** Taigh nam Mòrairean *m* **the Lord's Prayer** Ùrnaigh an Tighearna *f*
lorry *n* làraidh *f*
lose *v* caill
loss *n* call *m*
lost *a* air chall, caillte
lot *n* (*amount*) mòran *m*, tòrr *m*; (*in life*) crannchur *m* **cast lots** tilg croinn
lotion *n* cungaidh *f*
lottery *n* crannchur *m* **the National L.** an Crannchur Nàiseanta
loud *a* àrd, faramach
loudspeaker *n* glaodhaire *m*
lounge *n* rùm-suidhe *m* *v* sìn
louse *n* mial *f*
lousy *a* grod; (*with lice*) mialach
lout *n* burraidh *m*
love *n* gaol *m*, gràdh *m*; (*tennis*) neoni *m* **my l.** m' eudail *v* gràdhaich, thoir gaol **l l. you** tha gaol agam ort **we l. skiing** 's fìor thoigh leinn sgitheadh, tha sinn fìor dhèidheil/mhiadhail air sgitheadh
lovely *a* bòidheach, àlainn, lurach, maiseach
lover *n* leannan *m*
lovesick *a* an trom-ghaol
loving *a* gràdhach, ionmhainn
low *a* ìosal, ìseal
low *v* geum, bi a' geumnaich
lower *v* ìslich, lùghdaich
lowing *n* geumnaich *f*
Lowlander *n* Gall *m*, (*female*) bana-Ghall *f pl* Goill
low water *n* muir-tràigh *f*
loyal *a* dìleas
loyalist *n* dìlseach *m*
loyalty *n* dìlseachd *f*
lubricate *v* lìomh, dèan sleamhainn, cuir ola air/an
lucid *a* soilleir
luck *n* sealbh *m*, fortan *m*, rath *m* **Good l.!** Gur(a) math a thèid dhut/leat!
lucky *a* sealbhach, fortanach
lucrative *a* airgeadach

ludicrous *a* amaideach, gòrach

luggage *n* bagaichean *m pl*, màileidean *f pl*

lukewarm *a* meadh-bhlàth, flodach

lull *v* meall; (*to sleep*) cuir a chadal

lullaby *n* tàladh *m*

lumbago *n* leum-droma *m*

lumber *n* treal(l)aich *f*, seann àirneis *f*

luminous *a* soillseach, deàlrach

lump *n* cnap *m*; (*geog*) meall *m* **a l. sum** cnap airgid *m*

lumpy *a* cnapach

lunacy *n* euslaint-inntinn *f*; (*met*) mullach an amaideis *m*

lunatic *n* euslainteach-inntinn *m*

lunch *n* lòn *m*, diathad *f* **l. break** tràth-bìdh *m*, biadh meadhain-latha *m*

lung *n* sgamhan *m*

lurch *n* tulgadh *m*, siaradh *m* *v* dèan tulgadh/siaradh

lure *v* buair, breug

lurid *a* eagalach, sgràthail, oillteil

lurk *v* falaich, siolp

luscious *a* sòghmhor

lush *a* mèath

lust *n* ana-miann *f m*, drù(i)s *f* *v* **l. after/for** sanntaich, miannaich

lustre *n* deàlradh *m*, gleans *m*, lainnir *f*; (*met*) mòr-chliù *m*

luxurious *a* sòghail

luxury *n* sògh *m*, sòghalachd *f*

lying *n* (*phys*) laighe *f*; (*telling lies*) innse bhreug *f* *a* (*untruthful*) breugach

lynch *v* croch (gun chùirt)

lyric *n* liric *f*, ealaidh *f*

lythe *n* liugha *f*, liùgh *f*

M

machination *n* innleachd *f*

machine *n* inneal *m*

machinery *n* innealradh *m*; (*met*) modhan-obrach *f pl*

mackerel *n* rionnach *m*

mad *a* às a c(h)iall/rian *etc*; (*slang*) cracte **he was mad** (*angry*) bha an cuthach air

madam *n* bean-uasal *f*

madden *v* (*anger*) cuir an cuthach air

madness *n* dìth-cèille *f m*; (*slang*) crac *m*

magazine *n* iris *f*; (*quarterly*) ràitheachan *m*; (*arms store*) armlann *f*; (*of gun*) cèis-bhiathaidh *f*

maggot *n* cnuimh *f*

magic *n* draoidheachd *f* *a* draoidheil

magician *n* draoidh *m*

magistrate *n* bàillidh *m*, maigh(i)stir-lagha *m*

magnanimous *a* fial-inntinneach, fialaidh

magnet *n* magnait *m*, clach-iùil *f*

magnificent *a* òirdheirc

magnify *v* meudaich; (*extol*) àrdaich

magpie *n* pitheid *f*, pioghaid *f*

maid(en) *n* maighdeann *f*, gruagach *f*; (*servant*) searbhanta *f*

mail *n* post *m*, litrichean *f pl* **m.-order** òrdugh tron phost *m* *v* post(aig), cuir sa phost

maim *v* ciorramaich, leòn, ciùrr

main *a* prìomh **m. road** rathad-mòr *m*

mainland *n* tìr-mòr *f m*, mòr-thìr *f*

mainly *adv* anns a' mhòr-chuid, gu beagnaich

maintain *v* (*keep*) glèidh, cùm; (*support*) cùm suas; (*in argument*) cùm a-mach, tagair

maintenance *n* gleidheadh *m*, cumail suas *f*; (*of person*) beathachadh *m*

maize *n* cruithneachd Innseanach *f m*

majestic *a* flathail

majesty *n* mòrachd *f*, rìoghachd *f*

major *n* (*mil*) màidsear *m*; (*sport*) prìomh fharpais *f*

major *a* mòr, cudromach; (*greater*) ... as/a bu motha

majority *n* mòr-chuid *f*, tromlach *f*, a' chuid as/a bu motha *f*

make *n* seòrsa *m* **m.-up** rìomhadh (gnùis(e)) *m*; (*met*) dèanamh *m*, nàdar *m* *v* dèan; (*compel*) thoir

air, co-èignich; (*bed*) càirich **m.**
for (*head for*) dèan air **m.**
believe leig air/oirre *etc* **we'll m.**
it nì sinn a' chùis
male *n* fireannach *m* *a* fireann
malevolent *a* gamhlasach, le
droch rùn
malice *n* mì-rùn *m*, droch rùn *m*,
droch mhèinn *f*
malicious *a* droch-rùnach, droch-
mhèinneach
malign *v* mì-chliùthaich
malignant *a* millteach; (*of cancer*)
cronail, nimheil
mallard *n* lach riabhach *f*
malleable *a* so-chumte, a ghabhas
cumadh
malnutrition *n* dìth beathachaidh
f m, cion a' bhìdh *m*
malpractice *n* mì-chleachdadh *m*,
droch ghiùlan *m*
malt *n* braich *f* **m. whisky** mac na
braiche *m*
maltreat *v* droch-làimhsich, dèan
droch ghiollachd air
maltreatment *n* droch-
làimhseachadh *m*, droch
ghiollachd *m*
mammal *n* sineach *m*, mamal *m*
man *n* duine *m*, fear *m*,
fireannach *m*; (*husband*) duine
manage *v* stiùir; (*be able to*) dèan
a' chùis
manageable *a* so-riaghladh, so-
stiùireadh, a ghabhas dèanamh
management *n* stiùireadh *m*,
riaghladh *m*; (*personnel*) luchd-
stiùiridh *m*
manager *n* manaidsear *m*,
ceannbhair *m*
manageress *n* bana-mhanaidsear
f, bana-cheannbhair *f*
mandate *n* òrdugh *m*, àithne *f*;
(*electoral*) ùghdarras *m*
mandatory *a* do-sheachanta,
èigneachail
mane *n* muing *f*
manfully *adv* gu duineil, gu dian
mangle *v* reub, dèan ablach de
manhood *n* fearalas *m*
mania *n* boile-cuthaich *f*
maniac *n* neach-cuthaich *m*,
caochanach *m*

manic *a* fon chuthach
manicure *n* grinneachadh làimhe
m *v* grinnich làmhan
manifest *a* follaiseach, soilleir
v taisbean, nochd, foillsich
manipulate *v* obraich
mankind *n* an cinne-daonna *m*
manliness *n* duinealas *m*,
fearalachd *f*
manly *a* duineil, fearail
manner *n* modh *f m*, seòl *m*,
dòigh *f*
mannerism *n* cleachdadh *m*, cleas
m, cuinse *f*
mannerly *a* modhail
manners *n* modh *f m*
manoeuvre *n* eacarsaich *f*; (*mil*)
gluasad (airm) *m*; (*met*)
innleachd *f*, cleas *m*
manpower *n* sgiobachd *f*
manse *n* mansa *m*
mansion *n* taigh/aitreabh mòr *m*,
àros *m*
mantlepiece *n* breus *m*
manual *a* làimhe **m. work** obair
làimhe *f* *n* leabhar-
làimhe/mìneachaidh *m*
manufacture *v* dèan
manure *n* todhar *m*, mathachadh
m, innear *f*
manuscript *n* làmh-sgrìobhainn *f*
Manx *n* Gàidhlig Mhanainneach *f*
a Manainneach
Manxman *n* Manainneach *m*
Manxwoman ban-
Mhanainneach *f*
many *n* mòran *m* *a* iomadh,
iomadach **m. people** mòran
dhaoine **m. a time** ... 's iomadh
uair ... **as m. again** uiread eile
so m. a leithid de, uiread de
twice as m. a dhà uimhir
map *n* map(a) *m*, clàr-dùthcha
m
mar *v* mill
marble *n* màrmor *m*; (*ball*)
marbal *m*, mìrleag *f*
March *n* am Màrt *m*
march *n* màrsail *f*, mèarrsadh *m*;
(*tune*) caismeachd *f* *v* dèan
màrsail/mèarrsadh, mèarrs
mare *n* làir *f*
margarine *n* margarain *m*

margin *n* oir *f m*, iomall *m*
marginal *a* iomallach,
  leathoireach
marigold *n* a' bhile bhuidhe *f*
marine *a* mara
mariner *n* maraiche *m*
maritime *a* cuantach
mark *n* comharra *m*; (*trace*)
  làrach *f m*, lorg *f*; (*currency*)
  marc *m v* comharraich;
  (*notice*) thoir fa-near, gabh
  beachd air
market *n* fèill *f*, margadh *f m*,
  margaid *f* **m. place** ionad
  margaidh *m*
marketing *n* margaideachd *f*
marmalade *n* marmalaid *m*
marquee *n* puball *m*, pàillean *m*
marquis *n* marcas *m*
marriage *n* pòsadh *m*
married *a* pòsta **m. couple** càraid
  phòsta *f*
marrow *n* smior *m*; (*veg*) mearag *f*
marry *v* pòs
marsh *n* boglach *f*, fèith *f*
  m.-marigold lus buidhe
  Bealltainn *m*
marshal *v* cuir an òrdugh, trus
mart *n* ionad margaidh *m*
martial *a* gaisgeanta
Martinmas *n* an Fhèill
  M(h)àrtainn *f*, Latha Fhèill
  Màrtainn *m*
martyr *n* martarach *m*
marvel *n* iongnadh *m*, mìorbhail
  f v gabh iongnadh
marvellous *a* mìorbhaileach,
  iongantach
Marxist *n, a* Marcsach *m*
mascot *n* suaichnean *m*
masculine *a* fearail; (*gram*) fireannta
mash *v* pronn
mashed *a* pronn
mask *n* aghaidh-choimheach *f*,
  aodannan *m*
mason *n* clachair *m*
masonry *n* clachaireachd *f*
mass *n* tomad *m*; (*great
  quantity*) meall *m*, tòrr *m*;
  (*majority*) mòr-chuid *f*; (*relig*)
  aifreann *f m*
massacre *n* casgradh *m*
  v casgair, murt

massage *n* suathadh/taosgnadh-
  bodhaig *m*
massive *a* tomadach, àibheiseach
mast *n* crann *m*
master *n* maigh(i)stir *m*; (*of ship*)
  sgiobair *m* **m. of ceremonies**
  fear an taighe *m v* (*subdue*)
  ceannsaich; (*become proficient
  in*) fàs suas ri
masterly *a* ealanta, sgaiteach
masterpiece *n* sàr obair *f*, euchd
  m
mat *n* brat *m*
match *n* maids(e) *m*, lasadair *m*;
  (*sport*) maids(e) *m*; (*equal*) seise
  m, samhail *m* **m.-box** bogsa/
  bucas-mhaidseachan *m*
  v freagair, co-fhreagair, maids
mate *n* cèile *m*, companach *m*;
  (*rank*) meat(a) *m*
material *n* stuth *m*
materialistic *a* saoghalta
maternal *a* màithreachail
maternity *a* màthaireil **m. hospital**
  ospadal mhàthraichean *m*
  m. leave fòrladh màthaireil *m*
mathematical *a* matamataigeach
mathematics *n* matamataig *m*
matrimony *n* dàimh-pòsaidh *f m*
matrix *n* machlag *f*; (*maths*)
  meatrags *f*
matron *n* bean-phòsta *f*; (*rank*)
  ban-cheannard *f*
matter *n* stuth *m*, brìgh *f*; (*affair*)
  gnothach *m*, cùis *f* **what's the
  m.?** dè tha ceàrr? *v* **it does not
  m.** chan eil e gu diofar
mattress *n* bobhstair *m*
mature *a* abaich, inbheach, air
  tighinn gu ìre *v* abaich
maturity *n* abaichead *m*, ìre *f*
maul *v* pronn, lidrig
mauve *n* liath-phurpaidh *m*
maximize *v* barraich
maximum *a* … as motha **the m.**
  a' chuid as motha *n* os-mheud
  m
May *n* an Cèitean *m*, a' Mhàigh *f*
  May Day Latha (Buidhe)
  Bealltainn *m*
may *v* (*permission*) faod;
  (*perhaps*) faod, 's dòcha **may I
  go?** am faod mi falbh? **they**

may not chan fhaod iad **she may come** faodaidh i tighinn; (*perhaps*) faodaidh gun tig i, 's dòcha gun tig i

mayday *n* gairm èiginn *f*

mayor *n* àrd-bhàillidh *m*, ceannard baile *m*

maze *n* ioma-shlighe *f*

me *pron* mi, (*emph*) mise

meadow *n* lòn *m*, faiche *f*, dail *f*, lèana *f*

meagre *a* gann, lom

meal *n* biadh *m*; (*flour*) min *f*

mean *a* spìocach; (*of spirit*) suarach, tàireil; (*stat*) meadhanail

mean *v* ciallaich; (*intend*) cuir romhad

meaning *n* ciall *f*, seagh *m*, brìgh *f*

meaningful *a* ciallach, brìoghmhor

meanness *n* spìocaireachd *f*; (*of spirit*) suarachas *m*

meantime *adv* an-dràsta **in the m.** anns an eadar-àm

meanwhile *adv* aig a' cheart àm

measles *n* a' ghriùthrach *f*, a' ghriùthlach *f*

measure *n* tomhas *m*; (*portion*) cuid *f*, roinn *f*; (*action*) ceum *m* *v* tomhais

measurement *n* tomhas *m*

meat *n* feòil *f*

mechanic *n* meacanaig *f*

mechanical *a* meacanaigeach

mechanism *n* uidheam *f*; (*means*) meadhan *m*, dòigh *f*

medal *n* bonn *m* **gold medal** bonn òir

meddle *v* buin ri, cuir làmh an, gabh gnothach ri

media, the *n* na meadhanan *m pl*

mediate *v* rèitich, rach san eadraiginn, eadar-mheadhanaich

mediation *n* eadraiginn *f*, eadar-ghuidhe *f*

mediator *n* eadar-mheadhanair *m*

medical *a* lèigh, meidigeach

medication *n* cungaidh leighis *f*

medicine *n* ìocshlaint *f*, cungaidh *f*; (*science*) eòlas-leighis *m*

medieval *a* meadhan-aoiseil

mediocre *a* meadhanach

meditate *v* beachdaich, beachd-smaoinich, meòraich

Mediterranean *n* a' Mhuir Mheadhan-thìreach *f* *a* Meadhan-thìreach

medium *a* meadhanach **m.-sized** meadhanach mòr **m. wave** bann meadhanach *m* *n* meadhan *m*

meek *a* macanta, ciùin

meet *v* coinnich, tachair; (*gather*) cruinnich; (*fulfil*) coilean

meeting *n* coinneamh *f*; (*act of*) coinneachadh *m*

melancholy *n* leann-dubh *m* *a* dubhach, fo leann-dubh

mellifluous *a* binn, milis

mellow *a* tlàth, làn-abaich

melodic/melodious *a* binn, fonnmhor

melody *n* fonn *m*

melon *n* meal-bhuc *m*

melt *v* leagh

member *n* ball *m* **MP** BP (Ball Pàrlamaid) *m* **MSP** BPA (Ball Pàrlamaid na h-Alba) **MEP** BPE (Ball Pàrlamaid Eòrpach)

membership *n* ballrachd *f*

membrane *n* meamran *m*

memento *n* cuimhneachan *m*

memoir(s) *n* eachdraidh-beatha *f*

memorable *a* ainmeil, fada air chuimhne

memorandum/memo *n* meòrachan *m*

memorial *n* cuimhneachan *m* **m. stone** clach-chuimhne *f* **m. cairn** càrn cuimhne *m* **m. service** seirbheis cuimhneachaidh *f*

memorize *v* cùm air chuimhne

memory *n* cuimhne *f*

menace *n* bagradh *m*, maoidheadh *m* **he's a m.** 's e plàigh a th' ann *v* bagair, maoidh

mend *v* càirich **be on the m.** rach am feabhas, thig air adhart

menial *a* sgalagail, seirbheiseil

meningitis *n* fiabhras eanchainn(e) *m*, teasach eanchainn *f*

mental a inntinneil **m. hospital** ospadal inntinn m

mention n iomradh m, luaidh m v ainmich, thoir iomradh/tarraing air, dèan luaidh air

menu n clàr-bìdh m, cairt-bìdh f; (computer) clàr-iùil m

mercenary n (mil) amhasg m, buanna m

mercenary a sanntach, miannach air airgead

merchandise n bathar m

merchant n ceannaiche m, marsanta m **the M. Navy** an Cabhlach Marsantach m

merciful a tròcaireach, iochdmhor

merciless a gun tròcair, an-iochdmhor

mercury n airgead-beò m

mercy n tròcair f, iochd f

merely adv a-mhàin, dìreach

merge v rach còmhla, coimeasg, dèan cothlamadh

merger n coimeasg(adh) m, aonadh m

meringue n mearang m

merit n luach m, airidheachd f v toill, bi airidh air

mermaid n maighdeann-mhara f

merriment n aighear m, mire f

merry a aighearach, mear

mesh n mogal m

mesmerize v dian-ghlac, cuir fo gheas

mess n bùrach m, butarrais f; (staff) seòmar-comaidh m

message n teachdaireachd f

messenger n teachdaire m

metabolism n meatabolachd f, fàs-atharrachadh m

metal n meatailt f **m. work** obair mheatailt f

metamorphose v cruth-atharraich

metaphor n meatafor m

metaphorical a meataforach

metaphysical a feallsanachail

meteor n dreag f, rionnag-earbaill f

meteorite n aileag f, sgeith-rionnaig f

meteorological a dreagach **Met.**
Office Oifis na Sìde f

meteorology n eòlas-sìde m

meter n inneal-tomhais m

method n dòigh f, seòl m, modh f m; (order) rian m

methodical a òrdail, rianail

methodology n dòigh-obrach f, modh-obrach f m

metre n meatair m; (of poetry) rannaigheachd f, meadrachd f

metric a meatrach

metrical a rannaigheachd, meadrachail

metro n trèan fo thalamh m

metropolitan a prìomh-bhailteach

mettle n smioralachd f

mew v dèan miathalaich/ miamhail

Michaelmas n an Fhèill M(h)ìcheil f, Latha Fhèill Mìcheil m

microbe n bitheag f, meanbhag f

microbiology n meanbh-bhith-eòlas m

microphone n maicreafòn m

microscope n maicreasgop m

microwave n meanbh-thonn f; (oven) àmhainn mheanbh-thonnach f

midday n meadhan-latha m

midden n sitig f, òcrach f, òtrach f

middle n meadhan m **m.-aged** sa mheadhan-latha **(the) M. Ages** na Meadhan-Aoisean f pl **m.-class** eagar meadhanach m a meadhan, meadhanach

midge n meanbh-chuileag f

midnight n meadhan-oidhche m

midriff n (an) sgairt f

midsummer n meadhan (an t-) samhraidh m; (St John's Day) Latha Fèill Eòin m

midway adv letheach-slighe, sa mheadhan

midwife n bean-ghlùine f

midwifery n banas-glùine m

might n cumhachd m, neart m, spionnadh m

might v faod, 's dòcha; (ought) bu choir dhut **a seat belt m. have saved his life** dh'fhaodadh gum biodh/gun robh crios-

sàbhalaidh air a chumail beò
you m. have apologized to her
bha coir agad a bhith air
mathanas iarraidh oirre
mighty *a* cumhachdach,
foghainteach
migrate *v* dèan imrich
migration *n* imrich *f*; (*overseas*)
imrich cuain
mild *a* màlda, ciùin, tlàth
mildew *n* clòimh-liath *f*
mile *n* mìle *f m* **mileage** astar
mhìltean *m* **milestone** clach-
mhìle *f*
militant *n* mìleantach *m*, cathach
m *a* mìleanta, cathachail
military *a* cogail, armailteach
militate *v* (*against*) obraich an
aghaidh
militia *n* mailisidh *m*
milk *n* bainne *m* *v* bleoghain(n)
mill *n* muileann *f m* **millstone**
clach-mhuilinn *f*; (*met*) eallach *m*
millennium *n* mìle bliadhna *f m*
milligram *n* mìlegram *m*
millilitre *n* mìleliotair *m*
millimetre *n* mìlemeatair *m*
million *n* millean *m*
millionaire *n* milleanair *m*
mime *n* mìm *f* *v* dèan mìm
mimic *v* dèan atharrais (air)
mince *n* mions *m*
mind *n* inntinn *f*, aigne *f*, ciall *f*
keep in m. cuimhnich *v* **what did
you have in m.?** dè bh' agad san
amharc? **he is out of his m.** tha
e às a chiall *v* thoir an aire,
thoir fa-near; (*remember*)
cuimhnich
mindful *a* cuimhneachail,
cùramach
mine *n* mèinn *f* **coal m.** toll-guail
m *v* cladhaich; (*plant mines*)
cuir mèinnean (an)
mine *pron* leamsa, agamsa **that's
m.** 's ann leamsa a tha sin **this
memory of m.** a' chuimhne seo
agamsa
miner *n* mèinneadair *m*, mèinnear
m
mineral *n* mèinnir *m*
a mèinnireach **m. water** uisge
mèinnireach *m*

mingle *v* measgaich, coimeasg,
cuir an ceann a chèile; (*with
people*) rach an lùib
minibus *n* bus beag *m*
minimal *a* fìor bheag; (*least*) as/a
bu lugha
minimize *v* lùghdaich, ìslich
minimum *n* a' chuid as/a bu
lugha *f*, ìos-mheud *m* *a* as/a bu
lugha
minister *n* ministear *m* *v* fritheil,
ministrealaich
ministry *n* ministre(al)achd *f* **the
M. of Defence** Ministre(al)achd
an Dìon *f*
mink *n* minc *m*
minor *a* beag, as lugha, fo-
n òg-aoisear *m*
minority *n* mion/beag-chuid *f*;
(*age*) òg-aois *f* **m. language**
mion-chànan *f m*
mint *n* meannt *m*; (*place*) taigh-
cùinnidh *m* **he made a m.** rinn e
fortan
minus *prep* às aonais (+ *gen*);
(*math*) thoir air falbh
minute *n* mionaid *f*; (*of meeting*)
geàrr-chunntas *m*
minute *a* meanbh, mion, beag
bìodach
miracle *n* mìorbhail *f*
miraculous *a* mìorbhaileach
mirage *n* mearachadh sùla *m*
mire *n* poll *m*, eabar *m*
mirror *n* sgàthan *m*
mirth *n* mire *f*, sùgradh *m*
misadventure *n* mì-shealbh *m*,
sgiorradh *m*
misbehave *v* bi ri mì-mhodh, bi
mì-mhodhail
misbehaviour *n* mì-mhodh *m*,
droch ghiùlan *m*
miscalculate *v* àireamhaich ceàrr;
(*met*) dèan co-dhùnadh ceàrr
miscall *v* càin
miscarriage *n* (*med*) asaid
anabaich *f*; (*general*) dol a dhìth
m **m. of justice** iomrall ceartais *m*
miscarry *v* asaid an-abaich;
(*general*) rach a dhìth
miscellaneous *a* measgaichte,
eugsamhail
miscellany *n* measgachadh *m*

mischief *n* luathaireachd *f*;
(*serious*) aimhleas *m*, miastadh
m
mischievous *a* luathaireach
misconception *n* mì-thuigsinn *f*,
claon-bheachd *m*
misconduct *n* mì-mhodh *m*,
droch ghiùlan *m*
misdemeanour *n* eucoir *f*,
mì-ghnìomh *m*
miser *n* spìocaire *m*
miserable *a* truagh, brònach
misfit *n* faondraiche *m*
misfortune *n* mì-fhortan *m*,
mì-shealbh *m*
misgiving(s) *n* teagamh(an) *m* (*pl*)
misguided *a* neo-ghlic, cearbach
mishap *n* mì-thapadh *m*, tubaist *f*
misinform *v* thoir fios meallta/
ceàrr
misinterpret *v* mì-bhreithnich, tog
ceàrr
misjudge *v* thoir mì-bhreith (air),
tuig ceàrr
mislay *v* caill
mislead *v* meall, mì-threòraich,
cuir ceàrr/air seachran
misleading *a* meallta
mismatch *n* neo-ionannachd *f*
misplace *v* caill
misprint *n* mearachd clò *f*
misrepresent *v* thoir claon-aithris
misrule *n* mì-riaghladh *m*;
(*anarchy*) mì-riaghailt *f*
Miss *n* A' Mhaighdeann *f* (*abb*)
A' Mh.
miss *v* ionndrainn; (*train etc*)
caill; (*target etc*) ana-cuimsich
missile *n* tilgean *m*, astas *m*
missing *a* a dhìth,
a dh'easbhaidh; (*person*) air
chall, gun lorg
mission *n* misean *f*; (*purpose*) rùn
m **m. statement** aithris rùin *f*
missionary *n* miseanaraidh *m*
mist *n* ceò *f m*, ceathach *m*
mistake *n* mearachd *f*, iomrall *m*
Mister (Mr) *n* Maigh(i)stir (Mgr) *m*
mistletoe *n* uil-ìoc *m*
mistress *n* bana-mhaighstir *f*;
(*lover*) coimhleapach *f m*,
boireannach eile *m* **Mrs** A' Bh.
misty *a* ceòthach, ceòthar

misunderstand *v* tog ceàrr
misunderstanding *n* mì-thuigse *f*,
togail ceàrr *f*
misuse *n* mì-bhuileachadh *m*
mite *n* fineag *f*
mitigating *a* lasachaidh,
maothachaidh
mitigation *n* lasachadh *m*,
maothachadh *m*
mix *v* measgaich, cuir an lùib a
chèile, cothlaim
mixed *a* measgaichte, measgte
mixer *n* measgaichear *m*, inneal-
measgachaidh *m*
mixture *n* measgachadh *m*
moan *n* gearan *m*; (*sound*) acain
f, osna *f* *v* gearain; (*sound*)
dèan acainn/osna
mob *n* gràisg *f*
mobile *a* gluasadach **m. phone** *n*
fòn-làimhe *f m*
mobility *n* gluasadachd *f*,
cothrom gluasaid *m*
mock *v* mag (air), dèan fanaid
(air)
mockery *n* magadh *m*, fanaid *f*
mod *n* mòd *m* **the National Mod**
am Mòd Nàiseanta **local m.**
mòd ionadail
mode *n* modh *f m*, dòigh *f*, seòl
m, rian *m*
model *n* modail *m*, cruth *m*,
samhail *m*; (*make*) seòrsa *m*;
(*fashion*) modail *m* *a* m.
employee brod an obraiche
v deilbh, cum, dealbhaich **m.
oneself on** lean eisimpleir
(+ *gen*)
modem *n* mòdam *m*
moderate *a* cuibheasach,
meadhanach; (*disposition*)
stuama, riaghailteach *v* (*of
weather*) ciùinich; (*exams*)
co-mheas
moderation *n* stuaim *f*,
riaghailteachd *f*; (*of exams*)
co-mheasadh *m*
moderator *n* co-mheasadair *m*;
(*eccl*) moderàtor *m*
modern *a* ùr, nuadh, nodha
modernize *v* ùraich, nuadhaich
modest *a* nàrach, màlda,
socharach

modesty *n* beusachd *f*, màldachd *f*, socharachd *f*
modify *v* atharraich, leasaich
module *n* modal *m*
moist *a* tais, bog
moisten *v* taisich, bogaich
moisture *n* taiseachd *f*, fliche *f*
mole *n* (*animal*) famh *f*; (*on skin*) ball-dòrain *m*; (*insider*) ruamharaiche *m* **molehill** dùnan-faimh *m*
molecule *n* moileciuil *m*
molest *v* (*accost*) thoir ionnsaigh air; (*annoy*) cuir dragh air
mollify *v* maothaich, ciùinich
molten *a* leaghte
moment *n* tiota(n) *m*, mòmaid *f*
momentary *a* car tiota
momentous *a* fìor chudromach
momentum *n* cumhachd gluasaid *m*; (*velocity*) luaths *m*
monarch *n* monarc *m*
monarchist *n* monarcach *m*
monarchy *n* monarcachd *f*
monastery *n* manachainn *f*
Monday *n* Diluain *m*
monetary *a* ionmhasail
money *n* airgead *m*
mongol *n* mongolach *m*
mongrel *n*, *a* eadar-ghnè *f*
monitor *v* cùm sùil air, sgrùd
monk *n* manach *m*
monkey *n* muncaidh *m*
mono- *pref* aon-
monopolize *v* lèir-shealbhaich, gabh thairis
monopoly *n* monopolaidh *f m*, lèir-shealbhachd *f*
monotonous *a* aon-duanach, liosta
monotony *n* an aon duan *m*, liostachd *f*
monster *n* uilebheist *f m*
monstrous *a* sgriosail, oillteil
month *n* mìos *f m*
monthly *a* mìosail
monument *n* carragh-cuimhne *f*, càrn-cuimhne *m*
mood *n* sunnd *m*, gleus *f m*, triom *f*; (*gram*) modh *f m*
moody *a* caochlaideach, greannach, frionasach
moon *n* gealach *f m* **moonlight**

solas na gealaich *m* **the man in the m.** bodach na gealaich *m*
moor *n* mòinteach *f*, monadh *m* **m. fire** falaisg *f*
moor *v* acraich
moorhen cearc-fhraoich *f*
moose *n* lon *m*
mop *n* mop *m*, sguab-fhliuch *f*
mope *v* bi fo ghruaimean
moral *a* moralta, beusach *n* (*of story*) teagasg *m*, teachdaireachd *f* **morals** *n* beusan *f pl*
morale *n* misneachd *f*, spiorad *m*
morality *n* moraltachd *f*
morass *n* bog(l)ach *f*
morbid *a* mì-fhallain, dubhach
more *n* tuilleadh *m*, barrachd *f* *adv* **any m.** tuilleadh, nas mò
morning *n* madainn *f*
moron *n* lethchiallach *m*
morose *a* gruamach, mùgach
morphia, morphine *n* moirfin *f*
morsel *n* mìr *f*, criomag *f*, bìdeag *f*
mortal *a* bàsmhor
mortar *n* aol-tàthaidh *m*
mortgage *n* morgaids(e) *m*
mosaic *n* breac-dhualadh *m*
Moslem *n*, *a* See Muslim
mosque *n* mosg *m*
mosquito *n* mosgìoto *f*
moss *n* (*bot*) còinneach *f*; (*topog*) bog(l)ach *f*
most *n* a' mhòr-chuid *f*, a' chuid as motha *f* *a* as motha/a bu mhotha, a' chuid as motha/a bu mhotha
mostly *adv* mar as trice, sa mhòr-chuid
moth *n* leòmann *m*
mother *n* màthair *f* **m.-in-law** màthair-chèile *f*
motion *n* gluasad *m*; (*at meeting*) moladh *m* **set in m.** cuir a dhol *v*
motivate *v* spreag, brod
motivation *n* togradh *m*
motive *n* adhbhar *m*, ceann-fàth *m*
motley *a* ioma-sheòrsach, ioma-dhathach
motor *n*, *a* motair *m* **m. bicycle** motair-baidhsagal *m* **m.-cycle** motair-rothair *m*

motorist *n* motairiche *m*
motorway *n* mòr-rathad *m*
motto *n* faca(i)l-suaicheantais *m*
mould *n* molldair *m*; (*form*) cruth *m* **blue m.** clòimh-liath *f v* com
moult *v* cuir/tilg na h-itean, cuir fionnadh/gaoisid
mound *n* tom *m*, tòrr *m*
mount *v* dìrich, streap; (*horse*) rach air muin eich; (*set up*) cuir air dòigh
mountain *n* beinn *f*, monadh *m*
mountaineer *n* streapadair (beinne) *m*
mountaineering *n* streapadaireachd *f*, streap nam beann *m*
mourn *v* caoidh
mournful *a* brònach, tiamhaidh
mourning *n* bròn *m*, caoidh *f*, tuireadh *m* **in m.** a' caoidh, ri bròn
mouse *n* luch *f*
moustache *n* stais *f*
mouth *n* beul *m*; (*large*) craos *m* **m.-music** port-à-beul *m* **m.-organ** òrgan-beòil *m*
mouthful *n* làn-beòil *m*, balgam *m*
move *v* gluais, caraich; (*propose*) cuir air adhart, mol **m. house** dèan imrich/imprig
movement *n* gluasad *m*
moving *a* (*emotion*) drùidhteach
mow *v* geàrr, buain
mower *n* lomaire *m*
much *adv* mòran; (*with a*) fada **as m. again** uimhir eile **as m. as** uiread ri/agus **too m.** cus **that is m. better** tha sin fada/cus/ mòran nas fheàrr *n* mòran *m*
muck *n* salchar *m*, eabar *m*; (*manure*) buachar *m*, innear *f*
mucky *a* salach
mucus *n* ronn *m*
mud *n* poll *m*, eabar *m*
muddle *n* bùrach *m*, troimh-a-chèile *f m v* cuir troimh-a-chèile
muddy *a* eabarach, fo eabar/pholl
muffle *v* (*wrap up*) còmhdaich; (*deaden*) mùch
mug *n* muga *f m*; (*fool*) gloidhc *f*
mug *v* dèan braid-ionnsaigh

mugging *n* braid-ionnsaigh *f*
muggy *a* bruthainneach
Mull person *n* Muileach *m*, (*female*) ban(a)-Mhuileach *f*
multi- *pref* ioma-
multicoloured *a* ioma-dhathach
multicultural *a* ioma-chultarach
multilateral *a* ioma-thaobhach
multilingual *a* ioma-chànanach
multimedia *n* ioma-mheadhan *m*
multinational *a* ioma-nàiseanta
multiple *a* ioma-sheòrsach, iomadach
multiplication *n* iomadachadh *m*, meudachadh *m*
multiply *v* iomadaich, meudaich; (*genetically*) sìolaich, fàs lìonmhor
multitude *n* mòr-shluagh *m*
mum(my) *n* mamaidh *f*
mumble *v* bi a' brunndail
mumps *n* an t-at-busach *m*, an tinneas-plocach *m*
munch *v* cagainn
mundane *a* àbhaisteach, làitheil
mural *n* dealbh-balla *m*
murder *n* murt *m v* dèan murt
murderer *n* murtair *m*
murmur *n* (*of nature*) monmhar *m*, torman *m*, crònan *m*; (*person*) brunndail *f*
muscle *n* fèith *f*
muscular *a* fèitheach
museum *n* taigh-tasgaidh *m*
mushroom *n* balgan-buachair *m*
music *n* ceòl *m*
musical *a* ceòlmhor, binn; (*person*) math air ceòl **m. instrument** *n* inneal-ciùil *m*
musician *n* neach-ciùil *m*
Muslim *n, a* Muslamach *m*, (*female*) ban-Mhuslamach *f*
mussel *n* feusgan *m*
must *v* feumaidh, bi aig … ri, 's èiginn do, 's fheudar do
mustard *n* (*bot*) sgeallan *m*; (*condiment*) mustard *m*
muster *v* cruinnich, trus
musty *a* tungaidh, fuaraidh
mutation *n* mùthadh *m*, atharrachadh *m*
mute *a* balbh, tostach
mutilate *v* ciorramaich, geàrr

mutiny *n* ceannairc *f*, ar-a-mach *m* *v* dèan ceannairc/ar-a-mach
mutter *v* dèan dranndan/gearan
mutton *n* muilt-fheòil *f*, feòil caorach *f*
mutual *a* co-aontach, a rèir a chèile
muzzle *v* cuir glas-ghuib air
my *poss pron* mo, (*before vowels*) m', agam(sa) **my key** an iuchair agam
myself *pron* mi fhèin/fhìn
mysterious *a* dìomhair
mystery *n* dìomhaireachd *f*, rùn dìomhair *m*
mystical *a* fàidheanta
mystify *v* cuir an imcheist
myth *n* miotas *m*, uirsgeul *m*
mythical *a* miotasach
mythology *n* miotas-eòlas *m*

N

nag *v* dèan cànran
nail *n* tarrag *f*; (*finger/toe*) ìne *f*
  n.-file lìomhan-ìnean *m*
  n. varnish bhàrnais ìnean *f*
naive *a* neo(i)chiontach, sìmplidh
naked *a* lomnochd, rùisgte
name *n* ainm *m*; (*reputation*) cliù *m* *v* ainmich **give a n. to** thoir ainm air
nap *n* norrag *f*, snuachdan *m*, cadalan *m*; (*on cloth*) caitean *m*
napkin *n* nèapaigin *m*
nappy *n* badan *m*
narrate *v* aithris
narration *n* aithris *f*, iomradh *m*, seanchas *m*
narrator *n* neach-aithris *m*, seanchaidh *m*
narrow *a* cumhang, caol
  n.-minded cumhang
nasty *a* mosach, suarach
nation *n* nàisean *m*, dùthaich *f*, rìoghachd *f*
national *a* nàiseanta **n. insurance** *n* àrachas nàiseanta *m* **the N. Health Service** Seirbheis Nàiseanta na Slàinte *f*
nationalism *n* nàiseantachas *m*
nationalist *n, a* nàiseantach *m*
nationality *n* nàiseantachd *f*

nationalize *v* stàit-shealbhaich, cuir an seilbh na stàite
native *n* dùthchasach *m* **n. of** neach a mhuinntir ... *m* (+ *gen*) *a* dùthchasach, san dualchas **n. speaker** fileantach ((bh)o dhùthchas) *m*
natural *a* nàdarra(ch)
naturalist *n* neach-eòlais-nàdair *m*
naturally *adv* gu nàdarra(ch)
nature *n* nàdar *m*, gnè *f*, seòrsa *m* **n. reserve** tèarmann nàdair *m*
naught *n* neoni *m*
naughty *a* dona, mì-mhodhail
nausea *n* òrrais *f*, neoshannt *m*
nautical *a* seòlaidh, maraireachd
navel *n* imleag *f*
navigate *v* (*plot course*) tog cùrsa; (*make passage*) seòl
navigation *n* mara(irea)chd *f*
navy *n* cabhlach *m*, nèibhidh *m*
navy-blue *a* dubh-ghorm
neap-tide *n* conntraigh *f*
near *a* faisg (air), dlùth (air), teann (air)
nearly *adv* faisg/dlùth air; (*almost*) cha mhòr nach (+ *v*)
neat *a* grinn, sgiobalta, cuimir
necessary *a* riatanach, deatamach, do-sheachanta
necessity *n* riatanas *m*, deatamachd *f* **dire n.** an dubh-èiginn *f*
neck *n* amha(i)ch *f*, muineal *m*
necklace *n* seud-muineil *m*, usgar-bràghad *m*, paidirean *m*
need *n* feum *m*; (*want*) dìth *f m*, easbhaidh *f*; (*poverty*) airc *f* *v* bi feumach air; (*must*) feum(aidh); (*want*) bi a dhìth air **we n. money** tha sinn feumach air airgead **we'll n. to go** feumaidh sinn falbh **what do you n.?** dè tha dhìth ort? **you n. not do that** cha leig/ruig thu a leas sin a dhèanamh
needle *n* snàthad *f*
needless *a* gun adhbhar
needy *a* ainniseach, easbhaidheach *n* **the n.** na feumaich *m pl*
negative *a* àicheil

neglect *n* dearmad *m* *v* dèan dearmad (air), bi gun diù (mu)
negligence *n* dearmadachd *f*, mì-chùram *m*, cion diù *m*
negligent *a* dearmadach, mì-chùramach
negligible *a* suarach, neonitheach
negotiate *v* barganaich, dèan gnothach (ri), co-rèitich
negotiation *n* barganachadh *m*, co-rèiteachadh *m*
neigh *v* dèan sitir/sitrich, sitrich
neighbour *n* nàbaidh *m*, coimhearsnach *m*
neighbourhood *n* nàba(idhea)chd *f*, coimhearsnachd *f*
neither *a, pron* a h-aon *conj* cha mhò *adv* nas mò **n. of them stayed** cha do dh'fhuirich a h-aon aca/fear seach fear aca/tè seach tè aca **she doesn't drive and n. does he** cha dèan ise dràibheadh 's cha mhò a nì esan
neo- *pref* nuadh-
nephew *n* mac peathar/bràthar *m*
nerve *n* fèith-mhothachaidh *f*, nearbh *f* **what a n.!** abair aghaidh! **he lost his n.** chaill e a mhisneachd
nervous *a* iomagaineach, nearbha(sa)ch
nest *n* nead *f m* *v* neadaich
net *n* lìon *m* **the Net** an Lìon
netball *n* ball-lìn *m*
nettle *n* deanntag *f*, feanntag *f*
network *n* lìon *m*, lìonra *m* *v* dèan lìonra; (*met*) dèan eadar-cheanglaichean
neuter *a* (*gram*) neodrach
neutral *a* neo-phàirteach, gun taobh
never *adv* (*with neg v*) a-chaoidh, gu bràth, uair sam bith; (*in past*) (a-)riamh **n. mind!** *interj* coma leat!
nevertheless *adv* an dèidh sin, a dh'aindeoin sin
new *a* ùr, nuadh **New Year** a' Bhliadhn' Ur *f* **N. Year's Day** Latha na Bliadhn' Uire *m* **Happy New Year!** Bliadhna Mhath Ùr!
news *n* naidheachd *f*, fios *m*

newspaper pàipear-naidheachd *m*
next *a* an ath (+ *len*), ... as fhaisge/a b' fhaisge *adv* a-nis **n. week** an ath sheachdain **what next!** dè nis!, dè an ath rud!
nibble *v* criom, creim
nice *a* gasta, laghach, snog
niche *n* cùil *f*, oisean *m*
nick *n* eag *f* **in the n. of time** dìreach na uair/ann an tide *v* eagaich; (*steal*) goid
nickname *n* far-ainm *m*, frith-ainm *m*
niece *n* nighean peathar/bràthar *f*
night *n* oidhche *f* **all n.** fad na h-oidhche **at n.** air an oidhche **the n. before last** a' bhòn-raoir **last n.** a-raoir **tonight** a-nochd **tomorrow n.** an ath-oidhch'
nightgown/nightie *n* gùn-oidhche *m*
nightmare *n* trom-laighe *f m*
nil *n* neoni *m*
nimble *a* clis, sgiobalta
nine *n* a naoi *a* naoi, naodh **n. people** naoinear, naodhnar *f m*
nineteen *n, a* naoi-deug, naodh-deug **n. points** naoi puingean deug
ninety *n, a* ceithir fichead 's a deich, naochad *m*
ninth *a* naoidheamh, naodhamh
nip *n* bìdeadh *m*, teumadh *m*; (*of whisky*) tè bheag *f* *v* bìd, teum
nit *n* mial *f*
no *neg response* cha/chan *plus verb used in question* **will you be there? no** am bi thu ann? cha bhi **will she tell him? no** an innis i dha? chan innis *a* sam bith, gin, sgath **it was of no benefit to him** cha robh buannachd sam bith ann dha **we have no milk** chan eil sgath bainne againn **there were no children** cha robh gin a chloinn ann *adv* càil/dad nas ... (*with neg v*) **he is no better** chan eil e càil/dad nas fheàrr
nobility *n* uaislean *m pl*, maithean *m pl*; (*quality*) uaisleachd *f*
noble *n, a* uasal *m*

nobody/no one *n* (*after neg v*)
aon *m*, duine *m* **there was n. to
be seen** cha robh duine/neach
(sam bith) ri fhaicinn
nod *n* gnogadh cinn *m*
v gnog/crom (do cheann) **she
nodded off** rinn i norrag
noise *n* fuaim *f m*
noisy *a* fuaimneach, gleadhrach,
faramach
nominal *a* san ainm
nominate *v* ainmich
nomination *n* ainmeachadh *m*
nominative *a* ainmneach **the n.
case** an tuiseal ainmneach *m*
non- *pref* neo-
non-stop *a*, *adv* … gun stad
nonchalant *a* gun chùram
none *pron* (*after neg v*) aon
duine *m*, neach (sam bith) *m*,
gin *f*, sgath *m*
nonsense *n* amaideas *m*
nook *n* cùil *f*, iùc *f*
noon *n* nòin *m*, meadhan-latha *m*
nor *conj* no, cha mhò
norm *n* àbhaist *f*
normal *a* riaghailteach,
àbhaisteach, gnàthach
normally *adv* am bitheantas, anns
a' chumantas
Norse *a* Lochlannach
north *n*, *a* (an) tuath *m*, an àird a
tuath *f* **in the n.** mu thuath **n. of**
tuath air **n.-east** (an) ear-thuath
m **n.-west** (an) iar-thuath *m*
Norwegian *n*, *a* Nirribheach *m*,
(*female*) ban-Nirribheach *f*
nose *n* sròn *f* **nosebleed**
leum-sròine *m*
nostalgia *n* cianalas *m*
not *adv* cha, chan, na, nach **we
will not go there** cha tèid sinn
ann **I will not leave it** chan fhàg
mi e **do not move it** na gluais e
**he said that he would not do
that** thuirt e nach dèanadh e sin
notable *a* ainmeil, sònraichte
notch *n* eag *f*
note *n* nota *f*; (*letter*) sgrìobag *f*;
(*mus*) pong *m* *v* thoir fa-near,
comharraich
noted *a* ainmeil, cliùiteach
nothing *n* neoni *m*; (*with neg*)

nì/rud sam bith **she would think
n. of it** cha shaoileadh i dad
dheth
notice *n* fios *m*, brath *m*;
(*written*) sanas *m*; (*warning*)
rabhadh *m* *v* mothaich, thoir
fa-near, thoir an aire
notify *v* leig fhaicinn do, thoir
fios (do)
notion *n* beachd *m*, smaoin *f*;
(*concept*) bun-bheachd *m*
notorious *a* suaicheanta, le droch
cliù
noun *n* ainmear *m* **verbal n.**
ainmear gnìomhaireach
nourish *v* àraich, beathaich, tog
nourishment *n* beathachadh *m*
novel *n* nobhail *f*, uirsgeul *m*
novel *a* nuadh, annasach
novelty *n* annas *m*
November *n* an t-Samhain *f*
now *adv* a-nis(e), an-dràsta, an
ceartuair
nowadays *adv* an-diugh, san là
an-diugh
nowhere *adv* (*after neg v*) an àite
sam bith
nozzle *n* soc *m*, smeachan *m*
nuclear *a* niùclasach **n. power**
cumhachd niùclasach *f m*
n. waste sgudal niùclasach *m*
n. weapons armachd niùclasach
f
nucleus *n* niùclas *m*
nude *a* rùisgte, lomnochd
nudge *v* put
nuisance *n* dragh *m*
null *a* gun stàth, gun bhrìgh
n. and void falamh gun èifeachd
numb *a* meilichte, rag le fuachd,
anns an eighealaich **n. with cold**
air a lathadh *etc* *v* meilich,
ragaich
number *n* àireamh *f* **phone n.**
àireamh-fòn *v* cunnt(ais),
àireamhaich
numeral *n* figear *m*
numerate *a* àireamhachail
numerical *a* àireamhach
numerous *a* lìonmhor, iomadach
(*precedes n*)
nun *n* bean-chràbhaidh *f*,
cailleach-dhubh *f*

nurse *n* banaltram *f*, nurs *f m*,
v nurs(aig), altraim
nursery *n* seòmar-altraim *m*;
(*school*) sgoil-àraich *f*; (*bot*)
planntlann *f*
nursing *n* banaltramachd *f*,
nursadh *m*; (*of child*) altramas
m **n.-home** taigh-altraim *m*
nurture *v* àraich, oileanaich
nut *n* (*food, mech*) cnò *f*
nutrition *n* beathachadh *m*,
mathas *m*
nylon *n* nàidhlean *m*

O

oak *n* darach *m* *a* daraich
oar *n* ràmh *m*
oasis *n* innis-fàsaich *f*
oatcake *n* aran-coirce *m*
oath *n* bòid *f* **oaths** mionnan *f m*
pl
oatmeal *n* min-choirce *f*
oats *n* coirce *m*
obdurate *a* rag-mhuinealach
obedience *n* ùmhlachd *f*
obedient *a* umhail
obese *a* reamhar, tiugh, sultmhor
obey *v* bi umhail (do)
obituary *n* iomradh-bàis *m*;
(*death notice*) sanas bàis *m*
object *n* nì *m*, rud *m*; (*objective*)
adhbhar *m* **o. of ...** cùis- ... *f*,
cuspair *m* (+ *gen*); (*gram*)
cuspair *m*
object *v* cuir an aghaidh
objection *n* cur an aghaidh *m*,
gearan *m*
objective *n* amas *m*, ceann-uidhe
m *a* cothromach, neo-
eisimeileach
obligation *n* comain *f*, dleastanas
m
oblige *v* (*require*) cuir mar
fhiachaibh air; (*do a favour to*)
cuir fo chomain
obliging *a* èasgaidh, deònach
obliterate *v* dubh a-mach
oblong *a* cruinn-fhada
obnoxious *a* gràineil
obscene *a* draosta, drabasta
obscure *a* doilleir; (*met*)
dìomhair *v* dèan doilleir, cuir

fo sgleò, falaich
observant *a* forail, mothachail,
aireil
observatory *n* amharclann *f*
observe *v* amhairc, coimhead,
thoir an aire; (*keep*) cùm, glèidh
observer *n* neach-coimhid *m*,
neach-amhairc *m*
obsession *n* beò-ghlacadh *m*
obsolete *a* à cleachdadh, (bh)o
fheum
obstacle *n* cnap-starra *m*, bacadh
m
obstinate *a* rag-mhuinealach,
fada na c(h)eann fhèin *etc*
obstruct *v* bac, cuir bacadh air
obstruction *n* cnap-starra *m*,
bacadh *m*
obtain *v* faigh
obvious *a* follaiseach, soilleir,
nochdte
occasion *n* (*event*) tachartas *m*;
(*reason*) adhbhar *m*; (*time*) uair
f, turas *m* **on one o.** aon
uair/turas
occasionally *adv* corra uair, an-
dràsta 's a-rithist, (bh)o àm gu
àm
occupation *n* obair *f*, dreuchd *f*;
(*of property*) gabhail thairis *m*
occupy *v* gabh sealbh/
còmhnaidh; (*space*) lìon; (*time*)
cuir seachad tìde; (*property*)
gabh thairis
occur *v* tachair **o. to** thig a-steach
air
occurrence *n* tachartas *m*
ocean *n* cuan *m*, fairge *f*
octagon *n* ochd-shliosach *m*
octave *n* ochdad *m*
October *n* an Dàmhair *f*
octopus *n* ochd-chasach *m*,
gibearnach-meurach *m*
odd *a* neònach, àraid; (*number*)
còrr **o. one out** (an) conadal *m*
odds *n* còrrlach *m*; (*leftovers*)
fuidheall *m* **against the o.** an
aghaidh an t-sruth **it makes no
o.** is coma, chan eil e gu diofar
ode *n* duan *m*
odour *n* boladh *m*, boltradh *m*
of *prep* de/dhe, à **one of these
days** latha dhe na lathaichean

many of us mòran againn/dhinn
think of it smaoinich air/mu
dheidhinn (*often conveyed by
gen form*) **a sum of money** sùim
airgid) **of course it is** nach eil
fhios gu bheil
off *prep* de, dhe, bhàrr/far (+ *gen*)
the car went off the road chaidh
an càr bhàrr an rathaid/dhen
rathad   *adv* dheth **he put off the
light** chuir e dheth an solas **they
made off** rinn iad às **come off it!**
thalla is thoir ort! **it's gone off**
(*gone bad*) tha e air fàs grod
offence *n* oilbheum *m*, coire *f*;
(*criminal*) eucoir *f*
offend *v* dèan/thoir oilbheum do;
(*criminally*) dèan eucoir
offender *n* eucorach *m*, ciontach
m
offensive *a* oilbheumach;
(*attacking*) ionnsaigheach
offer *n* tairgse *f*, tathann *m*
   v tairg, dèan/thoir tairgse,
tathainn
offhand *a* coma, beag-sùim
office *n* oifis *f*, oifig *f*; (*role*)
dreuchd *f*
officer *n* oifigear *m*
official *n* oifigeach *m* *a* oifigeil
   o. opening fosgladh oifigeil *m*
offspring *n* sliochd *m*, àl *m*
often *adv* (gu) tric, (gu) minig
oil *n* ola *f* *v* cuir ola air **oilfield**
raon-ola *m* **oilrig** crann-ola *m*
   oil-tanker tancair ola *m*
oily *a* olach, ùilleach
ointment *n* acfhainn *f*, aolmann
m
old *a* sean, aosta **old-fashioned**
seann-fhasanta **old man** bodach
m **old woman** cailleach *f*
olive *n* (*tree*) crann-ola *m*; (*fruit*)
meas a' chroinn-ola *m*, dearc-
ola *m* **o.-oil** ola a' chroinn-ola *f*
omen *n* manadh *m*
ominous *a* droch-fhàistinneach
omission *n* dearmad *m*
omit *v* dèan dearmad, fàg às
omnipotent *a* uile-chumhachdach
on *prep* air; (*after*) an dèidh *adv*
air; (*onwards*) air adhart **off
and on** air is dheth, thuige 's

bhuaithe
once *adv* uair, aon uair/turas
one *n* a h-aon; (*person*) neach *m*,
fear *m*, tè *f*; (*one thing*) aon(an)
m
one *a* aon **one-way** aon-
shligheach
onerous *a* trom, sàrachail
onion *n* uinnean *m*
on-line *n* air loidhne
only *a* aon **the o. way** an aon
dòigh *adv* a-mhàin *conj* (*after
neg v*) ach **he o. wanted to help
her** cha robh e ach airson a
cuideachadh
onus *n* uallach *m*
onward *adv* air adhart
ooze *v* sil
opaque *a* doilleir, do-lèirsinneach
open *v* fosgail *a* fosgailte;
(*frank*) fosgarra
opener *n* fosglair *m*
opening *n* fosgladh *m*, beàrn *f m*
openly *adv* gu fosgailte
opera *n* opara *f pl* oparathan
operate *v* obraich; (*med*) dèan
opairèisean, cuir fon sgithinn
operation *n* obair *f*, gnìomhachd
f; (*med*) opairèisean *f m*
opinion *n* barail *f*, beachd *m*
   o. poll cunntas-bheachd *m*
opinionated *a* rag-bharalach, fada
na c(h)eann fhèin *etc*
opponent *n* cuspairiche *m*, neach-
dùbhlain *m*
opportune *a* fàbharach
opportunity *n* cothrom *m*
oppose *v* cuir an aghaidh
opposite *n* ceart-aghaidh *f* *prep*
(+ *gen*) fa chomhair, mu
choinneamh
opposition *n* cur an aghaidh *m*,
dùbhlan *m*; (*polit*) **the O.** am
Partaidh Dùbhlanach *m*
oppress *v* claoidh, dèan fòirneart
air
oppression *n* ainneart *m*,
fòirneart *m*
oppressive *a* ainneartach,
fòirneartach; (*weather*) trom,
murtaidh
opt for *v* tagh **opt out** tarraing
a-mach/às

optician n fradhairciche m, neach nan sùilean m

optimism n so-aigne f

optimistic a so-aigneach

option n roghainn f m

optional a roghnach, ri roghnachadh

opulence n saidhbhreas m, toic f

or conj no, air neo

oral a labhairteach, beòil
 o. tradition beul-aithris f

orange n orainsear m **o. juice** sùgh orains m a orains

orator n òraidiche m

orbit a reul-chuairt f, cuairt f

Orcadian n, a Arcach m, (female) ban-Arcach f

orchard n ubhal-ghort m

orchestra n orcastra f

ordain v socraich, sònraich; (relig) cuir an dreuchd

ordeal n cruaidh-dheuchainn f

order n òrdugh m, òrdan m; (relig) riaghailt f **in o. that** air chor ('s gu) **out of o.** briste; (met) mì-iomchaidh

order v òrdaich; (arrange) cuir an òrdugh

orderly a òrdail, riaghailteach

ordinary a àbhaisteach, cumanta

ore n clach-meinnir f

organ n (body) ball m; (mus) òrgan m

organic a fàs-bheairteach

organist n òrganaiche m

organization n buidheann f m; (act of) eagrachadh m

organize v cuir air dòigh, eagraich

organizer n neach-eagrachaidh m, eagraiche m

orgy n ruidhtearachd f

oriental a earach

orifice n fosgladh m

origin n tùs m, bun m, màthair-adhbhar f

original a tùsail, prìomh, bun-

originate v tàrmaich, tòisich

ornament n òrnaid f

ornamental a òrnaideach

ornate a mòr-mhaisichte, mòr-sgeadaichte

ornithology n eun-eòlas m

orphan n dìlleachdan m

orthodox a gnàthach; (relig) ceart-chreideach

osprey n iolair-uisge f

ostrich n struth m

other pron eile **the o. day** an latha roimhe **one after the o.** fear/tè às dèidh fir/tè **the others** càch **they gave each o. gifts** thug iad tiodhlacan dha chèile

otherwise adv a chaochladh, air mhodh eile; (or else) no

otter n biast-dhubh f, dòbhran m

ouch! exclam aobh!, aobhag!

ought v is còir, tha còir aig **she o. to do it** is còir dhi a dhèanamh/ tha còir aice a dhèanamh **you o. to have done it** bu chòir dhut a bhith air a dhèanamh/bha còir agad a bhith air a dhèanamh

ounce n unnsa m

our poss pron ar, ar n- (before vowels), againne **our father** ar n-athair **our house** an taigh againne

ourselves pron sinn fhèin/fhìn

oust v cuir às

out adv a-muigh; (motion outwards) a-mach **O. you/we go! Mach à seo!**

outcast n dìobarach m

outcome n buil f, toradh m

outcry n iolach f, gàir m

outdoors adv a-muigh, air a' bhlàr a-muigh

outer a a-muigh, a-mach

outfit n trusgan m, aodach m

outing n splaoid f, cuairt f

outlaw n neach-cùirn m, neach fon choill m v cuir fon choill

outline n dealbh-iomaill f m; (met) cnàmhan m pl v thoir cunntas air

outlook n sealladh m

out-of-date a à fasan, às an fhasan; (past sell-by date) seachad air a' cheann-latha

output n cur a-mach m, toradh m

outrage n cùis-uabhais f

outrageous a uabhasach

outright adv (gu) buileach, (gu) tur

outset n fìor thoiseach m, ciad

dol a-mach *m*
outside *n* an taobh/leth a-muigh
m adv a-muigh; (*motion*)
a-mach
outsize *n, a* mòr-thomhas *m*,
mòr-mheud *m*
outskirts *n* iomall (baile) *m*
outspoken *a* fosgarra, a-mach leis
outstanding *a* barraichte, air
leth ...
outward *a* air an taobh a-muigh;
(*met*) faicsinneach
outwardly *adv* (bh)on taobh
a-muigh, (bh)o shealladh
dhaoine
outwit *v* thoir an car à/às
oval *a* air chumadh uighe, ugh-
chruthach *n* ugh-chruth *m*
ovation *n* mòr-bhualadh-bhas *m*
oven *n* àmhainn *f*
over *prep* (*above*) os cionn
(+ *gen*); (*beyond*) thar (+ *gen*);
(*across*) thairis air, tarsainn air
adv (*hither*) a-null; (*yonder*)
a-nall; (*past*) seachad;
(*additional*) a bharrachd,
a bhàrr air; (*left over*) a chòrr
pref ro- (+ *len*)
overall *a* iomlan
over-anxious *a* ro chùramach
overcharge *v* iarr/cuir tuilleadh 's
a' chòir (+ *air*)
overcome *v* thoir buaidh air,
ceannsaich
overdo *v* dèan tuilleadh 's
a' chòir
overdraft *n* for-tharraing *f*
overdue *a* fadalach
overflow *n* cur thairis *m* *v* cuir
thairis
overhead *adv* os cionn, gu h-àrd
overheads *n* cosgaisean a
bharrachd *f pl*
overhear *v* dèan farchluais
overload *v* an-luchdaich, cuir cus
air
overlook *v* seall thairis air;
(*forget*) dèan dearmad air
overnight *a* tron oidhche
overrule *v* bac, diùlt
overrun *v* cuir fo smachd; (*time*)
ruith thairis air ùine
overseas *a* thall thairis *adv* thall

thairis; (*motion*) a-null thairis
overshadow *v* cuir fo sgàil
oversight *n* dearmad *m*;
(*supervision*) stiùireadh *m*
overt *a* nochdte, follaiseach
overtake *v* beir air, rach seachad
air
overthrow *v* tilg sìos, cuir às do
overtime *n* ùine a bharrachd *f*,
còrr ùine *f*
overturn *v* cuir car de, cuir bun-
os-cionn
overweight *a* ro throm
owe *v* bi fo fhiachan aig;
(*gratitude*) bi an comain
(+ *gen*) **I o. him £20** tha fichead
not aige orm **he owes me £20**
tha fichead not agam air
owl *n* cailleach-oidhche *f*,
comhachag *f*
own *pron* fhèin/fèin
own *v* sealbhaich; (*admit*) gabh
ri, aidich
owner *n* neach-seilbhe *m*,
sealbhadair *m*
ownership *n* sealbh *m*
ox *n* damh *m*
oxter *n* achlais *f*
oxygen *n* ogsaidean *m*
oyster *n* eisir *m*
oystercatcher *n* trilleachan *m*
ozone *n* òson *m*, àile *m*

P

pace *n* ceum *m*; (*speed*) astar *m*
v ceumnaich, spaidsirich
pacifist *n* sìochantair *m*
pacify *v* sìthich, ciùinich
pack *n* paca *m*; (*a large number
of*) dròbh *f m* **a pack of lies** tòrr
bhreug(an) *v* pacaig; (*fill up*)
lìon
package *n* pasgan *m*, pacras *m*
p. deal tairgse iomlan *f*
packaging *n* pacaigeadh *m*,
còmhdach *m*
packet *n* pacaid *f*
packing *n* pacadh *m*, pacaigeadh
m
pact *n* cùmhnant *m*,
còrdadh *m*
pad *n* pada *f*; (*residence*) cùil *f*

paddle n pleadhag f, pleadhan m
v grunnaich, plubraich; (boat)
pleadhagaich
pagan n, a pàganach m
paganism n pàganachd f
page n duilleag f, taobh-
duilleig(e) m; (boy) gille-
frithealaidh m
pageant n taisbeanadh-gluasaid
m
pail n peile m, cuinneag f
pain n cràdh m, pian m
painful a cràiteach, piantach
painstaking a saothrachail,
mionaideach
paint n peant(a) m v peant
painter n peantair m; (boat's
rope) ball m
painting n peantadh m;
(a picture) dealbh f m
pair n càraid f, paidhir f m
v dèan càraid/paidhir
Pakistani n, a Pagastànach m,
(female) ban-Phagastànach f
pal n companach m
palace n lùchairt f
palatable a blasta
palate n càirean m, mullach-beòil
m; (met) càil f
pale a bàn
palm n bas/bois f; (tree) craobh-
phailm f
palpable a follaiseach; (tangible)
a ghabhas fhaireachdainn
palpitation n plosgartaich f
paltry a suarach
pamper v dèan cus de, peataich
pamphlet n duilleachan m, bileag
f
pan n pana m p. loaf
lof(a)-phan(a) f
pan- pref uil(e)-
panacea n uil-ìoc m
pancake n foileag f
pancreas n am brisgean milis m
pander (to) v riaraich
pane n l(e)òsan m, glainne f
panel n pannal m; (section) clàr
m
pang n biorgadh m, guin m
panic n clisgeadh m, breisleach m
pant v plosg
panther n pantar m

panting n plosgartaich f **he was
p.** bha anail na uchd, bha
aonach air
pantomime n pantomaim m
pantry n stòr-bìdh m, preas(a)-
bìdh m
pants n drathais f, pants f pl;
(trousers) briogais f
papal a pàpach
paper n pàipear m **p.-clip**
greimear-pàipeir m
v pàipearaich, boltaig
par n co-ionannachd f; (golf) an
cuibheas m **feeling below par**
gun a bhith gu math
parable n cosamhlachd f
parachute n paraisiut m
parade n (march) caismeachd f
v spaidsir
Paradise n Pàrras m
paradox n frith-bharail f, dubh-
fhacal m
paraffin n paireafain m
paragon n sàr-eisimpleir f m
paragraph n paragraf m
parallel n (line) sgrìob cho-shìnte
f; (met) samhailt f a co-shìnte;
(met) ionann
paralysis n pairilis f m
parameter n paraimeatair m,
crìoch f
paramount a os cionn gach nì,
fìor chudromach
parapet n uchd-bhalla m
paraphrase n ath-innse f; (relig)
laoidh m
parasite n dìosganach m,
faoighiche m
parasol n sgàilean-grèine m
paratrooper n saighdear
paraisiut m
parcel n parsail m, pasgan m,
trusachan m
parched a pàiteach, gus
teuchdadh/tiachdadh
pardon n mathanas m v math,
thoir mathanas **p. me** gabh mo
leisgeul
pare v beàrr, snaigh
parent n pàrant m
parish n sgìre f, paraiste f
parity n co-ionannachd f
park n pàirc(e) f **car p.** pàirc(e)

chàraichean *f* *v* parc; (*set down*) càirich
parking place *n* ionad/àite-parcaidh *m*
Parliament *n* Pàrlamaid *f*
parochial *a* sgìreachdail, sgìreil; (*met*) beag-seallaidh
parody *n* atharrais *f*
parole *n* paròil *m*
parrot *n* pitheid *f*, pearraid *f*
parry *v* dìon o bhuille; (*met*) cuir seachad
parsimonious *a* cruaidh, spìocach
parsley *n* peirsill *f*
parsnip *n* curran geal *m*
part *n* pàirt *f m*, cuid *f*, roinn *f*, cuibhreann *f m*; (*in drama*) pàirt *m* **for my p.** air mo shonsa *v* sgar, dealaich, tearb
partake *v* compàirtich
partial *a* ann an cuid; (*biased*) leth-bhreitheach **p. to** dèidheil/titheach air
participant *n* compàirtiche *m*
participate *v* compàirtich, gabh pàirt (an)
particle *n* gràinean *m*, mìrean *m*; (*gram*) mion-fhacal *m*
particular *a* àraidh, sònraichte; (*fastidious*) faiceallach
parting *n* dealachadh *m*
partisan *a* aon-taobhach, leth-bhreitheach
partition *n* balla-tarsainn *m*, tallan *m*, cailbhe *m*; (*polit*) roinn *f* *v* roinn
partly *adv* gu ìre, ann an cuid
partner *n* companach *m*; (*in business*) neach-compàirt *m* *v* rach cuide ri, rach an co-bhonn ri
partnership *n* companas *m*; (*in business*) compàirteachas *m*
partridge *n* cearc-thomain *f*
party *n* partaidh *m*; (*group*) buidheann *f m*
pass *n* (*topog*) bealach *m*; (*in games*) pas *m*
pass *v* rach/gabh seachad; (*in sport*) pas(aig); (*exam*) dèan a' chùis, pas(aig); (*eg salt*) thoir/sìn do; (*law*) dèan lagh **p. away** eug, siubhail **p. the time**

cuir seachad ùine
passage *n* turas *m*, slighe *f*; (*text*) earrann *f* **passageway** trannsa *f*
passenger *n* neach-siubhail *m pl* luchd-siubhail
passing place *n* àite-seachnaidh *m*
passion *n* boile *f*, dìoghras *m*; (*of Christ*) fulangas (Chrìosd) *m*
passionate *a* dìoghrasach
passive *a* neo-ghnìomhach; (*gram*) fulangach
passport *n* cead-siubhail *f*
password *n* facal-faire *m*
past *a* seachad **p. tense** an tràth caithte *m* *n* an t-àm a dh'fhalbh *m* *prep* seach, seachad air
paste *n* taois *f*; (*glue*) glaodh *m* *v* glaodh
pasteurize *v* paistiuraich
pastime *n* cur-seachad *m*
pastor *n* aoghair *m*
pastoral *a* (*relig*) aoghaireil; (*way of life*) treudach
pastry *n* pastraidh *m*
pasture *n* ionaltradh *m*, feurach *m*
pat *v* clapranaich
patch *n* brèid *m*, tuthag *f* *v* cuir tuthag air, cuir pìos ùr air
patently *adv* gu follaiseach
paternal *a* athaireil
path *n* starran *m*, ceum *m*, frith-rathad *m*
pathetic *a* truagh; (*awful*) cianail **a p. soul** culaidh-thruais *f*
pathology *n* galar-eòlas *m*
pathos *n* drùidhteachd *f*, truasachd *f*
patience *n* foighidinn *f*
patient *n* euslainteach *m* *a* foighidneach
patiently *adv* gu foighidneach
patriotism *n* gràdh-dùthcha *m*
patrol *n* freiceadan-faire *m*
patron *n* neach-taice *m*
patronymic *n* sloinneadh *m*
patter *n* briog-brag *m*; (*talk*) goileam *m*
pattern *n* pàtran *m*
paucity *n* gainne *f*
paunch *n* maodal *f*

pauper *n* ainnis *m*, bochd *m*
pause *n* stad *m*, anail *f* *v* stad,
fuirich
pavement *n* cabhsair *m*
pavilion *n* pàillean *m*
paw *n* spòg *f*, màg *f*
pawn *v* cuir dhan phàn
pay *n* pàigheadh *m*, tuarastal *m*
v pàigh; (*met*) dìol **p. attention
to** thoir aire (do) **you'll pay for it
yet** dìolaidh tu air fhathast
payable *a* ri p(h)àigheadh
payment *n* pàigheadh *m*
pea *n* peasair *f pl* peasraichean
peace *n* sìth *f*, fois *f*, tàmh *m*
peaceful *a* sìtheil, ciùin
peach *n* peitseag *f*
peacock *n* peucag *f*, coileach-
peucaig *m*
peak *n* (*hill*) stùc *f*, binnean *m*;
(*summit*) mullach *m*
peal *n* torrann *m*, bualadh *m*
peanut *n* cnò-thalmhainn *f*
pear *n* peur *f*
pearl *n* neamhnaid *f*
peasant *n* neach-tuatha *m*
peat *n* mòine *f*; (*single*) fàd *m*
p.-bank poll-mòna(ch)/mòna(dh)
m **p.-stack** cruach-mhòna(ch)/
mhòna(dh) *f*
pebble *n* molag *f*
peck *v* pioc; (*kiss*) thoir pògag
peculiar *a* àraid, neònach
pedal *n* casachan *m*, troighean *m*
pedantic *a* rag-fhoghlamach
peddle *v* reic, malairtich
pedestal *n* bun-carraigh *m*, bonn
m
pedestrian *n* coisiche *m*
p. precinct àrainn-choisichean *f*
a coise; (*uninspiring*) mu làimh
p. way ceum coise *m*
pedigree *n* sinnsearachd *f*
peel *n* rùsg *m*, plaosg *m* *v* rùisg
peeled *a* air a rùsgadh
peep *n* caogadh *m*, dìdeadh *m*
v caog, dìd
peer *n* (*noble*) morair *m*; (*in age*)
comhaois *m*; (*equal*) seise *m*,
co-inbheach *m*
peeved *a* leamh, tàmailteach
peewit *n* curracag *f*
peg *n* cnag *f*, ealchainn *f*

pelican *n* peileagan *m*
pellet *n* gràinnean *m*
pelt *n* bian *m*, seiche *f*
pelt *v* caith … air
pen *n* peann *m*; (*fold*) crò *m*,
buaile *f*
penalize *v* peanasaich, cuir
peanas air
penalty *n* peanas *m* **p. kick** breab
peanais *f*
pence *n* sgillinnean *f pl*
pencil *n* peansail *m* **p. sharpener**
geuraiche peansail *m*
pendant *n* crochadan *m*
pending *a* a' feitheamh, ri
t(h)ighinn
pendulum *n* cudrom-siùdain *m*
penetrate *v* drùidh, faigh tro
penetrating *a* drùidhteach; (*met*)
geurchuiseach
penguin *n* ceann-fionn *m*
penicillin *n* peinisilean *m*
peninsula *n* leth-eilean *m*
penis *n* bod *m*
penitence *n* aithreachas *m*
penitent *a* aithreachail
penknife *n* sgian-p(h)òcaid *f*
pennant *n* bratachag *f*
penniless *a* gun sgillinn
penny *n* sgillinn *f*
pension *n* peinnsean *m*
pensioner *n* peinnseanair *m*,
neach-peinnsein *m*
pensive *a* fo throm-smaoin
pentagon *n* còig-cheàrnach *m*
Pentecost *n* a' Chaingis *f*
penthouse *n* bàrr-àros *m*
penultimate *a* leth-dheireannach
people *n* sluagh *m*, muinntir *f*
pepper *n* piobar *m*
per capita *adv* gach pearsa/neach
perceive *v* mothaich, thoir fa-
near
per cent *adv* sa cheud
percentage *n* ceudad *m*, ìre sa
cheud *f*
perceptible *a* nochdte
perception *n* tuigse *f*, lèirsinn *f*
perceptive *a* lèirsinneach,
breithneachail, geurchuiseach
perch *n* spiris *f*, spàrr *m*; (*fish*)
creagag *f* *v* rach air spiris
percolate *v* sìolaidh

percolator *n* sìol(t)achan *m*
  coffee p. sìol(t)achan cofaidh
percussion *n* bualadh *m*, faram *m*
peremptory *a* obann, sparrail; (*decisive*) do-atharraichte
perennial *a* bliadhnail; (*long-lasting*) maireannach
perfect *a* coileanta, foirfe *v* dèan coileanta/foirfe
perfection *n* foirfeachd *f*, coileantachd *f*
perfectionist *n* foirfiche *m*
perforate *v* toll, cuir tuill an
perform *v* (*carry out*) dèan, coilean; (*in play*) cluich; (*stage*) cuir air àrd-ùrlar
performance *n* (*execution*) coileanadh *m*, cur an gnìomh *m*; (*on stage etc*) cluich *f* **p. indicator** comharra coileanaidh *m*
performer *n* cluicheadair *m*, cleasaiche *m*
perfume *n* cùbhrachd *f*
perhaps *adv* is dòcha (gu), math dh'fhaodte/is mathaid (gu)
peril *n* gàbhadh *m*
perilous *a* gàbhaidh
perimeter *n* cuairt-thomhas *m*
period *n* ùine *f*; (*era*) àm *m*; (*punct*) stad-phuing *f*; (*menstruation*) fuil-mìos *f*
periodically *adv* (bh)o àm gu àm
periodical *n* ràitheachan *m*, iris *f*
peripheral *a* iomallach, air an oir; (*met*) neo-chudromach
periphery *n* iomall *m*, oir *f m*
periscope *n* pearasgop *m*
perish *v* rach a dhìth, rach às an rathad
perjure *v* thoir fianais-bhrèige/mionnan-eithich
perjury *n* eitheach *f m* **commit p.** *v* thoir fianais-bhrèige/mionnan-eithich
perky *a* bideanach
perm *n* pearm *m*
permanent *a* buan, maireannach
permeate *v* rach air feadh, rach tro
permissible *a* ceadaichte
permission *n* cead *m*
permit *n* bileag-cead *f*, ceadachd *f*

v ceadaich, leig le
permutation *n* iomlaid *f*, mùthadh *m*
pernicious *a* millteach
perpendicular *a* inghearach, dìreach suas/sìos
perpetrate *v* dèan, cuir an gnìomh
perpetual *a* sìor-mhaireannach
perpetuate *v* cùm a' dol, sìor chleachd
perplex *v* cuir imcheist air
perplexed *a* imcheisteach, an imcheist
perquisite *n* frith-bhuannachd *f*
persecute *v* geur-lean, dèan geur-leanmhainn air
persecution *n* geur-leanmhainn *m*
perseverance *n* leanaltas *m*, cumail aige *f*
persevere *v* lean air, cùm aig/ri
persist *v* lean air/ri, cùm a' dol
persistent *a* leanailteach, sìor-
person *n* neach *m*, pearsa *m*
  spokesperson neach-labhairt *m*
personable *a* tlachdmhor
personal *a* pearsanta
personality *n* pearsantachd *f*
  a p. pearsa ainmeil *m*
personification *a* pearsachadh *m*
personify *v* pearsaich
personnel *n* luchd-obrach *f*, sgioba *f*, sgiobachd *f* **P. Dept** Roinn na Sgiobachd *f*
perspective *n* (*standpoint*) sealladh *m*, beachd *m*; (*in art*) buaidh-astair *f* **from my p.** na mo shealladh-sa
perspiration *n* fallas *m*
perspire *v* cuir fallas de **he was perspiring** bha fallas air/bha e a' cur falla(i)s dheth
persuade *v* cuir ìmpidh air, thoir … a thaobh, thoir air
persuasion *n* ìmpidh *f*, toirt … a thaobh *m*; (*creed*) creideamh *m*; (*values*) feallsanachd *f*
persuasive *a* buadhmhor, a bheir neach a thaobh
pervasive *a* lìonsgarach, fad' is farsaing
pertain *v* buin do
pertinent *a* iomchaidh

perturb v buair, cuir dragh air
perturbed a draghail
peruse v leugh; (*scrutinise*) sgrùd, rannsaich
pervade v lìon, rach air feadh
perverse a claon
pervert n claonaire m v claon, cuir fiaradh an
pessimism n eu-dòchas m
pessimist n neach gun dòchas m
pessimistic a eu-dòchasach
pest n plàigh f **he's a p.** 's e plàigh a th' ann
pester v cuir dragh air
pesticide n puinnsean bhiastagan m
pet n peata m
petal n flùr-bhileag f
petition n athchuinge f, tagradh m, guidhe f m v dèan athchuinge, guidh, aslaich
petrified a a' dol à cochall mo chridhe, eagal mo bheatha orm
petrol n peatrail m **p.-pump** pump(a) peatrail m
petticoat n còta-bàn m
petty a beag, suarach
petulant a bleideil
pew n suidheachan m, treasta m
pewter n feòdar m
phallic a bodail, mar bhod
phantom n taibhs(e) m, tannasg m
pharmacy n eòlas-leigheasan m; (*shop*) bùth ceimigeir f
phase n ìre f **p. in** v thoir a-steach mean air mhean **p. out** v cuir às mean air mhean
pheasant n easag f
phenomenon n iongantas m, rud air leth m
phial n meanbh-bhotal m
philanthropy n deagh euchdachd f
philology n eòlas chànan m
philosopher n feallsanach m
philosophical a feallsanachail; (*stoical*) leagte ri
philosophy n feallsanachd f
phlegm n ronn m
phone n fòn f m v fòn(aig)
phonetic a fogharach
phoney a fallsa, breugach, gun bhrìgh n mealltaire m

phosphate n fosfat m
phosphorescence n caile-bianain m, teine-sionnachain m
phosphorus n fosfor m, sionn m
photocopier n lethbhreacadair m, copaidhear m
photocopy n lethbhreac m, copaidh f v dèan lethbhreac/copaidh
photograph n dealbh camara f m v tog dealbh
photographer n neach-togail-dhealbh m
photography n togail dhealbh f
phrase n abairt f
physical a corporra **p. education** foghlam corporra m
physician n lèigh m, lighiche m
physics n fiosaig f
physiotherapist n anaclair-cuirp m
physiotherapy n anacladh-cuirp m
physique n dèanamh m
pianist n cluicheadair piàna m
piano n piàna m
pibroch n ceòl-mòr m
pick n taghadh m; (*pickaxe*) pic m, piocaid f v (*choose*) tagh, roghnaich; (*lift*) tog; (*meat off bones*) pioc, spiol
picket n piceid m
pickle n picil f v saill, cuir ann am picil
pickpocket n mèirleach-pòcaid m
picky a àilgheasach
picnic n cuirm-chnuic f
Pict n Cruithneach m
picture n dealbh f m, pioctar m
picturesque a àillidh, mar dhealbh
pie n paidh m **pie chart** clàr-cearcaill m
piece n pìos m, mìr m, earrann f, bìdeag f; (*sandwich*) pìos m
piecemeal a (*unsystematic*) bìdeagach adv (*gradually*) mean air mhean
pier n cidhe m
pierce v toll
piercing a (*sound*) biorach
piety n cràbhadh m
pig n muc f **piglet** uircean m

pigsty fail-mhuc *f*
pigeon *n* calman *m*
pig-headed *a* ceann-dàna, rag
pike *n* pìc *f*; (*fish*) geadas *m*
pile *n* dùn *m*, càrn *m*, tòrr *m*
    v càrn, cruach
pilfer *v* dèan braide, goid
pilgrim *n* taistealach *m*
pilgrimage *n* taistealachd *f*,
    taisteal *m*
pill *n* pile *f m*, gràinnean *m*
pillage *v* creach, spùill
pillar *n* carragh *f*, colbh *m*
pillow *n* cluasag *f* **p.-case**
    cuibhrig(e)-cluasaig *f m*
pilot *n* neach-iùil *m*, paidhleat *m*
    p. scheme sgeama dearbhaidh
    m   v (*guide*) treòraich, stiùir;
    (*try out*) dèan dearbhadh air,
    feuch
pimple *n* guirean *m*, plucan *m*
pin *n* prìne *m*, dealg *f* **pin cushion**
    prìneachan *m* **pins and needles**
    cadal-deilgneach *m*
pincers *n* teanchair *m*
pinch *n* bìdeag *f*, gòmag *f*; (*small
    quantity*) gràinnean *m   v* thoir
    bìdeag/gòmag à
pine *n* giuthas *m* **p. forest**
    giùthsach *m*
pine *v* searg, caith **p. for** gabh
    fadachd airson
pineapple *n* anann *m*
pink *a* pinc, ban-dhearg
pinky *n* lùdag *f*
pinnacle *n* binnean *m*, bidean *m*
pint *n* pinnt *m* **a p. of beer** pinnt
    leann(a)
pioneer *n* tùsaire *m*
pious *a* cràbhach, diadhaidh
pipe *n* pìob *f   v* cluich/seinn
    a' phìob
pipeline *n* loidhne phìoban *f* **in
    the p.** sa bheairt
piper *n* pìobaire *m*
piping *n* pìobaireachd *f*
pirate *n* spùinneadair-mara *m*
pistol *n* daga *m*
piston *n* loinid *f*
pit *n* toll *m*, sloc *m*
pitch *n* (*tar*) bìth *f*; (*sound*) àirde
    f; (*sport*) raon-cluiche *m*
pitch *v* suidhich; (*throw*) tilg;

(*target*) amais **p. tent** cuir suas
    teanta
pitfall duilgheadas *m*
pith *n* glaodhan *m*; (*met*)
    spionnadh *m*, brìgh *f*
pitiful *a* truagh
pittance *n* sùim shuarach *f*
pity *n* truas *m*, iochd *f*,
    truacantas *m* **what a p.!** 's mòr
    am beud! *v* gabh truas de/ri
pivot *n* maighdeag *f*
pizza *n* piotsa *m*
placate *v* ciùinich
place *n* àite *m*, ionad *m* **p. name**
    ainm-àite *m   v* suidhich,
    socraich, càirich, cuir
placid *a* ciùin, sèimh
plagiarism *n* mèirle-sgrìobhaidh *f*
plague *n* plàigh *f*
plaice *n* lèabag/leòbag-mhòr *f*
plaid *n* breacan *m   a* breacain
plain *n* còmhnard *m*, faiche *f*
    a rèidh, còmhnard; (*clear*)
    soilleir, plèan; (*ordinary*) plèan
plaintive *a* tiamhaidh
plait *n* figheachan *m*
plan *n* plana *m*, innleachd *f*
    development p. plana
    leasachaidh *v* dealbh, innlich,
    planaig
plane *n* plèan(a) *m*, itealan *m*;
    (*tool*) locair *f*; (*abstr*) raon *m*
    v locair, locraich
planet *n* planaid *f*
plank *n* clàr *m*, dèile *f*
planner *n* neach-dealbh(ach)aidh *m*
planning *n* dealbh(ach)adh *m*,
    planadh *m* **p. permission** cead-
    dealbh(ach)aidh *m*
plant *n* lus *m*, luibh *f m*,
    planntrais *f*; (*mech*) uidheam *m*;
    (*factory*) factaraidh *f m   v* cuir,
    planntaich; (*place*) suidhich
plantation *n* (*place*) ionad
    cuir/cura *m*; (*trees etc*)
    planntachas *m*
plaster *n* plèastar *m*, sglàib *f*;
    (*med*) plàst *m*
plaster *v* plèastair
plasterer *n* plèastair *m*
plastic *n* plastaig *f* **p. surgery** *n*
    ath-dhealbhadh bodhaig *m   a*
    plastaig

plasticine n plastasan m
plate n truinnsear m; (sheet) pleit f
platform n àrd-ùrlar m
platter n truinnsear mòr m
plausible a beulach, beulchar
play n cluich(e) m, cleas m; (stage) dealbh-chluich f m v cluich
player n cluicheadair m
playful a beadrach, sùgrach
playground n raon-cluiche m
playgroup n cròileagan m
playleader n stiùiriche-cluiche m
playwright n sgrìobhaiche dràma m, dràmadaiche m
plea n guidhe f m; (law) tagradh m
plead v guidh air; (in law) tagair; (excuse) thoir mar leisgeul
pleasant a taitneach, tlachdmhor
please v toilich, riaraich; (intrans) còrd, taitinn **if you p.** mas e do thoil e, (pl & pol) mas e ur toil e
pleased a toilichte
pleasing a tlachdmhor, càilear
pleasure n tlachd f, toileachadh m
pleat n filleadh m, pleat f v figh, cuachaich, pleat
pleated a cuachach, pleatach
pledge n geall m, gealladh m, barantas m v geall, rach an geall, thoir barantas
plenary a làn-, iomlan **p. session** làn-sheisean m
plentiful a pailt, lìonmhor
plenty n pailteas m adv gu leòr
pleurisy n an grèim mòr m, pliùrais m
pliable a sùbailte, subailte, so-lùbte
pliers n greimire m
plight n cor m, càradh m
plod v saothraich, imich gu trom
plot n (of ground) goirtean m, pìos talmhainn m; (scheme) innleachd f, guim m; (lit) plot(a) m v dèan innleachd/ guim; (track) lorg/lean slighe
plough n crann m **the P.** an Crann v treabh

ploughman n treabhaiche m
plover n feadag f
ploy n plòidh f; (tactic) cleas m
pluck v spìon, buain
plucky a tapaidh
plug n plucan m, pluga m, cnag f; (in boat) tùc m **plughole** toll-sìolaidh m v dùin, plucaich; (of product) put
plum n pluma(i)s m
plumb v feuch doimhneachd
plumb a dìreach **p.-line** sreang-dhìreach f
plumber n plumair m
plummet v tuit gu grad
plump a reamhar, tiugh, sultmhor
plunder n creach f, cobhartach f m v spuinn, creach
plunge n tumadh m v tùm; (thrust) sàth
plural a iomarra n, a iolra m
plus prep agus, le, a thuilleadh air
ply v saothraich; (supply) cùm ... ri; (shipping) ruith
pneumonia n am fiabhras-clèibhe m, teasach sgamhain f
poach v poidsig; (food) slaop
poacher n poidsear m
pocket n pòcaid f **p.-money** airgead-pòcaid m v cuir na p(h)òcaid etc, pòcaidich
pod n plaosg m
poem n dàn m, duan m
poet n bàrd m, filidh m
poetess n bana-bhàrd f
poetry n bàrdachd f
poignant a tiamhaidh
point n puing f; (headland) rubha m; (of pencil) gob m; (of view) barail f, sealladh m **what's the p.?** dè am feum a th' ann? v comharraich, seall
pointed a biorach; (remark) geur
poise n giùlan grinn m; (balance) co-chothrom m
poised a an co-chothrom, air mheidh **p. to ...** deiseil gu ...
poison n puinnsean m, nimh m v puinnseanaich
poisonous a puinnseanach, puinnseanta, nimheil
poke n (bag) poca m

poke *v* brod(an)aich; *(prod)* stob
  p. about rùraich
poker *n* brod-teine *m*, pòcair *m*
polar bear *n* mathan bàn *m*
polarize *v* pòlaraich, cuir calg-
  dhìreach an aghaidh a chèile
pole *n* pòla *m*, pòile *m*, cabar *m*
  the North P. am Pòla a Tuath
  the South Pole am Pòla a Deas
Pole *n* Pòlainneach *m*, *(female)*
  ban-Phòlainneach *f*
polecat *n* taghan *m*
police *n* poileas *m* **p. car** càr
  poilis *m* **p. officer** oifigear poilis
  m **p. station** stèisean poilis *m*
policeman *n* poileas *m*,
  poileasman *m*
policewoman *n* ban-phoileas *f*
policy *n* poileasaidh *m*
polish *n* lìomh *f*, lìomhadh *m* *v*
  lìomh, cuir lìomh air, lìomhaich
Polish *a* Pòlainneach
polished *a* lìomhte
polite *a* modhail
politic *a* glic, gleusta
political *a* poilitigeach **p. asylum**
  comraich phoilitigeach *f*
  p. party partaidh poilitigeach *m*
politically correct *a* ceart gu
  poilitigeach
politician *n* neach-poilitigs *m*
politics *n* poilitigs *f*
poll *n* cunntas cheann *m*; *(vote)*
  bhòtadh *m*; *(election)* taghadh
  m **p. tax** *n* cìs cheann *f*
pollen *n* poilean *m*
pollute *v* truaill, salaich
polluted *a* truaillte, air a
  t(h)ruailleadh *etc*
pollution *n* truailleadh *m*
polygon *n* ioma-cheàrnach *f*
pomp *n* greadhnachas *m*
pomposity *n* mòrchuis *f*
pompous *a* mòrchuiseach
pond *n* linne *f*, lòn *m*
ponder *v* beachd-smaoinich,
  cnuasaich, meòraich
ponderous *a* trom
pontificate *v* cuir às do chorp,
  dèan searmon de
pontoon *n* pontùn *m*
pony *n* pònaidh *m*
pool *n* linne *f*, glumag *f*, lòn *m*

poor *a* bochd, truagh
pop *n* *(sound)* brag *m* **p. music**
  ceòl pop *m*
Pope *n* am Pàp(a) *m*
poplar *n* pobhlar *m*
poppy *n* crom-lus *m*
popular *a* measail (aig daoine)
popularity *n* measalachd *f*
population *n* sluagh *m*; *(number)*
  àireamh-sluaigh *f*
porch *n* poirdse *m*
porcupine *n* gràineas *m*
pore *n* pòr *m*
pork *n* muicfheòil *f*, feòil muice *f*
pornography *n* drùiseantachd *f*
porous *a* pòrach, còsach
porpoise *n* pèileag *f*, cana *m*
porridge *n* lite *f*, brochan *m*
port *n* port *m*, caladh *m*, baile-
  puirt *m*; *(wine)* fìon-poirt *m*;
  (naut) clì *m*, an taobh clì *m*
portable *a* so-ghiùlan, a ghabhas
  giùlan
portent *n* comharra *m*, manadh *m*
porter *n* portair *m*, dorsair *m*;
  (drink) portair *m*
portion *n* earrann *f*, roinn *f*, cuid
  f
portrait *n* dealbh (neach) *f m*
portray *v* dèan cunntas/dealbh
Portuguese *n* Portagaileach *m*,
  (female) ban-Phortagaileach *f*;
  (lang) Portagaileis *f*
  a Portagaileach
pose *v* suidhich (thu *etc* fhèin),
  rach ann an cruth/riochd;
  (question) cuir ceist; *(problem)*
  adhbhraich; *(impersonate)* leig
  air/oirre a bhith na *etc*
posh *a* spaideil
position *n* suidheachadh *m*; *(in*
  contest) àite *m*; *(rank)* inbhe *f*,
  ìre *f*
positive *a* dòchasach,
  deimhinneach; *(certain)* dearbh-
  chinnteach; *(genuine)* dìreach,
  sònraichte **p. discrimination**
  leth-bhreith thaiceil *f*
possess *v* sealbhaich, gabh seilbh
  (de) **I don't even p. a watch** chan
  eil fiù 's uaireadair agam
possession *n* seilbh *f* **my**
  possessions mo chuid *f*

possessive *a* seilbheach
possibility *n* comas *m*,
comasachd *f*, cothrom *m*
possible *a* comasach **it is not
p. to do that** cha ghabh
sin dèanamh, tha sin
do-dhèanta
possibly *adv* is dòcha (gu), math
dh'fhaodte (gu)
post *n* post *m*; (*position*) dreuchd
f **postcode** còd puist *m* **p. office**
oifis/oifig a' phuist *f* *v* post,
cuir sa phost
postage *n* postachd *f*
postal *a* puist **p. vote** bhòt tron
phost *f*
postcard *n* cairt-p(h)uist *f*
poster *n* postair *m*
postgraduate *n* iar-cheumnaiche *m*
a iar-cheumnach
posthaste *adv* an làrach nam
bonn
postman/postwoman *n* post(a) *m*
postpone *v* cuir dàil an, cuir
dheth
postscript *n* fo-sgrìobhadh *m*
posture *n* giùlan *m*; (*polit*)
seasamh *m*
pot *n* poit *f*, prais *f*
potassium *n* potasaidheam *m*
potato *n* buntàta *m*
potbellied *a* bronnach
potent *a* cumhachdach, làidir
potential *n* comas *m* *a* comasach
air a bhith, san t-sealladh
potion *n* deoch *f*
potter *n* crèadhadair *m*
pottery *n* crèadhadaireachd *f*;
(*place*) ionad-crèadhaidh *m*
pouch *n* pòcaid *f* **tobacco p.**
spliùchan *m*
poultice *n* fuar-lit *f*
poultry *n* cearcan *f pl*
pounce *v* leum air
pound *n* punnd *m*; (*money*) nota
m **p. sterling** punnd Sasannach *m*
pound *v* pronn; (*impound*)
punnd, cuir ann am punnd;
(*strike*) buail
pour *v* (*trans*) dòirt **it poured with
rain** bha dìle uisge ann
pout *v* cuir bus/gnoig air/oirre *etc*
poverty *n* bochdainn *f*

powder *n* fùdar *m*, pùdar *m*
v cuir fùdar air; (*pulverize*)
min-phronn
power *n* cumhachd *f m*;
(*authority*) ùghdarras *m*
powerful *a* cumhachdach
powerless *a* gun chumhachd, lag
practical *a* practaigeach; (*skilled*)
deas-làmhach
practice *n* cleachdadh *m*;
(*performance*) cur an gnìomh
m; (*instrument etc*) dol thairis
air *m*
practise *v* bi ri ...; (*perform*) cuir
an gnìomh; (*instrument etc*)
rach thairis air
pragmatic *a* pragmatach
pragmatism *n* pragmatachas *m*
prairie *n* prèiridh *m*
praise *n* moladh *m*, cliù *m* *v* mol
praiseworthy *a* ionmholta, ri
m(h)oladh *etc*
pram *n* pram *m*
prance *v* leum, geàrr sùrdag
prank *n* cleas *m*
prattle *v* dèan cabadaich/
gobaireachd
prawn *n* muasgan-caol *m*
pray *v* dèan ùrnaigh *Also vn* ag
ùrnaigh
prayer *n* ùrnaigh *f* **p. meeting**
coinneamh-ùrnaigh *f*
pre- *pref* ro-
preach *v* searmonaich, teagaisg
preacher *n* searmonaiche *m*
preamble *n* facal-toisich *m*
precarious *a* cugallach
precaution *n* earalas *m*
precede *v* rach/thig ro
precedent *n* ro-shampall *m*,
eisimpleir *f m*
preceding *a* roimhe
precentor *n* neach togail fuinn *m*,
neach cur a-mach na loidhne *m*
precept *n* àithne *f*, reachd *m*
precinct *n* crìoch(an) *f pl*, àrainn
f; (*district*) ceàrn *f* **shopping p.**
àrainn bhùthan
precious *a* prìseil, luachmhor
p. stone seud *m*
precipice *n* bearradh *m*, stùc *f*
precipitate *v* (*hasten*) cabhagaich;
(*cause*) adhbhraich

precipitate *a* bras, cabhagach
precipitous *a* cas
precise *a* pongail, mionaideach
precisely *adv* gu cruinn ceart
precision *n* pongalachd *f*,
mionaideachd *f*
preclude *v* bac, dùin a-mach
precocious *a* ro-abaich,
comasach ron àm
preconception *n* ro-bheachd *m*
predator *n* sealgair *m*
predatory *a* creachach,
reubainneach
predecessor *n* neach a bh' ann
roimhe *m*
predetermine *v* ro-rùnaich
predicament *n* càs *m*, teinn *f*
predict *v* ro-inn(i)s, dean
fàisneachd air
predictable *a* ro-innseach, ris a
bheil dùil
prediction *n* fàisneachd *f*
predominant *a* as bitheanta,
buadhach
pre-empt *v* caisg ro-làimh
prefabricated *a* togte ro-làimh
preface *n* ro-ràdh *m* *v* can sa
chiad dol a-mach
prefer *v* prefers 's fheàrr le ...
preferable *a* nas fheàrr
preference *n* roghainn *m*
preferential *a* am fàbhar (neach)
prefix *n* ro-leasachan *m*
pregnancy *n* leatrom *m*
pregnant *a* trom, torrach, air
turas
prehistoric *a* ro-eachdraidheil
prejudge *v* ro-bhreithnich, thoir
ro-bhreith air
prejudice *n* claon-bhàidh/bhreith
f *v* claon-bharailich; (*damage
case etc*) dochainn, mill
prejudiced *a* le claon-bharail
preliminary *a* tòiseachail
prelude *n* ro-thachartas *m*
premature *a* an-abaich, ron àm
premeditated *a* ro-bheachdaichte
premier *n* prìomhaire *m*
a prìomh (+ *len*)
premiere *n* ciad shealladh *m*
premise *n* tùs-bheachd *m*
premises *n* aitreabh *f*, togalach *m*
on the p. san àite (fhèin)

premium *n* (*eg insurance*)
tàilleabh *m*
premonition *n* ro-fhaireachdainn
f, rabhadh *m*
prenatal *a* ro bhreith
preoccupation *n* cùram *m*
pre-ordain *v* ro-òrdaich
preparation *n* ullachadh *m*,
deasachadh *m*
prepare *v* ullaich, deasaich
prepared *a* ullaichte, deasaichte
preposition *n* roimhear *m*
prepositional pronoun *n* ro-
riochdair *m*
preposterous *a* gun sgot/chiall
prerequisite *n* riatanas *m*
Presbyterian *n*, *a* Clèireach *m*
presbytery *n* clèir *f*
prescribe *v* òrdaich, comharraich
prescribed *a* òrdaichte,
comharraichte
prescription *n* òrdugh *m*,
riaghailt *f*; (*med*) òrdugh-
cungaidh *m*
prescriptive *a* òrdachail
presence *n* làthaireachd *f*
present *n* (*time*) an t-àm (a) tha
(an) làthair *m*; (*gift*) tiodhlac *m*
at p. an ceartuair the p. day an
là an-diugh *m* the p. tense an
tràth làthaireach *m* *a* an
làthair, làthaireach
present *v* nochd, taisbean; (*give*)
thoir do, thoir seachad do,
builich (air)
presentation *n* taisbeanadh *m*;
(*gift*) tabhartas *m*
preservation *n* gleidheadh *m*
preserve *v* glèidh, cùm; (*food*)
grèidh
presidency *n* uachdranachd *f*
president *n* ceann-suidhe *m*
press *n* (*printing*) clò *m*;
(*newspapers*) na pàipearan *m*;
(*journalists*) luchd-naidheachd
m; (*cupboard*) preas *m*
p. conference coinneamh
naidheachd *f* p. release fios
naidheachd *m* p. statement
brath naidheachd *m*
press *v* fàisg, brùth, put; (*point*)
leig cuideam air; (*urge*) cuir
ìmpidh air, spàrr (air)

pressing *a* deatamach
pressure *n* bruthadh *m*,
teannachadh *m*; (*stress*)
èiginn *f*, eallach *m*; (*atmos*)
tomhas-bruthaidh *m*
p. group buidheann-tagraidh
f m
pressurize *v* cuir/leig cuideam air
prestige *n* cliù *m*, ainm *m*, teist *f*
prestigious *a* cliùiteach, a
sheallas inbhe
presumably *adv* 's fheudar (gu), a
rèir coltais
presume *v* gabh air/oirre *etc*,
rach dàn; (*assume*) bi dhen
bheachd
presumptuous *a* ladarna, dalma
presuppose *v* bi dhen bheachd;
(*imply*) gabh ris gu bheil
pretence *n* leisgeul *m*, leigeil air
m
pretend *v* leig air/oirre *etc*, cuir
an ìre
pretext *n* leisgeul *m*
pretty *a* brèagha, bòidheach *adv*
an ìre mhath
prevail *v* buadhaich **p. upon** thoir
air
prevailing *a* (*usual*) àbhaisteach
p. wind gnàth-ghaoth *f*
prevalent *a* cumanta, bitheanta
prevaricate *v* dèan breug, bi ri
mealltaireachd
prevent *v* bac, caisg
prevention *n* bacadh *m*, casg *m*
preview *n* ro-shealladh *m*
previous *a* eile
previously *adv* mu thràth, mar
tha, ro-làimh
pre-war *a* ron chogadh
prey *n* creach *f*, cobhartach *f m*
v spùinn, creach **p. upon** gabh
brath air
price *n* prìs *f* **p. list** liosta
phrìsean *f v* cuir prìs air
priceless *a* thar luach, prìseil thar
tomhais
prick *v* bior, cuir bior an; (*met*)
bior, brod, stuig
prickly *a* biorach; (*irritable*)
calgach, crosta
pride *n* pròis *f*, uaill *f*, àrdan *m*;
(*justified*) moit *f*

priest *n* sagart *m*
prim *a* ro ghrinn, ro fhìnealta
primarily *adv* sa chiad àite, gu
h-àraid
primary *a* ciad, prìomh **p. school**
bun-sgoil *f*
primate *n* àrd-easbaig *m*; (*biol*)
prìomhaid *m*
prime *a* prìomh (+ *len*) **p.**
example fìor dheagh eisimpleir
f m **P. Minister** Prìomhaire *m*
n làn-bhlàth *m*; (*phys*) trèine a
neairt *f*
prime *v* cuir air ghleus
primitive *a* prìomhadail
primrose *n* sòbhrach *f*, sòbhrag *f*
prince *n* prionnsa *m*
princess *n* bana-phrionnsa *f*
principal *n* prionnsapal *m*,
ceann(ard) *m* *a* prìomh (+ *len*)
principally *adv* gu sònraichte, gu
h-àraid
principle *n* prionnsapal *m*
principled *a* prionnsapalta, le
prionnsapail
print *n* clò *m*; (*footprint*) lorg *f*
v clò-bhuail, cuir an clò
printer *n* clò-bhualadair *m*
prior *a* ro-làimh *adv* roimhe **p. to**
their arrival mun do ràinig iad
prioritize *v* prìomhaich, dèan
prìomhachas air
priority *n* prìomhachas *m*
prison *n* prìosan *m*
prisoner *n* prìosanach *m*
pristine *a* fìorghlan, gun mheang
privacy *n* uaigneas *m*
private *a* uaigneach, dìomhair,
prìobhaideach **p. eye** lorgaire *m*
p. sector roinn phrìobhaideach
f n saighdear cumanta *m*
in p. ann an dìomhaireachd
privately *adv* gu dìomhair, os
ìosal, gu prìobhaideach
privilege *n* sochair *f*
privileged *a* fo shochair
prize *n* duais *f v* meas, cuir luach
air
proactive *a* for-ghnìomhach
probable *a* coltach
probably *adv* is dòcha
(gu/gun/gum/nach)
probation *n* pròbhadh *m*; (*period*)

àm dearbhaidh *m*
probationer *n* neach fo
dhearbhadh *m*
probe *n* (*implement*) bior-
tomhais *m*; (*inquiry*)
rannsachadh *m*; (*space*) sireadh
m *v* rannsaich, sir
problem *n* ceist *f*, duilgheadas *m*;
(*maths*) cuistean *m*
problematic *a* na cheist/
dhuilgheadas
procedure *n* modh *f m*, dòigh *f*,
dòigh-obrach *f*
proceed *v* rach air adhart, gluais,
lean (air/oirre *etc*)
proceedings *n* dol air adhart *m*,
cùisean *f pl*; (*leg*) cùis-lagha *f*
proceeds *n* teachd a-steach *m*,
toradh *m*
process *n* giullachd *f*, modh-
obrachaidh *f m*, cùrsa *m*
v làimhsich, dèilig ri
procession *n* caismeachd *f*, triall
m
proclaim *v* aithris gu follaiseach
proclamation *n* aithris
fhollaiseach *f*
procrastinate *v* dèan maill(e),
màirnealaich, cuir dheth
procrastination *n* dàil *f*, maill(e) *f*,
màirneal *m*
procreate *v* gin, sìolaich
procurator *n* procadair *m* **p. fiscal**
neach-casaid a' Chrùin *m*,
fiosgal *m*
procure *v* faigh, solaraich
prod *v* brod, stob; (*encourage*)
brosnaich
prodigal *a* strùidheil, stròdhail
the P. Son am Mac Stròdhail *m*
prodigious *a* anabarrach
produce *n* toradh *m*, cinneas *m*
produce *v* dèan; (*show*) nochd,
taisbean, thoir am follais; (*eg*
film) riochdaich
producer *n* (*eg film*) riochdaire *m*
product *n* toradh *m*; (*result*) buil
f
production *n* dèanamh *m*;
(*artistic*) riochdachadh *m*
productive *a* torrach, tarbhach
profane *a* mì-naomha
profess *v* cuir an cèill, aidich

profession *n* dreuchd *f*, obair *f*;
(*relig*) aidmheil *f*
professional *a* dreuchdail,
proifeiseanta
professor *n* (àrd-)ollamh *m*,
proifeasair *m*
proficiency *n* comas *m*, alt *m*, liut
m
proficient *a* comasach, ealanta
profile *n* leth-aghaidh *f*; (*article*)
geàrr-iomradh *m*; (*image*)
iomhaigh *f* **she has a high p.** tha
i gu mòr san fhollais
profit *n* prothaid *f*, buannachd *f*
v prothaidich, dèan prothaid à,
faigh buannachd à
profitable *a* prothaideach,
buannachdail
profligate *a* ana-caithteach, mì-
stuama
profound *a* domhainn
profuse *a* pailt
profusion *n* mòr-phailteas *m*,
sgaoilteach *f*
prognosis *n* fàisneas *m*,
ro-thuaiream *f*
programme *n* prògram *m*
v prògram
progress *n* adhartas *m* **p. report**
aithisg adhartais *f* *v* rach air
adhart
progression *n* gluasad *m*;
(*continuity*) leantainneachd *f*
progressive *a* adhartach
progressively *adv* mean air
mhean
prohibit *v* toirmisg
prohibited *a* toirmisgte
prohibition *n* toirmeasg *m*,
bacadh *m*
prohibitive *a* toirmeasgach;
(*price*) ro dhaor
project *n* pròiseact *f m*
project *v* stob a-mach; (*on*
screen) tilg; (*estimate*) dèan
ro-mheasadh
projection *n* stob *m*; (*on screen*)
tilgeil *f*; (*estimate*) ro-mheasadh *m*
projector *n* proiseactair *m*
proliferate *v* sìolaich, fàs
lìonmhor
prolific *a* torrach; (*rich in*)
beairteach

prolong v sìn a-mach, cuir
dàil an
promenade n promanàd m;
(walk) sràidireachd f
prominent a follaiseach, nochdte;
(to the fore) inbheach
promiscuous a iol-fheiseach
promise n gealladh m, gealltanas
m v geall, thoir gealladh
promising a gealltanach
promontory n rubha m, sròn f,
àird f
promote v cuir air
adhart/aghaidh; (at work)
àrdaich, thoir àrdachadh do
promotion n cur air adhart m;
(at work) àrdachadh (inbhe) m
prompt a clis, sgiobalta v spreig;
(remind) cuir an cuimhne
prone a dual, buailteach do;
(lying) air a b(h)eul fodha etc
pronoun n riochdair m **personal
p.** riochdair pearsanta
pronounce v fuaimnich; (leg)
thoir a-mach binn
pronunciation n fuaimneachadh
m
proof n dearbhadh m
prop n taic f, cùl-taic f v cùm
suas, thoir taic do, cuir taic ri
propaganda n propaganda m
propel v iomain
propeller n proipeilear m
proper a iomchaidh, cubhaidh,
dòigheil, ceart
properly adv gu cubhaidh, gu
dòigheil, (gu) ceart
property n cuid f, seilbh f;
(attribute) buadh f
prophecy n fàisneachd f,
fàidheadaireachd f
prophesy v fàisnich, dèan
fàidheadaireachd
prophet n fàidh m
propitious a fàbharach
proportion n cuid f, earrann f;
(symmetry) cumadh m,
cunbhalachd f, co-rèir m **in p.
to** a rèir
proportional a co-rèireach,
co-roinneil **p. representation**
riochdachadh co-roinneil m
proposal n (offer) tairgse f;

(motion) moladh m; (of
marriage) tairgse-pòsaidh f
propose v tairg; (motion) mol
proposition n tairgse f; (phil)
smaoineas m v (sexual) tairg
feis
proprietor n sealbhadair m
propriety n freagarrachd f,
iomchaidheachd f
propulsion n iomain f
prosaic a lom, tioram, neo-
bheothail
proscribe v toirmisg, caisg
proscribed a toirmisgte
prose n rosg m
prosecute v tog casaid an
aghaidh, cuir casaid às leth
prosecution n casaideachadh m;
(service) luchd-casaid m
prospect n (view) sealladh m;
(met) dùil f **in p.** san amharc
prospective a san amharc, ri
teachd
prospectus n ro-shealladh m;
(institutional) leabhran-iùil
oilthigh/colaiste/sgoile m
prosper v soirbhich
prosperity n soirbheachadh m
prosperous a soirbheachail
prostitute n siùrsach f, strìopach f
prostitution n siùrsachd f,
strìopachas m; (of talents) mì-
bhuileachadh m
prostrate a sleuchdte, sìnte
protect v dìon, teasraig
protection n dìon m
protective a dìona
protein n pròtain m
protest n gearan m, casaid f
v gearain, tog casaid; (against)
tog fianais an aghaidh (+ gen)
Protestant n, a Pròstanach m,
(female) ban-Phròstanach f
protester n neach-togail-fianais
m, casaidiche m
protocol n pròtacal m
protractor n protractair m
protrude v bi na stob a-mach, bi
faicsinneach
proud a pròiseil, uailleil,
àrdanach; (justifiably) moiteil
prove v dearbh; (test) feuch
proved, proven a dearbhte

proverb *n* seanfhacal *m*, gnàth-fhacal *m*

provide *v* solair, solaraich

providence *n* freastal *m*

province *n* roinn *f*

provincial *a* roinneil, a bhuineas dhan tuath; (*attitude*) beag-sheallach

provision *n* ullachadh *m*, solar *m* **provisions** lòn *m*

provisional *a* (*temporary*) sealach, car ùine; (*conditional*) air chùmhnant

proviso *n* cumha *f*, cùmhnant *m*

provocation *n* buaireadh *m*, stuigeadh *m*, cùis-fheirge *f*

provocative *a* buaireasach, buaireanta

provoke *v* cuir thuige, cuir conas air, stuig; (*engender*) adhbhraich

provost *n* pròbhaist *m*

prowess *n* comas *m*; (*in battle*) gaisge *f*

prowl *v* liùg

proximity *n* fagasachd *f*

proxy *n* neach-ionaid *m*, neach a ghabhas àite *m*

prude *n* neach nàrach *m*

prudence *n* crìonnachd *f*, faiceall *f*

prudent *a* crìonna, faiceallach, ciallach

prune *n* prùn *m*

prune *v* sgath, beàrr

psalm *n* salm *f m*

psalmody *n* salmadaireachd *f* **p. class** sgoil fhonn *f*

psalter *n* salmadair *m*

psyche *n* aigne *f*

psychiatrist *n* lighiche-inntinn *m*

psychiatry *n* leigheas-inntinn *m*

psychic *a* leis an dà shealladh; (*of psyche*) aignidheil

psychological *a* inntinn-eòlach

psychologist *n* eòlaiche-inntinn *m*

psychology *n* eòlas-inntinn *m*

ptarmigan *n* tàrmachan *m*

pub *n* taigh-seinnse *m*

puberty *n* inbhidheachd *f*

public *n* poball *m*, mòr-shluagh *m* *a* poblach **p. conveniences** goireasan poblach *m pl* **p.**

holiday saor-latha poblach *m*, latha fèille *m* **p. house** taigh-seinnse *m* **p. inquiry** rannsachadh poblach *m*

publican *n* òstair *m*

publication *n* foillseachadh *m*

publicity *n* follaiseadh *m*

publicize *v* thoir am follais

publish *v* foillsich, cuir a-mach

publisher *n* foillsichear *m*

publishing *n* foillseachadh *m*

pudding *n* (*sweet*) mìlsean *m* **black/white p.** marag dhubh/gheal *f*

puddle *n* lòn *m*

puff *n* (*of wind*) osag *f*, oiteag *f*

puffin *n* buthaid *f*

pugnacious *a* buaireanta, cogail

puke *v* sgeith, cuir a-mach

pull *n* tarraing *f*, slaodadh *m*, draghadh *m* *v* tarraing, slaod, dragh

pullet *n* eireag *f*

pulley *n* ulag *f*

pulp *n* glaodhan *m*, taois *f*, pronnach *f*

pulpit *n* cùbaid *f*

pulse *n* (*med*) buille cuisle *f*

pulverize *v* mìn-phronn

pump *n* pump(a) *m*; (*dancing shoe*) bròg-dannsa *f* *v* tarraing, pump

pun *n* cainnt-chluich *f m*, geàrr-fhacal *m*

punch *n* dòrn *m*, buille *f*; (*tool*) tollair *m*; (*drink*) puinnse *m*

punctual *a* pongail, na uair, ris an uair

punctuation *n* puingeachadh *m*, pungadh *m*

puncture *n* toll *m*, tolladh *m* *v* toll

pungent *a* searbh, geur, guineach

punish *v* peanasaich, cronaich

punishment *n* peanas *m*, cronachadh *m*

punitive *a* peanasach

puny *a* crìon, beag

pup *n* cuilean *m*

pupil *n* sgoilear *m*; (*of eye*) clach na sùla *f*

puppet *n* pupaid *f m*, gille-mirein *m*

puppy *n* cuilean *m*
purchase *v* ceannaich
pure *a* fìorghlan
purgative *n* purgaid *f*
purge *v* glan, cairt, purgaidich
purification *n* glanadh *m*
purify *v* glan
purity *n* fìorghlaine *f*
purple *a* purpaidh, corcair
purport *v* leig ort, cùm a-mach
purpose *n* adhbhar *m*, rùn *m*
purposely *adv* a dh'aon ghnotha(i)ch
purr *v* dèan crònan
purse *n* sporan *m*
pursue *v* rach às dèidh/air tòir (+ *gen*); (*met*) lean
pursuit *n* tòir *f*, ruaig *f*; (*pastime*) cur-seachad *m* **in p. of** air tòir (+ *gen*)
pus *n* iongar *m*, brachadh *m*
push *n* putag *f* *v* put; (*press*) brùth
pushchair *a* carbad-leanaibh *m*
pushy *a* aghach
put *v* cuir **put aside** cuir mu seach, cuir an dàrna taobh **put off (the light)** cuir às/dheth (an solas) **put on clothes** cuir ort/umad *etc* aodach
putrid *a* grod, lobhte
putt *v* (*golf*) amais **putting the shot** putadh na cloiche *m*
putty *n* potaidh *m*, botaidh *f*
puzzle *n* tòimhseachan *m*, dubh-fhacal *m* *v* cuir fo imcheist; (*intrans*) bi an imcheist
pygmy *n* luchraban *m*, troich *f m*
pyjamas *n* deise-leapa *f*
pylon *n* crann-dealain *m*
pyramid *n* pioramaid *f*

Q

quadrangle *n* ceithir-cheàrnag *f*
quadruple *v* ceathraich
quadruplets *n* ceathrar (san aon bhreith) *m*
quagmire *n* bog(l)ach *f*, sùil-chrithteach/chruthaich *f*
quaich *n* cuach *f*
quaint *a* neònach, seann-fhasanta
quake *v* rach air chrith, criothnaich

qualification *n* (*formal*) teisteanas *m*; (*attribute*) feart *m*; (*caveat*) ceist *f*, teagamh *m*
qualified *a* (*formally*) le teisteanas; (*equipped*) uidheamaichte; (*with caveat*) le ceist/teagamh
qualify *v* thoir a-mach teisteanas; (*be eligible*) bi freagarrach (airson)
quality *n* buadh *f*, feart *m*, gnè *f*
quandary *n* imcheist *f* **in a q.** fo imcheist, eadar dhà bharail
quango *n* cuango *m*
quantify *v* àirmhich, tomhais meud
quantity *n* meud *m*, uiread *m*, uimhir *f*
quarrel *n* aimhreit *f*, còmhstri *f*, trod *f m* *v* rach far a chèile, troid, bi ag aimhreit
quarrelsome *a* aimhreiteach, connspaideach
quarry *n* cuaraidh *f m*; (*prey*) creach *f*
quarter *n* cairteal *m*, ceathramh *m*; (*of year*) ràith(e) *f*; (*area*) ceàrn *m*; (*mercy*) tròcair *f*
q. past one cairteal/ceathramh an dèidh uair
quarterly *n* (*magazine*) ràitheachan *m* *adv* ràitheil, gach ràith(e), uair san ràith(e)
quarters *n* àite-fuirich *m*, cairtealan *m pl*
quartet(te) *n* (*group*) ceathrar *m*; (*mus piece*) ceòl-ceathrar *m*
quash *v* mùch, caisg, cuir an dara taobh
quatrain *n* ceathramh *m*, rann *m*
quaver *n* crith *f*; (*mus*) caman *m*
quay *n* cidhe *m*
queen *n* banrigh *f*
queer *a* neònach
quell *v* ceannsaich, mùch
quench *v* bàth, cuir às
quern *n* brà *f*
query *n* ceist *f*
quest *n* tòir *f*, iarraidh *m*, sireadh *m*
question *n* ceist *f*; (*doubt*) amharas *m* **q. mark** comharra-ceiste *m* *v* ceasnaich, faighnich,

feòraich; (*doubt*) cuir teagamh an
questionable *a* teagmhach, a' togail ceist
questioning *n* ceasnachadh *m*
questionnaire *n* ceisteachan *m*
queue *n* ciudha *f*
quibble *n* gearan beag-seagh *m* *v* gearain mu nithean beag-seagh
quick *a* luath, ealamh, clis
quickly *adv* gu luath, gu h-ealamh, gu clis
quid *n* nota *f*
quiet *a* sàmhach, tostach **be q.!** (e)ist! *n* sàmhchair *f*, tost *m*
quieten *v* ciùinich; (*intrans*) fàs sàmhach
quietness *n* sàmhchair *f*, ciùineas *m*
quilt *n* cuibhrig(e) *f m*
quit *v* sguir, falbh, leig seachad; (*place*) fàg
quite *adv* (*fairly*) gu math, rudeigin, lethchar; (*completely*) gu tur, gu lèir, gu h-iomlan, buileach (*with neg*) **it wasn't q. ready** cha robh e buileach deiseil
quiver *v* crith, dèan ball-chrith
quiz *n* ceasnachadh *m*, farpais-cheist *f*
quorum *n* àireamh riaghailteach *f*, cuòram *m*
quota *n* cuid *f*, cuota *m*
quotation *n* (*extract*) pìos air a thogail à *m*, às-earrann *f*; (*estimate*) tuairmeas *m*; (*valuation*) luach *m* **q. marks** cromagan turrach *f pl*
quote *n* briathran (a labhradh) *m pl*; (*estimate*) tuairmeas *m* *v* (*extract*) tog à; (*cite*) tog mar ùghdarras; (*estimate*) thoir tuairmeas

R

rabbit *n* coineanach *m*, rabaid *f*
rabble *n* gràisg *f*
rabid *a* (*lit*) cuthachail; (*met*) dearg (+ *n/a & len*)
rabies *n* fibin *f*
race *n* rèis *f*; (*ethnic*) cinneadh *m*; (*genetic*) gineal *f* **racecourse** cùrsa-rèis *m* **racehorse** steud-each *m* **r. relations** dàimh cinnidh *m* *v* ruith
racial *a* cinneadail **r. discrimination** leth-bhreith chinneadail *f*
racing *n* rèiseadh *m* **r. car** càr-rèisidh *m*
racism *n* gràin-cinnidh *f*
racist *n* neach a tha ri gràin-cinnidh *f* *a* gràin-c(h)innidheach
rack *n* ealchainn *f*; (*for torture*) inneal pianaidh *m* **going to r. and ruin** a' dol a Thaigh Iain Ghròt(a)
racket *n* (*noise*) gleadhraich *f*; (*sport*) racaid *f*
radar *n* rèidear *m*
radiant *a* lainnireach, boillsgeach, deàlrach
radiate *v* deàlraich
radiation *n* rèididheachd *f*
radical *a* radaigeach, freumhail, bunasach
radio *n* rèidio *m*, radio *m*
radioactive *a* rèidio-beò
radiography *n* rèidiografaidh *m*
radiology *n* rèidio-eòlas *m*
radiotherapy *n* gath-leigheas *m*
radish *n* meacan-ruadh *m*
radium *n* rèidium *m*
radius *n* rèidius *m*, spòg *f*
raffle *n* crannchur-gill *m*
raft *n* ràth *m*
rafter *n* cabar *m*, taobhan *m*, tarsannan *m*
rag *n* luideag *f*, clobhd(a) *m*
rage *n* boile *f*, cuthach *m*
ragged *a* luideagach
raging *a* fon chuthach, air bhoil(e)
raid *n* ruaig *f*, ionnsaigh *f*, creach *f* *v* ruag, thoir ionnsaigh (air)
raider *n* creachadair *m*, neach-ionnsaigh *m*
rail *n* rèile *f*
railway *n* rathad-iarainn *m* *a* rèile
rain *n* uisge *m* **raincoat** còta-froise *m* **rainfall** uisge *m* **rainforest** coille-uisge *f* *v* sil; (*heavily*) dòirt **it's raining** tha an t-uisge ann

rainbow *n* bogha-froise *m*
raise *v* tog, àrdaich **r. awareness** dùisg mothachadh, tog aire
raisin *n* rèiseid *f*
rake *n* ràcan *m*; (*person*) raidhc *m*, ràcaire *m* *v* ràc
rally *n* (*gathering*) cruinneachadh *m* *v* misnich, thoir cruinn; (*intrans*) ath-chruinnich; (*from illness*) ath-bheothaich
ram *n* reithe *m*, rùda *m*
ramble *n* cuairt *f*, fàrsan *m* *v* bi a' cuairtearachd/rèabhaireachd; (*in talk*) bi ri blabhdaireachd
rambler *n* ramalair *m*, fàrsanach *m*, rèabhair(e) *m*
rambling *a* fàrsanach; (*talk*) sgaoilte; (*bot*) streapach
ramification *n* ioma-bhuaidh *f*, buil *f*
ramp *n* ramp *m*
rampant *a* gun srian, gun cheannsachadh
ranch *n* rains(e) *f*
rancid *a* breun
rancour *n* gamhlas *m*
random *a* air thuaiream, tuaireamach
randy *a* macnasach
range *n* raon *m*; (*of mountains*) sreath bheanntan *f m*
rank *n* inbhe *f*; (*row*) rang *f m*, sreath *f m* **the r. and file** a' mhòr-chuid chumanta *f*, na mithean *m pl* *v* rangaich, cuir an òrdugh *a* (*intens*) tur, buileach; (*odour*) breun
rankle *v* fàg cais/ainmein air
ransack *v* rùraich; (*plunder*) creach
ransom *n* èirig *f* *v* saor/fuasgail (air èirig)
rant *v* bi ri blaomadaich **ranting and raving** ag èigheach 's ag uabhas
rap *n* buille *f*, sgailc *f*; (*on door*) gnogadh cruaidh *m* **take the rap** faigh/gabh a' choire
rape *n* èigneachadh *m* *v* èignich
rapid *a* bras, clis
rapids *n* bras-shruth *m*
rapport *n* co-bhàidh *f*
rapturous *a* mòr-aoibhneach

rare *a* tearc, ainneamh; (*in cooking*) gann-bhruich
rascal *n* blaigeard *m*, rasgal *m*
rash *n* broth *m* *a* bras, gun tùr
rasher *n* sliseag *f*
raspberry *n* subh-craoibh *m*
rat *n* radan *m*
rate *n* ìre *f*; (*speed*) astar *m* **r. of interest** ìre an rèidh *f* **the rates** na reataichean *m pl* *v* meas
rather *adv* rudeigin, car **r. than** seach, an àite (+ *gen*) **I'd r. go** b' fheàrr leam falbh
ratify *v* daingnich
ratio *n* co-mheas *m*
ration *n* cuibhreann *f m* *v* cùm ri cuibhreann
rational *a* ciallach, reusanta
rationale *n* feallsanachd *f*
rationalize *v* dèan leisgeul; (*operation etc*) cuir air stèidh ùr
rattle *n* gliogan *m*, glag *m*, glagadaich *f*; (*toy*) gliogan *m*
ravage *v* spùill, creach, cuir fàs
rave *n* hòro-gheallaidh *f m* *v* bi air bhoil(e) **r. about** dèan othail mu dheidhinn
raven *n* fitheach *m*
ravenous *a* cìocrach, gu fannachadh
ravine *n* mòr-ghil *f*
ravish *v* èignich
raw *a* amh **r. material** bun-stuth *m*
ray *n* gath *m*, leus *m*
raze *v* leag gu làr
razor *n* ealtainn *f*, ràsar *m* **r.-fish** muirsgian *f*
re- *pref* ath-
reach *v* ruig **r. for** sìn a dh'iarraidh (+ *gen*)
react *v* gluais, gabh ri, freagair **he reacted badly to it** chaidh e dona dha
reaction *n* gluasad *m*, gabhail ris *m*, freagairt *f*; (*chem*) iom-obrachadh *m*
reactor *n* reactar *m*
read *v* leugh
reader *n* leughadair *m*
readily *adv* gu toileach; (*quickly*) gu sgiobalta
reading *n* leughadh *m*

ready *a* deiseil, ullamh
reaffirm *v* daingnich
real *a* fìor
realistic *a* ciallach, practaigeach
reality *n* fìrinn *f*, fìorachd *f* **in r.**
an dà-rìribh
realize *v* tuig; (*fulfil*) thoir gu
buil; (*sell*) reic
really *adv* gu dearbh; (*sceptically*)
seadh?
realm *n* rìoghachd *f*
reap *v* buain
reaper *n* buanaiche *m*; (*mech*)
inneal-buana *m*
rear *n* deireadh *m*
rear *v* tog, àraich, altraim
reason *n* ciall *f*, reusan *m*; (*cause*)
adhbhar *m*, fàth *m*
v reusanaich
reasonable *a* reusanta, ciallach,
coltach
reasoning *n* reusanachadh *m*
reassurance *n* fois-inntinn *f*
reassure *v* thoir fois-inntinn do
reassuring *a* fois-inntinneach
rebate *n* lasachadh *m*
rebel *n* reubaltach *m* *v* dèan
ar-a-mach **r. against** rach an
aghaidh (an t-sruth)
rebellion *n* ar-a-mach *m*
rebellious *a* ceannairceach
rebound *v* leum air ais **it will r. on
him** thig e air ais air
rebuff *n* diùltadh *m*
rebuild *v* tog às ùr, ath-thog
rebuke *v* thoir achmhasan (do),
cronaich
rebut *v* dearbh ceàrr, breugnaich
recall *v* cuimhnich air, bi cuimhn'
aig; (*bring back*) thoir air ais
recap *n* ath-shùil *f*
recede *v* rach air ais, sìolaidh
receipt *n* (*written*) cuidhteas *m*
receive *v* faigh; (*react to*) gabh ri;
(*welcome*) fàiltich
recent *a* ùr, o chionn ghoirid
recently *adv* o chionn ghoirid
reception *n* gabhail ri *m*; (*in
hotel etc*) fàilteachadh *m*;
(*event*) cuirm *f*
receptionist *n* fàiltiche *m*
receptive *a* fosgailte (ri)
recess *n* cùil *f*; (*vacation*)

fosadh *m*
recession *n* crìonadh *m*, seacadh
m
recipe *n* reasabaidh *m*
recipient *n* neach-faighinn *m*,
neach a gheibh *m*
reciprocal *a* air gach taobh
reciprocate *v* dèan dha rèir
recitation *n* aithris *f*
recite *v* aithris
reckless *a* neo-chùramach
reckon *v* cunnt; (*consider*) meas
reclaim *v* thoir air ais; (*recover*)
faigh/iarr air ais
recline *v* sìn, laigh
recluse *n* aonaran *m*
reclusive *a* aonaranach,
leathoireach
recognize *v* aithnich; (*admit*)
aidich
recoil *v* leum air ais **r. from** clisg
(bh)o
recollect *v* cuimhnich
recollection *n* cuimhne *f*
recommend *v* mol
recommendation *n* moladh *m*
recommended *a* air a
m(h)oladh *etc*
recompense *n* ath-dhìoladh *m*,
èirig *f*
reconcile *v* (*bring together*) thoir
gu chèile; (*figures etc*) rèitich
they were reconciled thàinig iad
gu rèite
reconciliation *n* (*bringing
together*) toirt gu chèile *f*;
(*figures etc*) rèite *f*
reconsider *v* ath-bheachdaich
reconstruction *n* ath-thogail *f*,
ath-chruthachadh *m*
record *n* cunntas *m*, clàr *m*;
(*disc*) clàr *m* *v* clàraich, cùm
cunntas (air); (*express*) cuir an
cèill; (*mus*) cuir air clàr
recorder *n* clàradair *m*; (*mus*)
reacòrdair *m*
recording *n* clàr *m*, clàradh *m*
recount *v* aithris; (*vote*)
ath-chunnt
recoup *v* faigh air ais
recover *v* (*get back*) faigh air ais;
(*improve*) fàs nas fheàrr, rach
am feabhas

recovery *n* faighinn/faotainn air
ais *f*; (*in health*) fàs nas fheàrr
m, dol am feabhas *m*
re-create *v* ath-chruthaich
recreation *n* cur-seachad *m*
recruit *v* tog
rectangle *n* ceart-cheàrnag *f*
rectangular *a* ceart-cheàrnach
rectify *v* ceartaich, cuir ceart
rector *n* (*educ*) ceannard *m*;
(*university*) reachdair *m*; (*relig*)
ministear *m*
recuperate *v* slànaich, rach am
feabhas
recur *v* tachair a-rithist
recurrent *a* tillteach
recycle *v* ath-chleachd, ath-
chuartaich
recycling *n* ath-chleachdadh *m*,
ath-chuartachadh *m*
red *a* dearg; (*hair*) ruadh
redeem *v* (*save*) saor, fuasgail;
(*fin*) ath-cheannaich
redirect *v* ath-sheòl
redistribute *v* ath-riaraich
redouble *v* (*efforts*) dèan spàirn is
ath-spàirn
redraft *v* ath-dhreachd
redress *n* (*fin*) ath-dhìoladh *m*;
(*leg*) furtachd *f*
reduce *v* lùghdaich, ìslich
reduced *a* lùghdaichte, air a
lùghdachadh
reduction *n* lùghdachadh *m*,
beagachadh *m*, ìsleachadh *m*
redundancy *n* pàigheadh dheth
m; (*superfluity*) anbharr *m*
r. pay airgead pàigheadh
dheth *m*
redundant *a* anbharra, gun
fheum; (*idle*) gun obair **they
were made r.** chaidh am
pàigheadh dheth
reed *n* cuilc *f*; (*mus*) ribheid *f*
reef *n* bodha *m*, sgeir *f*; (*a sail*)
riof *f*
reek *v* (*smell*) cuir fàileadh
dheth/dhith *etc*; (*smoke*) cuir
smùid/toit dheth/dhith *etc*
reel *n* r(u)idhle *m*; (*of thread*)
piorna *f m*
re-elect *v* ath-thagh
re-examine *v* ath-sgrùd

refectory *n* biadhlann *f*
refer (to) *v* thoir iomradh/tarraing
air; (*pass to*) cuir gu; (*send
back*) till air ais
referee *n* rèitire *m*; (*for job*)
teistiche *m*
reference *n* iomradh *m*, tarraing
f; (*testimonial*) teisteanas *f* **with
r. to** a thaobh (+ *gen*) **r. book**
leabhar-fiosrachaidh *m*
referendum *n* reifreann *m*,
referendum *m*
refine *v* glan; (*met*) grinnich
reflect *v* tilg air ais; (*think*)
meòraich, cnuasaich
reflection *n* faileas *m*; (*in mirror*)
dealbh-sgàthain *f m*; (*thought*)
meòrachadh *m*, cnuasachadh *m*
reflective *a* meòrachail,
breithneachail
reflex *a* neo-shaor-thoileach
reform *n* leasachadh *m*, ath-
leasachadh *m* *v* leasaich, ath-
leasaich
reformation *n* ath-leasachadh *m*
the R. an t-Ath-Leasachadh
refrain *v* cùm (bh)o, sguir
refresh *v* ùraich
refreshment *n* (*drink*) deoch *f*;
(*renewal*) ùrachadh *m*
refrigerator *n* inneal-
fionnarachaidh *m*, frids *m*
refuel *v* ath-chonnaich, lìon le
connadh a-rithist
refuge *n* tèarmann *m*, dìdean *m*
refugee *n* fògarrach *m*
refund *n* airgead air ais *m*
v pàigh air ais, ath-dhìol
refuse *n* sgudal *m*, sprùilleach *m*
refuse *v* diùlt
refute *v* dearbh ceàrr, breugnaich
regain *v* ath-choisinn,
ath-shealbhaich
regal *a* rìoghail
regard *n* meas *m*, sùim *f*, spèis *f*
with kind regards leis gach
deagh dhùrachd **as regards**
a thaobh (+ *gen*) *v* (*consider*)
meas; (*esteem*) thoir spèis
do; (*pay heed to*) thoir aire
do
regardless *adv* a dh'aindeoin
(sin)

regatta *n* rèisean shoithichean *f pl*
regenerate *v* ath-nuadhaich
regeneration *n* ath-nuadhachadh *m*
regime *n* riaghladh *m*; (*system*) rèim *f*
regiment *n* rèisimeid *f*
region *n* roinn *f*, ceàrn *f*
regional *a* roinneil, roinne
register *n* clàr *m* **cash r.** clàradair airgid *m v* clàraich; (*reveal*) leig ris; (*show up*) nochd
registrar *n* neach-clàraidh *m*
registration *n* clàradh *m*
registry *n* ionad-clàraidh *m*
regret *n* aithreachas *m*; (*sorrow*) duilichinn *f v* gabh aithreachas; (*be sorry*) bi duilich
regrettable *a* na adhbhar aithreachais; (*sad*) duilich
regular *a* cunbhalach, riaghailteach
regularity *n* cunbhalachd *f*
regulate *v* riaghlaich, rèitich
regulation *n* riaghailt *f*; (*act of*) riaghladh *m*
rehearsal *n* ruith thairis *f*
rehearse *v* ruith thairis air; (*go through*) ath-aithris
reign *n* rìoghachadh *m*
reimburse *v* pàigh air ais (airson)
rein *n* srian *f*
reindeer *n* rèin-fhiadh *m*
reinforce *v* daingnich, neartaich
reinstate *v* ath-shuidhich
reissue *v* cuir a-mach às ùr, ath-sgaoil
reiterate *v* ath-aithris
reject *v* diùlt
rejoice *v* dèan gàirdeachas/ aoibhneas
rekindle *v* ath-bheothaich
relapse *n* tuiteam air ais *m*; (*med*) tilleadh tinneis *m*
relate *v* innis, aithris
related (to) *a* co-cheangailte ri; (*family*) càirdeach (do), an dàimh ri **r. by marriage** ann an cleamhnas
relation *n* co-cheangal *m*; (*relative*) neach-dàimh *m*, dàimh *m* **in r. to** ann an dàimh ri
relationship *n* càirdeas *m*, dàimh

m **be in a r. with ...** a bhith a' falbh le ...
relative *n* neach-dàimh *m, pl* luchd-dàimh *m*, càirdean *m a* dàimheach **r. to** an coimeas ri
relaunch *v* cuir air bhog a-rithist
relax *v* gabh fois; (*rules etc*) lasaich, fuasgail
relaxation *n* fois *f*, tàmh *m*; (*pastime*) cur-seachad *m*
relaxed *a* socrach
relay *n* sreath (mu seach) *f m* **r. race** rèis phàirteach *f v* (*news etc*) sgaoil
release *v* fuasgail, leig às, cuir/leig mu sgaoil
relegate *v* cuir sìos
relent *v* taisich, gabh truas
relentless *a* gun sgur, gun abhsadh; (*implacable*) neo-thruacanta
relevance *n* buntainneas *m*
relevant *a* buntainneach, a' buntainn ri
reliable *a* earbsach
reliance *n* earbsa *f*, muinighin *f*
relief *n* fao(tha)chadh *m*, furtachd *f*; (*help*) cobhair *f*, cuideachadh *m*
relieve *v* furtaich, thoir fao(tha)chadh do; (*help*) cuidich **we were relieved** fhuair sinn fao(tha)chadh
religion *n* creideamh *m*
religious *a* cràbhach, diadhaidh
relinquish *v* leig/thoir seachad
relish *v* gabh fìor thlachd de/an
relocate *v* gluais (gu àite eile)
reluctant *a* ain-deònach **I was r. to do that** bha leisg(e) orm sin a dhèanamh
rely *v* cuir earbs(a) (an/ri)
remain *v* fuirich, fan
remainder *n* fuidheall *m*, còrr *m*
remains *n* fuidhleach *m*; (*corpse*) dust, duslach *m*
remark *n* iomradh *m*, facal *m v* thoir iomradh air; (*notice*) thoir fa-near
remarkable *a* sònraichte, suaicheanta, iongantach
remedial *a* leasachail

remedy *n* (*med*) leigheas *m*,
ìocshlaint *f*; (*solution*)
leasachadh *m* *v* leighis,
slànaich; (*solve*) leasaich
remember *v* cuimhnich
remind *v* cuir an cuimhne,
cuimhnich do
reminisce *v* cuimhnich (air)
remiss *a* dearmadach,
neo-shuimeil
remit *n* raon-dleastanais/
ùghdarrais *m*
remit *v* cuir air falbh; (*refer back*)
till, cuir air ais; (*cancel*) math
remittance *n* pàigheadh *m*, sùim
airgid *f*
remnant *n* fuidheall *m*, iarmad *m*
remorse *n* dubh-aithreachas *m*,
agartas-cogais *m*
remorseful *a* làn aithreachais
remote *a* iomallach, cian, fad' às
removal *n* gluasad *m*; (*flitting*)
imrich *f*
remove *v* thoir air falbh; (*move*)
gluais
remunerate *v* ìoc do, pàigh
renaissance *n* ath-bheothachadh
m **the R.** Linn an
Ath-Bheothachaidh *f m*
rend *v* srac, reub
render *v* (*pay*) ìoc, liubhair;
(*make*) dèan
rendezvous *n* àite-coinneachaidh
m
renew *v* ath-nuadhaich, ùraich
renewal *n* ath-nuadhachadh *m*,
ùrachadh *m*
rennet *n* binid *f*
renounce *v* leig bhuat, trèig, cuir
cùl ri
renovate *v* ùraich, nuadhaich
renovation *n* nuadhachadh *m*,
ùr-sgeadachadh *m*
renown *n* cliù *m*
renowned *a* cliùiteach,
iomraiteach
rent *n* sracadh *m*, reubadh *m*;
(*fin*) màl *m* *v* gabh air mhàl
rented *a* air mhàl
re-open *v* fosgail às ùr
reorganization *n* ath-eagrachadh
m, ath-òrdachadh *m*
reorganize *v* ath-eagraich, cuir

rian ùr air
repair *v* càirich **r. to** tog air/oirre
etc gu
repay *v* pàigh air ais
repayment *n* pàigheadh air ais *m*
repeal *v* cuir à bith
repeat *v* can a-rithist, ath-aithris
repeatedly *adv* uair is uair
repel *v* till; (*be offensive to*)
sgreamhaich, cuir sgàig air
repent *v* dèan/gabh aithreachas
repercussion *n* toradh *m*, buil *f*
repetition *n* ath-aithris *f*, ath-
innse *f*
repetitive *a* a-rithist is a-rithist
replace *v* gabh àite (+ *gen*)
r. ... with ... cuir ... an àite ...
re-plant *v* cuir a-rithist, ath-chuir
replay *n* ath-chluich *f*
v ath-chluich
replenish *v* ath-lìon
replete *a* làn, buidheach
replica *n* mac-samhail *m*
reply *n* freagairt *f* *v* freagair
report *n* aithisg *f*, iomradh *m*
v thoir cunntas/iomradh (air),
dèan aithisg (air)
reporter *n* neach-naidheachd *m*
repossess *v* ath-shealbhaich,
thoir air ais (bh)o
represent *v* riochdaich
representation *n* riochdachadh *m*
representative *n* riochdaire *m*
a riochdachail, samhlach
repression *n* mùchadh *m*,
ceannsachadh *m*
reprieve *n* allsachd *f*
reprimand *n* achmhasan *m* *v*
cronaich, thoir achmasan do
reprint *v* ath-chlò-bhuail
reprisal *n* dìoghaltas *m*
reproach *n* cronachadh *m*;
(*disgrace*) masladh *m* **beyond r.**
gun choire sam bith
reproduce *v* gin; (*copy*) mac-
samhlaich
reproduction *n* gintinn *m*; (*copy*)
mac-samhlachadh *m*
reptile *n* pèist *f*, snàgair *m*
republic *n* poblachd *f*
republican *n, a* poblachdach *m*
repudiate *v* cuir cùl ri, diùlt
gabhail ri

repulse *v* ruaig, cuir ruaig air
repulsive *a* gràineil, oillteil
reputable *a* le deagh chliù, measail
reputation *n* cliù *m*, ainm *m*
request *n* iarrtas *m* *v* iarr
require *v* feum; (*ask*) iarr
requirement *n* riatanas *m*, feumalachd *f*
requisite *a* riatanach, air a bheil feum
rescue *n* sàbhaladh *m*, teasairginn *f* *v* sàbhail, teasairg
research *n* rannsachadh *m*, sgrùdadh *m* *v* rannsaich, dèan sgrùdadh
researcher *n* neach-rannsachaidh *m*, rannsaiche *m*
resemble *v* bi coltach ri
resent *v* fairich searbh mu, gabh san t-sròin
resentful *a* searbh, tàmailteach
resentment *n* tàmailt *f*
reservation *n* (*doubt*) cumha *f m*, teagamh *m*; (*booking*) ro-chlàradh *m*
reserve *v* glèidh, taisg
reserved *a* fad' às, dùinte; (*place, polit*) glèidhte
reservoir *n* tasgadh-uisge *m*; (*met*) stòr *m*, stòras *m*
reside *v* fuirich, gabh còmhnaidh an
residence *n* àite/ionad-còmhnaidh *m*, àros *m*
resident *n* neach-còmhnaidh *m*
residential *a* còmhnaidheach
residue *n* fuidheall *m*, còrr *m*
resign *v* leig dheth/dhith *etc* dreuchd, thoir suas; (*yield*) gèill, bi leagte ri
resignation *n* leigeil dheth/dhith *etc* dreuchd *m*; (*yielding*) gèilleadh *m*
resilient *a* fulangach
resin *n* ròiseid *f*, bìth *f*
resist *v* strì, cuir an aghaidh
resistance *n* strì *f*, cur an aghaidh *m*
resolute *a* seasmhach, gramail
resolution *n* (*outcome*) fuasgladh *m*; (*decision*) rùn *m*; (*resolve*) seasmhachd *f*

resolve *n* rùn suidhichte *m* *v* cuir romhad, rùnaich; (*solve*) fuasgail, rèitich
resonant *a* ath-fhuaimneach; (*met*) a' dùsgadh …
resort *n* baile turasachd *m*; (*recourse*) innleachd *f*, dòigh *f*
resource *n* goireas *m*, stòras *m*; (*ingenuity*) innleachd *f*; (*fin*) ionmhas *m* **r. centre** ionad ghoireasan *m*
resourceful *a* innleachdach
respect *n* spèis *f*, urram *m* **with r. to** a thaobh (+ *gen*) *v* thoir spèis/urram do
respectable *a* measail, coltach
respectful *a* modhail, suimeil
respectively *adv* fa leth
respite *n* fao(tha)chadh *m*, anail *f* **r. care** cùram fao(tha)chail *m*
respond *v* (*answer*) freagair; (*act on*) dèilig ri
response *n* freagairt *f*
responsibility *n* dleastanas *m*, cùram *m*, uallach *m*
responsible *a* cùramach; (*accountable*) cunntachail; (*behaviour*) ciallach **r. for** an urra ri
responsive *a* freagairteach, mothachail
rest *n* fois *f*, tàmh *m*; (*mus*) clos *m* **the r.** (*persons*) càch; (*things*) an còrr *v* gabh fois, leig anail
restaurant *n* taigh-bìdh *m*
restful *a* socair, foiseil
restless *a* an-fhoiseil, mì-stòlda, luasganach, idrisgeach
restore *v* dèan suas às ùr; (*give back*) thoir air ais; (*of health*) aisig gu slàinte
restrain *v* bac, caisg, ceannsaich
restrained *a* sriante, fo srian
restraint *n* (*curb*) bacadh *m*, casg *m*; (*self-control*) smachd *m*
restrict *v* cuingealaich, cuibhrich
restricted *a* cuingealaichte
restriction *n* cuingealachadh *m*, cuibhreachadh *m*
result *n* buil *f*, toradh *m* **you'll see the r.!** bidh a' bhuil ann!
resume *v* tòisich a-rithist; (*recover*) gabh air ais

resurgence *n* ath-bheothachadh *m*, dùsgadh *m*

resurrection *n* aiseirigh *f*

resuscitate *v* ath-bheothaich

retail *a* bùtha

retailer *n* ceannaiche *m*, marsanta *m*

retain *v* cùm, glèidh

retaliate *v* dìoghail, sabaidich air ais

retaliation *n* dìoghaltas *m*, sabaid air ais *f*

retard *v* bac, cùm air ais

retch *v* sgeith

retention *n* cumail *f*, gleidheadh *m*

retentive *a* glèidhteach

reticent *a* dùinte, diùid

retire *v* rach air chluainidh, leig dheth/dhith dreuchd *etc* **I retired** leig mi dhìom mo dreuchd

retired *a* air chluaineas/chluainidh

retirement *n* cluaineas *m*, leigeil dheth/dhith *etc* dreuchd *m*

retort *n* freagairt gheur *f* *v* freagair gu geur/bras

retrace *v* rach air ais air

retract *v* tarraing air ais

retreat *n* ionad dìomhair *m*; (*eccl*) tèarmann *m*; (*mil*) ratreut *m* *v* teich, tarraing air ais

retrieve *v* faigh air ais; (*met*) leasaich

retrograde *a* ais-cheumach **a r. step** ceum air ais *m*

retrospect *n* coimhead/sealltainn air ais *m* **in r.** le sùil air ais

retrospective *a* ais-sheallach

return *n* tilleadh *m*; (*fin*) prothaid *f* **r. fare** faradh gach rathad *m* *v* till; (*give back*) cuir/thoir air ais

reunion *n* ath-choinneachadh *m*

reveal *v* nochd, taisbean, foillsich, leig ris

revealing *a* nochdte, follaiseach

revelation *n* taisbeanadh *m*; (*eyeopener*) sùileachan *m* **Book of Revelations** Leabhar an Taisbeanaidh *m*

revelry *n* fleadhachas *m*

revenge *n* dìoghaltas *m* **take r. on** *v* dèan dìoghaltas air

revenue *n* teachd a-steach *m* **Inland R.** Oifis nan Cìsean *f*

reverberate *v* ath-ghairm; (*affect*) thoir buaidh air

reverence *n* urram *m*, ùmhlachd *f*

reverend *a* urramach **the Rev** an t-Urramach (an t-Urr)

reverent *a* a' nochdadh spèis/urraim

reverse *v* rach air ais; (*overturn*) cuir car de

revert *v* till (gu)

review *n* breithneachadh *m*; (*arts*) lèirmheas *m*, sgrùdadh *m* *v* dèan breithneachadh air; (*arts*) dèan lèirmheas air, sgrùd

reviewer *n* lèirmheasaiche *m*

revise *v* ath-sgrùd, thoir sùil air ais air

revision *n* ath-sgrùdadh *m*, sùil air ais *f*

revitalise *v* ath-bheothaich

revival *n* ath-bheothachadh *m*; (*relig*) dùsgadh *m*

revive *v* ath-bheothaich, dùisg; (*trans*) ùraich

revoke *v* tarraing air ais

revolt *n* ar-a-mach *m*

revolting *a* gràineil, sgreamhail

revolution *n* car *m*, cuairt iomlan *f*; (*polit*) reabhlaid *f*, ar-a-mach *m*; (*met*) cruth-atharrachadh *m*, làn-thionndadh *m*

revolutionary *n* reabhlaideach *m*, neach ar-a-mach *m* *a* gu tur ùr; (*polit*) reabhlaideach

revolve *v* rach mun cuairt

revulsion *n* sgàig *f*

reward *n* duais *f* *v* thoir duais

rewrite *v* ath-sgrìobh

rhetoric *n* ùr-labhairt *f*, deaschainnt *f*; (*pej*) glòireis *f*

rhetorical *a* ùr-labhrach, deaschainnteach; (*pej*) glòireiseach

rheumatism *n* lòinidh *f m*

rhinoceros *n* sròn-adhairceach *m*

rhododendron *n* ròs-chraobh *f*

rhubarb *n* rùbarab *m*, ruadh-bhàrr *m*

rhyme *n* comhardadh *m* **internal r.** uaithne *m* *v* dèan comhardadh; (*compose a verse*) dèan rann

rhythm *n* ruitheam *m*, ruith *f*
rib *n* asna *f m pl* asnaichean, aisean *f pl* aisnean
ribbon *n* ribean *m*, ribinn *f*
rice *n* rus *m*
rich *a* beairteach, saidhbhir; (*soil*) torrach
riches *n* beairteas *m*, saidhbhreas *m*
rick *n* coc *f m*, cruach *f*
rid *v* saor, fuasgail **get r. of** faigh cuidhteas (+ *nom*)
riddle *n* tòimhseachan *m*; (*agric*) ruideal *m*, criathar garbh *m*
ride *v* marcaich
rider *n* marcaiche *m*
ridge *n* druim *m*
ridicule *n* sgeig *f*, fanaid *f v* dèan fanaid air, dèan cùis-bhùirt de
ridiculous *a* gòrach, amaideach, luideach
riding *n* marcachd *f*
rife *a* pailt, lìonmhor
rifle *n* raidhfil *f*, isneach *f*
rift *n* sgoltadh *m*; (*between people*) sgaradh *m*
rig *n* rioga *f*; (*agric*) feannag *f* **oilrig** crann-ola *m v* (*equip*) uidheamaich, beartaich; (*manipulate*) claon
right *n* còir *f*, dlighe *f*; (*justice*) ceartas *m a* ceart; (*hand etc*) deas **r. away** sa bhad *v* cuir ceart
righteous *a* ionraic, fìreantach
rightful *a* dligheach
rights *n* còraichean *f pl* **civil r.** còraichean catharra
rigid *a* rag, do-lùbaidh
rigorous *a* cruaidh, mion
rigour *n* cruas *m*
rim *n* oir *f m*, bile *f*, iomall *m*
rind *n* rùsg *m*
ring *n* fàinne *f m*; (*area*) cearcall *m*, buaile *f* **r. finger** mac an aba *m* **r.-road** cuairt-rathad *m v* seirm **r. the bell** brùth an clag
rink *n* rinc *m* **ice r.** rinc deighe *m*
rinse *v* sgol, sruthail
riot *n* ùpraid *f*, iorghail *f*
riotous *a* ùpraideach, iorghaileach; (*prodigal*) stròdhail
rip *v* srac, reub

ripe *a* abaich
ripen *v* abaich
ripple *n* crith *f*, luasgan *m*, caitean *m*
rise *v* èirich
risk *n* cunnart *m v* feuch; (*put at risk*) cuir an cunnart
risky *a* cunnartach
ritual *n* deas-ghnàth *m*
rival *n* co-dheuchainniche *m*, co-fharpaiseach *m*
rivalry *n* còmhstri *f*, farpais *f*
river *n* abhainn *f*
riveting *a* aire-tharraingeach, drùidhteach
road *n* rathad *m* **r. sign** soidhne rathaid *f*
roam *v* rach air fàrsan
roar *n* beuc *m*, glaodh *m*, bùirean *m v* beuc, glaodh
roast *n* ròst *f m* **r. beef** mairtfheòil ròsta *f v* ròist
rob *v* robaig, creach, goid air
robber *n* robair *m*, gadaiche *m*
robbery *n* goid *f*, robaireachd *f*, gadachd *f*
robe *n* fallaing *f*, trusgan *m*
robin redbreast *n* brù-dhearg *m*
robust *a* calma, làidir, foghainteach
rock *n* creag *f*, carraig *f*; (*substance*) clach *f*
rock *v* luaisg, tulg
rocket *n* rocaid *f*
rocking chair *n* sèithear-tulgaidh *m*
rocking horse *n* each-tulgach *m*
rock music *n* ceòl rog *m*
rocky *a* creagach
rod *n* slat *f*
rodent *n* criomach *m*
roe *n* earb *f*, ruadhag *f*; (*of fish*) iuchair *f*, glasag *f* **roebuck** boc-earba *m*
rogue *n* slaightear *m*, rògaire *m*
role *n* pàirt *f m*; (*in org*) dreuchd *f*; (*in society*) àite *m* **r.-play** gabhail riochd *m*
roll *n* roile *f m v* roilig, cuir car air char; (*fold*) paisg, fill
roller *n* roilear *m* **r.-coaster** roilear-còrsair *m* **r.-skate** bròg-roth *f*

Roman *n*, *a* Ròmanach *m*,
(*female*) ban-Ròmanach *f*
Roman Catholic *n*, *a* Caitligeach
m, (*female*) ban-Chaitligeach *f*
romance *n* romansachd *f*; (*story*)
sgeul romansach *m*; (*love affair*)
suirghe *f*
romantic *a* romansach
romp *v* bi a' ruideal
rone *n* guitear *m*, ròn *f*
roof *n* mullach *m*
rook *n* ròca(i)s *f*
room *n* rùm *m*, seòmar *m*;
(*space*) àite *m*, rùm *m*
roomy *a* rùmail, farsaing
roost *n* spàrr *m*, spiris *f*
root *n* freumh *m*, bun *m*
rope *n* ròp(a) *m*, ball *m*
rosary *n* a' chonair(e) *f*, paidirean
m
rose *n* ròs *m*
rot *n* grodadh *m*, lobhadh *m*
v grod, lobh
rota *n* clàr-dleastanais *m*
rotate *v* cuir mun cuairt; (*intrans*)
rach mun cuairt
rotten *a* grod, lobhte, breun
rotter *n* trustar *m*
rotund *a* cruinn
rough *a* garbh; (*hairy*) molach;
(*temper*) garg
roughness *n* gairbhead *m*, gairge
f
round *n* cuairt *f*, car *m* *a* cruinn
adv mun cuairt, timcheall
roundabout *n* timcheallan *m*,
cearcall-rathaid *m*
rouse *v* dùisg; (*stimulate*)
brosnaich, piobraich
rousing *a* brosnachail,
spreigearra
rout *n* ruaig *f*, sgiùrsadh *m*
v rua(i)g, sgiùrs
route *n* rathad *m*, slighe *f*
routine *n* gnàth-chùrsa *m*
a gnàthach
rove *v* bi a' ruagail, bi
a' rèabhaireachd
row *n* (*line*) sreath *f m*
row *n* (*quarrel*) sabaid *f*, trod *m*
v trod
row *v* (*boat*) iomair
rowan *n* caorann *m*

rowdy *a* gleadhrach
rowing *n* iomradh *m* **r. boat** bàta-
ràmh *m*, geòla *f*
royal *a* rìoghail **the R. Family** an
Teaghlach Rìoghail *m*
royalty *n* rìoghalachd *f*; (*fin*)
dleasadh ùghdair *m*
rub *v* suath
rubber *n* rubair *m*
rubbish *n* sgudal *m*, treal(l)aich *f*
it's just r. chan eil ann ach
frachd **r. bin** biona-sgudail *m*
r. dump lagais *f*, òtrach *m*
ruby *n* ruiteachan *m*, rùbaidh *f*
rucksack *n* màileid-droma *f*
rudder *n* stiùir *f*, falmadair *m*
ruddy *a* ruiteach, ruadh
rude *a* mì-mhodhail
rudeness *n* mì-mhodh *m*
rudimentary *a* tòiseachail
rue *v* gabh aithreachas mu
rueful *a* dubhach, brònach, leamh
ruffian *n* brùid *f m*
ruffle *v* dèan ain-rèidh; (*met*) cuir
colg air
rug *n* ruga *m*, brat-ùrlair *m*
rugby *n* rugbaidh *m*
rugged *a* garbh, corrach
ruin *n* sgrios *m*; (*site*) làrach *f m*,
tobhta *f* *v* sgrios, mill
rule *n* riaghailt *f*; (*exercise of*)
ceannas *m* **as a r.** mar as trice
v riaghail, riaghlaich
ruler *n* riaghladair *m* **rulers**
luchd-riaghlaidh *m pl*;
(*measuring*) rùilear *m*
rum *n* ruma *m*
rumble *v* dèan torrann; (*stomach*)
bi a' rùchdail
rumbling *n* torrann *m*, brùnsgal *f*;
(*stomach*) rùchdail *f*
rummage *v* rùraich
rumour *n* fathann *m*
rump *n* dronn *f*, rumpall *m*
run *n* ruith *f*; (*transport*) slighe *f*
v ruith; (*flee*) teich; (*melt*) leagh
runner *n* neach-ruith *m*
running *n* ruith *f* **r. costs** cosgais
ruith *f*
runway *n* raon-laighe *m*
rupture *v* bris(t), sgàin, sgaoil
rural *a* dùthchail
ruse *n* innleachd *f*, clìc *f*

rush *n* dian-ruith *f*, sitheadh *m*, roid *f v* dèan cabhag/sitheadh **r. out** brùchd a-mach
rushes *n* luachair *f*
Russian *n*, *a* Ruiseanach *m*, *(female)* ban-Ruiseanach *f*; *(lang)* Ruisis *f*
rust *n* meirg *f v* meirg(ich)
rustic *a* dùthchail
rustling *n* siosarnaich *f*
rusty *a* meirgeach
rut *n* clais *f*; *(of deer)* dàmhair (nam fiadh) *f* **in a rut** san aon imire/eag
ruthless *a* cruaidh; *(pitiless)* gun iochd
rye *n* seagal *m*

S

Sabbath *n* an t-Sàbaid *f* **S. Day** Latha na Sàbaid *m*
sabotage *n* sabotàis *f*
sack *n* poca *m*, sac *m* **s.-race** rèis a' phoca *f*
sack *v (from work)* cuir à obair; *(destroy)* sgrios, creach
sacred *a* naomh, coisrigte
sacrifice *n* ìobairt *f v* ìobair
sacrilege *n* ceall-shlad *m*, airchealladh *m*
sad *a* brònach, dubhach, muladach; *(pitiful)* truagh
sadden *v* cuir bròn air, dèan dubhach
saddle *n* dìollaid *f*
sadness *n* bròn *m*, mulad *m*
safe *a* sàbhailte, tèarainte **s. and sound** slàn sàbhailte *n* ciste-tasgaidh *f*
safeguard *n* dìon *m v* dìon, geàrd
safety *n* sàbhailteachd *f*, tèarainteachd *f* **s.-belt** crios-sàbhalaidh *m* **s.-pin** prìne (banaltraim) *m*
sag *v* tuit
saga *n* sgeulachd *f*, mòr-sgeul *m*
sage *n (bot)* slàn-lus *m*; *(person)* saoi *m*
sail *n* seòl *m v* seòl, bi a' seòladh
sailor *n* seòladair *m*, maraiche *m*
saint *n* naomh *m*

saithe *n* saoithean *m*
sake *n* sgàth *m* **for the s. of** air sgàth (+ *gen*)
salad *n* sailead *m* **s. dressing** annlann sailead *m*
salary *n* tuarastal *m*
sale *n* reic *m*; *(reduced prices)* reic-saor *m* **s. of work** fèill-reic *f*
salesman fear-reic *m*
salesperson neach-reic *m*
saliva *n* seile *m*
salivate *v* seilich
sallow *a* lachdann
salmon *n* bradan *m*
salon *n* ionad *m* **beauty s.** ionad maise
salt *n* salann *m* **s. cellar** saillear *m* **s.-water** sàl *m a* saillte *v* saill
saltire *n* bratach na croise *f*
salty *a* saillte
salubrious *a* greadhnach
salutary *a* tairbheach **a s. warning** rabhadh feumail *m*
salute *n (mil)* nochdadh urraim *m v* nochd urram; *(acknowledge)* fàiltich, cuir fàilte air
salvage *v* dèan sàbhaladh air
salvation *n* teàrnadh *m*, saoradh *m*, slàinte *f* **Salvation Army** Arm an t-Saoraidh *m*
same *a* ionann, ceudna, ceart, aon
sameness *n* co-ionannachd *f*
sample *n* eisimpleir *f m*, sampall *m*; *(abstr)* taghadh *m v* feuch, blais
sanctify *v* naomhaich
sanctimonious *a* feall-chràbhach
sanction *n (approval)* aontachadh *m*, ùghdarras *m*; *(ban)* smachd-bhann *m*, òrdugh *m v (approve)* ceadaich, ùghdarraich; *(ratify)* daingnich
sanctuary *n (relig)* ionad coisrigte *m*; *(refuge)* comraich *f*, tèarmann *m*
sand *n* gainmheach *f* **s. dune** coilleag *f*, dùn gainmhich *m*
sandbank oitir-ghainmhich *f*, banca-gainmhich *m*
sandpaper pàipear-gainmhich *m* **sandstone** clach-ghainmhich *f*

sandal n cuaran m
sandpiper n fìdhlear m
sandwich n ceapaire m
sandy a gainmheil, gaineamhach
sane a ciallach
sanguine a dòchasach
sanitary a slàinteil, slàinte
sanitation n slàintealachd f
sanity n ciall f
Santa Claus n Bodach na Nollaig m
sap n snodhach m, sùgh m v sùgh, traogh
sapphire n gorm-leug f
sarcasm n searbhas m, searbh-chainnt f, leamhachas m
sarcastic a searbh, leamh, beumnach
sardine n sàrdain m
sardonic a sgaiteach
sash n crios m, bann m
Satan n Sàtan m, an Donas m, an Droch Fhear m
satanic a diabhlaidh, deamhnaidh
satellite n saideal m
satin n sròl m a sròil
satire n aoir f
satirical a aoireil
satirize v aoir, dèan aoireadh
satisfaction n riarachadh m, sàsachadh m, toileachadh m
satisfactory a dòigheil, mar as còir
satisfied a riaraichte, sàsaichte, toilichte
satisfy v riaraich, sàsaich, toilich
satisfying a sàsachail
saturate v trom-fhliuch; (met) lèir-sgaoil
saturated a bog fliuch, trom-fhliuch; (met) loma-làn
Saturday n Disathairne m
sauce n sabhs m, leannra m
saucepan n sgeileid f
saucer n sàsar m, flat m
saucy a beadaidh
sauna n teaslann (smùide) f
saunter v spaidsirich
sausage n isbean m
savage a allaidh, borb
savagery n buirbe f
save v sàbhail, caomhain

saved a saorte, air a s(h)àbhaladh
saving(s) n sàbhaladh m, tasgadh m **s. bond** bann tasgaidh m
Saviour n an Slànaighear m
savour v feuch blas
savoury a blasta
saw n sàbh m **sawdust** min-sàibh f **sawmill** muileann-sàbhaidh f m v sàbh(aig)
saxifrage n lus nan cluas m
saxophone n sagsafòn m
say v can, abair
saying n ràdh m, facal m
scab n sgreab f, càrr f
scabies n am piocas m
scaffolding n sgafallachd f
scald v guail, sgald
scale n tomhas m; (size) meud m; (mus, geog) sgèile f; (on fish) lann f
scale v (climb) streap
scallop n creachan(n) m
scalp n craiceann a' chinn m
scalpel n sgian lèigh f, lannsa f
scamper n ruith, thoir ruaig, teich
scampi n muasgain-chaola m
scan v sgrùd; (metr) bi a rèir meadrachd, meadaraich
scandal n sgainneal m, tuaileas m
scandalize v sgainnealaich
scandalous a maslach, tàmailteach, sgainnealach
Scandinavian n, a Lochlannach m
scanner n sganair m
scant(y) a gann, tearc
scapegoat n cùis-choireachaidh f
scar n làrach f m, leòn m
scarce a gann, tearc, ainneamh
scarcely adv air èiginn, is gann gu
scarcity n gainnead m, teirce f
scare n eagal m v cuir eagal air
scarecrow n bodach-ròcais/feannaig/starraig m
scarf n sgarfa f, stoc m
scarlet n sgàrlaid f **s. fever** an teasach sgàrlaid f
scatter v sgap, sgaoil
scattered a sgapte
scene n (view, drama) sealladh m; (place) ionad m
scenery n sealladh m
scent n fàileadh m, boladh m,

cùbhras *m*
scented *a* cùbhraidh
sceptic *n*, *a* eas-creidmheach *m*
sceptical *a* eas-creidmheach
scepticism *n* eas-creideamh *m*
schedule *n* clàr(-ama) *m* **ahead of
s.** ron àm, tràth **on s.** ris an uair
behind s. fadalach, air
d(h)eireadh *v* cuir air clàr(-ama)
scheme *n* sgeama *m*, innleachd *f*,
dòigh *f* *v* dèan sgeama/
innleachd
schism *n* sgaradh *m*
scholar *n* sgoilear *m*
scholarship *n* sgoilearachd *f*,
foghlam *m*
school *n* sgoil *f* **s.house** taigh-
sgoile *m* **s.master** maigh(i)stir-
sgoile *m* **s.mistress** ban-sgoilear,
bana-mhaigh(i)stir-sgoile *f*
sciatica *n* siataig *f*
science *n* saidheans *m*
scientific *a* saidheansail
scientist *n* neach-saidheans *m*
scissors *n* siosar *m*
sclerosis *n* sglearòis *f*
scoff *v* mag, dèan fanaid (air)
scold *v* càin, cronaich
scone *n* sgona *f m*, bonnach *m*
scoop *n* liagh *f*, ladar *m*, taoman
m v cladhaich a-mach, tog
a-mach
scope *n* comas *m*; (*opportunity*)
cothrom *m*; (*extent*) raon *m*,
farsaingeachd *f*
score *n* (*sport*) sgòr *m*; (*twenty*)
fichead *m*; (*cut*) sgrìob *f*
v (*sport*) cuir/faigh tadhal;
(*cut*) sgrìob
scorn *n* tàir *f*, dìmeas *m v* dèan
tàir/dìmeas air; (*opportunity*)
leig seachad
scornful *a* tàireil
scorpion *n* sgairp *f*
Scot *n* Albannach *m*
Scots *n* (*language*) Albais *f*,
Beurla Ghallda *f*
Scottish *a* Albannach **S. Arts
Council** Comhairle Ealain na
h-Alba **S. Executive** Riaghaltas
na h-Alba **S. Parliament**
Pàrlamaid na h-Alba
scoundrel *n* balgaire *m*

scour *v* sgùr
scourge *v* sgiùrs
scout *n* beachdair *m*
scowl *v* bi fo ghruaim, cuir
drèin/mùig air/oirre *etc*
scraggy *a* reangach
scramble *v* bi a' sporghail;
(*climb*) streap
scrap *n* criomag *f*, mìr *f*; (*fight*)
sabaid *f*, tuasaid *f*
scrape *v* sgrìob **s. together** trus le
èiginn
scratch *n* sgrìobadh *m*, sgrìob *f*,
sgrìoch *f v* sgròb, sgrìob; (*itch*)
tachais
scrawl *n* sgròbaireachd *f v* dèan
sgròblaich
scream *n* sgiamh *f m*, sgreuch *m*
v dèan sgiamh/sgreuch
screech *n* sgread *m*, sgreuch *m*
v dèan sgread/sgreuch
screen *n* sgàilean *m*, sgrion *m*
v (*shelter*) dìon, sgàilich;
(*examine*) cuir fo sgrùdadh
screw *n* sgriubha *m*
v sgriubh(aig)
screwdriver *n* sgriubhaire *m*
scribble *n* sgròbail *m* **a. quick s.**
sgrìobag ghoirid *f v* dean
sgròbail
scribe *n* sgrìobhaiche *m*
script *n* sgrìobhadh *m*, clò *m*;
(*handwriting*) làmh-
sgrìobha(i)dh *f*
scripture *n* sgriobtar *m*
scroll *n* rolla *f v* roilig
scrub *v* sgùr, nigh gu math
scruffy *a* piollagach, loireach
scruple *n* teagamh *m*, imcheist *f*
scrupulous *a* fìor chùramach,
mion-fhaiceallach
scrutinize *v* sgrùd
scrutiny *n* sgrùdadh *m*
scuffle *n* buaireas *m*
scullery *n* sguilearaidh *f m*,
cùlaist *f*
sculptor *n* snaigheadair *m*
sculpture *n* snaigheadh *m*; (*a
piece of*) ìomhaigh shnaighte *f*
scum *n* rèim *m*, sgùm *m*; (*slang*)
salchair *m pl*
scurrilous *a* sgainnealach,
tuaileasach

scythe n speal f v speal
sea n muir f m, cuan m, fairge f
seabed n grunnd na mara m,
  aigeann m
seagull n faoileag f
seal n ròn m; (document) seula
  m v seulaich; (close) dùin
seam n (clothing) dùnadh m,
  fuaigheal m
seaman n maraiche m, seòladair m
search n lorg m, sireadh m
  searchlight solas-siridh m
  v lorg, sir
seashore n cladach m, tràigh f
seasick a leis an tinneas-mhara,
  le cur na mara
seasickness n an tinneas-mara
  m, cur na mara m
season n ràith(e) f, seusan m;
  (time) aimsir f, tràth m
season v (wood etc) seusanaich,
  grèidh; (food) cuir blas ri
sea-spray n siaban m, marcan-
  sìne m
seat n suidheachan m, cathair f,
  àite-suidhe m; (residence) àros
  m; (in Parliament) seat f **s. belt**
  crios-suidheachain m
sea trout n bànag f, gealag f
seaweed n feamainn f
secede v bris(t) air falbh, trèig
secluded a uaigneach,
  leathoireach
second n diog m
second a dara, dàrna
second v cuir taic ri; (to post)
  fo-fhastaich
secondary a dàrnacha, dhen
  dàrna ìre **s. school** àrd-sgoil f
seconder n neach-taice m
secondhand a ri/air ath-reic
secondly adv anns an dara h-àite,
  anns an dàrna àite
secrecy n dìomhaireachd f, cleith f
secret n rùn-dìomhair m, sgeul-
  rùin m a dìomhair, falaichte,
  falchaidh
secretariat n clèireachas m,
  rùnachas m
secretary n clèireach m, ban-
  chlèireach f; (personal) rùnaire
  m **S. of State** Rùnaire (na) Stàite
  m

secretive a falchaidh, ceilteach
secretly adv os ìosal, gun fhiosta
  (do dhaoine)
sect n dream m, treubh f
sectarian a dreamail, treubhail
section n roinn f, earrann f
sector n roinn f, raon m
secular a saoghalta
secure a tèarainte, seasgair
  v dèan cinnteach; (lock)
  gla(i)s; (obtain) faigh
security n (abstr) tèarainteachd f,
  dìon m; (personnel) luchd-dìon
  m **s. of tenure** còir-gabhaltais f
  s. guard geàrd-faire m
sedate a ciùin, stòlda
sedative n cungaidh stòlaidh f
sedge n seisg f
sediment n grùid f
seduce v thoir a thaobh, breug
seduction n toirt a thaobh f,
  breugadh m
see v faic **see you soon** chì mi (a)
  dh'aithghearr thu
seed n sìol m, fras f; (offspring)
  sliochd m, gineal m, iarmad m
  v sìolaich, cuir fras de
seek v iarr, sir, lorg
seem v bi mar ... , leig air/oirre
  etc (a bhith)
seemly a iomchaidh, cubhaidh,
  coltach
seep v sìolaidh tro
seer n fiosaiche m, fàidh m
seethe v (met) bi fo chuthach
segment n gearradh-cuairteig m,
  roinn f
segregate v dealaich, sgar, tearb
segregation n dealachadh m,
  sgaradh m, tearbadh m
seize v glac, cuir làmh an,
  greimich air
seizure n glacadh m, grèim m
seldom adv ainneamh, gu tearc,
  gu h-ainmig
select v tagh, roghnaich
selection n taghadh m, roghainn
  f m
selective a roghnach
self pron fhèin, fèin
self-confidence n fèin-
  mhisneachd f
self-confident a fèin-mhisneachail

self-denial *n* fèin-àicheadh *m*
self-employed *a* ag obair air a c(h)eann fhèin *etc*, fèin-fhastaichte
self-explanatory *a* fèin-mhìneachail
self-government *n* fèin-riaghladh *m*
self-interest *n* fèin-bhuannachd *f*
selfish *a* fèineil, fèinchuiseach
selfishness *n* fèinealachd *f*
self-respect *n* fèin-mheas *m*
self-satisfied *a* fèin-riaraichte
self-service *n* fèin-fhrithealadh *m*
self-same *a* ceart, ionann
sell *v* reic
seller *n* reiceadair *m*, neach-reic *m*
semblance *n* samhla *m*, coltas *m*
semi- *pref* leth-
semi-circle *n* leth-chearcall *m*
semi-colon *n* leth-chòilean *m*, leth-stad *m*
semi-detached *a* leth-dhealaichte
seminal *a* mòr-bhuadhach; (*phys*) sìolach
seminar *n* co-chonaltradh *m*
senate *n* seanadh *m*
senator *n* seanadair *m*
send *v* cuir **s. word** cuir fios (gu) **s. for** cuir a dh'iarraidh
senile *a* seanntaidh
senior *a* as sine, nas sine, àrd-(+ *len*), prìomh (+ *len*)
sensation *n* mothachadh *m*, faireachdainn *f m*
sense *n* (*wits*) ciall *f*, toinisg *f*; (*meaning*) brìgh *f*, seagh *m*; (*faculty*) ceudfath *f*, mothachadh *m*
senseless *a* gun chiall/sgot; (*phys*) gun mhothachadh
sensibility *n* mothachas *m*
sensible *a* ciallach, tùrail
sensitive *a* mothachail; (*contentious*) frionasach
sensory *a* mothachaidh
sensual *a* feòlmhor, collaidh
sensuous *a* ceudfathach
sentence *n* seantans *f*, rosgrann *m*; (*leg*) binn *f*, breith *f* *v* thoir binn, dìt
sentiment *n* (*thought*) smaoin *f*;

(*emotion*) faireachdainn *f m*
sentimental *a* maoth-inntinneach
separate *a* dealaichte, sgaraichte, air leth, leis fhèin *v* dealaich, sgar, tearb, roinn
separation *n* dealachadh *m*, sgaradh *m*
sept *n* fine *f*
September *n* an t-Sultain *f*
septic *a* lionnraichte, iongarach
sequel *n* na leanas **the s. to** a leanas
sequence *n* leanmhainn *m*, ruith *f* **in s.** an sreath a chèile
serene *a* soineannta, ciùin, suaimhneach
serenity *n* soineanntachd *f*, ciùineas *m*, suaimhneas *m*
sergeant *n* sàirdseant *m*
serial *n* leansgeul *m*
series *n* sreath *f m*
serious *a* cudromach, trom-chuiseach; (*person*) dùrachdach
seriously *adv* an da-rìribh
sermon *n* searmon *m* **preach s.** searmonaich, dèan searmon
serpent *n* nathair *f*
serrated *a* eagach
servant *n* searbhanta *f*, seirbheiseach *m*, sgalag *f*
serve *v* (*food*) fritheil, riaraich; (*in office*) dèan seirbheis **s. one's time** thoir a-mach ceàird
service *n* seirbheis *f*, frithealadh *m*; (*relig*) seirbheis *f*; (*dom*) muinntireas *f m* **s.-station** stèisean-frithealaidh *m*
serviceable *a* feumail, iomchaidh
serviette *n* nèapaigin-bùird *f m*
servile *a* tràilleil
session *n* seisean *m*
set *n* seat(a) *m* *a* suidhichte, stèidh(ich)te; (*usual*) gnàthach; (*ready*) deiseil
set *v* suidhich, socraich, stèidhich, cuir; (*sun*) laigh, rach fodha **s. apart** cuir air leth **s. fire to** cuir na theine, cuir teine ri **s. off/out** tog air/oirre *etc* **s. out** (*outline*) mìnich; (*resolve*) cuir roimhe/roimhpe *etc* **s. up** cuir air bhonn/chois **s. table** deasaich/seat am bòrd

settee n seidhs(e) f m
setter n cù-eunaich/luirg m
setting n suidheachadh m,
seatadh m **s. of sun** dol fodha
na grèine m
settle v seatlaig, socraich;
(intrans) sìolaidh; (argument)
rèitich; (inhabit) tuinich, àitich
settled a stèidhichte, seatlaigte
settlement n socrachadh m;
(resolution) rèite f, rèiteachadh
m; (habitation) tuineachadh m
settler n tuiniche m, neach-
tuineachaidh m
seven n a seachd a seachd **s.
people** seachdnar m
seventeen a seachd-deug **s. cards**
seachd cairtean deug
seventh a seachdamh
seventy n trì fichead 's a deich m,
seachdad m
sever v sgar, dealaich
several a iomadh, iomadach
severe a cruaidh; (intense) dian;
(of person) gnù, gnuath,
gruamach; (criticism) feanntach
severity a cruas m, teinne f
sew v fuaigh, fuaigheil
sewage n giodar m, òtrachas m
sewer n sàibhear m
sewing n fuaigheal m **s. machine**
beairt-fuaigheil f
sex n gnè f, cineal m; (act) feis(e)
f **sex appeal** tarraing chorporra
f **sex discrimination** leth-bhreith
(a thaobh) gnè f
sexist a gnè-thaobhach
sexual a gnèitheasach, gnèitheach
sexy a seagsaidh
shabby a robach; (treatment)
suarach
shack n bothag f
shackle n geimheal m, ceangal m
v geimhlich, cuingealaich
shade n sgàil f, dubhar m
shadow n faileas m, sgàil f,
dubhar m
shadowy a faileasach, sgàileach
shady a dubharach; (met)
a' togail amharais/teagaimh,
mì-chneasta
shaft n cas f, samhach f; (mech)
crann m; (of light) gath m; (lift,

mine) toll m
shaggy a molach, ròmach
shake n crith f v crath, luaisg;
(intrans) crith **s. hands with**
beir/breith air làimh air
shaky a critheanach
shallow a ao-domhainn, tana;
(met) staoin
sham n mealladh m
shambles n bùrach m
shame n nàire f, masladh m,
tàmailt f **it's a s.** 's e call a
th' ann v nàraich, maslaich
shameful a nàr, maslach
shameless a lugha-nàire, beag-
nàrach
shampoo n siampù m, failcean m
v failc
shamrock n seamrag f
shank n lurg(a) f, cas f
shape n cumadh m, cruth m v
cum, dealbh, thoir cumadh air
shapeless a gun chumadh; (not
shapely) neo-chuimir
shapely a cuimir, cumadail
share n roinn f, cuid f,
cuibhreann f m, earrann f
v roinn, pàirtich, riaraich **s. in**
gabh pàirt an **s. and s. alike**
dèan roinn a' mhic is an athar
air **shareholder** neach-
earrannan m pl luchd-
earrannan
shark n siorc m **basking s.**
cearban m
sharp a geur, biorach; (of person)
geurchuiseach; (of practice)
carach
sharpen v geuraich, faobharaich
shatter v bris(t) na mhìrean,
bloighdich
shave n bearradh m, lomadh m
he had a close s. (met) chaidh
fìor shàbhaladh air v beàrr,
lom(aich)
shawl n seàla f, guailleachan m
she pron i, (emph) ise
sheaf n sguab f m
shear v rùisg, lomair, beàrr
shearing n rùsgadh m, lomadh
m, bearradh m
shears n deamhais f m
sheath n truaill f, duille f

shed *n* bothan *m*, sead(a) *f m*
shed *v* dòirt, sil; (*staff*) leig dheth
sheen *n* lainnir *f*
sheep *n* caora *f* **sheepdog**
cù-chaorach *m* **sheepskin**
craiceann-caorach *m*
sheepish *a* (*met*) similidh
sheer *a* fìor; (*steep*) cas
sheet *n* siota *m*; (*bed*) braith-lìn
f; (*of paper*) duilleag *f*; (*sail*)
sgòd-siùil *m* **ice-s.** clàr-deighe *m*
shelduck *n* cràdh-ghèadh *m*
shelf *n* sgeilp *f*; (*of rock*) sgeir *f*
shell *n* slige *f*, plaosg *m*
shellfish *n* maorach *m*
shelter *n* fasgadh *m*, dìon *m* **bus**
s. ionad-fasgaidh bus *m*
v (*take*) gabh fasgadh; (*give*)
thoir fasgadh do
sheltered *a* fasgach
shepherd *n* cìobair *m*
sheriff *n* siorram *m*, siorraidh *m*
s. court cùirt an t-siorraim *f*
sherry *n* searaidh *m*
shield *n* sgiath *f* *v* dìon, glèidh
shift *v* caraich, gluais
shifty *a* seòlta, carach
shilling *n* tastan *m*
shin *n* lurg *f*, lurgann *f*
shine *n* deàlradh *m*, gleans(a) *m*
v deàlraich, soillsich, deàrrs
shingle *n* mol *m*, morghan *m*
shingles *n* deir *f*
shining *a* deàlrach, deàrrsach,
boillsgeach
shinty *n* iomain *f*, camanachd *f*
s. stick caman *m*
shiny *a* deàlrach, gleansach
ship *n* bàta *m*, soitheach *f m*,
long *f* *v* (*load*) cuir air bòrd;
(*transport*) giùlain; (*water*) leig
a-steach uisge
shipbuilding *n* togail shoithichean
f
shipyard *n* gàrradh-iarainn *m*
shire *n* siorr(am)achd *f*
shirk *v* seachain
shirt *n* lèine *f* **s.-sleeve**
muilicheann lèine *m*
shiver *n* crith *f*, gaoir *f* *v* crith, bi
air chrith; (*with cold*) bi ga
lathadh *etc*
shivering *a* air chrith

shoal *n* tanalach *m*; (*of fish*)
sgaoth *m*
shock *n* clisgeadh *m*, sgànradh
m; (*horror*) oillt *f*; (*of hair*)
cnuaic *f*, cràic *f* *v* (*startle*) cuir
clisgeadh air, sgànraich;
(*horrify*) uabhasaich
shocking *a* sgriosail
shoddy *a* bochd, suarach, mu
làimh
shoe *n* bròg *f*; (*horse*) crudha
(*eich*) *m*
shoelace *n* barrall *m*
shoemaker *n* greusaiche *m*
shoot *n* faillean *m*, ògan *m*
shoot *v* (*gun*) loisg; (*in game*)
srad, amais air an lìon
shooting *n* losgadh *m*
shop *n* bùth *f*
shopkeeper *n* neach-bùtha *m*
shopping centre *n* ionad bhùthan
m
shore *n* cladach *m*, tràigh *f*
short *a* goirid, geàrr **s.-cut**
aithghearrachd *f* **s. leet** liosta
thaghte *f* **shortlived** diombuan
s.-sighted geàrr-sheallach
s. story sgeulachd ghoirid *f*
s.-tempered cas, aithghearr
(san nàdar) **s.-term** *n* geàrr-ùine
f *a* geàrr-ùineach
shortage dìth *f m*, gainne *f*
shortbread *n* aran-milis *m*
shortcoming *n* easbhaidh *f*
shorten *v* giorraich
shorthand *n* geàrr-sgrìobhadh *m*
shortly *adv* a dh'aithghearr
shorts *n* briogais ghoirid *f*
shot *n* (*of gun*) urchair *f*
shotgun *n* gunna-froise *m*
shoulder *n* gualainn *f*, slinnean *m*
shout *n* èigh *f*, glaodh *m* *v* èigh,
glaodh
shove *n* putadh *m*, putag *f* *v* put
shovel *n* sluasaid *f* *v* obraich le
sluasaid/spaid
show *n* sealladh *m*, taisbeanadh
m; (*entertainment*) cuirm-
chluich *f* *v* seall, nochd,
foillsich, taisbean
shower *n* fras *f*, meall *m*;
(*appliance*) frasair *m* **what a s.!**
abair seat! *v* fras, dòirt, sil

showery *a* frasach
showroom *n* seòmar-taisbeanaidh *m*
shred *n* mìr *m*, bìdeag *f*, criomag *f* *v* cuir na stiallan
shrewd *a* glic, teòma, gleusta, geurchuiseach
shriek *n* sgread *m*, sgreuch *m* *v* dèan sgread/sgreuch
shrill *a* sgalanta, sgairteil
shrimp *n* carran *m*
shrine *n* ionad coisrigte *m*
shrink *v* seac; (*recoil*) bi fo gheilt, tarraing air ais (bh)o
shrivel *v* crìon, searg
shrivelled *a* seargte
shroud *n* marbhphaisg *f*; (*naut*) cupaill *m* *pl*
shrub *n* preas *m*
shrubbery *n* preasarnach *f*
shrug *n* crathadh guailne *m* *v* crath guailnean
shudder *n* ball-chrith *f*, criothnachadh *m* *v* criothnaich
shuffle *v* (*cards etc*) measgaich; (*gait*) dragh do chasan
shun *v* seachain
shut *v* dùin *a* dùinte
shutter *n* còmhla (uinneige) *f*
shuttle *n* spàl *m* **shuttlecock** gleicean *m*
shy *a* diùid, socharach
sick *a* tinn, bochd, meadhanach
sicken *v* fàs tinn/bochd, gabh tinneas; (*trans*) dèan tinn
sickle *n* corran *m*
sickness *n* tinneas *m*, bochdainn *f* **s. benefit** sochair tinneis *f*
side *n* taobh *m*, cliathach *f* **s.-road** frith-rathad *m* **s.-street** frith-shràid **sidewalk** cabhsair *m* *f* **s. with** gabh taobh (+ *gen*) **sidetrack** thoir a thaobh
sideboard *n* preasa-tasgaidh *m*
sideline *n* iomall *m*; (*another activity*) frith-obair *f* *v* cuir gus an oir/an t-iomall
sidestep *v* (*met*) seachain; (*phys*) gabh ceum às an rathad
sideways *adv* air fiaradh, an comhair a t(h)ao(i)bh *etc*
sidle *v* siolp
siege *n* sèist *f m*

sieve *n* criathar *m*
sift *v* criathraich, rèitich
sigh *n* osna *f*, osann *f* *v* leig osna/osann, osnaich
sight *n* sealladh *m*; (*faculty*) fradharc *m* **out of s.** às an t-sealladh **second s.** an dà shealladh
sightseeing *n* siubhal sheallaidhean *m*
sign *n* comharra *m*, soidhne *m*
signpost post-seòlaidh *m*, post-soidhne *m* *v* soidhnig, cuir ainm ri; (*indicate*) dèan comharra
signal *n* comharra *m*, soidhne *m*
signature *n* ainm-sgrìobhte *m*
signet *n* fàinne seula *f*
significance *n* brìgh *f*; (*importance*) cudromachd *f*
significant *a* brìgheil; (*important*) cudromach
signify *v* comharraich, ciallaich
Sikh *n* Siog *m*, (*female*) ban-Siogach *f* *a* Siogach
silence *n* sàmhchair *f*, tost *m*
silent *a* sàmhach, na t(h)ost *etc*
silhouette *n* sgàil-riochd *m*
silicon *n* sileagon *m*
silk *n*, *a* sìoda *m*
silk(y)/silken *a* sìodach
sill *n* sòl *f*
silliness *n* gòraiche *f*, faoineas *f*
silly *a* gòrach, faoin
silt *n* eabar *m*
silver *n* airgead *m* *a* airgid, airgeadach
similar *a* coltach, ionann
similarity *n* coltas *m*, ionannachd *f*; (*resemblance*) suaip *f*
simile *n* samhla *m*
simmer *v* earr-bhruich
simple *a* sìmplidh; (*in mind*) slac, baoth
simplify *v* sìmplich
simplistic *a* ro shìmplidh
simply *adv* dìreach
simulate *v* leig ort
simultaneous *a* còmhla, mar-aon, aig an aon àm, co-amail
sin *n* peacadh *m* *v* peacaich
since *adv* (bh)o *conj* a chionn

gu(n) *prep* (bh)o, o chionn
(+ *gen*)
sincere *a* treibhdhireach,
dùrachdach
sincerity *n* treibhdhireas *m*,
dùrachd *f*
sinew *n* fèith *f*
sing *v* seinn, gabh òran
singe *v* dàth
singer *n* seinneadair *m*; (*female*)
ban-sheinneadair *f*
single *a* singilte; (*not married*)
gun phòsadh **s.-handed**
leis/leatha (*etc*) fhèin, gun
chuideachadh
singular *a* singilte; (*unusual*)
sònraichte, àraid
sinister *a* (*threatening*)
bagarrach; (*evil*) olc
sink *n* sinc(e) *f m*
sink *v* (*trans*) cuir fodha;
(*intrans*) rach fodha
sinner *n* peacach *m*
sinuous *a* lùbach
sip *n* balgam *m*, drudhag *f*
v gabh balgam/drudhag
siphon *n* pìob-èalaidh *f*
sir *n* an ridire *m*, sir *m*
siren *n* (*hooter*) dùdach *f m*,
conacag *f*
sister *n* piuthar *f* **s.-in-law**
piuthar-chèile *f*
sit *v* suidh, dèan suidhe
site *n* làrach *f m*, ionad *m*
v suidhich
sitting-room *n* seòmar-suidhe *m*,
rùm-suidhe *m*
situated *a* suidhichte, air a
s(h)uidheachadh **well s.** air a
dheagh shuidheachadh
situation *n* suidheachadh *m*
six *n, a* sia **s. people** sianar *m*
sixteen *n* a sia, *a* sia-deug *m* **s.
letters** sia litrichean deug
sixth *a* siathamh
sixty *n, a* trì fichead *m*, seasgad
m
sizeable *a* meadhanach mòr,
meudmhor
size *n* meud *m*, meudachd *f*,
tomhas *m*
skate *n* (*fish*) sgait *f*; (*ice*) spèil *f*,
bròg-spèilidh *f v* spèil

skating *n* spèileadh *m*
skeleton *n* cnàimhneach *m*
skelp *n* sgailc *f*
skerry *n* sgeir *f*
sketch *n* sgeidse *f v* dèan sgeidse
ski *n* sgì *f pl* sgithean *v* sgì
skid *v* sleamhnaich
skiff *n* coit *f*, sgoth *m*
skiing *n* sgitheadh *m*
skilful *a* sgileil, ealanta
skill *n* sgil *f m*
skilled *a* sgileil, ealanta
skim *v* (*eg milk*) thoir uachdar
de; (*intrans*) falbh air
uachdar/bàrr (+ *gen*); (*read*)
dèan bloigh leughaidh (air)
skin *n* craiceann *m*; (*of animals*)
bian *m*, seiche *f* **by the s. of
one's teeth** dìreach air èiginn
v feann, thoir an craiceann de
skinny *a* caol, tana
skip *n* leum *m*, sùrdag *f*;
(*rubbish*) tasgan sgudail *m*
v leum, dean sùrdag
skipper *n* sgiobair *m*
skipping *n* sgiob(aige)adh *m*
s. rope ròp(a)-sgiobai(gi)dh *m*
skirt *n* sgiort(a) *f*
skulk *v* bi a' cùiltearachd
skull *n* claigeann *m*
sky *n* adhar *m*, speur *m* **skylight**
fàirleus *f m* **skyline** fàire *f*
Skyeman *n* Sgitheanach *m*
Skyewoman ban-Sgitheanach *f*
skylark *n* uiseag *f*
slab *n* leac *f*
slack *a* slac, flagach; (*not busy*)
sàmhach, slac; (*lax*) lag
slacken *v* slac, lasaich
slam *v* slàraig, thoir slaic air;
(*met*) càin, thoir slaic air
slander *n* cùl-chàineadh *m*,
tuaileas *m v* cùl-chàin,
sgainnealaich
slanderous *a* sgainnealach
slang *n* mith-chainnt *f*
slant *n* (*phys, met*) claonadh *m*,
fiaradh *m*
slanted *a* air a chlaonadh, le
fiaradh ann; (*biased*) claon, fiar
slap *n* sgailc *f*, pais *f v* thoir
sgailc/pais do
slapdash *a* leibideach, gun diù

slash n gearradh m, sgath f
v geàrr, sgath
slate n sglèat m v sglèat, cuir
sglèat air
slater n sglèatair m
slaughter n marbhadh m,
casgairt f **slaughterhouse** taigh-
spadaidh m v spad, casgair,
marbh
Slav/Slavonic n, a Slàbhach m,
(female) ban-Slàbhach f
slave n tràill f m
slavery n tràillealachd f,
braighdeanas m
slay v marbh
sledge n càrn-slaoid m, slaodan
m
sleek a slìom, mìn
sleep n cadal m **short s.** norrag f
v caidil, dèan cadal
sleeping bag n poca-cadail m
sleepless a gun chadal
sleepy a cadalach
sleet n flin(ne) m
sleeve n muilicheann m,
muinichill m
slender a tana, seang
slice n slis f, sliseag f v slis,
slisnich
sliced a sliseagach
slick a ealanta, le liut
slide n sleamhnag f v slaighd,
sleamhnaich
slight n dìmeas m, tàire f a beag,
aotrom
slim a tana, seang, caol v fàs
seang/caol, caill cuideam
slime n làthach f m, clàbar m
sling n (med) iris gàirdein f;
(weapon) crann-tabhaill m
slink v siap
slip n (phys, met) tuisleadh m;
(error) mearachd f v tuislich
s. up dèan mearachd
slipper n sliopair f m, slapag f
slippery a sleamhainn
slipshod a mu làimh
slipway n cidhe m; (for
launching) leathad cur air bhog
m
slit n sgoltadh m v sgoilt, geàrr
slogan n sluagh-ghairm f
slope n leathad m, bruthach f m

sloping a ag aomadh
sloppy a bog; (untidy) mì-
sgiobalta; (shoddy) leibideach,
lapach
slot n beulag f
sloth n leisg(e) f
slothful a leisg
slovenly a robach, rapach
slow a slaodach, màirnealach
sludge n eabar m, làthach f m
slug n seilcheag f
sluggish a slaodach, trom, gun
sgoinn
slum n sluma m, bochd-cheàrn f
slump v tuit nad chnap; (fin) tuit
gu mòr
slur n (insult) aithis f; (of speech)
slugadh m, mabladh m v (of
speech) sluig facail/faclan **cast a
s.** aithisich
slush n sneachd(a) leaghte m
slut n luid f, sgliùrach f
sly a carach, slìogach
smack n dèiseag f
small a beag
smallpox n a' bhreac f
smart a grinn, spaideil; (clever)
geur
smash n bris(t)eadh m; (accident)
bualadh na chèile m v bris(t);
(tennis) smoidsig
smashing a (met) sgoinneil
smear v smeur, liacair, smiùr
smell n fàileadh m, boladh m
v (trans) feuch/tog fàileadh **it
smells** tha fàileadh dheth
smelt v leagh
smile n fiamh-ghàire m, snodha-
gàire m, faite-gàire f v dèan
fiamh-ghàire, dèan snodha/
faite-gàire
smirk n plìon(as) m v **he smirked**
thàinig plìonas air
smith n gobha m
smock n lèine f
smoke n ceò f m, toit f, deatach f
v (tobacco) gabh ceò/smoc,
smoc(aig)
smoky a ceòthach
smooth a mìn, rèidh, còmhnard
smoothe v dèan rèidh
smother v mùch, tachd
smoulder v cnàmh-loisg

smudge *n* smal *m*, spuaic *f*
v smalaich, cuir spuaic air
smug *a* riaraichte (leis/leatha
fhèin *etc*)
smuggle *v* dèan cùl-
mhùtaireachd
smuggler *n* cùl-mhùtaire *m*
smut *n* drabastachd *f*
smutty *a* drabasta
snack *n* blasad bìdh *m*, greimeag
f
snag *n* duilgheadas *m*
snail *n* seilcheag *f*
snake *n* nathair *f*
snap *v* bris(t) le brag; (*bite*) dèan
glamhadh
snapshot *n* mion-dhealbh *f m*;
(*met*) dealbh aithghearr *f m*
snare *n* ribe *f*   *v* rib
snarl *v* dèan dranndan
snatch *v* glac, beir (air)
sneak *n* sniag *m*, lìogaire *m*
v sniag, liùg, èalaidh
sneaky *a* sniagach, lìogach
sneer *v* dèan fanaid, cuir an
neo-shùim
sneeze *n* sreothart *m*   *v* dèan
sreothart
sniff *n* boladh *m*, fàileadh *m*
v gabh fàileadh/boladh **s. at**
dèan tarcais air
snigger *n* siot-ghàire *f*
snip *v* geàrr le siosar
snipe *n* naosg *f m*
snob *n* sodalan *m*, mòrchuisiche
m
snobbery *n* sodalachd *f*,
mòrchuiseachd *f*
snobbish *a* mòrchuiseach,
sodalach
snooze *n* norrag *f*, snuachdan *m*
v dèan norrag/snuachdan
snore *n* srann *f m*   *v* dèan srann
snort *n* srannartaich *f*   *v* bi
a' srannartaich
snotty *a* spliugach
snout *n* soc *m*, sròn *f*
snow *n* sneachd(a) *m* **snowball**
ball-sneachd(a) *m* **snowdrift**
cith(e) *m* **snowflake** pleòideag *f*,
bleideag *f*, lòineag *f* **snowman**
bodach-sneachd(a) *m*
snowstorm stoirm s(h)neachd(a)

f m   *v* cuir sneachd(a)
snowdrop *n* gealag-làir *f*
snuff *n* snaoisean *m* **s.-box**
bogsa/bucas snaoisein *m*
snug *a* seasgair, clùthmhor
snuggle *v* teann dlùth ri
so *adv* cho; (*like this*) mar seo;
(*therefore*) mar sin **so long as**
cho fad 's a **so-and-so** a leithid
seo a dhuine **s. much** uimhir
interj seadh
soak *v* drùidh; (*eg clothes*) cuir
am bogadh
soaking/soaked *a* bog fliuch
soap *n* siabann *m* **TV s.** siabann
telebhisein
soar *v* itealaich gu h-àrd; (*fin*)
àrdaich gu mòr
sob *n* glug caoinidh *m*
sober *a* sòbarra; (*moderate*)
stuama, measarra   *v* sòbraich,
fuaraich, dèan/fàs sòbarra
soccer *n* ball-coise *m*
sociable *a* cuideachail, càirdeil
social *a* sòisealta, caidreabhach,
comannach **S. Democrat**
Deamocratach Sòisealta *m*
s. security tèarainteachd
shòisealta *f* **s. work** obair
shòisealta *f*
socialism *n* sòisealachd *f*
socialist *n, a* sòisealach *m*
society *n* an comann-sòiseanta *m*,
sòisealtas *m*; (*body*) comann *m*
sociology *n* eòlas sòisealtais *m*
sock *n* stocainn *f*, socais *f*;
(*blow*) sgleog *f*
socket *n* socaid *f* **electrical s.**
bun-dealain *m*
sod *n* fòid *f*, sgrath *f*
soda *n* sòda *f m*
sodden *a* bog fliuch
sodium *n* sòidium *m*
sofa *n* sòfa *f*, langasaid *f*
soft *a* bog, maoth, socair
s.-hearted tais-chridheach
soften *v* bogaich, maothaich
softness *n* buige *f*, maothachd *f*
software *n* bathar bog *m*
soggy *a* bog fliuch
soil *n* ùir *f*, talamh *m*
soil *v* salaich, truaill
soiled *a* loireach

solace n cofhurtachd f, furtachd f

solan goose n sùlaire m **young s.g.** guga m

solar a na grèine

sold a air a reic etc

solder v sobhdraich, solldraig

soldier n saighdear m

sole n bonn na coise m; (fish) lèabag/leòbag-cheàrr f

sole a aon

solely adv a-mhàin

solemn a sòlaimte

solicit v (request) iarr

solicitor n neach-lagha m

solid n teann-stuth m a teann, cruaidh, daingeann; (sound) susbainteach

solidarity n dlùth-phàirteachas m, dìlseachd f

solidify v cruadhaich

solitary a aonranach, uaigneach

solitude n uaigneas m

solo n (song) òran aon-neach m, (instrumental) cluich aon-neach f a leis/leatha etc fhèin

soloist n òranaiche m, neach-ciùil aona(i)r m

soluble a so-sgaoilte

solution n fuasgladh m; (substance) eadar-sgaoileadh m

solve v fuasgail

solvent n lionn-sgaoilidh m

solvent a comasach air pàigheadh

sombre a dubhach, gruamach; (of dress) dorch(a)

some n cuid f, roinn f, pàirt f m; (people) feadhainn f, cuid f

somebody pron cuideigin f, neacheigin m

somehow adv air dòigh air choreigin, air dòigheigin

someone n cuideigin f, neacheigin m

somersault n car a' mhuiltein m v dèan car a' mhuiltein

something pron rudeigin m, nìtheigin m

sometime adv uaireigin

sometimes adv uaireannan

somewhat adv rudeigin, beagan, car, lethchar

somewhere adv an àiteigin, am badeigin

son n mac m, gille m **son-in-law** cliamhainn m

song n òran m, amhran m

soon adv a dh'aithghearr, gu grad, an ùine ghoirid/ghearr

soot n sùith(e) f m

soothe v (calm) ciùinich; (assuage) thoir fao(tha)chadh do

soothing a sèimheachail

sophisticated a soifiostaigeach

sordid a suarach, salach

sore a goirt, cràiteach; (resentful) leamh n creuchd f, lot m

sorrow n bròn m, mulad m, tùrsa f

sorrowful a brònach, muladach, tùrsach

sorry a duilich

sort n seòrsa m, gnè f v cuir an òrdugh, seòrsaich; (fix) cuir air dòigh

so-so a, adv mu làimh, meadhanach

soul n anam m **we didn't see a s.** chan fhaca sinn duine beò

sound n fuaim m; (topog) caolas m a (healthy) slàn, fallain; (reliable) earbsach; (advice) glic **s. asleep** na s(h)uain etc chadail **s.-proof** fuaim-dhìonach v dèan fuaim; (alarm) gairm rabhadh; (instrument) sèid, seinn **s. out** faigh beachd (bh)o **that sounds fine/reasonable** tha sin taghta/reusanta

soup n brot m, eanraich f

sour a goirt, geur, searbh

source n màthair-adhbhar m, bun m, freumh m **s. of river** bun aibhne m

south n, a deas f **the s.** an (àird a) deas f **the s.-east** an (àird an) ear-dheas f **the s.-west** an (àird an) iar-dheas f

southerly a, adv deas, à deas

southern a mu dheas, a deas

souvenir n cuimhneachan m

sovereign n rìgh m àrd-uachdaran m; (coin) sòbhran m a uachdarail, neo-eisimeileach

sovereignty n uachdaranachd f

sow *n* muc *f*, cràin *f*
sow *v* cuir (sìol)
space *n* rùm *m*, rèidhleach *m*,
farsaingeachd *f*; (*atmos*) fànas
m; (*gap*) beàrn *f* **spaceship**
soitheach-fànais *f m* **s. shuttle**
spàl-fànais *m*
spacious *a* farsaing, mòr, rùmail
spade *n* spaid *f*, caibe m
span *n* rèis *f*; (*lifetime*) rèis *f*,
saoghal *m*; (*interval*) greis *f*
Spaniard *n* Spàinn(t)each *m*,
(*female*) ban-Spàinn(t)each *f*
spaniel *n* cù-eunaich *m*
Spanish *n* (*lang*) Spàinn(t)is *f*
a Spàinn(t)each
spanner *n* spanair *m*
spare *a* a chòrr, a bharrachd
s. part pàirt-càraidh *f*
spare *v* caomhain, cumhain
spared *a* air a s(h)àbhaladh *etc* **if**
we are s. ma bhios sinn air ar
caomhnadh/cùmhnadh
spark *n* sradag *f*
sparkle *n* lainnir *f*, deàlradh *m*
v lainnrich, deàlraich
sparkling *a* deàlrach, drìlseach
sparrow *n* gealbhonn *m*
sparrow-hawk *n* speireag *f*
sparse *a* gann
spasm *n* crupadh fèithe *m*
spasmodic *a* an-dràsta 's a-rithist
spastic *n*, *a* spastach *m*
spate *n* lighe *f*; (*met*) meall *m*
spawn *n* sìol *m*, cladh *m*
v sìolaich, cladh
speak *v* abair, bruidhinn, labhair
speaker *n* neach-labhairt *m*,
òraidiche *m*; (*mus etc*)
labhradair *m* **the S.** an
Labhraiche *m*
spear *n* sleagh *f*, gath *m*
special *a* àraidh, sònraichte
specialism *n* speisealachd *f*
specialist *n* speisealaiche *m*,
fìor-eòlaiche *m a* speisealta
specialize *v* speisealaich
specialized *a* speisealaichte
species *n* seòrsa *m*, gnè *f*
specific *a* sònraichte, àraid
specification *n* sònrachadh *m*,
mion-chomharrachadh *m*
specified *a* sònraichte,

comharraichte
specify *v* sònraich, comharraich
specimen *n* sampall *m*, ball-
sampaill *m*
specious *a* meallta
speck *n* smùirnean *m*, sal *m*,
smal *m*
speckled *a* breac, ballach
spectacle *n* sealladh *m*
spectacles *n* speuclairean *m pl*,
speuclair *m*, glainneachan *f pl*
spectator *n* neach-amhairc/
coimhid *m*
spectre *n* tannasg *m*
spectrum *n* speactram *m*
speculate *v* beachdaich, dèan
tuairmeas air; (*fin*) cuir airgead
sa mhargadh
speculation *n* beachdachadh *m*,
tuairmeas *m*
speculative *a* beachdachail,
tuairmeasach
speech *n* cainnt *f*; (*oration*) òraid
f **s. therapy** leasachadh cainnt *m*
speechless *a* gun chainnt, balbh
speed *n* luaths *m*, astar *m* **s. limit**
casg astair *m v* rach luath,
greas
spell *n* (*of time*) greis(eag) *f*;
(*charm*) seun *m*
spell *v* litrich
spelling *n* litreachadh *m*
spend *v* caith, cosg
spendthrift *n* caithtiche *m*
a caithteach
sperm *n* sìol(-ginidh) *m*
spew *v* cuir a-mach, sgeith
sphere *n* cruinne *m*; (*met*) raon
m
spherical *a* cruinn
spice *n* spìosradh *m*
v spìosraich, dèan spìosrach
spicy *a* spìosrach
spider *n* damhan-allaidh *m*
spike *n* spìc *f*, bior *m*
spill *v* dòirt
spin *v* snìomh; (*wheel*) cuir caran
s. around grad-thionndaidh *n*
(*met*) snìomh *m*
spinach *n* bloinigean-gàrraidh *m*
spindle *n* dealgan *m*, fearsaid *f*
spindrift *n* cathadh-mara *m*,
siaban *m*

spine *n* cnàimh-droma *m*
spinner *n* (*person*) snìomhadair
  m; (*mech*) uidheam-snìomh *f*
spinning *n* snìomh *m*, calanas *m*
  s.-wheel cuibheall-shnìomh *f*
spinster *n* maighdeann *f*,
  boireannach gun phòsadh *m*
spiral *n* snìomhan *m*
  a snìomhanach
spire *n* stìopall *m*, binnean *m*
spirit *n* spiorad *m*, aigne *f*;
  (*mettle*) meanmna *m*,
  misneachd *f*; (*ghost*) tannasg *m*
spirited *a* aigeannach,
  misneachail, meanmnach
spirits *n* (*drink*) deoch-làidir *f*
spiritual *a* spioradail
spit *n* smugaid *f*; (*roasting*) bior-
  ròstaidh *m   v* tilg smugaid
spite *n* gamhlas *m*, miosgainn *f*
  in s. of a dh'aindeoin (+ *gen*)
spiteful *a* gamhlasach
spittle *n* seile *m*, ronn *m*
splash *n* steall *f*, splais *f   v* steall,
  splaisig
splay-footed *a* spleadhach,
  pliutach
spleen *n* (*anat*) an dubh-chlèin *f*;
  (*spite*) gamhlas *m*
splendid *a* gasta, taghta;
  (*imposing*) greadhnach
splendour *n* greadhnachas *m*
splice *v* spla(o)idhs
splint *n* cleithean *m*
splinter *n* sgealb *f*, spealg *f*
  v spealg
split *n* sgoltadh *m   v* sgoilt
splutter *v* (*person*) bi
  a' sgeamhadaich
spoil *v* mill, cuir a dholaidh
spoils *n* creach *f*, cobhartach *f m*
spoilt *a* air a m(h)illeadh *etc*,
  millte
spoke *n* spòg *f*, tarsannan *m*
spokesperson *n* neach-labhairt
  m, labhraiche *m* **spokesman**
  fear-labhairt *m* **spokeswoman**
  tè-labhairt *f*
sponge *n* spong *m*; (*cake*)
  spuinnse *f*
sponsor *n* neach-urrais *m*,
  goistidh *m   v* rach mar neach-
  urrais, bi mar ghoistidh

sponsorship *n* urrasachd *f*,
  goistidheachd *f*
spontaneous *a* saor-thoileach,
  deònach
spoon *n* spàin *f*
sporadic *a* corra uair
spore *n* spòr *m*
sport *n* spòrs *f*
sporting *a* spòrsach
sports *n* lùth-chleasan *m pl*,
  geamachan *m pl* **s. centre** ionad
  spòrs *m*
sportsman *n* neach-spòrs *m*
spot *n* spot *f m*; (*place*) àite *m*,
  bad *m*; (*stain*) smal *m* **on the s.**
  (*time*) an làrach nam bonn
  v (*notice*) mothaich do
spotless *a* gun smal
spotted *a* ballach, breac
spotty *a* guireanach
spouse *n* cèile *f m*, cèile-p(h)òsta
  f m
spout *n* srùb *m*, spùt *m   v* spùt;
  (*whale*) sèid; (*hold forth*) cuir
  dheth/dhith *etc*
sprain *n* snìomh *m*, sgochadh *m*,
  siachadh *m   v* cuir snìomh an,
  sgoch
sprawl *v* sìn a-mach; (*of person*)
  bi nad shlèibhtrich
spray *n* (*sea*) cathadh-mara *m*;
  (*water*) sradadh *m*; (*aerosol*)
  frasadair *m*; (*bot*) fleasg *f*
  v srad (air)
spread *v* sgaoil, sgap, sìn a-mach
spreadsheet *n* cliath-dhuilleag *f*
spree *n* (*drinking*) daorach *f*
  shopping s. splaoid ceannaich *f*
sprig *n* faillean *m*
sprightly *a* (*of mood*) beothail,
  suigeartach; (*phys*) frogail,
  spraiceil
spring *n* earrach *m*; (*water*)
  fuaran *m*; (*leap*) grad-leum *m*;
  (*mech*) sprionga *m*, cuairteag *f*
  s.-tide reothart *m   v* grad-leum
  s. from thig/sruth (bh)o
springboard *n* (*met*) stèidh *f*
sprinkle *v* crath
sprinkling *n* craiteachan *m*
sprint *n* roid *f*, deann-ruith *f*;
  (*race*) dian-rèis *f   v* dian-ruith,
  ruith le roid

sprout *n* buinneag *f* **Brussels sprouts** buinneagan Bruisealach *f pl*
spruce *n* giuthas Lochlannach *m*
spruce *a* deas, speiseanta
spur *n* spor *m*, brod *m*; (*met*) spreigeadh *m* *v* brod, stuig; (*met*) spursaig, spreig, piobraich
spurious *a* breugach
spurn *v* diùlt le tàir
spurt *n* briosgadh *m*, cabhag *f*; (*of liquid*) stealladh *m*
spy *n* beachdair *m*, neach-brathaidh *m*, brathadair *m* *v* bi ri beachdaireachd
squabble *n* connsachadh *m*, tuasaid *f*
squad *n* sguad *m*
squalid *a* robach, salach
squall *n* sgal/cnap-gaoithe *m*
squander *v* caith, dèan ana-caitheamh air, mì-bhuilich
square *n* ceàrnag *f* *a* ceithir-cheàrnach, ceàrnagach
squash *v* brùth, pronn
squat *v* crùb
squatter *n* sguatair *m*
squeak *n* bìog *m* *v* bi a' bìogail
squeal *n* sgiamh *f* *v* dèan sgiamh
squeamish *a* òrraiseach
squeeze *n* fàsgadh *m*, bruthadh *m* *v* fàisg, brùth
squid *n* gibearnach *m*
squint *n* claonadh *m*, fiaradh *m* *a* claon, fiar **s.-eyed** cam/fiar-shùileach **it is s.** tha e cam, tha fiaradh ann *v* seall claon
squirrel *n* feòrag *f*
squirt *v* steall, spùt
stab *v* sàth, stob
stabbing *n* sàthadh *m*, stobadh *m*
stabilize *v* bunailtich, cùm air bhunailt
stable *a* bunailteach, seasmhach
stable *n* stàball *m*
stack *n* stac(a) *m*, càrn *m*; (*of hay, peat etc*) cruach *f* *v* cruach, càrn; (*shelves*) cuir air sgeilp
stadium *n* lann-cluiche *f*
staff *n* luchd-obrach *m*; (*stick*) bata *m* **staffroom** seòmar luchd-obrach *m*

stag *n* damh (fèidh) *m*
stage *n* àrd-ùrlar *m*; (*in process*) ìre *f*
stagger *v* rach mu seach; (*amaze*) cuir fìor iongnadh air
staggering *a* (*met*) iongantach
stagnant *a* marbh, neo-ghluasadach
stagnate *v* bi/fàs marbhanta
staid *a* stòlda, suidhichte
stain *n* sal *m*, smal *m* *v* salaich, cuir/fàg smal air
stair *n* staidhre *f*
stake *n* post *m*; (*betting wager*) airgead-gill *m*
stalactite *n* aol-chluigean *m*
stalagmite *n* aol-charragh *f*
stale *a* sean, goirt
stalemate *n* closadh *m*, glasadh *m*
stalk *n* gas *f*
stalk *v* bi a' stalcaireachd **s. person** lean neach mun cuairt
stalker *n* stalcaire *m*; (*of person*) lorgair *m*
stall *n* stàile *f*
stall *v* cuir maill air
stallion *n* àigeach *m*
stalwart *a* sgairteil, calma, làidir
stamina *n* cùl *m*, smior *m*, cumail ris *m*
stammer *n* (s)gagachd *f*, stad *m* **she has a s.** tha stad na cainnt *v* bi (s)gagach
stamp *n* stamp(a) *f*; (*met*) comharra *m* *v* (*feet*) stamp; (*of letters*) cuir stampa air **s. out** cuir às do
stance *n* (*met*) seasamh *m*; (*phys*) dòigh-seasaimh *f*; (*site*) làrach *f m*
stand *n* seasamh *m*; (*stance*) ionad *m*; (*display*) taisbeanadh *m* *v* seas; (*endure*) fuiling, cuir suas ri; (*in election*) seas san taghadh
standard *n* inbhe *f*, ìre *f*, bun-tomhas *m*; (*flag*) meirghe *f* **s. of living** cor beòshlaint *m* *a* cumanta, cunbhalach, coitcheann **S. Grade** an Ìre Choitcheann *f*
standardize *v* cunbhalaich, dèan cunbhalach

standing n (met) seasamh m,
inbhe f a na s(h)easamh etc **s.
committee** gnàth-chomataidh
etc f **s. orders** gnàth-riaghailtean
f pl **s. stones** tursachan m pl
standstill n stad m **at a s.** na
stad/t(h)àmh etc
stanza n rann m
staple n stìnleag f
staple a prìomh
star n rionnag f, reul f
v comharraich le reul; (in
performance) gabh prìomh
phàirt
starboard n deas-bhòrd m
starch n stalc m, stuthaigeadh m
v stalcaich, stuthaig
stare v geur-amhairc, spleuchd
starfish n crosgan m
stark a rag; (absolute) tur, fìor **s.
naked** dearg-rùisgte
starling n druid f
starry a rionnagach, làn
rionnagan
start n toiseach m **a sudden s.**
clisgeadh m v tòisich; (be
startled) clisg; (sudden move)
leum
starter n neach-tòiseachaidh m;
(in engine) inneal-spreigidh m
startle v clisg, cuir clisgeadh air
starvation n gort(a) f
starve v leig gort(a) air **s. to
death** (intrans) bàsaich leis
a' ghort **we were starving** bha
an t-acras gar tolladh
state n staid f, cor m; (country)
stàit f
state v can, cuir an cèill
stately a stàiteil
statement n aithris f, cunntas m
statesman n stàitire m
static a na stad, gun ghluasad
station n stèisean m; (in life) staid
f, inbhe f
stationary a na stad, gun
ghluasad
stationery n stuth-sgrìobhaidh m,
pàipearachd f
statistical a staitistigeil,
àireamhail
statistics n staitistearachd f
statue n ìomhaigh f

stature n àird f
status n inbhe f
statute n reachd m
statutory a reachdail, a rèir an
lagha
staunch a daingeann, dìleas
staunch v caisg
stay v fuirich, fan
steadfast a daingeann, dìleas
steady a seasmhach, daingeann,
socraichte v socraich,
daingnich
steak n staoig f
steal n goid f, mèirle f v goid,
dèan mèirle **s. away** (intrans)
liùg air falbh
stealing n goid f, mèirle f
steam n toit f, smùid f
steed n steud f, steud-each m
steel n cruaidh f, stàilinn f
a dhen chruaidh, dhen stàilinn
steep a cas; (price) anabarrach
daor
steep v bog, cuir am bogadh,
tùm
steeple n stìopall m
steer v stiùir, treòraich **s. clear of**
cùm clìoras (+ nom)
steering n stiùireadh m **s.
committee** comataidh stiùiridh f
stem n (bot) gas f
stench n boladh m, breuntas m
step n step m; (a pace) ceum m **s.
by s.** ceum air cheum **take steps**
(met) cuir mu dheidhinn
step a leth- **s.-brother** leth-
bhràthair m **s.-sister** leth-
phiuthar f **s.-daughter** nighean-
cèile f **s.-son** dalta m **s.-father**
oide m **s.-mother** muime f
stereotype n gnàth-iomhaigh f
sterile a seasg, aimrid; (ground)
fàs; (med) sgaldach
sterilize v seasgaich; (ground)
fàsaich; (med) sgald
sterling n airgead Bhreatainn m **a
pound s.** not(a) Breatannach m
sterling a fìor, foghainteach
stern n deireadh m
stern a gruamach, dùr
stethoscope n steatasgop m
stew n stiubha f v stiùbhaig
steward n stiùbhard m

stewardess ban-stiùbhard *f*
stick *n* maide *m*, bioran *m*
  walking s. bata *m*
stick *v* (*adhere to*) steig; (*become caught*) rach an sàs; (*endure*) fuiling
sticker *n* steigear *m*
sticky *a* steigeach; (*problem*) righinn
stiff *a* rag
stiffen *v* ragaich
stiffness *n* raige *f*
stifle *v* mùch
stigma *n* adhbhar nàire *m*; (*bot*) stiogma *m*
stigmatize *v* dèan cùis-nàire de
still *n* poit-dhubh *f*, stail *f*
still *a* sàmhach, balbh; (*weather*) ciùin, fèathach
still *adv* an dèidh sin, a dh'aindeoin sin; (*of time*) fhathast
stimulant *n* stuth beothachaidh *m*
stimulate *v* brosnaich, spreig
stimulating *a* brosnachail, togarrach
stimulus *n* brosnachadh *m*, spreagadh *m*
sting *n* gath *m*, guin *m* *v* cuir gath ann, guin
stinginess *n* spìocaireachd *f*
stingy *a* spìocach
stink *n* tòchd *m*, samh *m*
stinking *a* breun, malcaidh
stipend *n* tuarastal *m*
stipulate *v* sònraich, cùmhnantaich
stir *n* othail *f*, ùinich *f*
stir *v* (*food*) cuir mun cuairt; (*move*) gluais; (*stimulate*) brosnaich **s. up** dùisg
stirk *n* gamhainn *m*
stirring *a* togarrach, brosnachail
stitch *n* (*med, sewing*) grèim *m*; (*knitting*) lùb *f*; (*pain*) grèim *m*; (*of clothing*) stiall *f* *v* fuaigh, fuaigheil
stoat *n* neas gheal *f*
stock *n* stoc *m* **s.-taking** cunntas stoc *m* *v* stocaich
stock exchange *n* margadh nan earrannan *m*
stockbroker *n* margaiche

earrannan *m*
stocking *n* stocainn *f*
stocks *n* (*fin*) earrannan *f pl*
stodgy *a* trom
stoical *a* strìochdte
stoke *v* cùm connadh ri
stolen *a* air a g(h)oid *etc*
stomach *n* stamag *f*, goile *f*, maodal *f*
stone *n* clach *f* **S. Age** Linn na Cloiche *m* *a* cloiche
stonechat *n* clacharan *m*
stonemason *n* clachair *m*
stook *n* adag *f*, suidheachan *m*
stool *n* stòl *m*, furm *m*
stoop *v* crom, lùb, crùb
stooped *a* crom
stop *n* stad *m*; (*ban*) toirmeasg *m*
  s.-cock goc *m* **s.-gap** neach/nì a lìonas beàrn *m* *v* stad, cuir stad air; (*cease*) sguir, stad
stoppage *n* stad *m*, stopadh *m*, grabadh *m*
stopper *n* àrc *f*, ceann *m*
storage *n* stòradh *m*, tasgadh *m*
store *n* stòr *m*; (*resources*) stòras *m* *v* stòir, taisg
storey *n* lobhta *f m*, làr *m*
stork *n* corra-bhàn *f*
storm *n* stoirm *f m*, doineann *f*, gailleann *f* *v* thoir ionnsaigh air
stormy *a* stoirmeil, doineannach, gailbheach
story *n* sgeul *m*, sgeulachd *f*, stòiridh *f* **s.-teller** sgeulaiche *m*, seanchaidh *m*
stout *n* leann dubh *m*
stout *a* garbh, tiugh; (*brave*) tapaidh
stove *n* stòbh(a) *f m*
straddle *v* rach gòbhlachan/casa-gòbhlagain air
straggler *n* slaodaire *m*
straight *a* dìreach **s. away** *adv* sa mhionaid, gun dàil
straighten *v* dìrich
strain *n* strèan *m*; (*phys*) teannachadh *m*, snìomh *m*; (*mental*) uallach *m* *v* strèan; (*phys*) teannaich, snìomh; (*filter*) sìolaidh
strainer *n* sìol(t)achan *m*; (*for fence*) strèanair *m*

straitjacket n cuing-cuirp f
strait(s) n caol m, caolas m;
(distress) cruaidh-theinn f
stramash n hù-bhitheil f m,
ùpraid f
strand n dual m; (shore) tràigh f
strange a neònach, iongantach,
coimheach
stranger n coigreach m,
srainnsear m
strangle v tachd, mùch
strap n strap m, iall f v strapaig,
cuir strap/bann air
strapping a tapaidh, mòr, calma
stratagem n cuilbheart f
strategic a ro-innleachdail
strategy n ro-innleachd f
strath n srath m
straw n connlach f, fodar m; (for
drinking) sràbh m **s. poll**
beachd air thuairmse m
strawberry n sùbh-làir m
stray a conadail, fuadain;
(wayward) air seachran
v rach air seachran
streak n stiall f, srianag f
stream n sruth m
streamline v sìmplich
street n sràid f
strength n neart m, spionnadh m,
lùths m
strengthen v neartaich
strenuous a dian, saothrachail
stress n (phys) cuideam m;
(mental) uallach m, eallach m
v cuir/leig cuideam air
stretch v sìn, sgaoil, leudaich
strict a teann, cruaidh
stride n sìnteag f, searradh m
v sìnteagaich, dèan searradh
strife n strì f, còmhstri f
strike n (ind) stailc f v buail; (go
on strike) rach air stailc
striker n stailcear m; (football)
neach-ionnsaigh m
striking a comharraichte,
sònraichte
string n sreang f; (mus) teud m
stringent a teann
strip n stiall f v thoir dheth/dhith
etc d' aodach
stripe n srianag f, sgrìob f
striped a srianach, sgrìobach

stripped a rùisgte, lomnochd
strive v dèan spàirn/strì
stroke n stràc f m, buille f; (med)
stròc m v slìob
stroll v gabh cuairt/ceum, spaidsir
strong n làidir, treun
structure n structair m, dèanamh
m, togail f v structair
struggle n gleac m, spàirn f, strì f
v gleac, dèan spàirn/strì
strut v falbh gu stràiceil
stub n bun m
stubble n asbhuain f; (facial) bun
feusaig m
stubborn a rag, rag-mhuinealach
stubbornness n raigeann m,
rag-mhuinealas m
stubby a cutach, bunach
stuck a an sàs, steigte
stud n stud f; (horses) greigh f
student n oileanach m
studio n stiùidio f
studious a dèidheil air foghlam
study n ionnsachadh m; (room)
seòmar-sgrùdaidh m
v ionnsaich (mu); (research)
sgrùd, cnuasaich; (consider)
beachdaich (air)
stuff n stuth m v lìon, dinn
stumble n tuisleadh m v tuislich
stumbling-block n ceap-tuislidh
m, cnap-starra m
stump n bun m, stoc m
stun v cuir an tuaineal, cuir
tuainealaich air
stunt n cleas m
stupid a amaideach, gòrach
stupidity n amaideas m, gòraiche
f
stupor n tuaineal m, neul m
sturdy a bunanta, gramail
stutter v bi manntach/gagach
stye n (s)leamhnagan m
style n stoidhle f, modh f m;
(fashion) fasan m, stoidhle f;
(title) tiotal m **with s.** le
snas/loinn
stylish a fasanta, spaideil
sub- pref fo- (+ len)
sub-committee n fo-chomataidh f
subconscious n fo-mhothachadh
m
sub-contract v fo-chunnraich

subdivide *v* fo-roinn
subdue *v* ceannsaich, cìosnaich
sub-heading *n* fo-thiotal *m*
subject *n* cuspair *m*; (*of talk etc*)
ceann-labhairt/teagaisg *m*,
cuspair *m*; (*citizen*) ìochdaran
m
subject *v* ceannsaich, cuir fo
smachd (+ *gen*) **s. to** ... cuir fo ...
subjective *a* pearsanta,
suibseigeach
subject to *a* umhail do, fo
smachd (+ *gen*), an urra ri
subjugate *v* ceannsaich
subjunctive *a* (*gram*) eisimeileach
sublime *a* òirdheirc
submarine *n* bàta-aigeil *m*
submerge *v* tùm; (*trans*) cuir
fodha; (*intrans*) rach fodha
submission *n* (*lodged*) tagradh *m*;
(*yielding*) ùmhlachd *f*, gèill *f*
submissive *a* umha(i)l
submit *a* (*lodge, argue*) cuir
a-steach, (t)agair; (*yield*) gèill,
strìochd
subordinate *a* ìochdarach, fo-
(+ *len*)
subscribe *v* fo-sgrìobh **s. to**
gabh/thoir taic do
subscription *n* fo-sgrìobhadh *m*,
sìnteas *m*
subsequent *a* a leanas, an dèidh
làimhe
subsequently *adv* mar sin, na
dhèidh sin, an dèidh làimhe
subside *v* sìolaidh, traogh, tràigh
subsidence *n* dol sìos *m*,
traoghadh *m*, ìsleachadh *m*,
fo-thuiteam *m*
subsidiary *a* ìochdaireil,
cuideachail, fo- (+ *len*)
subsidize *v* thoir
subsadaidh/tabhartas do
subsidy *n* subsadaidh *m*,
tabhartas *m*
subsistence *n* teachd-an-tìr *m*
substance *n* susbaint *f*, brìgh *f*;
(*material*) stuth *m*
substantial *a* susbainteach, làidir,
tàbhachdach
substantiate *v* dearbh, fìrinnich
substitute *n* stuth/nì-ionaid *m*
(an) ionad *m*; (*person*) neach-

ionaid *m*, riochdaire *m* *v* cuir
an àite **s. for** gabh àite (+ *gen*)
sub-title *n* fo-thiotal *m*
subtle *a* seòlta
subtlety *n* seòltachd *f*
subtract *v* thoir (air falbh) (bh)o
suburb *n* iomall baile *m*
subversive *a* ceannairceach
subway *n* fo-shlighe *f*
succeed *v* soirbhich, rach le;
(*follow*) lean
success *n* soirbheachadh *m*,
buaidh *f*
successful *a* soirbheachail
successive *a* leantainneach, an
dèidh a chèile
successor *n* neach-ionaid *m*,
neach a thig an àite/às dèidh ...
m (+ *gen*)
succinct *a* geàrr, cuimir
succulent *a* brìoghmhor, blasta
succumb *v* gèill, strìochd
such *a*, *pron* (a) leithid, mar,
dhen t-seòrsa **as s.** ann/innte
fhèin
suck *v* deothail, deoc, sùigh
sudden *a* obann, grad, aithghearr
suddenly *adv* gu h-obann, gu
grad, gu h-aithghearr
sue *v* thoir gu lagh
suet *n* geir *f*
suffer *v* fuiling; (*permit*) ceadaich
suffering *n* fulangas *m*
suffice *v* foghain
sufficient *a* leòr, cuibheasach
suffix *n* (iar-)leasachan *m*
suffocate *v* mùch
suffuse *v* sgaoil air feadh
sugar *n* siùcar *m*
suggest *v* mol, comhairlich, cuir
an inntinn (+ *gen*)/air shùilibh
do
suggestion *n* moladh *m*, cur an
inntinn (+ *gen*)/air shùilibh *m*
suicide *n* fèin-mhurt *m* **commit s.**
cuir às dhut fhèin
suit *n* deise *f*; (*law*) cùis(-lagha) *f*
suit *v* freagair
suitable *a* freagarrach, iomchaidh
suitcase *n* màileid *f*, baga *m*
suite *n* (*rooms*) sreath *f m*;
(*furniture*) suidht *f*; (*mus*)
sreath *f m*

suitor

suitor
274

suitor *n* suirghiche *m*
sullen *a* dùr, gnù
sully *v* salaich, truaill, cuir smal
air
sulphur *n* pronnasg *m*
sulphuric *a* pronnasgach
sultry *a* bruthainneach
sum *n* àireamh *f*, sùim *f*
summarize *v* thoir geàrr-chunntas
air, giorraich
summary *n* geàrr-chunntas *m*,
giorrachadh *m*
summer *n* samhradh *m* **s. school**
sgoil shamhraidh *f*
summit *n* mullach *m*, bàrr *m*
s. meeting àrd-choinneamh *f*
summon *v* gairm; (*leg*) sumain
summons *n* gairm *f*; (*leg*) bàirlinn
f, sumanadh *m*
sumptuous *a* sòghail
sums *n* cunntadh *m*
sun *n* grian *f* **sundial** uaireadair-
grèine *m* **sunflower** neòinean-
grèine *m* **sunrise** èirigh na
grèine *f* **sunset** dol fodha na
grèine *m*, laighe na grèine *f m*
sunshine deàrrsadh na grèine *m*
sunbathe *v* gabh a' ghrian,
blian (thu/e/i *etc* fhèin) **sunburnt**
a loisgte aig a' ghrèin
Sunday *n* Didòmhnaich *m*,
Latha/Là na Sàbaid *m*
sundry *a* iomadaidh, measgaichte
sunk *a* air a dhol fodha
sunny *a* grianach
super *a* sgoinneil, barraichte *pref*
os-, an(a)-
superannuation *n*
peinnseanachadh *m*
superb *a* barraichte, sgoinneil
superficial *a* staoin, gun
doimhneachd
superfluous *a* iomarcach, thar
a' chòrr
superhuman *a* os-daonna
superintendent *n* stiùireadair *m*,
àrd-neach-stiùiridh *m*
superior *n* uachdaran *m*
a uachdarach, àrd
superiority *n* uachdarachd *f*, bàrr
m, ceannas *m*
superlative *a* còrr, barraichte;
(*gram*) feabhasach

supermarket *n* mòr-bhùth *f*
supernatural *a* os-nàdarra(ch)
supersede *v* gabh àite (+ *gen*),
cuir às àite
superstition *n* saobh-chràbhadh
m
superstitious *a* saobh-chràbhach
supervise *v* stiùir, cùm sùil air
supervision *n* stiùireadh *m*,
cumail sùil air *f*
supervisor *n* neach-stiùiridh/
coimhid *m*
supper *n* suipear *f*
supple *a* sùbailte, subailte
supplement *n* leasachadh *m*
supplementary *a* a bharrachd,
leasachail **s. benefit** sochair-
leasachaidh *f*
supplier *n* solaraiche *m*
supply *n* solarachadh *m*, solar *m*
v solaraich, cùm ri **do s. work**
obraich an àite cuideigin
support *n* taic *f*, tacsa *m*, cùl-taic
m *v* thoir taic do, cuir/cùm taic
ri, cuidich
supporter *n* neach-taic(e) *m*;
(*sport*) neach-leantail/leantainn
m
supportive *a* taiceil
suppose *v* saoil
suppress *v* cùm fodha, mùch
suppression *n* cumail fodha *f*,
mùchadh *m*
supremacy *n* ceannasachd *f*,
àrd-cheannas *m*
supreme *a* àrd-, sàr, barraichte
supremo *n* àrd-cheannard *m*
surcharge *n* for-chìs *f* *v* leag for-
chìs air
sure *a* cinnteach, deimhinnte
surely *adv* is cinnteach, gu
fìrinneach
surf *n* ròd *m*, rùid *m* *v* marcaich
tuinn **s. the net** tràl an lìon
surface *n* uachdar *m*, leth
a-muigh *m*
surfeit *n* sàth *m*, cus *m*
surge *n* onfhadh *m* *v* at, bòc
surgeon *n* lannsair *m*
surgery *n* obair-lannsa *f*; (*place*)
ionad an dotair *m*; (*polit*)
freastal-lann *f*
surly *a* gnù, greannach

surmise *v* saoil, bi dhen bharail
surmount *v* rach/faigh os cionn
(+ *gen*)
surname *n* cinneadh *m*,
sloinneadh *m*
surpass *v* thoir bàrr air
surplus *n* còrr *m*
surprise *n* iongnadh *m*, iongantas
m *v* cuir iongnadh/iongantas
air **s. someone** thig gun fhios air
surprising *a* iongantach, neònach
surrender *v* (*intrans*) strìochd,
gèill; (*trans*) thoir suas
surround *v* cuartaich, iadh mu
thimcheall
survey *n* tomhas *m*, sgrùdadh *m*
v tomhais, sgrùd; (*look at*) gabh
beachd air
surveyor *n* neach-tomhais/
sgrùdaidh *m*
survive *v* mair beò, tàrr às **s. on**
thig beò air
survivor *n* neach a tha beò/
maireann *m*, neach a thàrr
às *m*
susceptible *a* buailteach (do)
suspect *n* neach fo amharas *m*
v bi/cuir an amharas **I s.** tha
amharas agam (gu)
suspected *a* fo amharas
suspend *v* (*hang*) croch; (*defer*)
cuir dàil an; (*from work*) cuir à
dreuchd rè ùine
suspense *n* teagamh *m* **in s.** fo
theagamh, a' feitheamh, air
bhioran
suspension *n* crochadh *m*; (*from
work*) cur à dreuchd rè ùine *m*
s. bridge drochaid crochaidh *f*
suspicion *n* amharas *m*
suspicious *a* amharasach
sustain *v* cùm suas; (*suffer*)
fuiling
sustainable *a* buan, seasmhach
sustenance *n* lòn *m*,
beathachadh *m*
swallow *n* gòbhlan-gaoithe *m*
swallow *v* sluig
swamp *n* fèith *f*, bog(l)ach *f*
swan *n* eala *f*
swarm *n* sgaoth *m*
swarthy *a* doimhearra, ciar
sway *n* riaghladh *m*, seòladh *m*

v luaisg; (*opinion*) gluais,
buadhaich
swear *v* (*vow*) mionnaich, thoir
mionnan, bòidich; (*curse*) bi ri
guidheachan/mionnan
swearing *n* (*avowing*)
mionnachadh *m*; (*cursing*)
guidheachan *f m pl*
sweat *n* fallas *m* *v* cuir fallas
(dheth/dhith *etc*)
sweatshirt *n* lèine spòrs *f*
sweaty *a* fallasach
Swede *n* Suaineach *m*, (*female*)
ban-S(h)uaineach *f*
Swedish *a* Suaineach *n* (*lang*)
Suainis *f*
sweep *v* sguab
sweeper *n* sguabaire *m*
sweet *n* mìlsean *m* *a* milis;
(*scent*) cùbhraidh; (*sound*) binn
sweeten *v* mìlsich, dèan milis
sweetheart *n* leannan *m*, eudail *f*
sweets *n* suiteis *m pl*, siùcaran *m*
pl
swell *v* at, sèid, bòc
swelling *n* at *m*, cnap *m*, bòcadh *m*
sweltering *a* brothallach,
bruthainneach
swerve *v* claon, lùb, rach a
thaobh
swift *n* gobhlan-gainmhich *m*
swift *a* luath, grad, siùbhlach,
ealamh
swim *n* snàmh *m* *v* snàmh
swimmer *n* snàmhaiche *m*
swimming *n* snàmh *m* **s.-pool**
amar-snà(i)mh *m*
swindle *v* thoir an car à, dèan
foill (air)
swine *n* mucan *f pl*; (*slang*)
trustar *m*
swing *n* (*action*) luasgadh *m*; (*for
playing*) dreallag *f*; (*pendulum*)
siùdan *m*; (*polit*) gluasad *m*;
(*golf*) dòigh-bualaidh *f* **in full s.**
fo làn-sheòl *v* luaisg; (*of
pendulum*) dean siùdan; (*polit*)
gluais
swingeing *a* cruaidh
swipe *n* sgailc *f*
Swiss *n*, *a* Eilbheiseach *m*,
(*female*) ban-Eilbheiseach *f*
switch *n* suidse *f m*; (*wand*) slat *f*

switch *v* atharraich
swivel *n* udalan *m*, fulag *f*
swollen *a* air at/sèid
swoon *v* rach an neul, rach am paiseanadh
swoop *v* thig le roid/sitheadh
  s. for sguab leat, grad-ghlac
sword *n* claidheamh *m* **s.-dance** danns a' chlaidheimh *m*
swot *v* ionnsaich gu dian
syllable *n* lideadh *m*
syllabus *n* clàr-obrach *m*
symbol *n* samhla *m*
symbolical *a* samhlachail
symbolism *n* samhlachas *m*
symbolize *v* samhlaich, riochdaich
symmetrical *a* ceart-chumadail, cothromaichte
sympathetic *a* co-fhaireachail, truasail
sympathize *v* nochd co-fhaireachdainn
sympathy *n* co-fhaireachdainn *f*
symphony *n* (*mus piece*) siansadh *m*
symptom *n* comharra *m*
synchronize *v* co-thìmich
syndicate *n* comann iomairt *m*; (*media*) buidheann naidheachdais *f m*
synod *n* seanadh *m*
synonym *n* co-fhacal *m*
synopsis *n* geàrr-iomradh *m*, giorrachadh *m*
syntax *n* co-chàradh *m*
synthesis *n* co-chur *m*, co-thàthadh *m*
synthetic *a* co-thàthte; (*artificial*) fuadain
syphon *n* sùghachan *m*, lìonadair *m*
syringe *n* steallair(e) *m*
syrup *n* siorap *f m*
system *n* siostam *m*, seòl *m*
systematic *a* rianail, òrdail, eagarach

T

table *n* bòrd *m*; (*figures*) clàr *m*
  t.-tennis teanas-bùird *m*
  tablecloth anart-bùird *m*,
  tubhailt(e) *f m*
tablet *n* pile *f*; (*block*) clàr *m*
tacit *a* gun ainmeachadh, gun a ràdh
tack *n* tacaid *f*; (*naut*) tac(a) *f*; (*lease*) tac *f*
tackle *n* acfhainn *f*, uidheam *f*; (*in sport*) dol an sàs *m*
tactic *n* innleachd *f*, seòl *m*
tactical *a* innleachdail
tactile *n* beantainneach, beanailteach
tadpole *n* ceann-phollan *m*, ceann-simid *m*
tail *n* earball *m*, eàrr *f m*, feaman *m* **tailback** ciudha charbadan *m*
tailor *n* tàillear *m*
tainted *a* trothach, air a t(h)ruailleadh *etc*, millte
take *v* gabh, thoir **it takes a long time** tha e a' toirt ùine mhòr
  t. a photograph tog dealbh
takeover *n* gabhail thairis *m*
takings *n* teachd-a-steach *m*
tale *n* sgeulachd *f*, sgeul *m*
talent *n* tàlant *m*, comas *m*, buadh *f*
talented *a* tàlantach, comasach
talk *n* bruidhinn *f*, cainnt *f*; (*chat*) còmhradh *m*; (*lecture*) òraid *f* *v* bruidhinn; (*chat*) dèan còmhradh
talkative *a* còmhraideach, bruidhneach, cabach
talking *n* bruidhinn *f*, labhairt *f*
tall *a* àrd
tallow *n* geir *f*, blona(i)g *f*, crèis *f*
tally *n* cunntas *m*, àireamh *f*
talon *n* spuir *m*, ionga *f*
tame *a* soitheamh, call(d)a, ceannsaichte *v* callaich, ceannsaich
tamper *v* buin/bean ri, mill
tan *n* dubhadh (-grèine) *m* *v* gabh a' ghrian; (*leather*) cairt
tang *n* blas geur *m*
tangent *n* beantan *m* **going off at a t.** a' dol bhàrr do sgeòil
tangible *a* so-bheantainn, susbainteach, a ghabhas làimhseachadh
tangle *n* troimh-a-chèile *f m*; (*fishing line*) rocladh *m*;

(*seaweed*) stamh *m* *v* rach an sàs/an lùib a chèile; (*fishing line*) rocail
tank *n* tanca *f m*
tanker *n* tancair *m*
tantalize *v* cùm air bhioran, leamhaich
tantamount *a* co-ionann, ionann
tantrum *n* prat *m*, dod *m*
tap *n* goc *m*, tap *f m*; (*sound*) gnogag *f* *v* (*sound*) thoir gnogag do; (*access*) tarraing air/à
tape *n* teip *f* **t.-measure** teip-tomhais *f* **t.-recorder** teip-chlàradair *m* *v* teip, cuir teip air; (*record*) cuir air teip, clàraich
taper *v* (*intrans*) fàs barra-chaol; (*trans*) dèan caol
tapestry *n* brat-grèise *m*
tar *n* teàrr *f*, bìth *f* *v* teàrr
tardy *a* athaiseach, màirnealach, slaodach
target *n* targaid *f* **t. audience** luchd-amais sònraichte *m* *v* cuimsich air
tariff *n* cìs *f*; (*prices*) clàr-phrìsean *m*
tarnish *v* smalaich, dubhaich
tarpaulin *n* cainb-thearra *f*
tart *n* pigheann *m*
tart *a* searbh, geur
tartan *n* tartan *m*, breacan *m*
task *n* obair *f*, gnìomh *m* **t.-force** buidheann-gnìomha *f m*
tassel *n* cluigean *m*, babag *f*
taste *n* blas *m*; (*judgement*) breithneachadh *m* *v* blais, feuch
tasteless *a* neo-bhlasta, gun bhlas; (*met*) neo-chubhaidh, mì-chiatach
tasty *a* blasta
tattle *n* goileam *m*
tattoo *n* tatù *m*
taunt *n* beum *m*, magadh *m*, tilgeil air *f* *v* beum, mag, tilg air
taut *a* teann
tawdry *a* suarach, gun snas
tawny *a* lachdann, ciar
tawse *n* strap *m*, stràic *f*

tax *n* cìs *f*, càin *f* **income tax** cìs cosnaidh **tax office** oifis chìsean *f* *v* leag cìs, cuir cìs air
taxation *n* leagail cìse *m*, cìs *f*
taxi *n* tagsaidh *f m*
taxman *n* cìs-mhaor *m*
taxpayer *n* neach-pàighidh cìse *m*
tea *n* tì *f*, teatha *f* **teacup** cupa tì *m*, copan teatha *m* **teapot** poit-tì/teatha *f* **teaspoon** spàin-tì/teatha *f*
teach *v* teagaisg, ionnsaich
teacher *n* tidsear *f m*, neach-teagaisg *f*
teaching *n* teagasg *m*
teal *n* crann-lach *f*
team *n* sgioba *f m*
tear *n* deur *m*; (*rent*) sracadh *m* *v* srac, reub
tease *v* tarraing à, farranaich; (*comb out*) cìr
teat *n* sine *f*
technical *a* teicneòlach, teicnigeach
technician *n* teicneòlaiche *m*
technique *n* alt *m*, dòigh *f*
technological *a* teicneòlach
technology *n* teicneòlas *m*
tedious *a* sàrachail, sgìtheil, ràsanach
teeming *a* loma-làn, a' cur thairis
teenager *n* deugaire *m*
telecommunications *n* tele-chonaltradh *m*
telephone *n* fòn *f m*, teilefòn *m* **t. directory** leabhar a'/na fòn *m* *v* fòn(aig)
telephonist *n* neach-freagairt fòn *m*
telescope *n* prosbaig *f*, teileasgop *f*
teletext *n* tele-theacsa *m*
television *n* telebhisean *f m*
tell *v* innis, abair
telltale *n* cabaire *m*
temerity *n* ladarnas *m*
temper *n* nàdar *m*
temperament *n* nàdar *m*, càil *f*
temperance *n* measarrachd *f*, stuamachd *f*
temperate *a* measarra, stuama; (*atmos*) eadar-mheadhanach
temperature *n* teòthachd *f*

temple *n* teampall *m*; (*head*)
lethcheann *m*
tempo *n* luaths *m*
temporarily *adv* airson ùine
ghoirid, rè tamaill
temporary *a* sealach, airson ùine
ghoirid, rè seal
tempt *v* buair, tàlaidh
temptation *n* buaireadh *m*
ten *n* a deich *a* deich **ten people**
deichnear *f m*
tenable *a* reusanta, a ghabhas
seasamh
tenacious *a* leanailteach, righinn,
greimeil
tenacity *n* leanailteachd *f*,
rìghneas *m*
tenancy *n* gabhaltas *m*
tenant *n* neach-gabhail *m*
tend *v* fritheil, àraich; (*incline*)
aom, bi buailteach
tendency *n* aomadh *m*,
buailteachd *f*
tender *n* tairgse *f v* tairg,
tabhann
tender *a* maoth, caoin
tenderness *n* maothalachd *f*,
caomhalachd *f*
tenement *n* teanamaint *m*
tennis *n* teanas *m*
tenor *n* brìgh *f*, seagh *m*; (*mus*)
teanor *m*
tense *n* tràth *m* **present/future/
past t.** an tràth làthaireach/
teachdail/caithte
tense *a* teann, rag
tension *n* teannachadh *m*,
ragachadh *m*; (*stress*) strì *f*
tent *n* teant(a) *f m*
tentacle *n* greimiche *m*
tentative *a* teagmhach,
mì-chinnteach
tenth *n* deicheamh *m*, an
deicheamh cuid *f a* deicheamh
tenuous *a* (*flimsy*) lag; (*fine*) tana
tenure *n* còir-fearainn *f*,
gabhaltas *m*
tepid *a* flodach; (*met*) meadh-
bhlàth
term *n* (*of time*) teirm *f*; (*end*)
crìoch *f*, ceann *m*; (*condition*)
cùmhnant *m*, cumha *f m*;
(*verbal*) facal *m*, briathar *m*

terminal *a* (*med*) crìche
terminate *v* cuir crìoch air,
crìochnaich
termination *n* crìochnachadh *m*;
(*med*) casg-breith *f*
terminology *n* briathrachas *m*
tern *n* steàrnan *m*
terrible *a* eagalach, uabhasach,
sgràthail
terrier *n* abhag *f*
terrify *v* oilltich, cuir oillt/eagal
air
terrifying *a* eagalach, oillteil
territory *n* tìr *f*, fonn *m*, fearann
m
terror *n* eagal *m*, oillt *f*; (*person*)
cùis-eagail *f*
terrorism *n* ceannairc *f*
terse *a* geàrr, cuimir
test *n* deuchainn *f*, ceasnachadh
m
testament *n* tiomnadh *m* **the Old
T.** an Seann Tiomnadh **the New
T.** an Tiomnadh Nuadh
testicle *n* magairle *f m*,
magairlean *m*, clach *f*
testify *v* thoir fianais
testimonial *n* teisteanas *m*
testimony *n* teisteas *m*, fianais *f*
tetchy *a* frionasach
tether *n* teadhair *f*, feist(e) *f*
text *n* teacsa *m*; (*sermon*) ceann-
teagaisg *m* **textbook** teacs-
leabhar *m*
textile *n* aodach fighte *m*
texture *n* dèanamh *m*, inneach *m*
than *conj* na **more t.** barrachd air
other t. ach, a thuilleadh air
thank *v* thoir taing/buidheachas
thankful *a* taingeil, buidheach
thankless *a* gun taing;
(*ungrateful*) mì-thaingeil,
neo-ar-thaingeil
thanks *n* tapadh leat/leibh *m*
many t. mòran taing
that *dem a* sin, siud *dem pron*
sin, ud *rel pron* a **all t.** na *conj*
gu, gum, gun *adv* cho **is it that
late?** a bheil e/i cho anmoch
sin?
thatch *n* tughadh *m v* tugh
thaw *n* aiteamh *m v* bi ag
aiteamh, leagh

the *def art* (*singular forms*) an,
am (+ *b, f, m, p*), a' (+ *len*), an
t- (+ *vowels*); (*plural*) na, na
h- (+ *vowels*) (*See Forms of the
article in Grammar*)
theatre *n* taigh-cluiche *m*
theft *n* mèirle *f*, goid *f*, braide *f*
their *poss pron* an, am, ... aca
them *pers pron* iad, (*emph*)
iadsan
theme *n* cuspair *m*; (*mus*) ùrlar *m*
themselves *emph pron* iad fhèin
then *adv* an sin, an uair sin;
(*afterwards*) an dèidh sin; (*in
that case*) mar sin, a-rèist(e)
thence *adv* às a sin, às an àite
sin, (bh)o sin
theology *n* diadhachd *f*
theoretical *a* teòiridheach,
beachdail
theory *n* teòiridh *f*, beachd *m*,
beachd-smuain *m*
therapist *n* neach-slànachaidh *m*,
leasaiche *m* **speech t.** leasaiche
cainnt *m*
therapy *n* slànachadh *m*,
leasachadh *m*
there *adv* an sin, an siud
thereabouts *adv* mu thimcheall sin
thereafter *adv* an dèidh sin, an
uair sin
thereby *adv* le sin, leis a sin
therefore *adv* mar sin, air an
adhbhar sin
thermal *a* tearmach
thermometer *n* teas-mheidh *f*
these *dem pron* iad seo
thesis *n* tràchdas *m*
they *pers pron* iad, (*emph*) iadsan
thick *a* tiugh, garbh
thicken *v* dèan nas tighe;
(*intrans*) fàs nas tighe
thicket *n* doire d(h)ùmhail *f m*
thickness *n* tighead *m*
thief *n* mèirleach *m*, gadaiche *m*
thieve *v* goid, dèan mèirle
thigh *n* sliasaid *f*
thimble *n* meuran *m*
thin *a* tana, caol; (*scarce*) gann
v tanaich
thing *n* nì *m*, rud *m* **how are
things?** ciamar a tha cùisean?
think *v* smaoinich, saoil, meas

thinness *n* tainead *m*, caoilead *m*
third *n* trian *m*, treas cuid *f*
a treas, tritheamh
thirdly *adv* san treas àite
thirst *n* pathadh *m*, tart *m*,
iota(dh) *m*
thirsty *a* pàiteach, tartmhor,
ìotmhor **are you t.?** a bheil am
pathadh ort?
thirteen *n, a* trì-deug **t. minutes**
trì mionaidean deug
thirteenth *a* treas ... deug
thirty *n, a* deich air fhichead,
trithead *m*
this *dem a* seo
thistle *n* cluaran *m*, fòghnan *m*
thole *v* fuiling
thong *n* iall *f*
thorn *n* dris *f*, droigheann *m*
thorny *a* driseach, droighneach;
(*difficult*) connspaideach,
ciogailteach
thorough *a* mionaideach,
domhainn; (*complete*) fìor
those *dem pron* iad sin, iad siud
though *conj* ge, ged **as t.** mar
gu/gun/gum
thought *n* smaoin *f*, smuain *f*
thoughtful *a* smaointeach;
(*considerate*) tuigseach
thoughtless *a* beag diù, gun
smaoin(eachadh)
thousand *n, a* mìle *m*
thrash *v* slaic, sgiùrs; (*grain*)
buail
thread *n* snàthainn *m*, snàithlean
m
threadbare *a* lom
threat *n* bagairt *f*, maoidheadh *m*
threaten *v* bagair, maoidh
threatening *a* bagarrach
three *n a* trì *a* trì **t. people** triùir *m*
t.-legged trì-chasach **t.-quarters**
trì chairteil *m pl*
thresh *v* buail
threshold *n* stairs(n)each *f*,
maide-buinn *m*
thrift *n* cùmhntachd *f*
thrifty *a* cùmhntach, glèidhteach
thrill *n* gaoir *f* *v* cuir gaoir an
thriller *n* gaoir-sgeul *m*
thrilling *a* fìor thogarrach, gad
chur nad b(h)oil *etc*

thrive *v* soirbhich
throat *n* amha(i)ch *f*, sgòrnan *m*
throb *v* dèan plosgartaich
thrombosis *n* trombòis *f*,
   cleiteachd-fala *f*
throne *n* rìgh-chathair *f*
throng *n* sluagh mòr *m*, co-long *f*
   v dùmhlaich/lìon àite **t. to**
   còmh(dha)laich
throttle *v* tachd, mùch
through *prep* tro, tre, trìd **t. other**
   troimh-a-chèile
throughout *adv* o cheann gu
   ceann, feadh gach àite
throw *n* tilgeadh *m*, tilgeil *m*,
   sadail *m*, caitheamh *m* *v* tilg,
   sad, caith **t. up** dìobhair
thrush *n* smeòrach *f*; (*med*) craos-
   ghalar *m*
thrust *n* sàthadh *m*, sparradh *m*;
   (*of argument*) prìomh phuing *f*
   v sàth, spàrr
thud *n* turtar *m*
thug *n* ùmaidh *m*
thumb *n* òrdag *f*
thump *n* buille *f*, slaic *f*; (*noise*)
   trost *m* *v* buail, thoir slaic do
thunder *n* tàirneanach *m* **t. and
   lightning** tàirneanaich is
   dealanaich
thunderbolt *n* beithir *f m*
Thursday *n* Diardaoin *m*
thus *adv* mar seo, air an dòigh
   seo
thwart *v* cuir bacadh air
thyme *n* lus an rìgh *m*
tick *n* (*sound*) diog *m*, buille *f*;
   (*moment*) diog *m*; (*mark*)
   strìochag *f*; (*insect*) gartan *m*,
   mial-chaorach *f*
ticket *n* tiogaid *f*, tigead *f*
tickle *v* diogail
tide *n* làn *m*, seòl-mara *m*, tìde-
   mhara *f* **high t.** muir-làn *f m*
   low t. muir-tràigh *f m*
tidy *a* sgiobalta *v* sgioblaich
tie *n* bann *m*; (*necktie*) tàidh *f*
   v ceangail
tier *n* sreath *f m*, ìre *f*
tiger *n* tìgear *m*
tight *a* teann
tighten *v* teannaich
tights *n* stocainnean-teann *f pl*

tile *n* leacag *f*, tàidhl *f* *v* leacaich,
   tàidhl
till *prep* gu, gu ruig(e) *conj* gus
tiller *n* (f)ailm *f*, falmadair *m*; (*of
   soil*) treabhaiche *m*
tilt *v* aom
timber *n* fiodh *m* *a* fiodha
time *n* àm *m*, uair *f*; (*period of*)
   ùine *f*, tìde *f*; (*abstr*) tìm *f* **a
   long t. ago** o chionn f(h)ada **any
   t.** uair sam bith **for a long t.**
   airson ùine mhòir **from t. to t.**
   b(h)o àm gu àm **in a week's t.**
   an ceann seachdain **in t.** na uair
   it's high t. you ... tha làn-
   àm/thìde agad ... **on t.** ris an
   uair **plenty of t.** ùine/tìde gu leòr
   what's the t.? dè 'n uair a tha e?
   at times uaireannan *v* tomhais
   an ùine
timely *adv* an deagh àm
timetable *n* clàr-ama *m* *v* dèan
   clàr-ama
timid *a* gealtach, meata
timing *n* tomhas-ama *m*
timorous *a* eagalach, sgeunach,
   sgàthach
tin *n* staoin *f*; (*can*) tiona *m*,
   canastair *m* **tin-opener** fosglair
   chanastairean *m*
tinge *n* lìth *f*, fiamh *m* *v* dath
tingle *n* biorgadaich *f* *v* (*feel a
   tingling*) fairich biorgadh
tinker *n* ceàrd *m*
tinkle *v* dèan/thoir gliong
tinsel *n* tionsail *f*
tint *n* fiamh-dhath *m*, bàn-dhath
   m, tuar *m* *v* dath
tiny *a* bìodach, meanbh, crìon
tip *n* bàrr *m*; (*money*) bonn-boise
   m
tipple *v* dèan pòit, gabh deoch
tipsy *a* air leth-mhisg, froganach
tiptoe *n* corra-biod(a) *m* **on t.** air
   chorra-biod(a)
tirade *n* sruth-cainnt *m*
tire *v* sgìthich, sàraich; (*intrans*)
   fàs sgìth, sgìthich
tired *a* sgìth
Tiree person *n* Tiristeach *m*,
   (*female*) ban-Thiristeach *f*
tiresome *a* sàrachail, leamh
tiring *a* sgìtheil

tissue *n* (*cell*) stuth (cealla) *m*; (*muscle*) maothran *m* **paper t.** nèapaigin pàipeir *m*
tit *n* (*bird*) gocan *m*, smutag *f*; (*slang*) cìoch *f*
tit-bit *n* grèim blasta *m*
title *n* tiotal *m*; (*leg*) còir *f*, dlighe *f*
to *prep* do (+ *len*), (*to a*) gu, (*to the*) chun (+ *gen*); (*before verbs and place names*) a (+ *len*); (*after verbs*) ri **are you going to the shop?** a bheil thu a' dol dhan bhùtha? **she went to a meeting** chaidh i gu coinneimh **are they going to the wedding?** a bheil iad a' dol chun na bainnse? **we are going to play football** tha sinn a' dol a chluich ball-coise **she spoke to him** bhruidhinn i ris *adv* **to and fro,** a-null 's a-nall
toad *n* muile-mhàgag *f*
toast *n* tost *m*; (*drink*) deoch-slàinte *f* *v* tost(aig); (*drink*) òl deoch-slàinte
toaster *n* tostair *m*
tobacco *n* tombaca *m*
today *adv* an-diugh
toddler *n* pàiste *m*
toe *n* òrdag coise *f*
toffee *n* tofaidh *m*
together *adv* còmhla, le chèile
toil *n* saothair *f*, dubh-chosnadh *m* *v* saothraich
toilet *n* taigh-beag *m* **t. roll** roile toidhleit *f m*
token *n* comharra *m*; (*memento*) cuimhneachan *m*
tolerable *a* a ghabhas fhulang; (*fairly good*) meadhanach math
tolerance *n* fulangas *m*; (*patience*) foighidinn *f*
tolerant *a* fosgailte; (*patient*) foighidneach
tolerate *v* fuiling, ceadaich, bi fosgailte do
toll *n* cìs *f*
tomato *n* tomàto *m*
tomb *n* uaigh *f*, tuam *m*
tomcat *n* cat fireann *m*, cullach *m*
tome *n* leabhar mòr *m*
tomorrow *adv* a-màireach
ton *n* tunna *m*

tone *n* (*sound*) fuaim *m*; (*mus*) tòna *f*; (*of voice*) dòigh-labhairt *f* **t.-deaf** *a* ceòl-bhodhar
tongs *n* clobha *m*
tongue *n* teanga *f*; (*lang*) cainnt *f*, cànan *f m*
tonic *n* ìocshlaint *f*; (*uplift*) togail *f*
tonight *adv* a-nochd
tonsil *n* tonsail *f*
too *adv* ro (+ *len*); (*also*) cuideachd, mar an ceudna **too black** ro dhubh **too much** cus, tuilleadh 's a' chòir
tool *n* inneal *m*, ball-acfhainn *m*
tooth *n* fiacail *f* **back t.** fiacail-cùil **toothache** an dèideadh *m*
toothbrush bruis-fhiaclan *f*
toothpaste uachdar-fhiaclan *m*
top *n* mullach *m*, bàrr *m*, uachdar *m* **spinning t.** dòtaman *m* **on t. of** air muin (+ *gen*) **top-heavy** bàrr-throm *v* thoir bàrr air
topic *n* cuspair *m*, ceann(-còmhraidh) *m*
topical *a* àmail, sna naidheachdan
topsy-turvy *a*, *adv* bun-os-cionn, dromach-air-thearrach
torch *n* toirds *f m*, biùgan *m*
torment *n* àmhghar *f m*, dòrainn *f* *v* lèir
torpedo *n* spaileart *m*
torrent *n* tuil *f*, bras-shruth *m*, beum-slèibhe *m*
torrid *a* loisgeach; (*met*) fìor dhian
torso *n* colann *f*, com *m*
tortoise *n* sligeanach *m*
tortuous *a* snìomhach, toinnte, lùbach
torture *n* cràdh *m*, pianadh *m* *v* cràidh, ceus
Tory *n* Tòraidh *m* **the T. Party** am Partaidh Tòraidheach *m*
toss *v* luaisg; (*throw*) tilg; (*of a coin*) cuir croinn
total *a* iomlan, uile *n* sùim (iomlan) *f*
totally *adv* gu lèir, gu h-iomlan, gu tur
touch *v* bean do, suath an, buin ri, làimhsich; (*with emotion*) drùidh air, maothaich

touching *a (emotive)* drùidhteach, maothach
touchy *a* frionasach
tough *a* cruaidh, righinn; *(of meat etc)* righinn
toughen *v* cruadhaich, rìghnich
tour *n* turas *m*, cuairt *f*
tourism *n* turasachd *f*
tourist *n* neach-turais *m pl* luchd-turais **t. information centre** ionad fiosrachaidh turasachd *m* **t. office** oifis turasachd *f*
tow *v* slaod, dragh
towards *prep* a dh'ionnsaigh (+ *gen*); gu, chun (+ *gen*); *(purpose)* a chum (+ *gen*)
towel *n* searbhadair *m*, tubhailt(e) *f m*
tower *n* tùr *m*
town *n* baile *m*, baile-mòr *m* **t. council** comhairle baile *f* **t. hall** talla baile *m*
township *n* baile *m*
toy *n* dèideag *f v* cluich
trace *n* lorg *f v* lorg
track *n* lorg *f*; *(path)* frith-rathad *m*, ceum *m*
tracksuit *n* deise-spòrs *f*
tract *n* leabhran *m*, tràchd *f m*; *(of land)* raonach *m*
tractor *n* tractar *m*
trade *n* malairt *f*; *(craft)* ceàird *f* **t. fair** fèill-mhalairt *f* **t. mark** comharra malairt *m* **t. union** aonadh-ciùird *m v* dèan malairt, malairtich
trader *n* neach-malairt *m*
tradition *n* dualchas; *(oral)* beul-aithris *f*
traditional *a* dualchasach, traidiseanta, beul-aithriseach
traffic *n* trafaig *f* **t. jam** stopadh trafaig *m*
traffic *v* dèan malairt
tragedy *n* cùis-mhulaid *f*; *(liter)* bròn-chluich *f*
tragic *a* muladach, cianail, dòrainneach
trail *n* lorg *f*, slighe *f v* bi air lorg (+ *gen*); *(drag)* slaod; *(intrans)* bi slaodach **t. after** triall às dèidh (+ *gen*)
trailer *n* trèilear *m*

train *n* trèan(a) *f*; *(bride's)* sguain *f v* trèan(aig), teagaisg, ionnsaich; *(intrans)* trèanaig, ionnsaich
trainee *n* foghlamach *m*, neach fo thrèanadh *m*
trainer *n* neach-trèanaidh *m*
trainers *n* brògan-trèanaidh *f pl*
training *n* trèanadh *m*, ionnsachadh *m*
trait *n* stil *f*
traitor *n* neach-brathaidh *m*, brathadair *m*
tramp *n (person)* deòra(i)dh *m*; *(walk)* ruaig *f v* coisich le ceum trom
trample *v* saltair, stamp
trance *n* neul *m*
tranquil *a* ciùin, sìochail, sèimh
tranquillity *n* ciùineas *m*, sìth-thàmh *m*
tranquillizer *n* ciùineadair *m*, tàmhadair *m*
transaction *n* gnothach *m*
transcend *v* rach thairis air, thoir bàrr air
transcribe *v* cuir an sgrìobhadh
transcript *n* riochd sgrìobhte *m*
transfer *n* gluasad *f*, aiseag *m v* gluais, aisig; *(intrans)* gluais gu
transfix *v (met)* beò-ghlac
transform *v* cruth-atharraich
transformation *n* cruth-atharrachadh *m*
transgress *v* bris(t) riaghailt/lagh, peacaich
transgression *n* bris(t)eadh riaghailt/lagh(a) *m*, peacadh *m*
transient *a* diombuan, neo-mhaireann
transition *n* caochladh *m*, eadar-ghluasad *f*
transitional *a* trastach, san eadar-àm, eadar-amail
translate *v* eadar-theangaich; *(move)* gluais
translation *n* eadar-theangachadh *m* **simultaneous t.** eadar-theangachadh mar-aon
translator *n* eadar-theangair *m*
transmission *n* sgaoileadh *m*; *(broadcast)* craobh-sgaoileadh *m*, craoladh *m*
transmit *v* sgaoil; *(broadcast)*

craobh-sgaoil, craol
transmitter *n* uidheam-sgaoilidh
m; (*mast*) crann-sgaoilidh *m*
transparency *n* trìd-shoilleireachd
f; (*met*) follaiseachd *f*
transparent *a* trìd-shoilleir; (*met*)
follaiseach
transpire *v* thig am follais;
(*happen*) tachair
transplant *n* ath-chur *m* **liver t.**
ath-chur air grùthan *v* ath-
chuir
transport *n* giùlan *m*, còmhdhail
f **T. Dept** Roinn na Còmhdhail
v giùlain, iomchair
transpose *v* atharraich òrdugh;
(*mus*) cuir an gleus eile
transverse *a* tarsainn, trasta
trap *n* ribe *f* *v* rib, glac
trash *n* sgudal *m*, smodal *m*
travel *n* siubhal *m*, taisteal *m*
t. agency buidheann-siubhail *f*
m **t. centre** ionad siubhail *m*
v siubhail
traveller *n* neach-siubhail *m*,
taistealaiche *m*
travelling *n* siubhal *m*
a siùbhlach **t.-people** luchd-
siubhail *m pl*
traverse *v* triall, rach tarsainn
trawl *n* lìon-sguabaidh *f*
v sgrìob, tràl(aig); (*search*)
dèan sireadh farsaing
trawler *n* tràlair *m*, bàta-
sgrìobaidh *m*
tray *n* treidhe *m*, sgàl *m*
treacherous *a* cealgach, foilleil;
(*dangerous*) cunnartach
treachery *n* cealg/ceilg *f*, foill *f*
treacle *n* trèicil *m*
tread *v* saltair
treason *n* brathadh *m*, feall *f*
treasure *n* ionmhas *m*, ulaidh *f* *v*
cuir luach mòr air **he treasured
her** bha meas a chridhe aige oirre
treasurer *n* ionmhasair *m*
treat *n* treat *f*, sòlas *m*; (*event*)
cuirm *f* *v* thoir aoigheachd do;
(*deal with*) dèilig ri, làimhsich;
(*med*) thoir aire do **t. someone
to ...** seas do làmh
treatment *n* làimhseachadh *m*,
giullachd *f*

treaty *n* cùmhnant *m*, còrdadh *m*,
cunnradh *m*
treble *a* trì-fillte; (*of voice*) àrd
tree *n* craobh *f*
trefoil *n* trì-bhileach *m*
tremble *v* criothnaich, bi air
chrith
trembling *a* critheanach
tremendous *a* àibheiseach,
sgoinneil **a t. loss** call cianail *m*
a t. help cuideachadh mòr *m*
tremor *n* crith *f*
tremulous *a* critheanach;
(*anxious*) iomagaineach
trench *n* clais *f*; (*in war*) trainnse *f*
trenchant *a* geur, cumhachdach
trend *n* claonadh *m*, gluasad *m*
trepidation *n* geilt *f*; (*phys*) crith-
eagail *f*
trespass *v* rach thar chrìochan;
(*sin*) peacaich
trial *n* deuchainn *f*, dearbhadh *m*;
(*leg*) cùirt *f*
triangle *n* triantan *m* **equilateral t.**
triantan ionann-thaobhach
isosceles t. triantan co-chasach
triangular *a* triantanach
tribe *n* treubh *f*, sliochd *m*
tribulation *n* trioblaid *f*, àmhghar
f m
tribunal *n* tribiùnal *m*
tribute *n* moladh *m*; (*payment*)
càin *f*
trick *n* car *m*, cleas *m* *v* thoir an
car à/às, meall
trickle *n* beag-shileadh *m*, beag-
shruth *m* *v* sil, sruth
tricycle *n* trì-rothach *m*,
traidhsagal *m*
trifle *n* faoineas *m*, rud beag *m*;
(*sweet*) mìlsean-measgaichte *m*,
traidhfeal *m*
trifling *a* beag, suarach
trigger *n* iarann-leigidh *m*
trim *a* sgiobalta, cuimir, grinn
v geàrr, lomaich; (*decorate*)
snasaich
Trinity *n* Trianaid *f* **T. College**
Colaiste na Trianaid *f*
trinket *n* faoin-sheud *m*
trio *n* triùir *f m*; (*mus*) ceòl-triùir *m*
trip *n* turas *m*, cuairt *f*, sgrìob *f*;
(*stumble*) tuisleadh *m* *v* tuislich

triple a trì-fillte v trìoblaich
triplets n triùir f m
tripod n trì-chasach m
trite a beag seagh
triumph n buaidh f; (exultation)
buaidh-chaithream m v thoir
buaidh, buadhaich
triumphant a (victorious)
buadhmhor; (exultant)
caithreamach
trivial a suarach, gun fhiù
trolley n troilidh f
trombone n trombòn m
troop n buidheann f m,
cuideachd f, trùp m **t. of horses**
greigh each f v triall
trophy n cuach buaidhe f
tropic n tropaig f **the Tropics** na
Tropaigean f pl
tropical a tropaigeach
trot v dèan trotan, trot
trouble n dragh m, saothair f;
(dispute) trioblaid f, buaireas m
v cuir dragh air, buair
troublemaker n buaireadair m,
neach-buairidh m
troublesome a draghail; (causing
trouble) buaireasach
trough n amar m
trounce v liodraig
trousers n briogais f
trout n breac m **sea t.** bànag f
trowel n sgreadhail f
truancy n seachnadh-sgoile m
truant n seachnaiche(-sgoile) m
truce n fosadh (còmhraig) m
truck n truga f **have no t. with** na
gabh gnothach ri
truculent a ceacharra
trudge v ceumnaich gu trom
true a fìor, fìrinneach; (faithful)
dìleas; (right) ceart **a t.**
understanding fìor thuigse
truly adv gu fìrinneach, gu
dearbh, gu deimhinn(e) **yours t.**
le dùrachd
trumpet n trombaid f
truncate v giorraich
truncheon n plocan m
trunk n stoc m, bun-craoibhe m;
(for storage) ciste f; (of animal)
sròn f, gnos m; (anat) com m
t. road prìomh-rathad m

trust n earbsa f, creideas m;
(company) urras m **the National
T.** an t-Urras Nàiseanta v earb
à, cuir muinighin an, thoir
creideas do
trustee n urrasair m
trusting a earbsail
trustworthy a earbsach
truth n fìrinn f **in t.** gu fìrinneach
to tell the t. a dh'innse na fìrinn
try v feuch
trying a deuchainneach
tryst n dàil f, coinneamh f;
(place) àite-coinneachaidh m
tub n tuba f m, ballan m
tube n pìoban m, feadan m, tiùb
f
tuberculosis n a' chaitheamh f
tuck v trus
Tuesday n Dimàirt m
tuft n dos m, topan m
tug n tarraing f, draghadh m;
(naut) tuga f v tarraing, dragh,
spìon
tuition n teagasg m, oideachadh
m, ionnsachadh m
tulip n tiuilip f
tumble n tuiteam m **t. dryer** n car-
thiormaichear m v tuit
tummy n brù f
tumour n at m, màm m, meall m
tumult n iorghail f, onghail f
tumultuous a iorghaileach,
onghaileach
tune n fonn m, port m v gleus,
cuir air ghleus
tuneful a ceòlmhor, fonnmhor
tuner n neach-gleusaidh m
tunnel n tunail f m
tup n reithe m, rùda m
turbine n roth-uidheam f
turbot n turbaid f
turbulence n buaireas m,
luaisgeachd f
turbulent a buaireasach,
luaisgeach
turf n (ground) bàrr-talmhainn
m; (a sod) sgrath f, fò(i)d f
turgid a air at; (style) trom,
iom-fhaclach
Turk n Turcach m, (female) ban-
T(h)urcach f
turkey n eun-Frangach m, cearc

Fhrangach *f*
Turkish *a* Turcach; (*lang*) Turcais *f*
turmoil *n* troimh-a-chèile *f m*
ùpraid *f*
turn *n* tionndadh *m*, car *m*, lùb *f*;
(*in sequence*) cuairt *f* **she took a
t.** thàinig cuairt oirre
v tionndaidh, cuir mun cuairt
turnip *n* tui(r)neap *m*, snèap *f*
turnout *n* na nochd
turnover *n* luach na malairt *m*;
(*of staff etc*) atharrachadh *m*
turquoise *a* tuirc-ghorm
turret *n* turaid *f*
turtle *n* turtar *f*
tusk *n* starr-fhiacail *f*, tosg *m*
tussle *n* tuasaid *f*, strì *f*
tut! *interj* t(h)ud!
tutor *n* oide *m*
tutorial *n* tràth-oideachaidh *m*
twang *n* gliong *m*; (*lang*) blas *m*
tweak *v* cuir car de; (*met*) dèan
atharrachadh beag air
tweed *n* clò (mòr) *m* **Harris T.** an
Clò Mòr/Hearach *m*
tweezers *n* greimiche *m*
twelfth *a* dara ... deug
twelve *n* a dhà-dheug *a* dà ...
dheug **t. disciples** dà dheisciobal
dheug *m*
twentieth *a* ficheadamh
twenty *n*, *a* fichead *m*
twice *adv* dà uair, dà thuras
twig *n* faillean *m*, slat *f*
twilight *n* eadar-sholas *m*,
camhanaich *f*, ciaradh *m*
twin *n* leth-aon *m* *pl* leth-aonan,
càraid *f*
twine *v* toinn
twinge *n* biorgadh *m*
twinkle/twinkling *n* priobadh *m*;
(*in eye*) drithleann *m* **in the t. of
an eye** ann am priobadh na sùla
v priob
twirl *n* roithleagan *m*; (*act*)
ruidhleadh *m* *v* ruidhil mun
cuairt
twist *n* toinneamh *m*, car *m*,
snìomh *m* *v* toinn; (*story*) cuir
car an; (*ankle*) cuir snìomh an
twisted *a* snìomhte, toinnte;
(*nature*) coirbte
twit *n* amadan *m*, gloidhc *f*

twitch *n* spadhadh *m*, strangadh
m
twitter *v* ceilearaich
two *n* a dhà *a* dà **two people**
dithis *f* **two-dimensional** dà-
sheallach **two-faced** dà-
aodannach, leam-leat **two-fold**
dà-fhillte, dùbailte **two-ply**
dà-dhualach
tycoon *n* toicear *m*, saidhbhriche *m*
type *n* seòrsa *m*; (*typ*) clò *m*
v clò-sgrìobh, taidhp
typhoid *n* am fiabhras breac *m*
typhus *n* am fiabhras ballach *m*
typical *a* coltach, dualach **that's t.
of him** tha sin cho coltach ris
typify *v* riochdaich, bi na (h-) *etc*
eisimpleir de
typing *n* clò-sgrìobhadh *m*
typographical *a* clò-bhualaidh **t.
error** mearachd clò-bhualaidh *f*
tyrannical *a* aintighearnail
tyrannize *v* dèan ainneart air
tyranny *n* aintighearnas *m*
tyrant *n* aintighearna *m*
tyre *n* tàidhr *f*, taidhear *f*

U

ubiquitous *a* sa h-uile h-àite,
uile-làthaireach
ugly *a* grànda
Uist person *n* Uibhisteach *m*,
(*female*) ban-Uibhisteach *f*
ulcer *n* neasgaid *f*
ulterior *a* ìochdarach; (*met*)
neo-fhollaiseach
ultimate *a* deireannach, mu
dheireadh
ultimatum *n* rabhadh deireannach
m
ultra *a* ro, sàr-, fìor, buileach
umbrage *n* oilbheum *m*
umbrella *n* sgàilean *m*
umpire *n* rèitire *m*, britheamh *m*
unable *a* eu-comasach **u. to** gun
chomas
unacceptable *a* ... ris nach
fhaodar gabhail
unaccompanied *a* na (h-)aonar
etc; (*mus*) gun taic-ciùil
unaccustomed *a* neo-chleachdte
(ri)

unadulterated *a* neo-thruaillte
unaided *a*, *adv* gun chuideachadh
unambiguous *a* (*lit*) aon-seaghach; (*met*) gun cheist
unanimous *a* aon-ghuthach, a dh'aon inntinn
unanimously *adv* gu h-aon-ghuthach
unappetizing *a* neo-bhlasta, mì-chàilear
unarmed *a* gun armachd, neo-armaichte
unassuming *a* iriosal
unattainable *a* do-ruighinn, thar ruigse
unattended *a* gun neach na c(h)ois *etc*
unauthorized *a* gun ùghdarras, neo-cheadaichte
unavailing *a* gun tairbhe
unavoidable *a* do-sheachanta
unaware *a* gun fhios/mhothachadh
unbalanced *a* mì-chothromach
unbearable *a* do-fhulang
unbeatable *a* nach gabh beatadh
unbecoming *a* mì-chneasta
unbelief *n* eas-creideamh *m*
unbiased *a* gun chlaonadh
unborn *a* gun bhreith
unbreakable *a* nach gabh bris(t)eadh
unbroken *a* gun bhris(t)eadh
unbutton *v* fuasgail
unceasing *a* gun sgur/stad/abhsadh
uncertain *a* mì-chinnteach
uncertainty *n* mì-chinnt *f*
unchanging *a* neo-chaochlaideach
uncivil *a* gun mhodh
uncivilized *a* neo-shìobhalta, borbarra
uncle *n* bràthair-athar/màthar *m*, uncail *m*
unclean *a* neòghlan
uncombed *a* gun chìreadh
uncomfortable *a* mì-chofhurtail
uncommon *a* neo-àbhaisteach, neo-chumanta
uncomplaining *a* neo-ghearaineach
unconcerned *a* gun chùram, gun dragh

unconditional *a* gun chùmhnantan/chumhachan
unconfirmed *a* gun daingneachadh
unconnected *a* gun cheangal, neo-cheangailte
unconscious *a* gun mhothachadh/fhaireachadh
unconstitutional *a* neo-reachdail
uncontested *a* gun fharpais
uncontrollable *a* thar smachd(achaidh)
uncooked *a* amh, gun chòcaireachd
uncouth *a* neo-ghrinn, amh
uncover *v* rùisg; (*met*) thoir gu follais
undecided *a* mì-chinnteach
undeniable *a* do-àicheadh
under *prep* fo *adv* fodha **it went u.** chaidh e/i fodha
undercurrent *n* fo-shruth *m*; (*met*) faireachdainn *f m*
undercut *v* cuir air prìs nas ìsle
underestimate *v* meas fo luach
undergo *v* rach/theirig tro, fuiling
underground *a* fo thalamh **u. train** trèan(a) fo thalamh *f*
underhand *a* cealgach, clìceach
underline *v* (*lit*) cuir sgrìob/loidhne fo; (*met*) comharraich, dearbh
undermine *v* (*lit*) cladhaich fo; (*met*) lagaich
underneath *prep* fo *adv* shìos, gu h-ìosal/ìseal
underpass *n* bealach fo thalamh *m*
underskirt *n* cota-bàn *m*
underspend *n* caiteachas fon t-sùim shuidhichte *m v* caith fon t-sùim shuidhichte
understand *v* tuig
understanding *n* tuigse *f*, breithneachadh *m*; (*accord*) còrdadh *m*
understanding *a* tuigseach
undertake *v* gabh os làimh
undertaker *n* neach-adhlacaidh *m*, adhlaicear *m*
undertaking *n* gnothach *m*, iomairt *f*
underway *a* fo sheòl, ga c(h)ur an

gnìomh
underwear *n* fo-aodach *m*
undeserved *a* neo-thoillte
undisputed *a* gun chonnspaid,
gun cheist, dearbhte
undo *v* fuasgail; (*unpick*) sgaoil;
(*abstr*) mill
undoubtedly *adv* gun teagamh
undress *v* cuir/thoir aodach
dheth, dhìth *etc* **I undressed**
chuir mi dhìom (m' aodach)
undue *a* neo-dhligheach;
(*excessive*) cus
uneasy *a* mì-shaorsainneil
uneconomic *a* neo-eaconamach
uneducated *a* neo-
fhoghlaim(ich)te, gun fhoghlam
unemployed *a* gun obair
unemployment *n* cion cosnaidh
m, dìth obrach *f m* **u. benefit**
sochair cion cosnaidh *f*
unequal *a* neo-ionann
uneven *a* mì-chothrom,
mì-chòmhnard
unexpectedly *adv* gun dùil
ris/rithe *etc*
unfair *a* mì-cheart,
mì-chothromach
unfaithful *a* mì-dhìleas, neo-
dhìleas
unfamiliar *a* coimheach
u. surroundings àite far nach
eil/robh mi *etc* eòlach
unfashionable *a* neo-fhasanta
unfasten *v* fuasgail
unfavourable *a* neo-fhàbharach
unfinished *a* neo-chrìochnaichte,
gun chrìochnachadh
unfit *a* (*phys*) gun spionnadh;
(*unsuitable*) mì-fhreagarrach,
neo-iomchaidh; (*unworthy*)
neo-airidh
unforeseen *a* gun dùil ris/rithe *etc*
unfortunate *a* mì-fhortanach,
mì-shealbhach
unfortunately *adv* gu mì-
fhortanach, gu mì-shealbhach
unfriendly *a* neo-chàirdeil, fad' às
ungainly *a* liobasta, cliobach,
spàgach
ungodly *a* ain-diadhaidh
ungrateful *a* mì-thaingeil
unhappy *a* mì-thoilichte,

mì-shona
unhealthy *a* mì-fhallain
unholy *a* mì-naomh(a); (*met*)
mì-chneasta
uniform *n* èideadh *m*, deise
dreuchd *f* **firefighter's u.** èideadh
smàladair *m* *a* aon-fhillte;
(*consistent*) cunbhalach
unify *v* co-aonaich
unilateral *a* aon-taobhach
unimportant *a* neo-chudromach
that is u. chan fhiach sin
bruidhinn air
uninformed *a* aineolach, gun
eòlas
uninspired *a* neo-thogarrach,
marbhanta
unintentionally *adv* gun fhiosta,
gun a bhith an rùn
uninterested *a* gun ùidh
uninvited *a* gun chuireadh/
fhiathachadh
union *n* aonadh *m* **trade u.**
aonadh luchd-ciùird
unique *a* gun choimeas, air leth
it was u. cha robh a leithid ann
unison *a* aon-ghuthach
unit *n* aonad *m*
unite *v* aonaich
united *a* aonaichte **the U.
Kingdom** an Rìoghachd
Aonaichte *f* **the U. States** na
Stàitean Aonaichte *f pl* **the U.
Nations** na Dùthchannan
Aonaichte *f pl*
unity *n* aonachd *f*
universal *a* uile-choitcheann,
coitcheann
universe *n* cruinne *m* (*f in gen*),
cruinne-cè *m* (*f in gen*), domhan
m
university *n* oilthigh *m*
unjust *a* mì-cheart
unkind *a* mosach, gun choibhneas
unknown *a* neo-aithnichte
unlawful *a* mì-laghail
unleaded *a* gun luaidhe
(ann/innte) **u. petrol** peatrail
gun luaidhe *m*
unless *conj* mur(a), nas lugha na
unlicensed *a* gun cheadachd
unlike *a* ao-coltach (ri)
unlikely *a* mì-choltach

unlimited *a* gun chrìoch, neo-chrìochnach
unload *v* thoir an luchd de
unlock *v* fosgail (glas)
unlucky *a* mì-shealbhach
unmarried *a* gun phòsadh
unmistakable *a* do-àicheanta
unnatural *a* mì-nàdarra(ch)
unnecessary *a* neo-riatanach, gun fheum air
unobtainable *a* nach gabh faighinn, do-ruighinn
unobtrusive *a* neo-fhollaiseach/nochdte
unoccupied *a* falamh, bàn
unofficial *a* neo-oifigeil
unorthodox *a* neo-ghnàthach
unpack *v* falmhaich, thoir às
unpaid *a* gun phàigheadh/tuarastal
unpalatable *a* mì-bhlasta/chàilear
unpardonable *a* nach fhaodar a mhathadh
unplayable *a* nach gabh cluich(e), do-chluiche
unpleasant *a* mì-thlachdmhor
unpopular *a* gun mheas air/oirre *etc*
unprecedented *a* gun choimeas, nach do thachair roimhe
unprepared *a* mì-dheiseil, neo-ullaichte
unproductive *a* gun tairbhe, neo-thorrach, neo-tharbhach
unprofessional *a* mì-phroifeiseanta
unprofitable *a* gun bhuannachd, neo-phrothaideach
unprotected *a* gun dìon
unqualified *a* gun teisteanas; (*total*) iomlan, fìor
unquestionably *adv* gun cheist
unravel *v* (*trans*) rèitich; (*intrans*) sgaoil
unreal *a* neo-fhìor
unrealistic *a* neo-phractaigeach
unreasonable *a* mì-reusanta
unrelated *a* gun bhuntainneas/cheangal
unreliable *a* neo-earbsach
unrest *n* an-fhois *f*; (*civil*) buaireadh *m*

unrestricted *a* gun bhacadh/chuing
unripe *a* an-abaich
unrivalled *a* gun choimeas, gun samhail
unruly *a* mì-rianail, tuasaideach; (*of children*) luathaireach
unsafe *a* mi-shàbhailte, cunnartach
unsatisfactory *a* neo-iomchaidh
I found it u. cha robh mi riaraichte leis
unsavoury *a* (*taste*) mì-bhlasta; (*met*) mì-chneasta
unseemly *a* mì-chiatach
unselfish *a* neo-fhèineil
unsettled *a* neo-shuidhichte, mì-sheatlaigte
unsightly *a* grànda, mì-mhaiseach
unsophisticated *a* sìmplidh
unspecified *a* neo-ainmichte
unspoiled *a* gun mhilleadh
unstable *a* cugallach, neo-sheasmhach
unsteady *a* cugallach, mì-chothromach
unsuccessful *a* neo-shoirbheachail
unsuitable *a* mì-fhreagarrach
unsuspecting *a* gun amharas
unsympathetic *a* neo-fhaireachail, neo-thruasail, gun cho-fhaireachdainn
untested *a* gun dearbhadh/fheuchainn
unthinkable *a* nach gabh smaoineachadh (air)
untidy *a* mì-sgiobalta
untie *v* fuasgail
until *prep* gu *conj* gus **u. she returns** gus an till i
unto *prep* gu, do, chun (+ *gen*)
untrue *a* neo-fhìrinneach, fìor (*preceded by neg v*) **that's quite u.** chan eil sin idir fìor
untruth *n* breug *f*
untruthful *a* neo-fhìrinneach, neo-fhìor
unusual *a* neo-àbhaisteach, annasach
unused *a* gun chleachdadh, nach deach a chleachdadh
unveil *v* leig ris, taisbean

unwanted *a* gun iarraidh
unwarranted *a* gun adhbhar cothromach
unwell *a* tinn, bochd, meadhanach
unwieldy *a* doirbh a ghiùlain, lòdail, liobasta
unwilling *a* ain-deònach, mì-dheònach
unwind *v* thoir às an toinneamh, fuasgail; (*relax*) gabh fois
unwise *a* neo-ghlic, gòrach
unworthy *a* (*person*) neo-airidh; (*motive*) suarach
unwrap *v* thoir còmhdach de
up *prep* suas *adv* shuas **up the hill** suas an cnoc **were you up?** an robh thu shuas? **we were up until 2 o'clock** bha sinn an-àird(e) gu dà uair
upbringing *n* togail *f*, àrach *m*
update *n* cunntas às ùr *m* *v* ùraich, clàraich às ùr, thoir cunntas as ùr do
uphold *v* glèidh, thoir taic do, cùm suas
uplift *v* (*phys*) tog (suas); (*mental*) tog inntinn/meanmna
uplifting *a* brosnachail, a thogas meanmna
upon *prep* air, air muin (+ *gen*), air uachdar (+ *gen*)
upper *a* shuas, uachdrach
upright *a* dìreach; (*met*) dìreach, treibhdhireach, ceart
uproar *n* ùpraid *f*
uproot *v* spìon on fhreumh/bhun
upset *n* troimh-a-chèile *f m*, bun-os-cionn *m* *v* cuir troimh-a-chèile/bun-os-cionn
upshot *n* bun a bh' ann *m*, buil *f*
upside-down *adv* bun-os-cionn, a c(h)asan os a c(h)ionn *etc*
upstairs *a, adv* shuas an staidhre *adv* shuas an staidhre **going u.** a' dol suas an staidhre
up-to-date *a* an là an-diugh **u. fashions** fasain an là an-diugh
upwards *adv* suas
urban *a* baile
urbane *a* furm(h)ailteach
urge *n* miann *f m* *v* brosnaich,

spàrr, cuir ìmpidh air
urgency *n* deatamachd *f*, èiginneachd/èigeannachd *f*, cabhag *f*
urgent *a* èiginneach/èigeannach
urgently *adv* gu cabhagach, na (h-)èiginn *etc*
urine *n* mùn *m*
us *pron* sinn, *emph* sinne
usage *n* cleachdadh *m*, gnàths *m*
use *n* cleachdadh *m*, ùisneachadh *m*; (*usefulness*) feum *m* **what use is it?** dè am feum a th' ann? *v* cleachd, cuir gu feum, cuir an sàs, ùisnich
useful *a* feumail, gu feum
useless *a* gun fheum
user *n* neach-cleachdaidh *m*
usher *n* treòraiche *m* *v* treòraich a-steach
usual *a* àbhaisteach **as u.** mar as àbhaist, (*past tense*) mar a b' àbhaist
usually *adv* gu h-àbhaisteach, mar as/(a) bu trice
usurp *v* gabh/glèidh gun chòir
utensil *n* soitheach *f m,* uidheam *f,* inneal *m*
uterus *n* machlag *f*
utility *n* goireas *m,* feum *m*
utilize *v* cleachd, cuir gu feum, cuir an sàs, ùisnich
utmost *a* as fhaide a-mach **I will do my u.** nì mi m' uile dhìcheall
utter *v* abair, can, labhair
utterly *adv* gu tur, uile-gu-lèir
U-turn *n* làn-char *m,* tur-atharrachadh *m*

V

vacancy *n* àite bàn/falamh *m,* beàrn *f m*
vacant *a* falamh, bàn, fàs
vacate *v* falmhaich, fàg
vacation *n* saor-làithean *m pl,* làithean-saora *m pl*
vaccination *n* banachdach *f*
vaccinate *v* thoir banachdach do
vacillate *v* bi eadar dhà bharail, bi sa bhonnalaich
vacuous *a* falamh, baoth
vacuum *n* falamhachd *f*

vacuum-cleaner *n* glanadair-sùghaidh *m*

vagina *n* faighean *m*

vagrant *n* siùbhlach *m*, faondrach *m*

vague *a* neo-shoilleir

vain *a* (*futile*) dìomhain, faoin; (*proud*) mòr às/aiste *etc* fhèin

valiant *a* calma, treubhach, foghainteach

valid *a* dligheach; (*of time*) a' seasamh

validate *v* dearbh

valley *n* gleann *m*; (*wide, with river*) srath *m*

valour *n* gaisge *f*

valuable *a* luachmhor, prìseil

valuation *n* meas *m*, luachadh *m*

value *n* luach *m*, fiach *m* *v* meas, cuir luach air, luach

valve *n* còmhla *f*, bhalbh *f m*

van *n* bhan(a) *f*; (*front*) toiseach *m*, tùs *m*

vandal *n* milltear *m*, sgriosadair *m*

vandalism *n* milleadh *m*, sgriosadh *m*

vanish *v* rach às an t-sealladh

vanity *a* dìomhanas *m*, faoineas *m*

vapour *n* deatach *f*, smùid *f*

variable *a* caochlaideach *n* caochladair *m*

variant *n* riochd eile *m*

variation *n* atharrachadh *m*, caochladh *m*; (*mus*) tionndadh *m*

varicose veins *n* fèithean borrach *f pl*

varied *a* eadar-dhealaichte

variety *n* (*mixture*) measgachadh *m*, caochladh *m*; (*kind*) seòrsa *m*, gnè *f*

various *a* iomadh, iomadach, eug-samhail

varnish *n* falaid *m*, bhàrnais *f* *v* cuir falaid/bhàrnais air, falaidich

vary *v* atharraich, caochail

vase *n* bhàs(a) *f*

vaseline *n* bhasailin *m*

vast *a* ro mhòr, àibheiseach

vault *n* (*cellar*) seilear *m*; (*tomb*) tuam *m*

vault *v* leum thairis air, geàrr sùrdag

veal *n* feòil-laoigh *f*

veer *v* gabh fiaradh, tionndaidh

vegetable(s) *n* glasraich *f*

vegetarian *n* glasraichear *m*, feòil-sheachnair *m*

vegetation *n* fàs-bheatha *f*

vehemence *n* dèineas *m*

vehement *a* dian, dealasach

vehicle *n* carbad *m*; (*means*) seòl *m*

veil *n* (*on person*) sgàile *f*, brat-gnùise *m* *v* còmhdaich, ceil, cuir fo sgàil

vein *n* cuisle *f*, fèith-fala *f* **in that v.** air a' mhodh sin

velvet *n* meileabhaid *f*

veneer *n* snas-chraiceann *m*; (*met*) còmhdach uachdair *m*, sgeadachadh *m*

venerate *v* thoir mòr-spèis do

venereal *a* muineil **v. disease** a' bhreac Fhrangach *f*

vengeance *n* dìoghaltas *m*

venison *n* sitheann(-fèidh) *f m*

venom *n* nimh *m*, puinnsean *m*

venomous *a* nimheil

vent *n* fosgladh *m*, luidhear *m* *v* leig a-mach, leig ruith le

ventilate *v* fionnaraich, èadhraig

ventilation *n* fionnarachadh *m*, èadhraigeadh *m*

venture *n* iomairt *f*, oidhirp *f* *v* meantraig

venue *n* àite *m*, ionad *m*

Venus *n* Bheunas *f*

verb *n* gnìomhair *m*

verbatim *adv* facal air an fhacal

verbose *a* briathrach, ro bhriathrach, cabach

verdant *a* gorm, feurach

verdict *n* breith *f*

verge *n* oir *f m*; (*of road*) fàl *m* **on the v. of ...** an impis ... (+ *vn*)

verify *v* dearbh, fìrinnich, dèan cinnteach

veritable *a* fìor, cinnteach

vermin *n* (*lice*) mialan *f pl*; (*rodents*) criomairean *m pl*

versatile *a* iol-chomasach, làmhcharach

verse *n* rann *m*, earrann *f*;

(*poetry*) bàrdachd *f*
version *n* (*draft*) dreach *m*; (*of events*) cunntas *f m*; (*alternative*) tionndadh *m*
versus *prep* an aghaidh (+ *gen*)
vertebrae *n* cnàmhan an droma *m pl*
vertebrate *n* druim-altach(an) *m*
vertical *a* dìreach
vertigo *n* tuaineal *m*, tuainealaich *f*
very *a* fìor (+ *len*), anabarrach; (*same*) ceart, dearbh (*both* + *len*) *adv* glè, fìor, ro (*all* + *len*)
vessel *n* soitheach *f m* **blood v.** balg fala *m*
vest *n* fo-lèine *f*; (*waistcoat*) siosacot *m*
vestibule *n* for-dhoras *m*
vestige *n* lorg *f*, comharra *m*
vet *n* lighiche-sprèidh *m*, bheat *m*
vet *v* sgrùd, breithnich
veteran *n* seann eòlach *m*; (*soldier*) seann saighdear *m* *a* seann, sean, eòlach
veto *n* crosadh *m*, bacadh *m*, bhèato *m* *v* cros, bac, dèan bhèato air
vex *v* leamhaich, buair, sàraich
vexation *n* leamhachas *m*, buaireadh *m*, sàrachadh *m*
via *prep* taobh (+ *gen*), tro
viability *n* comas obrachaidh *m*
viable *a* a ghabhas obrachadh
vial *n* searrag ghlainne *f*, meanbh-bhotal *m*
vibrate *v* crith, cuir air chrith, triob(h)uail
vibration *n* crith *f*, triob(h)ualadh *m*
vicar *n* piocair *m*, biocair *m*
vice *n* dubhailc *f*; (*tool*) bithis *f*, teanchair *m*
vice- *pref* iar-, leas- **vice-president** iar-cheann-suidhe *m*
vice-versa *adv* agus a chaochladh
vicinity *n* àrainn *f*, nàbachas *m*
vicious *a* guineach, garg
victim *n* fulangaiche *m*, neach a dh'fhuiling(eas) *m*
victorious *a* buadhach, buadhmhor

victory *n* buaidh *f*
video *n* bhidio *f* **videotape** teip bhidio *f* **v. conference** co-labhairt bhidio *f*
vie *v* strì (ri)
view *n* sealladh *m*; (*opinion*) beachd *m* *v* seall air, faic
viewer *n* neach-amhairc/coimhid *m*
viewpoint *n* àite-seallaidh/amhairc/coimhid *m*; (*opinion*) beachd *m*
vigil *n* faire *f* **keeping a v.** ri faire
vigilant *a* furachail
vigorous *a* sgairteil, calma
vigour *n* spionnadh *m*, sgairt *f*, treòir *f*
vile *a* gràineil, sgreataidh
vilify *v* màb, dubh-chàin
villa *n* taigh mòr *m*, taigh air leth *m*
village *n* baile beag *m*, clachan *m*
villain *n* slaightear *m*, eucorach *m*; (*liter*) droch fhear *m*
vindicate *v* dearbh; (*justify*) fìreanaich
vindictive *a* dìoghaltach
vine *n* fìonan *f m*, crann-fìona *m* **vineyard** fìon-lios *m*
vinegar *n* fìon geur *m*
violate *v* mill, bris(t)
violation *n* milleadh *m*, bris(t)eadh *m*; (*of person*) èigneachadh *m*
violence *n* fòirneart *m*, ainneart *m*
violent *a* fòirneartach, ainneartach **v. storm** gailleann *f*, doinnean *f* **he has a v. temper** tha leum eagalach na nàdar
violet *n* sail/dail-chuach *f*, bròg na cuthaige *f*
violin *n* fidheall *f*
violinist *n* fìdhlear *m*
viper *n* nathair-nimhe *f*
virgin *n* òigh *f*, maighdeann *f*
virginity *n* òigheachd *f*, maighdeannas *m*
virile *n* fearail, duineil
virtual *a* mas fhìor **v. reality** mas-fhìorachd *f*
virtually *adv* an impis (+ *vn*) **it's v. finished** cha mhòr nach eil e ullamh

virtue n subhailc f, deagh-bheus f, feart m
virtuous a subhailceach, beusach
virulent a nimhneach, geur
virus n bhìoras m
visa n bhìosa f
visage n aghaidh f, gnùis f
vis-à-vis prep a thaobh (+ gen); (opposite) aghaidh ri aghaidh
visibility n faicsinneachd f
visible a faicsinneach
vision n (sight) fradharc m, lèirsinn f; (insight) sealladh m, lèirsinn f; (dream) bruadar m, aisling f
visionary n neach le lèirsinn m a lèirsinneach
visit n tadhal m, cèilidh f m v tadhail, dèan cèilidh
visitor n neach-tadhail m, aoigh m, cèiliche m
visor n cidhis f
vista n sealladh m
visual a fradharcach, lèirsinne
visualize v dèan samhla sùla, dèan dealbh san inntinn
vital a beò, beathail; (important) ro chudromach
vitality n beathalachd f
vitamin n beothaman m
vitriol n (acid) searbhag loisgeach f; (rancour) nimhealachd f
vituperation n aithiseachadh m
vivacious a aigeannach, beothail
vivid a beò, boillsgeanta
vixen n sionnach boireann m
viz adv is e sin, 's e sin ri ràdh
vocabulary n (of person) stòr fhaclan m, (glossary) faclair m
vocal a guthach; (outspoken) àrd-ghuthach
vocation n (work) dreuchd f, ceàird f; (calling) gairm beatha f
vocative a gairmeach **v. case** an tuiseal gairmeach m
vociferous a sgairteach
vodka n bhodca m
vogue n fasan m **in v.** san fhasan
voice n guth m v cuir am briathran/an cèill
void n fàsalachd f; (outer space) fànas a falamh, fàs
volatile a cugallach,

caochlaideach, luaineach
volcano n beinn-theine f, b(h)olcàno m
volition n toil f
volley n (of gun) làdach m; (sport) bhòilidh f
volleyball n ball-làmhaich m
volt n bholt(a) m
voltage n bholtaids f, bholtachd f
voluble a sruth-chainnteach
volume n (book) leabhar m; (capacity) tomhas-lìonaidh m; (size) tomad m
voluntary a saor-thoileach **v. organization** buidheann s(h)aor-thoileach f m
volunteer n saor-thoileach m v tairg
voluptuous a (shape) làn-chumadail
vomit(ing) n cur a-mach m, sgeith m, dìobhairt m v cuir a-mach, sgeith, dìobhair
voracious a cìocrach, gionach, craosach
vote n bhòt(a) f **postal v.** bhòt(a) tron phost v bhòt
voter n neach-bhòtaidh m, bhòtair m
voting n bhòtadh m **v. system** siostam/modh bhòtaidh m
vouch v dearbh, thoir fianais
voucher n bileag fianais f, bileag-theist f
vow n bòid f, gealladh m v bòidich, mionnaich
vowel n fuaimreag f
voyage n turas-mara m, bhòidse f
vulgar a mì-chneasta, gràisgeil
vulnerable a (to attack) fosgailte (gu ionnsaigh); (person) so-leònte, dualach a g(h)oirteachadh etc
vulture n fang f

W

wade v grunnaich
wafer n abhlan m, slisneag f
waffle n (met) baoth-chòmhradh m, cainnt gun bhrìgh f
wag n àbhachdaiche m, sgeigire m

wage(s) *n* tuarastal *m*, duais *f*
wager *n* geall *m* *v* cuir geall, rach an urras
wagtail *n* breac-an-t-sìl *m*, breacan-buidhe *m*
wail(ing) *n* caoineadh *m*, gal *m*, burralaich *f*
waist *n* meadhan *m*
waistcoat *n* siosacot *m*, peitean *m*
wait *n* feitheamh *m*, stad *m* **they had a long w.** bha iad fada a' feitheamh *v* fuirich, feith, fan; (*serve*) fritheil
waiting-list *n* liosta-feitheimh *f*
waiting-room *n* seòmar-feitheimh *m*
waiter *n* fear-frithealaidh *m*
waitress *n* tè-fhrithealaidh *f*
waive *v* cuir an dàrna taobh
wake *n* faire *f*, taigh-fhaire *m*
wake(n) *v* dùisg
walk *n* cuairt *f*, ceum *m* *v* coisich, gabh ceum
walking-stick *n* bata *m*
wall *n* balla *m*; (*dyke*) gàrradh *m*
wallet *n* leabhar-pòcaid *m*
wallpaper *n* pàipear(-balla) *m*, bolt *m* *v* pàipearaich, boltaig
walnut *n* gall-chnò *f*
walrus *n* each-mara *m*, uàlras *m*
wand *n* slat *f*, slatag *f*
wander *v* rach air shiubhal; (*go astray*) rach air seachran; (*in mind*) rach iomrall
wanderer *n* siùbhlaiche *m*
wane *v* lùghdaich, crìon, searg
want *n* (*lack*) easbhaidh *f*, dìth *f* *m*; (*poverty*) bochdainn *f* *v* iarr; (*lack*) bi a dh'easbhaidh (+ *gen*)
wanton *a* drùiseil; (*reckless*) dalma
war *n* cogadh *m* **war memorial** cuimhneachan-cogaidh *m* *v* cog, cathaich
ward *n* (*hospital*) uàrd *m*; (*division*) roinn *f* **w. of court** neach fo chùram (cùrtach) *m*
warden *n* neach-gleidhidh *m*
warder *n* neach-faire *m*
wardrobe *n* preas-aodaich *m*
warehouse *n* taigh-bathair *m*
warfare *n* cogadh *m*
warm *a* blàth; (*personality*)

coibhneil *v* blàthaich, gar
warmth *n* blàths *m*; (*personality*) tlàths *m*
warn *v* thoir rabhadh (do)
warning *n* rabhadh *m*
warp *v* claon, seac
warrant(y) *n* barantas *m*
warren *n* broclach *f*, toll *m*
warrior *n* laoch *m*, gaisgeach *m*, curaidh *m*
warship *n* long-chogaidh *f*
wart *n* foinne *f m*
wary *a* faiceallach, cùramach
was *v* bha (*See verb* **to be** *in Grammar*)
wash *n* nighe *m*, glanadh *m*, ionnlad *m* *v* nigh, ionnlaid
washer *n* (*mech*) cearclan *m*
washing *n* nigheadaireachd *f* **w. machine** inneal nigheadaireachd *m* **w.-powder** fùdar nigheadaireachd *m* **w.-up-liquid** stuth-nighe shoithichean *m*
wasp *n* speach *f*, connspeach *f*
waste *n* (*misuse*) ana-caitheamh *m*; (*destruction*) sgrios *m*; (*rubbish*) sgudal *m* **w. of time** cosg tìde/ùine *m* **w.-paper basket** basgaid sgudail *f* *a* fàs *v* dèan mì-fheum de, dèan ana-caitheanaich; (*spoil*) mill
wasteful *a* caithteach, strùidheil
wasteland *n* talamh fàs *m*, àite fàsail *m*
waster *n* strùidhear *m*; (*slang*) duine gun fheum *m*
watch *n* faire *f*, caithris *f*; (*timepiece*) uaireadair *m* *v* cùm sùil air; (*TV etc*) coimhead; (*be careful*) thoir an aire **keep w.** *v* dèan/cùm faire, caithris
watchman *n* neach-faire *m*
water *n* uisge *m*, bùrn *m* **w. level** àird(e) an uisge *f* **w.-lily** duilleag-bhathte *f* **w.-mill** muileann-uisge *f m* **w.-pipe** pìob-uisge *f* *v* uisgich, fliuch
watercress *n* biolaire *f*
waterfall *n* eas *m*
waterproof *a* uisge-dhìonach
watershed *n* (*geog*) druim-uisge *m*; (*met*) àm/adhbhar-tionndaidh *m*

watertight *a* dìonach
waulking *n* luadh *m*, luadhadh *m*
  w. song òran-luaidh *m*
wave *n* tonn *m*, stuagh *f*
wave *v* crath **w. (to)** smèid (ri)
waveband *n* bann *m* **Medium Wave** am Bann Meadhain
wavelength *n* bann *m* **on the same w.** air an aon ràmh
wavy *a* (*hair*) dualach
wax *n* cèir *f* *v* cèirich, cuir cèir air; (*grow*) fàs
way *n* (*route*) slighe *f*, rathad *m*; (*method*) dòigh *f* **w. of life** dòigh-beatha *f*
waylay *v* dèan feall-fhalach
wayward *a* claon, fiarach, frithearra
we *pron* sinn, (*emph*) sinne
weak *a* lag, fann, anfhann, lapach
weaken *v* lagaich; (*intrans*) fannaich
weakling *n* lagach *m*, meathach *m*
weakness *n* laigse *f*, anfhannachd *f*
wealth *n* beairteas *m*, saidhbhreas *m*, ionmhas *m*
wealthy *a* beairteach, saidhbhir
wean *v* cuir bhàrr na cìche
weapon *n* ball-airm *m*, inneal-cogaidh *m*
wear *v* (*clothes*) caith, cuir umad/ort **w. out** cosg
weariness *n* sgìths *f m*, claoidh *f*
weary *a* sgìth, claoidhte *v* sgìthich, claoidh, sàraich **w. for** gabh fadachd ri
weasel *n* neas *f*
weather *n* aimsir *f*, sìde *f*
  w. forecast tuairmse sìde *f* **under the w.** gun a bhith ann an sunnd *v* (*met*) seas ri, cùm ri; (*geol*) caith, caoinich
weave *v* figh
weaver *n* breabadair *m*, figheadair *m*
weaving *n* breabadaireachd *f*, figheadaireachd *f*
web *n* lìon *m*, eige *f* **the World-Wide Web** Lìon na Cruinne *m*
website *n* làrach-lìn *f m*

wed *v* pòs
wedder *n* molt *m*
wedding *n* banais *f*, pòsadh *m*
  w. day latha na bainnse *m*
wedge *n* geinn *m* *v* cuir geinn an
Wednesday *n* Diciadain *m*
wee *a* beag
weed *n* luibh *f m* *v* glan, priog
weedkiller *n* puinnsean luibhean *m*
week *n* seachdain *f* **this w. (coming)** an t-s. seo/sa (tighinn) **last w.** an t-s. seo/sa chaidh
weekend *n* deireadh seachdain *m*
weekly *a* gach seachdain, seachdaineach *adv* gach seachdain
weep *v* caoin, guil, dèan caoineadh/gal
weeping *n* caoineadh *m*, gal *m*, gul *m*
weigh *v* cothromaich, cuir air mheidh, tomhais **w. up** breithnich **w. anchor** tog acair
weight *n* cudthrom *m*, cuideam *m*, truimead *m* **lose w.** *v* caill cuideam
weird *a* air leth neònach
welcome *n* fàilte *f*, furan *m* *a* di-beathte; (*of development*) ris an dèanar toileachadh **you're w.** 's e do bheatha *v* (*person*) cuir fàilte air, fàiltich; (*development(s)*) dèan toileachadh ri
weld *v* tàth
welding *n* tàthadh *m*
welfare *n* sochair *f*, math *m*
  w. state stàit shochairean *f*
well *n* tobar *f m*, fuaran *m*
well *a* math, gasta; (*of health*) fallain *adv* gu math
well-behaved *a* modhail
well-dressed *a* spaideil, leòmach
well-informed *a* fiosrach
wellington *n* bòtann *f m*
well-known *a* ainmeil, iomraiteach
Welsh *a* Cuimreach *n* (*lang*) Cuimris *f*
Welshman *n* Cuimreach *m*
  Welshwoman ban-Chuimreach *f*
were *v* bha (*See verb* **to be** in

Grammar)

west *n* an iar *f*, an àird an iar *f*
  the w. side an taobh siar *m*
  a siar adv an iar
westerly *a* on iar, às an àird an iar
western *a* siar **the W. Isles** na
  h-Eileanan Siar/an Iar
wet *a* fliuch *v* fliuch
whale *n* muc-mhara *f*
what *int* dè? *rel pron* an rud a;
  (*all that*) na *exclam* abair …!
  w. a crowd! abair sluagh!
whatever *pron* às bith, ge b' e air
  bith, ge brith *a* sam bith
wheat *n* cruithneachd *f m*
wheel *n* cuibheall *f*, cuibhle *f*,
  roth *m* **w.-house** taigh-cuibhle
  m, taigh na cuibhle *m* *v* (*trans*)
  cuibhil, ruidhil; (*intrans*)
  tionndaidh mun cuairt
  wheelbarrow bara(-roth) *m*
  wheelchair sèithear-cuibhle *m*,
  cathair-chuibhle *f*
wheeze *n* pìochan, sèitean *m* *v*
  dèan pìochan, bi a' sèiteanaich
whelk *n* faochag *f*
when *int* cuin? *conj* nuair (a), an
  uair (a)
whence *adv* cò às, cò bhuaithe
whenever *adv* gach uair, ge b' e
  uair, àm sam bith
where *int* càite? *rel pron* far, san
  àite san
whereas *conj* ach; (*since*) a
  chionn ('s gu)
whereby *conj* leis, leis an do
wherever *adv* ge b' e càite, às
  bith càite, ge brith càite
whereupon *adv* le sin, leis a sin
whet *v* geuraich, faobharaich;
  (*appetite*) brod càil
whether *conj* co-dhiù, a/an/am
  (+ *v*)
which *int* cò, cò aca? *rel pron* a;
  (*neg*) nach
whichever *pron* ge b' e cò, às
  bith cò, ge brith cò
whiff *n* aithneachadh (fàil(e)idh)
  m; (*air*) oiteag *f*
while *n* treis *f*, greis *f*, tacan *m*
  v cuir seachad (an) ùine
  adv fhad 's, am feadh 's
whim *n* baog *f*, baogaid *f*,

saobh-smaoin *f*
whimper *n* cnead *m*, sgiùgan *m*
whin *n* conasg *m*
whine *v* caoin, dèan caoidhearan;
  (*complain*) sìor ghearan
whinge *v* dèan cànran
whingeing *a* cànranach
whip *n* cuip *f* *v* cuip, sgiùrs
whiphand *n* làmh-an-uachdair *f*
whirl *n* cuairt *f*, cuartag *f*
whirligig *n* gille-mirein *m*
whirlpool *n* ioma-shruth *m*,
  cuairt-shruth *m*
whirlwind *n* ioma-ghaoth *f*
whisk *v* sguab, sgiot
whisky *n* uisge-beatha *m*
whisper *n* cagar *m*, sanais *m*
  v cagair, cuir cagar
whispering *n* cagarsaich *f*,
  sainnsearachd *f*
whistle *n* fead *f*; (*mus*) feadag *f*,
  fìdeag *f* *v* dèan fead/feadaraich
white *a* geal; (*pale*) bàn **w.-board**
  bòrd-geal *m* **W. Paper** Pàipear
  Geal *m*
whitewash *n* aol-uisg(e) *m*,
  gealachadh *m*; (*met*) dreach
  eile/glan *m* *v* gealaich; (*met*)
  cuir dreach eile/glan air
whiting *n* cuidhteag *f*
who *int pron* cò? *rel pron* a;
  (*neg*) nach
whoever *pron* ge b' e cò, às bith
  cò, ge brith cò; neach sam bith
  int pron cò idir?
whole *a* slàn, iomlan, uile, gu
  lèir; (*healthy*) fallain
wholehearted *a* làn-(+ *a*), le (h-)
  uile *etc* chridhe
wholesale *n* mòr-dhìol *m*, mòr-
  reic *m*
wholesome *a* slàn, fallain
wholly *adv* gu h-iomlan/buileach
whooping cough *n* an triuthach *f*
whose *int pron* cò leis?
why *int* carson? *adv* carson
wick *n* siobhag *f*, buaic *f*
wicked *a* olc, aingidh
wickedness *n* olc *m*,
  aingidheachd *f*
wide *a* farsaing, leathan(n)
  w.-ranging farsaing
widely *adv* fad' is farsaing

widen v leudaich; (intrans only) fàs farsaing
widespread a (common) bitheanta, fad' is farsaing
widow(er) n bantrach f (m)
width n leud m
wield v làimhsich, obraich
wife n bean f, bean-phòsta f
wig n gruag f, pioraraig f
wild a fiadhaich, allaidh
wilderness n fàsach m
wildlife n fiadh-bheatha f
wile n cuilbheart f, car m
wilful a fada na c(h)eann etc, ceann-làidir
will n toil f, rùn m, deòin f; (leg) tiomnadh m
willing a deònach, toileach
willingly a gu deònach/toileach
willow n seileach m
willy-nilly adv a dheòin no (a) dh'aindeoin
wily a seòlta, carach
win v buannaich, coisinn, buinig
wind n gaoth f; (breath) anail f **w. direction** àird na gaoithe f
wind v (around) suain, toinn, fill; (clock) rothaig **w. up** thoir gu crìch; (tease) bi a' tarraing à
windfall n (fin) clabag f
winding a lùbach, cam, cama-lùbach
windmill n muileann-gaoithe f m
window n uinneag f **w.-pane** l(e)òsan (uinneige) m **w.-sill** sòl uinneige m
windpipe n pìob-sgòrnain f
windscreen n sgùl m, sgàile-gaoithe m
windsurfing n marcachd thonn f
windward n fuaradh m, taobh an fhuaraidh m
windy a gaothach, gailbheach, garbh
wine n fìon m **red w.** fìon dearg **white w.** fìon geal **w.-list** clàr-fìona m
wing n sgiath f
wink n priobadh m, caogadh m, sùil bheag f v priob, caog, dèan sùil bheag
winner n neach-buannachaidh m, buadhaiche m

winnow v fasgain
winter n an geamhradh m v geamhraich
wintry a geamhrachail
wipe v suath **w. off** glan dheth
wiper n suathair m
wire n uèir f, teud m **barbed w.** uèir-bhiorach/stobach f
wiry a seang
wisdom n gliocas m
wise a glic
wish n miann f m, toil f, togradh m, dùrachd f v miannaich, togair, luthaig, rùnaich
wisp n sop m
wistful a cianail, tiamhaidh
wit n eirmseachd f, geur-labhairt f; (sense) toinisg f
witch n bana-bhuidseach f
witchcraft n buidseachd f
with prep le, cuide ri, còmhla ri, leis (+ art)
withdraw v thoir air ais/falbh, tarraing a-mach/air ais
wither v searg, seac, crìon
withered a seargte, seacte, crìon
withhold v cùm air ais
within adv a-staigh prep taobh a-staigh (+ gen)
without prep gun, às aonais (+ gen)
withstand v seas ri
witness a (abstr) fianais f v thoir fianais
witty a eirmseach, geur
wizard n buidseach m, draoidh m
woeful a muladach, truagh
wolf n madadh-allaidh m
woman n bean f, boireannach m
womb n machlag f, bolg f, brù f
wonder n iongnadh m, iongantas m v gabh iongantas
wonderful a iongantach
woo v bi a' suirghe (air)
wood n fiodh m; (forest) coille f
wooden a fiodha
woodland n fearann coillteach m
woodpecker n snagan-daraich m
woodwork n saorsainneachd f
woodworm n (insect) raodan m; (condition) raodanas m
wool n clòimh f, olann f; (knitting) snàth m

woollen *a* clòimhe
woolly *a* clòimhe; (*met*) ceòthach, doilleir
word *n* facal *m*; (*promise*) gealladh *m* **w. for w.** facal air an fhacal **w. processing** rianachadh fhaclan *m* **w.-processor** rianadair fhaclan *m*
work *n* obair *f*, saothair *f* **workforce** luchd-obrach *m* **workshop** bùth-obrach *f* *v* obraich, saothraich
worker *n* obraiche *m*, neach-obrach *m*
working-party *n* buidheann-obrach *f m*
works *n* (*place*) ionad-obrach *m* **gasworks** ionad a' ghas *m*
world *n* saoghal *m*, cruinne *m* (*f in gen*)
worldly *a* saoghalta
worm *n* boiteag *f*, cnuimh *f*, durrag *f*
worn *a* caithte, breòite
worried *a* draghail, fo iomagain, fo chùram
worry *n* dragh *m*, iomagain *f*, cùram *m* *v* dèan dragh do, cuir dragh/iomnaidh air **I w. too much** bidh cus cùraim orm (mu rudan)
worse *a* nas miosa
worsen *v* fàs nas miosa
worship *n* adhradh *m* **family w.** adhradh teaghlaich, gabhail an Leabhair *m* *v* dèan adhradh *Also vn* ag adhradh
worst *a* as miosa
worth *n* fiach *m*, luach *m* *a* fiù, airidh *air* **it is not w. bothering about** chan fhiach/cha d' fhiach bodraigeadh mu dheidhinn
worthless *a* gun luach, gun fhiù
worthy *a* airidh, fiùghail, fiachail
wound *n* lot *m*, leòn *m*, creuchd *f* *v* leòn, lot
wounded *a* leònte
wounding *a* guineach
wrangle *v* connsaich, troid
wrap *v* paisg, fill **w. around** suain
wrapping paper *n* pàipear-còmhdaich *m*
wrath *n* corraich *f*, fearg *f*

wreath *n* blàth-fhleasg *f*
wreck *n* (*naut*) long-bhriste *f*; (*of a person or article*) ablach *m* *v* sgrios, mill
wren *n* dreathan-donn *m*
wrench *v* spìon
wrest *v* tarraing (bh)o
wrestle *v* bi a' carachd, gleac
wrestler *n* caraiche *m*, gleacadair *m*
wrestling *n* carachd *f*, gleac *m*
wretch *n* truaghan *m*
wretched *a* truagh, àmhgharach
wriggle *v* rach an lùban, toinneamhaich
wring *v* fàisg
wrinkle *n* preas *m*, roc *f*
wrinkled *a* preasach, liorcach, rocach
wrist *n* caol an dùirn *m* **wristband** bann dùirn *m* **wristwatch** uaireadair làimhe *m*
writ *n* sgrìobhainn-cùirte/cùrtach *f*
write *v* sgrìobh **w. up** dèan cunntas air **w. off** meas gun luach, dubh às
writer *n* sgrìobhadair *m*, sgrìobhaiche *m*
writhe *v* snìomh, bi gad aonagraich fhèin
writing *n* sgrìobhadh *m* **w.-paper** pàipear-sgrìobhaidh *m*
written *a* sgrìobhte
wrong *n* coire *f*, eucoir *f*, euceart *m* *a* ceàrr; (*culpable*) coireach, eucorach *v* dèan eucoir air
wry *a* cam, fiar, claon

X

xenophobia *n* gamhlas do choigrich *m*
Xmas *n* an Nollaig *f*
x-ray *n* x-ghath *m* *a* x-ghathach *v* x-ghathaich
xylophone *n* saidhleafòn *m*

Y

yacht *n* sgoth-seòlaidh *f*, gheat *f*
yak *n* iac *m*

yank *v* spìon
yap *v* (*dog*) dèan comhart; (*talk*) bleadraig
yard *n* slat *f*; (*enclosure*) gàrradh *m*, lios *f* yardstick slat-t(h)omhais *f*
yarn *n* snàth *m*; (*story*) sgeulachd *f*, naidheachd *f*
yawn *n* mèaran *m*, mèanan *m* *v* bi a'/dèan mèaranaich/mèananaich *Also vn* a' mèaranaich, a' mèananaich
yawning *n* mèaranaich *f*, mèananaich *f*
year *n* bliadhna *f* this y. am-bliadhna next y. an ath-bhliadhna last y. an-uiridh the y. before last a' bhòn-uiridh
yearn *v* miannaich gu làidir, bi fo fhadachd airson
yearning *n* iarraidh *f m*, fadachd *f*
yeast *n* beirm *f*
yell *n* glaodh *m*, sgal *m*, sgairt *f* *v* glaodh
yellow *n*, *a* buidhe *m*
yelp *n* sgiamh *f m*; (*of dog*) tathann *m* *v* dèan sgiamh; (*dog*) dèan tathann
yes *adv a* *Yes answer is represented by the positive form of the verb used in a question, eg* a bheil thu sgìth? tha an e saor a th' ann? 's e am faca tu an gèam? chunnaic; (*in argument*) seadh
yesterday *adv* an-dè the day before y. a' bhòn-dè
yet *conj* an dèidh sin, ach *adv* fhathast yet again aon uair eile
yew *n* iubhar *m*
yield *n* toradh *m* *v* thoir a-mach toradh; (*submit*) gèill, strìochd
yoga *n* ìoga *f*
yoghurt *n* iogart *m*
yoke *n* (*phys, met*) cuing *f* *v* (*ready*) beairtich; (*oppress*) cuingich
yolk (*of egg*) *n* buidheagan *m*
yon(der) *adv* thall, ud, an siud
you *pron* thu, (*emph*) thusa, (*pl & pol*) sibh, (*emph*) sibhse
young *a* òg younger than nas òige

na youngest as òige *n* àl (òg) *m*; (*people*) òigridh *f*
youngster *n* òganach *m*
your *poss pron* do, d', t', (*pl & pol*) bhur, ur
yours *poss pron* leat, (*emph*) leatsa, (*pl & pol*) leibh, (*emph*) leibhse
yourself *pron* thu fhèin, (*pl & pol*) sibh fhèin, sib' fhèin
youth *n* (*abstr*) òige *f*; (*person*) òigear *m*, òganach *m*; (*coll*) òigridh *f* y. centre ionad òigridh *m* y. club club-òigridh *m*, buidheann-òigridh *f m* y. hostel ostail òigridh *m*
youthful *a* òg, ògail
Yuch/Yuck *exclam* (A) ghia!
Yule *n* Nollaig *f*

Z

zany *a* cleasach, àraid
zeal *n* eud *m*, dealas *m*
zealot *n* eudmhoraiche *m*
zealous *a* eudmhor, dealasach
zebra *n* seabra *m* z. crossing trast-rathad seabra *m*
zenith *n* bàrr *m*
zero *n* neoni *f* z. tolerance nach ceadaich an cron as lugha
zest *n* fonn *m*, sunnd *m*
zigzag *a* cam-fhiarach
zinc *n* sinc *m*
zip *n* siop *m*
zodiac *n* grian-chrios *m*, crios na grèine *m*
zone *n* raon *m*, ceàrn *m*, sòn *m*; (*geog*) bann *m*, crios *m* *v* suidhich raon/sòn
zoo *n* sù *m*, sutha *f*
zoologist *n* ainmh-eòlaiche *m*
zoology *n* ainmh-eòlas *m*
zoom *v* falbh le roid

personal names

Surnames *Sloinnidhean*

The forms of surnames for women and men differ from each other in Gaelic. Where a man's surname begins with **Mac**, a woman's begins with **Nic**. Thus, **Dòmhnall MacLeòid** (Donald MacLeod) but **Oighrig NicLeòid** (Effie MacLeod). With surnames other than those beginning with **Mac/Nic**, the female form of the noun is lenited. Thus, **Seumas Caimbeul** (James Campbell) but **Màiri Chaimbeul** (Mary Campbell).

As will be seen below, there is more than one Gaelic version of some names, one with **Mac/Nic** and one without, like **MacFhearghais/Fearghasdan** (Ferguson). In addition, a form in **-ach** is often used when the person's surname and not his personal name is being used, eg '**Chunnaic mi an Granndach an-diugh**' ('I saw Grant today'). This practice is much less common with the surnames of women, but on the rare occasions on which it would be used, the female equivalent would be '**a' bhan-Ghranndach**'. In the case of a few names, this form is as common or commoner in speech than the **Mac/Nic** form is, and so it has has been listed below in addition to the other form.

For convenience, the English names have all been spelt with a capital after Mac, but it is recognized that there are many variations on this, and also in other aspects (MacNeil/ MacNeill etc). The same is true of Gaelic names, especially those which have the element **gille** (lad, servant) in them. Here we have rendered that element as **Ille** or **Ill**.

Beaton	*Peutan*	MacIntosh	*Mac an Tòisich*
Black	*MacIlleDhuibh*	MacIntyre	*Mac an t-Saoir*
Boyd	*Boidhd*	MacIver	*MacÌomhair*
Bruce	*Brus, Brusach*	MacKay	*MacAoidh*
Buchanan	*Bochanan*	MacKenzie	*MacCoinnich*
		MacKerlich	*MacTheàrlaich*
Cameron	*Camshron*	MacKinlay	*MacFhionnlaigh*
Campbell	*Caimbeul*	MacKinnon	*MacFhionghain*
Chisholm	*Siosal, Siosalach*	MacLean	*MacIllEathain*
		MacLellan	*MacIllFhaolain,*
Douglas	*Dùghlas*		*MacIllFhialain*
		MacLennan	*MacIllFhinnein*
Ferguson	*Fearghasdan,*	MacLeod	*MacLeòid*
	MacFhearghais	MacMillan	*MacIlleMhaoil,*
Finlayson	*Fionnlasdan,*		*Mac a' Mhaoilein*
	MacFhionnlaigh	MacNab	*Mac an Aba*
Fraser	*Friseal*	MacNeil	*MacNèill*
		MacPhail	*MacPhàil*
Gillies	*MacIllIosa*	MacPhee	*Mac-a-phì*
Graham	*Greum,*	MacPherson	*Mac a' Phearsain*
	Greumach	MacQuarrie	*MacGuaire*
Grant	*Grannd*	MacRae	*MacRath*
		MacRitchie	*MacRisnidh*
Johnson	*MacIain*	MacSween	*MacSuain*
		MacTaggart	*Mac an t-Sagairt*
Kennedy	*Ceanadach,*	MacVicar	*Mac a' Phiocair*
	MacUalraig	MacVurich,	*MacMhuirich*
		Currie	
MacAllister	*MacAlasdair*	Martin	*Màrtainn*
MacArthur	*MacArtair*	Montgomery	*MacGumaraid*
MacAskill	*MacAsgaill*	Morrison	*Moireasdan,*
MacAulay	*MacAmhlaigh*		*MacIlleMhoire*
MacBain	*MacBheathain*	Munro	*Rothach,*
MacBeth	*MacBheatha*		*Mac an Rothaich*
MacCorquodale	*MacCòrcadail,*	Murray	*Moireach*
	MacThòrcadail		
MacCrimmon	*MacCruimein*	Nicolson,	*MacNeacail*
MacDonald	*MacDhòmhnaill,*	MacNicol	
	Dòmhnallach		
MacDougall	*MacDhùghaill,*	Robertson	*Robasdan,*
	Dùghlach		*MacDhonnchaidh*
MacEachen	*MacEachainn*	Ross	*Ros*
MacEachern,	*MacEacharna*		
MacKechnie		Smith	*Mac a' Ghobhainn*
MacFadyen	*MacPhàidein*		
MacFarlane	*MacPhàrlain*	Thomson	*MacThòmais*
MacGregor	*MacGriogair*		
MacInnes	*MacAonghais*	Whyte	*MacIlleBhàin*

First names *Ciad ainmean*

Some of the names below are not etymologically related in the way that Alan and **Ailean** are but are used as equivalents, eg Claire/**Sorcha** and Kenneth/**Coinneach**.

Agnes	*Ùna*	Edward	*Eideard, Ìomhar*
Alan	*Ailean*	Effie, Euphemia	*Oighrig*
Alasdair,	*Alasdair*	Elizabeth	*Ealasaid*
Alexander		Ewan, Ewen	*Eògha(i)nn*
Alec, Alex, Alick	*Ailig*		
Alice	*Ailis, Ailios*	Farquhar	*Fearchar*
Andrew	*Anndra*	Fergus	*Fearghas*
Angus	*Aonghas*	Finlay	*Fionnlagh*
Ann(e), Anna	*Anna, Annag*	Flora	*Flòraidh,*
Archibald	*Gilleasbaig*		*Fionnghal*
Archie	*Eàirdsidh*		
Arthur	*Artair*	George	*Seòras, Deòrsa*
		Gilbert	*Gille-Brìghde*
Barbara	*Barabal*	Gordon	*Gòrdan*
Bessie	*Beasag*	Graham	*Greum*
Beth	*Beathag*		
Betty	*Beitidh*	Hector	*Eacha(i)nn*
		Helen	*Eilidh*
Cal(l)um,	*Calum*	Henry	*Eanraig*
Malcolm		Hugh	*Ùisdean, Aodh,*
Catherine,	*Catrìona*		*Eòghann*
Katherine			
Cathleen,	*Caitlin*	Ia(i)n	*Iain*
Kathleen		Innes	*Aonghas*
Charles	*Teàrlach*	Isobel, Ishbel	*Iseabail*
Chrissie	*Criosaidh, Ciorstag*	Ivor	*Ìomhar*
Christine,	*Cairistìona,*		
Christina	*Ciorstag,*	Jack, Jock	*Seoc*
Christoper	*Crìsdean*	James	*Seumas*
Claire	*Sorcha*	Jane	*Sìne*
Colin	*Cailean*	Janet	*Seònaid*
		Jessie	*Seasaidh*
David	*Daibhidh*	Joan	*Seonag*
Deirdre	*Deirdre*	John	*Iain, Seonaidh*
Derek, Der(r)ick	*Ruairidh*	Johnny	*Seonaidh*
Diarmid, Dermot	*Diarm(a)id*	Joseph	*Eòsaph, Iòsaph*
Dolina, Dolly	*Doileag, Doilìona,*	Julia	*Sìleas*
	Doilidh		
Donald	*Dòmhnall*	Kate	*Ceit, Ceiteag*
Donnie	*Donaidh*	Katie	*Ceitidh, Ceiteag*
Douglas	*Dùghlas*	Kenna	*Ceana*
Duncan	*Donnchadh*	Kenneth	*Coinneach*
		Kieran	*Ciaran*

Kirsty	*Ciorstaidh*
Lachlan	*Lachla(i)nn, Lachann*
Maggie	*Magaidh*
Margaret	*Mai(gh)read*
Marion	*Mòr*
Marjory	*Marsaili*
Mark	*Marc*
Mary	*Màiri*
May	*Màili*
Michael	*Mìcheal*
Morag	*Mòrag*
Murdo	*Murchadh*
Myles	*Maoilios, Maoileas*
Nancy	*Nansaidh*
Neil, Niall	*Niall*
Norman	*Tormod*
Patrick	*Pàdraig*
Paul	*Pòl*
Peggy	*Peigi*
Peter	*Peadar, Pàdraig*
Rachel	*Raonaid, Raghnaid*
Ranald, Ronald	*Raghnall*
Robert	*Raibeart, Rob*
Roderick	*Ruairidh*
Roy	*Ruadh*
Ruth	*Rut*
Samuel, Sorley	*Somhairle*
Sheena	*Sìne*
Sheila	*Sìle*
Stephen, Steven	*Steaphan*
Stewart	*Stiùbhart*
Susan	*Siùsaidh*
Thomas	*Tòmas*
Torquil	*Torca(i)ll*
Una	*Ùna*
William	*Uilleam*

place names

Aberdeen	*Obar Dheathain*	Bowmore	*Bogha Mòr*
Aberfeldy	*Obar Pheallaidh*	Braemar	*Bràigh Mhàrr*
Aberfoyle	*Obar Phuill*	Britain	*Breata(i)nn*
Africa	*Afraga*	Brittany	*A' Bhreata(i)nn*
Airdrie	*Àrd Ruighe*		*Bheag*
Albania	*Albàinia*	Brussels	*A' Bhruiseal*
America	*Ameireaga(idh)*	Bulgaria	*Bulgàiria*
Argyll	*Earra-Ghàidheal*	Bute	*Bòd*
Arran	*Arainn*		
Asia	*(An) Àisia*	the Cairngorms	*Am Monadh Ruadh*
the Atlantic Ocean	*An Cuan Siar*	Caithness	*Gallaibh*
Athens	*Baile na h-Àithne*	Callander	*Calasraid*
Australia	*Astràilia*	Campbeltown	*Ceann Loch*
Austria	*An Ostair*		*(Chille Chiarain)*
Aviemore	*An Aghaidh Mhòr*	Canada	*Canada*
Ayr	*Inbhir Àir*	Canna	*Canaigh*
		Cape Breton	*Ceap Breatann*
Badenoch	*Bàideanach*	Castlebay	*Bàgh a' Chaisteil*
Ballachulish	*Bail' a' Chaolais*	Coll	*Col(l)a*
Balmoral	*Baile Mhoireil*	Colonsay	*Colbhasaigh*
Bannockburn	*Allt a' Bhonnaich*	China	*Sìona*
Barra	*Barraigh*	Cornwall	*A' Chòrn*
Beauly	*A' Mhanachainn*	Craignure	*Creag an Iubhair*
Belfast	*Beul Feirste*	Crieff	*Craoibh*
Belgium	*A' Bheilg*	Croatia	*Croatia*
Benbecula	*Beinn na Fadhla/*	Cromarty	*Cromba(i)dh*
	Beinn a' Bhadhla	the Cuillins	*An Cuiltheann*
Ben Nevis	*Beinn Nibheis*	Culloden	*Cùl Lodair*
Bernera(y)	*Beàrnaraigh*	Cumbernauld	*Comar nan Allt*
Berwick	*Bearaig*	Czech Republic	*Poblachd nan Seic*
the Black Isle	*An t-Eilean Dubh*		
Blair Atholl	*Blàr (an) Athaill*	Denmark	*An Danmhairg*
the Borders	*Na Crìochan*	Dingwall	*Inbhir*
Bosnia	*Bosnia*		*Pheofharain*

Dublin	*Baile Àtha Cliath*	Huntly	*Hunndaidh*
Dumbarton	*Dùn Breatann*		
Dunfermline	*Dùn Phàrlain*	Iceland	*Innis Tìle*
Dumfries	*Dùn Phris*	India	*Na h-Innseachan*
Dunblane	*Dùn Blathain*	Inveraray	*Inbhir Aora*
Dundee	*Dùn Dèagh*	Invergordon	*Inbhir Ghòrdain*
Dunkeld	*Dùn Chailleann*	Inverness	*Inbhir Nis*
Dunoon	*Dùn Omhain*	Iona	*Ì (Chaluim Chille)*
Dunvegan	*Dùn Bheagain*	Iran	*Iran, Ioran*
		Iraq	*Iraq, Iorag*
East Kilbride	*Cille Bhrìghde*	Ireland	*Èirinn*
	an Ear	Islay	*Ìle*
Edinburgh	*Dùn Èideann*	Isle of Man	*Eilean Mhanainn*
Egypt	*An Èipheit*	Isle of Skye	*An t-Eilean*
Eigg	*Eige*		*Sgitheanach*
Elgin	*Eilginn*	Israel	*Israel, Iosarail*
England	*Sasa(i)nn*	Italy	*An Eadailt*
Eriskay	*Èirisgeigh*		
Estonia	*Estòinia*	Japan	*Iapan*
Europe	*An Roinn Eòrpa*	Jerusalem	*Ierusalem*
		Jordan	*Iòrdan*
Falkirk	*An Eaglais Bhreac*	Jura	*Diùra*
Fife	*Fiobha*		
Finland	*Fionnlainn*	Kenya	*Ceinia*
Forres	*Farrais*	Killin	*Cill Fhinn*
Fort Augustus	*Cille Chuimein*	Kilmarnock	*Cille Mheàrnaig*
Fort William	*An Gearastan,*	Kingussie	*Cinn a'*
	An Gearasdan		*Ghiùthsaich*
France	*An Fhraing*	Kinlochleven	*Ceann Loch*
Fraserburgh	*A' Bhrua(i)ch*		*Lìobhann*
		Kintyre	*Cinn Tìre*
Gairloch	*Geàrrloch*	Knoydart	*Cnòideart*
Galloway	*Gall-*	Kyle of Lochalsh	*Caol Loch Aills(e)*
	Ghàidhealaibh		
Germany	*A' Ghearmailt*	Lanark	*Lannraig*
Gigha	*Giogha*	Largs	*Na Leargaidh*
Glasgow	*Glaschu*		*Ghallda*
Glencoe	*Gleann(a) Comhann*	Latvia	*Latbhia*
Glenfinnan	*Gleann Fhionghain*	Leith	*Lìte*
Golspie	*Goillspidh*	Lewis	*Leòdhas*
Greece	*A' Ghrèig*	Libya	*Libia*
Greenock	*Grianaig*	Lismore	*Lios Mòr*
		Lithuania	*Lituàinia*
Harris	*Na Hearadh*	Lochaber	*Loch Abar*
the Hebrides	*Innse Gall*	Lochgilphead	*Ceann Loch Gilb*
Helmsdale	*Bun Ilidh*	Lochboisdale	*Loch Baghasdail*
the Highlands	*A' Ghàidhealtachd*	Lochinver	*Loch an Inbhir*
Holland	*An Òlaind*	Loch Lomond	*Loch Laomainn*
Hungary	*An Ungair*	Lochmaddy	*Loch nam Madadh*

Loch Ness	*Loch Nis*	River Tweed	*Abhainn Tuaidh*
London	*Lunnainn*	Romania	*Romàinia*
Lothian	*Lodainn, Lobhdaidh*	Rome	*An Ròimh*
		Ross	*Ros*
the Lowlands	*A' Ghalldachd*	Rothesay	*Baile Bhòid*
Luing	*Luinn*	Rum	*Rùm, Eilean Ruma*
Luxembourg	*Lugsamburg*	Russia	*An Ruis, Ruisia*
Mallaig	*Malaig*	Scalpay	*Sgalpaigh*
the Mediterranean	*A' Mhuir Mheadhan-thìreach*	Scandinavia	*Lochlann*
		Scotland	*Alba*
		Serbia	*Serbia*
the Minch	*An Cuan Sgìth*	Shetland	*Sealtainn*
Moidart	*Mùideart*	Sleat	*Slèite*
Morvern	*A' Mhorbhairne*	Slovakia	*Slobhagia*
Motherwell	*Tobar na Màthar*	Slovenia	*Slobhinia*
Muck	*Eilean nam Muc*		
Mull	*Muile*	South Africa	*Afraga a Deas*
		South Uist	*Uibhist a Deas*
Nairn	*Inbhir Narann*	Spain	*An Spàinn*
Ness	*Nis*	Staffin	*Stafainn, An Taobh Sear*
the Netherlands	*An Tìr Ìosal*		
Newtonmore	*Bail' Ùr an t-Slèibh*	St Andrews	*Cill Rìmhinn*
the North Sea	*An Cuan a Tuath*	Stirling	*Sruighlea*
North Uist	*Uibhist a Tuath*	Stornoway	*Steòrnabhagh*
Norway	*Nirribhidh*	Strathclyde	*Srath Chluaidh*
Nova Scotia	*Alba Nuadh*	Strathspey	*Srath Spè*
		Sweden	*An t-Suain*
Oban	*An t-Òban*	Switzerland	*An Eilbheis*
Orkney	*Arcaibh*		
		Tain	*Baile Dhubhthaich*
the Pacific Ocean	*An Cuan Sèimh*	Tarbert	*An Tairbeart*
Paisley	*Pàislig*	Thurso	*Inbhir Theòrsa*
Pakistan	*Pagastan*	Tiree	*Tiriodh, Tiridhe*
Perth	*Peairt*	Tobermory	*Tobar Mhoire*
Peterhead	*Ceann Phàdraig*	Tongue	*Tunga*
Pitlochry	*Baile Chloichrigh*	Torridon	*Toirbheartan*
Plockton	*Am Ploc*	the Trossachs	*Na Tròiseachan*
Poland	*A' Phòlainn*	Turkey	*An Tuirc*
Port Ellen	*Port Ilein*	Tyndrum	*Taigh an Droma*
Portree	*Port Rìgh, Port Ruighe*	Uig	*Ùige, Ùig*
Portugal	*Portagail*	Uist	*Uibhist*
		Ullapool	*Ulapul*
Raasay	*Ratharsair, Ratharsaigh*	the United States	*Na Stàitean Aonaichte*
River Clyde	*Abhainn Chluaidh*	Vatersay	*Bhatarsaigh*
River Forth	*Abhainn Foirthe*		
River Spey	*Abhainn Spè, Uisge Spè*	Wales	*A' Chuimrigh*
		Wick	*Inbhir Ùige*
River Tay	*Abhainn Tatha*		

grammar

Word order

In English, the subject precedes the verb. In Gaelic, the verb precedes the subject and is normally the first word in a sentence or question, eg

| bha sinn anmoch | we were late |
| an glas mi an doras? | shall I lock the door? |

In certain types of question, a question word precedes the verb:

| cò bha siud? | who was that? |

Another change in sequence between English and Gaelic arises with nouns and adjectives. Whereas in English the adjective precedes the noun, in Gaelic the noun generally precedes the adjective, eg

| latha math | (a) good day |

Adjectives are lenited if the noun they are qualifying is feminine in gender. Lenition is shown in the written form of a word by the insertion of an **h** after the first letter.

| oidhche mhath | good night |

There are a few exceptions to this convention. The adjectives **deagh** (good), **droch** (bad), **sàr** (excellent, supreme), **fìor** (true, absolute) and **seann** (old) are the main exceptions. These cause lenition, where applicable, of the following noun, eg

deagh bhiadh	good food
droch shìde	bad weather
sàr sheinneadair	an excellent singer
fìor charaid	a true friend
seann chù	an old dog

Adverbs

An adverb is formed by putting **gu** or **gu h-** before an adjective. **gu h-** is used when the adjective begins with a vowel, eg

mòr (great)	**gu mòr** (greatly)
àrd (high)	**gu h-àrd** (above)

Forms of the article

There is no indefinite article in Gaelic – 'a window' is **uinneag**, 'a jacket' is **seacaid**. There are, however, several forms of the definite article (equivalent to 'the' in English). The form of article used varies according to the gender, number and case of the noun. The main forms of the article are set out in the table below:

(a) Forms of the article with nouns in the nominative case

Gender & number	First letter of noun	Form of article	Example
Masculine singular	b, f, m, p a, e, i, o, u other letters	am an t- an	am bòrd an t-ubhal an leabhar
Feminine singular	b, c, g, m, p	a' + (len)	a' bhròg a' chaileag
	f	an + (len)	an fhreagairt an fhairge
	sl, sn, sr, s + vowel	an t-	an t-sràid an t-seacaid
	other letters	an	an nighean an sgoil an uinneag
Masculine, feminine plural	consonant	na	na leabhraichean na sgoilearan
	vowel	na h-	na h-òrdagan na h-uinneagan

(b) Forms of the article with nouns in the genitive case

Gender & number	First letter of noun	Form of article	Example
Masculine singular	b, c, g, m, p	a' + (len)	am post → oifis a' phuist
	f	an + (len)	am fraoch → dath an fhraoich
	sl, sn, sr, s + vowel	an t-	an salann → blas an t-salainn
	other letters	an	an rathad → ceann an rathaid
Feminine singular	consonant	na	a' chailleach → còta na caillich
	vowel	na h-	an eaglais → doras na h-eaglaise
Masculine, feminine plural	b, f, m, p	nam	na bàird → obair nam bàrd
	other letters	nan	na leabhraichean → Comhairle nan Leabhraichean

(c) Forms of the article with nouns in the dative case

Gender & number	First letter of noun	Form of article	Example
Masculine singular	b, c, g, m, p	a' + (len)	am balach → leis a' bhalach
	f	an + (len)	am feur → anns an fheur
	sl, sn, sr, s + vowel	an t-	an salm → anns an t-salm
	other letters	an	an taigh → air an taigh
Feminine singular	b, c, g, m, p	a' + (len)	a' ghealach → air a' ghealaich
	f	an + (len)	an fheòrag → aig an fheòraig

	sl, sn, sr, s + vowel	an t-	an t-sràid → air an t-sràid
	other letters	an	an trèan → air an trèan an uinneag → air an uinneig
Masculine, feminine plural	consonant	na	na bùithean → anns na bùithean
	vowel	na h-	na h-òrain → ris na h-òrain

Regular verbs

Gaelic verbs have three forms:

- independent – normally the first word in a sentence
- dependent – used in subordinate clauses or after particles
- relative – used after relative pronouns

The root of the verb is the second person singular imperative, eg *seall* (look), literally, 'look you'.

The verb 'to be' apart, Gaelic verbs have no simple present tense. The present tense is formed by combining the verb 'to be' with the verbal noun of the verb being used.

eg *tha iad a' cluich* – they are playing

The verbal noun, as the name implies, can act both as noun or as verb. It is marked in English by the *-ing* ending.

eg *bha sinn a' snàmh* – we were swimming
tha snàmh math dhut – swimming is good for you

Root	Verbal Noun	Infinitive	Subjunctive/ Conditional
bris *break*	a' briseadh *breaking*	a bhriseadh *to break*	bhrisinn *I would break*
cuir *put*	a' cur *putting*	a chur *to put*	chuirinn *I would put*
dùin *close/shut*	a' dùnadh *closing/shutting*	a dhùnadh *to close/shut*	dhùineadh e *he would close/shut*

freagair *answer*	a' freagairt *answering*	a fhreagairt *to answer*	fhreagradh i *she would answer*
gabh *take*	a' gabhail *taking*	a ghabhail *to take*	ghabhadh tu *you would take*
las *light*	a' lasadh *lighting*	a lasadh *to light*	lasainn *I would light*
mill *spoil*	a' milleadh *spoiling*	a mhilleadh *to spoil*	mhilleadh tu *you would spoil*
nigh *wash/clean*	a' nighe *washing/ cleaning*	a nighe *to wash/clean*	nigheamaid *we would wash/clean*
pòs *marry*	a' pòsadh *marrying*	a phòsadh *to marry*	phòsadh iad *they would marry*
ruith *run*	a' ruith *running*	a ruith *to run*	ruitheadh sibh *you (pl) would run*
suidh *sit*	a' suidhe *sitting*	a shuidhe *to sit*	shuidheadh i *she would sit*
tog *lift*	a' togail *lifting*	a thogail *to lift*	thogadh iad *they would lift*
aithnich *recognize*	ag aithn- eachadh *recognizing*	a dh'aithn- eachadh *to recognize*	dh'aithn- icheadh sibh *you (pl) would recognize*
èirich *rise*	ag èirigh *rising*	a dh'èirigh *to rise*	dh'èireamaid *we would rise*
ith *eat*	ag ithe *eating*	a dh'ithe *to eat*	dh'itheadh e *he would eat*
òl *drink*	ag òl *drinking*	a dh'òl *to drink*	dh'òlainn *I would drink*
ullaich *prepare*	ag ullachadh *preparing*	a dh'ullachadh *to prepare*	dh'ullaicheadh i *she would prepare*
fuirich *stay/wait*	a' fuireach *staying/waiting*	a dh'fhuireach *to stay/wait*	dh'fhuiricheadh iad *they would stay/wait*

Notes

- there are different ways of forming verbal nouns
- verbal nouns beginning in consonants are preceded by *a'*
- verbal nouns beginning in vowels are preceded by *ag*
- the infinitive ('to') forms are related to the verbal noun forms
- there is no apostrophe after the *a* in the infinitive
- infinitive forms of verbs beginning in consonants are lenited where possible
- infinitive forms of verbs beginning in *f* followed by a vowel begin with *dh'* and are lenited. The *fh* combination is not pronounced and the verb is treated as if it began in a vowel
- subjunctive/conditional forms vary according to the person being referred to, or subject. The following is an example of the different forms of one verb:

chuirinn	I would put	*chuireamaid*	we would put
chuireadh tu	you would put	*chuireadh sibh*	you (pl) would put
chuireadh e	he would put	*chuireadh iad*	they would put
chuireadh i	she would put		

- the first person singular and plural forms have special forms which include the pronoun, while the pronoun is added separately in the second and third persons. However, in some areas *sinn* is retained in the first person plural, eg *chuireadh sinn*
- *thu* appears as *tu* in the subjunctive/conditional
- subjunctive/conditional forms of verbs beginning in consonants are lenited
- subjunctive/conditional forms of verbs beginning in vowels or *f* followed by a vowel begin with *dh'*

Regular verbs: past tense

Root	Positive	Negative	Interrogative
bris	bhris	cha do bhris	an do bhris?
break	*broke*	*did not break*	*did ... break?*
cuir	chuir	cha do chuir	an do chuir?
put	*put*	*did not put*	*did ... put?*
dùin	dhùin	cha do dhùin	an do dhùin?
close/shut	*closed/shut*	*did not close/shut*	*did ... close/shut?*

freagair	fhreagair	cha do fhreagair	an do fhreagair?
answer	*answered*	*did not answer*	*did ... answer?*
gabh	ghabh	cha do ghabh	an do ghabh?
take	*took*	*did not take*	*did ... take?*
las	las	cha do las	an do las?
light	*lit*	*did not light*	*did ... light?*
mill	mhill	cha do mhill	an do mhill?
spoil	*spoilt*	*did not spoil*	*did ... spoil?*
nigh	nigh	cha do nigh	an do nigh?
wash/clean	*washed/ cleaned*	*did not wash/clean*	*did ... wash/clean?*
pòs	phòs	cha do phòs	an do phòs?
marry	*married*	*did not marry*	*did ... marry?*
ruith	ruith	cha do ruith	an do ruith?
run	*run*	*did not run*	*did ... run?*
suidh	shuidh	cha do shuidh	an do shuidh?
sit	*sat*	*did not sit*	*did ... sit?*
tog	thog	cha do thog	an do thog?
lift	*lifted*	*did not lift*	*did ... lift?*
aithnich	dh'aithnich	cha do dh'aithnich	an do dh'aithnich?
recognize	*recognized*	*did not recognize*	*did ... recognize?*
èirich	dh'èirich	cha do dh'èirich	an do dh'èirich?
rise	*rose*	*did not rise*	*did ... rise?*
ith	dh'ith	cha do dh'ith	an do dh'ith?
eat	*ate*	*did not eat*	*did ... eat?*
òl	dh'òl	cha do dh'òl	an do dh'òl?
drink	*drank*	*did not drink*	*did ... drink?*
ullaich	dh'ullaich	cha do dh'ullaich	an do dh'ullaich?
prepare	*prepared*	*did not prepare*	*did ... prepare?*
fuirich	dh'fhuirich	cha do dh'fhuirich	an do dh'fhuirich?
stay/wait	*stayed/waited*	*did not stay/wait*	*did ... stay/wait?*

Notes

- positive forms of the past tense are derived by leniting the root form, where possible. Verbs beginning in *l, n, r* and *sg, sm, sp, st* retain the root form
- positive forms of verbs beginning in vowels begin with *dh'*
- negative forms of the past tense are marked by *cha do*
- interrogative (question) forms of the past tense are marked by *an do*
- the interrogative forms are answered, as appropriate, by the positive (yes) and negative (no) forms
  eg *an do dh'aithnich thu iad? dh'aithnich/cha do dh'aithnich*
  did you recognize them?   yes   no

Regular verbs: future tense

Root	Positive	Negative	Interrogative
bris *break*	brisidh *will break*	cha bhris *will not break*	am bris ...? *will ... break?*
cuir *put*	cuiridh *will put*	cha chuir *will not put*	an cuir ...? *will ... put?*
dùin *close/shut*	dùinidh *will close/ shut*	cha dhùin *will not close/shut*	an dùin ...? *will ... close/shut?*
freagair *answer*	freagraidh *will answer*	cha fhreagair *will not answer*	am freagair ...? *will ... answer?*
gabh *take*	gabhaidh *will take*	cha ghabh *will not take*	an gabh ...? *will ... take?*
las *light*	lasaidh *will light*	cha las *will not light*	an las ...? *will ... light?*
mill *spoil*	millidh *will spoil*	cha mhill *will not spoil*	am mill ...? *will ... spoil?*
nigh *wash/clean*	nighidh *will wash/ clean*	cha nigh *will not wash/ clean*	an nigh ...? *will ... wash/ clean?*
pòs *marry*	pòsaidh *will marry*	cha phòs *will not marry*	am pòs ...? *will ... marry?*
ruith *run*	ruithidh *will run*	cha ruith *will not run*	an ruith ...? *will ... run?*

suidh	suidhidh	cha shuidh	an suidh ...?
sit	*will sit*	*will not sit*	*will ... sit?*
tog	togaidh	cha thog	an tog ...?
lift	*will lift*	*will not lift*	*will ... lift?*
aithnich	aithnichidh	chan aithnich	an aithnich ...?
recognize	*will recognize*	*will not recognize*	*will ... recognize?*
èirich	èiridh	chan èirich	an èirich ...?
rise	*will rise*	*will not rise*	*will ... rise?*
ith	ithidh	chan ith	an ith ...?
eat	*will eat*	*will not eat*	*will ... eat?*
òl	òlaidh	chan òl	an òl ...?
drink	*will drink*	*will not drink*	*will ... drink?*
ullaich	ullaichidh	chan ullaich	an ullaich ...?
prepare	*will prepare*	*will not prepare*	*will ... prepare?*
fuirich	fuirichidh	chan fhuirich	am fuirich ...?
stay/wait	*will stay/wait*	*will not stay/wait*	*will ... stay/wait?*

Notes

- positive forms of the future are generally derived by adding *-idh* or *-aidh* to the root form. The former is added when the last vowel in the root is *i* or *e,* and *-aidh* is added when the last vowel is *a, o* or *u*
- a few verbs, eg *freagair*, drop part of the second syllable before adding the *-(a)idh* element
- negative forms are marked by *cha* or *chan*. *Chan* is used before vowels and before *f* followed by a vowel
- interrogative (question) forms are marked by *an* or *am*. *Am* is used before verbs beginning in *b, f, m, p*
- the interrogative forms are answered, as appropriate, by the positive (Yes) and negative (No) forms
  eg *an gabh thu cofaidh?   gabhaidh/cha ghabh, tapadh leat*
  will you have a coffee?   yes/no, thank you
- some alternative forms not involving lenition of *d, s* and *t* are not listed above eg *cha suidh*

Irregular verbs

Root	Verbal Noun	Infinitive	Subjunctive/ Conditional
abair	ag ràdh	a ràdh	theirinn
say	*saying*	*to say*	*I would say*
beir	a' breith/	a bhreith/	bheireadh i
	a' beireachdainn	a bheireachdainn	
catch	*catching*	*to catch*	*she would catch*
cluinn	a' cluinntinn	a chluinntinn	chluinneamaid
hear	*hearing*	*to hear*	*we would hear*
dèan	a' dèanamh	a dhèanamh	dhèanainn
do, make	*doing, making*	*to do, make*	*I would do, make*
faic	a' faicinn	a dh'fhaicinn	chitheadh tu
see	*seeing*	*to see*	*you would see*
faigh	a' faighinn	a dh'fhaighinn	gheibheadh iad
get	*getting*	*to get*	*they would get*
rach	a' dol	a dhol	rachainn
go	*going*	*to go*	*I would go*
ruig	a' ruighinn/	a ruighinn/	ruigeadh sibh
	a' ruigsinn	a ruigsinn	
arrive, reach	*arriving, reaching*	*to arrive, reach*	*you would arrive, reach*
thoir/tabhair	a' toirt/	a thoirt/	thoireamaid
	a' tabhairt	a thabhairt	
give, take, bring	*giving, taking, bringing*	*to give, take, bring*	*we would give, take, bring*
thig	a' tighinn	a thighinn	thigeadh e
come	*coming*	*to come*	*he would come*

Irregular verbs: past tense

Root	Positive	Negative	Interrogative
abair	thuirt/	cha tuirt/	an tuirt/
	thubhairt	tubhairt	tubhairt ...?
say	*said*	*did not say*	*did ... say?*
beir	rug	cha do rug	an do rug ...?
catch	*caught*	*did not catch*	*did ... catch?*
cluinn	chuala	cha chuala	an cuala ...?
hear	*heard*	*did not hear*	*did ... hear?*

dèan	rinn	cha do rinn	an do rinn ...?
do, make	*did, made*	*did not do, make*	*did ... do, make?*
faic	chunnaic	chan fhaca	am faca ...?
see	*saw*	*did not see*	*did ... see?*
faigh	fhuair	cha d' fhuair	an d' fhuair ...?
get	*got*	*did not get*	*did ... get?*
rach	chaidh	cha deach	an deach ...?
go	*went*	*did not go*	*did ... go?*
ruig	ràinig	cha do ràinig	an do ràinig ...?
arrive, reach	*arrived, reached*	*did not arrive, reach*	*did ... arrive, reach?*
thoir/tabhair	thug	cha tug	an tug ...?
give, take, bring	*gave, took, brought*	*did not give, take, bring*	*did .... give, take, bring*
thig	thàinig	cha tàinig	an tàinig ...?
come	*came*	*did not come*	*did ... come?*

Irregular verbs: future tense

abair	their	chan abair	an abair ...?
say	*will say*	*will not say*	*will ... say?*
beir	beiridh	cha bheir	am beir ...?
catch	*will catch*	*will not catch*	*will ... catch?*
cluinn	cluinnidh	cha chluinn	an cluinn ...?
hear	*will hear*	*will not hear*	*will ... hear?*
dèan	nì	cha dèan	an dèan ...?
do, make	*will do, make*	*will not do, make*	*will ... do, make?*
faic	chì	chan fhaic	am faic ...?
see	*will see*	*will not see*	*will ... see?*
faigh	gheibh	chan fhaigh	am faigh ...?
get	*will get*	*will not get*	*will ... get?*
rach	thèid	cha tèid	an tèid ...?
go	*will go*	*will not go*	*will ... go?*
ruig	ruigidh	cha ruig	an ruig ...?
arrive, reach	*will arrive, reach*	*will not arrive, reach*	*will ... arrive, reach?*

thoir/tabhair	bheir	cha toir/ tabhair	an toir/ tabhair ...?
give, take, bring	*will give, take, bring*	*will not give, take, bring*	*will ... give, take, bring?*
thig	thig	cha tig	an tig ...?
come	*will come*	*will not come*	*will ... come?*

The verb 'to be'

There are two separate strands of the verb 'to be' in Gaelic. One is based on **bi** and the other, known as the assertive form, is based on **is**.

These strands are set out separately below:

bi forms

Root	Present positive	Present negative	Present interrogative
bi	tha	chan eil	a bheil?
	am, is, are	*am not, is not, are not*	*am?, is?, are?*

Past positive	Past negative	Past interrogative
bha	cha robh	an robh?
was, were	*was not, were not*	*was ... not?, were ... not?*

Future positive	Future negative	Future interrogative
bidh/bithidh	cha bhi	am bi?
will be	*will not be*	*will ... be?*

Present relative	Present dependent positive	Present dependent negative
a tha	gu bheil	nach eil
who/which/ that is	*that ... is*	*that ... is not*

Past relative	Past dependent positive	Past dependent negative
a bha	gun robh	nach robh
who/which/ that was/were	*that ... was/were*	*that ... was/ were not*

Future relative	Future dependent positive	Future dependent negative
a bhitheas/ a bhios	gum bi	nach bi
who/which/ that will be	*that ... will be*	*that ... will not be*

2nd pl. imp.	Infinitive	Subjunctive/ conditional dependent	Subjunctive/ conditional
bithibh *be (pl)*	a bhith *to be*	bhithinn *I would be*	gum bithinn *that I would be*
		bhiodh/ bhitheadh ... *you/he/she/it/ they would be*	gum biodh/ bitheadh *that he/she/it/ they would be*
		bhitheamaid, bhitheadh sinn *we would be*	gum bitheamaid, gum bitheadh sinn *that we would be*

Assertive forms

Present positive	Present negative	Present interrogative
is/'s *am, is, are*	cha(n) *am not, is not, are not*	an, am *am?, is?, are?*
Past positive & Conditional positive	**Past negative & Conditional negative**	**Past interrogative & Conditional interrogative**
bu/b' *was, were, would be*	cha bu, cha b' *was not, were not, would not be*	am bu? am b'? *was?, were?, would ... be?*
Present relative	**Present dependent positive**	**Present dependent negative**
as *that am, that is, that are*	gur *that am, that is, that are*	nach *that am not, that is not, that are not*
Past relative & Conditional relative	**Past dependent positive & Conditional dependent positive**	**Past dependent negative & Conditional dependent negative**
(a) bu, b' *that was, that were, that would be*	gum bu, gum b' *that was, that were, that would be*	nach bu, nach b' *that was not, that were not, that would not be*

Is is often reduced to **'S** in pronunciation and in writing, while **Bu** becomes **B'** before a word beginning in a vowel.

The Assertive forms are used to highlight, identify and define a particular point, eg

's e àite snog a th' ann	*it's a nice place*
's ann à Ile a tha iad	*they are from Islay*
cha b' ise a bh' ann idir	*it wasn't her at all*
b' ann a-raoir a thachair e	*it was last night it happened*

'S and **B'** are followed by pronouns when the point being highlighted or identified is a person or thing. They are accompanied by **ann** when reference is being made to a place or time.

The various forms of **Is** and **Bu** feature in a number of phrases in combination with a noun or adjective and a prepositional pronoun. These phrases convey the meanings carried by certain verbs in English, eg

's toil/toigh leam	*I like*
's caomh leis	*he likes*
's fheàrr leatha	*she prefers*
's beag orm	*I dislike*
's lugha air	*he hates*
chan àbhaist dhomh	*I don't usually*
an urrainn dhut?	*can you?*
bu chòir dhi	*she should/ought to*
an aithne dhuibh?	*do you (pl) know?*

The prepositional pronouns

Preposition	Singular			
	1st	**2nd**	**3rd Masc**	**3rd Fem**
aig *at*	agam *at me*	agad *at you*	aige *at him/it*	aice *at her/it*
air *on*	orm *on me*	ort *on you*	air *on him/it*	oirre *on her/it*
ann *in*	annam *in me*	annad *in you*	ann *in him/it*	innte *in her/it*
às *out of*	asam *out of me*	asad *out of you*	às *out of him/it*	aiste *out of her/it*
bho *from* o	bhuam uam *from me*	bhuat uat *from you*	bhuaithe uaithe *from her/it*	bhuaipe uaipe *from her/it*
de *of, off*	dhìom *of me*	dhìot *of you*	dheth *of him/it*	dhith *of her/it*
do *to*	dhomh *to me*	dhut *to you*	dha *to him/it*	dhi *to her/it*

eadar *between*	-		-		-		-
fo *under*	fodham *under me*	fodhad *under you*	fodha *under him/it*	foidhpe/foipe *under her/it*
gu/chun *to*	thugam *to me*	thugad *to you*	thuige *to him/it*	thuice *to her/it*
le *with, by*	leam *with me*	leat *with you*	leis *with him/it*	leatha *with her/it*
mu *about*	umam *about me*	umad *about you*	uime *about him/it*	uimpe *about her/it*
ri *to*	rium *to me*	riut *to you*	ris *to him/it*	rithe *to her/it*
ro/roimh *before*	romham *before me*	romhad *before you*	roimhe *before him/it*	roimhpe *before her/it*
tro/troimh *through*	tromham *through me*	tromhad *through you*	troimhe *through him/it*	troimhpe *through her/it*
thar *over*	tharam *over me*	tharad *over you*	thairis (air) *over him/it*	thairte *over her/it*

	Plural		
	1st	**2nd**	**3rd**
aig *at*	againn *at us*	agaibh *at you*	aca *at them*
air *on*	oirnn *on us*	oirbh *on you*	orra *on them*
ann *in*	annainn *in us*	annaibh *in you*	annta *in them*
às *out of*	asainn *out of us*	asaibh *out of you*	asta *out of them*
bho *from* o	bhuainn *from us* uainn	bhuaibh *from you* uaibh	bhuat *from them* uat
de *of, off*	dhinn *of us*	dhibh *of you*	dhiubh *of them*
do *to*	dhuinn *to us*	dhuibh *to you*	dhaibh *to them*
eadar *between*	eadarainn *between us*	eadaraibh *between you*	eatarra *between them*
fo *under*	fodhainn *under us*	fodhaibh *under you*	fodhpa/fòpa *under them*
gu/chun *to*	thugainn *to us*	thugaibh *to you*	thuca *to them*
le *with, by*	leinn *with us*	leibh *with you*	leotha *with them*
mu *about*	umainn *about us*	umaibh *about you*	umpa *about them*
ri *to*	rinn/ruinn *to us*	ribh/ruibh *to you*	riutha *to them*
ro/roimh *before*	romhainn *before us*	romhaibh *before you*	romhpa *before them*
tro/troimh *through*	tromhainn *through us*	tromhaibh *through you*	tromhpa *through them*
thar *over*	tharainn *over us*	tharaibh *over you*	tharta *over them*

gaelic
boyd robertson & iain taylor

- Do you want to cover the basics then progress fast?
- Do you want to communicate in a range of situations?
- Do you want to reach a high standard?

Gaelic starts with the basics but moves at a lively pace to give you a good level of understanding, speaking and writing. You will have lots of opportunity to practise the kind of language you will need to be able to communicate with confidence and understand Gaelic culture.

teach® yourself

Afrikaans
Arabic
Arabic Script, Beginner's
Bengali
Brazilian Portuguese
Bulgarian
Cantonese
Catalan
Chinese
Chinese, Beginner's
Chinese Script, Beginner's
Croatian
Czech
Danish
Dutch
Dutch, Beginner's
Dutch Dictionary
Dutch Grammar
English, American (EFL)
English as a Foreign Language
English, Correct
English Grammar
English Grammar (EFL)
English for International Business
English Vocabulary
Finnish
French
French, Beginner's
French Grammar
French Grammar, Quick Fix
French, Instant
French, Improve your
French, One-Day
French Starter Kit
French Verbs
French Vocabulary
Gaelic
Gaelic Dictionary
German
German, Beginner's
German Grammar
German Grammar, Quick Fix

German, Instant
German, Improve your
German Verbs
German Vocabulary
Greek
Greek, Ancient
Greek, Beginner's
Greek, Instant
Greek, New Testament
Greek Script, Beginner's
Gulf Arabic
Hebrew, Biblical
Hindi
Hindi, Beginner's
Hindi Script, Beginner's
Hungarian
Icelandic
Indonesian
Irish
Italian
Italian, Beginner's
Italian Grammar
Italian Grammar, Quick Fix
Italian, Instant
Italian, Improve your
Italian, One-Day
Italian Verbs
Italian Vocabulary
Japanese
Japanese, Beginner's
Japanese, Instant
Japanese Script, Beginner's
Korean
Latin
Latin American Spanish
Latin, Beginner's
Latin Dictionary
Latin Grammar
Nepali
Norwegian
Panjabi
Persian, Modern

Polish
Portuguese
Portuguese, Beginner's
Portuguese Grammar
Portuguese, Instant
Romanian
Russian
Russian, Beginner's
Russian Grammar
Russian, Instant
Russian Script, Beginner's
Sanskrit
Serbian
Spanish
Spanish, Beginner's
Spanish Grammar
Spanish Grammar, Quick Fix
Spanish, Instant
Spanish, Improve your
Spanish, One-Day
Spanish Starter Kit
Spanish Verbs
Spanish Vocabulary
Swahili
Swahili Dictionary
Swedish
Tagalog
Teaching English as a Foreign Language
Teaching English One to One
Thai
Turkish
Turkish, Beginner's
Ukrainian
Urdu
Urdu Script, Beginner's
Vietnamese
Welsh
Welsh Dictionary
World Cultures:
  China
  England
  France
  Germany
  Italy
  Japan
  Portugal
  Russia
  Spain
  Wales
Xhosa
Zulu

available from bookshops and on-line retailers